THE A-Z OF

HITCHCOCK

THE A–Z OF
HITCHCOCK

HOWARD MAXFORD

B.T.BATSFORD · LONDON

First Published 2002

Text © Howard Maxford 2002

Volume © B. T. Batsford

The right of Howard Maxford to be identified as Author
of this work has been asserted to him in accordance with
the Copyright, Designs and Patents Act 1988.

Illustrations supplied by Joel Finler Collection

ISBN 07134 8738 0

A CIP catalogue record for this book is available from the
British Library.

Printed in country G. Canale & C. S.p.A., Italy
Typeset in Bembo
for the publishers

B T Batsford
64 Brewery Road
London N7 9NT
England
www.batsford.com

A member of the Chrysalis Group plc

'I suppose it all must have started at the age of six months when I was in my mother's arms and she turned to me and said, "Boo!"'

Alfred Hitchcock

'Any American director who says he hasn't been influenced by him is out of his mind.'

John Frankenheimer

For my English teacher Jim Burns (Davenport Lower School, Stockport), who loved 'the filums'.

For my imaginary friends Joe and Pasquale – thanks for being there during the bad times as well as the good.

And in memory of the ABC, Classic and Davenport cinemas in Stockport (all now sadly demolished) where I spent many happy hours as a child.

My thanks to the folk at Batsford for making this book number six; to my editor Tina Persaud for her patience during the writing of this project, which turned out to be bigger than either of us imagined; and to Joel Finler for access to his Aladdin's cave of stills.

INTRODUCTION

Like any self-respecting film fan, I've always had a place in my heart (and video collection) for the films of Alfred Hitchcock. In fact *North by Northwest* (1959) is my all-time favourite movie. I must have seen it coming up to one hundred times by now, which is an incredible amount of time to invest in a single film (and yes, out of curiosity, I even ordered a Gibson once – the cocktail Cary Grant orders on the Twentieth Century Limited – only to discover that it was a Martini with a white-skinned pickle in it!).

Consequently, when my proposal to write this book about the great man's movies was accepted by the good burghers of Batsford, I was more than a little thrilled, not least because of the number of books that have already been written about the Master. Mine, I was determined, was going to be different, though. The biography and the film-by-film chronology had already been done several times over. Consequently, I fixed upon the idea of an all-encompassing encyclopedia, taking in all of Hitchcock's films – from his work as a titles designer in the twenties through to his British and American classics – as well as *Who's Who*-style entries on all of the actors, writers, composers and technicians with whom he had collaborated over the 50-plus years of his astonishing (and astonishingly prolific) career.

Among this amazing roll call are such names as Cary Grant, Ingrid Bergman, James Stewart, producer David O Selznick, composer Bernard Herrmann, cinematographer Robert Burks and editor George Tomasini, with whom Hitchcock worked again and again. Indeed, Hitchcock seemed to be incredibly loyal to certain artists with whom he was comfortable working. Not all of them were major names, however. In the roll call are such lesser-mentioned but equally worthy talents as cinematographer Jack Cox, who photographed 12 of Hitchcock's early films, including *Blackmail* (1929) and *The Lady Vanishes* (1938); bit-part player Clare Greet, who worked with Hitchcock seven times between 1922 and 1939; and character actor Tom Helmore, who not only made a silent film with Hitchcock, *The Ring* (1927), but went on to feature in *Secret Agent* (1936), *Vertigo* (1958) and an episode of *Alfred Hitchcock Presents*, thus giving him credits in every phase of the director's career. In fact one actress, Elsie Randolph, impressed Hitchcock so much in *Rich and Strange* (1932) that he determined on using her again as soon as possible; unfortunately, she had to wait exactly 40 years before he did so in *Frenzy* (1972) – but at least he kept his promise!

You'll find all these names, plus many more familiar and not so familiar talents, listed throughout the book, along with reviews of all Hitchcock's films, the majority of which are accompanied by sourced quotations from the director, cast and crew, along with comments from the critics of the day (for convenience, the films are also star-rated in the established manner, from zero to four stars, with zero representing a poor or unavailable film, and four representing a major cinematic achievement). You'll also find all the relevant cast and credit information to hand, plus video, DVD and CD availability. A good many of the *Who's Who* entries feature quotes and reviews, too, along with a 'Hitchography' listing all of the films, television programmes and radio adaptations each artist made for the Master. Please note, however, the emphasis of this particular book is the film work of Hitchcock – consequently, there are no entries for actors who appeared solely in episodes of the director's television work.

Also note that the book is not meant for reading from cover to cover – it's meant for browsing. So dip in with a favourite star or movie and see where things lead you. For those not overly familiar with Hitchcock's work, a good starting place might be his own 'Hitchography', which lists all the films and television programmes he was associated with, from *The Great Day* (1920) to *Family Plot* (1976). There may even be a couple of surprises for those who think they know Hitchcock's credits inside out, such as *The Elastic Affair* (1930), a previously unmentioned and seemingly lost short, and *The Dark Intruder* (1965), the rejected pilot for an anthology series titled *Black Cloak*, which was made by Hitchcock's production company Shamley and subsequently released theatrically as a programme filler. Un-filmed Hitchcock will hopefully prove equally intriguing, while his other interests are explored in the entries on Radio, Television and Publishing. This compendium also includes entries on Sequels, Remakes and Homages.

Certain of Hitchcock's films are worthy of books in themselves, and this has actually been the case with *The Birds* (1963), *Blackmail* (1929), *Vertigo* (1958) and *Psycho* (1960), with *Vertigo* and *Psycho* already numbering two books each, plus countless newspaper and magazine features. That said, the reviews within cram in as much information about each film as space will allow, including plot synopses and analysis. Given that Hitchcock himself had an aversion to overly interpretational reviews of his work, I've tried to avoid becoming too esoteric in my comments, preferring to leave that brand of navel-gazing to others.

Hitchcock believed in 'The medium of pure cinema.' [1] For him, this was 'the assembly of pieces of film to create fright.' [2] He certainly succeeded, to the point that his work is still watched and discussed today, over 100 years after his birth and over 20 years after his death, with many of his films featured in top 100 lists the world over. The British Film Institute's top 100 British films of the 20th century includes Hitchcock entries, *The 39 Steps* (1935) ranked at number four, *The Third Man* (1949), *Brief Encounter* (1945) and *Lawrence of Arabia* (1962), which certainly isn't bad company. The American Film Institute's top 100 American films of the 20th century meanwhile numbers three Hitchcocks, with *Psycho* (1960) ranking highest at number eighteen.

Of course, not all Hitchcock's films are classics. Like any director, he occasionally fell below his own high standards, as was the case with *Marnie* (1964) and *Topaz* (1969). *Marnie* has since been re-evaluated in some quarters, though personally I feel that *Topaz* is more worthy of rediscovery. I also have a particular fondness for such underdogs as *The Paradine Case* (1947) and *Torn Curtain* (1966), the latter arguably Hitchcock's last truly great film. It would certainly feature in my own top ten which, for the record, is as follows: *North by Northwest* (1959), *Rear Window* (1954), *The 39 Steps* (1935), *Rebecca* (1940), *Psycho* (1960), *Foreign Correspondent* (1940), *Torn Curtain* (1966), *The Lady Vanishes* (1938), *Young and Innocent* (1937) and *The Lodger* (1926), with *Frenzy* (1972) along for the ride as a guilty pleasure.

However, I'm afraid there is no place for *Mr. and Mrs. Smith* (1941), *Rope* (1948), *Under Capricorn* (1949), *The Trouble with Harry* (1955) and the remake of *The Man Who Knew Too Much* (1956). Even though I have seen it over twenty times and have visited many of its locations, *Vertigo* (1958) also leaves me curiously cold, despite its brilliant Bernard Herrmann score, while *The Birds* (1963), despite some effective touches, seems particularly juvenile to me. But we're all entitled to our opinions, and this book represents mine, some of which will no doubt rankle. But I stick by them in the hope that they'll at least provoke discussion.

Incidentally, mention of *The Lady Vanishes* brings to mind an incident from my childhood. I was travelling by train once with my father, and the windows of the carriage were all steamed up. Leaning over, I used my forefinger to write the name FROY on the glass, as in the moment in the film when Miss Froy spells out her name for Iris Henderson. Having done this, I pointed out my handiwork to my father who, to my surprise, didn't laugh (not having seen the film) but took great umbrage. You see, his name is Roy, and he thought I was being incredibly rude!

But I digress, and now invite you to venture forth into Hitchcock territory. However, beware of the McGuffins – their bite is deadly.

Howard Maxford,
South London, May 2002

A

ACADEMY AWARDS Astonishingly, despite being regarded as one of the greatest film-makers ever, Alfred Hitchcock never actually won an Oscar, though he was nominated in the Best Director category five times during his lengthy career and once as a Best Picture producer. His films, however, won many awards, including Best Picture for *Rebecca* (1940) and Best Actress – Joan Fontaine – for *Suspicion* (1941). Hitchcock himself didn't go entirely unrecognized, for he was eventually presented with the Irving G Thalberg award in 1967 in recognition of his body of work. The chronological list below represents all the Oscar-nominated and Oscar-winning films in the Hitchcock cannon.

Rebecca (1940)
Winner: Best Picture (David O Selznick, producer)
Winner: Best Cinematography (George Barnes)
Nominated: Best Director (Alfred Hitchcock)
Nominated: Best Actor (Laurence Olivier)
Nominated: Best Actress (Joan Fontaine)
Nominated: Best Supporting Actress (Judith Anderson)
Nominated: Best Screenplay (Robert E Sherwood, Joan Harrison)
Nominated: Best Score (Franz Waxman)
Nominated: Best Editing (Hal C Kern)
Nominated: Best Interior Decoration (Lyle Wheeler)
Nominated: Best Special Effects (Jack Cosgrove, photographic; Arthur Johns, sound)

Foreign Correspondent (1940)
Nominated: Best Picture (Walter Wanger, producer)
Nominated: Best Supporting Actor (Albert Bassermann)
Nominated: Best Original Screenplay (Charles Bennett, Joan Harrison)
Nominated: Best Cinematography (Rudolph Mate)
Nominated: Best Interior Decoration (Alexander Golitzen)
Nominated: Best Special Effects (Paul Eagler, photographic; Thomas T Moulton, sound)

Suspicion (1941)
Winner: Best Actress (Joan Fontaine)
Nominated: Best Picture (Alfred Hitchcock)
Nominated: Best Score (Franz Waxman)

Shadow of a Doubt (1943)
Nominated: Best Original Story (Gordon McDonell)

Lifeboat (1944)
Nominated: Best Director (Alfred Hitchcock)
Nominated: Best Original Story (John Steinbeck)
Nominated: Best Cinematography (Glen MacWilliams)

Spellbound (1945)
Winner: Best Score (Miklos Rozsa)

Nominated: Best Picture (David O Selznick, producer)
Nominated: Best Director (Alfred Hitchcock)
Nominated: Best Supporting Actor (Michael Chekhov)
Nominated: Best Cinematography (George Barnes)
Nominated: Best Special Effects (Jack Cosgrove)

Notorious (1946)
Nominated: Best Supporting Actor (Claude Rains)
Nominated: Best Original Screenplay (Ben Hecht)

The Paradine Case (1947)
Nominated: Best Supporting Actress (Ethel Barrymore)

Strangers On a Train (1951)
Nominated: Best Cinematography (Robert Burks)

Rear Window (1954)
Nominated: Best Director (Alfred Hitchcock)
Nominated: Best Screenplay (John Michael Hayes)
Nominated: Best Cinematography (Robert Burks)
Nominated: Best Sound Recording (Loren L Ryder)

To Catch a Thief (1955)
Winner: Best Cinematography (Robert Burks)
Nominated: Best Art Direction/Set Decoration (Hal Pereira, Joseph McMillan Johnson, Sam Comer, Arthur Krams)
Nominated: Best Costume Design (Edith Head)

The Man Who Knew Too Much (1956)
Winner: Best Song (Jay Livingston, Ray Evans, for 'Que Sera, Sera')

Vertigo (1958)
Nominated: Best Art Direction/Set Decoration (Hal Pereira, Henry Bumstead, Sam Comer, Frank McKelvy)
Nominated: Best Sound (George Dutton)

North by Northwest (1959)
Nominated: Best Original Story and Screenplay (Ernest Lehman)
Nominated: Best Editing (George Tomasini)
Nominated: Best Art Direction/Set Decoration (William A Horning, Robert Boyle, Henry Grace, Merrill Pye, Frank McKelvy)

Psycho (1960)
Nominated: Best Director (Alfred Hitchcock)
Nominated: Best Supporting Actress (Janet Leigh)
Nominated: Best Cinematography (John L Russell)
Nominated: Best Art Direction/Set Decoration (Robert Clatworthy, George Milo)

The Birds (1963)
Nominated: Best Visual Effects (Ub Iwerks)

ACKER, JEAN (1893–1978) American actress. Best remembered for being the first wife of Rudolph Valentino

(1895–1926, real name Rodolpho d'Antonguolla), to whom she was married between 1919 and 1921, Acker also had a busy career as a supporting actress on both stage and screen. In films from 1915 with *Are You a Mason?* she went on to appear in the likes of *Arabian Knight* (1920), *Brewster's Millions* (1921), *The Girl Habit* (1931) and *My Favorite Wife* (1940). She can also be spotted as a nurse at the Green Mansions psychiatric institute in Hitchcock's *Spellbound* (1945). **Hitchography:** *Spellbound* (1945)

ACKLAND, RODNEY (1908–1991) British playwright and screenwriter. Ackland first met Hitchcock on the set of *The Skin Game* in 1931 and was coerced by him into making a brief appearance as an extra in the film. He subsequently worked with Hitch scripting a film version of John Van Druten's play *The Wall*, but it was never made. However, *Number Seventeen* (1932), based on J Jefferson Farjeon's 1925 play *Joyous Melodrama*, was made, which Ackland co-scripted with Hitchcock and Alma Reville. Ackland went on to author several key British films, among them *Bank Holiday* (1938), *49th Parallel* (1941), for which he was nominated for an Oscar with co-writer Emeric Pressburger, and *The Queen of Spades* (1948). He also acted in *The Case of Gabriel Perry* (1935) and directed *Thursday's Child* (1942). **Hitchography:** *The Skin Game* (1931), *Number Seventeen* (1932)

ADAM, ROLAND (1896–1979) British character star. Following experience as a chartered accountant, Adam turned his attention to the stage, both as an actor and playwright. He made his film debut in 1936 in *Song of Freedom*, which he followed with *The Drum* (1938), *Q Planes* (1939) and *The Lion Has Wings* (1939) among others. His career took a hiatus during the war years, during which he reached the level of Wing Commander in the RAF. After the war he went on to appear in well over 100 films, among them such classics as *Green for Danger* (1946), *Seven Days to Noon* (1950), *Private's Progress* (1955) and *Cleopatra* (1963), more often than not in authoritative roles. In 1949 he appeared briefly as Mr Riggs in Hitchcock's *Under Capricorn*. Unfortunately, it was a small role in one of the director's more minor films. Adam's last film was *The Last Tycoon* (1976). **Hitchography:** *Under Capricorn* (1949)

ADAMS, KATHRYN (1893–1959) American supporting actress. Adams was featured in a handful of films in the late 1930s and early 1940s, among them *Fifth Avenue Girl* (1939), *Argentine Nights* (1940) and Hitchcock's *Saboteur* (1942) as a 'Young Mother', though she was 49 at the time. **Hitchography:** *Saboteur* (1942)

ADDINSELL, RICHARD (1904–1977) British composer. Addinsell, who made his film debut in 1936 with *The Amateur Gentleman*, remains best known for his *Warsaw Concerto*, which featured in the film *Dangerous Moonlight* (1940), although he also contributed sterling work to *Goodbye, Mr Chips* (1939), *Gaslight* (1940), *Blithe*

Spirit (1945) and *The Prince and the Showgirl* (1957). In 1949, he also scored Hitchcock's first British film for ten years, *Under Capricorn*, for which he supplied a lush, string-led score and several engaging dance pieces for the ball sequence. A student of the Royal College of Music, Addinsell also worked much in the theatre, providing music for the revues of Andre Charlot. He composed several pieces for the concert platform too, among them *The Smokey Mountains Concerto* and *Journey to Romance*. An accomplished pianist, Addinsell accompanied Joyce Grenfell in a series of acclaimed concerts during the war years. **Hitchography:** *Under Capricorn* (1949)

ADDINSON, JOHN (1920–1998) British composer. An Oscar winner for his score for *Tom Jones* (1963), Addison entered films in 1948 following training at the Royal College of Music. His many films include *The Guinea Pig* (1949), *Seven Days to Noon* (1950), *I Was Monty's Double* (1958), *The Entertainer* (1960), *Smashing Time* (1967), *Sleuth* (1972), *A Bridge Too Far* (1977) and *Strange Invaders* (1983), as well as much television work, including the theme for *Murder, She Wrote* (1985–1997). Known for his quirky way with a melody, Addison was also hired to replace Bernard Herrmann on Hitchcock's *Torn Curtain* (1966), from which the composer had been sacked following a clash over the film's music. Addison was more than up to the challenge and penned one of his best scores, providing the film with a catchy *Main Title* and the love theme *Green Years* (which was released as a song to promote the film with lyrics by Jay Livingston and Ray Evans). **Hitchography:** *Torn Curtain* (1966)

ADRIAN, GILBERT (1903–1959, real name Adrian Adolph Greenberg) American costume designer. Known simply as Adrian, this costumier was, along with art director Cedric Gibbons, very much responsible for the MGM look of the 1930s. At the studio from 1928 to 1941 following experience in Paris and on Broadway, he designed for all the major stars of the day, notably Joan Crawford, Norma Shearer and Greta Garbo. After leaving MGM in 1941, Adrian set up his own fashion house, Adrian Ltd, which went on to enjoy great success, particularly in the ready-to-wear market. However, the designer still contributed to the occasional film, among them Hitchcock's *Shadow of a Doubt* (1943), on which he shared his credit with Vera West, and *Rope* (1948). In 1952, following a heart attack, Adrian retired to Brazil for a period with his wife, film star Janet Gaynor (1906–1984, real name Laura Gainer), but later returned to New York to work on two Broadway musicals: *At the Grand Hotel* and *Camelot*. Sadly, he suffered a second fatal heart attack during the latter show's pre-production, and the Tony award he won for it was presented posthumously. **Hitchography:** *Shadow of a Doubt* (1943), *Rope* (1948)

AHERNE, BRIAN (1902–1986) British actor. On stage from the age of 8, this British leading man went on to study architecture before finally returning to the stage in

1922. He made his film debut in 1924 with *The Eleventh Commandment*, and gradually gained popularity in the likes of *King of the Castle* (1925), *Safety First* (1926) and *A Woman Redeemed* (1927). He made his Broadway debut in 1931 in a production of *The Barretts of Wimpole Street*, which he followed with his Hollywood debut two years later opposite Marlene Dietrich in *Song of Songs*. Remaining in Hollywood, his subsequent films included *The Great Garrick* (1937), *Merrily We Live* (1938), *Forever and a Day* (1943), *The Locket* (1946) and Hitchcock's *I Confess* (1953), in which he played the Crown Prosecutor Willy Robertson, a fairly light-hearted role which brought some welcome relief to an otherwise doom-laden piece. Aherne's subsequent films include *Titanic* (1953), *The Swan* (1956), *Lancelot and Guinevere* (1963) and *Rosie* (1967), following which he retired from the big screen. His first wife was the actress Joan Fontaine (1917– , real name Joan de Havilland), to whom he was married from 1939 to 1944. She starred in Hitchcock's *Rebecca* (1940) and *Suspicion* (1941). His brother, Patrick Aherne (1901–1970), meanwhile appeared in Hitchcock's *The Paradine Case* (1947). **Hitchography:** *I Confess* (1953)

AHERNE, PATRICK (1901–1970) Irish actor Aherne began making films in Britain in the mid-1920s, among them *A Daughter in Revolt* (1925) and *Huntingtower* (1927). In America from 1936, he went on to appear in the likes of *Trouble Ahead* (1936), *Green Dolphin Street* (1947) and *The Court Jester* (1956). He can also be spotted in minor roles in Hitchcock's *The Paradine Case* (1947) and the remake of *The Man Who Knew Too Much* (1955). His brother was the actor Brian Aherne (1902–1986), who appeared in Hitchcock's *I Confess* (1953). **Hitchography:** *The Paradine Case* (1947), *The Man Who Knew Too Much* (1956)

AITBAAR Of all the remakes of Hitchcock's work, this 1985 Indian version of *Dial M for Murder* (1954) is the most elusive, and currently unavailable in Britain and America.

ALBERTSON, FRANK (1909–1964) American actor. In films from the age of 13 as an extra, Albertson had featured roles in such films as *Prep and Pep* (1928), *Just Imagine* (1931), *Fury* (1936) and *Bachelor Mother* (1939) among others. He later turned to character roles, his most famous being that of the boastful oil tycoon Tom Cassidy in Hitchcock's *Psycho* (1960), although the director had wanted Alan Reed for the role. **Hitchography:** *Psycho* (1960)

THE ALFRED HITCHCOCK HOUR see *Alfred Hitchcock Presents*

Alfred Hitchcock Presents
(US, 1955–1965, 268x25m, 93x55m, bw) ★★★

In the mid-1950s, audience attendance for movies began to fall dramatically owing to the increasing popularity of television. All the major studios turned their backs on the

Hitchcock prepares to make one of his comic introductions for his successful television series Alfred Hitchcock Presents *(1955–1962). Hitchcock is on the left.*

new medium, and instead tried to attract back the crowds with new fads and come-ons, among them widescreen, 3D and stereophonic sound. Some studios even refused to lease their back catalogue for television airings (thus losing out on a valuable source of revenue), while contracted stars were forbidden to work on the small screen for fear of diminishing their pulling power on the big.

Rather than ignoring television, Hitchcock embraced it and launched a half-hour anthology series titled *Alfred Hitchcock Presents*, in which he personally introduced a weekly twist-in-the-tail episode. The series debuted on 2 October 1955 and was an immediate success, with Hitchcock's jaunty intros and closing conclusions enhancing rather than diminishing his reputation. Commented co-producer Norman Lloyd, who had worked with Hitchcock before as an actor in *Saboteur* (1942) and *Spellbound* (1945): 'Hitch was The Star. And without Hitch it would just have been another show… Those lead-ins in which he appeared were *very* much part of the draw of the show.' [1]

Produced through Hitchcock's own company Shamley, and filmed for Universal at the Revue Television Studios, the series was overseen by Hitchcock himself, with the day-to-day producing chores in the hands of Hitchcock's longtime associate Joan Harrison (and also, later, Norman Lloyd). Of the 268 programmes produced between 1955 and 1962, 18 were directed by Hitchcock himself, including the opening episode, *Revenge*. (The others were *Breakdown*, *The Case of Mr Pelham*, *Back for Christmas*, *Wet Saturday*, *Mr Blanchard's Secret*, *One More Mile to Go*, *The Perfect Crime*, *Lamb to the Slaughter*, *Dip in the Pool*, *Poison*, *Banquo's Chair*, *Arthur*, *The Crystal Trench*, *Incident at a Corner*, *Mrs Bixby and the Colonel's Coat*, *The Horseplayer* and *Bang! You're Dead*.)

Broadcast on CBS, the programmes opened with a line drawing of Hitchcock's profile, accompanied by the theme tune, *Funeral March of the Marionette* by Charles Gounod. Then it was into Hitchcock's intro, all of which were written for him by Jimmy Allardice. Recalled co-producer Norman Lloyd: 'He [Hitchcock] would do anything that Jimmy asked him to do for the lead-ins. Thus you had Hitch inside a bottle, and you had Hitch in golfing knickers playing golf... You had Hitch playing his brother. You had Hitch with a lion. The lead-ins would come in and I'd show them to Joan Harrison and say, "He'll never do this. We'd better send it back!"' [2] Of course, Hitchcock always obliged, no matter how ludicrous the set-up (he even donned a mop-top wig and became 'The Fifth Beatle' in one memorable intro).

Given the Hitchcock name and the quality of the programmes, the series was able to attract some pretty major names, including Bette Davis, Vincent Price, Lillian Gish, Christopher Lee and Gloria Swanson. Many who had appeared in Hitchcock's movies also popped up, among them Joan Fontaine, Peter Lorre, Ann Todd, James Mason, Joseph Cotton, John Williams, Martin Landau, Pat Hitchcock and Claude Rains. Plenty of then-new talent got a push up the ladder by appearing in the shows too, including Steve McQueen, Robert Redford, Charles Bronson, Walter Matthau, Lee Majors, Joanne Woodward, James Coburn, Roger Moore, William Shatner, Peter Falk and John Cassavetes.

Established and up-coming directors were involved, among them Robert Stevenson, Paul Henreid, Robert Altman, Sydney Pollack, Don Taylor, Arthur Hiller, Stuart Rosenberg, Jack Smight, William Friedkin, John Brahm, Gordon Hessler, Don Weis, Boris Sagal and Robert Florey, while the stories – adapted by the likes of Stirling Silliphant, Robert C Dennis and Francis Cockrell – came from such renowned writers as Roald Dahl, Dorothy L Sayers, Robert Bloch, Ira Levin, Garson Kanin, Evan Hunter, Adela Rogers St John and A A Milne.

The series moved to NBC in 1960, then back to CBS in 1962 as *The Alfred Hitchcock Hour*, although the format remained the same. This time 93 episodes were produced, of which Hitchcock directed just one, *I Saw the Whole Thing*. The series returned to NBC in 1964 and concluded the following year, but has remained in syndication ever since. Its success has influenced many other anthology series over the years, including *Turn of Fate* (1957), *The Twilight Zone* (1959–1963), *Thriller* (1960–1961), *Journey to the Unknown* (1968), also produced by Joan Harrison and Norman Lloyd, *Night Gallery* (1969) and *Tales of the Unexpected* (1979–1984), the latter of which featured

remakes of several *Alfred Hitchcock Presents* episodes, including *The Man from the South*, *Mrs Bixby and the Colonel's Coat*, *Poison* and *Lamb to the Slaughter* (some episodes were also produced and directed by Norman Lloyd).

In 1985, *Alfred Hitchcock Presents* was revived in its half-hour format. Note that in 1957 Hitchcock was involved in another anthology series titled *Suspicion* (see separate entry), which he executive produced; he also helmed the opening episode, *Four O'Clock* (which was later re-made for the 1980s *Alfred Hitchcock Presents* series). Meanwhile, 1960 saw Hitchcock direct an episode of *Ford Startime* (see separate entry); titled *Incident at a Corner*, starring Vera Miles.

The original *Alfred Hitchcock Presents/The Alfred Hitchcock Hour* programmes are:

GENERAL CREDITS
Production company: Universal/Shamley/Revue
Executive producer: Alfred Hitchcock
Producers: Joan Harrison, Norman Lloyd
Writer (intros): Jimmy Allardice

EPISODE CREDITS

Revenge
Director: Alfred Hitchcock
Teleplay: A I Bezzerides, Francis Cockrell, based on a story by Samuel Blas
Cast: Vera Miles, Ralph Meeker, Ray Teal, Ray Montgomery, Frances Bavier

Premonition
Director: Robert Stevens
Cast: John Forsythe, Cloris Leachman, George Macready

Triggers in Leash
Director: Don Medford
Cast: Gene Barry, Darren McGavin

Don't Come Back Alive
Director: Robert Stevenson
Cast : Sidney Blackmer, Virginia Gregg

Into Thin Air (aka The Vanishing Lady)
Director: Don Medford
Cast : Patricia Hitchcock, Mary Forbes

Salvage
Director: Justus Addiss
Teleplay: Dick Carr, Fred Freidberger
Cast: Gene Barry, Nancy Gates, Elisha Cook Jr

Breakdown
Director: Alfred Hitchcock
Teleplay: Francis Cockrell, Louis Pollock, based on a story by Louis Pollock
Cast: Joseph Cotten, Raymond Bailey, Lane Chandler, Aaron Spelling, Forrest Stanley

Our Cook's a Treasure
Director: Robert Stevens
Teleplay: Robert C Dennis, from a story by Dorothy L Sayers
Cast: Beulah Bondi, Everett Sloane

The Long Shot
Director: Robert Stevenson
Cast: John Williams, Peter Lawford, Robert Warwick

The Case of Mr Pelham
Director: Alfred Hitchcock
Teleplay: Francis Cockrell, from a story by Anthony Armstrong
Cast: Tom Ewell, Raymond Bailey, Kay Stewart, John Compton, Kirby Smith

Guilty Witness
Director: Robert Stevens
Teleplay: Robert C Dennis
Cast: Joe Mantell, Judith Evelyn

Santa Claus and the Tenth Avenue Kid
Director: Don Weis
Teleplay: Marian Cockrell
Cast: Barry Fitzgerald, Arthur Space

The Cheney Vase
Director: Robert Stevens
Cast: Darren McGavin, Patricia Collinge, George Macready

A Bullet for Baldwin
Director: Justus Addiss
Cast: Sebastian Cabot

The Big Switch
Director: Don Weiss
Teleplay: Richard Carr, from the story by Cornell Woolrich
Cast: George E Stone, George Mathews

You Got to Have Luck
Director: Robert Stevens
Teleplay: Eustace Cockrell, Francis Cockrell
Cast: John Cassavetes, Ray Teal, Marisa Pavan

The Older Sister
Director: Robert Stevens
Teleplay: Robert C Dennis
Cast: Joan Lorring, Patricia Hitchcock, Carmen Mathews

Shopping for Death
Director: Robert Stevens
Teleplay: Ray Bradbury
Cast: Robert H Harris, Jo Van Fleet, John Qualen

The Derelicts
Director: Robert Stevenson
Teleplay: Robert C Dennis
Cast: Philip Reed, Robert Newton

And So Died Riabouchinska
Director: Robert Stevenson
Teleplay: Mel Dinelli, from a story by Ray Bradbury
Cast: Claude Rains, Charles Bronson, Claire Carleton, Charles Cantor, Iris Adrian, Lowell Gilmore, Harry Tyler, Bill Haade, Virginia Gregg (voice)

Safe Conduct
Director: Justus Addiss
Teleplay: Andrew Solt
Cast: Claire Trevor, Jacques Bergerac, Werner Klemperer

Place of Shadows
Director: Robert Stevens
Teleplay: Robert C Dennis
Cast: Everett Sloane, Mark Damon

Back for Christmas
Director: Alfred Hitchcock
Teleplay: Francis Cockrell, from a story by John Collier
Cast: John Williams, Gavin Muir, Isobel Elsom, A E Gould-Porter, Katherine Warren

The Perfect Murder
Director: Robert Stevens
Teleplay: Victor Wolfson, from a story by Stacy Aumonier
Cast: Hurd Hatfield, Philip Coolidge, Mildred Natwick

There Was an Old Woman
Director: Robert Stevenson
Teleplay: Francis Cockrell, Marian Cockrell
Cast: Estelle Winwood, Charles Bronson

Whodunit
Director: Francis Cockrell
Teleplay: Francis Cockrell, Marian Cockrell
Cast: John Williams, Alan Naples

Help Wanted
Director: James Neilson
Teleplay: Robert C Dennis
Cast: John Qualen, Lorne Greene, Madge Kennedy

Portrait of Jocelyn
Director: Robert Stevens
Teleplay: Harold Swanton
Cast: John Baragrey, Nancy Gates, Philip Abbott

The Orderly World of Mr Appleby
Director: James Neilson
Teleplay: Victor Wolfson
Cast: Robert H Harris, Louise Larrabee

Never Again
Director: Robert Stevens
Teleplay: Irwin Gielgud, Gwen Bagni, Sterling Silliphant, from a story by Adela Rogers St John
Cast: Phyllis Thaxter, Warren Stevens, Louise Allbritton

The Gentleman from America
Director: Robert Stevens
Teleplay: Francis Cockrell
Cast: Biff McGuire, Ralph Clanton

The Baby Sitter
Director: Robert Stevens
Teleplay: Sarett Rudley
Cast: Thelma Ritter, Carmen Mathews, Mary Wickes

The Belfry
Director: Herschel Daugherty
Teleplay: Robert C Dennis
Cast: Patricia Hitchcock, Dabbs Greer, Jack Mullaney

The Hidden Thing
Director: Robert Stevens
Teleplay: James P Cavanagh
Cast: Biff McGuire, Robert H Harris, Judith Ames

The Legacy
Director: James Neilson
Cast: Leora Dana, Alan Hewitt, Jacques Bergerac

Mink
Director: Robert Stevenson
Teleplay: Gwen Bagni, Irwin Gielgud
Cast: Ruth Hussey, Vinton Hayworth, Anthony Eustrel

Decoy
Director: Arnold Laven
Teleplay: Bernard C Schoenfeld
Cast: Cara Williams, Robert Horton

The Creeper
Director: Herschel Daugherty
Teleplay: James P Cavanagh
Cast: Steve Brodie, Constance Ford

Momentum
Director: Robert Stevens
Teleplay: Francis Cockrell
Cast: Joanne Woodward, Skip Homeier

Wet Saturday
Director: Alfred Hitchcock
Teleplay: Marian Cockrell, based on a story by John Collier
Cast: Sir Cedric Hardwicke, John Williams, Kathryn Givney, Jerry Barclay, Tita Purdom

Fog Closing In
Director: Herschel Daugherty
Cast: Phyllis Thaxter, George Grizzard

De Mortuis
Director: Robert Stevens
Cast: Cara Williams, Philip Coolidge

Kill With Kindness
Director: Robert Stevens
Teleplay: A J Russell
Cast: Hume Cronyn, James Gleason, Carmen Mathews

None Are So Blind
Director: Robert Stevens
Cast: Mildred Dunnock, Hurd Hatfield

Toby
Director: Robert Stevens
Cast: Jessica Tandy

Alibi Me
Director: Jules Bricken
Cast: Shirley Smith, Herb Vigran

Conversation Over a Corpse
Director: Jules Bricken
Teleplay: Norman Daniels
Cast: Dorothy Stickney, Ray Collins, Carmen Mathews

Crack of Doom
Director: James Neilson
Cast: Robert Middleton, Robert Horton

Jonathan
Director: John Meredyth Lucas
Teleplay: Bernard Shoenfeld
Cast: Corey Allen, Walter Kingsford, Douglas Kennedy

The Better Bargain
Director: Herschel Daugherty
Teleplay: Bernard Shoenfeld
Cast: Henry Silva, Robert Middleton

The Rose Garden
Director: Marian Cockrell
Cast: Evelyn Varden, John Williams

Mr Blanchard's Secret
Director: Alfred Hitchcock
Teleplay: Sarett Rudley, based on a story by Emily Neff
Cast: Mary Scott, Robert Horton, Meg Mundy, Eloise Hardt, Dayton Lummis

John Brown's Body
Director: Robert Stevens
Teleplay: Robert C Dennis
Cast: Hugh Marlowe, Russell Collins, Leora Dana

Crackpot
Director: John Meredyth Lucas
Teleplay: Harold Gast, Martin Berkeley
Cast: Biff McGuire, Robert Emhardt, Mary Scott

Nightmare in 4D
Director: Justus Addiss
Cast: Virginia Gregg, Henry Jones

My Brother Richard
Director: Herschel Daugherty
Cast: Bobby Ellis, Henry Townes

Manacled
Director: Robert Stevens
Teleplay: Sterling Silliphant
Cast: Gary Merrill, William Redfield

A Bottle of Wine
Director: Herschel Daugherty
Teleplay: Sterling Silliphant, from a story by Borden Deal
Cast: Herbert Marshall, Robert Horton, Jarma Lewis

Malice Domestic
Director: John Meredyth Lucas
Teleplay: Victor Wolfson, from a story by Philip MacDonald
Cast: Vinton Hayworth, Ralph Meeker, Phyllis Thaxter

Number Twenty-Two
Director: Robert Stevens
Teleplay: Joel Murcott, from a story by Evan Hunter
Cast: Rip Torn, Ray Teal, Russell Collins

The End of Indian Summer
Director: Robert Stevens
Teleplay: James P Cavanagh
Cast: Gladys Cooper

One for the Road
Director: Robert Stevens
Teleplay: Robert C Dennis
Cast: John Baragrey, Louise Platt

The Cream of the Jest
Director: Herschel Daugherty
Teleplay: Sarett Rudley, from a story by Freddie Brown
Cast: Claude Rains, James Gregory, Paul Picerni, Joan Banks, Johnny Silver, Don Garret, Carol Shannon, Tom Martin

I Killed the Count (three episodes)
Director: Robert Stevens
Cast: John Williams, Melville Cooper

One More Mile to Go
Director: Alfred Hitchcock
Teleplay: James P Cavanagh, based on a story by F J Smith
Cast: Norman Leavitt, David Wayne, Louise Larrabee, Steve Brodie

Vicious Circle
Director: Paul Henried
Teleplay: Bernard Shoenfeld, from a story by Evan Hunter
Cast: George Macready, Dick York

The Three Dreams of Mr Findlater
Director: Jules Bricken
Teleplay: Sarett Rudley, from a story by A A Milne
Cast: John Williams, Isobel Elsom

The Night the World Ended
Director: Justus Addiss
Teleplay: Bernard Shoenfeld
Cast: Russell Collins, Harold Stone, Edith Barrett

The Hands of Mr Ottermole
Director: Robert Stevens
Teleplay: Francis Cockrell
Cast: Theodore Bikel, Rhys Williams

A Man Greatly Beloved
Director: James Neilson
Teleplay: Sarett Rudley, from a story by A A Milne
Director: Sir Cedric Hardwicke, Hugh Marlowe

Martha Mason, Movie Star
Director: Justus Addiss
Teleplay: Robert C Dennis
Cast: Vinton Hayworth, Judith Evelyn, Robert Emhardt

The West Warlock Time Capsule
Director: Justus Addiss
Teleplay: Marian Cockrell
Cast: Mildred Dunnock, Henry Jones

Father and Son
Director: Herschel Daugherty
Teleplay: James P Cavanagh, from a story by Robert Burke
Cast: Edmund Gwenn, Charles Davis, Frederic Warlock

The Indestructible Mr Weems
Director: Justus Addiss
Cast: Ted Newton, Russell Collins, Robert Middleton

A Little Sleep
Director: Paul Henreid
Teleplay: Robert C Dennis
Cast: Vic Morrow, Barbara Cook

The Dangerous People
Director: Robert Stevens
Teleplay: Francis Cockrell
Cast: Albert Salmi, Ken Clarke, Robert H Harris

The Glass Eye
Director: Robert Stevens (Emmy winner)
Teleplay: Stirling Silliphant, from a story by John Keir
Cast: Jessica Tandy, William Shatner, Tom Conway

The Mail Order Prophet
Director: James Neilson
Teleplay: Robert C Dennis
Cast: E G Marshall, Jack Klugman

The Perfect Crime
Director: Alfred Hitchcock
Teleplay: Sterling Silliphant, from a story by Ben Ray Redman
Cast: James Gregory, Vincent Price, John Zaremba, Marianne Stewart, Gavin Gordon

Heart of Gold
Director: Robert Stevens
Teleplay: James P Cavanagh, from a story by Henry Slesar
Cast: Nehemiah Persoff, Mildred Dunnock, Darryl Hickman

Silent Witness
Director: Paul Henreid
Teleplay: Robert C Dennis
Cast: Patricia Hitchcock, Dolores Hart, Don Taylor

Reward to Finder
Director: James Neilson
Teleplay: Frank Gabrielson
Cast: Oscar Homolka, Claude Akins, Jo Van Fleet

Enough Rope for Two
Director: Paul Henreid
Teleplay: Joel Murcott
Cast: Steve Brodie, Jean Hagen, Steven Hill

Last Request
Director: Paul Henreid
Teleplay: Joel Marcott
Cast: Harry Guardino, Hugh Marlowe

The Young One
Director: Robert Altman
Teleplay: Sarett Rudley
Cast: Carol Lynley, Vince Edwards

The Diplomatic Corpse
Director: Paul Henreid
Teleplay: Robert C Harris, Alec Coppel
Cast: Peter Lorre, George Peppard

The Deadly
Director: Don Taylor
Teleplay: Robert C Dennis
Cast: Phyllis Thaxter, Craig Stevens

Miss Paisley's Cat
Director: Marian Cockrell
Teleplay: Marian Cockrell, from a story by Roy Vickers
Cast: Raymond Bailey, Dorothy Stickney

Night of the Execution
Director: Bernard Schoenfeld
Teleplay: Bernard Schoenfeld, from a story by Henry Slesar
Cast: Pat Hingle, Russell Collins

The Percentage
Director: James Neilson
Teleplay: Bernard Shoenfeld
Cast: Carmen Mathews, Alex Nicol, Nita Talbot

Together
Director: Robert Altman
Teleplay: Robert C Dennis, from a story by Alec Coppel
Cast: Joseph Cotten, Christine White

Sylvia
Director: Herschel Daugherty
Teleplay: James P Cavanagh, from a story by Ira Levin
Cast: Ann Todd, John McIntire

The Motive
Director: Robert Stevens
Cast: Skip Homeier, William Redfield, Carmen Mathews

Miss Bracegirdle Does Her Duty
Director: Marian Cockrell
Teleplay: Marian Cockrell, from a story by Stacy Aumonier
Cast: Mildred Natwick, Gavin Muir

The Equalizer
Director: James Neilson
Teleplay: Robert C Dennis
Cast: Leif Erickson, Martin Balsam

On the Nose
Director: James Neilson
Teleplay: Irving Elman
Cast: David Opatoshu, Carl Betz, Jan Sterling

Guest for Breakfast
Director: Paul Henreid
Teleplay: James P Cavanagh, B Guilford
Cast: Joan Tetzel, Scott McKay

The Return of the Hero
Director: Herschel Daugherty
Teleplay: Andrew Solt, Sterling Silliphant
Cast: Jacques Bergerac, Susan Kohner

The Right Kind of House
Director: Don Taylor
Teleplay: Robert C Dennis, from a story by Henry Slesar
Cast: Jeanette Nolan, Robert Emhardt

Foghorn
Director: Robert Stevens
Teleplay: Frank Gabrielson, from a story by Gertrude Atherton
Cast: Michael Rennie, Bartlett Robinson, Barbara Bel Geddes

Fight to the East
Director: Arthur Hiller
Teleplay: Joel Murcott
Cast: Anthony George, Gary Merrill, Patricia Cutts

Bull in a China Shop
Director: James Neilson
Teleplay: Sarett Rudley
Cast: Dennis Morgan, Estelle Winwood, Ellen Corby, Elizabeth Patterson, Ida Moore

Disappearing Trick
Director: Arthur Hiller
Teleplay: Kathleen Hite, from a story by Victor Canning
Cast: Robert Horton, Raymond Bailey, Betsy Von Furstenberg

Lamb to the Slaughter
Director: Alfred Hitchcock
Teleplay: Roald Dahl, based on a story by Roald Dahl
Cast: Barbara Bel Geddes, Harold Stone, Robert C Ross, Allan Lane, Ken Clark

Fatal Figures
Director: Don Taylor
Teleplay: Robert C Dennis
Cast: John McGiver, Vivian Nathan

Death Sentence
Director: Paul Henreid
Teleplay: Joel Murcott
Cast: James Best, Katherine Bard, Steve Brodie

The Festive Season
Director: Arthur Hiller
Teleplay: James P Cavanagh
Cast: Carmen Mathews, Edmon Ryan

Listen! Listen!
Director: Don Taylor

Teleplay: Bernard Shoenfeld
Cast: Adam Williams, Edgar Stehli, Dayton Lummis

Post Mortem
Director: Arthur Hiller
Teleplay: Robert C Dennis, from a story by Cornell Woolrich
Cast: Steve Forest, Edgar Peterson, Joanna Moore

The Crocodile Case
Director: Don Taylor
Teleplay: Robert C Dennis, from a story by Roy Vickers
Cast: Hazel Court, Denholm Elliott

Dip in the Pool
Director: Alfred Hitchcock
Teleplay: Francis Cockrell, from a story by Roald Dahl
Cast: Fay Wray, Keenan Wynn, Louise Platt, Philip Bourneuf, Doreen Lang

The Safe Place
Director: James Neilson
Teleplay: Michael Hogan
Cast: Robert H Harris, Wendell Holmes, Jerry Paris

The Canary Sedan
Director: James Neilson
Teleplay: Sterling Silliphant, from a story by Ann Bridge
Cast: Jessica Tandy, Owen Cunningham, Murray Matheson, Gavin Muir

The Impromptu Murder
Director: Paul Henreid
Teleplay: Francis Cockrell, from a story by Roy Vickers
Cast: Hume Cronyn, Doris Lloyd, Valerie Cossart

Little White Frock
Director: Herschel Daugherty
Teleplay: Stirling Silliphant, from a story by Stacy Aumonier
Cast: Julie Adams, Herbert Marshall

Poison
Director: Alfred Hitchcock
Teleplay: Casey Robinson, from a story by Roald Dahl
Cast: Arnold Moss, Wendell Corey, James Donald, Weaver Levy

Don't Interrupt
Director: Robert Stevens
Teleplay: Sidney Carroll
Cast: Cloris Leachman, Chill Wills, Biff McGuire

The Jokester
Director: Arthur Hiller
Teleplay: Bernard Schoenfeld, from a story by Robert Arthur
Cast: Roscoe Ates, Albert Salmi, James Coburn

The Crooked Road
Director: Paul Henreid
Teleplay: William Fay
Cast: Richard Kiley, Patricia Breslin, Walter Matthau

The $2,000,000 Defense
Director: Norman Lloyd
Teleplay: William Fay
Cast: Lori March, Barry Sullivan, Leslie Nielsen

Design for Loving
Director: Robert Stevens
Teleplay: Ray Bradbury
Cast: Barbara Baxley, Norman Lloyd, Marian Seldes

A Man with a Problem
Director: Robert Stevens
Teleplay: Joel Murcott
Cast: Ken Lynch, Gary Merrill, Mark Richman, Elizabeth Montgomery

Safety for the Witness
Director: Norman Lloyd
Teleplay: William Fay
Cast: Doris Lloyd, Art Carney, Robert Bray, James Westerfield

Murder Me Twice
Director: David Swift
Teleplay: Irving Elman
Cast: Alan Marshall, Phyllis Thaxter, Tom Helmore

Tea Time
Director: Robert Stevens
Teleplay: Kathleen Hite
Cast: Marsha Hunt, Murray Matheson, Margaret Leighton

And the Desert Shall Blossom
Director: Arthur Hiller
Teleplay: Bernard Schoenfeld
Cast: Ben Johnson, William Demarest, Roscoe Ates

Mrs Herman and Mrs Fenimore
Director: Arthur Hiller
Teleplay: Robert C Dennis
Cast: Mary Astor, Russell Collins, Doro Merande

Six People, No Music
Director: Norman Lloyd
Teleplay: Richard Berg, from a story by Garson Kanin
Cast: Howard Smith, John McGiver

The Morning After
Director: Herschel Daugherty
Teleplay: Rose Simon Kohn, Robert C Dennis
Cast: Robert Alda, Fay Wray, Jeanette Nolan, Dorothy Provine

A Personal Matter
Director: Paul Henreid
Teleplay: Joel Murcott, from a story by Brett Halliday
Cast: Wayne Morris, Frank Silvera, Joe Maross

Out There, Darkness
Director: Paul Henreid
Teleplay: Bernard Schoenfeld
Cast: Frank Albertson, Bette Davis, James Congdon

Total Loss
Director: Don Taylor
Teleplay: J E Selby
Cast: Barbara Lord, Nancy Olson, Ralph Meeker

The Last Dark Step
Director: Herschel Daugherty
Teleplay: William Fay
Cast: Robert Horton, Fay Spain

The Morning of the Bride
Director: Arthur Hiller
Teleplay: Kathleen Hite
Cast: Patricia Hitchcock, Barbara Bel Geddes, Don Dubbins

The Diamond Necklace
Director: Herschel Daugherty
Teleplay: Sarett Rudley
Cast: Betsy Von Furstenberg, Claude Rains, Alan Hewitt, Stephen Benassy, Selmer Jackson, Peter Walker, Dorothea Lord, Norman DuPont

Relative Value
Director: Paul Almond
Teleplay: Francis Cockrell, from a story by Milward Kennedy
Cast: Torin Thatcher, Denholm Elliott, Tom Conway, Frederic Warlock

The Right Price
Director: Arthur Hiller
Teleplay: Bernard Schoenfeld
Cast: Eddie Foy Jr, Allyn Joslyn

I'll Take Care of You
Director: Robert Stevens
Teleplay: William Fay
Cast: Elisabeth Fraser, Ida Moore, Ralph Meeker, Russell Collins

The Avon Emeralds
Director: Robert Stevens
Teleplay: William Fay
Cast: Hazel Court, Alan Napier, Roger Moore

The Kind Waitress
Director: Paul Henreid

Teleplay: William O' Farrell
Cast: Olive Deering, Celia Lovsky, Rick Jason

Cheap is Cheap
Director: Bretaigne Windust
Teleplay: Albert S Lewin, Burt Styler
Cast: Dennis Day, Alice Backes

The Waxwork
Director: Robert Stevens
Teleplay: Casey Robinson, from a story by M Burrage
Cast: Everett Sloan, Barry Sullivan

The Impossible Dream
Director: Robert Stevens
Teleplay: Meade Roberts
Cast: Mary Astor, Franchot Tone, Carmen Mathews

Banquo's Chair
Director: Alfred Hitchcock
Teleplay: Francis Cockrell, from a story by Rupert Croft-Cooke
Cast: John Williams, Kenneth Haig, Max Adrian, Reginald Gardiner, Tom P Dillon

A Night With the Boys
Director: John Brahm
Teleplay: Bernard Schoenfeld
Cast: Joyce Meadows, John Smith

Your Witness
Director: Norman Lloyd
Teleplay: William Fay
Cast: Brian Hutton, Brian Keith, Leora Dana

The Human Interest Story
Director: Norman Lloyd
Teleplay: Frederic Brown
Cast: Steve McQueen, Tyler McVey, Arthur Hill

The Dusty Drawer
Director: Herschel Daugherty
Teleplay: Halsted Welles
Cast: Dick York, Philip Coolidge

Curtains for Me
Director: Leonard Horn
Teleplay: Robert C Dennis, from a story by Anthony Gilbert
Cast: Robert Webber, Kent Smith, Madge Kennedy, Jane Greer

Touché
Director: John Brahm
Teleplay: William Fay
Cast: Hugh Marlowe, Robert Morse, Paul Douglas, King Calder

Invitation to an Accident
Director: Don Taylor
Teleplay: Robert C Dennis
Cast: Gary Merrill, Joanna Moore

Arthur
Director: Alfred Hitchcock
Teleplay: James P Cavanagh, based on a story by Arthur Williams
Cast: Patrick Macnee, Laurence Harvey, Robert Douglas, Hazel Court, Barry G Harvey

The Crystal Trench
Director: Alfred Hitchcock
Teleplay: Sterling Silliphant, from a story by A E W Mason
Cast: Patricia Owens, James Donald, Patrick Macnee, Ben Astar, Werner Kemperer

Appointment at Eleven
Director: Robert Stevens
Teleplay: Evan Hunter
Cast: Clint Kimbrough, Michael J Pollard, Clu Gulager

Coyote Moon
Director: Herschel Daugherty
Teleplay: Harold Swanton
Cast: Macdonald Carey, Colin Wilcox, Edgar Buchanan

No Pain
Director: Norman Lloyd
Teleplay: William Fay
Cast: Joanna Moore, Brian Keith

Anniversary Gift
Director: Norman Lloyd
Teleplay: Harold Swanton, from a story by John Collier
Cast: Harry Morgan, Jackie Coogan, Barbara Baxley

Dry Run
Director: John Brahm
Teleplay: Bill S Ballinger
Cast: Walter Matthau, Robert Vaughn

The Blessington Method
Director: Herschel Daugherty
Teleplay: Halsted Welles
Cast: Elizabeth Patterson, Henry Jones, Dick York

Dead Weight
Director: Stuart Rosenberg
Teleplay: Jerry Stohl
Cast: Joseph Cotten, Julie Adams

Special Delivery
Director: Norman Lloyd
Teleplay: Ray Bradbury
Cast: Beatrice Straight, Steve Dunne

Road Hog
Director: Stuart Rosenberg
Teleplay: Bill S Ballinger
Cast: Raymond Massey, Richard Chamberlain, Robert Emhardt

The Specialty of the House
Director: Robert Stevens
Teleplay: Victor Wolfson
Cast: Robert Morley

An Occurrence at Owl Creek Bridge
Director: Robert Stevenson
Teleplay: Harold Swanton
Cast: Juano Hernandez, Ronald Howard, James Coburn

Graduating Class
Director: Herschel Daugherty
Teleplay: Sterling Silliphant
Cast: Gigi Perreau, Wendy Hiller

Man from the South
Director: Norman Lloyd
Teleplay: William Fay, from the story by Roald Dahl
Cast: Steve McQueen, Peter Lorre

The Ikon Elijah
Director: Paul Almond
Teleplay: Norah Perez, Victor Wolfson
Cast: Sam Jaffe, Oscar Homolka

The Cure
Director: Herschel Daugherty
Teleplay: Michael Pertwee
Cast: Cara Williams, Nehemiah Persoff

Backward, Turn Backward
Director: Stuart Rosenberg
Teleplay: Charles Beaumont
Cast: Paul Maxwell, Tom Tully, Alan Baxter

Not the Running Type
Director: Arthur Hiller
Teleplay: Jerry Stohl
Director: Paul Hartman, Wendell Holmes, Robert Bray

The Day of the Bullet
Director: Norman Lloyd
Teleplay: Bill S Ballinger
Cast: Barry Gordon, John Graven, Glenn Walken

Hitch Hike
Director: Paul Henreid
Teleplay: Bernard Schoenfeld
Cast: John McIntire, Read Morgan, Suzanne Pleshette, Robert Morse

Across the Threshold
Director: Arthur Hiller
Teleplay: Charlotte Armstrong
Cast: Barbara Baxley, George Grizzard. Patricia Collinge

Craig's Will
Director: Gene Reynolds
Teleplay: Albert E Levin, Burt Styler
Cast: Dick Van Dyke, Paul Stewart, Stella Stevens

Mme Mystery
Director: John Brahm
Teleplay: William Fay, from a story by Robert Bloch
Cast: Joby Baker, Audrey Totter, Harp McGuire

The Little Man Who Was There
Director: George Stevens, Jr.
Teleplay: Gordon Russell, Larry Ward
Cast: Clegg Hoyt, Norman Lloyd, Arch Johnson, Read Morgan, Robert Armstrong

Mother, May I Go Out to Swim?
Director: Herschel Daugherty
Teleplay: James P Cavanagh, from a story by Q Patrick
Cast: Jessie Royce Landis, William Shatner, Gia Scala

The Cuckoo Clock
Director: John Brahm
Teleplay: Robert Bloch
Cast: Patricia Hitchcock, Beatrice Straight, Fay Spain, Don Beddoe

Forty Detectives Later
Director: Arthur Hiller
Teleplay: Henry Slesar
Cast: Jack Weston, James Franciscus

The Hero
Director: John Brahm
Teleplay: Bill S. Ballinger, from a story by H DeVere Stackpoole
Cast: Irene Tedrow, Oscar Homolka

Insomnia
Director: John Brahm
Teleplay: Henry Slesar
Cast: Al Hodge, Dennis Weaver, James Milhollin

I Can Take Care of Myself
Director: Alan Crosland Jr
Teleplay: Thomas Grant
Cast: Linda Lawson, Pat Harrington, Myron McCormick

One Grave Too Many
Director: Arthur Hiller
Teleplay: Eli Jerome
Cast: Jeremy Slate, Biff Elliott, Neile Adams

Party Line
Director: Hilton A Green
Teleplay: Eli Jerome
Cast: Judy Canova, Arch Johnson

Cell 227
Director: Paul Henreid
Teleplay: Bill S Ballinger
Cast: James Westerfield, Brian Keith

The Schartz-Metterlume Method
Director: Richard Dunlap
Teleplay: Marian Cockrel, from a story by Saki
Cast: Patricia Hitchcock, Elspeth March, Hermione Gingold, Doris Lloyd, Norma Varden, Tom Conway

Letter of Credit
Director: Paul Henreid
Teleplay: Helen Neilsen
Cast: Theodore Newton, Bob Sweeney, Robert Bray

Escape to Sonoita
Director: Stuart Rosenberg
Teleplay: James A Howard, Bill S Ballinger
Cast: Burt Reynolds, James Bell

Hooked
Director: Norman Lloyd
Teleplay: Thomas Grant
Cast: Anne Francis, Robert Horton

Mrs Bixby and the Colonel's Coat
Director: Alfred Hitchcock
Teleplay: Halsted Welles, from the story by Roald Dahl
Cast: Audrey Meadows, Les Tremayne, Stephen Chase, Sally Hughes, Bernie Hamilton

The Doubtful Doctor
Director: Arthur Hiller
Teleplay: Jerry Stohl
Cast: Michael Burns, Dick York, Gena Rowlands

A Very Moral Theft
Director: Norman Lloyd
Teleplay: Allan Gordon
Cast: Walter Matthau, Sam Gilman, Karl Swenson, Betty Field

The Contest of Aaron Gold
Director: Norman Lloyd
Teleplay: William Fay
Cast: Frank Maxwell, Barry Gordon, Sydney Pollack

The Five Forty-Eight
Director: John Brahm
Teleplay: Charlotte Armstrong, from the story by John Cheever
Cast: Zachary Scott, Phyllis Thaxter

Pen Pal
Director: John Brahm
Teleplay: Hilary Murray
Cast: Clu Gulager, Roy Montgomery, Katherine Squire

Outlaw in Town
Director: Herschel Daugherty
Teleplay: Michael Fessier
Cast: Ricardo Montalban, Arch Johnson, Constance Ford

Oh, Youth and Beauty!
Director: Norman Lloyd
Teleplay: Halsted Welles, from a story by John Cheever
Cast: David Lewis, Gary Merrill, Patricia Breslin

The Money
Director: Ida Lupino
Cast: Doris Dowling, Wolfe Barzell

Sybilla
Director: Ida Lupino
Teleplay: Charlotte Armstrong
Cast: Barbara Bel Geddes, Alexander Scourby

The Man with Two Faces
Director: Stuart Rosenberg
Teleplay: Henry Slesar
Cast: Spring Byington, Bethel Leslie

The Baby Blue Expression
Director: Arthur Hiller
Teleplay: Helen Nielsen
Cast: Peter Walker, Sarah Marshall

The Man Who Found the Money
Director: Alan Crosland Jr
Teleplay: Allan Gordon
Cast: Lucy Prentiss, R G Armstrong, Rod Cameron, Arthur Hill

Change of Heart
Director: Robert Florey
Teleplay: Robert Bloch
Cast: Anne Helm, Abraham Sofaer, Nicholas Pryor

Summer Shade
Director: Ida Lupino
Teleplay: Harold Swanton
Cast: John Hoyt, Julie Adams, James Franciscus

A Crime for Mothers
Director: Ida Lupino
Teleplay: Henry Selsar
Cast: Howard McNear, Patricia Smith, Biff Elliott, Claire Trevor

The Last Escape
Director: Paul Henreid

Teleplay: Henry Slesar
Cast: Jan Sterling, Keenan Wynn

The Greatest Monster of them All
Director: Robert Stevens
Teleplay: Robert Bloch
Cast: Robert H Harris

The Landlady
Director: Paul Henreid
Teleplay: Robert Bloch, from a story by Roald Dahl
Cast: Laurie Main, Dean Stockwell, Patricia Collinge

The Throwback
Director: John Brahm
Teleplay: Henry Slesar
Cast: Scott Marlowe, Murray Matheson, Joyce Meadows

The Kiss-Off
Director: Alan Crosland Jr
Teleplay: Talmadge Powell
Cast: Rip Torn, Bert Freed, Mary Munday

The Horseplayer
Director: Alfred Hitchcock
Teleplay: Henry Slesar, based on a story by Henry Slesar
Cast: Claude Rains, Ed Gardner, Percy Helton, Kenneth MacKenna, William Newell, David Carle, Ada Murphy

Incident in a Small Jail
Director: Norman Lloyd
Teleplay: Henry Slesar
Cast: John Fiedler, Ron Nicholas, Richard Jaekel

A Woman's Help
Director: Arthur Hiller
Teleplay: Henry Slesar
Cast: Geraldine Fitzgerald, Scott McKay

Museum Piece
Director: Paul Henreid
Teleplay: Harold Swanton
Cast: Myron McCormick, Bert Convy, Larry Gates

Coming, Mama
Director: George Stevens Jr
Teleplay: James P Cavanagh
Cast: Don DeFore, Eileen Heckart

Deathmate
Director: Alan Crosland Jr
Teleplay: Bill S Ballinger
Cast: Lee Philips, Gia Scala, Les Tremayne

Gratitude
Director: Alan Crosland Jr
Teleplay: William Fay
Cast: Clegg Hoyt, Peter Falk, Paul Hartman

The Pearl Necklace
Director: Don Weis
Teleplay: Peggy Shaw, Lou Shaw
Cast: Ernest Truex, Hazel Court, Jack Cassidy

You Can't Trust a Man
Director: Paul Henreid
Teleplay: Helen Nielsen
Cast: Polly Bergen, Frank Albertson, Joe Maross

The Gloating Place
Director: Alan Crosland Jr
Teleplay: Robert Bloch
Cast: Susan Harrison, King Calder, Henry Brandt

Self-Defense
Director: Paul Henreid
Teleplay: John T Kelley
Cast: Selmer Jackson, George Nader, Audrey Totter

A Secret Life
Director: Don Weis
Teleplay: Jerry Stohl, based on a story by Nicholas Monsarrat
Cast: Arte Johnson, Ronald Howard, Patricia Donahue

Servant Problem
Director: Alan Crosland Jr
Teleplay: Henry Slesar
Cast: Jo Van Fleet, John Emery

Coming Home
Director: Alf Kjellin
Teleplay: Henry Slesar
Cast: Gil Perkins, Crahan Denton, Jeanette Nolan

Final Arrangements
Director: Gordon Hessler
Teleplay: Robert Arthur
Cast: Slim Pickens, Martin Balsam

Make My Death Bed
Director: Arthur Hiller
Teleplay: Henry A Cogge
Cast: Diana Van Der Vlis, James Best, Biff Elliott, Jocelyn Brando

Ambition
Director: Paul Henreid
Teleplay: Joel Murcott
Cast: Leslie Nielsen, Harry Landers, Harold Stone, Ann Robinson

The Hat Box
Director: Alan Crosland Jr
Teleplay: Henry Slesar
Cast: Paul Ford, Billy Gray

Bang! You're Dead
Director: Alfred Hitchcock
Teleplay: Harold Swanton, based on a story by Margery Vosper
Cast: Billy Mumy, Marta Kristen, Biff Elliott, Lucy Prentiss, Steve Dunne, Kelly Flynn

Maria
Director: Boris Sagal
Teleplay: John Collier, from a story by John Wyndham
Cast: Kreg Martin, Norman Lloyd, Nita Talbot

Cop for a Day
Director: Paul Henreid
Teleplay: Henry Slesar
Cast: Susan Brown, Walter Matthau, Glenn Cannon

Keep Me Company
Director: Alan Crosland Jr
Teleplay: Henry Slesar
Cast: Jack Ging, Anne Francis, Edmund Hashim

Beta Delta Gamma
Director: Alan Crosland Jr
Teleplay: Calvin Clements
Cast: Burt Brinkerhoff, Severn Darden

You Can't Be a Little Girl All Your Life
Director: Norman Lloyd
Teleplay: Helen Nielsen, from a story by Stanley Ellin
Cast: Ted de Corsia, Dick York, Caroline Kearney

The Old Pro
Director: Paul Henreid
Teleplay: Calvin Clements
Cast: Sarah Shane, Richard Conte

I, Spy
Director: Norman Lloyd
Teleplay: John Collier, based on the play by John Mortimer
Cast: Eric Barker, Kay Walsh, Cecil Parker, William Kendall

Services Rendered
Director: Paul Henreid
Teleplay: William Link, Richard Levinson
Cast: Steve Dunne, Hugh Marlowe

The Right Kind of Medicine
Director: Alan Crosland Jr
Teleplay: Henry Slesar
Cast: Robert Redford, Russell Collins

A Jury of Her Peers
Director: Robert Florey
Teleplay: James P Cavanagh
Cast: Robert Bray, Ann Harding

The Silk Petticoat
Director: John Newland
Teleplay: Halsted Welles, Norman Ginsberg, from a story by Joseph Shearing
Cast: Michael Rennie, Antoinette Bower

Bad Actor
Director: John Newland
Teleplay: Robert Bloch
Cast: Robert Duvall, Carole Eastman, David Lewis

The Door Without a Key
Director: Herschel Daugherty
Teleplay: Irving Elman, based on a story by Norman Daniels
Cast: Billy Mumy, Claude Rains, John Larch, Connie Gilchrist, David Fresco, Sam Gilman, Andy Romano, Jeff Parker, Jimmy Hawkins

The Case of M J H
Director: Alan Crosland Jr
Teleplay: Henry Slesar
Cast: Barbara Baxley, Richard Gaines, Robert Loggia

The Faith of Aaron Menefee
Director: Norman Lloyd
Teleplay: Ray Bradbury, based on a story by Stanley Ellin
Cast: Olan Soule, Robert Armstrong, Sidney Blackmer, Andrew Prine

The Woman Who Wanted to Live
Director: Alan Crosland Jr
Teleplay: Bryce Walton
Cast: Charles Bronson, Lola Albright

Strange Miracle
Director: Norman Lloyd
Teleplay: Halsted Welles
Cast: David Opatoshu, Fran De Kova

The Test
Director: Boris Sagal
Teleplay: Henry Slesar
Cast: Brian Keith, Eduardo Ciannelli, David Opatoshu

Burglar Proof
Director: John Newland
Teleplay: Henry Slesar
Cast: Whit Bissell, Robert Webber, Paul Hartman

The Big Score
Director: Boris Sagal
Teleplay: Bryce Walton
Cast: Evan Evans, Tom Gilleran, Rafael Campos

Profit Sharing Plan
Director: Bernard Girard

Teleplay: William Link, Richard Levinson
Cast: Rebecca Sand, Henry Jones, Ruth Storey

Apex
Director: Alan Crosland Jr
Teleplay: John T Kelley
Cast: Patricia Breslin, George Kane, Mark Miller, Vivienne Segal

The Last Remains
Director: Leonard Horn
Teleplay: Henry Slesar
Cast: Ed Gardner, John Fiedler

Ten O'Clock Tiger
Director: Bernard Girard
Teleplay: William Fay
Cast: Karl Lukas, Frankie Darro, Robert Keith

Act of Faith
Director: Bernard Girard
Teleplay: Nicholas Monsaratt, based on a story by Eric Ambler
Cast: Dennis King, George Grizzard

The Kerry Blue
Director: Paul Henreid
Teleplay: Henry Slesar
Cast: Carmen Mathews, Rob Reiner, Gene Evans

The Matched Pearl
Director: Bernard Girard
Teleplay: Henry Slesar
Cast: Ernest Truex, John Ireland

What Frightened You, Fred?
Director: Paul Henreid
Teleplay: Joel Murcott
Cast: Adam Williams, Ed Asner, R G Armstrong

Most Likely to Succeed
Director: Richard Whorf
Teleplay: Henry Slesar
Cast: Joanna Moore, Howard Morris, Jack Carter

Victim Four
Director: Paul Henreid
Teleplay: Talmadge Powell
Cast: John Lupton, Peggy Ann Garner, Paul Comi

Golden Opportunity
Director: Robert Florey
Teleplay: Bryce Walton, Henry Slesar
Cast: Rebecca Sand, Richard Long, Colleen Gray

The Twelve-Hour Caper
Director: John Newland
Teleplay: Harold Swanton

Cast: Sarah Marshall, Dick York

The Children of Alda Nuova
Director: Robert Florey
Teleplay: Robert Wallstein
Cast: Christopher Dark, Jack Carson

First Class Honeymoon
Director: Don Weis
Teleplay: Henry Slesar
Cast: Marjorie Bennett, Robert Webber, Jeremy Slate, John Abbott

The Big Kick
Director: Alan Crosland Jr
Teleplay: Robert Bloch
Cast: Wayne Rogers, Anne Helm, Brian Hutton

Where Beauty Lies
Director: Robert Florey
Teleplay: James P Cavanagh
Cast: Cloris Leachman, George Nader

The Sorcerer's Apprentice
Director: Joseph Leytis
Teleplay: Robert Bloch
Cast: Diana Dors, Brandon De Wilde, Larry Kert, David J Stewart

THE ALFRED HITCHCOCK HOUR

Piece of the Action
Director: Bernard Girard
Cast: Gig Young, Robert Redford

Don't Look Behind You
Director: John Brahm
Cast: Jeffrey Hunter, Vera Miles

Night of the Owl
Director: Alan Crosland Jr
Cast: Philip Coolidge, Brian Keith

I Saw the Whole Thing
Director: Alfred Hitchcock
Teleplay: Henry Slesar, based on a story by Henry Cecil
Cast: Kent Smith, John Forsythe, John Fiedler, Philip Ober, William Newell

Captive Audience
Director: Alf Kjellin
Cast: James Mason, Ed Nelson

Final Vow
Director: Norman Lloyd
Cast: Carol Lynley, Clu Gulager

Annabel
Director: Paul Henreid
Cast: Dean Stockwell, Susan Oliver

House Guest
Director: Alan Crosland Jr
Cast: Billy Mumy, Macdonald Carey

The Black Curtain
Director: Sydney Pollack
Cast: Lee Philips, Richard Basehart

Day of the Reckoning
Director: Jerry Hopper
Cast: Claude Akins, Louis Hayward

Ride the Nightmare
Director: Bernard Griard
Cast: Olan Soule, Gail Bonney

Hangover
Director: Bernard Girard
Cast: Jayne Mansfield, Tony Randall

Bonfire
Director: Joseph Pevney
Cast: Craig Duncan, Peter Falk

The Tender Poisoner
Director: Leonard Horn
Cast: Howard Duff, Dan Dailey

The 31st of February
Director: Alf Kjellin
Cast: David Wayne, William Conrad

What Really Happened
Director: Jack Smith
Cast: Gladys Cooper, Anne Francis

Forecast: Low Clouds and Coastal Fog
Director: Charles Haas
Cast: Dan O'Herlihy, Inger Stevens

A Tangled Web
Director: Alf Kjellin
Cast: Robert Redford, Barry Morse

To Catch a Butterfly
Director: David Lowell Rich
Cast: Bradford Dillman

The Paragon
Director: Jack Smight
Cast: Joan Fontaine, Gary Merrill

I'll Be the Judge, I'll Be the Jury
Director: James Sheldon
Cast: Albert Salmi, Peter Graves

Diagnosis: Danger
Director: Sydney Pollack
Cast: Michael Parks, Charles McGraw

The Lonely Hour
Director: Jack Smight
Cast: Juanita Moore, Nancy Kelly

The Star Juror
Director: Herschel Daugherty
Cast: Betty Field, Dean Jagger

The Long Silence
Director: Robert Douglas
Cast: Michael Rennie, Phyllis Thaxter

An Out for Oscar
Director: Bernard Girard
Cast: Larry Storch, Linda Christian

Death and the Joyful Woman
Director: John Brahm
Cast: Gilbert Roland, Laraine Day

Last Seen Wearing Blue Jeans
Director: Alan Crosland Jr
Cast: Katherine Crawford, Randy Boone

The Dark Pool
Director: Jack Smight
Cast: Madlyn Rhue, Anthony George

Dear Uncle George
Director: Joseph Newman
Cast: Gene Barry, Dabney Coleman

Run for Doom
Director: Bernard Girard
Cast: Diana Dors, John Gavin

Death of a Cop
Director: Joseph Newman
Cast: Victor Jory, Richard Jaeckel

A Home Away from Home
Director: Herschel Daugherty
Music: Bernard Herrmann
Cast: Ray Milland, Claire Griswald

A Nice Touch
Director: Joseph Pevney
Cast: Anne Baxter, Harry Townes

Terror at Northfield
Director: Harvey Hart
Music: Bernard Herrmann
Cast: Jacqueline Scott, Dick York

You'll Be the Death of Me
Director: Robert Douglas
Music: Bernard Herrmann
Cast: Barry Atwater, Robert Loggia

Blood Bargain
Director: Bernard Girard
Cast: Richard Kiley, Anne Francis

Nothing Ever Happens in Linvale
Director: Herschel Daugherty
Music: Bernard Herrmann
Cast: Fess Parker, Gary Merrill

Starring the Defense
Director: Joseph Pevney
Cast: Teno Pollick, Richard Basehart

The Cadaver
Director: Alf Kjellin
Music: Bernard Herrmann (stock)
Cast: Joby Baker, Michael Parks

The Dividing Wall
Director: Bernard Girard
Cast: Simon Scott, James Gregory

Goodbye, George
Director: Robert Stevens
Cast: Patricia Barry, Robert Culp

How to Get Rid of Your Wife
Director: Alf Kjellin
Cast: Bob Newhart, Bill Quinn

Three Wives Too Many
Director: Joseph Newman
Cast: Dan Duryea, Teresa Wright

The Magic Shop
Director: Robert Stevens
Cast: Leslie Nielsen, David Opatoshu

Beyond the Sea of Death
Director: Alf Kjellin
Music: Bernard Herrmann (stock)
Cast: Diana Hyland, Mildred Dunnock

Night Caller
Director: Alf Kjellin
Music: Bernard Herrmann (stock)
Cast: Bruce Dern, David White

The Evil of Adelaid Winters
Director: Laslo Benedek
Cast: John Larkin, Kim Hunter

The Jar
Director: Norman Lloyd
Music: Bernard Herrmann
Cast: James Best

Final Escape
Director: William Whitney
Cast: Edd Byrnes, Robert Keith

Murder Case
Director: John Brahm
Cast: Ben Wright, John Cassavetes

Anyone for Murder?
Director: Leo Penn
Music: Bernard Herrmann (stock)
Cast: Dick Dawson, Barry Nelson

Beast in View
Director: Joseph Newman
Cast: Joan Hackett, Kevin McCarthy

Behind the Locked Door
Director: Robert Douglas
Music: Bernard Herrmann
Cast: James McArthur, Gloria Swanson

A Matter of Murder
Director: David Lowell Rich
Cast: Darren McGavin, Telly Savalas

The Gentleman Caller
Director: Joseph Newman
Cast: Roddy McDowell, Diane Sayer

The Ordeal of Mrs Snow
Director: Robert Stevens
Music: Bernard Herrmann (stock)
Cast: June Vincent, Patricia Collinge

Ten Minutes from Now
Director: Alf Kjellin
Cast: Lou Jacobi, Donnelly Rhodes

Sign of Satan
Director: Robert Douglas
Cast: Gia Scala, Christopher Lee

Who Needs an Enemy?
Director: Harry Morgan
Cast: Richard Anderson, Steven Hill

Bed of Roses
Director: Philip Leacock

Music: Bernard Herrmann (stock)
Cast: Torin Thatcher, Patrick O'Neal

Second Verdict
Director: Lewis Teague
Cast: Frank Gorshin, Martin Landau

Isabel
Director: Ralph Kjellin
Music: Bernard Herrmann (stock)
Cast: Les Tremayne, Bradford Dillman

Body in the Barn
Director: Joseph Newman
Music: Bernard Herrmann
Cast: Kent Smith, Lillian Gish

The Return of Verge Likens
Director: Arnold Laven
Music: Bernard Herrmann (stock)
Cast: Peter Fond, Sam Reese

Change of Address
Director: David Friedkin
Music: Bernard Herrmann
Cast: Phyllis Thaxter, Arthur Kennedy

Water's Edge
Director: Bernard Girard
Music: Bernard Herrmann
Cast: Ann Sothern, John Cassavetes

The Life Work of Juan Diaz
Director: Norman Lloyd
Music: Bernard Herrmann
Cast: Larry Donasin, Alejandro Rey

See the Monkey Dance
Director: Joseph Newman
Cast: Patricia Medina, Efrem Zimbalist Jr

Lonely Place
Director: Harvey Hart
Cast: Bruce Dern, Teresa Wright

The McGregor Affair
Director: David Friedkin
Music: Bernard Herrmann
Cast: John Hoyt, Andrew Duggan

Misadventure
Director: Joseph Newman
Music: Bernard Herrmann
Cast: Lola Albright, George Kennedy

Triumph
Director: Harvey Hart
Cast: Ed Begley, Jeanette Nolan

Memo from Purgatory
Director: Joseph Penvey
Cast: Walter Koenig, James Caan

Consider Her Ways
Director: Robert Stevens
Music: Bernard Herrmann
Cast: Gladys Cooper, Barbara Barrie

The Crimson Witness
Director: David Friedkin
Cast: Alan Baxter, Peter Lawford

Where the Woodbine Twineth
Director: Alf Kjellin
Music: Bernard Herrmann
Cast: Juanita Moore, Margaret Leighton

Final Performance
Director: John Brahm
Music: Bernard Herrmann (stock)
Cast: Franchot Tone, Roger Perry

Thanatos Palace Hotel
Director: Laslo Benedek
Cast: Angie Dickinson, Steven Hill

One of the Family
Director: Joseph Pevney
Cast: Olive Deering, Lilia Skala

An Unlocked Window
Director: Joseph Newman
Music: Bernard Herrmann
Cast: John Kerr, Dana Wynter

The Trap
Director: John Brahm
Music: Bernard Herrmann (stock)
Cast: Anne Francis, Donnelly Rhodes

Wally the Beard
Director: James Brown
Music: Bernard Herrmann
Cast: Larry Blydett, Katherine Squire

Death Scene
Director: Harvey Hart
Music: Bernard Herrmann
Cast: Vera Miles, John Carradine

The Photographer and the Undertaker
Director: Alex March
Music: Bernard Herrmann (stock)
Cast: Harry Townes, Jack Cassidy

Thou Still Un-ravished Bride
Director: David Friedkin

Music: Bernard Herrmann (stock)
Cast: David Carradine, Ron Randell

Completely Foolproof
Director: Alf Kjellin
Music: Bernard Herrmann (stock)
Cast: J D Cannon, Patricia Barry

Power of Attorney
Director: Harvey Hart
Music: Bernard Herrmann (stock)
Cast: Richard Johnson, Geraldine Fitzgerald

The World's Oldest Motive
Director: Joseph Newman
Cast: Henry Jones, Kathleen Freeman

The Monkey's Paw – A Re-telling
Director: Joseph Newman
Cast: Lee Majors, Jane Wyatt

The Second Wife
Director: Joseph Newman
Music: Bernard Herrmann (stock)
Cast: John Anderson, June Lockhart

Night Fever
Director: Herbert Coleman
Music: Bernard Herrmann (stock)
Cast: Colleen Dewhurst, Richard Bull

Off Season
Director: William Friedkin
Music: Bernard Herrmann (stock)
Cast: Tom Drake, John Gavin

Video availability: Universal
DVD availability: Universal
CD availability: *Hitchcock – Master of Mayhem* (Proarte), *Psycho – The Essential Alfred Hitchcock* (Silva Screen), *A History of Hitchcock – Dial M for Murder* (Silva Screen), all of which contain *Funeral March of the Marionette*, aka *The Alfred Hitchcock Theme* by Charles Gounod

ALFRED HITCHCOCK PRESENTS ★
In 1985, *Alfred Hitchcock Presents* was revived on NBC, complete with colourized versions of Hitchcock's intros. Produced by Andrew Mirisch, the series contained many new stories, but several from the old series were made over, including *The Man from the South* (also remade for *Tales of the Unexpected*), *Bang! You're Dead*, *Incident in a Small Jail*, *Night Fever*, *An Unlocked Window* and *Revenge*. Some familiar faces from the Hitchcock back catalogue came along for the ride, including Tippi Hedren, Martin Landau and Kim Novak, as well as such names as Martin Sheen, Andy Garcia, George Lazenbey, Ned Beatty, Jeff Fahey, Anthony Newley, David McCallum, Arsenio Hall, Van Johnson, Lindsay Wagner and Mark Hamill. Directors

included Joel Oliansky, Randa Haines, Fred Walton, Steve de Jarnatt and Tim Burton (who helmed a remake of *The Jar*). The series ran to 80 episodes, moving from NBC to the USA Cable Network after the first 24. Not everyone was keen on the idea, among them Norman Lloyd, who'd been much involved in the original series as an actor, director and producer: 'I wouldn't go near it,' he said of the new series. 'They… took Hitch's lead-ins, put them in colour and used *those*! Disgusting… Terrible idea!' [3] Despite Lloyd's reservations, the series was nevertheless a popular enough time filler. The titles are:

ALFRED HITCHCOCK PRESENTS: THE MOVIE
(which is comprised of four episodes, later shown separately: *Incident in a Small Jail*, *The Man from the South*, *Bang! You're Dead* and *An Unlocked Window*)
Revenge
Night Fever
Wake Me When I'm Dead
Final Escape
The Night Caller
Method Actor
The Human Interest Story
Breakdown
Prisoners
Gigolo
The Gloating Place
The Right Kind of Medicine
Beast in View
A Very Happy Ending
The Canary Sedan
Enough Rope for Two
The Creeper
Happy Birthday
The Jar
Deadly Honeymoon
Four O'Clock
Road Hog
The Initiation
Conversation Over a Corpse
Man on the Bridge
If the Shoe Fits
The Mole
Anniversary Gift
The Impatient Patient
When This Man Dies
The Specialty of the House
Final Twist
Tragedy Tonight
The World's Oldest Motive
Deathmate
Very Careful Rape
Animal Lovers
Prism
A Stolen Heart
Houdini on Channel Four
Killer Takes All
Hippocratic Oath

Prosecutor
If Looks Could Kill
You'll Die Laughing
Murder Party
Twist
User Deadly
Career Move
Full Disclosure
Kandinsky's Vault
There Was a Little Girl…
Twisted Sisters
The Thirteenth Floor
The Hunted (two episodes)
Fogbound
Pen Pal
Ancient Voices
Survival of the Fittest
The Big Spin
Don't Sell Yourself Short
For Art's Sake
Murder in Mind
Mirror, Mirror
Skeleton in the Closet
In the Driver's Seat
Driving Under the Influence
In the Name of Science
Romance Machine
Diamonds Aren't Forever
My Dear Watson
Night Creatures
The Man Who Knew Too Little
Reunion
South by Southeast

ALLEN, JAY PRESSON (1922–   ) American play-wright and screenwriter. She came to films with Hitchcock's *Marnie* (1964), which she was asked to work on following her success with her stage adaptation of Muriel Spark's novel *The Prime of Miss Jean Brodie* (Allen was in fact the film's third writer, following Joseph Stefano and Evan Hunter). Her other plays include *The First Wife* (which was filmed in 1963 as *Wives and Lovers*) and *Tru* (sic), while for the screen she has penned *The Prime of Miss Jean Brodie* (1968), *Cabaret* (1972) and *Prince of the City* (1981), all of which earned her Oscar nominations. She has also executive produced a number of films, including *It's My Turn* (1980) and *Deathtrap* (1982). Her husband was the director Lewis M Allen (1905–1986), best known for *The Uninvited* (1943). **Hitchography:** *Marnie* (1964)

ALLEN, PATRICK (1927–   ) British-born but Canadian-raised supporting actor. Known to television audiences of the 1960s as Richard Crane in the action series *Crane* (1963–1965), Allen is also well known for his commercial appearances and voice-overs, among them a long-running campaign for Barratt Homes. In films in Hollywood from 1953 with *World for Ransom*, Allen's sec-ond screen appearance was as Pearson in Hitchcock's *Dial M for Murder* (1954). His many other appearances include *I Was Monty's Double* (1958), *Puppet on a Chain* (1970), *The Wild Geese* (1978) and *The Sea Wolves* (1980). He also dubbed Leon Greene in *The Devil Rides Out* (1968), and narrated several films, including *Erotic Fantasies* (1971) and *The Sword and the Geisha* (1971). He has been married to the actress Sarah Lawson (1928–   ) since 1956. **Hitchography:** *Dial M for Murder* (1954)

ALLGOOD, SARA (1883–1950) Irish-born actress. Though one of the busiest character actresses working in Britain and, later, in Hollywood, Allgood actually made her film debut in Australia in 1918 in *Just Peggy*. She did-n't work in films again until 1929, when she landed the role of Mrs White in Hitchcock's sound debut, *Blackmail*. Following *To What Red Hell*, also made in 1929, she returned to Hitchcock for his screen adaptation of Sean O'Casey's *Juno and the Paycock* (1930) in which she played the leading role of Juno Boyle, the role she'd created in the original stage production at Dublin's Abbey Theatre, of which she was long a member (her sister, actress Maire O'Neill (1887–1952) was also in the play and film as Mrs Madigan). A slew of films followed, among them *Lily of Killarney* (1934), *Storm in a Teacup* (1937) and *Sixty Glorious Years* (1938). She also popped up in an un-credited cameo in Hitchcock's *Sabotage* (1936). Then, in 1940, she went to Hollywood to appear in *That Hamilton Woman* for pro-ducer-director Alexander Korda, for whom she'd made several films back in Britain. A flourishing career Stateside followed, including appearances in *Dr Jekyll and Mr Hyde* (1941), *How Green Was My Valley* (1941), which earned her a best supporting actress Oscar nomination, *Roxie Hart* (1942), *Jayne Eyre* (1943), *The Spiral Staircase* (1946) and *Cheaper by the Dozen* (1950). She also appeared in the remake of *The Lodger* (1944). She once described Hitchcock as being a 'cheap, second-rate director,' [4] although one hopes she was attempting to be ironic. **Hitchography:** *Blackmail* (1929), *Juno and the Paycock* (1930), *Sabotage* (1936)

ALPER, MURRAY (1904–1984) American support-ing actor. Alper was busy from the early 1930s onwards in such varied and variable films as *The Royal Family of Broadway* (1930), *Seven Keys to Baldpate* (1935), *The Maltese Falcon* (1941), *The Devil's Canyon* (1953) and *The Nutty Professor* (1963). Perhaps his finest moment came in Hitchcock's *Saboteur* (1942), in which he played the wisecracking truck driver who gives the hero a lift. Commented the *Monthly Film Bulletin* of the film: 'Performances are good. Some are so good – Norman Lloyd, Otto Kruger, Murray Alper – that they scarcely seem to be acting'. Alper returned to the Hitchcock fold for *Strangers on a Train* (1951) in which he played the fairground boatman who helps to save Farley Granger's Guy Haines from being convicted of murdering his wife. **Hitchography:** *Saboteur* (1942), *Strangers on a Train* (1951)

Always Tell Your Wife
(GB, 1923, 20m approx, bw, silent)

CREDITS
Production company: Seymour Hicks
    Productions/Wardour and F
Producer: Seymour Hicks
Screenwriter: Seymour Hicks, based on the
    play *Always Tell Your Wife* by
    E Temple Thurston
Directors: Hugh Croise, Alfred
Hitchcock

CAST
Seymour Hicks (James Chesson), Ellaline Terriss (Mrs Chesson), Gertude McCoy (Mrs Hawks), Stanley Logan (Jerry Hawkes), Ian Wilson (Office boy)

Made in early 1923, this lost black-and-white one-reel silent about a husband who fakes a cold so as to meet a blackmailing girl provided Hitchcock with his second job of directing following the aborted *Number 13* (1922). Made at Islington Studios, it starred Seymour Hicks, a noted theatrical *farceur* who had appeared in the play version many times. Unfortunately, Hicks, who was also financing the film, had a disagreement with his director, Hugh Croise, and so replaced him with Hitchcock, who had remained on at Islington following the departure of Famous Players-Lasky, for whom he'd been working as a graphic artist, designing inter-titles. Thus Hitchcock steered the film to completion for Hicks, though apparently he didn't receive a credit for his efforts. The film also starred Hicks' wife, Ellaline Terriss, a stage star in her own right. Interestingly, this was the second film version of *Always Tell Your Wife* that Hicks and Terriss had appeared in, the first having been directed by Leedham Bantock in 1914, making it the first of five remakes Hitchcock was involved in, the others being *The Manxman* (1929), which had previously been filmed in 1916, *The Skin Game* (1931), which had been filmed in 1920, *Number Seventeen*, which had been filmed in Germany in 1928, and *The Man Who Knew Too Much* (1956), which Hitch himself had already made in 1934. One could also argue that both *Dial M for Murder* (1954) and *The Wrong Man* (1956) are remakes, given that they were first broadcast on television.

AMANN, BETTY (1907–1990) German-born actress. Born to American parents, Amann began her film career in Germany with such films as *Asphalt* (1928), after which she moved to Britain, where she appeared in films such as *Temptation* (1929), *The Perfect Lady* (1931) and Hitchcock's *Rich and Strange* (1932), in which she played the fake princess who absconds with the hero's money. She later moved to America, where she appeared in several minor films, among them *In Old Mexico* (1939), *Nancy Drew – Reporter* (1939) and *Isle of Forgotten Sins* (1944). **Hitchography:** *Rich and Strange* (1932)

ANDERSON, ERNEST American supporting actor. In bit parts from the early 1940s, Anderson can be seen in such films as *In This Our Life* (1942), Hitchcock's *North by Northwest* (1959), in which he plays a porter on the 20th Century Limited, and *Whatever Happened to Baby Jane?* (1962). **Hitchography:** *North by Northwest* (1959)

ANDERSON, JOHN (1922–1992) American supporting actor. In films from 1952 with *Against All Flags* following experience on stage on a Mississippi riverboat, Anderson notched up around 100 appearances in films such as *Last Train from Gun Hill* (1959), *Welcome to Hard Times* (1967), *Soldier Blue* (1970) and *Eight Men Out* (1988), although he is perhaps best remembered for playing California Charlie, the used car salesman in Hitchcock's *Psycho* (1960), with whom Janet Leigh's Marion Crane hurriedly exchanges her car ('It's the first time the customer ever high pressured the salesman'). He also appeared in an episode of *The Alfred Hitchcock Hour*. **Hitchography:** *Psycho* (1960), *The Second Wife* (1965, TV)

ANDERSON, DAME JUDITH (1898–1992, real name Frances Margaret Anderson) Australian-born character actress. This star will forever be remembered for her Oscar nominated supporting role as the malevolent housekeeper Mrs Danvers in Hitchcock's *Rebecca* (1940). On stage in Australia from 1915 and in America from 1918, she made her film debut in 1930 in the short *Madame of the Jury*. Film work was scant in the 1930s, during which she concentrated on her stage career, which included performances as Gertrude in *Hamlet* (opposite John Gielgud) and Lady Macbeth in *Macbeth*. Following *Rebecca*, Anderson's film career finally took off, and she went on to appear in *King's Row* (1942), *Laura* (1944), *And Then There Were None* (1945), *Cat on a Hot Tin Roof* (1958) and *Cinderfella* (1960). She was made a Dame in 1960. Her other films include *A Man Called Horse* (1970), *Star Trek III: The Search for Spock* (1983), *Hitchcock, il Brivido del Genio* (1985) and *Impure Thoughts* (1986). She also appeared in the television soap opera *Santa Barbara* (1984). **Hitchography:** *Rebecca* (1940)

ANDERSON, MARY (1920–) American actress. Anderson had supporting roles in a number of major Hollywood movies of the late 1930s and early 1940s, including *Gone with the Wind* (1939), *The Song of Bernadette* (1944), *Wilson* (1944) and *To Each His Own* (1946). Perhaps her best part was as the nurse in Hitchcock's *Lifeboat* (1944), during the making of which she allegedly asked the director, 'Which do you think is my best side, Mr Hitchcock?' To which came the reply, 'You're sitting on it!' [5] **Hitchography:** *Lifeboat* (1944)

ANDERSON, MAXWELL (1888–1959) American playwright. Following experience as a teacher and journalist, Anderson went on to become one of America's most acclaimed playwrights, among his works being *What Price Glory*, *Mary of Scotland*, *Winterset*, *Key Largo*, *Joan of Arc* and *The Bad Seed*. He also turned his hand to screenwriting on occasion, penning *All Quiet on the Western Front* (1930), *Rain* (1932), *We Live Again* (1934), *So Red the Rose* (1935) and *Joan of Arc* (1948). In 1956 he worked on Hitchcock's *The Wrong Man* (1956), and was re-hired, at a fee of $65,000, to adapt *Vertigo* for the screen. Unfortunately, Hitchcock was less than impressed with Anderson's efforts and he was subsequently replaced. **Hitchograhy:** *The Wrong Man* (1956), *Vertigo* (1958)

ANDERSON, MILO American costume designer. Long at Warner Bros., Anderson designed the wardrobe for such films as *The Adventures of Robin Hood* (1938), *To Have and Have Not* (1945) and Hitchcock's *Stage Fright* (1950), although the latter's more glamorous creations were designed by an un-credited Christian Dior for Marlene Dietrich. **Hitchography:** *Stage Fright* (1950)

ANDREWS, DAME JULIE (1935– , real name Julia Wells) British actress and singer. Created a Dame in 2000, Andrews made her radio debut as a singer on *Monday Night at Eight* (1946), prior to which she had appeared on stage in her mother and step-father's music act, the highlight of which had been a performance in front of Queen Elizabeth (later the Queen Mother) at the Stage Door Canteen. She soon became a radio staple, and was a regular guest on *Educating Archie* (1950). She made her Broadway debut in 1954 in the musical *The Boy Friend*, and consolidated her stardom in 1956 by playing Eliza Dolittle opposite Rex Harrison's Professor Henry Higgins in the original Broadway run of *My Fair Lady*. When it came to making the film version of *My Fair Lady* (1964), producer Jack Warner famously cast the non-singing Audrey Hepburn instead (who had to be dubbed by Marni Nixon); however, Andrews had the last laugh, for she was cast by Walt Disney as the title character in the blockbusting fantasy musical *Mary Poppins* (1964) which won her a best actress Oscar (Hepburn wasn't even nominated, natch!).

The Americanization of Emily (1964) and *The Sound of Music* (1965) followed, by which time Andrews was a top box office draw. Her casting as Sarah Sherman, who follows Paul Newman's defecting Professor Michael Armstrong to East Berlin in Hitchcock's *Torn Curtain* (1966), was seen by many as an attempt by the star to break away from her established screen image ('I don't want to be thought of as wholesome,' [6] she said at the time). Unfortunately, she didn't seem entirely comfortable making the film, for which she was paid a whopping $750,000, and her performance doesn't rank as among her best (commented *The Times* of Newman and Andrews' casting, '[Both are] pretty wasted on pasteboard roles'). She also came in for some criticism from the National Roman Catholic Office for Motion

Pictures for a scene in which she shares a bed with her fiancée onboard a freezing Norwegian cruiser. 'Parents should be aware that the 'Mary Poppins' image of the female lead, shattered in this film, cannot serve as any criterion of the film's acceptability for their children,' commented the Board's review. Said Andrews of making the film: 'I did not have to act in *Torn Curtain*. I merely went along for the ride. I don't feel that the part demanded much of me, other than to look glamorous, which Mr Hitchcock can always arrange better than anyone. I did have reservations about this film, but I wasn't agonized by it. The kick of it was working for Hitchcock. That's what I did it for, and that's what I got out of it.' [7]

Andrews' subsequent films include *Hawaii* (1966), *Thoroughly Modern Millie* (1967), *The Tamarind Seed* (1974), '*10*' (1979), *Victor/Victoria* (1982), *Relative Values* (2000) and *The Princess Diaries* (2002). She was married to her first husband, production designer Tony Walton (1934–), between 1959 and 1967. She married her second husband, director Blake Edwards (1922– , real name William Blake McEdwards), in 1969. **Hitchography:** *Torn Curtain* (1966)

ANGEL, HEATHER (1909–1986) British-born actress. In Hollywood from 1932 following a handful of British films, among them *City of Song* (1930) and *A Night in Montmatre* (1931), Angel went on to appear in all manner of films, from main features such as *The Informer* (1935) and *The Last of the Mohicans* (1936), to B fillers such as the *Bulldog Drummond* series, of which she appeared in five installments. She also had the small role of Ethel in Hitchcock's *Suspicion* (1941) and the more substantial role of Mrs Higgins in *Lifeboat* (1944), in which she memorably clings to her dead baby. Her other films include *Cry Havoc* (1943), *The Saxon Charm* (1948) and *The Premature Burial* (1962). She also provided the vocals for a couple of Disney cartoons: *Alice in Wonderland* (1950), as Alice's sister, and *Peter Pan* (1953), as Mother Darling. The first of her three husbands was actor Ralph Forbes (1902–1951), to whom she was married between 1934 and 1942. **Hitchography:** *Suspicion* (1941), *Lifeboat* (1944)

ANYS, GEORGETTE French character actress. Anys is perhaps best remembered for playing Germaine, the housekeeper to John Robey (Cary Grant) in Hitchcock's *To Catch a Thief* (1955), whom we learn is as adept at making quiche Lorraine as she was at strangling enemies of the French Resistance during the war. Her other films include *Fanny* (1961), *Jessica* (1962), *Bon Voyage* (1962), *Love Is a Ball* (1963) and *Moment to Moment* (1966). **Hitchography:** *To Catch a Thief* (1955)

Appearances
(GB, 1921, 53m approx, bw, silent)

CREDITS

Production company:	Famous Players-Lasky
Director:	Donald Crisp
Screenplay:	Margaret Turnbull, based on the play by Edward Knoblock
Inter-titles:	Alfred Hitchcock

CAST

Langhorne Burton (Lord Thornton), Mary Glynne (Kitty Marshall), David Powell (Herbert Seaton), Marjorie Hume (Agnes), Percy Standing (Percy Dawkins), Mary Dibley (Lady Rutherford)

This lost black-and-white silent, directed by Donald Crisp, had inter-titles designed by the young Alfred Hitchcock. Made for Famous Players-Lasky at Islington Studios, it told the story of an English lord who gives the married woman he's in love with a blank cheque, only for her husband to fill it in for the then-staggering sum of £500.

ARCHIBALD, WILLIAM (1917–1970) West-Indian-born actor, dancer, playwright and screenwriter. A real 'all-rounder' he also worked on a handful of screenplays, notably Hitchcock's *I Confess* (1953). **Hitchography:** *I Confess* (1953)

ARNOLD, TOM British independent producer. Little seems to be known about Arnold, save that he financed Hitchcock's failed Strauss musical, *Waltzes from Vienna* (1933) and a number of Sandy Powell comedies, among them *It's a Grand Old World* (1936). **Hitchography:** *Waltzes from Vienna* (1933)

ARNOLD, WILFRED British art director. Beginning with *The Pleasure Garden* in 1925, Arnold (who is sometimes credited as C W Arnold) went on to design many of Hitchcock's early films, including such key and early works as *The Lodger* (1926) and *Blackmail* (1929), the latter involving the re-creation of sections of the British Library for the film's chase climax. His other films include *The Saint in London* (1939), *Horrors of the Black Museum* (1959) and *Walk a Crooked Path* (1969). **Hitchography:** *The Pleasure Garden* (1925), *The Lodger* (1926), *The Ring* (1927), *The Farmer's Wife* (1928), *Champagne* (1928), *The Manxman* (1929), *Blackmail* (1929), *Number Seventeen* (1932)

ASHCROFT, DAME PEGGY (1907–1991) British actress. One of the most acclaimed stage actresses of her generation, Ashcroft made all too few film appearances, beginning with *The Wandering Jew* in 1933. In her second film, Hitchcock's *The 39 Steps* (1935), she played the brief but telling role of the crofter's wife.

Ashcroft's other films include *Quiet Wedding* (1940), *Sunday, Bloody Sunday* (1971) and *A Passage to India* (1984), which earned her a best supporting actress Oscar for her performance as Mrs Moore. Her television work includes *Edward and Mrs Simpson* (1978), in which she played Queen Mary, and *The Jewel in the Crown* (1984). She was made a Dame in 1956, while in 1962 the newly built Ashcroft Theatre in Croydon was named after her. **Hitchography:** *The 39 Steps* (1935)

ATTERBURY, MALCOLM (1907–1992) American supporting actor. Atterbury appeared in all manner of films, from *Dragnet* (1954) to *I Was a Teenage Werewolf* (1957) to *Seven Days in May* (1964). However, he is perhaps best remembered for playing the nameless man Cary Grant's Roger Thornhill meets at a dusty prairie crossing in Hitchcock's *North by Northwest* (1959), in which he gets to utter the classic line, 'That's funny... that plane's dustin' crops where there ain't no crops.' He also re-appeared briefly in Hitchcock's *The Birds* (1963) as Al Malone. **Hitchography:** *North by Northwest* (1959), *The Birds* (1963)

ATWATER, BARRY (1918–1978) American supporting actor. Atwater appeared in minor roles in a handful of films in the 1950s and 1960s, among them *Nightmare* (1956), Hitchcock's *The Wrong Man* (1956), in which he played Mr Bishop, *Pork Chop Hill* (1959) and *Sweet Bird of Youth* (1962). He also appeared in an episode of *The Alfred Hitchcock Hour*. **Hitchography:** *The Wrong Man* (1956), *You'll Be the Death of Me* (1962, TV)

ATWATER, EDITH (1911–1986) American character actress. In films from the 1930s, Atwater numbered many movies during her lengthy career, among them *We Went to College* (1936), *Sweet Smell of Success* (1957), *True Grit* (1969) and Hitchcock's *Family Plot* (1976), in which she played Mrs Clay. Married three times, her husbands were the actors Joseph Allen Jr, Hugh Marlowe (1911–1982, real name Hugh Hipple) and Kent Smith (1907–1985). **Hitchography:** *Family Plot* (1976)

AUBER, BRIGITTE French actress. Auber is best remembered by English-speaking audiences for her performance as Danielle Foussard, revealed as the real thief at the end of Hitchcock's *To Catch a Thief* (1955). Recalled screenwriter John Michael Hayes of the young actress: 'She had a casual way of wearing a blouse, which exposed her bosom frequently. And Hitch, of course, was delighted. She brought a lot of humour and vivacity to the part.' [8] Auber's other films include *Sous le Ciel de Paris* (1951). **Hitchography:** *To Catch a Thief* (1955)

AULT, MARIE (1870–1951, real name Mary Cragg) British character actress. Ault first encountered Hitchcock on *Woman to Woman* in 1923, on which he was working as an assistant director. She obviously made an impression on Hitch, as he later hired her to play the suspicious landlady, Mrs Bunting, in his breakthrough film *The Lodger* (1926). Her other films include *Hobson's Choice* (1931), *Major Barbara* (1940), *Love on the Dole* (1941) and *Madness of the Heart* (1949). **Hitchography:** *Woman to Woman* (1923), *The Prude's Fall* (1924), *The Lodger* (1926)

Aventure Malgache
(GB, 1944, 31m, bw)

CREDITS

Production company:	Phoenix/Ministry of Information
Director:	Alfred Hitchcock
Cinematographer:	Gunther Krampf
Art director:	Charles Gilbert

CAST
The Moliere Players (all roles)

Video availability: Connoisseur

The second of two Ministry Information Films made in Britain by Hitchcock in 1944 (also see *Bon Voyage*), this French language short was intended to be shown in areas of France where the German occupation forces were weakening, so as to boost morale and shed favourable light on the activities of the Resistance. Unfortunately, the results were so lacklustre that the film didn't see the light of a projector until 1993, when it was aired on British television (BBC 2). Watching it today, one can well understand why, for it is among Hitchcock's poorest work.

In it, members of the Moliere Players (a refugee group of actors who had also featured in *Bon Voyage*) are preparing to go on stage, when one of them begins to recall his adventures with the Resistance in Madagascar, which involved manning an illegal radio station denouncing the Vichy regime, which was colluding with the Nazis. Flatly directed, the results are tedious to say the least, but are worth noting simply for Hitchcock's involvement, which doesn't seem to have been very enthusiastic in this case.

AYRTON, RANDLE (1869–1940) British actor. A respected supporting player in films from the late teens, Ayrton played the stern father Caesar Cregeen in Hitchcock's last silent drama *The Manxman* (1929). His other films include *My Sweetheart* (1918), *Chu Chin Chow* (1923) and *Talk of the Devil* (1936). **Hitchography:** *The Manxman* (1929)

B

BACON, IRVING (1893–1965) American supporting actor. In films from 1923 with *Anna Christie*, Bacon went on to appear in almost 300 films, from A features to B potboilers, among them *The Bowery* (1933), *The Glass Key* (1935), *Gone with the Wind* (1939), *Pin-Up Girl* (1944), *The Glenn Miller Story* (1953) and *Fort Massacre* (1958). In 1943 alone he appeared in 22 films, among them Hitchcock's *Shadow of a Doubt*, in which he can be spotted as the stationmaster. He also appears very briefly in *Spellbound* (1945), but his role is un-credited. **Hitchography:** *Shadow of a Doubt* (1943), *Spellbound* (1945)

BAGDASARIAN, ROSS (1919–1972) American supporting actor. Bagdasarian, also known as David Seville, appeared in a handful of 1950s films, among them *Alaska Seas* (1954), Hitchcock's *Rear Window* (1954), in which he played the composer, and *The Proud and the Profane* (1956). Also a music executive, he created the briefly popular singing Chipmunks, which involved speeded up recordings of his own voice. A cartoon series titled *Alvin and the Chipmunks*, produced by Bagdasarian, appeared in 1961 **Hitchography:** *Rear Window* (1954)

BAILEY, RAYMOND (1905–1980) American supporting actor. Familiar to television audiences as Milburn Drysdale in the long running sit-com *The Beverly Hillbillies* (1962–1970), Bailey also popped up in many feature films from the late 1930s onwards, including *Secret Service of the Air* (1939), *Picnic* (1955), *The Incredible Shrinking Man* (1957) and Hitchcock's *Vertigo* (1958) in which he played James Stewart's doctor. His other television work includes *My Sister Eileen* (1959) and *The Many Loves of Dobie Gillis* (1961–1962). He also appeared in four episodes of *Alfred Hitchcock Presents*, two of which, *Breakdown* (1955, TV) and *The Case of Mr Pelham* (1955, TV), were directed by Hitchcock himself. **Hitchography:** *Breakdown* (1955, TV), *The Case of Mr Pelham* (1955, TV), *Miss Paisley's Cat* (1957, TV), *The Disappearing Trick* (1958, TV), *Vertigo* (1958)

BAKALEINIKOFF, CONSTANTIN (1898–1966) Russian-born music director. Following studies at the Moscow Conservatory of Music, Bakaleinikoff moved to America, where he began his professional career with the Los Angeles Philharmonic. A music director for both Paramount and MGM in the 1930s, Bakalienikoff eventually headed RKO's music department from 1941 until 1952, during which period he conducted several hundred scores, including many by composer Roy Webb, among them that for Hitchcock's *Notorious* (1946). Bakaleinikoff's other credits include *Father and Son* (1929), *The Tuttles of Tahiti* (1942), *The Curse of the Cat People* (1944), *The Body Snatcher* (1945) and *I Remember Mama* (1948). **Hitchography:** *Notorious* (1946)

BAKER, ART (1898–1966, real name Arthur Shank) American actor. In supporting roles from the 1940s onwards, Baker can be spotted in such pictures as *Once Upon a Time* (1944), Hitchcock's *Spellbound* (1945), in which he played Lieutenant Cooley, *Living It Up* (1954) and *The Wild Angels* (1966). **Hitchography:** *Spellbound* (1945)

BAKER, DIANE (1938–) American actress. This intelligent leading lady made her film debut in 1959 in *The Diary of Anne Frank*, following which she took on a variety of roles, ranging from demure ingenue in *Journey to the Center of the Earth* (1959) to spiteful character support, a prime example of which can be found in Hitchcock's *Marnie* (1964), in which she plays Lil Mainwairing, sister-in-law to Sean Connery's Mark Rutland. Her many other films include *The Prize* (1964), *Krakatoa, East of Java* (1968), *A Tree Grows in Brooklyn* (1974, TV), *The Silence of the Lambs* (1991), *The Cable Guy* (1996) and *Hannibal* (2001), while her TV work includes the sit-com *Here We Go Again* (1973). She has also directed a documentary, *Ashyana* (1979), and produced a film, *Never Never Land* (1982). **Hitchography:** *Marnie* (1964)

BAKER, FAY American supporting actress. Busy throughout the 1940s and 1950s, Baker appeared in such films as *Tell It to the Judge* (1949), *The House on Telegraph Hill* (1951) and *Sorority Girl* (1957). She can also be spotted as Ethel in Hitchcock's *Notorious* (1946), although her role went un-credited. **Hitchography:** *Notorious* (1946)

BALCON, SIR MICHAEL (1896–1977) British producer and production executive. One of the major names in British films, Michael Balcon not only formed and/or headed such studios as Gainsborough, Gaumont-British and Ealing, he also gave several directors their first opportunities, most notable among them Alfred Hitchcock. Born in Birmingham, Balcon entered the film business in 1919 as a distributor, and later that same year he began producing his first films, a series of industrial shorts for Anglo-American Oil, which he made through Victory Motion Pictures, a company he co-founded with director Victor Saville (1897–1979).

In 1923 Balcon had a major commercial hit with his first feature film, *Woman to Woman*, which was directed by Graham Cutts, for whom Balcon went on to produce several more films in the 1920s, most notably *The Rat* (1925). More importantly, *Woman to Woman* introduced Balcon to the young Alfred Hitchcock, who not only co-wrote the film's script with Cutts, but was also its art director and assistant director. Hitchcock continued to work with Cutts and Balcon as a screenwriter/art director/assistant director on a further four films, after which Balcon finally gave him the chance to direct *The Pleasure Garden* in 1925. This was made for Gainsborough Pictures, which Balcon had formed the previous year with Cutts. However, internal wrangling, mostly engineered by Cutts, saw *The Pleasure Garden* shelved, along with Hitchcock's next film for the company, *The Mountain Eagle* (1925). Hitchcock's third film for Gainsborough, *The Lodger* (1926), also ran into trouble with Cutts, but was finally released to great acclaim following some re-editing.

Cutts left Gainsborough in the early 1930s, and while his career gradually declined as a consequence, Hitchcock's went from strength to strength, with Balcon producing his next two pictures. Hitchcock himself left Gainsborough in 1927 for British International Pictures, where he made a series of films for producer John Maxwell. In the meantime, Balcon was made director of production at Gaumont-British in 1931, and when Hitchcock became dissatisfied with his career at BIP, Balcon offered him a new contract with the studio, which led to Hitchcock's classic British period. This included such successes as *The Man Who Knew Too Much* (1934), *The 39 Steps* (1935) and *Sabotage* (1936), all of which Balcon personally produced.

Having left Gaumont-British in 1936 when it ceased production, Balcon was soon after appointed director of production for MGM-British, where his greatest success was *A Yank at Oxford* (1937). Greater things were to come, though, for between 1937 and 1959 Balcon was appointed chief of production at Ealing, where he went on to oversee such classics as *Dead of Night* (1945), *It Always Rains on Sunday* (1947), *The Lavender Hill Mob* (1950) *The Man in the White Suit* (1951) and *The Ladykillers* (1955) among others. His most successful year at Ealing was 1948, which saw him produce *Kind Hearts and Coronets*, *Scott of the Antarctic*, *Passport to Pimlico* and *Whisky Galore*. It was also the year he was knighted. Following his departure from Ealing, Balcon set up Bryanston Films in 1959 and, five years later, took over the running of British Lion. His daughter is the actress Jill Balcon (1925–) and his grandson the actor Daniel Day-Lewis (1957–), whose father was the poet laureate Cecil Day-Lewis. **Hitchography:** *Woman to Woman* (1923), *The White Shadow* (1924), *The Passionate Adventure* (1924), *The Prude's Fall* (1925), *The Blackguard* (1925), *The Pleasure Garden* (1925), *The Mountain Eagle* (1925), *The Lodger* (1926), *Downhill* (1927), *Easy Virtue* (1927), *The Man Who Knew Too Much* (1934), *The 39 Steps* (1935), *Secret Agent* (1936), *Sabotage* (1936)

BALFOUR, BETTY (1903–1978) British actress. Highly popular in the 1920s in the *Squibs* series of comedies about a Cockney flower girl, Balfour was regarded by many as Britain's answer to Mary Pickford. She made her film debut in 1920 in *Nothing Else Matters*, which she followed with *Mary, Find the Gold* (1921), *Squibs* (1921), *Squibs Wins the Calcutta Sweep* (1922), *Squibs, MP* (1923), *Squibs' Honeymoon* (1923) and *The Sea Urchin* (1925), the latter directed by Hitchcock's rival, Graham Cutts. In 1928 she took the leading role of Betty, the hapless millionaire's daughter, in Hitchcock's *Champagne*. Sadly, her popularity waned with the coming of sound, and she soon found herself playing supporting roles in films such as *Evergreen* (1934) and *My Old Dutch* (1934). She attempted a re-launch with a remake of *Squibs* in 1936, but her career in films was pretty much over, ending with *29, Acacia Avenue* in 1945. **Hitchography:** *Champagne* (1928)

BALSAM, MARTIN (1919–1996) American character actor. A best supporting actor Oscar winner for *A Thousand Clowns* (1965), Balsam made his screen debut in *On the Waterfront* in 1954, after which he notched up performances in *Twelve Angry Men* (1957), *Breakfast at Tiffany's* (1961), *Cape Fear* (1962), *The Carpetbaggers* (1964), *Summer Wishes, Winter Dreams* (1973), *Death Wish 3* (1985) and *Cape Fear* (1991), as well as the TV sit-com *Archie Bunker's Place* (1979–1981). However, he is perhaps best remembered for playing the private detective Milton Arbogast, who comes to a sticky end in the Bates house while looking for Janet Leigh's Marion Crane in Hitchcock's *Psycho* (1960). Among his best scenes in the film are his staccato interrogation of Anthony Perkins' Norman Bates ('Did you spend the night with her?'/'If it don't gell, it ain't aspic'), and his backwards, vertiginous fall down the Bates house staircase, having been fatally stabbed by 'Mother'. He also appeared in two episodes of *Alfred Hitchcock Presents*. **Hitchography:** *The Equalizer* (1958, TV), *Psycho* (1960), *Final Arrangements* (1961, TV)

BANKHEAD, TALLULAH (1903–1968) Glamorous American actress. Tallulah Bankhead was as well known for her tempestuous private life (which included drug taking and lesbian affairs) as for her stage and screen roles. The daughter of House of Representatives Speaker William Brockman Bankhead, she made her stage debut in 1918, the same year she made her first film, *When Men Betray*. A theatrical legend on both sides of the Atlantic by the end of the 1920s, she was also noted for her waspish wit, which could be brutal. Although she continued to make films throughout her career, among them *The Tarnished Lady* (1931), *Stage Door Canteen* (1943) and *Fanatic* (1965), the theatre remained her true home, where she had triumphs in *The Little Foxes* and *Private Lives*.

Her best film role was as the world weary journalist Constance Porter in Hitchcock's *Lifeboat* (1944), a part that made the most of her acerbic wit and carefully nurtured air of feigned ennui. Bankhead got on particularly well with Hitchcock, sharing his liking for vulgar jokes. During filming it became common knowledge that the actress never wore undergarments, much to the delight of the crew. When this news reached studio head Darryl Zanuck he told Hitchcock to remedy the situation, to which the director retorted, 'This will have to go through the correct channels, and I don't know which to go through: wardrobe or hairdressing.' [1] Amazingly, Bankhead's performance in the film didn't even rate a mention in *Variety's* review. Nevertheless, she went on to win the New York Film Critics' Circle Award for best actress for her role, which she re-created for radio in 1950. Bankhead was married to actor John Emery (1905–1964) between 1937 and 1941; he went on to have a supporting role in Hitchcock's *Spellbound* (1945).

Hitchography: *Lifeboat* (1944), *Lifeboat* (1950, radio)

BANKS, LESLIE (1890–1952, real name James Leslie Banks) British actor. Following his screen debut in Hollywood as the villainous Count Zaroff in *The Most Dangerous Game* in 1932, Banks returned to Britain where he starred in a string of popular home grown films, among them Hitchcock's *The Man Who Knew Too Much* (1934), in which he played Bob Lawrence, the hero whose daughter is kidnapped to ensure his silence about an impending assassination. His other films include *Sanders of the River* (1936), *Went the Day Well?* (1942), *Henry V* (1944), *The Small Back Room* (1948) and *Madeleine* (1950). In 1939, he played the role of Joss Merlyn, the bogus leader of the murderous smugglers in Hitchcock's *Jamaica Inn*, about which Graham Greene wrote of his performance in *The Spectator*: '[He] introduces some sense of real evil into a girl's dream of violent manhood.' **Hitchography:** *The Man Who Knew Too Much* (1934), *Jamaica Inn* (1939)

BANTON, TRAVIS (1894–1958) American costume designer. At Paramount between 1924 and 1938, Banton worked on such glamour-led films as *Morocco* (1930), *Shanghai Express* (1932), *The Scarlet Empress* (1934) and *The Devil Is a Woman* (1935), all of which starred Marlene Dietrich. In films from 1917 with *Poppy* following experience as a fashion designer, Banton's other films include *Intermezzo* (1938), *The Mark of Zorro* (1940), *Scarlet Street* (1945) and Hitchcock's *The Paradine Case* (1947). **Hitchography:** *The Paradine Case* (1947)

BARBOUR, JOYCE (1901–1977) British actress. Barbour popped up in minor parts in a number of 1930s films, among them Hitchcock's *Sabotage* (1936), in which she played Renee. Her other films include *Housemaster* (1938) and *Saloon Bar* (1940). **Hitchography:** *Sabotage* (1936)

BARING, NORAH (1907– , real name Norah Barker) British actress. Although her career is somewhat overlooked today, Baring had leading roles in several early British talkies, among them *Underground* (1928), *Cottage on Dartmoor* (1929), *At the Villa Rose* (1930) and Hitchcock's *Murder!* (1930), in which she played murder suspect Diana Baring, who only escapes the gallows after the intervention of a single jury member unconvinced of her guilt. Her other films include *Escape from Dartmoor* (1930), *Strange Evidence* (1932) and *The House of Trent* (1933). Her career seems to have fizzled out in the mid-1930s, after which she disappeared from view. **Hitchography:** *Murder!* (1930)

BARNES, GEORGE (1893–1953) American cinematographer. One of Hollywood's finest cinematographers, Barnes began his career in 1918 with *Vive La France*, which he co-photographed, following which he graduated to a number of major silent productions, among them *Desire* (1922), *The Eagle* (1925) and *The Son* *of the Sheik* (1926). A string of classic films followed in the 1930s and 1940s, among them *Footlight Parade* (1933), *Dames* (1934), *Stanley and Livingstone* (1939) and Hitchcock's *Rebecca* (1940), which earned Barnes a much-deserved Oscar for his moody chiaroscuro visuals. He teamed up with Hitchcock again with almost equal effect on *Spellbound* (1945), his work here involving the photographing of the memorable Salvador Dali-designed dream sequence. For his efforts, Barnes earned himself an Oscar nomination. His other films include *Jane Eyre* (1944), *Force of Evil* (1948), *The Greatest Show on Earth* (1952) and *War of the Worlds* (1953). Married an incredible seven times, his wives included comedienne Joan Blondell (1909–1979), to whom he was married between 1932 and 1936. **Hitchography:** *Rebecca* (1940), *Spellbound* (1945)

BARRETT, LAURINDA American stage actress. Barrett made but a few film appearances, among them Hitchcock's *The Wrong Man* (1956), in which she played Constance Willis, and *The Heart Is a Lonely Hunter* (1968). **Hitchography:** *The Wrong Man* (1956)

BARRY, JOAN (1903–1989) British actress. In films from the early 1920s as a supporting artist in such movies as *The Card* (1922), Barry gradually rose to leading lady status in the early 1930s, appearing in such productions as *The Outsider* (1931), *Rome Express* (1932) and *Mrs Drake's Defence* (1934). Her main claim to fame, however, is the fact that she dubbed the German-born actress Anny Ondra in Hitchcock's debut talkie *Blackmail* (1929). Given the primitive nature of sound recording at the time, Barry had to dub Ondra's lines live from the side of the camera, with Ondra miming to her voice. However, Barry's cut glass tones were just as unconvincing as Ondra's thick Czech accent, given that she was playing the daughter of a London shopkeeper. Perhaps by way of reward, Hitchcock cast Barry as the leading lady in his 1932 comedy drama *Rich and Strange*, the story of a young couple who come into money and travel round the world only to discover that they're happiest at home. Unlike *Blackmail*, the film was not a success. **Hitchography:** *Blackmail* (1929), *Rich and Strange* (1932)

BARRYMORE, ETHEL (1879–1959, real name Edith Blythe) American stage actress. Barrymore was considered one of the leading lights of her generation. On stage from the age of 14, she was a Broadway star by the age of 22. She began to make films as early as 1915 with *The Nightingale*, and although she continued to appear intermittently on screen, the stage remained her preference until she was well into her sixties, when she won a best supporting actress Oscar for her role as the dying mother in *None But the Lonely Heart* (1944). Well-suited to dowager types, she went on to appear in *The Spiral Staircase* (1946), Hitchcock's *The Paradine Case* (1947) and *Pinky* (1949), each of which earned her further Oscar nominations for best supporting actress. Her final films included

Deadline (1952), *Young at Heart* (1954) and *Johnny Trouble* (1957). Her brothers, Lionel (1878–1954, real name Lionel Blythe) and John (1882–1942, real name John Blythe), were equally acclaimed for their stage and screen work, and the lives of all three were spoofed in the 1927 play *The Royal Family of Broadway* by George S Kaufman and Edna Ferber. Barrymore's three children, Samuel (1910–1985), Ethel (1912–1977) and John-Drew (1913–1975), also had acting careers. **Hitchography:** *The Paradine Case* (1947)

BASEVI, JAMES (1890–1962) British-born art director. Basevi emigrated to America following experience in the army during World War I, in which he reached the rank of Colonel. He began his career as a designer at MGM in 1924, moving to Fox in 1937, where he remained for many years. He earned Oscar nominations for his work on *Wuthering Heights* (1939), *The Westerner* (1940), *The Gang's All Here* (1943) and *The Keys of the Kingdom* (1945), taking home the statuette for *The Song of Bernadette* (1943). One of his easiest assignments was Hitchcock's *Lifeboat* (1944), given that the entire film was set in the titular craft. Nevertheless, he shared his screen credit with Maurice Ransford. Rather more challenging was Basevi's work on Hitchcock's *Spellbound* (1945), for which he designed the interiors of the Green Mansions psychiatric institute and realized Salvador Dali's designs for the memorable dream sequence. **Hitchography:** *Lifeboat* (1944), *Spellbound* (1945)

BASS, ALFIE (1916–1987) British actor. Popular on television in the 1950s and 1960s in *The Army Game* (1957–1962) and *Bootsie and Snudge* (1960–1963, also 1974), comedy character actor Bass was also a reliable supporting actor, popping up in almost 100 films, beginning with *The Bells Go Down* in 1943. Although he appeared in several key productions, among them *Brief Encounter* (1945), *It Always Rains on Sunday* (1947) and Hitchcock's *Stage Fright* (1950), in which he played a cheery stagehand, it wasn't until he featured in *The Lavender Hill Mob* (1951) that he became a recognized name. His other films include *A Kid for Two Farthings* (1955), *A Tale of Two Cities* (1958) and *I Only Arsked!* (1959). He ended his film career as he began it, playing bit parts in the likes of *Death on the Nile* (1978) and *Moonraker* (1979). **Hitchography:** *Stage Fright* (1950)

BASS, SAUL (1920–1996) American graphic artist. Celebrated for his innovative main title designs, Bass formed his own design company – Saul Bass and Associates, Inc. – at the age of 26 following several years experience as a freelance artist. He went on to design the titles for many films, among them *Carmen Jones* (1955), *The Man with the Golden Arm* (1956) and *Around the World in Eighty Days* (1956), which were noted for their style and inventiveness. In 1958 Bass teamed up with Hitchcock for the first of three films, *Vertigo* (1958), for which he devised a series of spirograph-like swirls. Commented Bass of working with Hitch that first time: 'He seemed to like me for some reason. Working with Hitch was a wonderful learning experience… I can't tell you how marvelous it was to see my work for *Vertigo* for the first time with that Bernard Herrmann score.' [2] Explained Bass of the title sequence: 'I wanted to achieve that very particular state of unsettledness associated with vertigo and also a mood of mystery. I sought to do this by juxtaposing images of eyes with moving images of intense beauty. I used Lissajous figures, devised by a French mathematician in the nineteenth century to express mathematical formulae, which I had fallen in love with several years earlier. You could say I was obsessed with them for a while – so I knew a little of what Hitch was driving at.' [3]

Bass returned for Hitchcock's next film, *North by Northwest* (1959), in which he had the film's credits sweep across a grid-like pattern, which is revealed to be the facade of a Manhattan office block. Meanwhile, for *Psycho* (1960), Bass not only provided the film's main credits (in which the film's title breaks apart so as to suggest the mental state of its protagonist), but also storyboarded the celebrated shower sequence. However, Bass's later claims that he helped to direct the sequence did not sit well with Hitchcock. Recalled Bass: 'It came time to shoot it and he [Hitchcock] benignly waved me on. And that was how it came about.' [4] Yet this claim is refuted by everyone who worked on the film, among them costumier Rita Riggs, who recalled, 'The storyboards for that sequence were unbelievable, but Mr Hitchcock absolutely shot it himself.' [5] Script supervisor Marshall Schlom concurred, adding, 'I was on that set every second. *Nobody* directs Mr Hitchcock's pictures but Mr Hitchcock.' [6] However, Bass did come up with the idea of the swinging light bulb for Mother's discovery. Recalled Bass: 'It was a very simple idea. The swinging light caused the light to change on the face and gave it a sort of macabre animation that almost made the face look like it was doing something – laughing, screaming, whatever – when you knew it was dead.' [7]

Bass's many other title sequences include *Ocean's 11* (1960), *Exodus* (1960), *West Side Story* (1961), *It's a Mad, Mad, Mad, Mad World* (1963), *Broadcast News* (1987), *Cape Fear* (1991) and *The Age of Innocence* (1993). He also directed many television commercials as well as live action documentaries, among them *The Searching Eye* (1963) and *Why Man Creates* (1968), the latter winning him a best documentary short Oscar. He directed the second unit for a few films too, notably *Spartacus* (1960) and *Grand Prix* (1966), and directed one feature, *Phase IV* (1974). It should be noted that Bass's title designs for *Psycho* were re-used for the ill-fated 1998 re-make. **Hitchography:** *Vertigo* (1958), *North by Northwest* (1959), *Psycho* (1960)

BASSERMANN, ALBERT (1967–1952) German stage star. Bassermann began appearing in films as early as 1912 with *Der Andere*. Although the theatre remained the primary focus of his career, he continued to make films throughout the 1910s, 1920s and 1930s, among them *Der Konig* (1913), *Christopher Columbus* (1922), *Napoleon auf St*

Albert Bassermann's Van Meer is about to be murdered by Charles Wagenheim's assassin in Hitchcock's second American film Foreign Correspondent *(1940). Joel McCrea's Huntley Haverstock stands centre.*

Helena (1929) and *Letzte Liebe* (1938). Following the rise of the Nazis and the outbreak of World War II, Bassermann fled to America, where he resumed his film career in 1940 with *Dr Ehrlich's Magic Bullet*, which was closely followed by Hitchcock's *Foreign Correspondent*, in which he played the kidnapped Dutch diplomat Van Meer, earning himself a best supporting actor Oscar nomination for his efforts. His other American films include *The Shanghai Gesture* (1941), *The Moon and Sixpence* (1942) and *Rhapsody in Blue* (1945). His last film was Powell and Pressburger's *The Red Shoes* (1948), which he made in Britain. **Hitchography:** *Foreign Correspondent* (1940)

BATES, FLORENCE (1888–1954, real name Florence Rabe) American-born actress. Following careers as a lawyer and businesswoman, Bates turned to acting in her forties, making her film debut in 1937 in *The Man in Blue*. She didn't make another film for three years, when she was cast as the monstrous New York matron Edythe Van Hopper in Hitchcock's *Rebecca* (1940). She stole the opening Monte Carlo-set scenes, along with all the best lines (commented *Variety*: 'Florence Bates provides many light moments in the early portion as a romantically inclined dowager'). Subsequently an audience favourite, she played variations on Mrs Van Hopper for years to come. Her many other films include *Love Crazy* (1941), *The Moon and Sixpence* (1942). *His Butler's Sister* (1943), *Portrait of Jennie* (1948) and *On the Town* (1949). **Hitchography:** *Rebecca* (1940)

BATES, MICHAEL British character actor. Best remembered for playing the wallah Rangi Ram in the sit-com *It*

Ain't Half Hot, Mum (1974–1977), Bates also popped up in several films, frequently as a policeman, as was the case in Hitchcock's *Frenzy* (1972), in which he played Sergeant Spearman. His other films include *I'm Alright, Jack* (1959), *Here We Go Round the Mulberry Bush* (1967) and *A Clockwork Orange* (1971), as well as further sit-com work in *Mr Digby, Darling* (1970–1971) and *Last of the Summer Wine* (1973–1975). **Hitchography:** *Frenzy* (1972)

Bates Motel
(US, 1987, 96m, colour TV)

CREDITS
Production company: Universal
Director: Richard Rothstein
Screenplay: Richard Rothstein

CAST
Bud Cort (Alex West), Moses Gunn (Henry Watson), Lori Petty (Willie), Gregg Henry (Tom Fuller), Kerrie Keane (Barbara Peters)

Between the release of *Psycho III* (1986) and *Psycho IV: The Beginning* (1990, TV), some bright spark at Universal came up with the idea of a weekly series set around the notorious Bates Motel, for which this tele-feature acted as a pilot. Perhaps wisely, Anthony Perkins managed to avoid becoming involved, thus the action centres round Bud Cort's Alex West, a former asylum inmate who has inherited the motel from his friend Bates. Cort, who specialized in disturbed young men – in movies *Brewster McCloud* (1970) and *Harold and Maude* (1971) – was ideally cast as West, but the project, poorly handled all round with no sense of irony or fun, simply couldn't maintain itself over a weekly format. Consequently, only a handful of episodes were made.

BATH, HUBERT (1883–1945) British conductor and arranger. Long at Gaumont as a composer, Bath worked, often un-credited, on three of Hitchcock's early productions, including his first sound film, *Blackmail* (1929), for which he arranged Campbell & Connely's score with John Reynders. His other films include *Kitty* (1929), *Chu Chin Chow* (1934), *A Yank at Oxford* (1937) and *Love Story* (1944), for which he penned his most celebrated composition, *Cornish Rhapsody*. **Hitchography:** *Blackmail* (1929), *Waltzes from Vienna* (1933), *The 39 Steps* (1935)

BAXTER, ALAN (1908–1976) American actor. On stage from 1932 and in films from 1935 with *Mary Burns, Fugitive*, Baxter went on to become a reliable support during the 1940s, frequently in cold roles, among them his memorable turn as Mr Freeman, one of the co-conspirators in Hitchcock's *Saboteur* (1942). His many other films include *Gangs of New York* (1938), *Winged Victory* (1944), *The True Story of Jesse James* (1957), *Judgment at Nuremberg* (1962) and *Willard* (1971). He also appeared in an episode of *Alfred Hitchcock Presents* and an episode of *The Alfred*

Hitchcock Hour. **Hitchography:** *Saboteur* (1942), *Backward, Turn Backward* (1960, TV), *The Crimson Witness* (1965, TV)

BAXTER, ANNE (1923–1985) American-born actress. Though she won a best supporting actress Oscar for her performance in *The Razor's Edge* (1946), Baxter is best remembered for her role as Eve Harrington in the waspish backstage drama *All About Eve* (1950), which earned her a second Oscar nomination, this time as best actress. On stage from the age of 11, she was appearing on Broadway as young as 13 (in *Seen but Not Heard*). She made her film debut at the age of 17 in *Twenty Mule Team* (1940), and this led to appearances in the likes of *Charley's Aunt* (1941), *The Magnificent Ambersons* (1942), *Five Graves to Cairo* (1943) and *Angel on My Shoulder* (1946). In 1953 she was cast as Montgomery Clift's romantic interest in Hitchcock's *I Confess* (1953), though she was actually the director's second, less preferred choice after the studio nixed his wish to cast Swedish actress Anita Bjork (1923–), best known for her performance in *Miss Julie* (1950). However, when Warner Bros. discovered that Bjork had a lover as well as an illegitimate child in tow, she was sent packing back to the fjords and was replaced by Baxter, who seemed slightly miscast (commented Hitchcock: 'When you compare Anita Bjork with Anne Baxter, wouldn't you say that was a pretty awkward substitution?' [8]).

Following *I Confess*, which was not a success, Baxter went on to appear in *The Blue Gardenia* (1953), *The Ten Commandments* (1956), *A Walk on the Wild Side* (1962), *The Family Jewels* (1965), *Jane Austen in Manhattan* (1980, TV) and *The Masks of Death* (1984, TV), etc. She was married to actor John Hodiak (1914–1955) between 1946 and 1953. He had starred in Hitchcock's *Lifeboat* (1944). During her marriage to her second husband Randolph Galt, to whom she was married between 1960 and 1968, Baxter went to live for several years on a cattle ranch in Australia, about which she wrote in her 1976 book *Intermission: A True Story*. In 1971, she appeared on Broadway in *Applause*, a musical version of *All About Eve*, although this time she played Margo Channing. Her last work was in the television series *Hotel*, in which she appeared between 1983 and 1985. Note that she also starred in an episode of *The Alfred Hitchcock Hour*. **Hitchography:** *I Confess* (1953), *A Nice Touch* (1963, TV)

BEL GEDDES, BARBARA (1922– , real name Barbara Geddes Lewis) American actress. Best known for playing Eleanor Southworth (Miss Ellie) in TV's long-running super soap *Dallas* (1978–1991), the perky Bel Geddes made her professional stage debut in 1940 and subsequently became something of a Broadway regular. In films from 1947 with *The Long Night*, she went on to appear in *I Remember Mamma* (1948), which earned her a best supporting actress Oscar nomination, *Blood on the Moon* (1947), *Caught* (1949), *Panic in the Streets* (1950), *Fourteen Hours* (1951) and Hitchcock's *Vertigo* (1958), in which she played commercial artist Midge Wood. Commented *Variety* of her work: 'Supporting players are all excellent, with Barbara Bel Geddes, in limited role of Stewart's down-to-earth girlfriend, stand out for providing early dashes of humour.' Recalled Bel Geddes of her experiences working with Hitchcock: 'He would say, "Don't act, don't act," and that was all. I think I knew what he meant and I tried very hard not to. He and Edith Head also gave me clothes that looked very well on me, little sweaters that I love, with little collars and simple skirts. I felt very secure in them, and it was just the way that Midge should look.' [9] Bel Geddes' subsequent films include *By Love Possessed* (1961) and *The Todd Killings* (1971). She also appeared in many television plays in the 1950s, including four episodes of *Alfred Hitchcock Presents*, one of which, *Lamb to the Slaughter* (1958, TV), was directed by the Master himself. **Hitchography:** *Vertigo* (1958), *Foghorn* (1958), *Lamb to the Slaughter* (1958, TV), *The Morning of the Bride* (1959, TV), *Sybilla* (1960, TV)

BENCHLEY, ROBERT (1899–1945) American actor. This noted American wit and member of the legendary Algonquin Circle also proved to be a popular supporting actor. He made his film debut in 1928 with a short titled *The Treasurer's Report*, which inaugurated a series of amusing lectures written and presented by Benchley on all manner of subjects, among them *The Sex Life of the Polyp* (1928), *How to Sleep* (1935), which earned a best short Oscar, and *The Courtship of the Newt* (1938). He began working as a supporting artist in features in 1933 with *Headline Shooter*, which led to appearances in *Piccadilly Jim* (1936), *The Broadway Melody of 1938* (1937) and, most memorably, Hitchcock's *Foreign Correspondent* (1940), in which he played the alcoholic London correspondent Stebbins. Benchley also contributed to the screenplay of *Foreign Correspondent*, providing much of his own dialogue. Said Benchley of his career as a writer: 'It took me fifteen years to discover that I had no talent for writing. But by then I couldn't give it up because I was too famous.' [10] Benchley's other films include *The Reluctant Dragon* (1941), *I Married a Witch* (1942), *It's in the Bag* (1945) and *Road to Utopia* (1945). His grandson is *Jaws* author Peter Benchley (1940–). **Hitchography:** *Foreign Correpondent* (1940)

BENDIX, WILLIAM (1906–1964) American actor. Following experience as a baseball player, the burly Bendix turned to the stage, making his Broadway debut in 1939. Films beckoned two years later with *Woman of the Year* (1941), although he had apparently already appeared in a Vitagraph film in 1911. Adept at playing both heavies and dumb bells, Bendix went on to appear in *Wake Island* (1942), which earned him a best supporting actor Oscar nomination, *The Blue Dahlia* (1946), *The Babe Ruth Story* (1948) and *Young Fury* (1964), while on television he was popular in *The Life of Riley* (1953–1958) and *The Overland Stage* (1960). In 1944 he appeared in Hitchcock's *Lifeboat*, in which he played jitterbug-obsessed seaman Gus Smith, who has to have his gangrenous foot amputated during a mid-Atlantic storm. *Variety* described his performance in the film as 'excellent'. **Hitchography:** *Lifeboat* (1944)

BENJAMIN, ARTHUR (1893–1960) British composer of Australian descent. Benjamin scored several films throughout his career, including *The Scarlet Pimpernel* (1934), *An Ideal Husband* (1948) and *Above Us the Waves* (1955). His best film work was for Hitchcock's *The Man Who Knew Too Much* (1934), which made excellent use of his cantata *Storm Clouds* during the Albert Hall sequence, in which an assassination is timed to coincide with a particularly loud passage of the music. In fact the piece was so successful that Hitchcock decided to re-use it in his 1956 remake (in which it is conducted onscreen by Bernard Herrmann). **Hitchography:** *The Man Who Knew Too Much* (1934), *The Man Who Knew Too Much* (1956)

BENNETT, CHARLES (1899–1995) British dramatist. Bennett had several stage successes with thrillers in the late 1920s and early 1930s, among them *The Last Hour* and *Blackmail*, the latter of which was adapted for the screen and became Hitchcock's first talkie in 1929. Although Bennett didn't work on the adaptation, he and Hitchcock got on well and decided to work together on an original screenplay. Titled *Bulldog Drummond's Baby*, it involved the kidnapping of Drummond's child. Unfortunately BIP, to whom Hitchcock was contracted at the time, did not like the script, so it was never made, although elements of the plot re-appeared in *The Man Who Knew Too Much* (1934), the success of which led to several more important projects, including such key works as *The 39 Steps* (1935), *Secret Agent* (1936), *Sabotage* (1936) and *Young and Innocent* (1937).

In 1940, Bennett followed Hitchcock to Hollywood, where he worked on *Foreign Correspondent* (1940), which earned him an Oscar nomination. His storyline for *The Man Who Knew Too Much* was also reworked (by John Michael Hayes) for Hitchcock's 1956 remake. In the 1990s, Bennett was said to be working on the remake script for *Blackmail*, although so far the film has yet to materialize. Bennett's other screen credits include *King Solomon's Mines* (1937), *Reap the Wild Wind* (1942), *The Lost World* (1960) and *War Gods of the Deep* (1965). He also directed two films: *Madness of the Heart* (1949) and *No Escape* (1953). Said Bennett of his working relationship with Hitchcock: 'I think more work was done on the script in the evening over cocktails than any other time!' [11] **Hitchography:** *Blackmail* (1929), *The Man Who Knew Too Much* (1934), *The 39 Steps* (1935), *Secret Agent* (1936), *Sabotage* (1936), *Young and Innocent* (1937), *Foreign Correspondent* (1940), *The Man Who Knew Too Much* (1956)

BENSON, SALLY (1900–1972) American novelist and screenwriter. Benson is best remembered for her novel *Meet Me in St. Louis*, which was successfully musicalized by MGM in 1944. Following experience as a bank teller, Benson turned to journalism and fiction, contributing to the *New Yorker* among others. Following the successful publication of both *Meet Me in St Louis* and *Junior Miss*, she turned to screenwriting, having been invited by Hitchcock to contribute to *Shadow of a Doubt* (1943). Her subsequent screenplays include *Anna and the King of Siam* (1946), which earned her an Oscar nomination, *The Farmer Takes a Wife* (1953) and *The Singing Nun* (1966). **Hitchography:** *Shadow of a Doubt* (1943)

BERADINO, JOHN American supporting actor. Also known as John Berardino, Beradino has just a few films to his credit, including *The World Was His Jury* (1957), *Seven Thieves* (1960) and *Do Not Fold, Spindle or Mutilate* (1971, TV). He can also be seen in Hitchcock's *North by Northwest* (1959) as the improbably named Sergeant Emile Klinger ('No, I didn't believe it either,' comments Cary Grant's Roger Thornhill to his mother, having told her the name over the telephone). **Hitchography:** *North by Northwest* (1959)

BERARDINO, JOHN see Beradino, John

DER BERGADLER see *The Mountain Eagle*

BERGMAN, INGRID (1915–1982) Swedish-born actress. One of the screen's great beauties, Bergman began her film career in her home country with *Munkbrogreven* in 1934 following training at Stockholm's Royal Dramatic Theatre School. However, it was her sixth film, *Intermezzo* (1936), which brought her to the attention of legendary Hollywood producer David O Selznick, who signed her to a long-term contract. Thus, following a further five films in Sweden, Bergman moved to America (where she was billed as 'Sweden's greatest export since Garbo') for the 1939 remake of *Intermezzo*, the success of which led to such films as *Dr Jekyll and Mr Hyde* (1941), *Casablanca* (1943), *For Whom the Bell Tolls* (1943), *Gaslight* (1944), which won her a best actress Oscar, and *The Bells of St Mary's* (1945).

In 1945 she worked with Hitchcock for the first time on *Spellbound*, in which she somewhat improbably played a psychiatrist who falls in love with an amnesiac (played by Gregory Peck) who might also have murdered a man. Though it had a variable reception from the critics, the film was a commercial smash, and Bergman's own reviews were among her best. 'Ingrid Bergman gives, in my opinion, the performance of her career so far,' praised Dylis Powell in the *Sunday Times*.

Following her success with *Spellbound*, Bergman turned her attention to *Saratoga Trunk* (1945), after which it was back to Hitchcock for *Notorious* (1946), in which she played Alicia Huberman, the daughter of a convicted Nazi sympathizer who is requested by the American government to help rout out further pro-Nazis in Brazil. Bergman shared several romantic scenes with Cary Grant in the film, among them one of the screen's longest seduction sequences. As a couple, Bergman and Grant were well matched. Yet when it came to Bergman's scenes with co-star Claude Rains, there were one or two problems, given Rains' diminutive stature. Commented Hitchcock: 'Claude Rains and Ingrid Bergman made a nice couple, but in the close shots the difference between them was so

marked that if I wanted them both in a frame, I had to stand Claude Rains on a box.' [12]

Another success, the film earned Bergman much praise. Wrote Dylis Powell in *The Sunday Times*: 'In a film consisting so largely of close-ups the burden on the players is heavy, and credit is due to Ingrid Bergman and in a smaller degree to Cary Grant for playing which, by shades of facial expression alone, indicates the emotional undertones of the narrative.'

Following *Notorious* (in which she performed in a radio version in 1948), Bergman went on to star in *Arch of Triumph* (1948) and *Joan of Arc* (1948), after which it was back to Hitchcock again, this time in Britain for *Under Capricorn* (1949), but the film was a commercial disaster of some significance, ending Hitchcock's dreams of becoming an independent filmmaker. In it, Bergman plays an Irish noblewoman who follows her commoner husband to Australia, where he has been deported for the alleged murder of her brother. Bergman's work recalls her performances in *Gaslight* (1944) and *Notorious* (1946), and though saddled with a vague Irish brogue, she manages to illicit some sympathy in an otherwise dull film. Commented *The Tatler*: 'Miss Bergman, struggling not quite in vain to translate her Swedish accent into a brogue, captures enough of the legendary glamour of the spirited Irish lady to make her humiliation genuinely touching.'

At the time, Bergman was the biggest star in the world, and for Hitchcock to have secured her services for an independent production was something of a coup, yet filming was not a happy experience for either director or star, who disagreed several times on set, chiefly concerning Hitchcock's insistence on lengthy takes, among them a 10-minute confession scene, to which Bergman had an aversion (following one altercation, Hitchcock allegedly said to the actress, 'It's only a movie, Ingrid!'). Consequently, despite their previous successes, they didn't work together again. Indeed, Hitchcock's displeasure with his star was further compounded when her adulterous affair with Italian director Roberto Rossellini following the completion of *Under Capricorn* prompted several Catholic organizations to boycott the film, thus further diminishing its box office chances (Bergman was even dubbed 'Hollywood's apostle of degradation' on the floor of the US Senate for having deserted her husband, Dr Peter Lindstrom, and her daughter Pia for the arms of Rossellini).

Following *Under Capricorn*, Bergman made *Stromboli* (1949) in Italy with Rossellini, whom she married in 1950. The union produced a son and twin daughters, one of whom, Isabella Rossellini (1952–), later became an actress herself. Several more films with Rossellini followed, among them *Europa 51* (1952) and *Viaggio in Italia* (1953), but their marriage didn't last and Bergman returned to Hollywood in 1954, where she had a personal triumph with *Anastasia*, which won her a second best actress Oscar as well as the forgiveness of the film world. Having divorced Rossellini in 1958 and married stage producer Lars Schmidt (whom she would divorce in

Ingrid Bergman discusses a scene with Hitchcock during the shooting of Notorious *(1946). The chair behind them belongs to cinematographer Ted Tetzlaff.*

1975), Bergman went on to appear in such films as *Indiscreet* (1958), *The Inn of the Sixth Happiness* (1958), *The Yellow Rolls Royce* (1964), *Cactus Flower* (1969), *Murder on the Orient Express* (1974), which won her a third Oscar as best supporting actress, *A Matter of Time* (1976) and *Autumn Sonata* (1978), as well as a television biopic of Israeli prime minister Golda Meir, *A Woman Called Golda* (1981). **Hitchography:** *Spellbound* (1945), *Notorious* (1946), *Notorious* (1948, radio), *Under Capricorn* (1949)

BERKELEY, BALLARD (1904–1988) British character actor. Known to television audiences the world over as Major Gowen in *Fawlty Towers* (1975–1979), Berkeley had by then already sustained a lengthy film career, beginning with *London Melody* in 1930 and going on to include *Trouble* (1933), *The Saint in London* (1939), *In Which We Serve* (1942), *Quiet Weekend* (1946) and Hitchcock's *Stage Fright* (1950), in which he played Sergeant Mellish, sharing a brief scene with Marlene Dietrich towards the end of the film. His many other appearances include *Men of Sherwood Forest* (1954), *Life is a Circus* (1958), *Confessions from the David Galaxy Affair* (1979) and *National Lampoon's European Vacation* (1985). He also did much stage work. **Hitchography:** *Stage Fright* (1950)

BERNSTEIN, SIDNEY (Lord Bernstein) (1899–1993) British producer. Bernstein is best known for establishing the Granada group, which included a chain of cinemas (begun as a family business in the 1920s) and an independent television company based in the North of England, which remains a major player in the ITV network to this day. Hitchcock first met Bernstein in 1923 during the filming of *Woman to Woman* (on which Hitch was working as a screenwriter, art director and assistant to director Graham Cutts), and the two became firm friends, both attending meetings of The Film Society, of which Bernstein was a founder member in 1925. Much more than a cinema exhibitionist in his early career, Bernstein had a genuine interest in the medium, and was the first executive to commission a national survey on the cinemagoing habits of British audiences. During the war years, he went on to become an advisor for the Ministry of Information, as which he persuaded Hitchcock to come to Britain and make a couple of French-speaking propaganda pieces – *Bon Voyage* (1944) and *Aventure Malgache* (1944) – for showing in those towns and cities in France where the occupying Germans had been defeated. Following the expiry of Hitchcock's seven-year contract with Hollywood producer David O Selznick in 1947,

Hitchcock and Bernstein set up their own independent film company, Transatlantic Pictures, the idea being that Hitchcock would now be able to make the kind of pictures he wanted to, with guaranteed artistic control. Unfortunately, the first two films made by the company – *Rope* (1948) and *Under Capricorn* (1949) – were not successes and the company was liquidated. Nevertheless, Hitchcock and Bernstein stayed on good terms, remaining friends until the end of their lives. **Hitchography:** *Bon Voyage* (1944), *Aventure Malgache* (1944), *Rope* (1948), *Under Capricorn* (1949)

BERWICK, RAY American animal trainer, specializing in birds. Berwick began his career as a scriptwriter, penning episodes of the long-running TV series *Lassie* (1954–1972). His many film credits include *The Birdman of Alcatraz* (1962), Hitchcock's *The Birds* (1963) and *Damien: Omen 2* (1978). As Berwick recalled, filming *The Birds* was no picnic: 'We had about twelve or thirteen crew members in the hospital in one day from bites and scratches. Some of them were absolutely terrified of the birds, and with good reason… The seagulls would deliberately go for your eyes. I got bitten in the eye region at least three times.' [13] Berwick returned to the Hitchcock fold for *Topaz* (1969), for which he was required to train some seagulls to carry some bread for a scene. **Hitchography:** *The Birds* (1963), *Topaz* (1969)

Beside the Bonnie Brier Bush
(GB, 1921, 45m approx, bw, silent)

CREDITS
Production company:	Famous Players-Lasky
Director:	Donald Crisp
Screenplay:	Margaret Turnbull, based on the play (and other sources) by James MacArthur and Augustus Thorne

CAST
Donald Crisp (Lachlan Campbell), Mary Glynne (Flora Campbell), Langhorne Burton (John Carmichael), Alec Fraser (Lord Donald Hay), Jerrold Robertshaw (Earl of Kilspindie), Dorothy Fane (Kate Carnegie)

Now seemingly lost, this black-and-white silent about a lord's son who prefers the affections of a peasant girl to those of his wealthy fiancée was directed by Donald Crisp, who also starred. Filmed in Devon (though set in Scotland), it had a screenplay by Margaret Turnbull that was apparently based on one novel and two plays. It also had inter-titles designed by Hitchcock. Some reference books list the film simply as *The Bonnie Brier Bush*.

BEST, EDNA (1900–1974) British actress. On stage from her teenage years, Best made her film debut in 1921 with *Tilly of Bloomsbury*, which she followed with *A Couple of Down and Outs* (1923), *Sleeping Partners* (1930) and the sound remake of *Tilly of Bloomsbury* (1930). In 1934 she was cast by Hitchcock as Jill Lawrence in *The Man Who Knew Too Much*, in which she memorably dispatches a villain with a single shot from a rifle. Following a further handful of British films, among them *South Riding* (1937) and *Prison without Bars* (1938), she went to Hollywood in 1939, where she appeared in the likes of *Intermezzo* (1939), *Swiss Family Robinson* (1940) and *The Ghost and Mrs Muir* (1947). She made her last film, *The Iron Curtain*, in 1948. Between 1928 and 1940, she was married to actor Herbert Marshall (1890–1966), who made *Murder!* (1930) and *Foreign Correspondent* (1940) for Hitchcock. **Hitchography:** *The Man Who Knew Too Much* (1934)

BEVAN, BILLY (1887–1957, real name William Bevan Harris) Australian-born comedian. Bevan moved to America in 1917 where, following his film debut in *Salome vs. Shenandoah* in 1919, he went on to become a star comic for producer Mack Sennett, appearing in countless shorts, among them *Gymnasium Jim* (1922), *Little Robinson Corkscrew* (1924) and *Peaches and Plumbers* (1927). With the coming of sound, he turned to character roles, often playing policemen, among them an un-credited appearance just prior to the inquest scene in Hitchcock's *Rebecca* (1940). He can also be spotted as a ticket collector in the opening scene of Hitchcock's *Suspicion* (1941). His many other films include *The Invisible Man Returns* (1941), *Mrs Miniver* (1942), the Hollywood remake of Hitchcock's *The Lodger* (1944), *The Picture of Dorian Gray* (1945), *The Woman in Green* (1945) and *The Fortunes of Captain Blood* (1950). He also co-directed one film: *The Quack Doctor* (1920). **Hitchography:** *Rebecca* (1940), *Suspicion* (1941)

BEVANS, CLEM (1879–1963, real name Clem Blevins) American actor. Though he didn't make his first film until the age of 56 with *Way Down East* (1935), Bevans went on to make almost 100 films, 20 of them in 1939 alone. Many of these were westerns in which he played grizzled townsfolk, among them *Dodge City* (1939), *The Oklahoma Kid* (1939), *Go West* (1940) and *The Paleface* (1948). He also appeared in Hitchcock's *Saboteur* (1942) as Nielson, the grizzled co-conspirator hiding out in the ghost town of Soda City. Bevans' other films include *Portrait of Jennie* (1948), *Captive of Billy the Kid* (1952) and *Davy Crockett and the River Pirates* (1956), after which he retired. **Hitchography:** *Saboteur* (1942)

BINNS, EDWARD (1916–1990) American supporting actor. In films from 1951 with *Teresa*, Binns appeared in such major movies as *Twelve Angry Men* (1957), *Judgment at Nuremberg* (1961), *Patton* (1969) and *The Verdict* (1982), although he is perhaps best remembered for his title role in the TV cop show *Brenner* (1959–1964). He can also be spotted in Hitchcock's *North by Northwest* as the incredulous Captain Junket ('Mr Thornhill has told us that he was brought to this house against his will last night and forcibly intoxicated by some of your husband's friends and then set out on the road. Did you know anything about this?'). **Hitchography:** *North by Northwest* (1959)

The Birds

(US, 1963, 119m, Technicolor) ★★

CREDITS

Production company:	Universal
Producer:	Alfred Hitchcock
Director:	Alfred Hitchcock
Screenplay:	Evan Hunter, based on the novella by Daphne Du Maurier
Cinematographer:	Robert Burks
Sound consultant:	Bernard Herrmann
Electronic sound effects:	Remi Gassman, Oska Sala
Editor:	George Tomasini
Production design:	Robert Boyle
Costumes:	Edith Head
Wardrobe supervisor:	Rita Riggs
Special effects:	Ub Iwerks, Lawrence A Hampton, Dave Fleischer, Albert Whitlock
Sound:	William Russell, Waldon . Watson
Titles:	James . Pollak
Bird trainer:	Ray Berwick

CAST

Tippi Hedren (Melanie Daniels), Rod Taylor (Mitch Brenner), Jessica Tandy (Lydia Brenner), Veronica Cartwright (Cathy Brenner), Suzanne Pleshette (Annie Hayworth), Ethel Griffies (Mrs Bundy, the ornithologist), Doreen Lang (Concerned mother), Charles McGraw (Sebastian Sholes), Ruth McDevitt (Mrs MacGruder), Malcolm Atterbury (Al Malone), Lonny Chapman (Deke Carter), Joe Mantell (Salesman), Doodles Weaver (Boatman), John McGovern (Post office clerk), Karl Swenson (Drunk in café), Bill Quinn (Farm hand), Morgan Brittany (Schoolgirl), Richard Deacon (Mitch's apartment neighbour)

Video availability: Universal
DVD availability: Universal

'The Birds is coming,' exclaimed Hitchcock, much to the chagrin of schoolteachers everywhere. Yet though this remains one of Hitchcock's most famous films alongside *North by Northwest* (1959) and *Psycho* (1960), the sad truth is that it is not one of the Master's greats. However, there are certainly good things in it (the set pieces still dazzle), as well as bad (40 years on, the Oscar–nominated effects, highly publicized at the time, seem somewhat fuzzy around the edges, while save for the attack sequences, the script is little more than a soap opera featuring two-dimensional characters about whom one cares very little). But at the time, Hitchcock was most enthusiastic about the project. Recalled screenwriter Evan Hunter: 'He confided to me that he was at the top of his form, that he was entering his Golden Age of filmmaking, and that everything was still ahead of him. And he was brimming all the

Hitchcock talks through a scene for The Birds *(1963) with Rod Taylor. Suzanne Pleshette takes it easy on the ground.*

time with ideas... Indeed, I felt he *was* at the top of his form.' [14]

Daphne Du Maurier's novella *The Birds*, set on a Cornish farm whose owners find themselves unaccountably attacked by flocks of birds, had first appeared in a collection of her short stories in 1952. It was later reprinted in a Hitchcock anthology, which is where the director discovered it. 'It was in one of those *Alfred Hitchcock Presents* books,' he revealed, adding, 'The basic appeal to me [was] that it had to do with ordinary, every day birds... I think that if the story had involved vultures, or birds of prey, I might not have wanted it.' [15] Of course, Hitchcock had adapted Du Maurier's work before – *Jamaica Inn* (1939) and *Rebecca* (1940) – but this story would be unlike any other he had filmed.

To work on the script, Hitchcock hired novelist and screenwriter Evan Hunter, known for such films as *Strangers When We Meet* (1961) and *The Young Savages* (1961), as well as such novels as *The Blackboard Jungle* (filmed in 1955) and the 87th *Precinct* crime series, which he penned under the pseudonym Ed McBain. He'd also had one of his short stories, *Vicious Circle*, filmed for the *Alfred Hitchcock Presents* TV series in 1957, while in 1959 he'd adapted Robert Turner's story *Appointment at Eleven* for the series. Originally, Hitchcock had intended to film *Marnie* after *Psycho*, and had begun work on the film's script with *Psycho* screenwriter Joseph Stefano. However, when Grace Kelly, who had expressed an interest in returning to the screen in the film, pulled out of the project, a dejected Hitchcock turned his attention to the Du Maurier story instead. Recalled Hunter: 'The call came my agent... I thought at first that Joan Harrison wanted me to adapt another story for Hitch's TV show. But no, it seemed Hitch had purchased motion picture rights to a Daphne Du Maurier novella titled *The Birds*, and he wanted me to write the screenplay for the movie he planned to make from it. I told my agent I would have to read the story before I decided. In truth, for the chance to work with Alfred Hitchcock on a feature film, I would have agreed to do a screenplay based on the Bronx telephone book.' [16]

The first thing Hitchcock did when he and Hunter began work on the script on 18 September 1961 was to junk Du Maurier's story, retaining only the title and a few incidents from it, among them a scene in which a flock of finches flies down a chimney and into the farm house. After all, opined Hitchcock, 'The only stars in this movie are the birds and me.' [17]

While working on the script, Hitchcock and Hunter quickly came to one inescapable conclusion: 'We both realized that by the time the movie opened, the audience would know well in advance that birds would be attacking people,' said Hunter. 'If not, then a multi-million dollar promotion and advertising campaign would have been a failure... The title and all the pre-opening hoopla would tell us what would be happening – birds were going to attack – but not *when*.' [18] Thus, with this suspense mechanism built in, Hitchcock and his writer decided to open the film in a light comedy vein. 'If we could start the audience laughing in the early part of the picture, and then suddenly cause them to choke on their own laughter, the suspense would turn to shock,' [19] the writer commented.

An admirable sentiment, but unfortunately it just doesn't work, for the opening sequence in which society gadfly Melanie Daniels (Tippi Hedren) meets lawyer Mitch Brenner (Rod Taylor) in a San Francisco pet shop – he mistaking her for a shop assistant, and she playing along with the misconception – is strained to say the least, lacking the required wit and sophistication to bring it off. Nevertheless, it gets the story rolling, which subsequently sees Daniels drive out to Brenner's farm near the Bodega Bay fishing township so as to deliver a pair of love birds to his sister Cathy (Veronica Cartwright) as a joke (audiences must have been rocking in their seats at this). However, having crossed the bay and delivered the birds by boat, Daniels is hit by a seagull on her return journey, thus introducing an escalating series of events which see the township, the nearby school and Brenner's farm attacked by birds of every variety, including gulls, crows and swallows.

The unfolding drama surrounding these attacks is strictly daytime television: Daniels falls for Brenner; Brenner's widowed mother Lydia (Jessica Tandy) sees Daniels as a threat; whilst schoolteacher Annie Hayworth (Suzanne Pleshette), with whom Daniels stays, gets to play the noble ex, given that she and Brenner once harboured feelings for each other. Unimaginatively shot and rather dully performed, these various dramas do little but pad out the running time between the attack sequences, which are brilliantly handled, among them a seagull attack at Cathy's birthday party, an attack by crows on the school and an attack on the township itself, which sees the local gas station go up in a fireball (at which Hitchcock cuts to an impressive aerial view of the carnage, into which even more birds glide, as if surveying the damage).

But the thrills are a long time coming, as critic Dwight MacDonald pointed out: 'We must sit through half an hour of pachydermous flirtation between Rod and Tippi before the seagull attacks, and another fifteen minutes of tedium before the birds attack again. If one adds later interrelations between mother, girlfriend and a particularly repulsive child actress, about two-thirds of the film is devoted to extraneous matters.' Stanley Kaufman was even more forthright, adding, 'The dialogue is stupid, the characters insufficiently developed to rank as cliché, [and] the story in-cohesive.'

Even Evan Hunter admitted that his script was far from perfect, but laid the blame on Hitchcock for failing to act on this: 'If there were weaknesses in my screenplay, they should have been pointed out to me before shooting began, and they would have been corrected... The concept of the film was to turn a light love story into a story of blind, unreasoning hatred. Since Hedren and Taylor could not handle the comedy at the top of the film, the audience became bored. They had come to see birds attacking people, so what was all this nonsense with these two people, one who can't act and the other who's so full of machismo you expect him to have a steer thrown over his shoulder? Bad acting and – for Hitchcock – incredibly bad directing.' [20] Hunter has even suggested that the script was altered during shooting: 'I think Hitch allowed his actors outrageous liberties with what I had written, and he juggled scenes and cut scenes and even *added* one scene, the writer of which still remains unknown to me,' [21] he revealed.

Having lost Grace Kelly to Prince Ranier and given up hope of turning the reluctant Vera Miles into his next leading lady, Hitchcock decided to cast an unknown as Melanie Daniels, whose look and performance he could subsequently mould to his satisfaction. He finally found her in Tippi Hedren, a model with very little acting experience whom he signed to a seven-year contract having spotted her in an ad for a Sego diet drink, in which she gets wolf-whistled by her young son. It was a bold step for the director to take, as Hedren herself has admitted: 'People said, "Hitch, how can you put this woman who's never acted, who isn't known, into your picture?" But Hitch gave me the assurance that he could do it.' [22]

Filming began on the $3 million production on 22 March 1962, by which time Hitchcock had assembled the team he had grown to rely upon, among them cinematographer Robert Burks, editor George Tomasini, costume designer Edith Head and composer Bernard Herrmann, who would this time be acting as the film's sound consultant, supervising the experimental electronic sound effects by Oskar Sala and Remi Gassman that Hitchcock wanted to use instead of a conventional score. Meanwhile, the effects were placed in the hands of Ub Iwerks, Dave Fleischer, Lawrence A Hampton and bird trainer Ray Berwick who, between them, would handle the attack scenes, while matte artist Albert Whitlock would provide a number of scenic foreground and background plates (Whitlock's 12 paintings for the film took over a year to complete).

Astonishingly, some $200,000 was spent on developing mechanical replicas of birds with motorized wings for the film before it was decided to rely on more tried and tested methods, including a mixture of travelling mattes, superimpositions, blue screen, trained live birds and stuffed dead ones (left over from *Psycho* perhaps?). Recalled associate editor Bud Hoffman: 'Some tests had been done at Universal using mechanical birds, but they were very phony looking… They [were] these strange-looking creatures that looked like model airplanes with wings that moved up and down. There was also a glider type of bird which came down on wire that was just about as laughable.' [23]

The location shooting, which lasted two months, took place at Bodega Bay itself, a pictorial hamlet up the coast from San Francisco, where the crew made full use of actual buildings – including the Tides restaurant and a dilapidated schoolhouse which was refurbished for the film – as well as purpose-built facades, among them the Brenner farm and Annie Hayworth's house. The production represented a steep learning curve for Hedren, who admitted, 'I learned so much from Hitchcock. He's an absolutely fascinating person. He has a mind like an IBM computer… He's a very psychological director. He works on you like putty.' [24]

Hedren's character begins the film looking every inch a glamour queen. However, like Tallulah Bankhead's character in Hitchcock's *Lifeboat* (1944), she has been brought down to earth by her ordeal by the end of the picture. In fact Hedren herself was completely exhausted by the time the film wrapped, thanks chiefly to the scene in which Daniels is attacked by ravens, crows and gulls in the attic of the Brenner farm. This sequence took several days to film using a mixture of live and stuffed birds, during which Hedren was reduced to a nervous wreck. She also suffered a severe cut below her eye. Commented the actress: 'I then considered the possibility that maybe this was one of the reasons why Hitchcock had chosen an unknown for the part – there *was* an element of danger in it, since the birds were not all nice guys.' [25]

The other major attack sequence to feature Daniels was filmed at the schoolhouse, where the crows famously amass behind her on the playground climbing-frame as she idly smokes a cigarette while waiting for Cathy to come out of school – though why Daniels and schoolteacher Hayworth subsequently endanger the children by taking them *out* of the school and exposing them to attack in the ensuing scene is never fully explained (unless this is by way of punishing them for having made us sit through several seemingly unending verses of the dismal roundelay *Ristle-tee Rostle-tee Now Now Now*). To film the attack on the children as they flee down the hill to the township, Hitchcock had them run on treadmills in front a blue screen, on to which the background was rear-projected while stuffed birds were flown at them on wires from overhead. This was then overlaid with shots of live birds to complete the effect.

Meanwhile, for the scene in the Brenner farmhouse where the finches come down the chimney to attack Daniels and the Brenners, the whole set was encased in polythene so that the birds could not escape between performing their duties.

One sequence that does *not* appear in the film, however, is the finale as written, which Hitchcock chose not to film. Following the final shot of Daniels and the Brenners escaping the farm in Mitch's car, the film was to have carried on for several more scenes, as writer Evan Hunter recalled. 'I don't know why Hitch did not shoot the ending as we'd discussed it and I wrote it. At least ten pages, and perhaps more, of the screenplay were not shot. In those ten pages, the Brenners and Melanie leave the house and drive through the town, where we see absolute chaos and realize that the bird attacks are not a personal vendetta on Melanie and the Brenners, but a widespread calamity… When I saw it for the first time in a theatre, people turned to each other and mumbled, 'Is it over? Is that it? Huh?' and words to that effect.' [26]

Despite the abrupt ending and the lukewarm reviews, the film turned a handsome profit when released on 28 March 1963, thanks to audience expectation about the story and the almost relentless publicity drive, which naturally featured Hitchcock himself at its centre ('If you have ever eaten a turkey drumstick, caged a canary or gone duck hunting, *The Birds* will give you something to think about,' he proclaimed in one radio spot, while on the poster he says of the movie, 'It could be the most terrifying motion picture I have ever made'). However, the director's attempts to pass the film off as some type of apocalyptic allegory have since been decried by Evan Hunter: 'I think Hitch is putting the world on when he pretends there is anything meaningful about *The Birds*. We were trying to scare the hell out of people. Period.' [27]

Note that *The Birds* was nominated for one Oscar, for best special effects (Ub Iwerks), which astonishingly, it lost out on to *Cleopatra* (1963). A belated TV sequel-cum-remake, *The Birds II: Land's End*, appeared in 1994, but was not a success.

Hitchcock cameo Hitchcock can be seen exiting Davidson's pet shop at the top of the film with two dogs. These were the director's own dogs, two prize Sealyham poodles named Stanley and Geoffrey, after whom he also named a company, Stanley Geoffrey, through which he produced his next film, *Marnie* (1964).

The Birds II: Land's End
(US, 1994, 82m, colour, TV)

CREDITS
Director: Alan Smithee
           (Rick Rosenthal)
Screenplay: Ken Wheat, Jim Wheat,
           Robert Eisele

CAST
Brad Johnson (Ted Hocken), Chelsea Field (May Hocken), Megan Gallacher (Joanna Hocken), Stephanie Milford (Jill Hocken), James Naughton (Frank Irving), Tippi Hedren (Helen Matthews), Jan Rubes (Karl)

In this dismal TV movie sequel-cum-remake, an unhappily married couple and their two children find themselves under attack by our feathered friends when they decide to take a vacation on Gull Island. A major disappointment, the film pales in the shadow of Hitchcock's less than perfect original, despite a cameo by that film's leading lady Tippi Hedren, who here plays Helen Matthews. In fact, so poor was the film that its director, Rick Rosenthal – *Halloween II* (1981), *Bad Boys* (1983) – had his credit replaced by the pseudonym Alan Smithee.

BLACK CLOAK see *Dark Intruder*

BLACK, (TED) EDWARD (1900–1948) British producer. One of Britain's busiest and most successful film producers in the 1930s and 1940s, Black was the son of George Black, who established one of Britain's first permanent cinemas, the Monkwearmouth Picture Hall in Sunderland, in 1905. [28] Following his father's death in 1910, Black and his brothers continued to operate the cinema, which soon grew into a circuit of 13. Black became an assistant production manager for Gaumont-British in 1930, and in 1935 he was appointed associate producer (along with Sidney Gilliat) on *Tudor Rose*, which was released the following year. 1935 also saw him produce *Boys Will be Boys*, the first of a series of successful Will Hay comedies, among them *Where There's a Will* (1936), *Oh, Mr Porter* (1937) and *Ask a Policeman* (1938). Meanwhile, in 1937, Black began a two-picture association with Alfred Hitchcock, for whom he produced *Young and Innocent* (1937) and *The Lady Vanishes* (1938), the latter regarded as one of Hitchcock's finest British films. Black's other films include *The Frozen Limits* (1939), *Kipps* (1941), *The Young Mr Pitt* (1942), *The Man in Grey* (1942), *Millions Like Us* (1943) and *Bonnie Prince Charlie* (1948). Astonishingly, few cinema reference books actually mention him.
Hitchography: *Young and Innocent* (1937), *The Lady Vanishes* (1938)

BLACK, KAREN (1942– , real name Karen Ziegler) American actress. In vogue as a star actress in the 1970s, leading lady Black came to films following stage experience, including training at the Actors' Studio. She made a splash in her debut film *You're A Big Boy Now* (1967), though she had appeared as an extra in *The Prime Time* (1959). Her subsequent films took in such successes as *Easy Rider* (1969), *Five Easy Pieces* (1970), which earned her a best supporting actress Oscar nomination, *The Great Gatsby* (1974), *Airport 1975* (1974), in which she memorably had to land a stricken jumbo jet, *The Day of the Locust* (1975) and *Nashville* (1975). In 1976 she starred in Hitchcock's last film *Family Plot* (1976) as Fran, whose kidnapping scam with boyfriend Arthur Adamson (William Devane) leads to some unexpected plot developments. Commented *Variety* of the actress' work: 'Karen Black gives a deep resonance to her relationship with the mercurial Devane.' Black's career began to slide in the early 1980s, but she always remains a welcome face. Her other films include *Killer Fish* (1978), *Capricorn One* (1978), *Come Back to the Five and Dime, Jimmy Dean, Jimmy Dean* (1982), *Invaders from Mars* (1985), *The Player* (1992), *Children of the Corn IV: The Gathering* (1996), *Waiting for Dr McGuffin* (1998) and *The Independent* (2000).
Hitchography: *Family Plot* (1976)

The Blackguard
(GB/Ger, 1925, 92m approx, bw, silent)

CREDITS
Production company: Gainsborough/UFA
Producer: Michael Balcon
Director: Graham Cutts
Screenplay: Alfred Hitchcock, based on the novel by Raymond Paton
Cinematographer: Theodor Sparkuhl
Art director: Alfred Hitchcock
Assistant director: Alfred Hitchcock
Associate producer: Erich Pommer
Continuity girl: Alma Reville

CAST
Walter Rilla (Michael Caviol, the Blackguard), Jane Novak (Princess Marie Idourska), Bernhard Goetzke (Adrian Levinski), Frank Stanmore (Pompouard), Rosa Valetti (Grandmother), Martin Hertzberg (Young Michael Caviol)

Made in 1925, this lost black-and-white silent was one of several films the young Alfred Hitchcock worked on in a variety of capacities prior to establishing his own directorial career. A co-production between Gainsborough and the German film company UFA (Universum Film Aktiengesellschaft), it told the story of a French violinist who saves a princess from the Russian Revolution, and was shot in Berlin at the Neubabelsberg Studios. The film's associate producer, Erich Pommer, was already an established producer in Germany, having made such classics as *The Cabinet of Dr Caligari* (1919) and *Variety* (1925). He would later produce Hitchcock's *Jamaica Inn* (1939).

Blackmail

(GB, 1929, 86m (sound version), 78m (silent version), bw)
★★

CREDITS

Production company:	British International Pictures/Gainsborough
Producer:	John Maxwell
Director:	Alfred Hitchcock
Screenwriters:	Alfred Hitchcock, Benn W Levy, based on the play by Charles Bennett
Cinematographer:	Jack Cox
Music:	Campbell & Connely
Musical directors:	Hubert Bath, Harry Stafford
Conductor:	John Reynders
Editor:	Emile de Ruelle
Art director:	Wilfred Arnold
Assistant director:	Frank Mills
Assistant cameraman:	Ronald Neame
Assistant camera operator:	Alfred Roome

CAST

Anny Ondra (Alice White), John Longden (Frank Webber), Donald Calthrop (Tracy), Cyril Ritchard (Crewe), Sara Allgood (Mrs White), Charles Paton (Mr White), Hannah Jones (Landlady), Harvey Braban (Chief Inspector), Joan Barry (voice of Alice), Phyllis Monkman (Neighbour), Percy Parsons (Crook), Phyllis Konstam

To fully appreciate the impact *Blackmail* had on both audiences and critics, one would have to travel back in time to 1929, because for present day viewers it seems painfully stilted and dated at times. Nevertheless, certain sequences retain an impact, while historically the film remains a major landmark in Hitchcock's developing career.

Following the success of *Don Juan* (1926) and *The Jazz Singer* (1927) in America, which featured a synchronized score and fragments of dialogue respectively, the talkie revolution was upon the world. However, owing to the cost of changing over to the new medium in both studios and cinemas, the conversion process was slow. Consequently, some films begun as silents had a talkie reel tacked on to the end of them, so as to jump on the sound bandwagon and reap the financial benefits, while other films were shot in two versions: one silent, for theatres that had yet to make the change over to sound, the second for theatres that had. *Blackmail* fell between these stools. Begun as a silent, it was completed and later released as such to non-sound theatres. Hitchcock also completely revised this silent version, adding dialogue scenes and a music score. And it was this version that was released first to great adulation (contrary to popular belief, *Blackmail*

Hitchcock listens to the sound during the filming of Blackmail *(1929), his first talkie. The camera was placed in a special soundproof booth so that its noise would not be picked up.*

was *not* Britain's first talkie; that honour went to an adaptation of the Edgar Wallace thriller *Clue of the New Pin*, which was released in March 1929, a full three months before *Blackmail*).

The focus of the story is Alice White (Anny Ondra), a shopkeeper's daughter who is dating a police detective, Frank Webber (John Longden). In the midst of a date in a busy tearoom, Alice ditches Frank so that she can meet a new beau, an artist named Crewe, with whom she returns to his studio on the top floor of a rooming house. They are spotted entering the house by a local scrounger named Tracy (Donald Calthrop), who tries to tap the artist for some money. Having brushed Tracy off, Crewe takes Alice upstairs where, after some serious flirting, he attempts to rape her. Grabbing a bread knife – conveniently left on the bedside table, along with a loaf of bread! – Alice stabs Crewe to death, following which she runs from the scene in panic, failing to notice that she has been spotted by Tracy, who is still skulking in the shadows outside. In a state of shock, Alice wanders the streets until dawn, finally reaching home and clambering into bed just as her mother enters her room with an early morning cuppa.

Naturally, the murder is big news the next day, and Alice can barely conceal her guilt. In an ironic twist, her boyfriend Frank is assigned to the case, and upon searching the artist's garret, he discovers one of Alice's gloves, with which he confronts her at her father's shop. However it transpires that Tracy, who also turns up at the shop, has retrieved the matching glove, with which he now attempts to blackmail Alice.

Luckily for Alice, Crewe's landlady reports that she saw Tracy lurking outside the house, and the police conclude that *he* must have murdered the artist. On hearing this information, Frank turns the tables on Tracy, who makes a run for it. A chase across London ensues, with the blackmailer finally plunging to his death through the roof of the British Museum. As far as the police are concerned, the case in now closed. But Alice doesn't yet know this, and not being able to bear her guilt any longer, she decides to turn herself in. However, when she gets to the police station, she is referred to Frank, who persuades her to accept the fact that Tracy has been blamed for the murder, and that she has got off Scott free.

Billed as 'Britain's all-talkie challenge to the world,' *Blackmail* was based on a stage play by Charles Bennett, which began a successful run at The Globe Theatre in London's West End in February 1928. This had starred Hollywood legend Tallulah Bankhead, who would later star in Hitchcock's *Lifeboat* (1943), and had been directed by the actor Raymond Massey, who would go on to star in such classics as *The Old Dark House* (1932), *Things to Come* (1936) and *East of Eden* (1955). The stage script was subsequently adapted for film by Hitchcock himself and Benn W Levy, who replaced Hitchcock's usual script collaborator Eliot Stannard who, aggrieved at not being offered the assignment, never worked with the director again.

The film went into production in early 1929 as a silent, with the Czech actress Anny Ondra, who'd starred in Hitchcock's previous film *The Manxman* (1929), in the role of Alice. But when it was decided to re-shoot much of the film with sound, it quickly became apparent that Ondra's heavy accent would be a problem, given that she was supposed to be playing the daughter of a London shopkeeper. Yet at the time dubbing techniques were practically non-existent. Consequently, it was decided to dub Ondra live on set. To this end, English actress Joan Barry stood by a microphone just off camera, reciting the lines for Ondra, who in turn mouthed them for the cameras. A clever idea at the time, the results unfortunately now look and sound rather primitive, especially as Ondra always opens her mouth just a couple of beats before she is supposed to speak, while the refined voice that issues from it is no more realistic for the daughter of a London shopkeeper than Ondra's own accent would have been (indeed, Joan Barry's voice is *so* cut glass it makes the queen sound like a navvy).

This inventive bit of dubbing was by no means Hitchcock's only experiment with sound in *Blackmail*. Elsewhere, in a celebrated scene, a gossipy neighbour prattles on about the murder while Alice and her family sit down to breakfast. As the neighbour (an un-credited Phyllis Monkman) continues to talk, the sound of her voice gradually diminishes, save for the word *knife*, the constant repetition of which sends Alice into an extreme state of agitation, causing her to drop the bread knife with which her father has asked her to cut a slice of bread.

The film also benefits from having its own musical score composed by Campbell and Connely (played by the British International Symphony Orchestra and 'Recorded by the RCA Photophone System' so the credit reads). Elsewhere, though, the new medium all too clearly limits the film. Crewe's seduction of Alice in his studio drags on for an eternity, and the dialogue is incredibly stilted. At one stage, actor Cyril Ritchard even begins to call Anny Ondra by her real name before correcting himself, so that her character's name comes out as 'An-Alice,' a slip up which amazingly wasn't spotted. The scenes with the blackmailer in the shop are also painfully slow by today's standards. Yet an early scene in which Frank and Alice visit a busy Lyon's Corner House tearoom is particularly well handled, the bustle and clatter of place effectively being relayed.

It is in the action sequences that the film truly comes alive, among them the opening sequence (shot as silent) in which Frank and a colleague arrest a crook in an East End slum. Hitchcock then meticulously follows the police procedure of interrogating, booking, fingerprinting and locking up the criminal (in a wry reference to this, Frank later informs Alice during their date at the tearoom that he wants to take her to the pictures to see a new police drama called *Fingerprints*, commenting, 'It should be amusing. They're bound to get all the detail wrong!').

The climactic chase is also expertly handled, particularly those parts of it supposedly shot in the British Museum. Unable to film in the museum itself owing to a lack of sufficient light, Hitchcock had a series of nine stills taken. As transparencies, these were then projected using the Schufftan Process. Explained Hitchcock: 'You set a mirror at an angle of 45 degrees and you reflect a full picture of the British Museum in it... Then we scraped the silvering away in the mirror in certain places corresponding to a décor prop we had built on the set. For instance, a doorframe through which one of the characters came in.' [29]

A variation on this process was used for the shot in which Tracy climbs to the top of the Museum's dome and crashes to his death. However, fearing that studio executives would be wary of the complicated processes involved to achieve these shots, Hitchcock worked in secret on them. Naturally, when the executives finally saw what Hitchcock had been up to, they were most impressed.

The opening and closing sequences aside, Hitchcock also exercises his style in a number of scenes elsewhere in the film. Among the more effective touches are a lengthy crane shot up an entire flight of stairs in Crewe's rooming house; the depiction of the passing of time via the increasing number of cigarette stubs seen in an ashtray; and a shock cut from Alice, screaming at the sight of a sleeping beggar who reminds her of the man she's just murdered, to Crewe's screaming landlady who has just discovered his body. Perhaps the subtlest touch comes towards the end of the film when Alice writes a note for Frank, telling him that she is going to the police to confess. Having finished the note, she stands up, and the light coming through the window casts a noose-like shadow round her neck.

Sadly, humour is a little thin on the ground in *Blackmail* save for one priceless exchange between Crewe's landlady and the policeman she's telephoned to report the murder to. Wanting to confirm the house number, the copper asks, 'What number did you say? Seven or eleven?' to which comes the reply, 'Thirty-one!'

Running at 86 minutes, the sound version of *Blackmail* was released in June 1929 with an 'A' for adult certificate (the silent version, running 75 minutes, followed in August), and the reaction of both the press and the cinema-going public was almost unanimously positive. 'Some of us are already beginning to say that talkies are an art,' enthused *Close Up*, while *The Bystander* described the film as being 'packed throughout with excitement and incident.' *Variety* went even further, labeling the film 'a landmark,' while the *London Evening News* dubbed Hitchcock 'The Talkie King.'

However, Hitchcock had little time to rest on his laurels. A German language version of *Blackmail* had to be prepared (again directed by Hitch), while pre-production on his next assignment, a musical, was also under way. Nevertheless, it must have been deeply gratifying to him that, with this major cinematic achievement under his belt, he was now regarded as Britain's most innovative director.

Also note that Michael Powell, the future director of *The Red Shoes* (1948), is said to have contributed to the script, while another future director, Ronald Neame, served as the film's clapperboy. Neame of course went on to direct *Tunes of Glory* (1960), *The Prime of Miss Jean Brodie* (1968) and *The Poseidon Adventure* (1972).

Hitchcock cameo Hitchcock makes his cameo appearance in an amusing little vignette on a tube train, in which he is disturbed from reading his book by a mischievous young boy.

BLOCH, ROBERT (1917–1994) American novelist. Best known for penning the pulp shocker *Psycho*, which was published in 1959, Bloch went on to become a successful screenwriter following Hitchcock's blockbusting 1960 adaptation of the book (for which the author received just $9000 for the screen rights). His subsequent screen credits include *The Cabinet of Dr Caligari* (1962), *Strait Jacket* (1963), *The Night Walker* (1964), *Asylum* (1972) and *The Dead Don't Die* (1975, TV). One of his stories, *Mme Mystery*, was adapted for the *Alfred Hitchcock Presents* TV series, of which he also penned eight episodes. Later, in 1982 he authored *Psycho 2*, but the book wasn't used as the basis for the 1983 film of the same name. **Hitchography:** *Mme Mystery* (1960, TV), *Psycho* (1960), *The Cuckoo Clock* (1960, TV), *Change of Heart* (1961, TV), *The Greatest Monster of Them All* (1961, TV), *The Landlady* (1961, TV), *The Gloating Place* (1961, TV), *Bad Actor* (1962, TV), *The Big Kick* (1962, TV), *The Sorcerer's Apprentice* (1962, TV)

BLYTHE, JOHN (1921–1993) British character actor. Specializing in 'spiv' roles, Blythe turned to films in 1939 with *Goodbye, Mr Chips* following experience as a stagehand. His second film was the French-language wartime short *Bon Voyage* (1944), directed by Hitchcock at the behest of the Ministry of Information, in which he plays John Dougal, the RAF officer recounting his adventures with the Resistance. His other films include *The Way Ahead* (1944), *This Happy Breed* (1944), *On the Beat* (1962) and *Keep It Up Downstairs* (1976) **Hitchography:** *Bon Voyage* (1944)

BOBRINSKOY, ALEXI Danish character actor. Much on stage in Copenhagen, Bobrinskoy was chosen by Hitchcock to play the Foreign Prime Minister who is almost assassinated in his remake of *The Man Who Knew Too Much* (1956). **Hitchography:** *The Man Who Knew Too Much* (1956)

BOLTON, GUY (1884–1979) British playwright. Born in Britain to American parents, Bolton went on to become a major name in musicals, penning the books for such classic shows as *Lady be Good, Rio Rita, Girl Crazy, Anything Goes* and *Rosalie*. He also translated Marcelle Maurette's celebrated play *Anastasia*. His screen credits include *Grounds for Divorce* (1925), *The Love Parade* (1930) and Hitchcock's *Waltzes from Vienna* (1933), which he adapted from his own stage success, itself based on the German play *Waltzkrieg* by Heinz Reichhart, A M Wilmer and Ernest Marischka. His other screenplay credits include *The Guv'nor* (1934), *The Morals of Marcus* (1935) and *Adorable Julia* (1962). **Hitchography:** *Waltzes from Vienna* (1933)

Bon Voyage
(GB, 1944, 26m, bw)

CREDITS

Production company:	Phoenix/Ministry of Information
Director:	Alfred Hitchcock
Screenplay:	Angus MacPhail, J O C Orton, Claude Dauphin
Story:	Arthur Calder-Marshall
Cinematographer:	Gunther Krampf
Art director:	Charles Gilbert

CAST

John Blythe (Sergeant John Dougal), The Moliere Players (all other roles)

Video availability: Connoisseur

Between the making of *Lifeboat* (1944) and *Spellbound* (1945) in Hollywood, Hitchcock travelled to Britain where he made two short films for the Ministry of Information at the behest of his friend Sidney Bernstein, of which this was the first. Said Hitchcock: 'I felt the need to make a little contribution to the war effort.' [30] Filmed in French, the idea was to show the films in those areas of France where the invading Germans were losing ground, thus giving the French an appreciation of the key role of the Resistance.

In this first film, RAF pilot Sergeant John Dougal (John Blythe) recounts to an officer of the French Free Force in London how he escaped from occupied territory with the help of a Polish Resistance fighter named Stefan Godowski. Recalling their various adventures, he reveals how Godowski had to kill a Vichy informer so as to save their skins. However, at the end of his story, Sergeant Dougal is informed that Godowski was in fact a Gestapo agent, using Dougal as a means to flush out as many Resistance fighters as possible, among them the Vichy informer whom he murdered, who was in fact another Resistance worker.

Made at the cramped Welwyn Studios, the film was written by Angus MacPail (with whom Hitchcock would work again in America) and J O C Orton, with the assistance of various French writers and artists working in London, among them the stage and screen star Claude Dauphin. Unfortunately, despite its intriguing plot, the film is for the most part un-inventively staged, and almost 60 years on seems somewhat slow and stilted. By no means a lost gem, it might just have passed muster as a half-hour TV show thanks to its twist, but disappoints on almost every other level. Yet compared to its sister film, *Aventure Malgache* (1944), it's practically a work of art!

THE BONNIE BRIER BUSH see *Beside the Bonnie Brier Bush*

BORRADAILE, OSMOND (1898–1999) Canadian–born cinematographer. This distinguished cinematographer began his career in Hollywood in 1916, although he is best known for his work in Britain in the 1930s and 1940s, when he did much work for producer Alexander Korda as a second unit cameraman on the likes of *The Private Life of Henry VIII* (1933), *Sanders of the River* (1935), *The Four Feathers* (1939) and *The Thief of Bagdad* (1940). His many other films include *The Overlanders* (1946), on which he was the sole cinematographer, and *Scott of the Antarctic* (1948), which he co-photographed with Geoffrey Unsworth and Jack Cardiff. He also photographed the European second unit sequences for Hitchcock's *Foreign Correspondent* (1940). **Hitchography:** *Foreign Correspondent* (1940)

BOULTON, MATTHEW (1883–1962) British actor. This workaday actor appeared in minor roles in a number of movies in the 1930s and 1940s, among them *The Brighton Strangler* (1945), *The Woman in Green* (1945) and *Bulldog Drummond Strikes Back* (1947). He also appeared as a jury member in Hitchcock's *Murder!* (1930), and had a small role in *Sabotage* (1936). **Hitchography:** *Murder!* (1930), *Sabotage* (1936)

BOYLE, ROBERT (1910–) American production designer. Following experience as an architect, Boyle began working as an extra in films when his firm went bust. He joined the art department at Paramount in 1933, where he gained experience as a draughtsman and design assistant. He received his first screen credit as an art director on Hitchcock's *Saboteur* in 1942 (which he shared with one of the studio's supervising art directors, Jack Otterson). Boyle went on to design for Hitchcock a further four times, his best work being his Oscar-nominated efforts for *North by Northwest* (1959), for which his tasks included re-creating the interior of the United Nations and the giant presidential sculptures of Mount Rushmore, across which Cary Grant and Eva Marie Saint clamber during the climax. His many other films include *Flesh and Fantasy* (1943), *It Came from Outer Space* (1953), *How to Succeed in Business Without Really Trying* (1967), *Fiddler on the Roof* (1971) and *Troop Beverly Hills* (1989). **Hitchography:** *Saboteur* (1942), *Shadow of a Doubt* (1943), *North by Northwest* (1959), *The Birds* (1963), *Marnie* (1964)

BRAITHWAITE, DAME LILIAN (1873–1948) British actress. On stage from 1897, Braithwaite became one of the leading actresses of her generation. She made her film debut in 1915 in *The World's Desire*. Further film appearances were rare, among them *The Woman Who Was Nothing* (1916), *Castles in Spain* (1920) and Hitchcock's *Downhill* (1927), in which she played the imperious Lady Berwick. She also appeared in silent and sound versions of *The Chinese Puzzle* (1919 and 1932). Her film career came to a close in 1947 with a role in *A Man About the House*. **Hitchography:** *Downhill* (1927)

BRIDIE, JAMES (1888–1951, real name Osborne Henry Mavor) Scottish playwright. Bridie, whose works include *A Sleeping Clergyman* and *It Depends What You Mean*, also contributed to the occasional screenplay, including three for Hitchcock, beginning with *The Paradine Case* (1947). It was originally intended that Bridie work in America on *The Paradine Case*. However, when he arrived in New York and no one was there to greet him at the airport, he reportedly boarded the next plane home, where he completed his work, which he then mailed to the film's producer David O Selznick. Bridie also wrote the screenplay for Hitchcock's *Under Capricorn* (1949), but the film was not a success, some of the blame for which the director placed at Bridie's door, commenting of the writer: 'He was a semi-intellectual playwright and not, in my opinion, a very thorough craftsman… He always had very good first and second acts, but he never succeeded in ending his plays.' [31] Nevertheless, this didn't prevent Hitchcock from using Bridie again on *Stage Fright* (1950), to which he added some pawky humour. **Hitchography:** *The Paradine Case* (1947), *Under Capricorn* (1949), *Stage Fright* (1950)

BRISSON, CARL (1895–1958, real name Carl Pedersen) Danish-born boxer and actor. Brisson made his screen debut as fairground fighter 'One Round' Jack Sander in Hitchcock's *The Ring* (1927), which led to a further leading role for Hitchcock in *The Manxman* (1929). During the filming of *The Ring*, Hitchcock made the very most of Brisson's sporting background to add to the film's verisimilitude. 'I exploited Brisson's knowledge of boxing,' confessed the director. 'I told him to box as he would if it were a genuine match.' [32] Consequently, during the climactic bout, he attacked his opponent, unsuspecting actor Ian Hunter, 'with the eye of a practiced athlete.' [33] Brisson's other films include *The American Prisoner* (1929), *Murder at the Vanities* (1934) and *All the King's Men* (1935). **Hitchography:** *The Ring* (1927), *The Manxman* (1929)

BRITISH INTERNATIONAL STUDIOS (BIP) Founded in 1925 by J D Williams, W Schlesinger and Herbert Wilcox, this studio, originally named British National Films and today known simply as Elstree, was bought by former distributor and exhibitor John Maxwell in 1927, after which it was renamed British International Studios (though insiders nicknamed it The Porridge Factory owing to Maxwell's Scottish parsimony). Among those put under contract to the new studio were Alfred Hitchcock, who went on to make 12 films there, of which he directed 11 and produced the twelfth. They were *The Ring* (1927), *The Farmer's Wife* (1928), *Champagne* (1928), *The Manxman* (1929), *Blackmail* (1929), *Elstree Calling* (1930), *Juno and the Paycock* (1930), *Murder!* (1930), *The Skin Game* (1931), *Number Seventeen* (1932), *Rich and Strange* (1932) and *Lord Camber's Ladies* (1932), the latter directed by Benn W Levy, who had co-scripted *Blackmail* for Hitchcock. Hitchcock left the studio in 1932 following a dispute over a proposed Bulldog Drummond film. However, he did return to direct *Jamaica Inn* there in 1939,

although the production company was Mayflower, which merely rented studio space from BIP.

BRITISH NATIONAL FILMS see British International Studios

BRITTANY, MORGAN (1951– , real name Suzanne Caputo) American actress. In films from a child, Brittany appeared in a number of 1960s' productions, including *Gypsy* (1962) and *Yours, Mine and Ours* (1968). She also appeared twice for Hitchcock, in *The Birds* (1963), in which she played one of the schoolchildren terrorized by the titular creatures, and *Marnie* (1964), in which she again played a schoolgirl. Her adult credits include *The Day of the Locust* (1974), *Gable and Lombard* (1976) and *The Prodigal* (1983), while on television her work includes *Dallas* (1981–1984) and *Glitter* (1984–1985). **Hitchography:** *The Birds* (1963), *Marnie* (1964)

BROOK, CLIVE (1887–1974, real name Clifford Brook) British-born stage star. Brook is today primarily remembered for one of his last films, the comedy *On Approval* (1944), which he also co-scripted and directed. In films from 1920 with *Trent's Last Case*, he later went to Hollywood, where he had major successes with *Shanghai Express* (1932) and *Cavalcade* (1933). In 1923, he was contracted to appear in three films for Balcon-Freedman-Saville, on which Alfred Hitchcock worked as an assistant director. Brook's other films include *East Lynne* (1931), *Convoy* (1940) and *The List of Adrian Messenger* (1963). Brook's daughter, actress Faith Brook (1922–), had an un-credited role in Hitchcock's *Suspicion* (1941). **Hitchography:** *Woman to Woman* (1923), *The White Shadow* (1924), *The Passionate Adventure* (1924)

BROOK, FAITH (1922–) British actress. The daughter of stage star Clive Brook (1887–1974, real name Clifford Brook), Brook began making films in Hollywood in the early 1940s, among her first un-credited roles being that of Alice Barham in Hitchcock's *Suspicion* (1941). Her other films include *The Jungle Book* (1942), *To Sir with Love* (1966) and *The Sea Wolves* (1980). She also appeared in the 1959 remake of Hitchcock's *The Thirty-Nine Steps* as the ill-fated Nanny. **Hitchography:** *Suspicion* (1941)

BROOKE, HILLARY (1914–1999, real name Beatrice Peterson) American model turned-actress. In films from 1937 with *New Faces of 1937* following experience as a model, this Hollywood blonde became a familiar face in B movies of the 1940s and 1950s, among them *Sherlock Holmes and the Voice of Terror* (1942), *The Woman in Green* (1945) and *Invaders from Mars* (1953). She can also be found in supporting roles in the likes of Hitchcock's *The Man Who Knew Too Much* (1956), in which she played Jan Peterson, the socialite friend of the McKennas (Doris Day, James Stewart) in a few brief scenes. She had perhaps her greatest success on television, however, in such shows as *My Little Margie* (1952–1955) and *The Abbott and Costello*

Show (1953–1954). She retired from the screen in 1960 following her second marriage to MGM's general manager Ray Klune. **Hitchography:** *The Man Who Knew Too Much* (1956)

BROWN, BERNARD B American sound recordist. Long at Universal, Brown recorded and/or supervised the sound for countless films, among them *Son of Frankenstein* (1939), *Sherlock Holmes and the Voice of Terror* (1942), *Son of Dracula* (1943), *Sherlock Holmes in Washington* (1943), *The Michigan Kid* (1947), *Pirates of Monteray* (1947) and *The Vigilantes Return* (1947). He also supervised the sound for two Hitchcock pictures. **Hitchography:** *Saboteur* (1942), *Shadow of a Doubt* (1943)

BROWN, CHARLES D (1887–1948) American-born supporting actor. Busy from the late 1920s onwards, Brown appeared in the likes of *The Dance of Life* (1929), *It Happened One Night* (1934) and *The Grapes of Wrath* (1940). Despite playing the Judge in the early scenes of Hitchcock's *Notorious* (1946), his role went un-credited. **Hitchography:** *Notorious* (1946)

BROWN, JOHN American supporting actor. John Brown made but a handful of films, among them Hitchcock's *Strangers on a Train* (1951), in which he played the drunken Professor Collins who fails to provide Farley Granger's Guy Haines with a much-needed alibi (although he does get to sing an amusing song about a man and a goat!). His other films include *Hans Christian Andersen* (1952) and *Master Spy* (1964). **Hitchography:** *Strangers on a Train* (1951)

BROWN, LEW American supporting actor. Lew Brown made a handful of films in the 1950s, 1960s and 1970s, among them *Crime and Punishment USA* (1959), Hitchcock's *Topaz* (1969), in which he played a US official, and *Grand Theft Auto* (1977). **Hitchography:** *Topaz* (1969)

BROWN, WALLY (1898–1961) American comedy actor. Wally Brown was familiar to moviegoers in the 1940s for a number of comedies in which he was teamed with Alan Carney (1911–1973), among them *Adventures of a Rookie* (1944), *Zombies on Broadway* (1945) and *Genius at Work* (1945). He also made solo appearances as a supporting actor, among them a brief turn as Mr Hopkins in Hitchcock's *Notorious* (1946). His other films include *The High and the Mighty* (1954), *The Absent-Minded Professor* (1961) and the TV series *Cimarron City* (1958). **Hitchography:** *Notorious* (1946)

BROWNE, ROSCOE LEE (1925–) African-American character actor. On stage from 1956 following experience as an athlete and teacher, Browne began appearing in films in the early 1960s, among them *The Connection* (1962), *Black Like Me* (1964) and *The Cool World* (1964). In 1969 he played undercover agent Philippe Dubois in a memorable segment of Hitchcock's *Topaz*. This made him only the second black actor to have a featured role in a Hitchcock film following Canada Lee's appearance as George Joe Spencer in *Lifeboat* (1944). Browne's other films include *The Liberation of L B Jones* (1970), *The Cowboys* (1972), *Logan's Run* (1976), *The Mambo Kings* (1992) and *Babe* (1995), which he narrated. Meanwhile, on television, he was a popular fixture on such shows as *McCoy* (1975–1976) and *Soap* (1980–1981). **Hitchography:** *Topaz* (1969)

BRUCE, NIGEL (1895–1953) Mexican-borne British actor. Fondly remembered for portraying the bumbling Dr Watson opposite Basil Rathbone's Sherlock Holmes in 14 screen adventures, Bruce made his screen debut in Britain in 1929 in *Red Aces*. Following a handful of further films, among them *The Squeaker* (1930), *Lord Camber's Ladies* (1932), which was produced by Hitchcock, and *The Scarlet Pimpernel* (1934), Bruce went to Hollywood in 1934, providing able support in *Becky Sharp* (1935), *The Charge of the Light Brigade* (1936) and *The Rains Came* (1939). In 1940 he appeared as the Watson-esque Major Giles Lacy in Hitchcock's *Rebecca*, which in turn led to the role of Beaky in *Suspicion* (1941). Bruce's other films include *Lassie Come Home* (1943), *The Corn is Green* (1945) and *World for Ransom* (1954). **Hitchography:** *Lord Camber's Ladies* (1932), *Rebecca* (1940), *Suspicion* (1941)

BRUNEL, ADRIAN (1892–1958) British director. Directing from 1917 with *The Cost of a Kiss*, Brunel worked at Gainsborough and then British International Pictures at the same time as Alfred Hitchcock in the late 1920s and early 1930s, yet he never quite achieved the same heights as his friendly rival, either commercially or artistically, though he did handle several popular productions, among them *Blighty* (1927), *The Vortex* (1927) and *The Constant Nymph* (1928). In 1930, Brunel co-wrote and directed several episodes in the musical revue *Elstree Calling*, on which Hitchcock also worked. Unfortunately, Brunel did not enjoy the experience, and following three years out of work, his career began to steadily decline, ending in 1940 with two Ministry of Information shorts: *Food for Thought* and *Salvage with a Smile*. His other films include *The Bump* (1920), *The Shimmy Sheik* (1923), *A Light Woman* (1928), *Variety* (1934) and *The Lion Has Wings* (1939). **Hitchography:** *Elstree Calling* (1930)

BUCHAN, JOHN (1875–1940) British novelist. Buchan is best known for his thriller *The 39 Steps*, which has been filmed three times to date, most notably by Hitchcock in 1935, although the screenplay paid scant attention to Buchan's narrative. The other versions followed in 1959 and 1978, while a television series, *Hannay*, based on the further exploits of the book's hero, Richard Hannay, appeared in 1988. The only other book of Buchan's to have been filmed is *Huntingtower* (1922). Not only a writer, Buchan was a Conservative MP (from 1927) and the Governor General of Canada (from 1935, the same year he was created Baron Tweedsmuir of Elsfield). Note that following the release of *Marnie* (1964), Hitchcock toyed with the idea of filming Buchan's *The Three Hostages*, which again features the exploits of Richard Hannay. **Hitchography:** *The 39 Steps* (1935)

BULL, PETER (1912–1984) British character actor. This heavy-set actor was equally at home in comedy and melodrama (in which he was often cast as the bad guy). He made his film debut in 1936 in *As You Like It*. Later the same year he made an un-credited appearance in Hitchcock's *Sabotage* as an anarchist. His other films include *Oliver Twist* (1948), *Tom Jones* (1963), *Dr Strangelove* (1964) and *Alice's Adventures in Wonderland* (1972). He was also an authority on teddy bears, and his vast collection included the bear used to 'play' Aloysius in *Brideshead Revisted* (1981, TV). **Hitchography:** *Sabotage* (1936)

BULLDOG DRUMMOND'S BABY see Un-filmed Hitchcock

BUMSTEAD, HENRY (1915–) American art director. An Oscar winner for his work on both *To Kill a Mockingbird* (1962) and *The Sting* (1973), Bumstead began his career in the late 1940s on the likes of *Saigon* (1948) and *Song of Surrender* (1949). However, he got his biggest break when Hitchcock's regular cinematographer Robert Burks, with whom he'd worked on *The Vagabond King* (1956), suggested him as one of the art directors for Hitchcock's next film, *The Man Who Knew Too Much* (1956). Recalled Bumstead: 'I was surprised and thrilled that I was going to be working for Mr Hitchcock. I had admired his work for many years, but in my wildest dreams I never expected I would ever work for him.' [34] Bumstead went on to work for Hitch a further three times, most notably on *Vertigo* (1958), which earned him an Oscar nomination. Bumstead's other films include *Father Goose* (1964), *Slaughterhouse Five* (1971), *The World According to Garp* (1982), *Cape Fear* (1991), *Absolute Power* (1997) and *Space Cowboys* (2000). He also designed the sets for *Psycho III* (1986). **Hitchography:** *The Man Who Knew Too Much* (1956), *Vertigo* (1958), *Topaz* (1969), *Family Plot* (1976)

BURKS, ROBERT (1910–1968) American cinematographer. This distinguished cinematographer, who won an Oscar for his glossy work on Hitchcock's *To Catch a Thief*

Cinematographer Robert Burks captured this iconographic image for Hitchcock's North by Northwest *(1959). Burks worked on a total of 12 films with the director.*

(1955), was the director's preferred cameraman in the 1950s and early 1960s. One of the Master's key collaborators, he worked on 12 of his films in all, from *Strangers on a Train* (1951), which earned him an Oscar nomination, through to *Marnie* (1964), with the exception of *Psycho* (1960), which was photographed by John L Russell.

Burks began his film career in the early 1940s as a special effects technician, working on such films as *In This Our Life* (1942), *Arsenic and Old Lace* (1944) and *Key Largo* (1948). He became a cinematographer proper in 1944 with *Make Your Own Bed*, following which he continued to blend effects work with cinematography for the rest of the decade. It was his association with Hitchcock that firmly established Burks' reputation, though. Despite meeting the challenges of photographing *Dial M for Murder* (1954) in 3D and *Rear Window* (1954) from the confines of a single set (earning himself another Oscar nomination in the process), his best work was for *North by Northwest* (1959), which has the slickest cinematography of any Hitchcock film (commented *Variety*, 'Robert Burks' photography, whether in the hot yellows of the prairie plain, or the soft green of South Dakota forests, is lucid and imaginatively composed'). Burks' other credits include *The Glass Menagerie* (1950), *The Enforcer* (1951), *The Desert Song* (1953), *The Music Man* (1962), *A Patch of Blue* (1966) and *Waterhole Three* (1967). Tragically, he died in a house fire at the height of his career. **Hitchography:** *Strangers on a Train* (1951), *I Confess* (1953), *Dial M for Murder* (1954), *Rear Window*

(1954), *To Catch a Thief* (1955), *The Trouble with Harry* (1955), *The Man Who Knew Too Much* (1956), *The Wrong Man* (1957), *Vertigo* (1958), *North by Northwest* (1959), *The Birds* (1963), *Marnie* (1964)

BURR, RAYMOND (1917–1993) Canadian actor. Following experience on stage and radio, Burr made his film debut in 1946 in *Without Reservations*, which he followed with the likes of *San Quentin* (1946), *Code of the West* (1947) and *Ruthless* (1948). His stocky appearance saw him frequently cast in villainous roles, his most famous being the wife murderer Lars Thorwald in Hitchcock's *Rear Window* (1954). Though Burr had very little dialogue in the film, he more than made up for this with his convincingly sinister presence. Burr's many other films include *Criss Cross* (1949), *Godzilla* (1956) and *Affair in Havana* (1957), although he is best remembered for the television series *Perry Mason* (1957–1965) and *Ironside* (1967–1974). He resurrected *Perry Mason* in 1985, making several feature-length TV movies beginning with *Perry Mason Returns*. **Hitchography:** *Rear Window* (1954)

BUTTOLPH, DAVID (1902–1983) American composer. In films from 1934 with his score for *The World Moves On*, Buttolph went on to work on all manner of pictures, but eventually became known chiefly for his western scores, among them *The Return of Frank James* (1940), *The Lone Ranger* (1950) and *Guns of the Timberland* (1960). In 1948 he adapted Francois Poulenc's *Perpetual Movement* for the opening credits of Hitchcock's *Rope*. The piece was no doubt chosen as an in-joke, given that the camera is perpetually in motion during the film. Buttolph's other films include *Pigskin Parade* (1936), *The Three Musketeers* (1939), *The House on 92nd St.* (1945) and *House of Wax* (1953). **Hitchography:** *Rope* (1948)

Buy War Bonds
(US, 1943, 2m, bw)

CREDITS
Producer: David O Selznick
Director: Alfred Hitchcock

CAST
Jennifer Jones

In 1943, while under contract to David O Selznick, Hitchcock was asked to direct this short appeal film encouraging Americans to buy war bonds. The film ran to less than 2 minutes and featured rising star Jennifer Jones, whose career Selznick would mould (he was also to marry the actress in 1949).

C

CADY, FRANK American supporting actor. Cady appeared in just a handful of important films, notably *Ace in the Hole* (1951) and Hitchcock's *Rear Window* (1954), in which (with Sara Berner) he played the unnamed couple who sleep on their fire escape. His other films include *Let's Make it Legal* (1951) and *Zandy's Bride* (1974). **Hitchography:** *Rear Window* (1954)

CAIN, SYD British art director and production designer. Cain has worked on a wide variety of films, among them *Dr No* (1962), *Summer Holiday* (1962), *Fahrenheit 451* (1966), *On Her Majesty's Secret Service* (1969), *The Sea Wolves* (1980) and *Supergirl* (1984). In 1972, he designed Hitchcock's last British film, *Frenzy*, which made use of several London locations, including the Covent Garden fruit market, which has since been redeveloped as a shopping arcade. **Hitchography:** *Frenzy* (1972)

CALHERN, LOUIS (1895–1956, real name Carl Henry Vogt) American actor. In films from 1921 with *The Blot*, Calhern matured into one of Hollywood's most respected character actors. Among his many credits are *20,000 Years in Sing Sing* (1933), *The Life of Emile Zola* (1938), *Up in Arms* (1944), *Annie Get your Gun* (1950), in which he made an unexpected Buffalo Bill, *The Prisoner of Zenda* (1952), *Julius Caesar* (1953), in which he played Caesar, and *Forever Darling* (1956). In 1946 he appeared in Hitchcock's *Notorious* as cheerful FBI boss Paul Prescott, seemingly unconcerned that he is sending Ingrid Bergman's Alice Huberman on a somewhat dangerous mission to Brazil to unearth a group of neo-Nazis. **Hitchography:** *Notorious* (1946)

The Call of Youth
(GB, 1920, 39m approx, bw, silent)

CREDITS
Production company: Famous Players-Lasky
Director: Hugh Ford
Screenplay: Eve Unsell, Ouida Bergere, Margaret Turnbull, based on the play *James the Fogey* by Henry Arthur Jones
Inter-titles: Alfred Hitchcock

CAST
Jack Hobbs (Hubert Richmond), Mary Glynne (Betty Overton), Ben Webster (Mark Lanton), Marjorie Hume (Joan Lanton), Malcolm Cherry (James Agar), Gertrude Sterroll (Mrs Lanton)

The second of several lost black-and-white silent films with inter-titles designed by Hitchcock, this 1920 romance about a poor girl who is pursued by a millionaire, despite her love for another, was directed by

American import Hugh Ford at Islington Studios and was based on the play *James the Fogey* by Henry Arthur Jones. This was adapted for the screen by Ouida Bergere, Margaret Turnbull and Eve Unsell, the latter having worked with Ford previously in America on the script for the first screen version of *Mrs Wiggs of the Cabbage Patch* in 1919.

CALTHROP, DONALD (1888–1940) British actor. In films from 1916 with *Wanted: A Widow*, Calthrop quickly grew into a respected character actor in such productions as *The Gay Lord Quex* (1917), *Shooting Stars* (1927) and *Clue of the New Pin* (1929), the latter being Britain's first talkie. More often than not Calthrop was called upon to play villainous roles, his most famous being that of the blackmailer in Hitchcock's first talkie *Blackmail* (1929). He made a further four films for Hitchcock, and also appeared in such popular fare as *The Ghost Train* (1931), *Rome Express* (1932) and *Fire Over England* (1936). He died of a heart attack on the set of *Major Barbara* (1940) following news that one of his sons had been killed. Said Hitchcock of Calthrop's contribution to *Blackmail*: 'He was superb on the set. He has more to give as a motion picture actor than most people I have ever handled. He has such a wide range of expression. He could be compared to a Wurlitzer organ, which can give you everything from tremendous volume to the softest notes.' [1] **Hitchography:** *Blackmail* (1929), *Elstree Calling* (1930), *Juno and the Paycock* (1930), *Murder!* (1930), *Number Seventeen* (1932)

CARDIFF, JACK (1914–   ) British cinematographer. This distinguished cinematographer, noted for his Technicolor expertise, began his career as an assistant on *The Informer* (1929), following which he graduated to operator on such films as *The Ghost Goes West* (1935) and *Knight Without Armour* (1937). Technicolor's first UK technical recruit, he operated the camera for *Wings of the Morning* (1937), Britain's first Technicolor production, which in turn led to his photographing a number of travelogues in the *World Window* series. Cardiff shot his first feature, *Western Approaches*, in 1944, and following second unit work on *The Life and Death of Colonel Blimp* (1943) and contributions to *Caesar and Cleopatra* (1945), he went on to become the lighting cameraman for director Michael Powell, for whom he shot such classics as *A Matter of Life and Death* (1946), *Black Narcissus* (1947), for which he won an Oscar, and *The Red Shoes* (1948).

Following work on *Scott of the Antarctic* (1948), Cardiff photographed *Under Capricorn* (1949), Hitchcock's first British film for a decade, which included vestiges of the ten-minute take the director had pioneered in his previous film *Rope* (1948). To achieve these lengthy, mobile takes, the studio floor had to be covered with a thick layer of felt and carpet to ensure that the camera's movements were silent. Given that the camera moved from room to room (and even floor to floor), lighting was a particular problem. Recalled Cardiff: 'More than two-hundred lamps had to be rigged so they could be altered for various sequences. My lights were fixed on old cranes, dollies and even on old mic booms, so that I could move them silently during the scene. It was a fantastic sight to see a lamp silently glide through a window, or even through a hole in the wall, twist and tilt and pan in several directions, then just as mysteriously disappear again.' [2] However, Cardiff did feel that the film was 'fatally inhibited' [3] by the frequently lengthy takes, which proved counter-productive to the building of tension. Cardiff's other films as a cinematographer include *The African Queen* (1951), *War and Peace* (1956), *The Vikings* (1958), *Death on the Nile* (1978), *Ghost Story* (1981) and *Rambo: First Blood Part II* (1985). He has also directed several films, among them *Intent to Kill* (1958), *Sons and Lovers* (1960), for which he was nominated for an Oscar, *The Liquidator* (1965) and *The Mutations* (1974). He received an honorary Academy Award in 2001 for his achievements as a cinematographer. **Hitchography:** *Under Capricorn* (1949)

CAREY, LEONARD (1893-1977) British character actor. In Hollywood from the early 1930s, Carey had supporting roles in a number of films, including *Laughter* (1930), *Merrily We Go to Hell* (1932), *Bombshell* (1933) and *Slightly French* (1949), although he is best remembered for playing mad Ben in Hitchcock's *Rebecca* (1940). He also appeared as a butler in Hitchcock's *Suspicion* (1941), although this time his performance went un-credited, as did his role in *Strangers on a Train* (1951), again as a butler. **Hitchography:** *Rebecca* (1940), *Suspicion* (1941), *Strangers on a Train* (1951)

CAREY, MACDONALD (1913–1994) American actor. In films from 1942 with *Dr Broadway*, this workaday American leading man began his career as a singer on both stage and radio. In 1943 he played detective Jack Graham in Hitchcock's *Shadow of a Doubt*, in which he is on the trail of Joseph Cotten's Merry Widow Murderer. His other films include *Variety Girl* (1947), *Blue Denim* (1959) and *It's Alive III: Island of the Alive* (1988), as well as such television series as the long-running soap *Days of Our Lives* (1973–1994). He also appeared in an episode of *Alfred Hitchcock Presents* and an episode of *The Alfred Hitchcock Hour*. **Hitchography:** *Shadow of a Doubt* (1943), *Coyote Moon* (1959, TV), *House Guest* (1962, TV)

CARRERE, EDWARD American art director. An Oscar-winner for his work on the musical *Camelot* (1967), Carrere also designed the sets for *White Heat* (1949), *The Sweet Smell of Success* (1957) and *The Wild Bunch* (1969). In 1954 he worked on Hitchcock's *Dial M for Murder*, for which he designed the elegant but cramped London flat of Tony and Margot Wendice, in which the action of the film is almost entirely set. **Hitchography:** *Dial M for Murder* (1954)

CARROLL, LEO G (1892–1972) British-born supporting actor. One of Hitchcock's favourite supporting actors, Carroll was equally adept at both kindly and sinister roles, both of which he played for Hitchcock, his murderous Dr Merchison in *Spellbound* (1945) and his kindly Professor in *North by Northwest* (1959) being particularly memorable. On stage in England from 1911, Carroll made his American debut the following year. He turned to films in 1934 with *Every Woman Knows*, which he followed with *The Barretts of Wimpole Street* (1934), *Wuthering Heights* (1939) and his first appearance for Hitchcock in *Rebecca* (1940), in which he briefly appears as Dr Baker towards the end of the film. His many other films include *The House on 92nd Street* (1945), *Forever Amber* (1947), *Father of the Bride* (1950), *Tarantula* (1955) and the Hitchcockian *The Prize* (1963). In the mid-1950s, he was known to television audiences for the fantasy series *Topper* (1953–1954), in which he played the title role, while in the mid-1960s he became a household name as Mr Waverly in *The Man from U.N.C.L.E.* (1964–1967), several episodes of which were edited together and released theatrically. In *North by Northwest* Carroll got to say perhaps his most memorable line, commenting to Cary Grant's hapless Roger Thornhill, who has asked him if he's a member of the CIA: 'FBI, CIA, ONI, we're all in the same alphabet soup!'

Hitchography: *Rebecca* (1940), *Suspicion* (1941), *Spellbound* (1945), *The Paradine Case* (1948), *Strangers on a Train* (1951), *North by Northwest* (1959)

CARROLL, MADELEINE (1906–1987, real name Marie Madeleine Bernadette O'Carroll) British actress. In films from 1927 with *The Guns of Loos*, Madeleine Carroll actually began her career as a schoolteacher, but following a stage appearance in 1927 was quickly snapped up for films. One of the most poised and elegant screen actresses of her generation, she was much admired for her work in *Young Woodley* (1929), *I Was a Spy* (1933) and, in Hollywood, *The Prisoner of Zenda* (1937). However, her most memorable role was in Hitchcock's *The 39 Steps* (1935), in which her character, the haughty Pamela, finds herself handcuffed to Richard Hannay (Robert Donat) for much of the film, and subjected to such indignities as being dragged over the Scottish moors. Though she later complained about the way she was treated on the film (Hitchcock apparently took a certain glee in seeing such a glamorous star soaked and covered in mud), this didn't prevent her from returning to the Hitchcock fold the following year for *Secret Agent*, in which she played Elsa

Madeleine Carroll takes comfort from John Gielgud while Peter Lorre takes a swig of the hard stuff following the train crash climax of Hitchcock's Secret Agent *(1936).*

Carrington, who finds herself involved in a wartime murder plot. This time, though, her character was merely decorative and barely essential to the plot. Carroll's other films include *Northwest Mounted Police* (1940), *My Favorite Blonde* (1942), in which she spoofed her Hitchcock image, and *The Fan* (1949). Married four times, her second husband was the actor Sterling Hayden (1916–1985), to whom she was married between 1942 and 1946. Commented Michael Powell of Carroll's rise to stardom: 'She soon became the brightest and most popular star in England, pure and ladylike, a schoolboy's dream, until she met Alfred Hitchcock and Robert Donat on *The 39 Steps* in 1935. They soon knocked the stuffing out of her demure, lifeless, saint-like image, and she revealed that she had a sense of humour.' [4] **Hitchography:** *The 39 Steps* (1935), *Secret Agent* (1936)

CARRUTH, MILTON American film editor. Carruth worked for much of his career at Universal, where he cut several of the studio's key horror films, among them *Dracula* (1930), *The Mummy* (1932), *Werewolf of London* (1935) and *The Mummy's Tomb* (1942), along with countless westerns, including *Kansas Raiders* (1950), *Apache Drums* (1951) and *The Man from Bitter Ridge* (1955). He also edited Hitchcock's *Shadow of a Doubt* (1943), which proved to be one of his most prestigious assignments. **Hitchography:** *Shadow of a Doubt* (1943)

CARSON, CHARLES (1885–1977) British actor. On stage from 1919 following experience as a civil engineer, Carson made his film debut in 1930 with *Dreyfus*. In later years he tended to specialize in authority figures, an early example of which can be found in Hitchcock's *Secret Agent* (1936) in which he plays 'R', the head of a secret government agency whose undercover operators are sent abroad to assassinate enemy agents (rather like 'M' would do in the later James Bond novels and films). Carson's other films include *Things to Come* (1936), *The Dam Busters* (1954), *The Trials of Oscar Wilde* (1960) and *Lady Caroline Lamb* (1972). His stage work meanwhile included much Shakespeare as well as work as a director for ENSA during World War II. **Hitchography:** *Secret Agent* (1936)

CARSON, JACK (1910–1963) Canadian-born comedy actor. In films from 1935 with the short *Knife No. 5*, Jack Carson carved a niche for himself as a beefy comedy star, although he was equally adept at dramatic roles when given the chance, as in *The Star is Born* (1954), in which he played studio publicist Matt Libby. His many other films include *Stage Door* (1937), *Carefree* (1938), *Destry Rides Again* (1939), *Mildred Pierce* (1945) and *Dangerous When Wet* (1953). He also played the supporting role of Chuck Benson in Hitchcock's comedy *Mr and Mrs Smith* (1941) and later starred in an episode of *Alfred Hitchcock Presents*. **Hitchography:** *Mr and Mrs Smith* (1941), *The Children of Alda Nuova* (1962, TV)

CARTWRIGHT, VERONICA (1949–) British-born actress. In films from 1958 with *In Love and War*, child actress Cartwright moved to Hollywood at an early age, where she went on to appear in such films as *The Children's Hour* (1962), *Spencer's Mountain* (1963) and *One Man's Way* (1964), although the best known of her early films is Hitchcock's *The Birds* (1963), in which she played Cathy Brenner who, along with her schoolmates, finds herself the subject of an attack by the title creatures. Despite suffering this trauma, she gets to utter the film's most amusing line, in which she describes a crime committed by one of her lawyer brother's clients: 'He has a client now who shot his wife in the head six times. Six times! Can you imagine it? I mean, even *twice* would have been overdoing it, don't you think?' As an adult performer, Cartwright re-emerged in such films as *Goin' South* (1978), *Invasion of the Body Snatchers* (1978), *Alien* (1979), *The Witches of Eastwick* (1987) and *Candyman 2: Farewell to the Flesh* (1995). She is married to the director Richard Compton; her sister is the actress Angela Cartwright (1952–), best known for playing Brigitta in *The Sound of Music* (1965). **Hitchography:** *The Birds* (1963)

THE CASE OF JONATHAN DREW see *The Lodger* (1926 version)

CASEY, TAGGART American supporting actor. Though he can be seen in Hitchcock's *North by Northwest* (1959) for less than 30 seconds, this gruff-looking actor gets one of the film's biggest laughs, observing Cary Grant's Roger Thornhill trying to shave in a station washroom with a miniature lady's razor. His other films include *Heller in Pink Tights* (1960), *Sex and the Single Girl* (1964) and *The Navy vs the Night Monsters* (1966). **Hitchography:** *North by Northwest* (1959)

CASSON, ANN (1915–1990) British actress. The theatrical pedigree of Ann Casson was impeccable, given that she was the daughter of Dame Sybil Thorndike (1882–1976) and Sir Lewis Casson (1875–1969). However, like her parents, she made only a few films, among them *Escape* (1930), *Dance, Pretty Lady* (1932) and Hitchcock's *Number Seventeen* (1932), in which she finds herself handcuffed to a banister, which subsequently breaks free and leaves her dangling several storeys in mid-air. Her mother later appeared in Hitchcock's *Stage Fright* (1950). **Hitchography:** *Number Seventeen* (1932)

CELLIER, FRANK (1884–1948) British supporting actor. Cellier appeared in countless British films in the 1930s and 1940s, among his more memorable appearances being that of the Sheriff in Hitchcock's *The 39 Steps* (1935), whose disbelief that his friend the Professor could be the leader of a ring of spies causes Robert Donat's Richard Hannay to go on the run a second time. Cellier's other films include *Dosshouse* (1933), *Rhodes of Africa* (1936) and *The Blind Goddess* (1947). **Hitchography:** *The 39 Steps* (1935)

Champagne
(GB, 1928, 80m (some sources state 90m and 100m), bw, silent film)

CREDITS
Production company:	British International Pictures
Producer:	John Maxwell
Director:	Alfred Hitchcock
Screenwriters:	Eliot Stannard, Alfred Hitchcock, based on the novel by Walter C Mycroft
Cinematographer:	Jack Cox
Art director:	C W Arnold
Assistant director:	Frank Mills
Stills:	Michael Powell

CAST
Betty Balfour (Betty), Gordon Harker (Betty's father), Jean Bradin (Betty's boyfriend), Claude Hulbert (Guest), Clifford Heatherley (Manager), Marcel Vibert (*Maitre d'hotel*), Phyllis Konstam, Jack Trevor, Theo Von Alten, Fredinand Von Alten, Hannah Jones, Balliol and Merton

Described by *The Bioscope* as 'bright entertainment' and by Hitchcock himself as 'probably the lowest ebb in my output,' [5] this fitfully effervescent comedy drama centres round Betty (Betty Balfour), the vivacious daughter of a millionaire (Gordon Harker) who falls in love with a penniless young man (Jean Bradin), with whom she absconds to France, much to her father's chagrin. In an attempt to make his daughter see sense, dad pretends to be bankrupt, thus forcing Betty to search for work, which she finds in a seedy cabaret. All ends happily, though, with father seeing sense and Betty married to her beau after all.

In this still taken by Michael Powell, Betty Balfour finds herself the centre of some unwanted attention in Hitchcock's Champagne *(1928).*

Despite Hitchcock's misgivings about the film, it contains several interesting touches, among them various shots through the bottoms of champagne glasses and a running gag involving a drunk onboard the ship Betty and her man take to France; when the sea is calm, the drunk staggers about the ship, yet when it hits rough waters, he's the only person able to walk straight!

Although mostly made by Hitchcock's then-regular crew (producer John Maxwell, writer Eliot Stannard, cinematographer Jack Cox), the film did offer work to one particular newcomer, stills cameraman Michael Powell, who of course went on to become a celebrated director in his own right. Recalled Powell of Hitchcock's feelings during the making of *Champagne*: 'Rumour said that he was far from happy. He had signed a long term contract with BIP after the success of *The Lodger* and *The Ring*, and was getting a big salary for the first time in his life. But he had no control or choice of subject: he had to make what the studio assigned him. He hated the frothy story *Champagne* [and] he hated Betty Balfour as a "piece of suburban obscenity".' [6]

Note that the film was also remade the following year in Germany with the same leading lady, though Hitchcock himself had nothing to do with the production.

Champagne
(GB/Ger, 1929, 80m approx, bw, silent film)

CREDITS
Production company:	BIP/Sascha Film
Director:	Gaza von Bolvary

CAST
Betty Balfour, Vivian Gibson, Jack Trevor, Marcel Vibert

Though this talkie German version of Hitchcock's 1928 silent starred the same leading lady, Betty Balfour, Hitchcock himself had nothing to do with the film, which was directed by Gaza von Bolvary. A co-production between British International Pictures and Sascha Film, it co-starred Vivian Gibson, Jack Trevor and Marcel Vibert, the latter also from Hitchcock's version. Sadly, little else is known about this apparently lost film.

CHANDLER, JOAN (1923–1979) American actress. Chandler was briefly popular in films in the 1940s, among them *Humoresque* (1947) and *The Street with No Name* (1948). She also played the wisecracking Janet Walker in Hitchcock's *Rope* (1948). **Hitchography:** *Rope* (1948)

CHANDLER, RAYMOND (1888–1959) American author. Acclaimed for his work in the detective genre, this acerbic author began his career as a journalist in England, where he'd spent much of his youth. However, it wasn't until the early 1930s, back in America following business experience in the oil industry, that he began writing short stories for magazines. His subsequent novels include such classics as *Farewell, My Lovely, The Big Sleep, The Long Goodbye, Lady in the Lake* and *The Little Sister*, all of which have been filmed in various guises. In Hollywood from the mid-1940s, Chandler contributed to the screenplays of *Double Indemnity* (1944), *And Now to Tomorrow* (1944), *The Unseen* (1945) and *The Blue Dahlia* (1946). Sadly, the time he spent writing *Strangers on a Train* (1951) for Hitchcock was an unhappy experience for both parties. Complained Chandler to his agent, future producer Ray Stark: 'Hitchcock seems to be a very considerate and polite man, but he is full of little suggestions and ideas which have a cramping effect on a writer's imagination... He is always ready to sacrifice dramatic logic (in so far as it exists) for the sake of a camera effect or a mood effect... He knows that in almost all his pictures there is some point where the story ceases to make any sense whatever and becomes a chase, but he doesn't mind. This is very hard on a writer, especially on a writer who has any ideas of his own, because [he] not only has to make sense out of the foolish plot, if he can, but he has to do that and at the same time do it in such a way that any kind of camera shot or background shot that comes into Hitchcock's mind can be incorporated into it.' [7] **Hitchography:** *Strangers on a Train* (1951)

CHAPMAN, EDWARD (1901–1977) British actor. Though remembered today chiefly for playing Mr Grimsdale in a series of films with comedian Norman Wisdom, there was much more than this to the career of Edward Chapman. He began performing on stage in 1924 following experience as a bank clerk. He made his film debut six years later in Hitchcock's adaptation of Sean O'Casey's *Juno and the Paycock*, in which he played the work shy 'Captain' Boyle, a role he inherited when the actor who originated it on stage, Arthur Sinclair, proved unavailable owing to a theatrical tour. Impressed by his performance, Hitchcock cast Chapman in his next two films, *Murder!* (1930) and *The Skin Game* (1931). Throughout the 1930s, 1940s and 1950s Chapman established himself as a thoroughly reliable character man, appearing in the likes of *Things to Come* (1936), *It Always Rains on Sunday* (1947) and *The October Man* (1947), in which he played a murderer. However, it was opposite Norman Wisdom in the likes of *The Square Peg* (1958) and *The Early Bird* (1965) that his talent for comedy came into its own. His last film was *The Man Who Haunted Himself* (1970). **Hitchography:** *Juno and the Paycock* (1930), *Murder!* (1930), *The Skin Game* (1931)

CHAPMAN, LONNY (1920–) American supporting actor. In films from 1954, Chapman has appeared in close to 50 films, among them *East of Eden* (1954), *Baby Doll* (1956), *Moving Violation* (1976) and *The China Lake Murders* (1990, TV). He can also be spotted in Hitchcock's *The Birds* (1963) as farmer Deke Carter. **Hitchography:** *The Birds* (1963)

Charters and Caldicott

(GB, 1985 6x50m TV episodes, colour) ★

CREDITS

Production company:	BBC/Network Seven
Producer:	Ron Craddock
Director:	Julian Amyes
Screenwriter:	Keith Waterhouse, based on the characters created by Sidney Gilliat and Frank Launder

CAST

Robin Bailey (Charters), Michael Aldridge (Caldicott)

The cricket-mad English gents Charters and Caldicott first appeared in Hitchcock's *The Lady Vanishes* (1938) and were played by Basil Radford and Naunton Wayne. The invention of one of the film's screenwriters, Sidney Gilliat (they do not appear in *The Wheel Spins*, the Ethel Lina White novel on which the films is based), they proved so popular with audiences that they went on to appear in two further films: *Night Train to Munich* (1940), again written by Sidney Gilliat and Frank Launder, and *Crook's Tour* (1941). They also had their own radio series in the 1940s, while Radford and Wayne subsequently went on to partner each other in a total of 11 films, including *Dead of Night* (1945) and *It's Not Cricket* (1949), the latter co-directed by Alfred Roome, who had edited *The Lady Vanishes*. In the 1979 remake of *The Lady Vanishes*, Charters and Caldicott were played by Arthur Lowe and Ian Carmichael, while in 1985, they re-appeared yet again in their own television series in the guise of Robin Bailey and Michael Aldridge, their various adventures this time including murder.

CHEKHOV, MICHAEL (1891–1955) Russian character actor. A relative of the celebrated dramatist Anton Chekhov (1860–1904), Michael Chekhov made his film debut in America in *Song of Russia* in 1944, prior to which he had been involved in establishing drama schools in both London and New York. His films were few, among them *In Our Time* (1944), *Spectre of the Rose* (1946), *Arch of Triumph* (1947) and *Rhapsody* (1954), although he is best remembered for playing psychiatrist Dr Brulov in Hitchcock's *Spellbound* (1945), a role which earned him a best supporting actor Oscar nomination. He certainly had some of the film's best lines, among them such misogynist observations as, 'We both know that the mind of a woman in love is operating on the lowest level of the intellect.' **Hitchography:** *Spellbound* (1945)

CHESNEY, ARTHUR (1882–1949, real name Arthur Gwenn) British stage actor. This busy actor was used by Hitchcock to play the suspicious landlord Mr Bunting in his breakthrough film *The Lodger* (1926). Interestingly, Chesney's brother, character star Edmund Gwenn (1875–1959), who made several films for Hitchcock, played the same role in a 1940 radio broadcast of the story, which Hitchcock himself adapted from *The Lodger's* original shooting script. **Hitchography:** *The Lodger* (1926)

CIANNELLI, EDUARDO (1887–1969) Italian-born character actor. Ciannelli found much work in Hollywood in the 1930s and 1940s, often in unscrupulous roles, among them Mr Krug in Hitchcock's *Foreign Correspondent* (1940), which *Variety* described as, 'the usual hiss-able villain.' In films from 1917 with *The Gamblers*, he went on to appear in over 100 productions, among them *Reunion in Vienna* (1933), *Angels Wash Their Faces* (1939), *For Whom the Bell Tolls* (1943) and *Seven Keys to Baldpate* (1947). In 1949, he began to appear mostly in Italian films (or Hollywood films shot on Italian locations), among them *Patto con Diavolo* (1949), *Helen of Troy* (1954) and *La Collina degli Stivali* (1969). He also appeared in an episode of *Alfred Hitchcock Presents*. **Hitchography:** *Foreign Correspondent* (1940), *The Test* (1962, TV)

CLARE, MARY (1894–1970) British actress. On stage from 1910, and in films from 1920 with *The Black Spider*, Clare, like Martita Hunt, could be relied upon to bring a touch of dignity to the screen, even when playing slightly villainous roles. Her many films include *The Skin Game* (1922), which Hitchcock later remade in 1931, *Hindle Wakes* (1931), *Lorna Doone* (1935), *Oliver Twist* (1948) and, again, *Hindle Wakes* (1952). She is best remembered for her two roles for Hitchcock, as Erica's suspicious aunt in *Young and Innocent* (1937), in which she manages to turn a children's birthday party into an ordeal for the leading protagonists, and the imperious Baroness in *The Lady Vanishes* (1938), who, it transpires, is part of the plot to kidnap poor Miss Froy ('There has been no English lady here!'). **Hitchography:** *Young and Innocent* (1937), *The Lady Vanishes* (1938)

CLARK, CARROLL (1894–1968) American art director. Following experience at both Pathe and with David O Selznick, Clark served a long period at RKO, beginning in the early 1930s. During his time at the studio, Clark worked on such high profile productions as *King Kong* (1933), *Top Hat* (1935) and *Bachelor Mother* (1939). He also worked twice for Hitchcock, on *Suspicion* (1941) and *Notorious* (1946). When Clark left RKO in the 1950s, he went to work for Disney, designing many of the studio's live action films, among them *Old Yeller* (1957), *Babes in Toyland* (1961) and *Mary Poppins* (1964). **Hitchography:** *Suspicion* (1941), *Notorious* (1946)

CLATWORTHY, ROBERT American art director. An Oscar winner for his work on *Ship of Fools* (1965), Clatworthy began his career as a design assistant in the 1940s, one of his earliest jobs being that of assistant to Robert Boyle on Hitchcock's *Saboteur* (1942). His later credits include *Touch of Evil* (1958) and Hitchcock's *Psycho* (1960), both of which, ironically, feature Janet Leigh in peril at a run down motel. Clatworthy worked

on *Psycho* with Joseph Hurley, and the duo received an Oscar nomination for their efforts. Recalled Clatworthy: 'Even though Hitchcock was an art director himself originally, he spoke only very generally. On the Bates house, he didn't say he wanted any particular look – which was one of the great things about him. He let you present your ideas.' [8] The art director's other credits include *That Touch of Mink* (1962), *The Secret of Santa Vittoria* (1969) and *Carwash* (1976). **Hitchography:** *Saboteur* (1942), *Psycho* (1960)

CLIFT, MONTGOMERY (1920–1966) American actor. Before the likes of James Dean and Marlon Brando popularized the Method in the 1950s, Clift was practicing this naturalized style of acting as early as 1947, when he was one of the founder members of the Actors' Studio. On stage from the age of 14, he went on to appear in stock and on Broadway before going to Hollywood to make the western *Red River* (1948). However, due to the film's lengthy post-production, it was his second film, *The Search* (1948), which was released first, earning the actor an Academy Award nomination. Clift's subsequent films include *The Heiress* (1949), *The Big Lift* (1950), *A Place in the Sun* (1951) and Hitchcock's *I Confess* (1953), in which he plays Father Michael Logan, a Catholic priest who hears the confession of a murderer only to find himself accused of the crime himself, but unable to tell the truth owing to the sanctity of the confessional. The film was not a commercial success, although critics praised Clift's performance. Said *Variety*, 'Clift's ability to project mood with restrained strength is a high spot of the film… his work is flawless.' Clift subsequently appeared in *From Here to Eternity* (1953), *Indiscretion of an American Wife* (1954) and *Raintree County* (1957), during the filming of which he was involved in a major car crash. Following reconstructive surgery, Clift resumed his career, which included *The Young Lions* (1958), *Lonelyhearts* (1959), *Suddenly Last Summer* (1959), *Wild River* (1960), *The Misfits* (1961), *Judgment at Nuremberg* (1961), *Freud* (1962) and *The Defector* (1966). He died of a heart attack following years of drug and alcohol abuse. He was just 45. **Hitchography:** *I Confess* (1953)

CLIVE, E E (1878–1940, real name Edward Clive) Welsh-born actor. Although he didn't arrive in Hollywood until the age of 55, Clive certainly made up for time during the seven years he lived there, clocking up an amazing 87 films, 21 of them in 1936 alone! Familiar to audiences as Tenny, Bulldog Drummond's manservant in the series of popular second features, he can also be seen in *The Invisible Man* (1933), which marked his debut, *Charlie Chan in London* (1934), *Clive of India* (1935), *Mr Moto's Last Warning* (1939) and *The Hound of the Baskervilles* (1940). His last film was an uncredited appearance as Mr Naismith in Hitchcock's *Foreign Correspondent* (1940). **Hitchography:** *Foreign Correspondent* (1940)

COBURN, CHARLES (1877–1961) American character actor. Coburn was always a welcome addition to the cast of any film. Following experience as a stage manager, he turned to acting in the late 1890s, making his Broadway debut in 1901. He didn't make his first film until the age of 56 with *Boss Tweed* (1933), following which he went on to become a highly respected supporting actor in the likes of *King's Row* (1941), *In This Our Life* (1942), *Heaven Can Wait* (1943) and *The More the Merrier* (1943), the latter winning him a best supporting actor Oscar. In 1947 he played Sir Simon Flaquer in Hitchcock's *The Paradine Case*, and though he had only a few brief scenes, he left his mark on the film thanks to his jovial persona and his way with an artful putdown or two. His other credits include *Monkey Business* (1952), *Around the World in Eighty Days* (1956) and *Pepe* (1960). **Hitchography:** *The Paradine Case* (1947)

COLASANTO, NICHOLAS (?–1985) American character actor. Best known for playing the dim-witted Coach in the sit-com *Cheers* (1982–1985), Colasanto also popped up in the occasional film, among them *The Counterfeit Killer* (1968), *Fat City* (1972) and Hitchcock's *Family Plot* (1976), in which he played kidnap victim Constantine. **Hitchography:** *Family Plot* (1976)

COLEMAN, HERBERT American producer. Long at Paramount, Coleman worked with Hitchcock on several of his key 1950s films, beginning with *Rear Window* (1954), on which he was the assistant director. He next directed the second unit sequences for *To Catch a Thief* (1955), among them the impressive aerial shots of the Corniche. After this he graduated to the position of associate producer on *The Trouble with Harry* (1955), in which capacity he worked on another five Hitchcocks. He began his film career as a humble studio driver in 1927. **Hitchography:** *Rear Window* (1954), *To Catch a Thief* (1955), *The Trouble with Harry* (1955), *The Man Who Knew Too Much* (1956), *The Wrong Man* (1956), *Vertigo* (1958), *North by Northwest* (1959), *Topaz* (1969)

COLLIER, CONSTANCE (1878–1955, real name Laura Constance Hardie) British stage actress. This celebrated actress made her stage debut in 1881 at the age of 3. Following experience as a chorus girl, she developed into one of the leading lights of her generation, working in both the West End and on Broadway. She made her film debut in 1916 in *Intolerance*, which she followed with the likes of *Macbeth* (1916), *Bleak House* (1920) and *The Bohemian Girl* (1922). In old age she began to play increasingly imperious roles in the likes of *Stage Door* (1937), *Kitty* (1946) and *Whirlpool* (1950), following which she retired from the screen. She crossed paths with Hitchcock twice in her career: first as the co-author (with Ivor Novello) of the play *Downhill*, which was filmed in 1927 (and for which she and Novello used the *nom de plume* David Lestrange), and secondly as an actress in *Rope* (1948), in which she played Mrs Atwater. However, close

scrutiny of her performance in the latter reveals that she was far from comfortable with the ten-minute takes required for the film. **Hitchography:** *Downhill* (1927), *Rope* (1948)

COLLINGE, PATRICIA (1894–1974) Irish-born actress. On stage from 1904, Collinge made her Broadway debut in 1908. She didn't make her first film, *The Little Foxes*, until 1941, in which she re-created her stage role of Aunt Birdie, for which she was nominated for a best supporting actress Oscar. Her next film was Hitchcock's *Shadow of a Doubt* (1943) in which she played Emma Newton; she also made an un-credited contribution to the film's screenplay, penning the love scene between her character's daughter Charlie (Teresa Wright) and detective Jack Graham (MacDonald Carey). Collinge made just five further films: *Tender Comrade* (1944), *Casanova Brown* (1944), *Teresa* (1951), *Washington Story* (1952) and *The Nun's Story* (1959). However, she did appear in three episodes of *Alfred Hitchcock Presents* and an episode of *The Alfred Hitchcock Hour*. She was also a successful writer of short stories. **Hitchography:** *Shadow of a Doubt* (1943), *The Cheney Vase* (1955, TV), *Across the Threshold* (1960, TV), *The Landlady* (1961, TV), *The Ordeal of Mrs Snow* (1964, TV)

COLVIG, HELEN American costume designer. Colvig made her film debut with fellow costumier Rita Riggs on Hitchcock's *Psycho* (1960), prior to which they'd both worked on the director's TV show *Alfred Hitchcock Presents*. Recalled Colvig of her experiences on the film: 'I was kind of shaky, but I'd been told Hitchcock had it in his mind to do it [the film] as television – realism, speed, with a documentary feeling around the edges… His research was so pure. He laid out photographs for every major character. In Phoenix, he'd found a girl like Marion, went into her home, photographed everything from her closet, her bureau drawers, her suitcases.' [9] **Hitchography:** *Alfred Hitchcock Presents* (1955–1965, TV), *Psycho* (1960)

COMPSON, BETTY (1896–1974, real name Eleanor Compson) American-born comedy actress. Compson made her film debut in 1914 in the aptly titled *Wanted – A Leading Lady*. She quickly established herself in a number of one-reel comedies, among them *Her Steady Car Fare* (1915), *Cupid Trims His Lordship* (1915) and *Love and Vaccination* (1915). In 1919 she began to add drama to her repertoire, and appeared in *The Miracle Man* with Lon Chaney. In 1923, she travelled to London where she was contracted – at £1000 a week - to appear in three films for Balcon-Freedman-Saville, on which the young Alfred Hitchcock worked as an assistant director. The first of these was *Woman to Woman*, which Compson remade in 1929. Many years later in Hollywood, the now established Hitchcock directed Compson in a small role in his comedy *Mr and Mrs Smith* (1941). Compson's other films include *The Barker* (1928), which earned her an Oscar nomination, *A Slight Case of Murder* (1938) and *Here Comes Trouble* (1948). **Hitchography:** *Woman to Woman*

(1923), *The White Shadow* (1924), *The Prude's Fall* (1925), *Mr and Mrs Smith* (1941)

COMPTON, FAY (1894–1978, real name Virginia C Mackenzie) British stage actress. This respected actress occasionally ventured into films, more so in older age as a character actress. She made her film debut in 1914 in *She Stoops to Conquer*. Her other films include *A Bill for Divorcement* (1922), *Odd Man Out* (1946) and *The Virgin and the Gypsy* (1978). She also appeared in Hitchcock's *Waltzes from Vienna* (1933) as the Countess. Sadly, this was her only appearance for Hitch. Her brother was the celebrated author Sir Compton Mackenzie (1883–1972), best known for the novel and film of *Whisky Galore* (1948).
Hitchography: *Waltzes from Vienna* (1933)

CONNERY, SIR SEAN (1930– , real name Thomas Connery) Scottish actor. 'Sean Connery *is* James Bond' proclaimed film posters throughout the 1960s, and very early on the star realized he was in danger of being type cast. Consequently, he made a number of films in distinct contrast to his Bond image, the first of which was Hitchcock's *Marnie* (1964), made after he had completed his second Bond film *From Russia with Love* (1963). In it he plays Philadelphia businessman Mark Rutland, whose curious obsession with kleptomaniac Marion Edgar (Tippi Hedren) leads to some dramatic realizations and revelations. The film was not a success and Connery didn't seem entirely suited to his role, about which *Variety* commen-ted: 'Connery handles himself convincingly, but… greater interest would have resulted from greater facets of character as he attempts to explore femme's unexplained past.' Nevertheless, Connery seemed to enjoy working with the director: 'I adored and enjoyed Hitchcock tremendously. He never lost his patience or composure on the set, and he never looked through a viewfinder because he had every frame of the movie in his head from that first day of shooting.' [10]

Connery came to films in 1954 with a bit part in *Lilacs in the Spring*, prior to which he'd had military experience in the navy, worked as a milkman and a coffin polisher, had represented Scotland in the Mr Universe contest and broken into the theatre as a chorus boy in the London run of *South Pacific*. Television work followed, along with appearances in such films as *No Road Back* (1956), *Darby O'Gill and the Little People* (1959) and *On the Fiddle* (1961), but his career didn't skyrocket until he was cast as James Bond in *Dr No* (1962). A further six Bond films followed, including *Goldfinger* (1964), *Thunderball* (1965) and a belated return with *Never Say Never Again* (1983), along

Sean Connery and Diane Baker look on as Hitchcock instructs Tippi Hedren on how to play a scene in Marnie *(1964).*

with such diverse productions as *Shalako* (1968), *The Offence* (1973), *The First Great Train Robbery* (1978), *Outland* (1981), *The Name of the Rose* (1986), *The Untouchables* (1987), which earned him a best supporting actor Oscar, *Indiana Jones and the Last Crusade* (1989), *Rising Sun* (1993) and *Entrapment* (1999). He is the father of actor Jason Connery (1963–), from his marriage to actress Diane Cilento (1933–), to whom he was married between 1962 and 1973 (Cilento later married playwright Anthony Shaffer, who scripted Hitchcock's *Frenzy* (1972)). Connery married his second wife, painter Micheline Roqubrune in 1975. He was knighted in 1999. Commented Connery of Hitchcock: 'He always had an active mind, and he survived to 81 – pretty good for a man who never did any exercise, always weighed over 250 pounds, and had a fair whack at the booze.' [11] **Hitchography:** *Marnie* (1964)

CONWELL, CAROLYN American actress. Best remembered as the farmer's wife who has to help Paul Newman's Professor Michael Armstrong kill an East German agent in her kitchen in Hitchcock's *Torn Curtain* (1966), Conwell speaks but a few lines in German in the film, but is perfectly cast, looking as if she's emerged straight from a UFA film of the 1920s or 1930s. Her other films include *The Boston Strangler* (1968) and *Adam at 6 A.M.* (1970). **Hitchography:** *Torn Curtain* (1966)

COOK, WHITFIELD American playwright. Cook had a certain success with a series of short stories about a schoolgirl named Violet, which were published in *Red Book* in the early 1940s. These were subsequently turned into a play, also titled *Violet*, in which the young Patricia Hitchcock starred on Broadway in 1945. Cook's connection with the Hitchcock family didn't end there, though. He also penned the screenplay for Hitchcock's *Stage Fright* (1950) and worked on the adaptation of *Strangers on a Train* (1951), both of which featured cameos by Patricia Hitchcock. **Hitchography:** *Stage Fright* (1950), *Strangers on a Train* (1951)

COOPER, CHARLES American supporting actor. Cooper has but a few screen credits to his name, notable among them Hitchcock's *The Wrong Man* (1956), in which he played Detective Matthews. He can also be seen in *A Dog's Best Friend* (1960), *Gun Fight* (1961), *FBI Code 98* (1964) and *The Big Bounce* (1969). **Hitchography:** *The Wrong Man* (1956)

COOPER, DAME GLADYS (1888–1971) British actress. On stage from the turn of the century, Gladys Cooper became one of the most admired leading ladies of her generation. She began to dabble in films as early as 1913 with *The Eleventh Commandment*, which she followed with appearances in *Dandy Donovan* (1914), *My Lady's Dress* (1917), *The Bohemian Girl* (1922) and *The Iron Duke* (1935). It wasn't until she went to Hollywood, however, that her celluloid career blossomed, thanks to her role as

Beatrice Lacy, sister of Maxim de Winter (Laurence Olivier), in Hitchcock's *Rebecca* (1940), in which she made the most of several waspish one-liners. Her subsequent films include *Now, Voyager* (1942), which earned her a best supporting actress Oscar nomination, *The Song of Bernadette* (1943), which brought a second supporting actress nomination, *The Bishop's Wife* (1947) and *Separate Tables* (1958). In 1964, she re-created for the screen her stage role of Mrs Higgins in the musical *My Fair Lady*, earning herself a third supporting actress nomination. She also appeared in an episode of *Alfred Hitchcock Presents* and two episodes of *The Alfred Hitchcock Hour* respectively. Her last film was *A Nice Girl Like Me* (1969). Her third husband was the actor Philip Merivale (1886–1946), who appeared in Hitchcock's *Mr and Mrs Smith* (1941). **Hitchography:** *Rebecca* (1940), *The End of Indian Summer* (1957, TV), *What Really Happened* (1963, TV), *Consider Her Ways* (1964, TV)

COOPER, MELVILLE (1896–1973) British-born actor. Ideally cast in pompous roles, Cooper began his film career in Britain in 1930 in the short *All Riot on the Western Front*. Having graduated to featured roles in *The Private Life of Don Juan* (1934) and *The Scarlet Pimpernel* (1934), he made the move to Hollywood in 1935, where he went on to leave his mark in a handful of classic films, among them *The Adventures of Robin Hood* (1938), in which he played the Sheriff of Nottingham, Hitchcock's *Rebecca* (1940), in which he played the Coroner, and *Pride and Prejudice* (1940), in which he played the snooty Mr Collins. His many other films include *The Great Garrick* (1937), *Tovarich* (1937), *The Lady Eve* (1941), *Random Harvest* (1942), *Father of the Bride* (1950) and *From the Earth to the Moon* (1958). He also appeared in a three-part programme in the *Alfred Hitchcock Presents* TV series. **Hitchography:** *Rebecca* (1940), *I Killed the Count* (1957, TV)

COOPER, WILKIE (1911–) British cinematographer. Wilkie Cooper followed in the footsteps of his father, cameraman D P Cooper. Having gained experience as an operator in the 1930s, he photographed his first film, *Ships with Wings*, in 1941, which he followed with the likes of *The Foreman Went to France* (1942), *I See a Dark Stranger* (1945), *The Admirable Crichton* (1957), *Jason and the Argonauts* (1963) and *Please, Sir!* (1971). He worked with many top directors, among them Alberto Cavalcanti, Basil Dearden, Sidney Gilliat, Frank Launder, Val Guest, Richard Lester, Guy Hamilton and, of course, Hitchcock, for whom he photographed *Stage Fright* (1950), which includes an elaborate crane shot through an entire house. **Hitchography:** *Stage Fright* (1950)

COPPEL, ALEC (1910–1972) Australian playwright and novelist. Coppel had a number of his works filmed in both Britain and America, among them *Obsession* (1946) and *The Gazebo* (1959). Also a screenwriter, his credits include *Over the Moon* (1939), *Mr Denning Drives North* (1951), *The*

Captain's Paradise (1953), which earned him an Oscar nomination, and *The Bliss of Mrs Blossom* (1969). Coppel also worked on two Hitchcock films: first on *To Catch a Thief* (1955), for which he penned a few brief re-take scenes in the absence of screenwriter John Michael Hayes, who was by then working on another project, and *Vertigo* (1958), for which he shared his credit with Samuel Taylor. Coppel also co-wrote an episode of *Alfred Hitchcock Presents* with Robert C Harris, while another was based on his story *Together*. **Hitchography:** *To Catch a Thief* (1955), *Vertigo* (1958), *The Diplomatic Corpse* (1957, TV), *Together* (1958, TV)

CORBY, ELLEN (1913–1999, real name Ellen Hansen) American character actress. Best remembered for her role as Grandma in TV's *The Waltons* (1972–1979), Corby came to acting full time following 12 years' experience as a script girl. She made her film debut in 1933 in *Twisted Rails* and went on to appear in *Little Women* the same year, following which she didn't appear before the cameras again until *Twilight on the Trail* in 1941. Following another four-year gap, her film career began in earnest with *Cornered* (1945), which led to *It's a Wonderful Life* (1946), *The Spiral Staircase* (1946), *Forever Amber* (1947), *I Remember Mamma* (1948), for which she earned a best supporting actress Oscar nomination, *Angels in the Outfield* (1951) and Hitchcock's *Vertigo* (1958), in which she played the manageress of the McKittrick Hotel, to which Scottie (James Stewart) follows the mysterious Madeleine (Kim Novak). Corby's other credits include *Four for Texas* (1963), *The Glass Bottom Boat* (1966), *The Legend of Lylah Clare* (1968) and *A Wedding on Walton's Mountain* (1983, TV). She also appeared in an episode of *Alfred Hitchcock Presents*. **Hitchography:** *Vertigo* (1958), *Bull in a China Shop* (1958, TV)

COREY, WENDELL (1914–1968) American actor. On stage as a professional from 1935, Corey was signed to films in 1945 by producer Hal Wallis, and made his debut in *Desert Fury* in 1947. His subsequent films include *Sorry, Wrong Number* (1948), *The Great Missouri Raid* (1951) and Hitchcock's *Rear Window* (1954) in which he played policeman Thomas J Doyle. He also appeared in an episode of *Alfred Hitchcock Presents*, in which he was again directed by Hitchcock. Somewhat lacking in screen presence, the star's other films include *The Big Knife* (1955), *Alias Jesse James* (1959) and *The Astro-Zombies* (1968). He also had political ambitions, but ultimately failed to reach Congress. **Hitchography:** *Rear Window* (1954), *Poison* (1958, TV)

COSGROVE, JACK American effects artist and matte painter. This brilliant artist did much work for producer David O Selznick in the 1930s and 1940s, among his films being *The Garden of Allah* (1936), *A Star is Born* (1937), *Nothing Sacred* (1937), *Since You Went Away* (1944) and *Duel in the Sun* (1946), although his greatest achievement was his work for *Gone with the Wind* (1939), which earned him an Oscar nomination. He also contributed paintings and miniatures to Hitchcock's *Rebecca* (1940), including the gigantic model of Manderlay, and *Spellbound* (1945), for which he had to realize Salvador Dali's paintings for the dream sequence. Both films earned Cosgrove an Academy Award nomination. **Hitchography:** *Rebecca* (1940), *Spellbound* (1945)

COTTEN, JOSEPH (1905–1994) American actor. A former drama critic for the *Miami Herald*, leading man Cotten turned to acting in 1930. In 1937, he began a long association with Orson Welles, joining the actor-director's Mercury Theatre Company, leaving in 1939 to join Katharine Hepburn in the original Broadway run of *The Philadelphia Story*. He made his big screen debut in 1941 in Welles' *Citizen Kane* in which he played Jedediah Leland. After co-starring with Merle Oberon in *Lydia* (1941), two further films for Welles followed: *The Magnificent Ambersons* (1942) and *Journey into Fear* (1942), to which Cotten contributed to the latter's screenplay. In 1943, Cotten played Charlie Oakley, the Merry Widow Murderer, in Hitchcock's *Shadow of a Doubt*, a performance that *Variety* described as being 'excellent as the motivating factor of the proceedings.'

Following *Shadow of a Doubt*, Cotten went on to appear in films such as *Gaslight* (1944), *Since You Went Away* (1944), *Duel in the Sun* (1946), *Portrait of Jennie* (1948) and *The Third Man* (1949), in which he again co-starred with Orson Welles. The same year, Cotten was re-united with Hitchcock on the British-made *Under Capricorn*, but lightning failed to strike twice, and the film, a period piece about a now wealthy former convict (Cotten) who mentally tortures his wife (Ingrid Bergman), was not a success, although the two stars managed to escape criticism (commented *The Tatler*: 'Both Miss Bergman and Mr Cotten succeed, against probability, in investing their stock characters with dignity and feeling... Mr Cotten is authoritative enough to inspire respect as well as pity').

Cotten's other films include *Niagara* (1952), *Hush, Hush, Sweet Charlotte* (1964), *The Abominable Dr Phibes* (1971), *Soylent Green* (1973) and *Heaven's Gate* (1980). Meanwhile, on television, he appeared on *The Twentieth Century Fox Hour* (1955–1956), which he hosted, *The Joseph Cotten Show* (1956–1957) and *Hollywood and the Stars* (1963–1964). He also guest starred in *Eye of the Truth* (1958, TV), an episode of *Suspicion*, which was executive produced by Hitchcock, and three episodes of *Alfred Hitchcock Presents*, in one of which, *Breakdown* (1955, TV), he was again directed by Hitchcock. It should also be noted that Cotten performed in several radio adaptations of Hitchcock's films, including a version of *Shadow of a Doubt*. **Hitchography:** *Shadow of a Doubt* (1943), *Foreign Correspondent* (1946, radio), *Rebecca* (1946, radio), *Notorious* (1948, radio), *Spellbound* (1948, radio), *Shadow of a Doubt* (1948, radio), *The Paradine Case* (1949, radio), *Under Capricorn* (1949), *Spellbound* (1951, radio), *Breakdown* (1955, TV), *Together* (1958, TV), *Eye of the Truth* (1958, TV), *Dead Weight* (1959, TV)

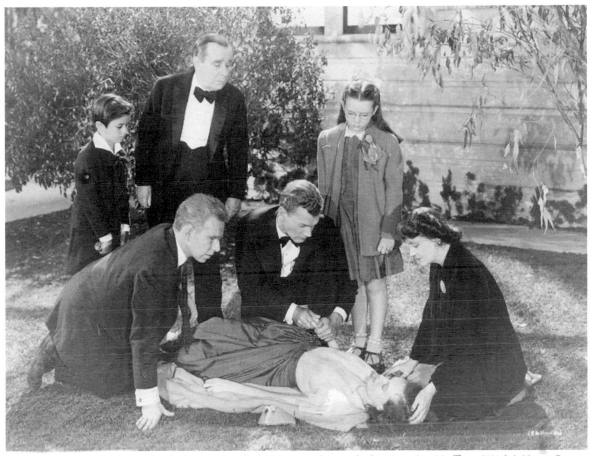

Can Joseph Cotten's kindly Uncle Charlie (centre) really have attempted to murder his niece, played by Teresa Wright? Hume Cronyn (kneeling), Charlie Bates, Henry Travers, Edna Mae Wonacott and Patricia Collinge look suitably concerned in Hitchcock's Shadow of a Doubt *(1943)*.

COURANT, CURT (1899–1968) German-born cinematographer. This busy cinematographer not only worked on the Continent, but also in Britain and America on such diverse films as *Quo Vadis?* (1924), *Perfect Understanding* (1933), *Broken Blossoms* (1936), *La Bete Humaine* (1938), *Monsieur Verdoux* (1947) and *It Happened in Athens* (1961). He also photographed one film for Hitchcock, *The Man Who Knew Too Much* (1934), but the association was apparently not an entirely happy one, given that Courant would often fail to carry our Hitchcock's instructions to the letter. **Hitchography:** *The Man Who Knew Too Much* (1934)

COX, JACK (1896–1960, real name John Jaffray Cox) British cinematographer. One of Hitchcock's most important early collaborators, Cox first worked with the director on *The Ring* (1927), a job he got following the departure of Hitchcock's usual cameraman, Claude L McDonnell, over financial terms. Cox began his career in 1913 as an assistant to director Lewin Fitzhamon and producer Cecil Hepworth. By 1921, Cox himself had become a cameraman, making his debut with *The Yellow Claw* for

director Réné Plaisetty, for whom he photographed several more films, among them *The Four Feathers* (1921) and *The Knave of Diamonds* (1921). However, it was his 11–film collaboration with director Maurice Elvey that raised his industry profile, among their output being *A Romance of Westdale* (1921), *The Passionate Friends* (1921), *Don Quixote* (1923) and *Hindle Wakes* (1927).

Equally prolific was Cox's lengthy collaboration with Hitchcock which, following *The Ring*, went on to include such landmarks as *Blackmail* (1929) and *The Lady Vanishes* (1938), both of which involved complex process photography. Recalled future director Michael Powell, who was the stills photographer on Cox's third film with Hitchcock, *Champagne* (1928): 'Jack Cox, the lighting cameraman, was a quick worker. He was a big, cheerful man, in a business suit like Hitch's and with an aggressive crest of dark hair. He opened his eyes very wide, which gave him a surprised expression. He was kind and genial.' [12]

Following Hitchcock's departure for America in 1939, Cox remained busy, among his many other films being *Charley's Big-Hearted Aunt* (1939), *The Ghost Train* (1941) and *The Wicked Lady* (1945). He finished his career by photographing several comedies for director John Paddy Carstairs, among them *One Good Turn* (1955), *Just My Luck* (1957) and *The Square Peg* (1958), bringing his grand total to an incredible 105 films (possibly more if one takes into consideration the foreign language versions of early talkies he also filmed, among them *Mary*, the German language version of Hitchcock's *Murder!*, which Hitchcock also directed). Of all the directors he worked with, Cox admired Hitchcock the most, for his 'quick mind, lively ideas, and workmanlike way of setting about the job.' [13] **Hitchography:** *The Ring* (1927), *The Farmer's Wife* (1928), *Champagne* (1928), *The Manxman* (1929), *Blackmail* (1929), *Juno and the Paycock* (1930), *Murder!* (1930), *Mary* (1930), *The Skin Game* (1931), *Rich and Strange* (1932), *Number Seventeen* (1932), *The Lady Vanishes* (1938)

CRIBBINS, BERNARD (1928–) British comedy character actor. This likeable actor began his career on stage at the age of 14, and by the mid-1950s he was a regular face in London revues. He made his film debut in 1957 in *The Yangtse Incident*, and went on to establish himself in such comedies as *Two Way Stretch* (1960), *The Wrong Arm of the Law* (1962), *Carry On, Jack* (1963) and *Carry On Spying* (1964). A recording artist, he also had a number of novelty song hits, among them *Right, Said Fred* and *Hole in the Ground*. In 1972, he took on the serious role of pub landlord Felix Forsythe in Hitchcock's *Frenzy*, but seemed uncomfortable in the hard man role and with the profanities he was compelled to utter. Cribbins' other films include *She* (1965), *Daleks – Invasion Earth 2150 AD* (1966), *The Railway Children* (1970), *The Water Babies* (1978) and *Carry On, Columbus* (1992). **Hitchography:** *Frenzy* (1972)

CRISP, DONALD (1880–1974) Scottish-born actor-director. Following experience as a soldier in the Boer War, Crisp emigrated to America in 1906, where he joined D W Griffith's Biograph company in 1908. Working as an actor at first, Crisp soon graduated to direction, helming his first film, *Her Father's Silent Partner*, in 1914. This proved to be the first of many directorial assignments for Biograph. He also assisted Griffith on such milestones as *The Birth of a Nation* (1915) in which he also appeared as General Grant.

Following further wartime experience, this time as a British spy in Russia during World War I, Crisp joined Famous Players-Lasky in 1920, helming three productions for the company's London arm, all of which had inter-titles designed by Hitchcock (he also directed an independently financed film, *Tell Your Children*, at Lasky's Islington Studios in London, on which Hitchcock also worked). These pictures completed, Crisp next travelled to India, where he supervised Lasky's Bombay arm. Back in America in 1923, he directed several large scale productions, among them *The General* (1924), which he co-directed with Buster Keaton, and *Don Q, Son of Zorro*

(1925). He directed his last film, *Runaway Bride*, in 1930, after which he concentrated on his acting career, appearing in such classics as *Red Dust* (1932), *Mutiny on the Bounty* (1935), *Wuthering Heights* (1939) and *How Green Was My Valley* (1941), the latter winning him a best supporting actor Oscar for his performance as Mr Morgan. He continued acting in films until 1963, his last appearance being in *Spencer's Mountain*. **Hitchography:** *The Princess of New York* (1921), *Appearances* (1921), *Beside the Bonnie Brier Bush* (1921), *Tell Your Children* (1922)

CRONYN, HUME (1911– , real name Hume Blake Cronyn) Canadian-born actor and screenwriter. Cronyn made his stage debut at the age of 19. He reached Broadway four years later, where he worked as both an actor and director. He made his film debut in 1943 in the supporting role of Herbie Hawkins in Hitchcock's *Shadow of a Doubt*, making a splash as the neighbour with a ghoulish relish for murder novels (commented *Variety*, 'Hume Cronyn gets attention as the small town amateur sleuth'). This led to a further role in Hitchcock's *Lifeboat* (1944) as the Cockney radio operator Stanley Garrett, one of the titular craft's sea-tossed survivors. This was by no means the end of Cronyn's association with the Master, though. He went on to work on the screenplays of both *Rope* (1948) and, un-credited, *Under Capricorn* (1949), and appeared in two episodes of *Alfred Hitchcock Presents*. Cronyn's other film credits include *Phantom of the Opera* (1943), *The Seventh Cross* (1944), which earned him a best supporting actor Oscar nomination, *The Parallax View* (1974), *Cocoon* (1985) and *The Pelican Brief* (1993). He was married to actress Jessica Tandy (1909–1994) from 1942, and frequently appeared in plays and films with her. She of course appeared in Hitchcock's *The Birds* (1963). Commented Cronyn of the Hitchcock style: 'He would get what would become almost an *idée fixe*, and he would pursue it. And if you didn't approve of it, you were free to walk away from it!' [14] **Hitchography**: *Shadow of a Doubt* (1943), *Lifeboat* (1944), *Rope* (1948), *Under Capricorn* (1949), *Kill with Kindness* (1956, TV), *The Impromptu Murder* (1958, TV)

CROSSLEY, SYD (1885–1960) British actor-singer-comedian. Known as 'The Long Comic', Crossley began his career in the music halls of Britain in 1899 as a comic singer. Following experience in America on the vaudeville circuit in the 1920s, he returned home and began appearing in movies, starting in 1925 with *Keep Smiling*. Before long he had established himself as a popular comedy support in such films as *Radio Parade of 1935* (1935), *Keep Your Seats, Please* (1936) and Hitchcock's *Young and Innocent* (1937), in which he can be spotted as one of the many coppers out to catch Robert Tisdall (Derrick De Marney). In 1937 alone Crossley appeared in 16 films. His other films include *Old Mother Riley* (1937), *Penny Paradise* (1938) and *Let the People Sing* (1942). **Hitchography:** *Young and Innocent* (1937)

CUMMINGS, ROBERT (1908–1990) American actor. This affable leading man began his career on stage in 1931, billing himself Blade Stanhope Conway. He made his first film appearance as an extra in 1933 in the Laurel and Hardy comedy *Sons of the Desert*. His first featured role followed in 1935 in *So Red the Rose*, after which he went on to appear in films such as *Three Cheers for Love* (1936), *Charlie McCarthy, Detective* (1939), *The Devil and Miss Jones* (1941) and *King's Row* (1942). He took the leading role of Barry Kane in Hitchcock's *Saboteur* (1942) after Gary Cooper turned the part down. Though adequate, he wasn't one of Hitchcock's more memorable leading men. Commented *Variety*: 'Robert Cummings lacks variation in his performance of the thick-headed, unjustly accused worker who crosses the continent to expose the plotters and clear himself; but his directness and vigour partly redeem that shortcoming.' Following *Forever and a Day* (1943), *The Accused* (1948) and *Marry Me Again* (1953) among others, Cummings worked for Hitchcock again, this time as Grace Kelly's love interest in *Dial M for Murder* (1953), about which *Variety* opined that he had 'a rather fruitless part in the resolution of the melodramatics.' Cummings's other films include *How to Be Very Popular* (1955), *Beach Party* (1963), *The Carpetbaggers* (1964) and *Partners in Crime* (1973, TV). He proved most popular on television in such series as *My Hero* (1952), *The Bob Cummings Show* (1955–1961) and *My Living Doll* (1964–1965). **Hitchography:** *Saboteur* (1942), *Dial M for Murder* (1953)

CUNNINGHAM, JACK British supporting actor This actor, with a penchant for authority roles, popped up in a number of minor parts in both Britain and Hollywood, among them Hitchcock's *Dial M for Murder* (1954), in which he played a copper, *Dublin Nightmare* (1958), in which he played an Inspector, and *The Quare Fellow* (1962), as a warden. **Hitchography:** *Dial M for Murder* (1954)

CURTIS, DONALD American actor. Curtis appeared in a variety of films in the 1940s and 1950s, among them Hitchcock's *Spellbound* (1945), in which he played Harry, *Phffft!* (1954), *It Came from Beneath the Sea* (1955) and *Earth vs the Flying Saucers* (1956). **Hitchography:** *Spellbound* (1945)

CURZON, GEORGE (1896–1976) British-born actor. Following experience in the navy, in which he reached the post of Lieutenant Commander, Curzon turned to acting, making his stage debut in 1924. He broke into films in the early 1930s, appearing in the likes of *The Impassive Footman* (1932), *Sexton Blake and the Hooded Terror* (1938), *Q Planes* (1939) and *Uncle Silas* (1947). In 1934 he was cast in the minor role of Gibson in Hitchcock's *The Man Who Knew Too Much*. This in turn led to the larger role of Guy, the twitching murderer in *Young and Innocent* (1937), for which he remains best known. He can also be spotted briefly in *Jamaica Inn* (1939) as one of Sir Humphrey Pengallan's guests. **Hitchography:** *The Man Who Knew Too Much* (1934), *Young and Innocent* (1937), *Jamaica Inn* (1939)

CUTTS, GRAHAM (1885–1958, real name Jack Graham Cutts) British director. Though now mostly forgotten, Cutts was Britain's leading commercial director in the 1920s. He began his film career in 1922 with *While London Sleeps* (1922), having previously been an exhibitor and, before that, a marine engineer. In 1923 he had a major international hit with *Woman to Woman*, the first of five films on which the young Alfred Hitchcock worked for Cutts in various capacities, including assistant director, art director and screenwriter. *Woman to Woman* was produced by Michael Balcon, with whom Cutts formed Gainsborough Pictures in 1924, for which Cutts went on to helm several other successes, most notably *The Rat* (1925) starring Mae Marsh and matinee idol Ivor Novello. However, Cutts left Gainsborough in the early 1930s, after which his career, unlike that of his former protégé, went into a gradual decline, resulting in such tepid fare as *Three Men in a Boat* (1933), *As Good as New* (1933) and *Oh, Daddy!* (1935). Although he continued to make features until 1939, Cutts was demoted to directing documentary shorts thereafter, among them *Air Transport Support* (1945) and *The 9.2 Inch Gun* (1947).

In fact by 1935, Cutts was also reduced to occasionally working as an assistant director, so desperate was he for money, and so low had his industry standing sunk. Among the films he worked on was Hitchcock's *The 39 Steps* (1935). This was particularly ironic, for Cutts had dismissed Hitchcock's early directorial efforts for Gainsborough, most notably *The Pleasure Garden* (1925), the release of which he'd helped to delay by two years. Recalled Hitchcock: 'When I was shooting *The 39 Steps*, there were some odd, extra shots to be done, and in order to speed up the production, the producer [Ivor Montagu] offered to get someone to do it. When I asked him whom he had in mind, he answered, "Graham Cutts." I said, "No, I won't have it. I used to work for him… How can I have him come on as my assistant?" And he answered, "Well, if you won't use him, you'll be doing him out of a job and he really needs the money." So I finally agreed. But it's a terrible thing, don't you think so?' [15]

Cutts' daughter, Patricia (1926–1974, also known as Patricia Wayne), was involved in the film industry too, initially as a child performer in films such as *Self Made Lady* (1931), then later as a leading lady in *Merry Andrew* (1958), *The Tingler* (1959) and *Private Road* (1971). She also appeared in *Fight to the East* (1958, TV), an episode of *Alfred Hitchcock Presents*. She committed suicide. **Hitchography:** *Woman to Woman* (1923), *The White Shadow* (1924), *The Passionate Adventure* (1924), *The Blackguard* (1925), *The Prude's Fall* (1925), *The 39 Steps* (1935)

D

D'AGOSTINO, ALBERT S (1893–1970) American art director. D'Agostino began his film career during the 1920s. His most prolific period was while working at RKO between 1936 and 1958, during which time he designed such films as *The Magnificent Ambersons* (1942), *The Curse of the Cat People* (1944), *Isle of the Dead* (1945) and Hitchcock's *Notorious* (1946). His many other credits include *Bedlam* (1946), *The Spiral Staircase* (1946) and *Androcles and the Lion* (1952). **Hitchography:** *Notorious* (1946)

DALE, ESTER (1885–1961) American character actress. Though she didn't make her first film until the age of 49 with *Crime without Passion* (1934), Dale went on to make over 100 films, her speciality being brusk nurses and housekeepers. Her many films include *The Awful Truth* (1937), *The Women* (1939), Hitchcock's *Mr and Mrs Smith* (1941), in which she played Carole Lombard's mother Mrs Krausheimer, *Margie* (1946) and *North to Alaska* (1960). She was also a regular in the *Ma and Pa Kettle* series of second features, playing Mrs Birdie Hicks. **Hitchography:** *Mr and Mrs Smith* (1941)

DALI, SALVADOR (1904–1989) Spanish artist. Celebrated for his surrealist work, about which he commented, 'Surrealism is an expression of the subconscious,' [1], Dali also occasionally dabbled in film,

Ingrid Bergman in a shot subsequently cut from the Salvador Dali-designed dream sequence in Hitchcock's Spellbound *(1945).*

co-writing and appearing in *Un Chien Andalou* (1928) and co-writing *L'Age d'Or* (1930), both of which were directed by Luis Bunuel. He also designed the celebrated dream sequence for Hitchcock's *Spellbound* (1945), for which he produced five paintings at a cost of $1000 each; these were then realized by art director James Basevi and effects technician Jack Cosgrove (the finished sequence cost $20,000). Said producer David O Selznick of Dali's work: 'It added an extra new facet to what I believe was the first film dealing with Freudian psychoanalysis.' [2] **Hitchography:** *Spellbound* (1945)

DALL, JOHN (1918–1971, real name John Jenner Thompson) American actor. Dall made his Broadway debut in 1941 in a minor part, but just three years later was appearing in leading roles (notably in *Dear Ruth*). He made his film debut in 1945, playing Morgan Evans to Bette Davis's Mrs Moffat in *The Corn is Green*, a role that earned him an Oscar nomination for best supporting actor. His other films include *Another Part of the Forrest* (1948), *Gun Crazy* (1950) and *Spartacus* (1960). In 1948 he played the murderous Brandon Shaw in Hitchcock's *Rope*, about which *Variety* noted, 'John Dall stands out as the egocentric who masterminds the killing and ghoulish wake.' **Hitchography:** *Rope* (1948)

Dangerous Lies
(GB, 1921, 66m approx, bw, silent)

CREDITS
Production company:	Famous Players-Lasky
Director:	Paul Powell
Screenplay:	Mary O'Connor, based on the novel by E Phillips Oppenheim
Inter-titles:	Alfred Hitchcock

CAST
Mary Glynne (Joan Farrant), David Powell (Sir Henry Bond), Minna Gray (Olive Farrant), Warburton Gamble (Leonard Pearce), Clifford Grey (Franklin Bond), Harry Ham (Phelps Westcott), Arthur Cullin (Eli Hodges)

Now apparently lost, this black-and-white silent, for which Hitchcock designed the inter-titles, told the story of a hapless widow who, following the death of her second husband, is visited by her violent first husband, who dies while assaulting her. Directed by Paul Powell, it was made for Famous Players-Lasky at Islington Studios.

DANO, ROYAL (1922–1994) American character actor. Perhaps best remembered as the Tattered Man in John Huston's *The Red Badge of Courage* (1951), this tall, gaunt-looking actor appeared in over 100 films, having made his debut in *Undercover Girl* in 1950. Frequently in bad guy roles in westerns, his credits take in *Johnny Guitar* (1954), *Death of a Gunfighter* (1969), *Something Wicked This Way Comes* (1983) and *Spaced Invaders* (1990). He also made a brief appearance as Calvin Wiggs in Hitchcock's *The Trouble with Harry* (1955). **Hitchography:** *The Trouble with Harry* (1955)

DARCY, GEORGINE American dancer. This pneumatic performer played the memorable role of 'Miss Torso' in Hitchcock's *Rear Window* (1954). Sadly, this seems to have been her only film. Recalled the actress of her experiences working on the giant apartment block set: 'It was a very quiet set, a very well organized set, and I remember a lot of people visiting the set. He [Hitchcock] was very proud of it. My little apartment had everything except running water and ice cubes!' [3] **Hitchography:** *Rear Window* (1954)

Dark Intruder
(US, 1965, 59m, bw) *

CREDITS

Production company:	Shamley
Producer:	Jack Laird
Director:	Harvey Hart
Screenplay:	Barre Lyndon
Cinematographer:	John F Warren
Music:	Lalo Schifrin
Editor:	Edward L Williams
Art director:	Lloyd S Papez
Make-up effects:	Bud Westmore

CAST

Leslie Nielsen (Brett Kingsford), Mark Richman (Robert Vandenburg), Werner Klemperer (Professor Malaki), Judi Meredith (Evelyn Lang), Charles Bolender (Nikola), Gilbert Green (Harvey Misback), Harriet Vinc (Hannah), Vaughn Taylor (Dr Burdett), Peter Brocco ('Chi Zang')

Something of a curiosity, this little-seen supernatural horror piece about a psychic criminologist who traces a series of murders to a Sumerian devil creature in turn-of-the-century San Francisco features future *Naked Gun* star Leslie Nielsen. The film was intended as a pilot for a new *Kolchak*-style anthology series titled *Black Cloak* (hence the brief running time), and was made by Hitchcock's Shamley production company, which had been responsible for *Alfred Hitchcock Presents* and *The Alfred Hitchcock Hour*, as well as *Psycho* (1960). When the series failed to be taken up by the networks, it was released theatrically as a supporting programme. Note that cinematographer John F Warren, who had also photographed several episode of *Alfred Hitchcock Presents*, went on to photograph Hitchcock's cold war thriller *Torn Curtain* (1966), so one must assume that Hitchcock had someting to do with this production even if it was only in an executive capacity.

DAUPHIN CLAUDE (1903–1978, real name Claude Franc-Nohan) French stage actor. This celebrated French star made his film debut in 1930 with *Langrevin Pére et Fils*, and went on to appear in such productions as *La Fortune*

(1931), *English Without Tears* (1944), *The Quiet American* (1958), *Barbarella* (1967) and *The Tennant* (1976). In 1944, while in London, he also contributed to the script of *Bon Voyage*, the first of two French-language Ministry of Information films Hitchcock made in Britain for the war effort. **Hitchography:** *Bon Voyage* (1944)

DAVENPORT, A BROMLEY (1867–1946) British character actor. On stage from 1892, Davenport made his film debut in 1920 in *The Great Gay Road*, following which he appeared as support in all manner of films, among them *Bonnie Prince Charlie* (1923), *When London Sleeps* (1932), *The Scarlet Pimpernel* (1934), *Love on the Dole* (1941) and *The Way Ahead* (1944). He also crossed paths with Hitchcock twice, appearing in *Lord Camber's Ladies* (1932), which Hitchcock produced and *Jamaica Inn* (1939), which Hitchcock directed. **Hitchography:** *Jamaica Inn* (1939)

DAVENPORT, HARRY (1866–1949) American actor. Although in later years he was known for playing grandfathers in the likes of *The Higgins Family* (1938) and *Meet Me in St Louis* (1944), the career of Harry Davenport reached back to the silent period, beginning with *Fogg's Millions* (1914) and, before that, the stage. His 100-plus films include *You Can't Take it with You* (1938), *The Hunchback of Notre Dame* (1939), *Gone with the Wind* (1939), *King's Row* (1940), *That Forsyte Woman* (1949) and *Riding High* (1950). He also directed 31 silent films between 1915 and 1917, including 18 installments in the *Jarr Family* series of comedy shorts, among them *Mr Jarr and the Lady Reformer* (1915), *Mrs Jarr and the Beauty Treatment* (1915) and *The Jarr Family Discover Harlem* (1915). In 1940, Davenport played Mr Powers, the editor of the *New York Daily Globe* in Hitchcock's *Foreign Correspondent*, his character's desire for news other than 'rumour and speculation' sending hero Johnny Jones (Joel McCrea) over to Europe to get the real low down on the war for the folks back home. **Hitchography:** *Foreign Correspondent* (1940)

DAW, MARJORIE (1902–1979) American actress. Billed as 'The girl with the nursery-rhyme name', Daw made her film debut at the age of 13 in *The Warrens of Virginia* (1915) for director Cecil B de Mille, for whom she also made *The Unafraid* (1915) and *Joan the Woman* (1916). Between 1917 and 1919 she made several popular films with Douglas Fairbanks Sr, including *A Modern Musketeer* (1918), *Mr Fix-It* (1918) and *The Knickerbocker Buckaroo* (1919). A major draw by the early 1920s, she went on to appear in *The Butterfly Girl* (1920), *Wandering Daughters* (1923) and *Revelation* (1924). In 1924 she travelled to Britain to make *The Passionate Adventure*, on which Hitchcock worked as a screenwriter, art director and assistant director. It was during the making of the film that Daw met the second of her three husbands, Myron Selznick (1898–1944), to whom she was married between 1925 and 1942. Selznick went on to become Hitchcock's agent. Daw's other films include *East Lynne* (1925), *Redheads Preferred* (1926) and *Spoilers of the West* (1927), following which she permanently retired from the screen. **Hitchography:** *The Passionate Adventure* (1924)

DAWSON, ANTHONY (1916–1992) British character actor. This severe-looking actor frequently found himself cast in sinister or villainous roles, the best of them being Swan Lesley, the oily murderer in Hitchcock's *Dial M for Murder* (1954), to which he brought an almost moustache-twirling intensity. In films from 1939 with *I Killed the Count*, Dawson's many other pictures include *The Way to the Stars* (1945), *Midnight Lace* (1960), *Curse of the Werewolf* (1961) and *Gamblers* (1990). He also made three Bond films, appearing as Professor Dent in *Dr No* (1962) and providing the voice of the unseen Blofeld in *From Russia with Love* (1963) and *Thunderball* (1965). He also appeared in the Bond spoof *Operation Kid Brother* (1967). **Hitchography:** *Dial M for Murder* (1954)

DAY, DORIS (1924– , real name Doris von Kappelhoff) American actress. This cheerful actress and recording artist began her career as a nightclub singer, gaining popularity with the Bob Crosby band in the early 1940s. Radio work followed, along with singles and LPs. Given her burgeoning popularity, it was inevitable that she would eventually turn to films, which she did in 1948 with the musical *Romance on the High Seas* (1948). Such hits as *On Moonlight Bay* (1951), *April in Paris* (1952) and *Calamity Jane* (1953) followed, although it was the star's dramatic work in *Storm Warning* (1950) that caught Hitchcock's eye, determining him to use the actress one day.

He eventually cast Day as singing star Jo McKenna in his remake of *The Man Who Knew Too Much* (1956), in which she and her husband, played by James Stewart, find

Doris Day and James Stewart fool around during a break on the set of Hitchcock's The Man Who Knew Too Much *(1956).*

themselves somewhat improbably involved in an assassination plot. By no means one of Hitchcock's better pictures, the film was nevertheless a commercial success, and introduced the Oscar-winning song *Que Sera Sera*, which went on to become a major hit for Day. Commented *Variety* of Day and Stewart's performances, 'Both draw vivid portraits of tortured parents when their son is kidnapped.' However, Day herself was beset by insecurity during the filming, as Hitchcock gave her little or no direction. 'Hitch never spoke to me before a scene to tell me how he wanted it played, and he never spoke to me afterward,' recalled Day. [4] Fearing that she wasn't pleasing her director, she eventually challenged him over the issue, only to be informed, 'Doris, you've done nothing to elicit comment from me… You have been doing what I felt was right for the film, and that's why I haven't told you anything!' [5] Consequently, Day finished the rest of filming feeling much happier about her work.

Day's many other films include *The Pajama Game* (1957), *Pillow Talk* (1959), the Hitchcockian thriller *Midnight Lace* (1960), *That Touch of Mink* (1962) and *Caprice* (1967), while her television work includes *The Doris Day Show* (1968–1972) and *Doris Day and Friends* (1985–1986). Known for her clean image, Groucho Marx once famously commented, 'I can remember Doris Day before she was a virgin.' She now devotes her time to animal welfare. **Hitchography:** *The Man Who Knew Too Much* (1956)

DAY, LARAINE (1917– , real name LaRaine Johnson) American actress. On stage from her teenage years, Day made her screen debut in *The Law Commands* in 1937, in which she was billed as Lorraine Hayes. She retained this name for her next film, *Doomed at Sundown* (1937), after which she became Laraine Johnson for *Stella Dallas* (1937) and a further six films, finally settling on Laraine Day with *Tarzan Finds a Son* (1939). Her next film, *Calling Dr Kildare* (1939) introduced her to the popular series of second features as Nurse Mary Lamont, the hero's fiancée, a role she would reprise a further six times, culminating with *Dr Kildare's Wedding Day* (1941). In 1940 she appeared in her then biggest role as Carol Fisher in Hitchcock's *Foreign Correspondent*, about which *Variety* commented of her performance, 'Laraine Day, virtually a fledgling in pictures, only in the most difficult sequences misses out as a top-grade dramatic player.' Day's other films include *Journey for Margaret* (1942), *The Story of Dr Wassell* (1944), *The High and the Mighty* (1954), *House of Dracula's Daughter* (1972) and *Murder on Flight 502* (1975, TV), since when she has devoted her life to the Mormon church, of which she has been a follower all her life. Note that she also appeared in an episode of *Alfred Hitchcock Presents*. **Hitchography:** *Foreign Correspondent* (1940), *Death and the Joyful Woman* (1963, TV)

DE BANZIE, BRENDA (1915–1981) British character actress. Best remembered for playing Maggie, the headstrong boot maker's daughter in *Hobson's Choice* (1954), De Banzie began her stage career in 1935, going on to make her film debut in 1951 in *The Long Dark Hall*. She is also remembered for playing the seemingly unassuming Englishwoman Mrs Drayton in Hitchcock's *The Man Who Knew Too Much* (1956), in which she turns out to be part of an elaborate assassination plot. Along with Bernard Miles, who played her husband, she was perhaps the best thing in this dull, widescreen fiasco. De Banzie's other credits include *The Thirty-Nine Steps*, the 1959 remake of Hitchcock's film of the same name, in which she played Nellie Lumsden, *The Entertainer* (1960), *The Pink Panther* (1963) and *Pretty Polly* (1967). **Hitchography:** *The Man Who Knew Too Much* (1956)

DE CASALIS, JEANNE (1896–1966, real name Jeanne de Casalis de Pury) British actress. Popular on stage and radio as the gossipy Mrs Feather, whom she played in the 1941 short *The Fine Feathers*, De Casalis made her first film appearance in 1925 in *Settled Out of Court*. She cameoed in several other films, among them *Nell Gwyn* (1933), Hitchcock's *Jamaica Inn* (1939), in which she played one of Sir Humphrey Pengallan's dinner guests, *The Turners of Prospect Road* (1947) and *The Twenty Questions Murder Mystery* (1949). She was married to the actor Colin Clive (1898–1937, real name Colin Clive Grieg). **Hitchography:** *Jamaica Inn* (1939)

DE CORDOBA, PEDRO (1881–1950) American actor. This gaunt American-born actor of Franco-Cuban parentage began his career as an opera singer, following which he began appearing in silent films in 1915 with *Carmen*. Many more followed, among them *Maria Rosa* (1916), *The Desert Sheik* (1924) and *The New Commandment* (1925). With the arrival of sound, he quickly established himself as a reliable support, frequently appearing in Latin roles in the likes of *Captain Blood* (1935), *Juarez* (1939), *The Sea Hawk* (1940) and *The Mark of Zorro* (1940). His most curious role was that of Bones the skeleton man in Hitchcock's *Saboteur* (1942), after which he went on to work in *For Whom the Bell Tolls* (1943), *The Song of Bernadette* (1943), *Samson and Delilah* (1949) and *Crisis* (1950). **Hitchography:** *Saboteur* (1942)

DE MARNEY, DERRICK (1906–1978) British actor. In films from 1928 with *The Little Drummer Boys*, De Marney went on to become an affable leading man in the 1930s, most notably in Hitchcock's *Young and Innocent* (1937) in which he played Robert Tisdall, one of Hitchcock's classic innocents on the run. His other films include *The Private Life of Henry VIII* (1933), *Things to Come* (1936), *Sixty Glorious Years* (1938), *Uncle Silas* (1947) and *The Projected Man* (1966). He also produced three films: *Latin Quarter* (1946), *She Shall Have Murder* (1950) and *Meet Mr Callaghan* (1954), each of which he also starred in. **Hitchography:** *Young and Innocent* (1937)

DE RUELLE, EMILE (1880–1948) American-born editor. In Britain in the 1920s, de Ruelle cut several films for Hitchcock, including his last silent, *The Manxman* (1929),

as well as his first talkie, *Blackmail* (1929), in which he had the added problem of seamlessly melding together already shot silent footage with newly filmed sound footage. He also cut *Mary* (1930), the German-language version of *Murder!* (1930). **Hitchography:** *The Manxman* (1929), *Blackmail* (1929), *Elstree Calling* (1930), *Juno and the Paycock* (1930), *Murder!* (1930), *Mary* (1930)

DE WOLFF, FRANCIS (1913–1984) British character actor. This bushy-browed actor had a busy career on stage, radio and in films, in which he made his debut in 1935 in *Sexton Blake and the Mademoiselle*. Frequently cast as villainous or authoritative types, he went on to appear in the likes of *Fire Over England* (1936), *Treasure Island* (1950), *Moby Dick* (1956), *From Russia with Love* (1963) and *Carry On, Cleo* (1964). He also made several Hammer horrors, among them *The Hound of the Baskervilles* (1959), *The Man Who Could Cheat Death* (1959), *The Two Faces of Dr Jekyll* (1960) and *Curse of the Werewolf* (1961). In 1949 he appeared as Major Wilkins in Hitchcock's *Under Capricorn* (1949). **Hitchography:** *Under Capricorn* (1949)

DEACON, RICHARD (1922–1984) American comedy character actor. This bald, supercilious-looking actor made over 50 films, beginning with *Them!* in 1954. His many appearances include *Abbott and Costello Meet the Mummy* (1955), *Invasion of the Body Snatchers* (1956), *That Touch of Mink* (1962), *Piranha* (1978) and *Bad Manners* (1984), while on television he could be found in such series as *Leave It to Beaver* (1957–1963) and *The Dick Van Dyke Show* (1961–1966). He also appeared as a concerned neighbour in Hitchcock's *The Birds* (1963), sending Melanie Daniels (Tippi Hedren) off to Bodega Bay to see Mitch Brenner (Rod Taylor) with the two lovebirds she has bought as a joke, thus setting in motion a series of catastrophic events. **Hitchography:** *The Birds* (1963)

DELANEY, MAUREEN British supporting actress. Delaney appeared in a handful of films in the 1940s and 1950s, among them *Another Shore* (1948), Hitchcock's *Under Capricorn* (1949), in which she played Flo, *Jacqueline* (1956) and *The Scamp* (1957). **Hitchography:** *Under Capricorn* (1949)

DENNY, REGINALD (1891–1967, real name Reginald Leigh Daymore) British-born actor. On stage from the age of 8, Denny began his film career in Hollywood in 1919 with *Bringing Up Betty*, which he followed with around 200 shorts and features, among them several *Bulldog Drummond* second features, in which he played Algy. His feature work includes *Of Human Bondage* (1934), *Anna Karenina* (1935) and Hitchcock's *Rebecca* (1940), in which he played estate manager Frank Crawley. His other films include *Sherlock Holmes and the Voice of Terror* (1942), *Mr Blandings Builds His Dream House* (1948) and *Batman* (1966). His interest in aviation saw him create his own aircraft company, among his successes being the first pilot-less radio-controlled aircraft. **Hitchography:** *Rebecca* (1940)

DERN, BRUCE (1936–) American actor. Adept at both manic comedy roles and psychos ('I've played more psychotics and freaks and dopers than anyone' [6]), American leading man Dern proved fashionable in the 1970s in such films as *The Cowboys* (1972), *Silent Running* (1972), *The Great Gatsby* (1974) and *Smile* (1975). He came to films in 1960 with a small part in *Wild River* (1960) following experience on stage, including Broadway. His subsequent films include *Bedtime Story* (1963) and Hitchcock's *Marnie* (1964), in which he played the sailor who comes to a sticky end in the flashback that reveals the cause of Marnie's psychosis. It was at this time that he also appeared in two episodes of *The Alfred Hitchcock Hour*. Appearances in *Hush, Hush… Sweet Charlotte* (1965), *Will Penny* (1968) and *They Shoot Horses, Don't They?* (1969) followed.

Dern returned to the Hitchcock fold for *Family Plot* in 1976, although by this time he'd graduated to leading man status, playing cab driver George Lumley, whose search for a missing heir with his girlfriend, the psychic Madame Blanche (Barbara Harris), inadvertently exposes a kidnapping plot. *Variety* described Dern's performance as 'oddly appealing,' although not everyone was impressed with his work. Wrote critic John Simon: '[Dern's] mugging now reaches a new low; even if Lumley is not meant to be brilliant, neither need he be a cretin whose facial muscles carry like a Shriners' convention.' The star's subsequent films include *Coming Home* (1978), which earned him a best supporting actor Oscar nomination, *Tattoo* (1980), *That Championship Season* (1982), *The 'burbs* (1988), *Diggstown* (1992), *Last Man Standing* (1996) and *All the Pretty Horses* (2000). He was once married to actress Diane Ladd (1939–, real name Rose D Ladnier) and is the father of actress Laura Dern (1966–). **Hitchography:** *Marnie* (1964), *Night Caller* (1964, TV), *Lonely Place* (1964, TV), *Family Plot* (1976)

DEVANE, WILLIAM (1937– , real name William Devaney) American actor. This handsome leading man with a killer smile proved popular in the 1970s and 1980s in both heroic and villainous roles. In films from 1967 with *In the Country* following stage experience, he went on to appear in *The Pursuit of Happiness* (1970) and *McCabe and Mrs Miller* (1971), although it was his performance as John F Kennedy in the TV drama *Missiles of October* (1974) that secured his fame, which he confirmed with another television hit, this time as John Henry Faulk in *Fear on Trial* (1975). He was subsequently cast as Arthur Adamson in Hitchcock's *Family Plot* (1976), replacing TV star Roy Thinnes mid-way through filming. One of Hitchcock's more urbane villains, *Variety* said of his performance, 'William Devane takes a high place in the roster of Hitchcockian rogues.' Devane played another memorable villain in his next film, the Hitchcockian *Marathon Man* (1976), which he has since followed with *Yanks* (1978), *Honky Tonk Freeway* (1981), *The President's Child* (1992, TV), *Payback* (1998) and *Space Cowboys* (2000), as well as stints on such TV series as *From Here to Eternity* (1979–1980), *Knott's Landing* (1983–1993) and *The Monroes* (1995). **Hitchography:** *Family Plot* (1976)

DEVLIN, WILLIAM British stage actor. Devlin seems to rate only a few film appearances, among them Hitchcock's *Jamaica Inn* (1939), in which he played one of Sir Humphrey Pengallan's tennants, *Blood of the Vampire* (1958) and *The Shuttered Room* (1967). **Hitchography:** *Jamaica Inn* (1939)

Dial M for Murder

Before Hitchcock filmed it in 1954, and even before it was seen in theatres, the BBC broadcast a version of Frederick Knott's classic play in 1952, with John Williams playing the role of Inspector Hubbard, as he also would in the subsequent stage and film versions. Long unseen, there is now every chance that the programme no longer exists.

Dial M for Murder
(US, 1954, 105m, Warnercolor, 3D film) ★★

CREDITS

Production company:	Warner Bros.
Producer:	Alfred Hitchcock
Director:	Alfred Hitchcock
Screenplay:	Frederick Knott, based on his play
Cinematographer:	Robert Burks
Music:	Dimitri Tiomkin
Editor:	Rudi Fehr
Art director:	Edward Carrere
Costumes:	Moss Mabry
Sound:	Oliver S Garretson

CAST

Ray Milland (Tony Wendice), Grace Kelly (Margot Wendice), Robert Cummings (Mark Halliday), Anthony Dawson (Swan Lesley/Captain Lesgate), Patrick Allen (Pearson), George Leigh (Williams), Leo Britt (Club bore), Robin Hughes (Sergeant), Guy Doleman (Detective), George Alderson (Detective), Jack Cunningham (Policeman)

Video availability: Warner Bros.
CD availability: *A History of Hitchcock – Dial M for Murder* (Silva Screen), which contains a *Suite* comprising of *Main Title*, *The Telephone*, *The Trap* and *Finale*; *Psycho – The Essential Hitchcock* (Silva Screen), which features a *Suite*

Hitchcock seemingly had little time for this generally compelling thriller based on the ingeniously plotted stage hit by Frederick Knott about an ageing tennis pro who wishes to do away with his wealthy wife in order to collect. Filmed in just 36 days, it was the last of four films Hitchcock was contracted to direct for Warner Bros. and was viewed simply as a means by which to conclude his obligations.

The play had originally aired on BBC television on 23 March 1952 before going on to notch up impressive runs in the West End and on Broadway. The film rights were

Hitchcock observes the filming of an early scene in Dial M for Murder *(1954). Note that the camera is placed in a hole in the studio floor, to help accentuate the film's theatrical origins.*

quickly sold to producer Alexander Korda for £1000. However, so determined was Hitchcock on making the film that he managed to persuade Warner Bros. in turn to buy the rights from Korda for a whopping £30,000. The play now his, as it were, Hitchcock worked with its author on the screenplay adaptation. Yet rather than 'open up' the drama, Hitchcock instead determined on emphasizing its theatrical origins, just as he had done with *Rope* (1948). Thankfully though, he at least abandoned the experimental ten-minute take that he'd saddled himself with on *Rope*; instead, he used every cinematic trick up his sleeve to make the most of the film's basic setting, that of a London flat in Maida Vale (hence the dialing code featured in the title).

'I just did my job, using cinematic means to narrate a story taken from a stage play,' [7] commented the director modestly. In fact, the 'cinematic means' Hitchcock used to film the picture originally included 3D, a process then briefly popular with audiences. Warner Bros. was keen to further exploit the gimmick, having already had a major commercial hit with it on *House of Wax* (1953). Unfortunately, by the time *Dial M for Murder* was released, the novelty value had worn off; consequently, although the film *did* play a few engagements in its 3D format, it was mostly released flat (3D versions of the film still exist and are occasionally programmed by film societies, such as the BFI in London).

Save for a few brief scenes, the action is confined most-

ly to the flat of Tony and Margot Wendice (Ray Milland and Grace Kelly). As the film opens, the couple are depicted in a scene of domestic bliss, eating breakfast together, although in a hint of the drama to come, Tony accidentally knocks over the salt, a sprinkling of which he throws over his shoulder to ward off bad luck. This superstitious act seems to have failed though, for seemingly unbeknownst to him, Tony is being cuckolded.

The culprit is an American mystery writer named Mark Halliday (Robert Cummings); an old flame of Margot's, he is currently visiting London, and is re-united with her at the flat while Tony is out. But as Margot goes on to reveal, her marriage with Tony has improved dramatically since she last saw Mark, and she's curious to know why. 'Tony's changed. He's a completely different person to the one I used to tell you about,' she informs her lover. She also tells Mark that, although she burned the love letters he previously sent her, she did keep hold of one ('You probably know the one I mean'), and it turns out that this letter has been stolen, and that Margot is being blackmailed for its return.

All is not is what it seems, though, for it is revealed that the letter was in fact stolen by Tony as part of an elaborate plot to do away with Margot. Having learned of her affair with Mark, he was concerned that he would lose his meal ticket. Consequently, he gave up his waning career on the tennis courts so as to concentrate on giving the impression that he was a devoted husband, thus averting a possible divorce and, more importantly, being excluded from his wife's will, said to be worth $90,000.

Having convinced Margot that she is being black-mailed, Tony gets in touch with a former school chum, one Swan Lesley (posing as Captain Lesgate), a disreputable chap whom he hopes to coerce into murdering his wife for a handsome return. In desperate need of money ('I'm almost resigned to living on what I can earn'), Swan eventually agrees to carry out the crime while Tony and Mark attend a stag dinner, thus giving Tony an alibi. Unfortunately for Tony things go wrong and it is Swan – who has been able to gain access to the flat with a key Tony has left for him under the stair carpet - who ends up dead, with a pair of Margot's sewing scissors in his back!

Undeterred, Tony manipulates the events, placing the stolen letter in the breast pocket of the dead man's jacket, so as to give the impression that Margot had premeditated his murder as revenge for Swan's supposedly blackmailing her. The police, led by Inspector Hubbard (John Williams), are initially deceived by Tony's plan, and Margot is subsequently sent to trial, where she is found guilty and sentenced to death. But there remains a nagging doubt in Hubbard's mind as to Margot's guilt. So, with the clock ticking for Margot, he eventually tricks Tony into revealing his involvement in the crime, which he does by getting him to inadvertently disclose the whereabouts of the latch key he left out for Swan; instead of keeping the key about his person, as Tony assumed he would, it transpires that Swan immediately replaced the key under the carpet *before* entering the flat. That Tony uses the key to enter the flat when locked out – thus revealing his knowledge of the key's whereabouts – is enough to convict him.

The rather convoluted business about the key aside (it is replaced, misplaced and misidentified once too often), *Dial M for Murder* grips from beginning to end, surprisingly so given that it is little more than a conversation piece which, according to *Variety*, 'talks up much more suspense than it actually delivers.' This is the result of the generally good performances, the best of them coming from John Williams, who obviously derives much pleasure from the sleuthing of the slightly eccentric Hubbard (the actor had already essayed the role on stage and in the television version). Anthony Dawson, who is suitably oily as the hired killer who comes to a sticky end, also leaves his mark, while Ray Milland manages to convince as the devious husband (more so than he does as a retired tennis player). Ditto the beautiful Grace Kelly who, in the first of three films for Hitchcock, effectively portrays Margot's increasing helplessness as the plot thickens and the hangman's noose threatens (to reflect this, her clothes become more and more sombre as the drama unfolds, progressing from a scarlet dress during her illicit clinches with Mark to a frumpy-looking charcoal two-piece once convicted). In fact the only false note comes from Robert Cummings as Margot's rather wooden lover (indeed, one frequently wishes that it is *his* murder that Tony is plotting).

Given the restricted setting, Hitchcock only had his camera angles to play with, but he and cinematographer Robert Burks generally keep things visually interesting with several expertly staged compositions, including an extremely effective high angle shot of Tony as he walks through his murderous plan for Swan. Meanwhile, rather than stage Margot's trial realistically, which would have slowed up the action, Hitchcock instead presents it stylistically, photographing Grace Kelly against a plain background as, on the soundtrack, we hear the lawyers sum up and the judge pass sentence, all of which is achieved in about 20 seconds!

Hitchcock does get to stage one major set piece, though: Swan's attempted murder of Margot. Like the later shower sequence in *Psycho* (1960), the director spent a great deal of time making sure every cut and angle had the desired impact, from the close-up of Swan as he tentatively stands behind the unsuspecting Margot, his silk scarf at the ready to strangle her, through to the iconographic shot of Margot's out-stretched hand grasping for the scissors (one of Hitchcock's few genuine sops to the 3D process). And of course, everyone remembers the shot of the scissors glinting in Swann's back and the way they plunge into him further as he falls on them. To achieve the low angle shot of Swan falling to the ground, Hitchcock had the floor of the set raised, so that the camera could be placed in a special cut out looking upwards, which again emphasizes the theatricality of the piece by giving the impression of being shot from the stalls.

However, during this sequence, sharp-eyed video watchers – pause buttons at the ready – should note an error: as Margot clutches the scissors ready to plunge them into her assailant's back, the light very briefly catches the tip of *another* pair of scissors already pre-placed in Swan's back. There is no possibility, from the way she stabs him, that the scissors will go into Swann's back at the angle we subsequently see them, so Hitchcock had Kelly *pretend* to stab Dawson, throw her scissors to the ground behind him, then have Dawson turn to reveal the pre-placed scissors in his back, all in one shot. Accompanied by Dimitri Tiomkin's violently brassy music, the effect is genuinely disturbing, despite this minor glitch (this is by no means the only glitch in the film, though: the shadow of the boom mic can be spotted at least twice during the action, once over a picture during the set up scene between Tony and Swann, and later, after the murder, over the bedroom door).

The carefully composed visuals aside, the screenplay also turns up several amusing moments: 'I was planning to palm you off with an indifferent port, but let's see what we have here,' says Tony as he prepares a drink for Swan during the set up sequence, while Hubbard's exasperation at Mark's interference during the investigation prompts him to comment, 'May the saints preserve us from the gifted amateur!' The best exchange, however, is between Margot and Mark at the fade out: 'What's the matter with me, Mark? I don't seem to able to feel anything,' says Margot, once her husband's plot has been exposed and she has been spared the hangman's noose. Comes his reply, 'Don't worry, darling. In a couple of days you're going to have the most wonderful breakdown!'

Note the giant wooden finger on the telephone dial when Tony phones Margot; Hitchcock couldn't get the close-up he desired with the bulky 3D cameras, and so had a giant mock up of a phone and finger made! Note also that Cary Grant let it be known that he was interested in playing the role of Tony Wendice, but his salary demands had been too high (of course, this would have meant that the star would have been the villain of the piece, a situation that had previously caused all kinds of problems in *Suspicion* (1941)).

The original 1952 television production aside, *Dial M for Murder* has been remade three times: as a 1981 TV movie, as an Indian drama titled *Aitbaar* (1985) and as *A Perfect Murder* (1998). Its plot was also utilized for *The Fifth Stair*, an episode of the series *77, Sunset Strip* (1958–1963) starring Richard Long and Julie Adams.

Hitchcock cameo Hitchcock can be spotted in a photograph of a reunion dinner, which Tony takes down from the wall to show Swan.

Dial M for Murder
(US, 1981, 96m, colour, TVM)

CREDITS

Production company:	NBC/Time-Life
Producer:	Peter Katz
Executive producer:	Freya Rothstein
Director:	Boris Sagal
Screenplay:	John Gay, from the play by Frederick Knott
Cinematographer:	Michael Hugo
Music:	Billy Goldenberg

CAST

Christopher Plummer (Tony Wendice), Angie Dickinson (Margot Wendice), Ron Moody (Swan Lesley), Anthony Quayle (Inspector Hubbard), Michael Parks (Mark Halliday)

In this disappointing TV movie remake of the Hitchcock favourite, Christopher Plummer takes on the role of the financially strapped tennis player Tony Wendice who hatches an elaborate plan to murder his wife for her money. Though the production is just about adequate, it seems pale and pointless beside Hitchcock's obviously far superior version, with only Anthony Quayle's Inspector Hubbard leaving any lasting mark, despite the fact that director Boris Sagal had helmed several effective episodes of *Alfred Hitchcock Presents*, among them *Maria* (1961), *The Test* (1962) and *The Big Score* (1962).

DICK, DOUGLAS (1920–) American supporting actor. In films from the early 1940s, Dick appeared in such movies as *The Searching Wind* (1946), *The Red Badge of Courage* (1951) and *North to Alaska* (1960). In 1948 he played the rather thankless role of Kenneth Lawrence in Hitchcock's *Rope*, a part that pretty much saw him relegated to the sidelines of the action. In the mid-1960s Dick retired from the screen to become a psychologist. **Hitchography:** *Rope* (1948)

DIETRICH, MARLENE (1901–1992, real name Maria Magdalena von Losch) German-born actress. One of the movies' true glamour queens, Dietrich went on to become a major star in America having already established herself on screen in her homeland. Following experience as a chorus girl, Dietrich became a student of Max Reinhardt in 1922, which led to further stage work and, of course, films, beginning with a minor role in *Der Kleine Napoleon* in 1922. Subsequent homegrown films included *Tragodie der Liebe* (1923), *Kopf Hoch, Charly* (1926) and *Liebesnacht* (1929), although it was *The Blue Angel* (1930), directed by Josef von Sternberg, which launched her on the international scene. Once in Hollywood, von Sternberg continued to mould Dietrich's career, directing her in several classics, among them *Morocco* (1930), *Shanghai Express* (1932), *Blonde Venus* (1932) *The Scarlet Empress* (1934) and *The Devil is a Woman* (1935). Dietrich's post-Sternberg films include *Desire* (1936), *The Garden of Allah* (1936) and *Knight without Armour* (1937), during the making of which in England she was approached by the German ambassador Joachim von Ribbentrop at Adolf Hitler's personal

Every inch the glamour queen, Marlene Dietrich shows off her alluring figure in Hitchcock's Stage Fright *(1950). Jane Wyman looks on jealously, as well she might.*

request to return to Germany to become a leading star of Nazi cinema. Dietrich declined the offer and instead became an American citizen in 1939, going on to earn the Medal of Freedom for her tireless work entertaining the troops during the war.

Dietrich's other films include *Destry Rides Again* (1939), *Golden Earrings* (1947), *A Foreign Affair* (1949) and Hitchcock's *Stage Fright* (1950), in which she played the glamorous but cold-hearted stage star Charlotte Inwood, who seems more concerned about the box office takings than the murder of her husband: 'We were playing to capacity before all this happened. Now they're hanging on to the chandeliers! Fifty pounds up tonight! Goodness knows how they squeeze them in!' Meanwhile, when questioned about the murder prior to going on stage, she replies, 'The only murderer here is the orchestra leader!' after which she goes on to deliver a delicious version of Cole Porter's *The Laziest Girl in Town*, providing the film with one of its highlights. Commented *Variety* of the film, 'There's not a bad performance anywhere… but the choice femme spot goes to Dietrich.' Said Dietrich of working with Hitchcock: 'He frightened the daylights out of me! He knew exactly what he wanted, a fact that I adore, but I was never quite sure if I did right. After work he would take us to the Caprice restaurant and feed us with steaks he had flown in from New York, because he thought they were better than the British meat, and I always thought he did that to show that he was not disgusted with our work.' [8]

Following *Stage Fright*, Dietrich's film appearances became rarer, but included memorable roles in *Rancho Notorious* (1952), *Witness for the Prosecution* (1957), *Touch of Evil* (1958), *Judgment at Nuremberg* (1961) and *Just a Gigolo* (1978). Instead, she concentrated on her stage show, appearing at the world's top theatres and nightclubs, as well as at the casinos of Las Vegas. Her last film was a documentary on her life, *Marlene* (1984), in which she can be heard but not seen. Her daughter is the actress Maria Riva and her grandson the production designer J Michael Riva. **Hitchography:** *Stage Fright* (1950)

DIOR, CHRISTIAN (1905–1957) French fashion designer. This acclaimed designer contributed costumes to the occasional film, among them Marlene Dietrich's glamorous gowns for Hitchcock's *Stage Fright* (1950). His other credits include *The Indiscretion of an American Wife* (1954) and *The Ambassador's Daughter* (1954). **Hitchography:** *Stage Fright* (1950)

DOLEMAN, GUY (1923–1996) Australian-born character actor. Doleman, long in Britain, is perhaps best remembered for playing the sarcastic Major Ross in the three Harry Palmer films: *The Ipcress File* (1965), *Funeral in Berlin* (1966) and *Billion Dollar Brain* (1967). He began his film career in America in the early 1950s in films such as *Phantom Stockade* (1953) and Hitchcock's *Dial M for Murder* (1954), in which he had a minor role as a detective. In British films from 1957 with *The Shiralee*, his other

films include *Thunderball* (1965) and *The Idol* (1966), while his television work takes in *General Hospital* (1986–1987) and a remake of *The Shiralee* (1988, TV). **Hitchography:** *Dial M for Murder* (1954)

DONAT, ROBERT (1905–1958, real name Frederick Robert Donat) British actor. In films from 1932 with *Men of Tomorrow*, Donat went on to become one of Britain's most popular leading men, among his hits being Hitchcock's *The 39 Steps* (1935), in which he played innocent on the run Richard Hannay, and *Goodbye, Mr Chips* (1939), which earned him a best actor Oscar. Commented *Variety* of his performance in *The 39 Steps*, 'It's a creamy role for Donat and his performance, ranging from humour to horror, reveals acting ability behind that good looking facade.' Said Donat of his experience working with Hitchcock: '[We] understood each other so perfectly in the making of that film.' [9] His other films include *The Private Life of Henry VIII* (1933), *The Count of Monte Cristo* (1934), *The Ghost Goes West* (1935), *The Citadel* (1938), *The Magic Box* (1951) and *The Inn of the Sixth Happiness* (1958), soon after which he died. He also directed one film, *The Cure for Love* (1949). The second of his two wives was actress Rene Asherson (1920–), to whom he was married between 1953 and 1956. Hitchcock had hoped to work with Donat again on *Sabotage* (1936), in which he was to have taken the role of Police Sergeant Ted Spencer,

Robert Donat wakes up to a nasty surprise in Hitchcock's The 39 Steps *(1935).*

but alas Alexander Korda, to whom the actor was under contract at the time, wouldn't release him. Instead, the part went to John Loder. **Hitchography:** *The 39 Steps* (1935)

DONATH, LUDWIG (1900–1967) Viennese character actor. Remembered for playing Al Jolson's father in the biopics *The Jolson Story* (1946) and *Jolson Sings Again* (1949), Donath made his stage debut in 1924 and quickly went on to establish himself on the Berlin stage. He left Germany for America in 1933 following the rise of the Nazis, and re-emerged as a supporting actor in Hollywood in the early 1940s where, ironically, he was frequently cast as Nazis, including Hitler himself in *The Strange Death of Adolf Hitler* (1943). His other films include *Lady from Chungking* (1942), *The Story of Dr Wassell* (1944), *Gilda* (1946), *The Great Caruso* (1950) and Hitchcock's *Torn Curtain* (1966), in which he plays the crotchety Professor Gustav Lindt. Not one of Hitchcock's lighter efforts, Donath nevertheless had one of the film's best lines: while listening to a dance band over a drink with Paul Newman's professor Michael Armstrong, he comments, 'Ah, the Vienna waltz. Did I tell you my sister got knocked down by a tram in Vienna?' **Hitchography:** *Torn Curtain* (1966)

DOR, KARIN (1938–) German actress. Remembered for playing Helga Brandt in the James Bond epic *You Only Live Twice* (1967), in which she is eaten by piranha fish, Dor was briefly a glamorous fixture in several international films of the 1960s, among them *Treasure of Silver Lake* (1962), *The Face of Fu Manchu* (1965) and Hitchcock's *Topaz* (1969), in which she played the stunning Juanita de Cordoba. Commented *Variety*: 'Karin Dor as a Cuban spy… steals most of the thunder.' **Hitchography:** *Topaz* (1969)

Downhill

(GB, 1927, 74m (some sources state 105m), bw, silent) ★

CREDITS

Production company:	Gainsborough
Producer:	Michael Balcon
Director:	Alfred Hitchcock
Screenplay:	Eliot Stannard, based on the play by Ivor Novello and Constance Collier (writing as David Lestrange)
Cinematographer:	Claude L McDonnell
Editor:	Ivor Montagu

CAST

Ivor Novello (Roddy Berwick), Lillian Braithwaite (Lady Berwick), Norman McKinnell (Sir Thomas Berwick), Ian Hunter (Archie), Isabel Jeans (Julia), Robin Irvine (Tim Wakely), Sybil Rhoda (Sybil Wakeley), Jerrold Robertshaw (Reverend Henry Wakeley), Ben Webster (Dr Dowson), Violet Farebrother (Poetess), Barbara Gott (Madame Michet), Hannah Jones, Annette Benson

Following *The Lodger* (1926), Hitchcock next turned his attention to this melodrama about the downfall of a well-to-do schoolboy, Roddy Berwick, expelled from his private school following an accusation of theft, made all the worse given that he is the prized try-scoring captain of the rugby team. Disowned by his family, he makes his way to the Continent where he has an affair with an actress in Paris, becomes a dancer in a show so as to pay his way and, ultimately, descends into alcoholism in Marseilles. However, the happy ending is never really in doubt and the boy is eventually reunited with his family and revealed to be innocent after all.

As he had been in *The Lodger*, the star was Ivor Novello (34, though supposedly playing 18), upon whose play – co-written with Constance Collier under the pseudonym David Lestrange – the film is based. Said Hitchcock of the screenplay, the work of his regular writer Eliot Stannard, 'The dialogue was pretty dreadful in spots.' [10] Indeed, this is borne out by subtitles such as, 'Does this mean, sir, that I shall not be able to play for the Old Boys?' which Roddy pleads upon being expelled. Hitchcock was also dismissive of one of his effects in the film: 'When the boy is thrown out of the house by his father, to show the beginning of his downhill journey, I put him on an escalator going down.' [11] In fact the French poster for the film, designed by Pierre Pigeot, features Novello in a sketch of this very scene (it should also be noted that the French title of the film was the rather obvious *C'est la Vie*). Nevertheless, there are several other interesting touches in the film, among them a dream sequence and a couple of bravura camera moves, among them a clever shot, the composition of which leads the audience to believe that Roddy is working as a waiter, Hitchcock then pulls back to reveal that he is actually playing a waiter in a show.

DU MAURIER, DAPHNE (1907–1989) British writer. The daughter of actor-manager Gerald Du Maurier (1873–1934) and the granddaughter of novelist George Du Maurier, Daphne became a successful novelist herself, with many of her books filmed, among them *Frenchman's Creek*, *My Cousin Rachel* and *Don't Look Now*. The best known of her filmed works, however, are the three films directed by Alfred Hitchcock: *Jamaica Inn* (1939), which she described as 'a wretched affair', *Rebecca* (1940), which won the best picture Oscar of its year, and *The Birds* (1963), the latter much changed from the short story on which it was based (although it was at least better than the 1994 TV movie sequel *The Birds II: Land's End*, which she mercifully didn't live to see). Her husband was the army officer Sir Frederick 'Boy' Browning. **Hitchography:** *Jamaica Inn* (1939), *Rebecca* (1940), *The Birds* (1963)

DU MAURIER, GERALD (1873–1934) British actor. On stage from the age of 21, Du Maurier went on to become one of the leading actor-managers of his generation, noted for his casual style. He disliked making films, and his appearances before the cameras were consequently few, beginning with *Masks and Faces* in 1916. His other films include *Escape* (1930), *Catherine the Great* (1934) and *Jew Suss* (1934). In 1932, he made *Lord Camber's Ladies*, which was directed by Benn W Levy and produced by Alfred Hitchcock, with whom Du Maurier had struck up a friendship. Knighted in 1922, Du Maurier was the son of novelist George Du Maurier (1834–1896), best known for the much-filmed novel *Trilby*. His daughter was the authoress Daphne Du Maurier (1907–1989) who had several encounters with Hitchcock herself. **Hitchography:** *Lord Camber's Ladies* (1932)

DUNN, EMMA (1875–1966) British character actress. Long in America, Dunn appeared in countless Hollywood films, including *The Glass Key* (1935), *Son of Frankenstein* (1939), *The Great Dictator* (1940) and the Hitchcock comedy *Mr and Mrs Smith* (1941), in which she played the supporting role of Martha. Her other films include *Ladies in Retirement* (1941), *I Married a Witch* (1942) and *The Woman in White* (1948). **Hitchography:** *Mr and Mrs Smith* (1941)

DUNNOCK, MILDRED (1904–1991) American character actress. Following experience as a teacher, Dunnock turned to acting in the late 1920s, making her Broadway debut in 1931. Having played Miss Ronberry in the 1940 production of *The Corn is Green*, Dunnock went on to repeat the role for the 1945 film, which marked her screen debut, and led to a string of solid supporting roles in films

such as *Kiss of Death* (1947), *Death of a Salesman* (1951), which earned her a best supporting actress Oscar nomination, and *Viva Zapata!* (1952). In 1955 she appeared as storeowner Mrs Wiggs in Hitchcock's black comedy *The Trouble with Harry*. Sadly, despite valiant efforts by all concerned, the film was one of the director's weakest affairs. Dunnock's other credits include *Baby Doll* (1956), *The Nun's Story* (1959), *Sweet Bird of Youth* (1962), which earned her a second supporting actress Oscar nomination, *Seven Women* (1965) and *The Pick-Up Artist* (1987). She also appeared in three episodes of *Alfred Hitchcock Presents* and an episode of *The Alfred Hitchcock Hour*. **Hitchography:** *The Trouble with Harry* (1955), *None Are So Blind* (1956, TV), *The West Warlock Time Capsule* (1957, TV), *Heart of Gold* (1957, TV), *Beyond the Sea of Death* (1964, TV)

DYALL, FRANKLIN (1874–1950) British actor. On stage from the age of 20, Dyall began appearing in films in the late 1920s, among his early roles being that of the drunken husband in Hitchcock's *Easy Virtue* (1927). Dyall's other films include *Atlantic* (1930), *The Ringer* (1932), *The Private Life of Henry VIII* (1933) and *Bonnie Prince Charlie* (1949). He was the father of the velvet-voiced actor Valentine Dyall (1908–1985). **Hitchography:** *Easy Virtue* (1927)

E

EAGLER, PAUL (1890–1961) American special effects technician. An Oscar winner for his work on *Portrait of Jennie* (1948), Eagler also contributed to the effects sequences in Hitchcock's *Foreign Correspondent* (1940), on which he also did some second unit photography, and *Notorious* (1946). **Hitchography:** *Foreign Correspondent* (1940), *Notorious* (1946)

EAST OF SHANGHAI see *Rich and Strange*

Easy Virtue
(GB, 1927, 73m (some sources state 74m and 105m), bw, silent) ★

CREDITS
Production company: Gainsborough
Producer: Michael Balcon, C M Woolf
Director: Alfred Hitchcock
Screenwriter: Eliot Stannard, from the play by Noel Coward
Cinematographer: Claude McDonnell
Editor: Ivor Montague
Art director: Clifford Pember
Assistant director: Frank Mills
Continuity: Alma Reville

CAST
Isabel Jeans (Larita Filton), Franklyn Dyall (Mr Filton), Robin Irvine (John Whittaker), Violet Farebrother (Mrs Whittaker), Frank Elliot (Mr Whittaker), Ian Hunter (Plaintiff's counsel), Eric Bransby Williams (Claude Robson, the correspondent), Darcia Dean (Frank Elliot's sister), Dorothy Boyd (Frank Elliot's sister), Enid Stamp-Taylor (Sarah), Benita Hume (Telephonist)

The mix of Hitchcock and Noel Coward might seem a little incongruous at first, but *Easy Virtue* is not one of Coward's lighter than air comedies. Slightly controversial in its time, it revolves round the fall-out from a scandalous divorce, still a taboo subject in the 1920s. The convoluted and often melodramatic plot centres around Larita Filton (Isabel Jeans), who finds solace from her drunken husband (Franklin Dyall) in the arms of an artist, who commits suicide when the husband discovers them together. Divorce proceedings follow, after which Larita escapes to the Mediterranean, where she meets another beau, John Whittaker (Robin Irvine), the son of a well-to-do English family. However, her subsequent marriage to John also ends in the divorce courts when his mother learns of Larita's notorious past as a woman of supposed easy virtue.

Hitchcock and Coward didn't collaborate at all on *Easy Virtue*, which was being shot at Islington Studios more or less at the same time as an adaptation of Coward's 1924 play *The Vortex*, which was being helmed by one of Gainsborough's other contract directors, Adrian Brunel,

with Ivor Novello in the leading role. However, while *The Vortex* was tediously bound by its stage origins, Hitchcock at least broke free from the confines of the proscenium. Nevertheless, this didn't prevent *The Bioscope* from commenting, 'Not one of his more effective films,' though it did allow that the director's 'resourcefulness and occasional brilliance' shone through at times. Indeed, one of Hitchcock's most inventive sequences focuses on John's proposal to Larita, who promises to telephone him with her answer at midnight. However, Larita and John do not feature in the subsequent scene. Instead, Hitchcock concentrates on the reaction of an eavesdropping switchboard operator (Benita Hume) whose grinning face tells us that Larita's answer has been yes. Said Hitchcock of the scene: 'That switchboard operator is in suspense; she is filled with it. Is the woman on the end of the line going to marry the man whom she called? The switchboard operator is very relieved when the woman finally agrees; her own suspense is over. This is an example of suspense that is not related to fear.' [1]

According to Hitchcock, the film also contains the worst inter-title he ever wrote. As Larita is leaving the divorce courts for the second time, she cries to the waiting photographers, 'Shoot – there's nothing left to kill!'

Hitchcock cameo Hitchcock watchers can spot the director by a tennis court during a scene in the South of France.

EDOUART, FARCIOT (1895–1980) American special effects technician. Long with Paramount, Edouart worked on many of the studio's key films, among them *Alice in Wonderland* (1933), *The Ghost Breakers* (1940), *Sullivan's Travels* (1941), *Sunset Boulevard* (1950) and *Ace in the Hole* (1951). A process photography expert, he also worked three times for Hitchcock, beginning with *To Catch a Thief* (1955). He won Oscars for his work on *Spawn of the North* (1938), *I Wanted Wings* (1941) and *Reap the Wild Wind* (1942). **Hitchography:** *To Catch a Thief* (1955), *The Man Who Knew Too Much* (1956), *Vertigo* (1958)

EHE IN GEFAHR see *The Passionate Adventure*

An Elastic Affair
(GB, 1930, 10m approx, bw, silent film)

CREDITS
Production company: BIP
Director: Alfred Hitchcock

CAST
Aileen Despard, Cyril Butcher

In 1930, Hitchcock found time to direct this now seemingly lost black-and-white silent short, which featured two winners of the *Film Weekly* acting scholarship. Little else is known about the film, save that it was made for British International Pictures, to whom Hitchcock was contracted at the time (*The British Film Catalogue* lists the short as a February 1930 release, the same month *Elstree Calling*, on which Hitchcock also worked, was released, so ostensibly, the film could have been shot in late 1929).

ELLIOT, LAURA (1929–   ) American supporting actress. Elliot had her most memorable role in Hitchcock's *Strangers on a Train* (1951) as the despised Miriam, who comes to a sticky end at the hands of Robert Walker's psychopath Bruno Antony, her murder being reflected in her fallen glasses. Her other films include *Special Agent* (1949), *When Worlds Collide* (1952) and *About Mrs Leslie* (1954), but all of them pale besides her brief moment of glory with Hitchcock. **Hitchography:** *Strangers on a Train* (1951)

ELLIS, JUNE British actress. This cheerful actress appeared in minor supporting roles in a variety of films in the 1960s and 1970s, among them *The Devil-Ship Pirates* (1964), *Quatermass and the Pit* (1967), *Anne of the Thousand Days* (1969) and Hitchcock's *Frenzy* (1972), in which she played a barmaid. **Hitchography:** *Frenzy* (1972)

ELSOM, ISOBEL (1893–1981) British actress. On stage from the age of 18, Elsom went on to make a number of silent films, beginning with *A Prehistoric Love Story* in 1915, which she followed with *Milestones* (1916), *Dick Turpin's Ride to York* (1922) and *The Love Story of Aliette Brunton* (1924), etc. Following a handful of sound films, including *Stranglehold* (1931) and *The Primrose Path* (1934), she made the move to Hollywood, where she went on to enjoy success in a variety of matronly roles in films such as *Ladies in Retirement* (1941), *Forever and a Day* (1943), *Of Human Bondage* (1946) and Hitchcock's *The Paradine Case* (1947), in which she played a Yorkshire innkeeper. Her other films include *The Secret Garden* (1949), *Love Is a Many-Splendored Thing* (1955) and *My Fair Lady* (1964). She also appeared in two episodes of *Alfred Hitchcock Presents*, in one of which, *Back for Christmas* (1956, TV), she was again directed by Hitchcock. She was once married to the director Maurice Elvey (1887–1967), who directed the 1932 remake of Hitchcock's *The Lodger*. **Hitchography:** *The Paradine Case* (1947), *Back for Christmas* (1956, TV), *The Three Dreams of Mr Findlater* (1957, TV)

The Adelphi Girls look on as Cicely Courtneidge galumphs her way through a number in the musical revue Elstree Calling *(1930), for which Hitchcock directed a handful of sequences.*

Elstree Calling

(GB, 1930, 95m (some sources state 86m), bw/Technicolor) ★

CREDITS

Production Company:	British International Productions
Producer:	John Maxwell
Directors:	Alfred Hitchcock, Adrian Brunel, Andre Chartlot, Jack Hulbert, Paul Murray
Screenwriters:	Adrian Brunel, Walter C Mycroft
Story:	Val Valentine
Cinematographer:	Claude Friese-Greene
Songs:	Reg Casson, Ivor Novello, Vivian Ellis, Chick Endor, Jack Strachen, Douglas Furber, Rowland Leigh, Donovan Parsons
Music directors:	Teddy Brown, Sydney Baynes, John Reynders
Editors:	A C Hammond, Emile de Ruelle
Choreographers:	Jack Hulbert, Paul Murray, Andre Charlot
Sound:	Alex Murray

CAST

Tommy Handley, Gordon Harker, Jack Hulbert, Cicely Courtneidge, Will Fyffe, Lily Morris, Teddy Brown, Anna May Wong, Donald Calthrop, Jameson Thomas, John Longden, Helen Burnell, Lawrence Green, Ivor McLaren, Bobbie Comber, John Stuart, Nathan Shacknovsky, The Berkoffs, The Charlot Girls, The Adelphi Girls

In the late 1920s and early 1930s, in order to exploit the novelty value of sound and colour, several Hollywood studios staged a number of all-star musical revues. Extremely variably in quality, the hits included *Show of Shows* (1929) made by Warner Bros., *The Hollywood Revue of 1929* (1929) made by MGM and *King of Jazz* (1930) made by Universal. Not wanting to miss this bandwagon, British producer John Maxwell decided to put his own all-star revue into production. The result was this extremely variable ragbag of comedy sketches and musical numbers, presided over by a number of theatrical talents (impresario Andre Charlot, musical comedy star Jack Hulbert) and BIP contract directors (Alfred Hitchcock and Adrian Brunel).

The excuse for the revue is that a film studio is broadcasting its first television show, which a London family, led by character star Gordon Harker, unsuccessfully tries to tune in to. The broadcast is hosted by comedian Tommy Handley, future star of radio's *It's That Man Again*, and features a couple of sketches directed by Hitchcock. The first, titled *Thriller*, follows the exploits of a cuckolded husband,

while in the second a Shakespearian actor (Donald Calthrop), portraying Petruchio, attempts to perform a scene from *The Taming of the Shrew*, only to have his efforts thwarted by his Katherine (Anna May Wong), who has armed herself with custard pies. Elsewhere, numbers are performed by the likes of Jack Hulbert, Cicely Courtneidge and Lily Morris, while Will Fyffe provides a comic monologue.

Though parts of it are filmed in Technicolor, the film almost totally lacks cinematic technique, with many of the sequences photographed as if from the middle of the stalls (commented the *Kinematograph Weekly*, 'Seems short of inspiration in its presentation methods'). Nevertheless, the film does preserve some important talent from the period, and as such it will be worth a look for archivists and music hall specialists. Hitchcock fans will have a thin time of it, though. Even Hitchcock himself described the film as being 'of no interest whatsoever.' [2]

EMERY, JOHN (1905–1964) American actor. In films and on stage as a supporting actor and occasional lead, Emery began appearing in movies in the late 1930s with *The Road Back* (1937). His other films include *Here Comes Mr Jordan* (1941), Hitchcock's *Spellbound* (1945), in which he played the lovesick Dr Fleurot, *The Woman in White* (1948) and *Youngblood Hawke* (1964). He also appeared in an episode of *Alfred Hitchcock Presents*. He was married to actress Tallulah Bankhead (1903–1968) between 1937 and 1941; she starred in Hitchcock's *Lifeboat* (1944). **Hitchography:** *Spellbound* (1945), *Servant Problem* (1961, TV)

EMMETT, EVH (1902–1971) British broadcaster. Best remembered as the commentator of *Gaumont-British News* in the 1930s and *Universal News* in the 1950s, Emmett also worked as a screenwriter, in which capacity he contributed 'additional dialogue' to Hitchcock's *Sabotage* (1936). He later became an associate producer at Ealing, where he made *Passport to Pimlico* (1949) and *Dance Hall* (1950). He can also be heard as the narrator in *Carry On, Cleo* (1964). **Hitchography:** *Sabotage* (1936)

ESMOND, JILL (1908–1990) British actress. Esmond, who worked in both Britain and America, is perhaps best remembered for being the first wife of Laurence Olivier (1907–1989), to whom she was married from 1930 to 1940 (Olivier would go on to star in *Rebecca* for Hitchcock in 1940). Her films include *F.P.1* (1932), *The Pied Piper* (1942) and *A Man Called Peter* (1955). She also appeared as Jill Hillcrist in Hitchcock's early talkie *The Skin Game* (1931), although the role is not regarded as one of her better ones. **Hitchography:** *The Skin Game* (1931)

EVANS, RAY (1915–) American lyricist. Long in partnership with composer Jay Livingston, Evans began his film career in 1943 with *Footlight Glamour*, and went on to win three best song Oscars, for *Buttons and Bows* from *The Paleface* (1948), *Mona Lisa* from *Captain Carey USA* (1950) and *Que Sera Sera* from Hitchcock's remake of *The Man Who Knew Too Much* (1956), for which he and Livingston also penned *We'll Love Again*. The duo's other big screen credits include *Fancy Pants* (1950), *Tammy and the Bachelor* (1957) and *Tammy and the Doctor* (1963). They also provided the theme tunes for such TV shows as *Bonanza* (1960–1973) and *Mr Ed* (1962–1965). Meanwhile in 1958, Evans and Livingston composed a song to promote Hitchcock's *Vertigo*, which was recorded by Billy Eckstine, but it quickly disappeared. Later, in 1966, Evans and Livingston also provided lyrics for John Addison's love theme from Hitchcock's *Torn Curtain*; titled *Green Years*, the song (not heard in the film but featured on the soundtrack album) was again used to promote the film, but failed to make an impact in the charts. **Hitchography:** *The Man Who Knew Too Much* (1956), *Vertigo* (1958), *Torn Curtain* (1966)

EVANSON, EDITH American stage actress. Film credits for Evanson are few and far between, although she did make a splash as the wisecracking maid Mrs Wilson in Hitchcock's *Rope* (1948), a role that seems to have been the prototype for Thelma Ritter's turn as the mouthy Stella in *Rear Window* (1954). Evanson's other film credits include *Magnificent Yankee* (1950), *The Clown and the Kid* (1961), *Married Too Young* (1962) and *The Prize* (1963), as well as a second, briefer appearance for Hitchcock as Rita the deaf cleaner in *Marnie* (1964). **Hitchography:** *Rope* (1948), *Marnie* (1964)

EVELYN, JUDITH (1913–1967, real name Judith Evelyn Allen) American actress. Remembered for playing 'Miss Lonelyhearts' in Hitchcock's *Rear Window* (1954), Evelyn made a handful of films in the 1950s, among them *The 13ᵗʰ Letter* (1951), *The Egyptian* (1954), *Female on the Beach* (1955) and *The Tingler* (1959). She also appeared in two episodes of *Alfred Hitchcock Presents*. **Hitchography:** *Rear Window* (1954), *Guilty Witness* (1955, TV), *Martha Mason, Movie Star* (1957, TV)

EWING, JOHN American art director. Ewing worked on a couple of notable films for producer David O Selznick in the 1940s: Hitchcock's *Spellbound* (1945) and *Duel in the Sun* (1946). **Hitchography:** *Spellbound* (1945)

Barbara Harris in full "Madame" Blanche regalia in Hitchcock's last film, Family Plot *(1976).*

82

F

Family Plot

(US, 1976, 121m, Technicolor film) ★★

CREDITS

Production company:	Universal
Producer:	Alfred Hitchcock
Director:	Alfred Hitchcock
Screenplay:	Ernest Lehman, based on the novel *The Rainbird Pattern* by Victor Canning
Cinematographer:	Leonard J South
Music:	John Williams
Editor:	J Terry Williams
Production designer:	Henry Bumstead
Costumes:	Edith Head
Special effects:	Albert Whitlock
Sound:	Robert L Hoyt, James Alexander
First assistant director:	Howard Kazanjian

CAST

Barbara Harris ('Madame' Blanche Tyler), Bruce Dern (George Lumley), Karen Black (Fran), William Devane (Arthur Adamson), Cathleen Nesbitt (Julia Rainbird), Katherine Helmond (Mrs Maloney), Ed Lauter (Joseph Maloney), Warren J Kemmerling (Grandison), Edith Atwater (Mrs Clay), Alexander Lockwood (Pastor), Martin West (Sanger), Marge Redmond (Vera Hannagan), John Lehne (Andy Bush), William Prince (Bishop), Nicholas Colasanto (Constantine), Charles Tyner (Wheeler)

Video availability: Universal

DVD availability: Universal

CD availability: *Psycho – The Essential Alfred Hitchcock* (Silva Screen), which contains the *Finale*

'There's no body in the family plot,' exclaimed the posters for Hitchcock's 53rd and, as it turned out, final film. What there *is*, though (and there's a lot of it) is plot; scene after scene of it, all laboriously relayed by the two sets of characters around whom the action revolves. The screenplay was based on the novel *The Rainbird Pattern* by Victor Canning (whose story *Disappearing Trick* had been filmed for *Alfred Hitchcock Presents* back in 1958), and was adapted by Ernest Lehman, who had last collaborated with Hitch on the brilliant *North by Northwest* (1959). Unfortunately, despite Lehman's pedigree, *Family Plot* is one of his lesser efforts resulting in one of Hitchcock's talkiest productions (writing in the *New York Post*, Frank Rich described Lehman's work as 'shoddy and, at times, downright sleazy').

Work on the screenplay began in 1974, at which stage it was known as *One Plus One Equals One* and, a little later, *Deceit*. It was under this title that shooting on the £3.5 million production began. The script had altered the story's setting from England to California, while other elements had been either dropped, added or remoulded. Essentially, though, the basic narrative thrust remained the same: Blanche Tyler (Barbara Harris), a fake medium, has been hired by the incredibly wealthy Julia Rainbird (Cathleen Nesbitt) to find her illegitimate nephew, who had been given away as a baby to save the family name. Helping 'Madame Blanche' track down the now adult child, for which she will be paid $10,000 if successful, is her boyfriend, taxi driver George Lumley (Bruce Dern), whose detective work the medium relies upon to hoodwink her clients. ('Without my research, you're about as psychic as dry salami,' he protests at being taken for granted once too often, adding, 'I'm sick and tired of you having me by the crystal balls.')

Following a lead that the infant was given away to a friend of the family chauffeur's, Madame Blanche and Lumley proceed to search for the missing heir. Meanwhile, San Francisco is hit by a number of high profile kidnappings, for which the ransom demand is always a valuable gem. The mastermind behind these audacious operations is diamond broker Arthur Adamson (William Devane), who is assisted in his crimes by his girlfriend Fran (Karen Black), who always picks up the ransom in person, safe in the knowledge that as long as the victim is in their hands she won't be apprehended.

Ironically, it transpires that Adamson is the heir Madame Blanche and Lumley are looking for. Adopted by a couple named Shoebridge who had named him Edward, he had lived with them in their run-down home. However, all three Shoebridges seemingly perished in a mysterious house fire; but as Lumley notes, the mother and father are buried in a separate grave to their adopted son, whose own gravestone looks new by comparison. Is there actually a body in Edward Shoebridge's grave, wonders Lumley, and if not, who and where is he now?

Gradually, the two stories merge, with Madame Blanche held hostage by Shoebridge/Adamson when, having finally discovered his whereabouts, she pays him a visit, only to stumble across his and Fran's latest ransom plot, which happens to involve the kidnapping of a bishop who, many years ago, had been the humble parson who baptized Edward Shoebridge. Drugged by Adamson and placed in a purpose-built soundproofed room in his basement, the game now seems up for Blanche (in the novel she is murdered by the kidnappers); however, Lumley, who has been busy working in his cab, is soon at hand to rescue her. Creeping about the house as Adamson and Fran discuss their plans, he discovers the whereabouts of the basement room, in which he manages to lock Fran and Adamson when they attempt to remove the supposedly still-drugged Blanche; as Adamson tries to lift her, Blanche screams and runs for the door, which Lumley slams behind her, locking the two kidnappers in their own cell!

Filming began on 12 May 1975. At this stage, television star Roy Thinnes, best known for the series *The Invaders* (1966–1967), was in the role of Shoebridge/Adamson. In fact filming proceeded for a whole month before Hitchcock decided that the actor was wrong for the role.

An announcement was finally made on 13 June that, owing to a conceptual change, Thinnes would be replaced by William Devane. 'Artistic differences' would seem to have been the root of the problem ('When I'm directing a film, *I'm* directing a film, not some actor,' [1] Hitchcock is said to have commented). The film's 58-day schedule was subsequently revised to accommodate the casting change, yet this doesn't seem to have affected production too adversely (it should be noted that Universal also wanted Liza Minnelli to play Madame Blanche, but Hitchcock demurred).

Filming wrapped on 18 August 1975, just 13 days over schedule. By this time the film was known as *Family Plot*, and as such it was eventually released after a lengthy post-production period on 21 March 1976, going on to earn a domestic gross of $7.5 million. The critics were divided. 'It is atmospheric, characterful, precisely paced, intricately plotted, exciting and suspenseful, beautifully acted and, perhaps more than anything else, amusing,' wrote Charles Champlin in the *L.A. Times*, barely able to contain his enthusiasm. Others were less positive: 'A laborious piece of crinkum-crankum,' condemned Stanley Kauffmann, to which Richard Corliss added, 'To call this 'a Hitchcock' film is to be accessory to false advertising. *Family Plot* should be reported to the Consumer Protection Agency.'

In fact, Corliss's assessment is pretty much near the mark, for there is very little in *Family Plot* to identify it as a Hitchcock picture. The pacing and handling are gene-rally lethargic (an early conversation between Blanche and Lumley in their car goes on for an age), the cinematography is uninventive (the film has the look of a TV movie of the period), and the set pieces, such as they are, lack the expected pizzazz. Indeed, the kidnapping of the bishop lacks the flair one would normally expect of the Master, while a sequence in which Madame Blanche and Lumley career down a mountain having had their car brakes cut by Adamson's henchman Maloney (Ed Lauter) is just ludicrous. Even the graveyard scenes lack the required atmosphere. But then again, Hitchcock was by now old and tired. He was 75 when the film was released; he may once had been revered and emulated for his deftness of touch. Now his work seemed curiously old fashioned and out of step with the times – and made to seem even more so by the frequent use of fashionable profanity and sexual refe-rences in the script, almost as if the film were trying to endear itself to a younger generation, but instead only embarrassing itself in the attempt (the script contains several unnecessary 'shits' and 'bullshits' while Lumley comments of Blanche's sexual demands, 'I'm too pooped to pop'). Commented director Brian de Palma, who has made more than his fair share of Hitchcock pastiches, 'The man has clearly lost his sense of timing, of cinema. He's 75! You can't be a genius forever.'

But let us not condemn the film entirely. The performances, despite some over-playing, are generally likeable and accomplished, notably Devane's urbane Adamson and Harris's engagingly kooky Madame Blanche, which *Variety* described as 'sensational'. The occasional touch also manages to make itself felt, such as the lengthy tracking shot which accompanies the heavily disguised Fran as she makes her way

to collect the ransom for one of Adamson's hapless kidnap victims, and the montage sequence in which Blanche searches for Arthur Adamson by going to see all the A Adamsons in the phone book until she finds the right one. Then there's the finale in which Madame Blanche, in a seemingly genuine trance, is led to Adamson's cache of jewels, hidden in his hallway chandelier. Of course, she could have heard Adamson discussing the diamonds just after having been drugged ('Let's go and get the new diamond for our chandelier'), which would explain her knowing wink to the camera just prior to the end credits.

The movie also contains one of composer John Williams' most playful scores. In fact without it, the film would truly drag its heels. Madame Blanche's 'psychic' activities are accompanied by an ethereal choral theme, whil a sinister organ motif is employed during the more dramatic moments. Meanwhile, a bouncy, mock classical piece carried by harpsichord and full orchestra is referred to during the lighter moments, most notably during the closing credits following Madame Blanche's delightful wink, which perfectly brings to an end both the film and Hitchcock's career.

Note that during the scene in which Blanche and Lumley's car careens down a mountain road, a close-up shows black break fluid leaking out onto the road, yet in the rear projection shots, there is no fluid on the road.

Hitchcock cameo Hitchcock can be spotted in silhouette behind a door marked Registrar of Births and Deaths.

Hitchcock did attempt to get one final film off the ground. Titled *The Short Night*, it reached the scripting stage, but Hitchcock himself pulled the plug on the pro-ject in 1979 (see Un-filmed Hitchcock).

FAMOUS PLAYERS-LASKY Originally founded in 1912 by producer Adolph Zukor, this American company derived its name from its promise of 'Famous players in famous plays' following the successful US release of the French-made *Queen Elizabeth* (1912, aka *Les Amours de la Reine Elisabeth*) starring stage legend Sarah Bernhardt. In 1916 the company merged with Jesse L Lasky's Feature Play Company, which had made its mark in 1914 with the release of Cecil B de Mille's *The Squaw Man*. In 1919, the company opened up a London branch at Islington Studios known as Famous Players-Lasky British Producers Ltd. This went on to produce a busy programme of films, among them *The Great Day* (1920) and *Three Live Ghosts* (1922), many of which had inter-titles designed by the young Alfred Hitchcock. The company wound down its London arm in 1923, although in America it went from strength to strength, absorbing several other companies, among them two distribution companies: Artcraft and Paramount Pictures Corporation, the latter founded in 1914 by W W Hodgkinson. By 1927 the company had gained the unwieldy name of The Paramount Famous Lasky Corporation, which in turn became The Paramount Publix Corporation three years later. However, this company went bankrupt in 1933, but re-emerged as Paramount Pictures Inc. in 1935. In the 1950s, Hitchcock resumed his association with the company, directing several key films for it, among them *Rear Window* (1954), *To Catch a Thief* (1955) and *Vertigo* (1958). Also see Islington Studios.

FAREBROTHER, VIOLET (1888–1969) British supporting actress. Farebrother popped up in bit parts in all manner of films, from the late silent period through to the mid-1950s. She worked for Hitchcock three times during her busy career, although all of her roles were minor (for example, in *Murder!* she played a jury member). Her other films include *The Woman for Joe* (1955) and *Fortune is a Woman* (1956). **Hitchography:** *Downhill* (1927), *Easy Virtue* (1927), *Murder!* (1930)

The Farmer's Wife

(GB, 1928, 67m (some sources state 100m), bw, silent film)

CREDITS
Production company: British International Pictures
Producer: John Maxwell
Director: Alfred Hitchcock
Screenwriter: Eliot Stannard, based on the play by Eden Philpotts, itself based on Philpotts' 1913 novel *Widdicombe Fair*
Cinematographer: Jack Cox
Editor: Alfred Booth
Assistant director: Frank Mills

CAST
Jameson Thomas (Samuel Sweetland), Lillian Hall-Davies (Araminta Dench, the housekeeper), Gordon Harker (Churdles Ash), Louise Pounds (Louisa Windeatt), Olga Slade (Mary Hearn), Ruth Maitland (Mercy Bassett), Gibb McLaughlin (Henry Coaker), Maude Gill (Thirza Tapper), Antonia Brough (Susan), Mollie Ellis (Sibley Sweetland), Haward Watts (Dick Coaker)

Based on the long running play by Eden Philpotts, *The Farmer's Wife* follows the attempts by a widower farmer named Samuel Sweetland (Jameson Thomas) to find a new wife. However, after assessing the suitability of several prospective brides, he eventually settles on the woman who has been under his nose all the time – his loyal housekeeper.

As with *Easy Virtue*, Hitchcock's task with *The Farmer's Wife* was to disguise its theatrical origins as best he could. Said the director, 'We tried to avoid using titles and, wherever possible, to use pictorial expression instead.' [2] Consequently, the director attempted to keep the film's tempo upbeat, although as he admitted, he wasn't always successful. 'I had to film a little scene... six times... because the players took it too slowly to fit in with the mood of the picture.' [3] It didn't help that cinematographer Jack Cox was off ill for much of the production either, forcing Hitchcock himself to take over his duties, including the lighting and framing of shots. 'It wasn't actually very cinematic,' [4] said the director of his efforts. Nevertheless, he seems to have had fun with the film's comic moments, among them a riotous tea party in which character actor Gordon Harker steals the scene as Sweetland's farm hand Churdles Ash, whose lack of social graces quickly, and hilariously, become apparent.

The film was remade in 1940 by Norman Lee and Leslie Arliss, but was not a success. It's also worth noting that Hitchcock became a father during the production of *The Farmer's Wife*, his wife Alma giving birth to daughter Patricia on 7 July 1928.

The Farmer's Wife

(GB, 1940, 85m, bw film)

CREDITS
Production company: Associated British
Directors: Norman Lee, Leslie Arliss
Screenwriters: Norman Lee, Leslie Arliss, J E Hunter, based on the play by Eden Philpotts, itself based on Philpotts' 1913 novel *Widdicombe Fair*

CAST
Wilfred Lawson (Churdles Ash), Basil Sydney (Samuel Sweetland), Michael Wilding (Richard Coaker), Patricia Roc (Sibley), Nora Swinburne (Araminta Grey), Enid Stamp Taylor (Mary Hearne), Kenneth Griffith (George Smerdon), A Bromley Davenport (Henry Coaker), Edward Rigby (Tom Gurney), Betty Warren (Lovisa Windeatt), Viola Lyel (Thirza Tapper)

An adequate though now little seen remake of the 1928 Hitchcock film, whose interesting cast features Michael Wilding, who later starred in *Under Capricorn* (1949) and *Stage Fright* (1950) for Hitchcock. Other Hitchcock alumni in the cast include Edward Rigby and A. Bromley Davenport.

FARRELL, TOMMY American actor. An occasional support in the 1950s and 1960s, Farrell's credits include *At War with the Army* (1950), *Jail Bait* (1954), *Kissin' Cousins* (1964) and *A Guide for the Married Man* (1967). He can also be spotted in Hitchcock's *North by Northwest* (1959), in which he plays the elevator operator in the opening scene ('Say hello to the missus,' comments Cary Grant's Roger Thornhill, to which comes the resigned reply, 'We're not talking'). **Hitchography:** *North by Northwest* (1959)

FEAR O'GOD see *The Mountain Eagle*

FEHR, RUDI (1911–1999) German-born editor. This distinguished editor worked for Warner Bros. for 40 years, cutting many of the studio's top productions, including *Humoresque* (1946), *Key Largo* (1948) and the 3D *House of Wax* (1953). He began his career in Berlin in the early 1930s working for producer Sam Spiegel, with whom he also worked in Austria and Britain. In Hollywood (and at Warner Bros.) from 1940 with *My Love Came Back*, he went on to edit *All Through the Night* (1942), *Watch on the Rhine* (1943) and *The Inspector General* (1949). In the early 1950s, he cut two films for Alfred Hitchcock: *I Confess* (1953) and the 3D *Dial M for Murder* (1954), but the latter was eventually released 'flat' (though 3D versions survive and are shown at cinema clubs). Fehr's other credits include *The Desert Song* (1953), which he produced, *Land of the Pharaohs* (1955) and *Prizzi's Honour* (1985), for which he earned an Oscar nomination with his daughter Kaja Fehr, herself a film editor. Fehr also worked in Europe in the 1960s as the overseer of foreign language versions of Warner productions, while in the 1980s he de-camped to American Zoetrope, where he became head of post-production, working on films such as *One from the Heart* (1981). His wife was the actress Maris Wrixon (1917–). **Hitchography:** *I Confess* (1953), *Dial M for Murder* (1954)

FELMY, HANSJOERGE (1931–) German character actor. In films from 1956 with *Der Stein von Afrika*, Felmy went on to appear in the likes of *Wir Wunderkinder* (1958) and *Buddenbrooks* (1959), as well as such English-language films as *Station Six Sahara* (1963) and Hitchcock's *Torn Curtain* (1966), in which he played Professor Heinrich Gerhard, who helps to engineer the defection of Paul Newman's Professor Michael Armstrong to East Berlin, without realizing that he is in fact a double agent. **Hitchography:** *Torn Curtain* (1966)

FENNELLY, PARKER American supporting actor. Fennelly made few films, among them Hitchcock's *The Trouble with Harry* (1955), in which he appears at the end as the millionaire who buys up all of Sam Marlowe's abstract artwork. His other credits include *The Russians Are Coming, The Russians Are Coming* (1966), *Pretty Poison* (1968) and *Angel in My Pocket* (1969). **Hitchography:** *The Trouble with Harry* (1955)

FERGUSON, PERRY (1901–1963) American art director. Ferguson spent much of his career at RKO, where he designed such films as *A Bill of Divorcement* (1932), *Gunga Din* (1939) and *Citizen Kane* (1941). His occasional freelance assignments include Hitchcock's *Rope* (1948), for which he designed a luxurious New York apartment, complete with removable walls so that Hitchcock's roving camera could freely move about the set. **Hitchography:** *Rope* (1948)

FERREN, JOHN American artist. Ferren provided the abstract paintings by artist Sam Marlowe (John Forsythe) in Hitchcock's black comedy *The Trouble with Harry* (1955). Hitchcock was obviously impressed by Ferren's work, as he invited the artist back for *Vertigo* (1958), for which he designed the nightmare sequence; he also painted the portrait of Carlotta Valdes seen at The Palace of the Legion of Honor. **Hitchography:** *The Trouble with Harry* (1955), *Vertigo* (1958)

FIELDING, EDWARD (1879–1945) American actor. Credits available for Fielding are few, but he did manage four films for Hitchcock in the 1940s, playing Frith in *Rebecca*

(1940), an antiques shop proprietor in *Suspicion* (1941), a doctor on a train in *Shadow of a Doubt* (1943) and the real Dr Edwardes in *Spellbound* (1945). He can also be spotted in *The Major and the Minor* (1942) and *What a Woman!* (1943). **Hitchography:** *Rebecca* (1940), *Suspicion* (1941), *Shadow of a Doubt* (1943), *Spellbound* (1945)

FINCH, JON (1941–) British actor. On stage in rep from 1963, leading man Finch made his film debut in *The Vampire Lovers* (1970). Following further supporting roles in *The Horror of Frankenstein* (1970), *L'Affaire Martine Desclos* (1971) and *Sunday, Bloody Sunday* (1971), he shot to stardom in the title role of director Roman Polanski's gore-filled version of *Macbeth* (1971). Much sought after as a consequence, he went on to play ex-squadron leader Richard Blaney, who finds himself wrongly accused of a series of murders in Hitchcock's last British film, *Frenzy* (1972). Recalled Finch of being cast in the film: 'It's probably the only time I've actually had an agent do anything for me, because he actually sent along a copy of this film I'd made for Yorkshire television which Hitchcock saw. After he'd seen this, Hitch said, "At least he can act! What's he doing at the moment?" He was told I was doing *Macbeth*, and he said, "I suppose he might do! Can he come and see me?" So I got in the studio car and went up to London to see him. And he was so sweet and charming. He said, "I know you can act because I've seen this little film that you've done. I didn't like the film, but you were all right. Do you want to do this?" And I said, "For Christ's sake, yes!" Then he said, "Good! Now that we've got that out of the way let's go and have a nice lunch!" And that was it!' [5]

Finch's subsequent films include *Lady Caroline Lamb* (1972), *The Final Programme* (1973), *Diagnosis: Murder* (1974), *Breaking Glass* (1980), *Strange* (1987) and *Darklands* (1996), but he never again reached the heights he achieved in those few brief years in the early 1970s. Said Finch of *Frenzy*'s impact on his career, 'It probably sunk it completely. I made quite a few films afterwards in Spain, Italy and Germany, but as far as this country was concerned, my career seemed to be finished.' [6] **Hitchography:** *Frenzy* (1972)

FINE, HARRY Irish-born producer. With such films as *The Pleasure Girls* (1965), *The Vampire Lovers* (1970) and *Twins of Evil* (1971) to his credit, Fine started his career as a stage manager, casting director and occasional actor, as which he appeared in a handful of films, including *The Ghosts of Berkeley Square* (1947), *To Have and To Hold* (1951) and Hitchcock's *The Man Who Knew Too Much* (1956), in which he played the un-credited role of Edington. **Hitchography:** *The Man Who Knew Too Much* (1956)

FITZGERALD, BARRY (1888–1961) Irish-born actor. Remembered chiefly for his Oscar winning role as Father Fitzgibbon in *Going My Way* (1944), Fitzgerald played a variety of character parts in such Hollywood films as *How Green Was My Valley* (1941), *And Then There Were None* (1945), *Top o' the Morning* (1949) and *The Quiet Man* (1952). However, he made his film debut in England as the Orator in Hitchcock's adaptation of Sean O'Casey's *Juno and the Paycock* (1930), following lengthy experience with the Irish Players at the Abbey Theatre in Dublin, which he joined in 1915. He later appeared in an episode of *Alfred Hitchcock Presents*. **Hitchography:** *Juno and the Paycock* (1930), *Santa Claus and the Tenth Avenue Kid* (1955, TV)

FITZMAURICE, GEORGE (1885–1941) French-born director. Fitzmaurice emigrated to America in 1905, where he first worked as a stage designer, then, from 1908, as a screenwriter. He began directing in 1914 with *When Rome Ruled*, and went on to helm several key silent star vehicles, among them *The Cheat* (1923), starring Pola Negri and *The Son of the Sheik* (1926) starring Rudolph Valentino. In 1922, he was contracted by Famous Players-Lasky to make two films in London, for which the young Hitchcock provided the inter-titles. Fitzmaurice's sound work included *Mata Hari* (1932), *The Emperor's Candlesticks* (1937) and *Adventure in Love* (1940), which was his last film. **Hitchography:** *The Man from Home* (1922), *Three Live Ghosts* (1922)

FLAVIN, JAMES (1906–1976) American supporting actor. Specializing in cops, this actor from an Irish background popped up in all manner of films, including *King Kong* (1933), *The Grapes of Wrath* (1944), *Mighty Joe Young* (1949), *Mister Roberts* (1955) and *It's a Mad, Mad, Mad, Mad World* (1963). He also played the un-credited role of an escort in Hitchcock's comedy *Mr and Mrs Smith* (1941). **Hitchography:** *Mr and Mrs Smith* (1941)

FLEMING, RHONDA (1922– , real name Marilyn Louis) American actress. This flame-haired actress began her film career as an extra at the age of 21 in *In Old Oklahoma* (1943). She soon graduated to supporting roles, among them a memorable turn as the man-hating Mary Carmichael in Hitchcock's *Spellbound* (1945). It was in the 1950s, however, that she truly came into her own in a series of Technicolor extravaganzas, among them *The Redhead and the Cowboy* (1950), *Pony Express* (1953) and *The Courtesan of Babylon* (1954). Her other films include *The Big Circus* (1959), *Won Ton Ton, the Dog Who Saved Hollywood* (1976) and *The Nude Bomb* (1980). **Hitchography:** *Spellbound* (1945)

FONDA, HENRY (1905–1982) American actor. One of Hollywood's great star actors, Fonda began his film career in 1935 in *The Farmer Takes a Wife*, in which he repeated his Broadway role. He turned to acting following experience as an office boy, and was soon admired the world over for the sincerity and integrity of his work in such films as *Jezebel* (1938), *Young Mr Lincoln* (1939) and, most importantly, *The Grapes of Wrath* (1940). Commented Orson Welles of the actor: 'I look at Henry Fonda and I see the face of America,' [7] although the star was rather more humble about himself, saying: 'I ain't really Henry Fonda. Nobody could have *that* much integrity.' [8] The star's many other films include *The Ox-Bow Incident* (1943), *My Darling Clementine* (1946), *Mister Roberts* (1955), *Twelve Angry Men* (1957), which he also pro-

Joan Fontaine in a dramatic moment from the opening scene of Hitchcock's Rebecca *(1940). The actress earned an Oscar nomination for her performance and went on to win the award for her next film with the director,* Suspicion *(1941)*

duced, *The Best Man* (1964), *Once Upon a Time in the West* (1969), in which he played a rare villainous role, *The Swarm* (1978) and *On Golden Pond* (1981), which won him a best actor Oscar (1981 also saw him win an honorary Oscar 'in recognition of his brilliant accomplishments' [9]).

In 1956, Fonda starred in Hitchcock's *The Wrong Man*, playing Manny Balestrero, a New York musician who is wrongly arrested for the crimes of another man. The story was based on a true-life incident, and *Variety* praised the actor's 'stark kind of impersonation.' Married five times, Fonda's wives were actress Margaret Sullavan (1911–1960, real name Margaret Brooke), to whom he was married between 1931 and 1933; Frances Seymour Brokaw, between 1936 and 1950; Susan Blanchard, between 1950 and 1956; Baronessa Alfreda Franchetti, between 1957 and 1961; and Shirlee Adams, from 1965 until his death. He was the father of actress Jane Fonda (1937–) and actor Peter Fonda (1939–), and the grandfather of actress Bridget Fonda (1964–). **Hitchography:** *The Wrong Man* (1956)

FONTAINE, JOAN (1917– , real name Joan de Beauvoir De Havilland) British-born actress. With the opening narration to Hitchcock's *Rebecca* (1940), Joan Fontaine got to speak one of the cinema's most memorable lines: 'Last night I dreamed I went to Manderley again.' Though English, Fontaine was actually born in Tokyo, Japan. In films from the age of 18, she made her debut the same year as her elder sister, Olivia De Havilland, appearing in *No More Ladies* under the name of Joan Burfield. Adopting the name Fontaine (that of her step-father), she went on to appear in *Quality Street* (1937), *Gunga Din* (1939) and *The Women* (1939) among others, but true stardom was slow in coming. It finally arrived when she was cast as the timid, un-named second Mrs de Winter in Hitchcock's *Rebecca*, beating such contenders as Anne Baxter, Loretta Young, Vivien Leigh, Margaret Sullavan and her sister Olivia De Havilland for the part. However, producer David O Selznick had a hard time convincing everybody that Fontaine was up to the role, a concern he voiced during the lengthy casting process, commenting, 'I couldn't get anybody on the staff, except for [editor] Hal Kern, or anybody in the New York office, to agree with me about her... People kept calling her "the wooden woman"'. [10]

Of course Fontaine proved her detractors wrong, and went on to earn universal praise, and a best actress Oscar nomination, for her performance. Commented *Variety*: 'Joan Fontaine is excellent as the second wife, carrying through the transition of a sweet and vivacious bride to that of a bewildered woman marked by the former tragedy she finds hard to understand.' However, as Fontaine herself later admitted, Hitchcock's direction didn't exactly fill her with self-confidence: 'Hitch kept me off balance, much to his own delight... He would constantly tell me that no one thought I was very good, except himself.' [11]

Hitchcock must have been pretty impressed by Fontaine, for he cast her again in his 1941 film *Suspicion*, in which the actress played another timid wife, Lina McLaidlaw-Aysgarth, who suspects that her husband is trying to poison her to death. This time she actually won the best actress Oscar. Enthused *Variety* again: 'Joan Fontaine successfully transposes to the screen her innermost emotions and fears over the wastrel and apparently murderous antics of her husband.'

Fontaine's other films include *Jane Eyre* (1944), *Letter from an Unknown Woman* (1948), *Voyage to the Bottom of the Sea* (1961), *The Witches* (1966) and *Hitchcock, il Brivido del Genio* (1985). She also starred in a radio adaptation of *Rebecca* and an episode of *The Alfred Hitchcock Hour*. Married four times, her husbands included actor Brian Aherne (1902–1986), to whom she was married between 1939 and 1944; producer William Dozier (1908–1991), to whom she was married between 1946 and 1951; and writer Collier Young (1908–1980), to whom she was married between 1952 and 1961. Brian Aherne went on to co-star in Hitchcock's *I Confess* (1953). Fontaine married her final husband, Alfred Wright, in 1964, divorcing him the following year. Said the star of her various marriages, 'If you keep marrying as I do, you learn everybody's hobby.' [12] her sister, actress Olivia de Havilland (1919–), starred in a 1944 radio adaptation of *Suspicion*.

Hitchography: *Rebecca* (1940), *Suspicion* (1941), *Rebecca* (1946, radio), *The Paragon* (1963, TV)

FORBSTEIN, LEO F (1892–1948) American composer-conductor-musical director. Forbstein was long resident at Warner Bros., where he conducted literally hundreds of scores, including *I Am a Fugitive from a Chain Gang* (1932), *42nd Street* (1933), *Gold Diggers of 1933* (1933), *Footlight Parade* (1933), *In This Our Life* (1942) and *Casablanca* (1943). One of his last jobs was a freelance assignment, conducting David Buttolph's arrangement of Francois Poulenc's *Perpetual Movement* for Hitchcock's *Rope* (1948). **Hitchography:** *Rope* (1948)

FORD, HUGH American director. Following his success in America directing the first screen version of *Mrs Wiggs of the Cabbage Patch* for Famous Players-Lasky in 1919, Ford was invited to Britain by the company to helm *The Great Day* (1920), the first film for its British arm. It was also the first film on which Alfred Hitchcock ever worked (in the capacity of inter-title designer). Ford also directed *The Call of Youth* (1920) for Famous Players-Lasky, providing Hitchcock with his second inter-title job. **Hitchography:** *The Great Day* (1920), *The Call of Youth* (1920)

Ford Startime

(US, 1960, 50m, bw TV)

CREDITS
Production company:	Shamley/Universal.Revue
Executive producer:	Alfred Hitchcock
Producer:	Joan Harrison
Director:	Alfred Hitchcock
Teleplay:	Charlotte Armstrong, based on her novel

CAST
Vera Miles, George Peppard, Paul Hartman, Leora Dana, Bob Sweeney

In 1960, amid his own successful series *Alfred Hitchcock Presents*, Hitchcock took time out to direct this episode of the anthology series *Ford Startime*, which used the director's usual television staff, including producer Joan Harrison. Titled *Incident at a Corner*, the programme starred Vera Miles, who had recently co-starred in the then yet-to-be-released *Psycho* for Hitchcock.

FORD, WALLACE (1898–1966) British-born actor. Ford began his stage career in variety at the age of 11, having run away from a foster home (in the mid-1930s, he became headline news when he was finally re-united with his real parents). In America from 1930, he made his film debut in the short *Absent-Minded*, and went on to star in a handful of features, including the notorious *Freaks* (1932) and *The Lost Patrol* (1934) before gradually turning to character roles. His many other films include *Sanders of the*

Joel McCrea and Laraine Day are surprised by one of the many dramatic developments in Hitchcock's Foreign Correspondent *(1940).*

River (1935), *Harvey* (1950) and *A Patch of Blue* (1965). He can also be seen as Fred Saunders in Hitchcock's *Shadow of a Doubt* (1943), and the bore who pesters Ingrid Bergman's Dr Peterson at the Empire State Hotel in *Spellbound* (1945). **Hitchography:** *Shadow of a Doubt* (1943), *Spellbound* (1945)

Foreign Correspondent
(US, 1940, 120m bw film) ★★★★

CREDITS

Production company:	United Artists
Producer:	Walter Wanger
Director:	Alfred Hitchcock
Screenplay:	Charles Bennett, Joan Harrison, James Hilton, Robert Benchley, Ben Hecht (un-credited), John Lee Mahin (un-credited), Richard Maibaum (un-credited)
Cinematographer:	Rudolph Mate
Music:	Alfred Newman
Editors:	Dorothy Spencer, Otho Lovering
Art director:	Alexander Golitzen
Associate art director:	Richard Irving
Special production effects:	William Cameron Menzies
Special effects:	Paul Eagler, Thomas T Moulton, Lee Zavitz, Ray Binger
Sound:	Frank Maher
2nd unit cinematography:	Osmond Borradaile
Camera operator:	Burnett Guffey

CAST
Joel McCrea (Johnny Jones/Huntley Haverstock), Laraine Day (Carol Fisher), Herbert Marshall (Stephen Fisher), George Sanders (Scott ffolliott), Albert Basserman (Van Meer), Edmund Gwenn (Rowley), Eduardo Ciannelli (Krug), Robert Benchley (Stebbins), Harry Davenport (Mr Powers), Charles Halton (Bradley), Barry Bernard (Steward), Martin Kosleck (Tramp), Barbara Pepper (Dorine), Emory Parnell (Captain), Frances Carson (Mrs Sprague), Edward Conrad (Latvian Diplomat), Charles Wagenheim (Photographer/assassin), John Burton (Radio announcer), Holmes Herbert (Assistant Commissioner ffolliott), Roy Gordon (Mr Brood), Gertrude Hoffman (Mrs Benson), Marten Lamont (Plane captain), Leonard Mudie (Inspector McKenna), E E Clive (Mr Naismith), Joan Leslie (Johnny Jones' sister), Dorothy Vaughan (Johnny Jones' mother), Mary Young (Auntie Maude), Jane Novak (Miss Benson), Hilda Plowright (Miss Pimm)

Video availability: Universal

Following the commercial and critical success of *Rebecca* (1940) and the rigours of producing *Gone with the Wind* (1939), producer David O Selznick, to whom Hitchcock was contracted, decided to take a break. Said Selznick, 'I want to loaf, play, and write and love. I don't even want to try and make money during this period.' [13] However, with two blockbusters in the theatres, Selznick couldn't help but rake in the dough. He also earned himself a tidy profit on the salary he was paying Hitchcock by hiring him out to other studios. Thus, for his second American film, Hitchcock found himself working for another independent producer, Walter Wanger, who had a deal with United Artists to make a political thriller provisionally titled *Personal History*.

Wanger had obtained the rights to Vincent Sheean's book about an American newspaper reporter corresponding from a Europe on the brink of war for $10,000, and it was this that Hitchcock and his team of writers used as a starting point for their screenplay. Among those working on the script was Hitchcock's secretary-turned-writer Joan Harrison and his collaborator of old Charles Bennett, who had scripted six of Hitchcock's British films, including *Blackmail* (1929) and *The 39 Steps* (1935). Working closely together, they constructed an elaborate chase plot with multiple locations, through which politically naïve *New York Morning Globe* reporter Johnny Jones (Joel McCrea) pursues a group of enemy agents (for which read Nazis) who have kidnapped and faked the assassination of an elderly Dutch diplomat named Van Meer (Albert Basserman), the one person capable of averting the onset of war thanks to his sole knowledge of a top secret clause in a treaty (shades of *The Lady Vanishes* here). Said Hitchcock of the storyline, 'It's in line with my earlier films, the old theme of the innocent bystander who becomes involved in an intrigue.' [14]

For the role of the newspaper reporter, Hitchcock had his eye on western legend Gary Cooper, but Coop declined the offer (to his later regret), citing that he didn't make thrillers. Consequently, Hitchcock settled on easy-going leading man Joel McCrea, who proved perfect casting. Meanwhile, the supporting cast was a rich one, headed by Herbert Marshall as Stephen Fisher, leader of a European Peace Corps who, it is later revealed, is the brains behind the kidnapping of Van Meer. Playing Fisher's daughter Carol, with whom Johnny Jones falls in love, was Laraine Day, best know for her portrayal of Sister Mary Lamont in the *Dr Kildare* series of second features, while as the kidnapped diplomat Van Meer, Hitchcock cast the distinguished German character actor Albert Basserman, who had fled from his home country following the outbreak of hostilities in 1939. Also popping up briefly for cameos were Edmund Gwenn as Rowley, the assassin whom Fisher hires to push Jones off the top of Westminster Cathedral, Robert Benchley as Stebbins, the *Globe's* alcoholic London correspondent who hands Jones his assignment, Harry Davenport as Mr Powers, the *Globe's* frustrated managing editor, and George Sanders as Scott ffolliott, Carol Fisher's upper crust colleague at the Peace Corps, who helps Jones out of a tight spot or two.

The plot for *Foreign Correspondent* is for the most part irrelevant, simply providing a hanger for the various set pieces, among them several of Hitchcock's finest. Take, for example, the assassination of the fake Van Meer on the rainy steps outside the peace conference, surrounded by a sea of black umbrellas (and pity the poor lookalike who has to die in his place!). Or how about the sequence at a Dutch windmill, hideout of the secret agents, its sails turning against the wind by way of a signal to a landing plane? Of course, how the enemy agents managed to rig this is not alluded to, nor the fact that they could just as easily have put a light in the window – but as Hitchcock commented, 'The picture was pure fantasy, and, as you know, in my fantasies, plausibility is not allowed to rear its ugly head.' [15]

Then there's the spectacular crash landing at sea of the clipper plane on which Jones is attempting to return to America. To achieve the point of view shot of the cockpit seemingly hitting the water, Hitchcock dumped thousands of gallons of water through the back projection screen, which sharp-eyed viewers will be able to spot tearing. Even better is the seamless sequence in which the camera moves in from an aerial shot of the clipper plane, up and through one of its windows, then down the interior aisle, taking in the various character types onboard (this was achieved through an artfully manipulated blend of model work, back projection and front projection).

Hitchcock was clearly having fun with the talent and equipment at his disposal. Indeed, he collaborated with William Cameron Menzies, the Oscar-winning production designer of *Gone with the Wind* (1939), on some of the film's more technically elaborate sequences, such as the opening shot, in which, following the main titles, the camera pulls back from the giant globe atop the *New York Morning Globe's* building, pans down the skyscraper and then in through one of the windows, all in one seamless take.

The film's excellent technical touches aside, the script also bristles with wit, containing contributions from a team of additional writers, among them Robert Benchley (who penned much of his own dialogue), John Lee Mahin, Richard Maibaum and Ben Hecht (the latter the co-author of that greatest of newspaper comedy-dramas, *The Front Page*). For example, early on we learn from his editor that Johnny Jones is not a man to be messed with lightly. 'He beat up a policeman, didn't he, in the line of duty?' enquires the *Globe's* editor, Mr Powers. Later, at a luncheon at the Savoy hosted by the Peace Corps, at which Van Meer is expected to speak, a wag sitting at Joness table quips of Carol's own impending speech, 'The female of the speeches is deadlier than the male.' Meanwhile, when Jones visits the home of Fisher, the double agent obviously fears exposure, commenting, 'This is close to home. In fact this *is* my home.' Fisher also gets to explain the motives of his operators: 'They're fanatics. They combine a mad love of country with an equally mad indifference to life. Their own as well as others.' Jones even gets to utter the immortal line, 'Follow that car, quick,' following the assassination of the lookalike Van Meer.

However, it is on Jones' final speech across the airwaves to America amid a London blitz that Hitchcock requested his writers to place particular emphasis, hoping that it would help to encourage America into World War II. Says Jones at the fadeout: 'Hello, America. I've been watching a part of the world blown to pieces... Yours are the only lights left burning. Cover them with steel. Ring them with guns. Hang on to your lights. They're the only lights left in the world!' Cue a rousing rendition of *Home of the Brave, Land of the Free*.

Audiences flocked to the film, which was advertised as being 'The thrill spectacle of the year.' The critics agreed. Wrote Howard Barnes in the *New York Herald Tribune*: 'It should not be missed by anyone who cherishes the sheer sorcery of the medium... This juxtaposition of outright melodramatics with deadly serious propaganda is eminently satisfactory.' *Time* agreed, adding that the film was, 'easily one of the best of the year.' Dylis Powell, writing in the *Sunday Times*, was even more succinct, commenting, 'This film is worth fifty *Rebecca*s.' A copy of the film even made it over to Germany, where Joseph Goebbels no less described it as, 'A masterpiece of propaganda, a first class production which no doubt will make a certain impression upon the broad masses of the people in enemy countries.'

The film also impressed the Academy of Motion Picture Arts and Sciences, which nominated it for best picture (Walter Wanger), best screenplay (Charles Bennett, Joan Harrison), best supporting actor (Albert Basserman), best cinematography (Rudolph Mate), best art direction (Alexander Golitzen) and best special effects (Paul Eagler and Thomas T Moulton). Yet despite its six nominations, the film didn't bag a single statuette. Nevertheless, Hitchcock could console himself with the fact that he'd already been nominated as best director that year for *Rebecca* (which would go on to win the best picture award), and that his second American film was another commercial and critical success.

Hitchcock cameo: Hitchcock can be spotted about 10 minutes into the film, walking past Johnny Jones's London hotel with a newspaper. Also note that a radio adaptation of the film was broadcast in 1946.

FORSYTHE, JOHN (1918–   , real name John Freund) American actor. Following experience as a sports commentator on radio, Forsythe turned to the stage, briefly appearing on Broadway before making his film debut in *Destination Tokyo* in 1943. This was followed by *The Captive City* (1952), *The Glass Web* (1953), *It Happens Every Thursday* (1953) and *Escape from Fort Bravo* (1953), after which he was offered the role of artist Sam Marlowe in Hitchcock's black comedy *The Trouble with Harry* (1955). Though one of the director's lesser works, it was nevertheless a major coup for Forsythe to have been chosen for the film, especially given that Hitchcock had hoped to cast Cary Grant in the role, but had balked at the star's asking price.

Forsythe's other films include *The Ambassador's Daughter* (1956) and *In Cold Blood* (1967), while in 1969 he returned to the Hitchcock fold to star in *Topaz*, in which he played American agent Michael Nordstrom, who helps Per-Axel Arosenius's KGB official Boris Kusenov escape to the West, where his revelations launch a complex political plot involving America, France, Russia and Cuba. However, it is on television that Forsythe has known his greatest successes, among them such long-running series as *Bachelor Father* (1957–1961), *Charlie's Angels* (1976–1980) and, most importantly, *Dynasty* (1981–1989), in which he played the suave Blake Carrington. He also appeared in an episode of *Alfred Hitchcock Presents* and an episode of *The Alfred Hitchcock Hour*, and was again directed by Hitchcock in the latter. **Hitchography:** *The Trouble with Harry* (1955), *Premonition* (1955, TV), *I Saw the Whole Thing* (1962, TV), *Topaz* (1969)

FOSTER, BARRY (1931–2002) British stage actor. Best remembered for playing the Dutch detective Van der Valk in the TV series of the same name (1972–1973, 1977 and 1991–1992), Foster also made several films during his lengthy career, beginning with *The Battle of the River Plate* in 1956. His other films include *Robbery* (1967), *Twisted Nerve* (1968), *Ryan's Daughter* (1970), *Sweeney!* (1976), *Heat and Dust* (1982) and *Impromptu* (1990). His best film role, however, was in Hitchcock's *Frenzy* (1972), in which he played serial killer Robert Rusk. Recalled Foster of the film's key scene, in which he retrieves a monogrammed tiepin from the clutches of a stiffening corpse in a truck full of potatoes: 'The potato truck took... three days. That was the most amazing storyboard. It was made up of something like 114 shots, all of which had special labels stuck on the clapperboard. As you know, on a clapperboard they write the shot number. Well, in addition to that, they put a little yellow post-it with a sequence number too. And I must say, in that instance the storyboards were extremely helpful.

Because of them you knew exactly where you were in the sequence. From the drawings, for example, I could see the ridiculous grimace on Rusk's face when he gets the corpse's foot stuck under his chin. Straight away I knew Hitch wanted a laugh there! So it was useful. Then there was the gruesome business of breaking the fingers to get the pin! So yes, it was an amazingly complicated business, breaking it down into a shoot-able sequence. Very different from the straight dialogue sequences.' [16] **Hitchography:** *Frenzy* (1972)

FRANCE, C V (1868–1949) British character actor. This respected actor appeared as Mr Hillcrist, whose attempts to prevent an industrialist from building a factory on his land formed the focus of Hitchcock's early talkie *The Skin Game* (1931). His other films include *Scrooge* (1935), *Victoria the Great* (1937) and *The Halfway House* (1944). **Hitchography:** *The Skin Game* (1931)

FREND, CHARLES (1909–1977) British editor. Beginning with *Waltzes from Vienna* in 1933, Frend went on to cut several of Hitchcock's key British films of the 1930s, including *Secret Agent* (1936) and *Sabotage* (1936). His other films as a cutter include such major productions as *The Citadel* (1938), *Goodbye, Mr Chips* (1939) and *Major Barbara* (1940). In 1942 he turned to direction with *The Big Blockade*, and went on to helm such highly regarded films as *San Demetrio, London* (1943), which he also co-wrote, *Scott of the Antarctic* (1948) and *The Cruel Sea* (1953). In the 1960s Frend turned to television, and directed several episodes of *Danger Man*. He also directed the second unit for such films as *Guns in the Heather* (1968) and *Ryan's Daughter* (1970). **Hitchography:** *Waltzes from Vienna* (1933), *Secret Agent* (1936), *Sabotage* (1936), *Young and Innocent* (1937)

Frenzy
(GB, 1972, 116m, Technicolor film) ★★

CREDITS

Production company:	Universal
Producer:	Alfred Hitchcock
Associate producer:	William Hill
Director:	Alfred Hitchcock
Screenplay:	Anthony Shaffer, based on *Goodbye, Piccadilly, Farewell, Leicester Square* by Arthur La Bern
Cinematographer:	Gilbert Taylor
Music:	Ron Goodwin
Editor:	John Jympson
Production designer:	Syd Cain
Art director:	Bob Laing
Costumes:	Dulcie Midwinter
Special effects:	Albert Whitlock
Sound:	Gordon K McCallum, Peter Handford
Camera operator:	Paul Wilson

Jon Finch's Richard Blaney encounters Barry Foster's necktie killer Robert Rusk in Hitchcock's Frenzy *(1972). Lovely!*

CAST

Jon Finch (Richard Blaney), Barry Foster (Robert Rusk), Anna Massey (Babs Milligan), Barbara Leigh-Hunt (Brenda Blaney), Alec McCowen (Chief Inspector Oxford), Vivien Merchant (Mrs Oxford), Billie Whitelaw (Hettie Porter), Clive Swift (Johnny Porter), Bernard Cribbins (Felix Forsythe), Jean Marsh (Monica Barling), Michael Bates (Sergeant Spearman), Madge Ryan (Mrs Davidson), George Tovey (Mr Salt), John Boxer (Sir George), Elsie Randolph (Gladys), Jimmy Gardner (Coburg porter), Noel Johnson (Doctor), Gerald Sim (Mr Asher), June Ellis (Barmaid), Rita Webb (Mrs Rusk), Bunny May (Barman), Robert Keegan (Patient), Geraldine Cowper (Girl)

Video availability: Universal
DVD availability: Universal
CD availability: *A History of Hitchcock – Dial M for Murder* (Silva Screen), which contains the *London* theme; *Psycho – The Essential Alfred Hitchcock* (Silva Screen), which also contains the *London* theme; *The Great British Film Music Album – Sixty Glorious Years 1938–1998* (Silva Screen), which – surprise, surprise – contains the *London* theme

Having been persuaded by Universal into abandoning his long cherished project *Kaleidoscope Frenzy*, a thriller about a serial killer who is compelled to murder whenever near large bodies of water, Hitchcock instead turned his attention to Arthur La Bern's similarly themed 1966 novel *Goodbye, Piccadilly, Farewell, Leicester Square* about a serial

killer who rapes and then strangles his female victims with his ties. The director nevertheless retained the title *Frenzy*, believing it to have box office potential. (Revealed the film's screenwriter, Anthony Shaffer: 'Hitch wanted to call it *Frenzy*, so I pointed out to him that there was already a Swedish film called *Frenzy*. He said, "Did anyone ever hear of it?" I said I didn't think they did. So he said, "Well, that's what we're going to call it!"' [17]

La Bern's London-set novel was loosely based on the true-life crimes of Neville Cleavely Heath, a handsome and personable young man who brutally murdered a number of women just after the war. Here, the killer is Covent Garden fruit trader Bob Rusk (Barry Foster), a charming Jack-the-lad whose activities have the whole city intrigued (as one observer puts it, 'We haven't had a good, juicy series of sex murders since Christie. And they're so good for the tourist trade. Foreigners somehow expect the squares of London to be fog-wreathed, full of handsome cabs and littered with ripped whores, don't you think?').

However, in true Hitchcock fashion, the wrong man is suspected of the crimes ('Hitchcock has used this basic dramatic situation before,' sniffed *Variety*). This time it's a former squadron leader named Richard Blaney (Jon Finch); down on his luck, he has been reduced to working as a barman at The Globe public house in Covent Garden, where he has been living in with his barmaid girlfriend Babs (Anna Massey). Sacked by the landlord (Bernard Cribbins) for helping himself to a pick-me-up, Blaney is offered a place to stay by his friend Rusk ('You weren't pissing in the beer *again*?' Rusk asks him). Instead, though, Blaney goes to see his ex-wife Brenda (Barbara Leigh-Hunt), who runs a dating agency. But the meeting does not go well, as Brenda's secretary, Miss Barling (Jean Marsh), notes. However, the two manage to bury their differences and later go to dinner at Brenda's club, during which she manages to slip some money into her ex-husband's jacket pocket. Blaney doesn't discover the money until later that night when, grabbing some sleep at a doss house, he catches a fellow down-and-out trying to steal it.

The next day, while her secretary is out to lunch, Brenda receives a visit from one of her more problematic clients, one William Robinson, who has professed a liking for masochistic relationships. He goes on to reveal his ardour for *her*, but when she resists his increasingly demonstrative advances, he attacks, rapes and strangles her with his tie. Robinson is of course Rusk, but it is Blaney whom the police, led by Chief Inspector Oxford (Alec McCowen), suspect of the crime, for shortly after it has been committed, he visits his wife again, only to find her office locked. As he exits he is glimpsed by the returning Miss Barling who, having discovered the body and called the police, tells them of Blaney's visit as well as the damning story about his violent row with his ex-wife the previous day.

Meanwhile, with the money Brenda has given him, Blaney takes his girlfriend Babs to the Coburg Hotel in Bayswater as a treat. But when they arise the next morning and see the papers with Blaney's face plastered over them, they quickly make a run for it, hoping that they'll somehow be able to prove his innocence ('Do I *look* like a sex murderer to you?' Blaney asks Babs. 'Can you imagine me creeping around London, strangling all those women with ties? For a start, I only own two!').

With help from his friends Johnny and Hettie Porter (Clive Swift and Billie Whitelaw), Blaney manages to stay out of sight. However, returning to work, Babs also finds herself out of her job and board at The Globe, having arrived late for her shift. Like Blaney, she is offered somewhere to stay by Rusk, whom she likewise knows. Unlike her boyfriend, though, she makes the fatal error of taking the trader up on his seemingly kind offer, only to be raped, strangled and dumped in the back of a truck in a potato sack. Unfortunately for Rusk, he has to return to the body when he realizes that Babs has his monogrammed tiepin clutched in her hand, which he has to prize open as the truck by now makes its way down the motorway. Rusk manages to escape the vehicle undetected, which soon after sheds its load, including Babs' body, in front of a police car.

When the news makes the papers, Blaney is forced to leave his hideout with the Porters, Hettie surmising that he must have killed Babs, even though he has been with them all the time. Consequently, Blaney decides to take up Rusk's offer of a room for the night. But Rusk informs the police of Blaney's whereabouts, and he is subsequently arrested, tried for murder at the Old Bailey and sent to prison for life, despite his pleas that Rusk must surely be the killer. Case closed, it seems, but a nagging doubt remains in the mind of Chief Inspector Oxford, who decides to take another look at the evidence. Visiting the dating agency again, he questions Miss Barling, showing her a photograph of Rusk, whom she instead identifies as Mr Robinson, the strange man whose masochistic requirements the agency could not satisfy.

Meanwhile, Blaney has deliberately thrown himself down a flight of iron stairs in prison, which naturally requires that he be taken to the nearby hospital, from which he manages to escape. He subsequently makes his way to Rusk's flat to kill him, only to find the body of a strangled woman prone on the bed there. Chief Inspector Oxford arrives on the scene moments later, and it again looks like circumstantial evidence has played another cruel trick on Blaney. However, Rusk himself turns up shortly afterwards, dragging a large trunk. 'Mr Rusk – you're not wearing your tie,' observes Oxford, thus finally bringing to an end Blaney's nightmare…

Budgeted at $2 million, *Frenzy* was filmed in and around London (and at Pinewood Studios) over a seven-week period between August and October 1971, with Hitchcock and screenwriter Anthony Shaffer – hot from his stage success with *Sleuth* – making the most of the milieu. Like *Topaz* (1969), the director decided to cast comparative unknowns in the film; unlike *Topaz*, though, they came not from the international film scene, but mostly from the London stage. Recalled Barry Foster, who played Rusk: 'I was in a play by David Mercer called *After Haggerty* at the Criterion, and I was told that Hitchcock was out front one night. Then, the next day, my agent called and said that Hitchcock wanted to see me, [and] he offered me the part.' [18] The same thing happened to Alec McCowen, who played Chief Inspector Oxford: 'He'd seen me in a play called *The Philanthropist* by Christopher Hampton. Well, I got this invitation to go and see him, and I was so looking forward to it. I didn't think I'd got the part, because I don't often play detectives. Nevertheless, I thought it was a wonderful chance to meet Hitchcock, and at the interview I almost interviewed *him*! I had lots of questions to ask about the way he'd done certain scenes in his films. So we talked for an hour and we didn't mention *Frenzy* at all. Instead, we talked about *Foreign Correspondent* and *The Lady Vanishes*! So I was quite surprised when my agent rang me up a few days later to say that Mr Hitchcock wanted me to play the part!' [19]

Filming went smoothly, despite the heavy location shoot (note how dirty the buildings are prior to their 1980s clean-up). In fact the only major setback was a personal one for Hitchcock; his wife Alma suffered a stroke at their Claridge's hotel suite during production. Hitchcock was naturally beside himself with worry, but thankfully his wife responded to treatment, and the director, ever the professional, didn't allow his personal life to intrude upon the film's progress. Recalled Jon Finch, who played Blaney: 'He was always cracking jokes, drinking vodka and orange and just having a good time. He was a sweet man.' [20]

'From the Master of Shock, a shocking new master-piece,' boasted the poster for the film, which ended Hitchcock's run of bad luck at the box office. In fact *Frenzy* went on to make an exceptionally healthy $16 million worldwide, despite some mixed reviews. 'Were Hitchcock less evident throughout the film, *Frenzy* would be as unbearable as it probably sounds when I report that the killer has to break the fingers of the corpse. Yet it is something more than just bearable, because never for a minute does one feel the absence of the storyteller, raising his eyebrows in mock woe,' opined Vincent Canby in the *New York Times*. Jay Cocks in *Time* tended to agree: 'It is not at the level of his greatest work, but it is smooth and shrewd and dexterous.' In fact the only truly negative reaction came from Arthur La Bern, upon whose novel the film was based. Writing in the *Times*, he likened the 'appalling' dialogue to 'a curious amalgam of an old Aldwych farce, *Dixon of Dock Green* and that almost forgotten *No Hiding Place*.'

Indeed, for a film made and set in the early 1970s that makes much use of the laxer attitudes towards onscreen sex, profanity and violence, *Frenzy* has a dated, almost post-war air to it. 'It's just how I expected Covent Garden to be,' comments a passing girl at one point, despite Hitchcock's professed view that the film would not present a tourist eye view of London. In fact the film opens with an impressive aerial shot of the Thames and Tower Bridge that could have come straight from a travelogue; filmed from a helicopter and accompanied by composer Ron Goodwin's heraldic *London* theme, it progresses *under* the raised bridge and up river to County Hall, where an MP is making a speech to a gathered crowd about how clean the once-polluted river has now become. 'Let us rejoice that pollution will soon be banished from the waters of this river and there will soon be no foreign bodies…' at which Hitchcock cuts to Rusk's latest victim, a naked woman who has washed up on the shore below, a tie tightly wrapped round her neck.

The film's post-war air can also be discerned in the script, with Blaney supposedly an ex-squadron leader with a DFC ('From squadron leader to barman in one easy lesson,' he complains at one stage). Yet given Blaney's age (Finch was 31 when the film was released), he would had to have been a pretty young squadron leader in order to have flown during the Suez crisis as he at one point claims. Commented Jon Finch: 'I remember the first time I read the script I hated it, but there was no way I was going to turn it down. He [Hitchcock] didn't know I'd be fifteen years too young for the character.' [21]

The script also contains some curious Americanisms, presumably there to make the film more acceptable to the ears of States-side audiences. For example, the killings are continually referred to as 'neck-tie' murders instead of just simply tie murders. Meanwhile, the porter at the Coburg hotel enquires of Blaney, 'Can I get you anything from the pharmacy, sir?' instead of the chemist shop. Also, when giving the police a description of Blaney, Miss Barling describes his weight in pounds instead of stones.

There are several anomalies too, among them Miss Barley's failure to recognize Rusk and Robinson as one and the same person during Blaney's trial (even if the two hadn't met while giving evidence, surely she would have seen Rusk's photograph in the newspapers, given the high profile nature of the case, which we have been shown is receiving blanket coverage). Meanwhile, when Rusk hides Babs' body in the potato sack, which he later has to return to in order to retrieve his tiepin, we see that the sack also contains a good many potatoes, which would surely have made it even more difficult for Rusk to carry from his flat to the truck as we see him do.

The script also seems to contain an over abundance of unnecessary swearing and several blunt sexual references ('Half the time he's pulling your tits instead of pints,' says Blaney's boss to Babs, somewhat ungallantly). The general misogyny is pretty astonishing too, even if meant humorously ('He rapes them first, doesn't he?' asks a barmaid of two gents who are discussing the killer's *modus operandi*, to which comes the reply, 'Well, I suppose it's nice to know every cloud has a silver lining'). The plotting is also pretty broken-backed, with too many arbitrary developments, among them Blaney's bumping into his old friend Johnny Porter just when he needs somewhere to hide out.

Yet for all its faults the film remains curiously compelling, with several notable touches among the more pedestrian sequences. The rape and murder of Brenda Blaney is genuinely disturbing, particularly given Rusk's moans of, 'Lovely, lovely, *lovely*,' throughout her ordeal, while his recovery of the incriminating tiepin from Babs' stiffening fingers is about as darkly humorous as one can get. The domestic scenes between Oxford and his wife (Vivien Merchant), in which she presents him with a series of increasingly inedible meals from the *cordon bleu* course she's been taking but hasn't quite mastered, also add some lighter moments to the proceedings. There's also an interesting experiment with sound; as Babs leaves The Globe after being sacked, the peripheral sound fades completely, at which Rusk, who is standing unbeknownst behind her, asks, 'Got a place to stay?' The film's most memorable shot follows soon after; when Rusk takes Babs up to his flat, the camera pulls back down the stairs as he closes the door, and - in one, long, how-did-they-*do*-that move - continues out into the street where the bustle of the market disguises any screams that Babs might be making.

Performance-wise, the film benefits enormously from its theatre-trained cast. Jon Finch's Blaney isn't the most likeable of heroes ('He was a bit of a git,' [22] said the actor of the character), yet he makes the best of a variably sketched role. Rather more interesting is Barry Foster's blonde-haired lady-killer who, like many Hitchcock villains, is actually more appealing than the nominal hero ('He was a tremendous charmer, otherwise he couldn't do what he did,' [23] said Foster).

Alec McCowen and Vivien Merchant meanwhile make the most of their comic moments ('Those meal scenes were just a gift for an actor. Anthony Shaffer was persuaded to put them in by Hitchcock, otherwise a lot of what I had to say regarding the case would just have been spoken to my assistant at Scotland Yard,' [24] revealed McCowen). Billie Whitelaw and Clive Swift also make a mark in their few brief scenes as Blaney's friends the Porters, while Barbara Leigh-Hunt and Anna Massey make attractive victims, despite their dreadful early-1970s hairstyles (one is particularly sad to see Massey's Babs bumped off, as she's such a likeable character). The only real miscasting is that of comedy actor Bernard Cribbins, who doesn't quite pull off the hard man role of the heartless landlord (his description of Blaney as 'a bastard' doesn't quite ring true on his lips).

Frenzy is by no means the masterpiece some would have it be, nor is it 'Hitchcock's most stodgy piece since *Dial M for Murder*,' as critic William S Pechter maintained. What it *is*, though, is an intriguing thriller that doesn't quite make the most of its possibilities, but nevertheless provides a fair measure of ghoulish, not-to-be-taken-seriously fun along the way.

Keep an eye out for the body double of Babs at the Coburg (she looks nothing like Anna Massey), and the reference to Mrs S Cain in the racing paper with which Rusk offers Blaney a hot tip (Syd Cain was the film's designer). Also note that Henry Mancini provided a score for the film (the opening title theme for which can be heard on the Universal DVD), but Hitchcock deemed it inappropriate, and so had it replaced with a second one by Ron Goodwin. Recalled Mancini of the incident, 'One minute everything was going fine and Hitch was saying, "Yes, yes, very nice." Then, all of a sudden, it was, "No, no!" For some reason he changed his mind about my score and decided to replace it. I think you'll find that most composers have that happen to them at some stage in their career – having their score replaced. You may recall it happened to Bernard Herrmann on *Torn Curtain*, which was also a Hitchcock picture. Still, it *does* hurt when it happens.' [25]

Hitchcock cameo Hitchcock can be spotted in the crowd outside County Hall in the opening sequence (however, for the film's trailer, a life-size dummy of the director was made and filmed floating down the Thames).

FRESNAY, PIERRE (1897–1975, real name Pierre-Jules-Louis Laudenbach). French actor. On stage from 1912 and in films from 1915 with *France d'Abord*, Fresnay went on to star in several distinguished French films, among them *Marius* (1931), *Fanny* (1932), *Cesar* (1936) and *La Grande Illusion* (1937). In 1934, he made a rare English-speaking appearance in Hitchcock's *The Man Who Knew Too Much*, in which he played Louis Bernard, the government agent whose assassination on a dance floor in St Moritz sparks the film's plot. His other films include *Le Duel* (1940), which he also directed, *Monsieur Vincent* (1947) and *Les Vieux de la Vielle* (1960). **Hitchography:** *The Man Who Knew Too Much* (1934)

FRIEDHOFER, HUGO (1902–1981) American composer. Best known for his Oscar-winning score for *The*

Best Years of Our Lives (1946), Friedhofer began his career in music as a cellist. Work as an arranger and orchestrator for the theatre followed; this in turn led to a contract with Fox in 1929 as an arranger-orchestrator, beginning with the musical *Sunny Side Up*. Friedhofer successfully turned to composition in 1937 with *The Adventures of Marco Polo*, which he followed with the likes of the remake of Hitchcock's *The Lodger* (1944), *The Bishop's Wife* (1947), *Vera Cruz* (1954), *The Secret Invasion* (1964) and *Private Parts* (1972). In 1944 he also worked on Hitchcock's *Lifeboat*, but save for the opening and closing credits, the film had no music. **Hitchography:** *Lifeboat* (1944)

FULTON, JOHN P (1902–1966) American special effects technician. Fulton is best remembered for his many contributions to the Universal horror cycle of the 1930s and 1940s, his credits taking in such genre landmarks as *Frankenstein* (1931), *The Mummy* (1932), *The Old Dark House* (1932), *The Invisible Man* (1933), *The Bride of Frankenstein* (1935), *Son of Frankenstein* (1939), *Man-Made Monster* (1941) and *Frankenstein Meets the Wolf Man* (1943). At Universal from 1930, he later moved to Goldwyn and then Paramount, winning Oscars for his work on *Wonder Man* (1945), *The Bridges at Toko-Ri* (1954) and *The Ten Commandments* (1956). A former surveyor and electrical engineer, he began his film career in the late 1920s as a camera assistant, graduating to cinematographer with *Hell's Harbour* (1929), *Eyes of the World* (1930) and *The Great Impersonation* (1930), following which he sidelined into effects work. In the 1950s, he worked on several films for Hitchcock, beginning with *Rear Window* (1954). His work for this particular film involved creating the travelling matte depicting James Stewart's convincing fall from his window. Fulton's many other films include *Visit to a Small Planet* (1960), *Hatari!* (1962) and *The Heroes of Telemark* (1965). **Hitchography:** *Rear Window* (1954), *To Catch a Thief* (1955), *The Trouble with Harry* (1955), *The Man Who Knew Too Much* (1956), *Vertigo* (1958)

FURSE, ROGER K (1903–1972) British art director. Following experience as a portrait painter and a commercial artist, Furse began to turn his attention to the theatre in the early 1930s, where he went on to achieve acclaim for his work on several of Laurence Olivier's lauded Shakespearian productions at the Old Vic. Furse continued his association with Olivier in films, designing the costumes for *Henry V* (1945) and the sets for *Hamlet* (1948), which earned him an Oscar, *Richard III* (1956) and *The Prince and the Showgirl* (1957). His other films include *Odd Man Out* (1947), *Ivanhoe* (1952) and *The Roman Spring of Mrs Stone* (1961). He also designed the costumes for Hitchcock's Australian-set period melodrama *Under Capricorn* (1949). His wife Margaret (1911–1974) was also a noted costume designer, her credits including *Oliver Twist* (1948), *The Inn of the Sixth Happiness* (1958), *The Lion in Winter* (1965) and *Mary, Queen of Scots* (1972). **Hitchography:** *Under Capricorn* (1949)

G

GABEL, MARTIN (1912–1986) American character actor. On stage from 1933, Gabel began appearing in films in 1951 with *Fourteen Hours*, although prior to this he had directed a film, *The Lost Moment* (1947), starring Susan Hayward and Robert Montgomery (the latter having starred in Hitchcock's *Mr and Mrs Smith* (1941)). A successful stage producer and quiz show host – *With this Ring* (1951) – Gabel's other screen credits include *The Thief* (1952), *Tip on a Dead Jockey* (1957) and Hitchcock's *Marnie* (1964), in which he played the stern Sidney Strutt, whose safe is burgled at the top of the film ('Robbed, clean out. 9,967 dollars!') He was married to the actress Arlene Francis (1908– , real name Arlene Kazanjian) from 1946. **Hitchography:** *Marnie* (1964)

GAINSBOROUGH Formed in 1924 by producer Michael Balcon and director Graham Cutts, Gainsborough, first operated out of the Islington Studios and began production with *The Passionate Adventure* the same year. The film had a screenplay by the young Alfred Hitchcock, who made his directorial debut for the company the following year with *The Pleasure Garden* (1925). Though the film was shelved, along with Hitchcock's next two films, *The Mountain Eagle* (1925) and *The Lodger* (1926), their eventual release secured his reputation and led to two more films for the company: *Downhill* (1927) and *Easy Virtue* (1927). Following a break, during which he went to work for British International Pictures, Hitchcock returned to Gainsborough (by now a subsidiary of Gaumont-British) in 1932, and went on to have several notable successes with the company, among them *The Man Who Knew Too Much* (1934), *The 39 Steps* (1935) and *The Lady Vanishes* (1938). In the 1940s, Gainsborough became known as the home of the period drama, churning out such profitable pieces as *The Man in Grey* (1943), *The Wicked Lady* (1945) and *Jassy* (1947).

GARDNER, JIMMY British supporting actor. Gardner appeared in minor roles in many films in the 1960s and 1970s, including *The Curse of the Mummy's Tomb* (1965), *He Who Rides a Tiger* (1966), *The Murder Game* (1966) and *The Committee* (1968). He can also be spotted in Hitchcock's *Frenzy* (1972) as the nosey porter at the Coburg Hotel. **Hitchography:** *Frenzy* (1972)

GARMES, LEE (1898–1978) American cinematographer. In films from 1916 as a prop boy, Garmes went on to become one of the cinema's most distinguished cinematographers. Following work as an assistant cameraman, he began to co-photograph films from 1918 with *The Hope Chest*. In 1924 he went solo with *Find Your Man*, which led to such films as *The Garden of Allah* (1927), *Morocco* (1930) and *Shanghai Express* (1932), the latter earning him an Academy Award. Noted for his atmospheric lighting effects, Garmes added his distinctive look to such films as *Scarface* (1932), *Zoo in Budapest* (1933), *Lydia* (1941) and *Since You Went Away* (1944). In 1947, he photographed *The Paradine Case* for Hitchcock, adding his usual high sheen gloss to the production. Commented *Variety* of the film's cinematography: 'A very mobile camera helps give a feeling of movement to majority of scenes confined to the British courtroom.' Garmes' other films include *The Secret Life of Walter Mitty* (1947), *Land of the Pharaohs* (1953) and *How to Save a Marriage and Ruin Your Life* (1968). An occasional producer and director, he was involved in the direction of *Crime Without Passion* (1934), *The Scoundrel* (1935) and *Angels Over Broadway* (1939), and co-produced *Dreaming Lips* (1936), *The Lilac Domino* (1936) and *Lydia* (1941). He also photographed many of the early scenes for *Gone with the Wind* (1939), but his work went un-credited. **Hitchography:** *The Paradine Case* (1947)

GAUMONT-BRITISH Formed in 1928 by C M Woolfe, Gaumont-British grew from the impressario's interest in production following the success of his Gaumont cinema chain, which numbered 280 theatres by that year, and various other film-related interests. The Gainsborough production company was absorbed into Gaumont-British in 1928, through which it produced such popular fare as *Sunshine Susie* (1931), *The Ghost Train* (1931) and *Jack's the Boy* (1932). In the 1930s, Hitchcock directed some of his best British films for Gaumont-British/Gainsborough, among them *The Man Who Knew Too Much* (1934), *The 39 Steps* (1935) and *Young and Innocent* (1937).

GAVIN, JOHN (1928– , real name John Golenor) American actor. This handsome, iron-jawed leading man came to films in 1956 following experience as a press agent and a naval intelligence officer during the Korean war. His films include *Behind the High Wall* (1956), *Spartacus* (1960), *Midnight Lace* (1960), *Thoroughly Modern Millie* (1967), *Rich Man, Poor Man* (1976, TV) and *Sophia Loren: Her Own Story* (1980, TV), in which he played Cary Grant. He is best remembered for Hitchcock's *Psycho* (1960), in which he played Sam Loomis who, with Vera Miles' Lila Crane, goes to search for the missing Marion Crane at the Bates Motel. Unfortunately, Hitchcock didn't get on well with Gavin, and referred to him as 'The Stiff' behind his back after it took the actor many takes to perform the opening bedroom scene to the director's satisfaction. Nevertheless, Gavin went on to star in two episodes of *The Alfred Hitchcock Hour*, although neither of them were directed by Hitch. Since the 1980s, Gavin has pursued a diplomatic career, and between 1981 and 1986 he was the US Ambassador to Mexico. He is married to the actress Constance Towers (1931–). **Hitchography:** *Psycho* (1960), *Run for Doom* (1963, TV), *Off Season* (1965, TV)

GELIN, DANIEL (1921–) French actor. This distinguished actor began appearing in bit parts in French films in 1939. His subsequent work includes *Miquette* (1940),

Edouard et Caroline (1950), *La Ronde* (1950), *Les Dents Longues* (1952), which he also directed, *Le Testament d'Orphee* (1960), *The Longest Day* (1962), *Is Paris Burning?* (1966), *Mister Frost* (1990) and *Obsession* (1997). In 1956 he played the mysterious Frenchman Louis Bernard in Hitchcock's remake of *The Man Who Knew Too Much*, in which, disguised as an Arab, he is assassinated in a Marrakech market place. Gelin was married to the actress Daniele Delorme (1926– , real name Gabrielle Girard) between 1945 and 1954, and is the father of actor-director Xavier Gelin (1946–1999) and actress Maria Schneider (1952–). **Hitchography:** *The Man Who Knew Too Much* (1956)

GERAGHTY, THOMAS (TOM) American-born screenwriter. Geraghty came to Britain in 1920 with the Famous Players-Lasky company, for which he worked in the inter-title department with Alfred Hitchcock. Two years later he graduated to co-director on two films (with John S Robertson), both of which featured inter-titles by Hitchcock. Following these films, Geraghty returned to America to resume his writing career, scripting such films as *The Sporting Venus* (1925), *It's the Old Army Game* (1926) and *Fireman, Save My Child* (1927). **Hitchography:** *Perpetua* (1922), *The Spanish Jade* (1922)

GERAY, STEVEN (1899–1973, real name Stefan Gyergay) Russian-born character actor. Following experience in the Hungarian theatre, Geray moved to London in 1934, where he made his first film appearance in *Dance Band* (1935). Following a handful of other British films, including *The High Command* (1936) and *Inspector Hornleigh* (1939), he moved to America in 1941, where he resumed his film career, notching up around 100 films, among them *The Moon and Sixpence* (1942), *The Phantom of the Opera* (1943), Hitchcock's *Spellbound* (1945), in which he played Dr Graff, *Call Me Madam* (1953) and *Ship of Fools* (1965). **Hitchography:** *Spellbound* (1945)

GIELGUD, SIR JOHN (1904–2000, real name Arthur John Gielgud) British-born actor. Gielgud was one of the leading Shakespearean actors of his generation, his appearances as Romeo and Hamlet at the Old Vic in the 1930s becoming part of theatre legend. He also made many films, beginning with *Who is the Man?* in 1924. However, it wasn't until later in life, when he took on character roles in such productions as *Becket* (1964), *The Charge of the Light Brigade* (1968) and *Providence* (1977) that his screen persona finally came into its own. Indeed, his outings as an affable leading man in the 1930s now seem particularly disappointing, none more so than his portrayal of the indecisive British agent Ashenden in Hitchcock's *Secret Agent* (1936), about which even he confessed a certain regret, commenting, 'Hitch said he was offering me Hamlet in modern dress. But when we came to make it, all the psychological interest was dissipated.' [1] Sadly, Hitchcock and Gielgud didn't work together again following this disappointment. Gielgud's other films include *Murder on the Orient Express* (1974), *Caligula* (1978) and

Arthur (1981), which earned him a best supporting actor Oscar for his portrayal of a foul-mouthed butler, *Prospero's Books* (1991), *Shine* (1996) and *Elizabeth* (1998), while on television he shone in the likes of *Brideshead Revisited* (1981) and *War and Remembrance* (1988). **Hitchography:** *Secret Agent* (1936)

GILLESPIE, A ARNOLD (1899–1978) American effects technician. Long at MGM, Gillespie began his career as an art director in 1922 with *Manslaughter*. He joined MGM in 1924 where he designed such films as *Ben-Hur* (1925), *London After Midnight* (1927) and *Mutiny on the Bounty* (1935), after which he turned his hand to effects work, winning Oscars for *Thirty Seconds Over Tokyo* (1944), *Green Dolphin Street* (1947) and the remake of *Ben-Hur* (1959). He also provided the effects for Hitchcock's *North by Northwest* (1959). His other credits include *The Wizard of Oz* (1939), *Forbidden Planet* (1956) and the remake of *Mutiny on the Bounty* (1962). **Hitchography:** *North by Northwest* (1959)

GILLIAT, SIDNEY (1908–1994) British screenwriter. In the 1930s Gilliat worked on a number of Hitchcockian comedy thrillers, among them *Rome Express* (1933), *Friday the Thirteenth* (1933), *Bulldog Jack* (1935) and *Seven Sinners* (1936). The latter, a story about gunrunners who wreck trains to cover their tracks, was co-written with another young writer named Frank Launder (1907–1997), and together the two went on to form a writing partnership, their first major success being *The Lady Vanishes* (1938) for Hitchcock (although the film, originally titled *Lost Lady*, was to have been helmed by the American director Roy William Neill).

When Hitchcock received most of the praise for the movie, Gilliat and Launder decided to go into production themselves, and as writer-director-producers, they turned out some of the most important British films of the 1940s and 1950s, among them such classics as *Millions Like Us* (1943), *Waterloo Road* (1943), *The Rake's Progress* (1945), *Green for Danger* (1946), *State Secret* (1950) and *The Belles of St Trinian's* (1954). Recalled Gilliat of his work on *The Lady Vanishes*: 'Hitchcock had nothing to do with it initially. Ted Black had purchased the book, probably through Frank Launder. I was still freelancing at Gainsborough and I was commissioned to do it. I got as far as inventing Charters and Caldicott on my own, then Frank was freed by Ted Black and joined me... Hitch did work very closely to the screenplay, which he had read to him. He had a photographic memory and could visualize the whole thing in his head. I think he found the actual shooting boring. The journalist Jympson Harmon asked him how he'd thought of Charters and Caldicott and Hitch claimed full credit for them and wouldn't make any kind of retraction when the reviews for *The Lady Vanishes* picked up his remark.' [2] Minus Launder, Gilliat also contributed to the screenplay of Hitchcock's next film, *Jamaica Inn* (1939), after a first draft by novelist Clemence Dane proved unsatisfactory. **Hitchography:** *The Lady Vanishes* (1938), *Jamaica Inn* (1939)

GIST, ROBERT (1924–) American supporting actor. Gist had perhaps his most memorable role in Hitchcock's *Strangers on a Train* (1951), in which he played undercover cop Hennessy, whose job it is to trail tennis star Guy Haines (Farley Granger), who is suspected of having murdered his wife. Comments Barbara Morton (Patricia Hitchcock), Guy's sister-in-law to be: 'Guy, did you know Mr Hennessy helped crack that axe murder I was reading about? You know, the one where the body was cut up and hidden in a butcher's shop!' Gist's other films include *Jigsaw* (1949), *The Band Wagon* (1953) and *Operation Petticoat* (1959). He also directed one film, *An American Dream* (1966), and much television, including episodes of *The Virginian* (1962–1969). **Hitchography:** *Strangers on a Train* (1951)

GLASER, VAUGHAN (1872–1958) American stage actor. Glaser made few film appearances, among them the blind hermit Philip Martin who offers shelter to the innocent on the run in Hitchcock's *Saboteur* (1942). Other credits are hard to trace. **Hitchography:** *Saboteur* (1942)

GLASS, NED (1905–1984) American character actor. Remembered for the TV sit-com *Bridget Loves Bernie* (1973), Glass also appeared as a support in many films, among them *Storm Warning* (1950), *Experiment in Terror* (1962) and *Save the Tiger* (1973). He can be spotted in Hitchcock's *North by Northwest* (1959) as the suspicious ticket teller at Grand Central Station. ('Something wrong with your eyes?' he asks Cary Grant's Roger Thornhill, who is wearing sunglasses to avoid recognition. 'Yes. They're sensitive to questions,' comes the reply.) **Hitchography:** *North by Northwest* (1959)

GLYNNE, MARY (1898–1954) British actress. On stage from the mid-1910s, Glynne made her film debut in 1919 in *The Cry of Justice*. In the early 1920s she was contracted to the London arm of Famous Players–Lasky, and made several films for them at the Islington Studios, many of which the young Hitchcock worked on as a graphic artist. Glynne's other films include *The Good Companions* (1932), *Scrooge* (1935) and *The Heirloom Mystery* (1937), following which she retired from the screen. **Hitchography:** *The Call of Youth* (1920), *The Princess of New York* (1921), *Appearances* (1921), *Dangerous Lies* (1921), *The Mystery Road* (1921), *Beside the Bonnie Brier Bush* (1921)

GOLITZEN, ALEXANDER (ALEXANDRE) (1907–) Russian-born production designer. Golitzen emigrated to America in 1923 and, following training as an architect, entered films in 1933 as a production illustrator. He became a fully-fledged art director in 1935 with *The Call of the Wild* and went on to become one of Hollywood's most respected production designers, earning Oscars for his work on *The Phantom of the Opera* (1943), *Spartacus* (1960) and *To Kill a Mockingbird* (1962). In 1940, he worked with Hitchcock on *Foreign Correspondent*, among his designs being the working interior of windmill and a one-acre re-creation of a Dutch town, complete with tramcars and a drainage system, the latter needed to deal with the vast amounts of water required for the rain-soaked assassination sequence amid a sea of black umbrellas. For his efforts, Golitzen earned an Academy Award nomination. His many other films include *Letter from an Unknown Woman* (1948), *Gambit* (1966) and *Earthquake* (1974). **Hitchography:** *Foreign Correspondent* (1940)

GOODMAN, JOHN B American art director. Long at Universal, Goodman worked on many of the studio's horror films, among them *Son of Dracula* (1943), *The Phantom of the Opera* (1943), which won him an Oscar, *House of Frankenstein* (1944) and *House of Dracula* (1945). He also designed Hitchcock's *Shadow of a Doubt* (1943) with Robert Boyle. Later, at Paramount, he designed two further Hitchcock pictures: *The Trouble with Harry* (1955) and *The Man Who Knew Too Much* (1956). **Hitchography:** *Shadow of a Doubt* (1943), *The Trouble with Harry* (1955), *The Man Who Knew Too Much* (1956)

GOODWIN, BILL (1910–1958) American supporting actor. In radio from 1934, the amiable Bill Goodwin graduated to movies in 1940 with *Let's Make Music*, which he followed with appearances in *Blondie in Society* (1941), *Bathing Beauty* (1944), Hitchcock's *Spellbound* (1945), in which he played the friendly house detective at the Empire State Hotel, *The Jolson Story* (1946), *Jolson Sings Again* (1949) and *The Big Beat* (1958). **Hitchography:** *Spellbound* (1945)

GOODWIN, RON (1929–) British composer and arranger. Having trained at the Guildhall School of Music, Ron Goodwin gained experience as a copyist and arranger before forming his own orchestra in 1951, with which he did many radio concerts. He broke into films in 1959 with *Whirlpool*, and went on to provide memorable scores for *Murder, She Said* (1962), *633 Squadron* (1964), *Those Magnificent Men in Their Flying Machines* (1965), *Where Eagles Dare* (1969), *The Battle of Britain* (1969) and *Force Ten from Navarone* (1978). In 1972, Goodwin scored Hitchcock's *Frenzy*, his music replacing a rejected score by Henry Mancini. Goodwin came to the film on the recommendation of its editor John Jympson, who had previously worked with him on *Where Eagles Dare*.

Recalled Goodwin of his first encounter with Hitchcock: 'It was a bit like meeting God, going to see him about it. In fact when I got the first phone call I thought it was some kind of practical joke. But when I found it was for real I was delighted. [Hitchcock] was a very charming man, contrary to all reports and anecdotes; some people said he was a nasty bit of work, but I never found that to be true.' [3]

Goodwin also found that the director had some firm thoughts about the film's music. 'Oh, very firm. I went home with sheaves of notes that his secretary had typed up. It was quite interesting, because he used musical terms in a very incorrect way. He'd say, "I'd like the music in this scene to be very pizzicato!" I knew what he meant, though if I'd taken him at his word he wouldn't have been very pleased. He was very specific with certain scenes too. For instance, with the opening titles, he said he wanted the sort of music you'd find in a travelogue on London. He didn't want a hint of suspense or anything nasty that was going to happen. So I bowed to his judgement, he being the Master, and came up with this theme based on the chimes of Big Ben. And it worked – Hitch was right – because in a way it had the effect of being a musical red herring. It lulls the audience into a false sense of security before the first body comes floating down the river!' [4] **Hitchography:** *Frenzy* (1972)

GORDON, GAVIN (1906–1970) American actor. This supporting actor and occasional leading man appeared in a variety of productions from the late 1920s onwards, including *Romance* (1930), *The Scarlet Empress* (1932), *The Bride of Frankenstein* (1935) and *Knock on Wood* (1959). He can be seen in Hitchcock's *Notorious* (1946) as Ernest Waylin. He also popped up in an episode of *Alfred Hitchcock Presents*, in which he was again directed by Hitchcock. **Hitchography:** *Notorious* (1946), *The Perfect Crime* (1957, TV)

Farley Granger encounters a familiar face in Hitchcock's Strangers on a Train *(1951). Note the planks onto which Granger is stepping.*

GORDON, HAL (1894–1946) British comedy actor. This chirpy actor, in films from 1928 with *Adam's Apple*, played stooge to a number of comedians during the 1930s, most notably George Formby, with whom he appeared in *Keep Your Seats, Please* (1936), *It's in the Bag* (1936), *Keep Fit* (1937), *It's in the Air* (1938), *Come on, George* (1939), *Trouble Brewing* (1939), *Let George Do It* (1940) and *Spare a Copper* (1940). He also had small roles in two Hitchcock films: *Lord Camber's Ladies* (1932), which Hitchcock produced, and *Sabotage* (1936). His other films include *When Knights Were Bold* (1929), *Dusty Ermine* (1936) and *Old Mother Riley, Detective* (1943). **Hitchography:** *Lord Camber's Ladies* (1932), *Sabotage* (1936)

GORDON, LEO (1922–2000) American-born supporting actor and screenwriter. On screen Gordon tended to play heavies. In films from 1953 with *All the Brothers Were Valiant*, his credits include *Riot in Cell Block 11* (1954), *Ten Wanted Men* (1955), Hitchcock's *The Man Who Knew Too Much* (1956), in which he briefly appears as a chauffeur, *The Intruder* (1961) and *Maverick* (1994). His screenplays include *Black Patch* (1957), *Tower of London* (1962) and *Tobruk* (1966). **Hitchography:** *The Man Who Knew Too Much* (1956)

GOTELL, WALTER (1924–1997) British character actor. Best known for his appearances as Colonel Gogol in the James Bond films, Gotell appeared in over 100 films, beginning with *Tomorrow We Live* (1942) and including *The Wooden Horse* (1950), *Solomon and Sheba* (1959), *The Guns of Navarone* (1961), *From Russia with Love* (1963), as henchman Morzeny, and six appearances as Gogol in *The Spy Who Loved Me* (1977), *Moonraker* (1979), *For Your Eyes Only* (1981), *Octopussy* (1983), *A View to a Kill* (1985) and *The Living Daylights* (1987). Sharp-eyed viewers will also be able to spot him as an uncredited embassy guard in Hitchcock's remake of *The Man Who Knew Too Much* (1956). **Hitchography:** *The Man Who Knew Too Much* (1956)

GRAHAM, MORLAND (1891–1949) Scottish-born character actor. Though he only ever had one leading film role of note, that of Old Bill in *Old Bill and Son* (1941), Graham was familiar to audiences in the 1930s and 1940s in the likes of *The Scarlet Pimpernel* (1934), *The Ghost Train* (1941) and *Whisky Galore* (1948). He can also be spotted in Hitchcock's *Jamaica Inn* (1939) as the sea lawyer, Sydney. **Hitchography:** *Jamaica Inn* (1939)

GRANGER, FARLEY (1925– , real name Farley Earle) American actor. This handsome leading man made his film debut at the age of 18 in *North Star* (1943), having been spotted in a 'little theatre' production while he was still at high school. *The Purple Night* (1944) and *They Live by Night* (1947) followed, after which he made his first appearance for Hitchcock in the experimental *Rope* (1948), in which he played the murderous Philip Morgan. Said Granger of Hitchcock's approach to the

Things start to heat up for Cary Grant in Hitchcock's North by Northwest *(1959).*

film, which was shot in lengthy, 10-minute takes: 'He wanted to do a film that had no editing in it. He wanted it to look like it was all done in one take… I think he wanted to do something quite different and interesting.' [5]

Following *Rope*, Granger went on to appear in *Enchantment* (1948), *Roseanna McCoy* (1949), *Edge of Doom* (1950), *Side Street* (1950) and *Our Very Own* (1950), after which he returned to Hitchcock to play his most famous role, that of Guy Haines in *Strangers on a Train* (1951). Although his performance paled beside Robert Walker's flamboyant psychopath Bruno Antony, Granger was much praised for his work in the film. Commented *Variety*, 'Granger is excellent as the harassed young man innocently involved in murder.' Granger's subsequent films include *Hans Christian Andersen* (1952), *The Girl in the Red Velvet Swing* (1955), *The Serpent* (1972), *Arnold* (1975) and *The Whoopee Boys* (1986). **Hitchography:** *Rope* (1948), *Strangers on a Train* (1951)

GRANT, CARY (1904–1986) British-born actor. Superstar Grant is without doubt the most debonair leading man to grace the silver screen. Born plain old Archibald Leach in Bristol, he grew up in poverty, eventually running away from home at the age of 13 to join a travelling acrobatic troupe. He remained with the troupe for several years, eventually going to New York with them for a series of engagements, after which he stayed on as a lifeguard at Coney Island. In 1923 he was back in Britain, finding work in a number of musicals, but returned to the States in 1927, where he finally got a break, appearing in the musical *Golden Dawn* for producer Arthur Hammerstein. Roles in *Polly with a Past*, *Rosalie* and *The Last Flight* followed, during the latter of which he screen tested for and won a role in the short *Singapore Sue* (1932), in which he played a sailor on shore leave. Grant was soon after signed to Paramount, adopting his new name for his debut feature, *This Is the Night* (1932).

Grant thus began the slow climb to stardom, helped along by appearances in such high profile productions as

Blonde Venus (1932), *She Done Him Wrong* (1933) and *The Eagle and the Hawk* (1933). When his contract with Paramount expired in 1935, Grant began to work freelance, first making *Sylvia Scarlet* (1935) for RKO, in which he co-starred for the first time with Katharine Hepburn. Over the following years, Grant gradually confirmed his stardom with such hits as *Topper* (1937), *Holiday* (1938), *Bringing Up Baby* (1938), *Only Angels Have Wings* (1939), *Gunga Din* (1939), *His Girl Friday* (1940) and *The Philadelphia Story* (1940). Then, in 1941, came *Suspicion*, his first collaboration with Alfred Hitchcock. Though the film led to a further three collaborations between director and star, this first encounter was something of a hodge-podge, with Grant not entirely convincing as Johnnie Aysgarth, a suspected wife murderer. In fact the front office brass at RKO became so jittery about the prospect of Grant being found guilty at the climax (as per the Francis Iles book on which the film is based) that they ordered it to be changed, thus making the story seem like a lot of fuss over the foolish imaginings of a rather silly woman. Said Hitchcock: 'I'm not too pleased with the way *Suspicion* ends. I had something else in mind.' [6] Grant agreed with Hitchcock, commenting, 'I thought Hitch's original ending was marvellous. It was a perfect Hitchcock ending.' [7]

Nevertheless, the film was a commercial success, despite its faults. Indeed, *Variety* was clearly enthusiastic about Grant's performance, commenting, 'Cary Grant turns in a sparkling characterization as the bounder who continually discounts financial responsibilities and finally gets jammed over thefts from his employer.' James Agate, writing in *Tatler*, was less convinced, though: 'It asks us to imagine that Cary Grant is a charming and well-bred English ne'er-do-well moving in good society, whereas he isn't anything of the kind. His shoulders have the American campus written all over them, and his manners have obviously been learnt from some *palais de danse*… Which just shows how Hollywood's communications corrupt English manners.'

It would be five years before Grant worked with Hitchcock again, during which time he made such films as *The Talk of the Town* (1942), *None But the Lonely Heart* (1944) and *Night and Day* (1946). 1946 also saw him star in a radio adaptation of *Suspicion*. Then came Grant's first true classic for Hitchcock, *Notorious* (1946), in which he played government agent T R Devlin, who has to persuade Alicia Huberman (Ingrid Bergman), the daughter of a convicted Nazi sympathizer, to go undercover to Brazil to help rout out a group of pro-Nazis. The film contained a number of love scenes between the two stars, about which actor David Niven commented in a column he then wrote for the *Sunday Express*: 'The love scenes are the best, the most beautifully played and the best directed that I have ever seen on the screen.' [8]

It would be another nine years before Hitchcock and Grant collaborated again, by which time the star had made such classics as *The Bachelor and the Bobby-Soxer* (1947), *Mr Blandings Build His Dream House* (1948), *I Was a Male War Bride* (1949) and *Monkey Business* (1952). *Notorious* had

been one of Grant's darker films; by contrast, his next Hitchcock assignment couldn't have been brighter. Set on the sunny Cote d'Azur, *To Catch a Thief* (1955) is a fitfully entertaining piece of fluff about a retired cat burglar (Grant) who finds his liberty at peril when another thief begins to use his *modus operandi*, the result being that the police suspect him of having returned to his old ways. Grant insisted that he was semi-retired at the time, but the chance of working with Grace Kelly proved too enticing. A major commercial success when released, Grant thoroughly enjoyed working on the film. Commented the star: 'Hitch and I had a rapport and understanding deeper than words. He was a very agreeable human being, and we were very compatible. I always went to work whistling when I worked with him, because everything on the set was just as you envisioned it would be. Nothing ever went wrong. He was so incredibly well prepared.' [9] Indeed, the star's enthusiasm is visible throughout the film, prompting *Variety* to observe: 'Grant gives his role his assured style of acting, meaning the dialogue and situations benefit… his is a master of timing, getting laughs where a lesser talent would have drawn a blank.'

For Grant, *The Pride and the Passion* (1957), *An Affair to Remember* (1957), *Kiss Them for Me* (1957), *Indiscreet* (1958), which re-teamed him with Ingrid Bergman, and *Houseboat* (1959), followed (so much for retirement!), after which he returned to Hitchcock for his finest role in *any* film – that of Madison Avenue advertising executive Roger O Thornhill, who finds himself mistaken for a spy in the masterful *North by Northwest* (1959). *Variety* described the star's role for which he was paid $450,000 as 'debonair as a cigarette ad,' even though Grant was 55 when he made the film (Jessie Royce Landis, who plays his mother in the film, was actually 11 months his junior!). Commented Grant of his experiences on the film: 'In *To Catch a Thief* I dashed over sloping rooftops of four-storied French Riviera villas with no net below, while either trying to rob Grace Kelly or save her from *being* robbed; and in *North by Northwest* I heroically hung both up and down on replicas of sections of Mount Rushmore, rafter-high on the tallest soundstage of Hollywood. I've always felt queasily uncertain whether or not Hitchcock was pleased at seeing me survive each day's work. I can only hope it was as great a relief to him as it was a disappointment.' [10] The star's efforts were well worth it. Added *Variety*, 'Cary Grant brings technique and charm to the central character.'

Sadly, this was Grant's last outing for Hitchcock, following which he made just a further six films, among them *Operation Petticoat* (1959), the Hitchockian *Charade* (1963) and *Walk, Don't Run* (1966). Even in retirement from the screen, though, he continued to be a world player, becoming a spokesperson for Fabergé and Western Airlines. Married five times, his wives were actress Virginia Cherrill (1908–1996), to whom he was married between 1933 and 1935; heiress Barbara Hutton, to whom he was married between 1942 and 1945; actress Betsy Drake (1923–), to whom he was married between 1949 and

1959; actress Dyan Cannon (1937– , real name Samile Diane Friesen), to whom he was married between 1965 and 1968; and Barbara Harris, whom he married in 1981, and to whom he remained married until his death in 1986 at the the age of 82. Even at that age, he could still have won the girl! **Hitchography:** *Suspicion* (1941), *Suspicion* (1946, radio), *Notorious* (1946), *To Catch a Thief* (1955), *North by Northwest* (1959)

The Great Day
(GB, 1920, 37m approx, bw, silent film)

CREDITS
Production company:	Famous Players-Lasky
Director:	Hugh Ford
Screenplay:	Eve Unsell, based on the play by Louis N Parker and George R Sims
Inter-titles:	Alfred Hitchcock

CAST
Arthur Bourchier (Sir Jonathan Borstwick), Mary Palfrey (Susan Borstwick), Bertram Burleigh (Frank Beresford), Percy Standing (Paul Nikola), Marjorie Hume (Clara Beresford), Geoffrey Kerr (Dave Leeson)

Released in 1920, this lost black-and-white silent was the first production to be made at Islington Studios, the London home of Famous Players-Lasky. It was also the first film on which Alfred Hitchcock ever worked, designing the inter-titles. The story of a husband and wife who are re-united following World War I, during which both were thought to have been killed, it was directed by American import Hugh Ford.

GREEN, HILTON A American producer. Green began his career as an assistant director on Hitchcock's TV series *Alfred Hitchcock Presents*, which subsequently led to his working in the same capacity on *Psycho* (1960), on which several other members of the director's TV personnel also worked. Recalled Green: 'While he was doing *North by Northwest* at MGM, I was quietly called in and told, "He's thinking of doing a low-budget, quality film," and that I was going to be the assistant director. *North by Northwest* having been a rather expensive film for its day, he wanted to prove to his peers he could make a quality movie without spending a lot of money to do it. So he thought of his television crew because we were more accustomed to shorter schedules.' [11] Green's association with Hitchcock didn't end there; he was also the unit manager for *Marnie* (1964) and directed *Party Line* (1960, TV), an episode of *Alfred Hitchcock Presents*. Meanwhile, his association with Norman Bates didn't end with the Hitchcock film, as Green later went on to produce *Psycho 2* (1983) and *Psycho III* (1983) for the cinema, while in 1990 he executive produced *Psycho IV: The Beginning* for television, all of which starred Anthony Perkins. His other credits include *Sixteen Candles* (1984). **Hitchography:** *Psycho* (1960), *Party Line* (1960, TV), *Marnie* (1964)

GREER, HOWARD (1886–1964) American costume designer. Designing for films from 1923 with *The Spanish Dancer*, this costumier went on to become Paramount's head costume designer the following year, though from 1927 he operated independently. His many films include *The Ten Commandments* (1924), *Bringing Up Baby* (1938), Hitchcock's *Spellbound* (1945) and *The French Line* (1954). **Hitchography:** *Spellbound* (1945)

GREET, CLARE (1871–1939) British character actress. Greet appeared in Hitchcock's very first film as a director, the uncompleted two-reeler *Number 13* in 1922, Hitchcock having previously spotted her in *Three Lives Ghosts* (1922) on which he'd worked as a graphic artist, designing the inter-titles. Greet obviously made an impression on Hitch, as he re-used her in six subsequent films, although her roles were little more than cameo appearances, the best of them being the poor tenant who is granted a new roof from Sir Humphrey Pengallan (Charles Laughton) in *Jamaica Inn* (1939). **Hitchography:** *Three Live Ghosts* (1922), *Number 13* (1922), *The Ring* (1927), *The Manxman* (1929), *Murder!* (1930), *Lord Camber's Ladies* (1932), *Sabotage* (1936), *Jamaica Inn* (1939)

GREGG, VIRGINIA (?–1986) American supporting actress. This busy actress appeared in a good many films in the 1950s and 1960s, among them *Dragnet* (1954), *Love is a Many-Splendored Thing* (1955), *Joy in the Morning* (1965) and *Two on a Guillotine* (1965). One of her earlier appearances was as a clerk in Hitchcock's *Notorious* (1946), but her role went un-credited. She later appeared in three episodes of *Alfred Hitchcock Presents*. However, she is best known for another Hitchcock film, *Psycho* (1960), for which she supplied the voice of 'Mother'. Recalled the actress, 'Hitchcock rehearsed and coached me very carefully. I had thought of Mother as sounding pearly and wheedling, but he had something very fixed in his mind: old, loud, strident and monstrous.' [12] It should be noted that Jeanette Nolan also recorded several of Mother's lines. However, it was Gregg who returned to voice Mother for two of the sequels: *Psycho 2* (1983) and *Psycho III* (1986). **Hitchography:** *Notorious* (1946), *Don't Come Back Alive* (1955, TV), *And So Died Riabochinska* (1956, TV), *Nightmare in 4D* (1957, TV), *Psycho* (1960)

GRENFELL, JOYCE (1910–1979) British comedy actress. Toothy, angular and with a highly inimitable upper-class voice, this much-loved star began her stage career in 1939 as a comedy monologist following experience as a journalist for *The Observer*. In films from 1941 with the short *A Letter from Home*, she went on to appear in the likes of *The Lamp Still Burns* (1943), *While the Sun Shines* (1946) and *A Run for Your Money* (1949), though it was her appearance as a gauche shooting gallery proprietress at a rainy theatrical garden party in Hitchcock's *Stage Fright* (1950) that helped to firmly establish her as a favourite with cinema audiences. With her cry of 'Do come and shoot some lovely ducks! Only half-a-crown' she made the most of her brief cameo opposite Alastair Sim (her character is actually billed 'Lovely Ducks' in the end credits). She also has great fun describing the prizes on offer: 'They're lovely dolls, fully dressed,' at which she lifts the skirt of one, adding, 'Fully!' Grenfell subsequently went on to appear with her *Stage Fright* co-star Sim in several popular comedies of the 1950s, among them *The Happiest Days of Your Life* (1950), *Laughter in Paradise* (1951) and, most memorably, *The Belles of St Trinian's* (1954), in which she played policewoman Sergeant Ruby Gates, a role she would reprise a further two times. Her other films include *The Pickwick Papers* (1952), *Genevieve* (1953), *Blue Murder at St Trinian's* (1957), *The Pure Hell of St Trinian's* (1960) and *The Americanization of Emily* (1964). A popular stage draw, she toured the world with her one-woman show in the fifties and 1960s, and later repeated many of her classic monologues on record, television and radio. **Hitchography:** *Stage Fright* (1950)

GREY, ANNE (1907– , real name Aileen Ewing) British actress. This British leading lady was extremely popular in the early 1930s (she made ten films in 1933 alone). A former journalist, she made her screen debut in 1927 with *The Constant Nymph*, which she followed with the likes of *What Money Can Buy* (1928), *The Squeaker* (1930) and Hitchcock's *Number Seventeen* (1932), in which she played the young heroine, Nora. In the mid-1930s, she briefly moved to Hollywood with her then husband, actor Lester Matthews (1900–1975), where she made *Break of Hearts* (1935) and *Bonnie Scotland* (1936). Her other film credits include *Too Many Parents* (1937) and *Dr Sin Fang* (1937). She retired from the screen in 1938 after making *Chinatown Nights* **Hitchography:** *Number Seventeen* (1932)

GRIFFIES, ETHEL (1878–1975, real name Ethel Woods) British actress. Apparently on stage from the age of 2, Griffies spent a great deal of her career treading the boards, although she also found time to appear in almost 100 films in Britain and America, beginning with *The Cost of a Kiss* (1917) and going on to include *Hard Cash* (1921), *Old English* (1930), *Bulldog Drummond Strikes Back* (1934), *The Werewolf of London* (1935), *Saratoga Trunk* (1945) and *Bus Riley's Back in Town* (1965). She is perhaps best remembered for *Billy Liar* (1963), in which she played Billy's ailing grandmother, and Hitchcock's *The Birds* (1963), in which she played the doubting ornithologist Mrs Bundy ('I have never known birds of different species flock together. The very concept is unimaginable. Why, if that happened, we wouldn't have a chance. How could we possibly hope to fight them?') Some reference books also list Griffies as having appeared in Hitchcock's *Shadow of a Doubt* (1943), but this would seem to be an erroneous claim (although her scene could well have ended up on the editing room floor). **Hitchography:** *The Birds* (1963)

GUFFEY, BURNETT (1905–1983) American cinematographer. An Oscar winner for his work on both *From Here to Eternity* (1953) and *Bonnie and Clyde* (1967), this distinguished cinematographer began his career as a camera operator in 1923. As such he worked on many films, including *The Informer* (1935), Hitchcock's *Foreign Correspondent* (1940) and *Cover Girl* (1944), following which he became a fully-fledged lighting cameraman with *The Soul of a Monster* (1944). His other films include *My Name is Julia Ross* (1945), *Birdman of Alcatraz* (1962) and *The Great White Hope* (1970). He also handled the second unit photography for *The Iron Horse* (1924). **Hitchography:** *Foreign Correpondent* (1940)

GWENN, EDMUND (1875–1959) Welsh-born character star. Equally adept at sympathetic and villainous roles, Gwenn was a major stage draw in the 1920s. He made his film debut in 1916 in *The Real Thing at Last*, but didn't make another film until four years later. This was the first version of the *Skin Game* (1920), the remake of which he was asked to star in by Hitchcock in 1931. Gwenn worked with Hitchcock at three distinctive points in the director's career. Firstly he starred in two of Hitchcock's early British films: *The Skin Game* and *Waltzes from Vienna* (1933), playing Strauss the Elder in the latter. He then made a cameo appearance in Hitchcock's second major Hollywood production, *Foreign Correspondent* (1940). Finally he co-starred in *The Trouble with Harry* (1955), which was made at the height of Hitchcock's most successful period (though in itself, it was one of the director's weakest productions). Of these films, Gwenn is perhaps best remembered for *Foreign Correspondent*, in which he played the bodyguard Rowley who attempts to assassinate reporter Johnny Jones (Joel McRea) by pushing him off the top of Westminster Cathedral, only to spectacularly plunge to his own death. He also performed in Hitchcock's radio dramatization of *The Lodger* in 1940, his brother, actor Arthur Chesney (1882–1949, real name Arthur Gwenn), having appeared in the original 1926 film. Gwenn's many other films include *The Good Companions* (1933), *Anthony Adverse* (1936), *Pride and Prejudice* (1940) and *Them!* (1954), although he is most fondly remembered for playing Kris Kringle in *Miracle on 34th Street* (1947), which won him a best supporting actor Oscar. He also starred in an episode of *Alfred Hitchcock Presents*. **Hitchography:** *The Skin Game* (1931), *Waltzes from Vienna* (1933), *Foreign Correspondent* (1940), *The Lodger* (1940, radio), *The Trouble with Harry* (1955), *Father and Son* (1957, TV)

H

HAAS, DOLLY (1911–1994) German actress. Haas became a popular box office draw in her home country following many years' experience as a ballet dancer. In films from the early sound period, her work includes *Eine Stunde Gluck* (1930), *Dolly Macht Karriere* (1930, aka *Dolly's Way to Stardom*), *Der Page vom Dalmasse Hotel* (1933) and *Warum Lugt Fraulein, Kathe?* (1935). Her English-language films include *Broken Blossoms* (1936), *Spy of Napoleon* (1937) and Hitchcock's *I Confess* (1953) in which she played Alma Keller, the cold-eyed wife of murderer Otto Keller (O E Hasse). **Hitchography:** *I Confess* (1953)

HALE, JONATHAN (1891–1966, real name Jonathan Hatley) Canadian-born supporting actor. In films from 1934 following experience in the diplomatic service, Hale made his film debut in *Lightning Strikes Twice*. Over 100 films followed, among them *Alice Adams* (1935), *Fury* (1936), *And Now Tomorrow* (1944) and *Four for Texas* (1963), although he is perhaps best known for playing Mr Dithers in the *Blondie* second features, among them *Blondie Plays Cupid* (1940), *Blondie Goes Latin* (1941) and *Leave It to Blondie* (1945). He can also be seen briefly in Hitchcock's *Strangers on a Train* (1951) as the much-despised father of psychopath Bruno Antony (Robert Walker). **Hitchography:** *Strangers on a Train* (1951)

HALL, WILLIS (1929–) British playwright and screenwriter. Long in collaboration with Keith Waterhouse (1929–), Hall penned such films as *Whistle Down the Wind* (1961), *A Kind of Loving* (1962) and *Billy Liar* (1963), the latter based on Waterhouse's successful novel. The duo also did a re-write on Hitchcock's *Torn Curtain* (1966), but an arbitration brought about by the film's nominal writer Brian Moore saw their work go un-credited. **Hitchography:** *Torn Curtain* (1966)

HALL-DAVIS, LILLIAN (1896–1933) British actress. A star of the silent era from her teenage years, Hall-Davis appeared in such popular fare as *The Admirable Crichton* (1918), *The Better 'Ole* (1918) and *A Royal Divorce* (1923). Unfortunately, she was one of several actors who failed to successfully make the transition to sound, and consequently, she committed suicide. Among her more notable films were two Hitchcock silents: *The Ring* (1927) and *The Farmer's Wife* (1928), in both of which she played the romantic interest. Her other films include *Pagliacci* (1923), *Quo Vadis?* (1924) and *Volga Volga* (1933). **Hitchography:** *The Ring* (1927), *The Farmer's Wife* (1928)

HALTON, CHARLES (1876–1959) American actor. Though he didn't make his first film appearance until the age of 41, Halton went on to become one of Hollywood's most prolific supporting actors. Beginning in 1917 with *The Adventurer*, the actor went on to appear in over 200 films, among them such diverse titles as *Gold Diggers of 1937* (1936), *Swanee River* (1939), *Dr Cyclops* (1940), *To Be or Not to Be* (1942), *Wilson* (1944) and *High School Confidential* (1958). He also cameoed in four Hitchcock pictures, beginning with *Foreign Correspondent* (1940). **Hitchography:** *Foreign Correspondent* (1940), *Mr and Mrs Smith* (1941), *Saboteur* (1942), *Spellbound* (1945)

HAMER, ROBERT (1911–1963) British director. In films from the early 1930s, Hamer worked his way up the industry ladder, first graduating from clapper boy to assistant cutter and then to editor, in which capacity he worked on Hitchcock's *Jamaica Inn* (1939). In 1943 he turned to writing with *San Demetrio, London* and, two years later, to direction, with the haunted mirror sequence in *Dead of Night* (1945). Over the next decade he would helm such classics as *It Always Rains on Sunday* (1947), *Kind Hearts and Coronets* (1949) and *Father Brown* (1954). When alcoholism finally got the better of him, he returned to writing, penning *A Jolly Bad Fellow* (1963) and contributing un-credited work to *55 Days at Peking* (1963). **Hitchography:** *Jamaica Inn* (1939)

HAMILTON, WILLIAM (E) (1894–1942) American editor. At RKO from the early 1930s, Hamilton cut two of Hitchcock's films for the studio: *Suspicion* (1941) and *Mr and Mrs Smith* (1941). As well as being a top editor, Hamilton occasionally turned his hand to acting and screenwriting. He also co-directed a handful of films, among them *Freckles* (1935), *Seven Keys to Baldpate* (1935), *Murder on the Bridal Path* (1936) and *Bunker Bean* (1936), all of which were co-directed with Edward Killy, and *Call Out the Marines* (1941), which was co-directed with Frank Ryan. His editing credits include such classics as *Our Dancing Daughters* (1928), *The Gay Divorce* (1934) and *Top Hat* (1935). **Hitchography:** *Suspicion* (1941), *Mr and Mrs Smith* (1941)

HANDL, IRENE (1901–1987) British character comedienne. This delightfully eccentric British star made her stage debut as the maid in the Gerald Savory play *George and Margaret* in 1937, a role she repeated in the 1940 film. She made her first film, *Missing, Believed Married*, the same year as her stage debut, and though she would go on to specialize in Cockney types, among them maids and chars, she was actually from aristocratic stock. Her 100-plus films include appearances in *Brief Encounter* (1945), *The History of Mr Polly* (1948), *The Belles of St Trinian's* (1954), *I'm Alright, Jack* (1959), *Morgan – A Suitable Case for Treatment* (1966), *The Italian Job* (1969), *Come Play with Me* (1977) and *Absolute Beginners* (1986). She also had a brief walk on as the maid, Mrs Mason, in Hitchcock's *Stage Fright* (1950). A popular face on television, she starred in *For the Love of Ada* (1970–1972), which produced a movie spin-off in 1972, *Maggie and Her* (1978–1979) and *Metal Mickey* (1980–1983) among others. She was also a respected novelist, penning *The Sioux* and *The Gold-Tipped Phitzer*. **Hitchography:** *Stage Fright* (1950)

Hannay

(GB, 1988–1989, 60m episodes, colour TV) ★

CREDITS

Production company:	Thames
Producers:	Richard Bates,
	Robert Banks Stewart
Executive producer:	Lloyd Shirley

CAST

Robert Powell (Richard Hannay), Gavin Richards
(Count Von Schwabbing)

Ten years after the release of the third version of *The Thirty-Nine Steps* (1978) starring Robert Powell, the same actor returned to the role of Richard Hannay for this cheerful collection of hour-long adventures based on the John Buchan character. Set in 1912, the programmes had Hannay back in Britain after a 30-year spell in South Africa. This time he is up against the schemes of Imperial Germany, as mostly perpetrated by the nefarious Count Von Schwabbing (Gavin Richards). The results are reasonably entertaining, though the period production values are occasionally let down by some flat studio videography.

HARDWICKE, SIR CEDRIC (1893–1964) British-born actor. On stage from 1912, the plumy-toned Hardwicke went on to become one of the leading British stage actors of his generation, earning a knighthood in 1934. He made his first film, *Riches and Rogues* in 1913, but it wasn't until 1926 that he made his second, *Nelson*, and 1931 before he made his third, *Dreyfus*. *Rome Express* (1932) and *Nell Gwyn* (1934) followed, after which he made his first foray to Hollywood for *Les Miserables* (1935) and *Becky Sharp* (1935). Several more British films came next, among them *Things to Come* (1936) and *Tudor Rose* (1936). In 1938 he removed himself to Hollywood for a longer stay, establishing himself as a character actor of note in such films as *The Hunchback of Notre Dame* (1939), *Stanley and Livingstone* (1939) and *Tom Brown's School Days* (1940). He was somewhat wasted in Hitchcock's *Suspicion* (1941), in which he and Dame May Whitty popped up briefly as Joan Fontaine's parents, and fared little better in *Rope* (1948), in which he played Mr Kentley, the father of the murder victim David Kentley. Hardwicke's many other films include *The Ghost of Frankenstein* (1942), the Hollywood remake of Hitchcock's *The Lodger* (1944), *A Connecticut Yankee in King Arthur's Court* (1948) and, back in Britain, *Richard III* (1955) and *The Pumpkin Eater* (1964). In 1943, Hardwicke co-directed (and also appeared in) one film, *Forever and a Day*, which Hitchcock had originally planned to direct a sequence for. Hardwicke also starred in two episodes of *Alfred Hitchcock Presents*, in one of which, *Wet Saturday* (1956, TV), he was again directed by Hitchcock. He was the father of actor Edward Hardwicke (1932–), best known for playing Dr Watson opposite Jeremy Brett's Sherlock Holmes. **Hitchography:** *Suspicion* (1941), *Rope* (1948), *Wet Saturday* (1956, TV), *A Man Greatly Beloved* (1957, TV)

HARE, LUMSDEN (1875–1964) Irish-born character actor. In Hollywood from the late 1920s, Hare appeared in countless films, from second features such as *Charlie Chan Carries On* (1931) to top-class studio productions, among them *She* (1935), *Gunga Din* (1939), *Northwest Passage* (1940) and two Hitchcocks: *Rebecca* (1940) and *Suspicion* (1941), in which he had minor roles. His other films include the Hollywood remake of *The Lodger* (1944), previously filmed by Hitchcock in 1926, *Julius Caesar* (1953) and *The Four Skulls of Jonathan Drake* (1959). **Hitchography:** *Rebecca* (1940), *Suspicion* (1941)

HARKER, GORDON (1885–1967) British actor. Making his film debut in Hitchcock's *The Ring* in 1927, Harker went on to become one of Britain's most popular character actors, appearing in such comedy-thriller favourites as *The Frog* (1937) and *The Return of the Frog* (1938), not to mention three Inspector Hornleigh films in which he co-starred with Alastair Sim: *Inspector Hornleigh* (1938), *Inspector Hornleigh on Holiday* (1939) and *Inspector Hornleigh Goes to It* (1940). Making the most of his Cockney roots, he enlivened many-a film, including a further three for Hitchcock, in which he played key supporting roles. His other credits include *The Squeaker* (1931), *My Old Dutch* (1934) and *Small Hotel* (1957). **Hitchography:** *The Ring* (1927), *The Farmer's Wife* (1928), *Champagne* (1929), *Elstree Calling* (1930)

Harmony Heaven

(GB, 1930, 61m, bw/colour film)

CREDITS

Production company:	British International Pictures
Director:	Thomas Bentley
	(and Alfred Hitchcock?)
Screenplay:	Arthur Wimperis, Randall Faye
Cinematographer:	Theodor Sparkuhl
Songs:	Eddie Pola, Edward Brandt
Music director:	John Reynders
Editor:	Sam Simmonds
Art director:	John Mead

CAST

Stuart Hall (Bob Farrell), Polly Ward (Billie Breeze), Jack Raine (Stuart), Trilby Clark (Lady Violet Mistley), Philip Hewland (Beasley Cutting), Percy Standing (Producer), Aubrey Fitzgerald (Suggs), Gus Sharland (Stage manager)

According to some sources, Alfred Hitchcock was allegedly involved in the direction of certain scenes in this early musical about a girl who helps a composer win fame despite the interventions of a flirtatious socialite. Indeed, in the revised edition of *Hitchcock by Truffaut* (Paladin, 1984), the film is listed with his other credits (Hitchcock is credited with the film's direction, while Eddie Pola is credited with the film's 'musical part' and Edward Brandt with its 'lyrical part'). However, the entry in *Halliwell's Film Guide* (HarperCollins, 2001) lists only Thomas

Bentley as the director (with Pola and Brandt down solely as the songwriters). Bentley's directorial credit is further borne out by Alison J. Filmer and Andre Golay in *Harrap's Book of Film Directors and Their Films* (Harrap, 1989) and Denis Gifford in *The British Film Catalogue Volume I, 3rd Edition* (Fitzroy Dearborn, 2001). Meanwhile, John Russell Taylor's landmark biography *Hitch: The Life and Times of Alfred Hitchcock* (Berkley, 1980) doesn't mention the film at all. Bit of a mystery, then!

HARRIS, BARBARA (1935–) American actress. An expert at playing 'kooky,' leading lady Harris has left her mark in a handful of films, among them *A Thousand Clowns* (1965), *Plaza Suite* (1971) and *Freaky Friday* (1977), although she is perhaps best remembered for playing the psychic 'Madame' Blanche in Hitchcock's *Family Plot* (1976), a performance which *Variety* described as 'sensational'. However, critic John Simon was less impressed with her work in the movie, writing, 'Nothing can explain or excuse the frenzied overacting [by Barbara Harris] throughout, except the mistaken notion that an electric blender can whip up comedy even when it has nothing inside it.' On stage from 1961, Harris came to attention in 1967 when she won a Tony for her performance in *The Apple Tree*. Her other films include *Movie, Movie* (1978), *The North Avenue Irregulars* (1979), *Peggy Sue Got Married* (1986), *Dirty Rotten Scoundrels* (1988) and *Grosse Pointe Blanke* (1997). **Hitchography:** *Family Plot* (1976)

HARRISON, JOAN (1911–1994) British screenwriter and producer. Harrison began her career as a secretary to Hitchcock, graduating to his assistant, his screenwriter (beginning with *Jamaica Inn* in 1939) and, later, the producer of his television series *Alfred Hitchcock Presents* (1955–1962), and *The Alfred Hitchcock Hour* (1962–1965). Her scripts for Hitchcock include *Rebecca* (1940) and *Foreign Correspondent* (1940), both of which earned her Oscar nominations. Following her contribution to *Saboteur* (1942), she temporarily left the Hitchcock camp to pursue an independent career as a writer and producer on such films as *Dark Waters* (1944), which she wrote, and *Phantom Lady* (1944), *Ride the Pink Horse* (1947) and *Circle of Danger* (1951), all of which she produced. Her husband was the acclaimed author and screenwriter Eric Ambler (1909–1998), whose script for *The Wreck of the Mary Deare* Hitchcock had once planned to make (the film was eventually directed by Michael Anderson in 1959); however, his story *Act of Faith* (1962, TV) was adapted for an episode of *Alfred Hitchcock Presents*. **Hitchography:** *Jamaica Inn* (1939), *Rebecca* (1940), *Foreign Correspondent* (1940), *Suspicion* (1941), *Saboteur* (1942), *Alfred Hitchcock Presents* (1955 – 1962, TV), *The Alfred Hitchcock Hour* (1962 – 1965, TV)

HARTLEY, MARIETTE (1940–) American actress. In films with *Ride the High Country* (1962), prior to which she'd had much stage experience, including Shakespeare,

Hartley went on to appear in *Drums of Africa* (1963), *Marooned* (1969), *Improper Channels* (1981) and *Encino Man* (1992). She can also be seen as Susan Clabon in Hitchcock's *Marnie* (1964). Her television work includes *Peyton Place* (1965) and *WIOU* (1990–1991). **Hitchography:** *Marnie* (1964)

HARVEY, FORRESTER (1884–1945) Irish-born supporting actor. Harvey began his film career in Britain, appearing in the likes of *The Lilac Sunbonnet* (1922), *The Flag Lieutenant* (1926) and Hitchcock's *The Ring* (1927), in which he made his mark as a boxing promoter. By the early 1930s Harvey was in Hollywood, and went on to make appearances in such classics as *Tarzan the Ape Man* (1932), *Red Dust* (1932) and *The Mysterious Mr Moto* (1938). In 1940, he played the small role of Chalcroft in *Rebecca* for Hitchcock, after which he popped up in the likes of *A Chump at Oxford* (1940), *The Wolf Man* (1941) and *Random Harvest* (1942). **Hitchography:** *The Ring* (1927), *Rebecca* (1940)

HARVEY, PAUL (1883–1955) American supporting actor. In films from 1918 with *Men Who Have Made Love to Me*, Harvey went on to notch up well in excess of 100 film appearances in films such as *The Awful Truth* (1929), *The Petrified Forest* (1935), *High Sierra* (1941), Hitchcock's *Spellbound* (1945), in which he played Dr Hanish, *Bondie's Lucky Day* (1946), *Father of the Bride* (1950) and *The Ten Commandments* (1956). **Hitchography:** *Spellbound* (1945)

HASSE, O E (1903–1978) German character actor. Hasse turned to the stage following career plans to be a lawyer, working with the legendary Max Reinhardt at Munich's Kammerspiele. In films from 1932 with *Peter Voss – der Milionendieb*, he went on to appear in a wide variety of German and international productions, including *Peer Gynt* (1934), *Dr Crippen an Bord* (1942), *The Big Lift* (1950), *Betrayed* (1954), *Above Us the Waves* (1955), *Die Todesstrahlen des Dr Mabuse* (1964) and *Etat Siege* (1973). To English-speaking audiences he is perhaps best known for playing the murderer Otto Keller in Hitchcock's *I Confess* (1953), an intense, unsympathetic role in which he was entirely convincing. When he wasn't appearing on screen, he also worked as a vocal artist, dubbing American films into German, regularly providing the 'voices' of the likes of Paul Muni and Spencer Tracy. **Hitchography:** *I Confess* (1953)

HAWORTH, EDWARD S (TED) (1917–1993) American production designer. Haworth worked on many key films throughout his career, among them *Marty* (1954), *Invasion of the Body Snatchers* (1956), *Some Like it Hot* (1959), *The Longest Day* (1962), *The Getaway* (1972) and *Pat Garrett and Billy the Kid* (1973). In Hollywood from the late 1940s, his career received a boost when he was invited by Hitchcock to design two of his films, *Strangers on a Train* (1951) and *I Confess* (1953), the former noted for its *noir* look, the latter for its bleak-looking location work. Haworth's other credits include *Friendly Persuasion* (1956), *Half a Sixpence* (1967), *Poltergeist II: The Other Side* (1986) and *Batteries Not Included* (1987). He won an Oscar for his work on *Sayonara* (1957). **Hitchography:** *Strangers on a Train* (1951), *I Confess* (1953)

HAWTREY, CHARLES (1914–1988) British-born actor. *Carry On* star Charles Hawtrey in a Hitchcock film? You bet! While he would go on to appear in 23 of the *Carry Ons*, among them such favourites as *Carry On, Cleo* (1964), *Carry On Screaming* (1966) and *Carry On Camping* (1969), in the 1930s he often popped up as a schoolboy stooge to comedian Will Hay in the likes of *Good Morning, Boys* (1937) and *Where's That Fire?* (1939). It was in this guise that he also briefly appears, un-credited, in Hitchcock's *Sabotage* (1936), in which he can be seen in the aquarium scene, telling his girlfriend about the sexual habits of the oyster: 'After laying a million eggs the female oyster changes her sex,' he informs her, to which she responds, 'I don't blame her!' Hawtrey's other films include *A Canterbury Tale* (1944), *The Galloping Major* (1950) and *Brandy for the Parson* (1952). **Hitchography:** *Sabotage* (1936)

Hitchcock discusses a wardrobe matter with costume designer Edith Head during the filming of Family Plot *(1976). Head was one of the director's most frequent collaborators.*

HAY, IAN British novelist. Beginning with *The 39 Steps* in 1935, Hay penned the dialogue for a handful of Hitchcock's key 1930s pictures, although by the time the director came to make *Young and Innocent* (1937), Hay had been replaced by fellow novelist Gerald Savory in Hitchcock's favours. **Hitchography:** *The 39 Steps* (1935), *Secret Agent* (1936), *Sabotage* (1936)

HAYE, HELEN (1874–1957) British actress. On stage from 1898, Haye appeared in several films from the early 1920s onwards, usually in featured cameo roles, among them *Tilly of Bloomsbury* (1921), *Atlantic* (1930), *The Spy in Black* (1939) and *Richard III* (1956). One of her larger parts was in Hitchcock's early talkie *The Skin Game* (1931) in which she played the snooty Mrs Hillcrist, although she is better remembered for playing the wife of the traitorous Professor Jordan in *The 39 Steps* (1935), her seeming indifference to her husband's exploits helping to make her brief role memorable. **Hitchography:** *The Skin Game* (1931), *The 39 Steps* (1935)

HAYES, JOHN MICHAEL (1919–) American writer. Having penned over 1500 radio dramas for such series as *Sam Spade* and *Night Beat*, Hayes began to turn his attention to screenwriting with *Red Ball Express* in 1952, which he followed with *Thunder Bay* (1953) and *Torch Song* (1953). His industry standing skyrocketed when he was personally selected by Hitchcock to write *Rear Window* (1954), the director having been impressed with Hayes' work for the radio series *Suspense*. The two hit it off immediately, and Hayes was invited back to script Hitchcock's following three films, *To Catch a Thief* (1955), *The Trouble with Harry* (1955) and *The Man Who Knew Too Much* (1956). Sadly, a disagreement over Hayes' screen credit for *The Man Who Knew Too Much* brought the association to an end; Hayes took Hitchcock to arbitration over the director's assertion that Angus MacPhail also deserved a credit for contributions to the script during the development phase. Commented Hayes of the situation: 'Hitch had to have somebody to talk things over with and keep notes. But it was left up to me to finally write it. Angus was a perfectly nice man. He was a friend of Hitchcock's from the 1920s, and Hitch wanted to give him a credit because he said, 'He needs a credit. He needs the work.' [1] Hayes won his case, but never worked for the director again. His post-Hitchcock credits include *Peyton Place* (1957), *Butterfield 8* (1960), *Nevada Smith* (1966) and *Iron Will* (1994). **Hitchography:** *Rear Window* (1954), *To Catch a Thief* (1955), *The Trouble with Harry* (1955), *The Man Who Knew Too Much* (1956)

HEAD, EDITH (1907–1981) American costume designer. This much-Oscared costumier took home the golden statuette a total of eight times for her work on *The Heiress* (1949), *All About Eve* (1950), *Samson and Delilah* (1950), *A Place in the Sun* (1951), *Roman Holiday* (1953), *Sabrina* (1954), *The Facts of Life* (1960) and *The Sting* (1973). In films from the late 1920s following experience as an art teacher, she went on to become the head costume designer for Paramount in the 1930s and Universal in the 1960s. She worked with Hitchcock 12 times, beginning with *Notorious* in 1946. Her most elaborate work for the Master can be found in the costume ball sequence in *To Catch a Thief* (1955), which the director showcases with great care. For her efforts, Head was nominated for an Oscar. Recalled the costumier of her work on the film: 'When people ask me who my favourite actress is, who my favourite actor is, and what my favourite film is, I tell them to watch *To Catch a Thief* and they'll get all the answers. The film was a costume designer's dream. It had all the ingredients for being fun, a challenge, and a great product... The story revolved around a world of people with great taste and plenty of money. Even the extras were meticulously dressed. At the end of the picture we had a fancy masquerade ball... so every woman was running around looking like Marie Antoinette. That was the most expensive set up I've ever done. Grace [Kelly] wore a dress of delicate gold mesh, a golden wig, and a golden mask. Hitchcock told me that he wanted her to look like a princess. She did.' [2]

Meanwhile, for such films as *The Man Who Knew Too Much* (1956), *Vertigo* (1958), *The Birds* (1963) and *Torn Curtain* (1966), Head provided Hitchcock's leading ladies with a number of smartly cut business-style outfits (she also costumed Vera Miles in *Psycho* [1960], but without credit). However, perhaps Head's most glamorous work for Hitchcock was done for Grace Kelly in *Rear Window* (1954), for whom she provided several eye-catching evening dresses as befitting the character's job as a model. Head's many other films include *Love Me Tonight* (1932), *I Married a Witch* (1942), *Sunset Boulevard* (1950), *White Christmas* (1954), *Funny Face* (1957), *Hud* (1963), *Rooster Cogburn* (1975) and *Dead Men Don't Wear Plaid* (1982). She can also be spotted in *The Oscar* (1966) and the Columbo mystery *Requiem for a Falling Star* (1972, TV). **Hitchography:** *Notorious* (1946), *Rear Window* (1954), *To Catch a Thief* (1955), *The Trouble with Harry* (1955), *The Man Who Knew Too Much* (1956), *Vertigo* (1958), *Psycho* (1960), *The Birds* (1963), *Marnie* (1964), *Torn Curtain* (1966), *Topaz* (1969), *Family Plot* (1976)

HECHT, BEN (1894–1964) American playwright and screenwriter. This acerbic writer is best remembered for co-authoring (with Charles MacArthur) the celebrated newspaper drama *The Front Page*, which so far has been filmed four times, in 1931, 1940 (as *His Girl Friday*), 1974 and 1988 (as *Switching Channels*). His many screenplays include *Underworld* (1929), which earned him an Oscar, *The Scoundrel* (1935), which brought a second Oscar, *Nothing Sacred* (1937) and *Wuthering Heights* (1939). In the 1940s he worked on six films for Hitchcock, beginning with un-credited contributions to the script of *Foreign Correspondent* (1940). He followed this with the screenplays for *Spellbound* (1945) and *Notorious* (1946), earning an Oscar nomination for the latter. He also co-scripted the wartime propaganda film *Watchtower Over Tomorrow*

Tippi Hedren's Marnie pets her beloved horse Forio in Hitchcock's Marnie *(1964).*

(1945), on which Hitchcock directed a few scenes without credit, and made some un-credited contributions to the scripts for *The Paradine Case* (1947), *Rope* (1948) and *Strangers on a Train* (1951). Hecht himself directed a handful of films, among them *The Scoundrel* (1935), *Angels Over Broadway* (1940), *The Specter of the Rose* (1946) and *Actors and Sin* (1952). Apparently he believed that screenwriting 'required no more effort than a game of pinochle.' [3] **Hitchography:** *Foreign Correspondent* (1940), *Spellbound* (1945), *Watchtower Over Tomorrow* (1945), *Notorious* (1946), *The Paradine Case* (1947), *Rope* (1948), *Strangers on a Train* (1951)

HECKROTH, HEIN (1897–1970) German costume and production designer. Following the rise of the Nazis in 1933, Heckroth left his home country for Britain, where he continued his career as a stage and film designer (although this didn't prevent him from being interned as an enemy agent during World War II). He is best remembered for his fruitful collaboration with writer-directors Michael Powell and Emeric Pressburger, for whom he designed, among others, *A Matter of Life and Death* (1945), *Black Narcissus* (1947) and *The Red Shoes* (1948), the latter winning him an Oscar. His other credits include *Caesar and Cleopatra* (1945), *The Story of Gilbert and Sullivan* (1953) and Hitchcock's *Torn Curtain* (1966), for which he was required to present a drab view of life behind the Iron Curtain. **Hitchography:** *Torn Curtain* (1966)

HEDREN, TIPPI (1931–) American actress. Given that Grace Kelly had moved to Monaco to become a princess and Vera Miles hadn't worked out as his leading lady, Hitchcock was on the lookout for a new star to headline his movie *The Birds* (1963). He eventually spotted her in a Sego diet drink ad. Her name was Nathalie Kay Hedren, but everyone called her Tippi. Although she had experience as a model, she'd never acted before, and it was a major gamble for the director to cast a complete unknown in a major motion picture. But having just made *Psycho* (1960), Hitchcock was in a position to do pretty much as he pleased, and so the American-born Hedren became Melanie Daniels, the flighty high society girl whose trip to the picturesque Bodega Bay turns into an apocalyptic nightmare. Commented the film's production designer Robert Boyle: 'Hitchcock always liked women who behaved like well-bred ladies. Tippi generated that quality. He was quite taken by the way she walked.' [4]

'I had no idea that I would be associated with *The Birds*. I knew that it was being made, but it never occurred to me that I would be in it,' [5] Hedren admitted. In fact she didn't even know *who* she was auditioning for when she was sent for. 'They didn't tell me who the producer was, even when I got to Universal.' [6] This didn't remain a secret long, though, and Hitchcock went on to spend some $25,000 screen testing Hedren over a three-day period, having her play scenes from *Rebecca*, *Notorious* and *To Catch a Thief* with Martin Balsam. Following the successful completion of the tests (which subsequently had to be destroyed, as Hitchcock no longer held the copyright to the material), the director invited his new star to dinner at Chasen's with his wife, Alma, and the head of Universal/MCA, Lew Wasserman. Recalled Hedren when the news was broken that she would be Hitchcock's new leading lady: 'I cried and Alma cried. Even Lew Wasserman had tears rolling down his face. It was a lovely moment.' [7]

Insisting that she always be billed as 'Tippi' Hedren, Hitchcock moulded his new star's look and performance absolutely. 'A fascinating new personality,' proclaimed the film's poster, which featured a portrait of the debutant actress. Nevertheless, she was greeted with mixed reviews. *The Times* described her as 'Another of those cool-but-sizzling-underneath blondes that Hitchcock delights to feature in films, [but] less appealing than many; one takes the point that she is not meant to be a very agreeable character, but at least the qualities she does have might come over more vividly.' *Variety* was much more enthusiastic, however: 'Aside from the birds, the film belongs to Hedren, who makes an auspicious screen bow. She virtually has to carry the picture alone for the first 45-minute stretch.'

Making *The Birds* had been an enlightening experience for Hedren; it was also occasionally traumatic (the filming of the attic scene in which she is attacked by gulls and crows took three days and left her shocked and injured). Nevertheless, she and Hitchcock remained on good terms, and he subsequently cast her as the lead in his following film *Marnie* (1964), the story of a sexually repressed kleptomaniac, which had originally been intended as Grace Kelly's comeback vehicle. Unfortunately, during filming, cracks began to show in the relationship between director and star. Admitted Hedren: 'During the filming of *Marnie*, everything went fine until probably the last quarter of the shoot. It was a five-month shoot, and it eventually got to the point where I couldn't stand the control, or the *trying* to control, and I resented it so highly that I finally told him I couldn't bear it anymore. Demands were being put on me that I couldn't acquiesce to, and I said I needed to get out… And he literally said, "I'll ruin your career."' [8]

Following the release of *Marnie*, Hitchcock kept Hedren under contract for two years, paying her salary, but not allowing her to work elsewhere. When she finally appeared in Chaplin's *A Countess from Hong Kong* (1967), which was a flop, her career had been fatally harmed. Her subsequent film work includes *Tiger by the Tail* (1968), *The Harrad Experiment* (1973) and *Roar* (1981), a $17 million wildlife thriller featuring many of the 150 lions and tigers which she and her agent and then-husband Noel Marshall – who wrote, produced and directed the film – lived with at their California ranch. Hedren also appeared in a belated sequel to *The Birds* titled *The Birds II: Land's End* (1994, TV), but it was not a success. She is the mother of actress Melanie Griffith (1957–), who is named after Hedren's character in *The Birds*. **Hitchography:** *The Birds* (1963), *Marnie* (1964)

HEINDORF, RAY (1908–1980) American music director, conductor, orchestrator and occasional composer. Long at Warner Bros., Heindorf won Oscars for his orchestrations for *Yankee Doodle Dandy* (1942), *This Is the Army* (1943) and *The Music Man* (1962). His many other credits include *Big City Blues* (1932), *Captain Blood* (1935), *A Streetcar Named Desire* (1951), *Finian's Rainbow* (1968) and *1776* (1972). He also conducted three scores for Hitchcock: Miklos Rozsa's Oscar-winning *Spellbound* (1945), for which he didn't receive an onscreen credit, and Dimitri Tiomkin's *Strangers on a Train* (1951) and *I Confess* (1953). **Hitchography:** *Spellbound* (1945), *Strangers on a Train* (1951), *I Confess* (1953)

HELLO, EVERYBODY see *Elstree Calling*

HELMOND, KATHERINE (1934–) American supporting/character actress. Best remembered for playing Jessica Tate in the cult sit-com *Soap* (1977–1981), Helmond came to film and television after many years on stage. In films from 1971 with *Believe in Me*, she went on to appear in *The Hospital* (1971), *The Hindenberg* (1975), *Baby Blue Marine* (1976) and Hitchcock's *Family Plot* (1976), in which she played the rather dowdy-looking Mrs Maloney. Following the success of *Soap*, Helmond went on to appear in more high profile films, including

three for director Terry Gilliam: *Time Bandits* (1981), *Brazil* (1985) and *Fear and Loathing in Las Vegas* (1998). She also directed several episodes of the sit-com *Who's the Boss?* (1984–1990) in which she also co-starred.
Hitchography: *Family Plot* (1976)

HELMORE, TOM (1904–1995) British-born actor. Helmore is perhaps best remembered for playing the devious Gavin Elster in *Vertigo* (1958), whose complex plot to murder his wife propels the film's star, James Stewart, into some extraordinary situations. However, this was not the first time Helmore had worked for Hitchcock. In 1927 he had an un-credited role in *The Ring*, while in 1936 he played another un-credited role, that of Colonel Anderson, in *Secret Agent*. Consequently, he is one of the few actors to feature in all three stages of Hitchcock's career: silent, classic British and classic American. He even appeared in an episode of *Alfred Hitchcock Presents*. In America from the late 1930s – he made his Broadway debut in *No Time for Comedy* in 1939 – Helmore's other films include *Trouble Along the Way* (1953), *The Time Machine* (1960) and *Flipper and the Pirates* (1964).
Hitchography: *The Ring* (1927), *Secret Agent* (1936), *Vertigo* (1958), *Murder Me Twice* (1958, TV)

Tom Helmore sets the plot with James Stewart in Hitchcock's Vertigo *(1958). Helmore was one of the few actors to feature in every stage of Hitchcock's career, from the silent days through to* Alfred Hitchcock Presents.

HERBERT, HOLMES (1882–1956, real name Edward Sanger) British-born actor. The archetypal Englishman, Herbert emigrated to America following the outbreak of World War I, where he launched a movie career that would number in excess of 200 films, beginning with *Pere Goriot* in 1915. Among his other films are such classics as *Dr Jekyll and Mr Hyde* (1931), *The Mystery of the Wax Museum* (1933),

Mark of the Vampire (1935), *The Adventures of Robin Hood* (1938) and *The Adventures of Sherlock Holmes* (1939). He also popped up as Assistant Commissioner ffolliott in Hitchcock's *Foreign Correspondent* (1940), following which his career continued with *The Ghost of Frankenstein* (1942), *The Pearl of Death* (1944) and *Anne of the Indies* (1951).
Hitchography: *Foreign Correspondent* (1940)

HERRMANN, BERNARD (1911–1975) American composer and conductor. The film career of this justly celebrated composer and conductor is noted not only for its highly productive association with Hitchcock, but also for alliances with Orson Welles, Ray Harryhausen, Francois Truffaut and Brian de Palma. An Oscar winner for his work on *All That Money Can Buy* (1942), Herrmann began his professional career composing and conducting at CBS radio in 1934, prior to which he had trained at New York's prestigious Juilliard School of Music. It was while at CBS that Herrmann became a member of Orson Welles' legendary Mercury Theatre group, working on a variety of radio dramas, including the infamous 1938 broadcast of *The War of the Worlds*, which managed to panic much of America (the story of its broadcast was later dramatized in the 1975 TV movie *The Night That Panicked America*). When Welles went to Hollywood to make *Citizen Kane*, Herrmann was invited to follow, his score for the classic ranking among the best of his many subsequent film works, which included such diverse productions as *The Magnificent Ambersons* (1942), *Jane Eyre* (1943), *Hangover Square* (1945), *The Ghost and Mrs Muir* (1947), *The Day the Earth Stood Still* (1951), *Journey to the Center of the Earth* (1959), *Jason and the Argonauts* (1963), *Fahrenheit 451* (1966), *Sisters* (1973) and *Taxi Driver* (1976).

Though they had met briefly in 1942, Herrmann didn't work for Hitchcock until 1955 when he scored the black comedy *The Trouble with Harry*, Herrmann having been suggested to Hitchcock by his friend and fellow composer Lyn Murray, who at the time was scoring *To Catch a Thief* (1955) for Hitch. Herrmann followed *The Trouble with Harry* with the remake of Hitchcock's own *The Man Who Knew Too Much* (1956), the 1934 original of which had been scored by Arthur Benjamin, whose cantata, *Storm Clouds*, was retained for the new version. Featured during the Albert Hall climax, the piece was conducted in the film by Herrmann himself in a Hitchcock-like cameo (Herrmann's name can also be seen on the posters outside the concert hall).

Following the downbeat docudrama *The Wrong Man* (1957), the music for which makes effective use of double bass embellishments (Henry Fonda's character is a double bass player in the film), the Hitchcock-Herrmann association truly took flight with *Vertigo* (1958), for which Herrmann penned his most deliriously romantic score. Commented the composer of his working relationship with the Master: 'Hitchcock is an extraordinarily well organized man in the making of his films. The actual shooting process to him is already boring, because he has made the film in his head. For example, he will never give an actor direction how to walk in and out of a room. He will accept the fact that the man had to walk into the room, and if the actor walks in that way, and it's done with conviction, he's quite happy with it. And so to work with him with music is also a great deal that way. He'll say, 'I have left reel three for you.' [9]

Herrmann also revealed his technique when working on a Hitchcock picture: 'In Hitchcock one has to create a landscape for each film, whether it be the rainy night of *Psycho* or the turbulence of a picture such as *Vertigo*... Hitchcock deals rarely with character portrayal, or has little or no interest in people's emotions. [He] deals in situations that are generally of a suspenseful nature – his interest in music is only in relation to how the suspense can be heightened.' [10]

Following *Vertigo* came the fandango-like *North by Northwest* (1959), noted for its intense, driving rhythms ('He would smite the world with trombones!' [11] commented fellow composer David Raksin). This in turn was followed by the screeching *Psycho* (1960), which Herrmann scored for a strings only orchestra (he called the results 'black and white music'). Of the film's celebrated shower murder, remembered for its stabbing violin motif, the composer commented: 'The shower scene had been a scene of much discussion. Hitchcock didn't want music for it, and I said, "Well, leave it to me and go away on holiday." Well, he came back and we showed him the film *with* the music and he said, "Of course, we'll use that!" But I said, "Hitch, you said absolutely *no* music!" He said, "Wow, Improper suggestion!"' [12]

In 1963 Herrmann acted as the sound consultant on *The Birds*, which, although it didn't have a music score, featured an effects track of electronically manipulated bird calls. Following the vigorous *Marnie* (1964), Herrmann's collaboration with Hitch came to an abrupt end with *Torn Curtain* (1966). Sadly, the composer's bombastic score never made it to the screen, having been rejected by Hitchcock, who had instructed Herrmann to take a lighter approach. Recalled horn player Alan Robinson of the incident: 'Hitchcock walked in and he said, "What's this? What kind of music is this? This isn't what I want!" And so we just went home.' [13] The movie was subsequently re-scored by John Addison, although Herrmann's rejected music has subsequently been released on CD, while the documentary *Music for the Movies: Bernard Herrmann* shows how the film's main murder scene – played with no music in the finished film – would have run with Herrmann's blistering score; the Universal DVD also restores Herrmann's music in the extras section. Commented fellow composer David Raksin of the *Torn Curtain* incident, 'Hitchcock owed him [Herrmann] everything and had the loyalty of an eel.' [14]

In fact the *Torn Curtain* break up so upset Herrmann that he eventually uprooted and moved to London in 1972, from where he continued his career, which included a series of album recordings for Decca's Phase Four sub-division, among them suites from his classic Hitchcock scores. He also wrote the music for a handful of Hitchcock pastiches, among them *Twisted Nerve* (1969),

The Night Digger (1971), *Endless Night* (1972), *Sisters* (1973) and *Obsession* (1976). Herrmann finished recording the music for his final film, *Taxi Driver* (1976), on 23 December 1975. He died in his sleep in the early hours of Christmas Eve. Yet over a quarter of a century on from his death, his music continues to be appreciated both by critics and soundtrack enthusiasts, and much of it is available on CD. Commented fellow composer Elmer Bernstein, who has recorded an album of Herrmann's music and adapted his 1961 *Cape Fear* score for the 1991 remake: 'His work is unique. Yet in a strange way, it can be said *not* to have influenced anybody – which makes his style stand out all the more. He doesn't really have any imitators, which is quite curious in a way. He was an absolutely superb musician and had an extremely good classical training. But most importantly, he was a dramatist.' [15]

Note that, in addition to his film work, Herrmann wrote the music for many television shows, among them episodes of *The Twilight Zone* (1959–1963), *The Virginian* (1962–1971) and *The Alfred Hitchcock Hour* (1962–1965), of which he scored 17 episodes; a further 17 episodes also utilized stock music composed by Herrmann. Interestingly, not one of these 34 episodes was directed by Hitchcock himself. Also note that though the sequels to *Psycho* feature entirely new scores, *Psycho 2* (1983) opens with Herrmann's famous slashing violin motif, surely one of the cinema's most memorable and immediately identifiable pieces of music. His *Psycho* score was also re-worked by Danny Elfman for the misguided 1998 remake.

Hitchography: *The Trouble with Harry* (1955), *The Man Who Knew Too Much* (1956), *The Wrong Man* (1957), *Vertigo* (1958), *North by Northwest* (1959), *Psycho* (1960), *The Birds* (1963), *A Home Away from Home* (1963, TV), *Terror at Northfield* (1963, TV), *You'll Be the Death of Me* (1963, TV), *Nothing Ever Happens in Linvale* (1963, TV), *The Cadaver* (1963, TV, stock), *The Jar* (1964, TV), *Behind the Locked Door* (1964, TV), *Marnie* (1964), *Change of Address* (1964, TV), *Water's Edge* (1964, TV), *The Life Work of Juan Diaz* (1964, TV), *The McGregor Affair* (1964, TV), *Misadventure* (1964, TV), *Consider Her Ways* (1964, TV), *Beyond the Sea of Death* (1964, TV, stock), *Night Caller* (1964, TV, stock), *Anyone for Murder?* (1964, TV, stock), *The Ordeal of Mrs Snow* (1964, TV, stock), *Bed of Roses* (1964, TV, stock), *Isabel* (1964, TV, stock), *The Return of Verge Likens* (1964, TV, stock), *Where the Woodbine Twineth* (1965, TV), *An Unlocked Window* (1965, TV), *Wally the Beard* (1965, TV), *Death Scene* (1965, TV), *Final Performance* (1965, TV, stock), *The Trap* (1965, TV, stock), *The Photographer and the Undertaker* (1965, TV, stock), *Thou Still Un-ravished Bride* (1965, TV, stock), *Completely Foolproof* (1965, TV, stock), *Power of Attorney* (1965, TV, stock), *Second Wife* (1965, TV, stock), *Night Fever* (1965, TV, stock), *Off Season* (1965, TV, stock), *Torn Curtain* (1966, rejected score)

HICKS, SIR SEYMOUR (1871–1949) British stage *farceur* and playwright. The distinguished playwright also dabbled in film, appearing, writing, directing and occasionally producing, beginning in 1907 with *Seymour*

Magazine caricature of Hitchcock, 1935.

Hicks Edits the Tatler. A favourite subject seems to have been *Scrooge*, in which Hicks played the title role in 1913 and 1935. Another favourite was the stage play *Always Tell Your Wife* by E Temple Thurston, which he filmed in 1914 and again in 1923. Hicks financed and scripted the latter version, which was filmed at Islington Studios. Unfortunately, the film's original director, Hugh Croise, left the project before it had been completed, and Hicks invited the young Hitchcock to help him finish the picture, thus providing him with his second (albeit un-credited) directorial assignment. Hicks' other screen credits include *A Prehistoric Love Story* (1915), *The Secret of the Loch* (1934) and *The Lambeth Walk* (1939). His wife, stage star Ellaline Terriss (1871–1971, real name Ellen Lewin), appeared in many of his films, including *Seymour Hicks and Ellaline Terriss* (1913) and both versions of *Always Tell Your Wife*. **Hitchography:** *Always Tell Your Wife* (1923)

HILDYARD, JACK (1908–1990) British cinematographer. In films from 1932 as a clapper boy, this distinguished cinematographer graduated to operator by the late 1930s on such films as *The Divorce of Lady X* (1938), *Pygmalion* (1938) and Hitchcock's *Jamaica Inn* (1939). He photographed his first film, *School for Secrets*, in 1946, although it was his work on *The Sound Barrier* (1952) for director

David Lean that firmly established his reputation. Hildyard worked with Lean a further three times on *Hobson's Choice* (1954), *Summer Madness* (1955) and *The Bridge on the River Kwai* (1957), the latter winning him an Oscar. His other films include *Suddenly Last Summer* (1959), *The Sundowners* (1960), *55 Days at Peking* (1962) and *Casino Royale* (1967). In 1969 – 30 years after he'd last worked with him – Hildyard photographed *Topaz* for Hitchcock, which included location work in Germany, Denmark and America. Hildyard's other films include *Puppet on a Chain* (1970), *The Beast Must Die* (1974) and *The Wild Geese* (1978). **Hitchography:** *Jamaica Inn* (1939), *Topaz* (1969)

HILTON, JAMES (1900–1954) British novelist. This celebrated writer is remembered for such classics as *Knight without Armour*, *Goodbye, Mr Chips*, *The Lost Horizon* and *Random Harvest*, each of which has been filmed (twice in some cases). His credits as a screenwriter include *We Are Not Alone* (1939), based on his novel, and Hitchcock's *Foreign Correspondent* (1940), to which he contributed to the dialogue. **Hitchography:** *Foreign Correspondent* (1940)

HINES, HARRY American bit part player. Hines is best remembered for playing the old codger who crawls underneath the out-of-control merry-go-round at the climax of Hitchcock's *Strangers on a Train* (1951), the filming of which led the director to fear for Hines' life. His other credits include *The Interns* (1962). **Hitchography:** *Strangers on a Train* (1951)

HITCHCOCK, SIR ALFRED (1899–1980) British-born director. Born into the late Victorian era on 13 August 1899, the young Alfred Joseph Hitchcock was raised in a Catholic household by his mother Emma in the flat above the greengrocer's shop in Leytonstone, London, where his father William plied his trade. The last of three children, he was preceded by William Jr, born in 1890, and Nellie, born in 1892. Educated at a variety of Jesuit schools, the young Hitchcock was by all accounts a solitary and introspective child of average academic achievement. His hobbies included a fascination with bus and train timetables, which may perhaps explain his later fastidiousness when preparing his films, the making of which ran like clockwork. Said Hitchcock: 'Everything is decided on paper. I do not improvise whilst the picture is being made.' [16] A childhood incident also seems to have left its mark: at the age of 5, Hitchcock's father sent the boy down to the local police station with a note following some minor transgression; having read the piece of paper, the officer in charge locked the unfortunate child in a cell for five minutes, after which he was released with the caution, 'This is what we do to naughty boys.' For the rest of his life, Hitchcock had a fear of the police and frequently treated them disdainfully in his films.

Following the death of his father in 1915, Hitchcock went to study engineering at the School of Engineering and Navigation, where he received training as a draughtsman. This in turn led to a job as a technical clerk for an

Hitchcock is joined by a close relative during the filming of Frenzy *(1972). The wax effigy was used for the film's trailer, in which it can be seen floating down the Thames.*

electrical cable company (the W T Henley Telegraph Company). He managed to avoid military service during World War I (he was classified C3 at his army medical), although he did put his skills to use by joining the volunteer corps of the Royal Engineers. It was about this time that Hitchcock also began to take a great interest in the cinema, absorbing as much technical information as he could about the burgeoning medium.

By now Hitchcock was working as a graphic artist for the cable company, providing illustrations for brochures and copy for newspaper advertisements. Then, in 1919, he learned that the American film company Famous Players-Lasky was looking to expand its operations overseas. This would involve building a London-based studio in the suburb of Islington (in a former railway power station), thus allowing British and American artists and technicians to work together. Hitchcock saw this as his chance to break into the movies and, in 1920, having learned of the company's plans to film *The Sorrows of Satan* by Marie Corelli, he produced a series of title designs for the proposed film on spec. Hitchcock approached the company with his work, only to be told that they were instead going to film *The Great Day* by Louis N Parker and George R Sims. Undaunted, Hitchcock returned the

next day with a new set of designs and, having sufficiently impressed the personnel officer, was hired as a title designer on a part-time basis. *The Great Day* appeared in cinemas in November 1920. Hitchcock at last had broken into the movies.

By now employed full time, Hitchcock went on to provide the inter-titles for 12 films for Famous Players-Lasky, among them *The Call of Youth* (1920), *The Princess of New York* (1921), *Appearances* (1921) and *Perpetua* (1922). In 1922, he began to express an interest in directing, and he managed to get a film off the ground titled *Number 13* (aka *Mrs Peabody*). Unfortunately, the production ran into trouble and was not finished; Hitchcock's ambitions seemed to be thwarted before he had even started. Indeed, it was at this time that Famous Players-Lasky abandoned their interests in Islington, which nevertheless remained open as a studio for hire.

It was during this uncertain period that Hitchcock was hired by the actor-producer Seymour Hicks to help finish his film *Always Tell Your Wife* (1923) whose original director, Hugh Croise, had left under a cloud. Hicks, who was renting floor space at Islington, had seen Hitchcock about the studio, and had been suitably impressed by the young man's enthusiasm. Consequently, he took him on to help finish his film. Unfortunately, Hitchcock's work went un-credited.

Perhaps realizing he was attempting to run before he could walk, Hitchcock next got a job with Balcon-Freeman-Saville – who took over space at Islington – for whom he worked his way up the cinematic ladder in a variety of capacities, including screenwriter, art director and assistant director. Indeed, Hitchcock took on all three jobs on his first film for the company, *Woman to Woman* (1923), whose technical crew included a young woman named Alma Reville (1900–1982), who was working as the film's editor and continuity girl. Hitchcock and Reville had been aware of each other at the studio for some time, but given that he had heretofore been but a lowly graphic artist while she had been an editor, Hitchcock bided his time until he had achieved a job of more superior status before actually asking the young woman out.

Hitchcock continued to work with Reville on such films as *The White Shadow* (1924), *The Passionate Adventure* (1924), *The Prude's Fall* (1925) and *The Blackguard* (1925), all of which, like *Woman to Woman*, were directed by Graham Cutts. Hitchcock's involvement on these films again amounted to several jobs, among them screenwriter, art director and assistant director, which quickly gained him a reputation of being something of a wiz, much to Cutts' increasing annoyance.

Hitchcock and Reville eventually became engaged during the production of *The Blackguard*, after which Hitch finally got his chance to make his credited debut as a director with *The Pleasure Garden* (1925). Again, Reville was by his side as assistant director and continuity girl, as she was on his following film, *The Mountain Eagle* (1925). Unfortunately, the professional jealousy of Graham Cutts, which had now reached new heights, saw the films condemned as un-releasable, as was Hitchcock's third film, *The Lodger* (1926). However, following some reworking in the editorial department, the latter was eventually released to great acclaim in 1927, this success prompting the company to release Hitchcock's first two films, which were also well received. By this time, Hitchcock had married Reville (at Brompton Oratory on 2 December 1926), and the two would remain inseparable for the remainder of their lives.

Thanks to the success of *The Lodger* (in which the director also made the first of his legendary cameo appearances), Hitchcock's career truly took off, and films such as *Downhill* (1927), *The Farmer's Wife* (1928) – during the making of which his daughter Patricia was born – and *The Manxman* (1929) followed. Then in 1929 came another defining picture, *Blackmail*, which was filmed as a silent, but substantially re-shot and released in an acclaimed talkie version.

At this stage in his career, Hitchcock had yet to become solely identified with the thriller genre, and following *Blackmail* he went on to helm on a variety of pictures, among them musicals – *Elstree Calling* (1930), *Waltzes from Vienna* (1933) – and dramas, including several

stage and novel adaptations, such as *Juno and the Paycock* (1930), *Murder!* (1930) and *The Skin Game* (1934). But it was another thriller, *The Man Who Knew Too Much* (1934) that got Hitchcock out of a rut and led him on to his classic British period, which saw him direct the likes of *The 39 Steps* (1935), *Sabotage* (1936), *Young and Innocent* (1937) and *The Lady Vanishes* (1938).

By now internationally recognized, Hitchcock began to look farther a-field for employment, and in 1939 he readily accepted an offer from *Gone with the Wind* producer David O Selznick to go to Hollywood. The contract was for seven years and Hitchcock's inaugural American production was to be an account of the Titanic tragedy. However, when this fell through at the planning stage, Hitchcock instead filmed an adaptation of Daphne Du Maurier's bestseller *Rebecca* (1940), which went on to achieve enormous commercial and critical success, winning an Academy Award for best picture (for Selznick) in the process. Further hits in the guise of *Foreign Correspondent* (1940), *Suspicion* (1941), *Saboteur* (1942) and *Shadow of a Doubt* (1943) followed, although there were occasional missteps, such as the screwball comedy *Mr and Mrs Smith* (1941). By this time, Hitchcock was also making in-roads into radio with adaptations of his big screen successes, which went on to include *Lifeboat* (1944), *Spellbound* (1945) and *Notorious* (1947). He also found time to work on a handful of documentaries and propaganda films during the war years, among them *Men of the Lightship* (1941), *Bon Voyage* (1944), *Aventure Malgache* (1944) and *Watchtower Over Tomorrow* (1945).

Following *The Paradine Case* (1947), the final film made under his contract with Selznick, Hitchcock attempted to go independent, forming Transatlantic Pictures with his longtime friend Sidney Bernstein. Unfortunately, the two pictures made under the Transatlantic banner – the experimental *Rope* (1948) and the period drama *Under Capricorn* (1949) – were not successes, and the company was subsequently liquidated. But Hitchcock was soon back on track again with *Strangers on a Train* (1951) which led to his classic 1950s period, which took in *Dial M for Murder* (1954), *Rear Window* (1954), *Vertigo* (1958) and *North by Northwest* (1959). Yet despite working with major stars, including several glamorous females who came to be known as the Hitchcock blondes, the director himself remained sexually repressed (from the mid-1930s onwards, he was apparently celibate). Commented screenwriter Ernest Lehman: 'He had this secret repressed interest in females. Inside him he had a lot of guilt feelings. Not over what he had *done*, but what he would *like* to have done.' [17]

The 1950s also saw Hitchcock make his first forays into television with *Alfred Hitchcock Presents* (1955–1962), which he hosted and occasionally directed, and *Suspicion* (1957–1958). He also became involved with publishing in 1955 when he made a deal with magazine proprietor Richard E Decker to promote *The Alfred Hitchcock Mystery Magazine*, while in 1957 he was approached by Simon & Schuster to endorse a collection of short suspense and horror stories to be named after his TV show *Alfred*

Hitchcock Presents. Further deals with Random House and Dell followed, resulting in literally dozens of compilations.

Then, in 1960, Hitchcock made *Psycho* (1960), a low budget shocker, which went on to become his most famous (and commercially successful) film. Another major hit followed with *The Birds* (1963), while in 1962 *Alfred Hitchcock Presents* became *The Alfred Hitchcock Hour* (1962–1965). Sadly, the remainder of the decade was blighted by a string of commercial failures, among them *Marnie* (1964) and *Topaz* (1969), which saw his box office stock dwindle, while an attempt to launch a further anthology series, *Black Cloak*, met with failure, resulting in the pilot episode, *Dark Intruder* (1965), being released as a theatrical support. Nevertheless, Hitchcock had one last hurrah with *Frenzy* (1972), which he followed with *Family Plot* (1976). This proved to be his last film, although plans were afoot for another film titled *The Short Night*, which was subsequently abandoned in 1979. When asked what he would like his last film to be about, if he was given *carte blanche*, Hitchcock replied, 'I think it would be about murder, mayhem, violence, sex – beautifully pictorially expressed, with lovely costumes, perfect cutting and a joke or two.' [18]

Hitchcock received the American Film Institute's lifetime achievement award in 1979. By this time he'd also received the Irving G Thalberg award in tribute to his career in 1968, while the following year saw him created an officer of the French Order of Arts and Letters. Meanwhile, 1979 saw him knighted by Queen Elizabeth II for his contribution to British culture. Astonishingly, despite being nominated for a best director Oscar five times, Hitchcock never won the award. When he died on 29 April 1980, he was recognized the world over as the undisputed Master of Suspense. As Hitchcock himself put it, 'I've become a body of films, not a man; I *am* all those films.' [19] **Hitchography:** *The Great Day* (1920), *The Call of Youth* (1920), *Dangerous Lies* (1921), *The Princess of New York* (1921), *The Mystery Road* (1921), *Appearances* (1921), *Beside the Bonnie Brier Bush* (1921), *Spanish Jade* (1922), *Perpetua* (1922), *Three Live Ghosts* (1922), *Tell Your Children* (1922), *The Man from Home* (1922), *Number 13* (1922), *Always Tell Your Wife* (1923), *Woman to Woman* (1923), *The White Shadow* (1924), *The Passionate Adventure* (1924), *The Prude's Fall* (1925), *The Blackguard* (1925), *The Pleasure Garden* (1925), *The Mountain Eagle* (1925), *The Lodger* (1926), *Downhill* (1927), *The Ring* (1927), *Easy Virtue* (1927), *The Farmer's Wife* (1928), *Champagne* (1928), *The Manxman* (1929), *Blackmail* (1929), *An Elastic Affair* (1930), *Elstree Calling* (1930), *Juno and the Paycock* (1930), *Murder!* (1930), *The Skin Game* (1931), *Number Seventeen* (1932), *Rich and Strange* (1932), *Lord Camber's Ladies* (1932), *Waltzes from Vienna* (1933), *The Man Who Knew Too Much* (1934), *The 39 Steps* (1935), *Secret Agent* (1936), *Sabotage* (1936), *Young and Innocent* (1937), *The Lady Vanishes* (1938), *Jamaica Inn* (1939), *Rebecca* (1940), *The Lodger* (1940, radio), *Foreign Correspondent* (1940), *Suspicion* (1941), *Mr and Mrs Smith* (1941), *Men of the Lightship* (1941), *Target for Tonight* (1941), *Saboteur* (1942), *Buy War*

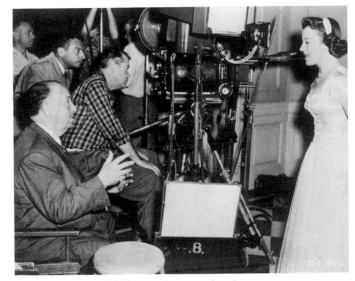

Hitchcock directs his daughter Pat in a scene from Strangers on a Train *(1951).*

Bonds (1943), *Shadow of a Doubt* (1943), *Bon Voyage* (1944), *Aventure Malgache* (1944), *Lifeboat* (1944), *Memory of the Camps* (1944), *Watchtower Over Tomorrow* (1945), *Spellbound* (1945), *Notorious* (1946), *The Paradine Case* (1947), *Rope* (1948), *Under Capricorn* (1949), *Stage Fright* (1950), *Strangers on a Train* (1951), *I Confess* (1953), *Dial M for Murder* (1954), *Rear Window* (1954), *To Catch a Thief* (1955), *Alfred Hitchcock Presents* (1955–1962), *Revenge* (1955, TV), *Breakdown* (1955, TV), *The Trouble with Harry* (1955), *The Case of Mr Pelham* (1955, TV), *Back for Christmas* (1956, TV), *Wet Saturday* (1956, TV), *The Man Who Knew Too Much* (1956), *Mr Blanchard's Secret* (1956, TV), *The Wrong Man* (1956), *One More Mile to Go* (1957, TV), *Four O'Clock* (1957, TV), *The Perfect Crime* (1957, TV), *Lamb to the Slaughter* (1958, TV), *Dip in the Pool* (1958, TV), *Poison* (1958, TV), *Vertigo* (1958), *Banquo's Chair* (1959, TV), *Arthur* (1959, TV), *The Crystal Trench* (1959, TV), *North by Northwest* (1959), *Incident at a Corner* (1960, TV), *Mrs Bixby and the Colonel's Coat* (1960, TV), *Psycho* (1960), *The Horseplayer* (1961, TV), *Bang! You're Dead* (1961, TV), *The Alfred Hitchcock Hour* (1962–1965), *I Saw the Whole Thing* (1962, TV), *The Birds* (1963), *Marnie* (1964), *Dark Intruder* (1965), *Torn Curtain* (1966), *Topaz* (1969), *Frenzy* (1972), *Family Plot* (1976)

HITCHCOCK, ALMA see Reville, Alma

HITCHCOCK, PATRICIA (PAT) (1928–) British-born actress. Given that her father was one of the world's most successful directors, Patricia could very well have exploited this to her advantage, yet she made only three films with her father, appearing in comedy cameo roles in *Stage Fright* (1950), as RADA student Chubby Bannister, *Strangers on a Train* (1951), in which she played the delightfully tactless Barbara Morton, and *Psycho* (1960), in which she appeared as Caroline, a mousy secretary. None of the roles were glamorous; indeed, all three are grotesques to a certain degree.

Born during the making of *The Farmer's Wife*, Patricia appeared in various amateur stage productions before making her professional debut in the John Van Druten play *Solitaire*, which had a three-week Broadway run in 1941. A second Broadway play, *Violet* by Whitfield Cook, followed in 1945, but again ran just three weeks. The burgeoning actress consequently decided to study acting seriously, and with her parents' consent moved to England to study drama at RADA in 1946. A third three-week Broadway run in *The High Ground* happened in 1951. However, following her 1952 marriage to businessman Joseph E O'Connell Jr, with whom she went on to have three daughters, she only periodically returned to acting, among her appearances being seven episodes of her father's television series *Alfred Hitchcock Presents*. Since her father's death, she has contributed to various documentaries about his career, among them the BBC's acclaimed two-parter *Reputations: Hitchcock* (1999) and Carlton's *Legends: Alfred Hitchcock* (2001), in which she revealed of her father's working methods: 'If he found a story, he'd take it back to my mother and ask if she thought it'd make a good picture, and if she said no, he didn't even touch it.' **Hitchography:** *Stage Fright* (1950), *Strangers on a Train* (1951), *Into Thin Air* (1955, TV), *The Older Sister* (1956, TV), *The Belfry* (1956, TV), *Silent Witness* (1957, TV), *The Morning of the Bride* (1959, TV), *The Cuckoo Clock* (1960, TV), *The Schartz-Metterlume Method* (1960, TV), *Psycho* (1960)

HODGES, HORACE (1865–1951) British character actor. Best remembered for his role as Sam Bishop, the washed up music hall star in the Gracie Fields vehicle *The Show Goes On* (1937), Hodges can also be spotted in *Escape* (1930) and *London Melody* (1937). In 1939 he was cast in the reasonably substantial role of Chadwick, butler to Sir Humphrey Pengallan (Charles Laughton), in Hitchcock's *Jamaica Inn*, a role in which he managed to invest some welcome humour. **Hitchography:** *Jamaica Inn* (1939)

HODGSON, LEYLAND American bit-part actor. Documented credits for Hodgson are few, but he can be spotted as the chauffeur during the climactic scenes of Hitchcock's *Rebecca* (1940), as well as in *Enter Arsene Lupin* (1944) and *Bedlam* (1946). **Hitchography:** *Rebecca* (1940)

HODIAK, JOHN (1914–1955) American actor. The career of Hodiak was tragically cut short at the age of 41 by a heart attack. A former stock clerk, he began performing on radio in the late 1930s, and went on to make his film debut in 1943 in *A Stranger in Town*. His subsequent films included *Sunday Dinner for a Soldier* (1944), *A Bell for Adano* (1945) and *Ambush at Tomahawk Gap* (1953), although his best work was in Hitchcock's *Lifeboat* (1944) as the rough and ready John Kovac, whose body is covered

with the tattooed initials of all his former girlfriends. He was married to actress Anne Baxter (1923–1985) between 1946 and 1953. She went on to star in Hitchcock's *I Confess* (1953). **Hitchography:** *Lifeboat* (1944)

HOFFMAN, BUD American editor. Following the death of his longtime editor George Tomasini, Hitchcock turned to Hoffman to cut his Cold War thriller *Torn Curtain* (1966), but it was the only time the two collaborated. **Hitchography:** *Torn Curtain* (1966)

HOMAGES The Hitchcock style has long been imitated, among the early examples being *Phantom Lady* (1944), a murder drama directed by Robert Siodmak and produced by Joan Harrison (the latter of whom had penned a handful of screenplays for Hitchcock in the early 1940s and would go on to produce his television series *Alfred Hitchcock Presents*). Another Siodmak film, *The Suspect* (1944), about a hen-pecked husband who murders his wife, also has a Hitchcockian air to it, as did the Harrison-scripted and produced *Dark Waters* (1944), a lady-in-peril thriller with a Louisiana swamp setting. The same could be said of several of the films of Roy William Neill; originally slated to direct *The Lady Vanishes* (1938), Neill went on to helm the majority of the episodes in Universal's celebrated Sherlock Holmes series, among them *The Pearl of Death* (1944), *The Scarlet Claw* (1944) and *Terror by Night* (1946), the latter a train-bound thriller very much in the manner of *The Lady Vanishes*. Meanwhile, the British comedy-thriller *My Learned Friend* (1944) followed the exploits of a shady lawyer attempting to track down a killer whose list of victims he is on. Produced by Michael Balcon and scripted by Angus MacPhail, both of whom had dealings with Hitchcock, the film climaxed with a thrill sequence on the face of Big Ben, which was later reworked into the 1978 remake of Hitchcock's *The 39 Steps*.

In the 1950s, it was *Les Diaboliques* (1954), the work of French director Henri-Georges Clouzot, which drew comparisons with Hitchcock. Indeed, Hitchcock had hoped to film the story himself, but he was beaten to the rights by Clouzot. Perhaps the most obvious of the early homages to Hitchcock came in 1961, when low budget producer-director William Castle exploited the success of *Psycho* (1960) by making his own transvestite shocker *Homicidal*, the story of a killer blonde and a strange young man who are never seen in the same room together! The film came complete with a 'fright break' gimmick and an opening murder – a vicious stabbing – that probably wouldn't have got past the censor prior to *Psycho*. *Psycho* also inspired a number of 'mini Hitchcocks' from British horror studio Hammer, among them *Taste of Fear* (1961), *Maniac* (1963), *Paranoiac* (1963), *Nightmare* (1964), *Hysteria* (1965) and *Crescendo* (1969). One should also perhaps mention Michael Powell's *Peeping Tom* (1959), in which a serial killer murders women while photographing their reactions, though it should be noted that this film appeared before *Psycho*, but proved equally controversial. Yet whereas *Psycho* was a major commercial success for

Is he a she or is she a he? Jean Arless serves up the soup du jour in William Castle's Psycho clone Homicidal *(1961).*

Hitchcock, *Peeping Tom* all but ruined Powell's career.

The 1960s also saw Hitchcock's glossy spy films pastiched by director Stanley Donen in *Charade* (1963), which starred Cary Grant, and *Arabesque* (1966), which starred Gregory Peck. Other spy pastiches included *The Prize* (1963), scripted by Ernest Lehman, *Blindfold* (1965) and *Mirage* (1965), the latter again starring Gregory Peck. Meanwhile, several more homages from France appeared, notably Francois Truffaut's *The Bride Wore Black* (1967), a revenge thriller with a Bernard Herrmann score, and Claude Chabrol's *Le Boucher* (1969), in which a young butcher goes on a killing spree in a small French village. Across the channel in England, the Boulting brothers made *Twisted Nerve* (1968), a controversial thriller about a young man who pretends to be retarded so as to get away with killing his hated father. Advertised with the strap line 'Enough to make even Hitchcock jump!' the film had a Bernard Herrmann score and featured Barry Foster and Billie Whitelaw, who would go on to star in Hitchcock's *Frenzy* (1972). Meanwhile, in Italy, director Dario Argento made *The Bird with the Crystal Plumage* (1969), the first of several visually flamboyant Hitchcockian thrillers that would go on to earn him the nickname of the Italian Hitchcock, among them *Cat O'Nine Tails*

(1971), *Four Flies on Grey Velvet* (1971), *Tenebrae* (1982) and *Sleepless* (2001).

In the 1970s, the floodgates truly opened, kicking off with *Endless Night* (1971); ostensibly an adaptation of an Agatha Christie novel about an American heiress who is frightened to death, the film was given a Hitchcockian air thanks to its Bernard Herrmann score and a couple of visual flourishes by writer-director Sidney Gilliat, who had of course co-written the screenplay for Hitchcock's *The Lady Vanishes* back in 1938. Then there was *The Night Digger* (1971); also known as *The Road Builder*, it told the story of a disturbed young man who commits a series of sex murders. Written by Roald Dahl (many of whose short stories had featured in *Alfred Hitchcock Presents*), the film again had a Bernard Herrmann score.

Indeed, a Herrmann score was almost a pre-requisite when doing a Hitchcock homage. At the suggestion of his editor Paul Hirsch, director Brian de Palma was persuaded to use the composer for his 1973 thriller *Sisters*, about a disturbed young woman who turns killer after being separated from her Siamese twin sister. The film readily borrowed from both *Psycho* and *Rear Window*, yet added a few twists of its own, plus a few visual flourishes that the Master himself would have been proud of (although he may have drawn the line at the gore). De Palma returned to Hitchcock territory with *Obsession* (1976), a loose refashioning of *Vertigo*, this time involving a widower who meets the double of his dead wife (who turns out to be his long lost daughter, who had been kidnapped as a child). As with *Sisters*, the score was by Bernard Herrmann. Sadly, Herrmann died before De Palma could mount his next Hitchcock homage. This was the masterful *Dressed to Kill* (1980), which drew heavily on the plot of *Psycho*, even down to having its leading lady, Angie Dickinson, murdered a third of the way through the movie by Michael Caine's transvestite psychiatrist Dr Elliott. De Palma has mined Hitchcock territory several times since, most notably with *Blow Out* (1981), *Body Double* (1984), *Raising Cain* (1992) and *Snake Eyes* (1998), although never quite with the same impact as *Dressed to Kill*, whose brutal murder scenes came in for some critical flak from feminist groups at the time of its release.

De Palma isn't the only director to venture into Hitchcock territory, though. Arthur Hiller had a stab at it with *Silver Streak* (1976), a train-bound comedy-thriller with echoes of *The Lady Vanishes* and *North by Northwest*. Jonathan Demme had a go too with *The Last Embrace* (1979), in which an investigator finds himself the subject of several assassination attempts. With its thrilling climax at Niagara Falls, the film also boasted a fine Miklos Rozsa score. The 1970s also saw a number of nature shockers inspired by *The Birds*. These ranged from *Jaws* (1975) to *Grizzly* (1976) to *Long Weekend* (1977) to *The Beasts Are on the Streets* (1978, TV) to *Prophecy* (1979).

The 1970s also produced perhaps the best-known Hitchcock parody, Mel Brooks' *High Anxiety* (1977), which includes take-offs of *Spellbound*, *Vertigo*, *North by Northwest*, *Psycho* and *The Birds* among others. By no means subtle, and far from consistently funny, the film nevertheless has a few cherishable moments (for example, instead of being attacked by birds, Brooks' Richard H Thorndyke is shat upon by them). However, it was incidents from Hitchcock's films rather than his cinematic style that were being sent up here, hence perhaps the film's overall failure (that said, John Morris' Herrmannesque score, complete with Moog effects, has its moments).

Meanwhile, the advent of the stalk-and-slash killer thriller in the seventies saw the shower scene in *Psycho* parodied and plundered in such films as *He Knows You're Alone* (1980), *Dressed to Kill* (1980), *Friday the 13th Part 2* (1981), *Blow Out* (1981) and *F/X 2: The Deadly Art of Illusion* (1991).

Since then Hitchcock homages have been fewer on the ground, among them *Still of the Night* (1982), a subdued but fairly skilful thriller by Robert Benton about a psychiatrist who tracks down a killer at an auction house. Meanwhile, *Henry: Portrait of a Serial Killer* (1990) and *The Silence of the Lambs* (1991) both entered *Psycho* territory to gruesome effect, as had the earlier *Texas Chainsaw Massacre* (1974) and *Eaten Alive* (1976) and the later *Ed Gein* (1999), while, *Le Confessional* (1995), an engaging mystery, chose as its setting Quebec during the filming of Hitchcock's *I Confess* (with Ron Burrage popping up as the Master). One also shouldn't forget the playful Australian thriller, *Road Games* (1981). Helmed by Richard Franklin, who had encountered Hitchcock while studying at the University of Southern California in 1967, it starred Stacy Keach as a trucker who tracks down a serial killer on the back roads of Oz. Stylishly made, the film also features a supporting role by Jamie Lee Curtis, (daughter Of *Psycho* star Janet Leigh), who plays a hitchhiker nicknamed Hitch. Finally, the supernatural shocker *What Lies Beneath* (2000) started out as a fairly straight *Rear Window* pastiche, while *Harry, He's Here to Help* (2000) has seen the psychological thriller taken to new levels. Add to these the many remakes of Hitchcock's own films, and one can see that his influence is both wide-ranging and far-reaching.

HOMOLKA, OSCAR (1898–1978) Austrian-born actor. On stage from 1918 and in films from 1926 with *Das Abenteuer eines Zehnmarkscheines*, Homolka went on to become typecast in both Britain and Hollywood as German spies and Russian generals during the Cold War era, most memorably in two Harry Palmer films: *Funeral in Berlin* (1966) and *Billion Dollar Brain* (1967), in which he played Colonel Stok. However, in his younger years he took on a number of important leading roles, key among them that of the saboteur Carl Verloc in Hitchcock's *Sabotage* (1936). Wrote Graham Greene of Homolka's performance, 'Mr Oscar Homolka, a slow, kindly, desperate Mr Verloc... raise[s] the melodrama at times to the tragic level.' Homolka's other films include *Rhodes of Africa* (1936), *Mission to Moscow* (1943), *War and Peace* (1956), *Song of Norway* (1970) and *The Tamarind Seed* (1974). He also appeared in three episodes of *Alfred*

Hitchcock Presents. He was married to the actress Joan Tetzel (1924–1977) from 1949 until her death. She appeared in a supporting role in Hitchcock's *The Paradine Case* (1947). **Hitchography:** *Sabotage* (1936), *Reward to Finder* (1957, TV), *The Ikon Elijah* (1960, TV), *The Hero* (1960, TV)

HORNING, WILLIAM A American art director. An Oscar winner for his work on both *Gigi* (1958) and *Ben-Hur* (1959), Horning spent much of his career at MGM, where he also worked on Hitchcock's *North by Northwest* (1959), designing the film with Robert Boyle and Merrill Pye. **Hitchography:** *North by Northwest* (1959)

HULBERT, CLAUDE (1900–1963) British character comedian and brother of comedy star Jack Hulbert. Claude Hulbert made his film debut in a minor role in Hitchcock's *Champagne* (1928), prior to which he'd had stage experience in revue. An expert at 'silly-ass' types, his other credits included *Thark* (1932), *The Ghost of St Michael's* (1941), *My Learned Friend* (1944) and *Not a Hope in Hell* (1960). He was long married to the actress Enid Trevor. **Hitchography:** *Champagne* (1928)

HULBERT, JACK (1892–1978) British musical comedy actor. This jaunty star of stage and screen, described by critic James Agate as being 'all silver lining and no cloud', made his screen debut in the musical extravaganza *Elstree Calling* (1930), segments of which he also directed, along with Hitchcock, Adrian Brunel, Paul Murray and Andre Charlot. Long married to comedy actress Cicely Courtneidge (1993–1980), with whom he often appeared, his other films include *Jack's the Boy* (1932), *Jack Ahoy!* (1934), *Jack of All Trades* (1934), *Under Your Hat* (1940) and *Not Now, Darling* (1973). His brother Claude (1900–1963) appeared in Hitchcock's *Champagne* (1928). **Hitchography:** *Elstree Calling* (1930)

HULL, HENRY (1890–1977) American actor. Hull began his career on stage in 1911, although experience as a prospector and a mining engineer followed. However, after his film debut in 1916 with *The Man Who Came Back*, he became a popular leading man on both stage and screen. His many subsequent films include *Little Women* (1919), *The Man Who Came Back* (1933), *Werewolf of London* (1935), *Babes in Arms* (1939) and *High Sierra* (1940). In 1944 he portrayed millionaire factory owner Charles D Rittenhouse in Hitchcock's *Lifeboat* (*Variety* described his performance as 'excellent'). His other films include *Objective Burma!* (1945), *Portrait of Jennie* (1948), *The Chase* (1966) and *A Covenant with Death* (1966), following which he retired from the big screen. **Hitchography:** *Lifeboat* (1944)

HUME, BENITA (1906–1967) British actress. On screen from 1924 with *The Happy Ending*, Hume made brief appearances in the likes of *They Wouldn't Believe Me* (1925) and *Second to None* (1926) before being spotted by Hitchcock for a cameo role as an eavesdropping telephonist in *Easy Virtue* (1927). Stardom beckoned, and over the next few years she appeared in such successes as *The Constant Nymph* (1928), *Balaclava* (1928) and *The Clue of the New Pin* (1929). In 1932, she returned to the Hitchcock fold for *Lord Camber's Ladies*, which Hitch produced and Benn W Levy directed, but it wasn't a success. In 1935 she moved to Hollywood, where she appeared in *The Divine Spark* (1935), *Tarzan Escapes* (1936) and *Peck's Bad Boy with the Circus* (1938), after which she retired to marry screen legend Ronald Colman (1891–1958). When he died, she married actor George Sanders (1906–1972), to whom she remained married between 1959 and 1967; he had starred in Hitchcock's *Rebecca* (1940) and *Foreign Correspondent* (1940). **Hitchography:** *Easy Virtue* (1927), *Lord Camber's Ladies* (1932)

HUNT, GRADY American costume designer and supervisor. Long at Universal, Hunt supervised the wardrobe for hundreds of the studio's TV movies and series in the 1970s, from *Columbo* to *Mystery Movie*. He also assisted Edith Head on Hitchcock's *Torn Curtain* (1966). **Hitchography:** *Torn Curtain* (1966)

HUNT, MARTITA (1900–1969) British character actress. This haughty-looking actress, born in the Argentine, is best remembered for playing Miss Havisham in David Lean's masterful version of *Great Expectations* (1946). Busy on stage throughout her career, she made her film debut in 1920 with *Rank Outsider*, which she followed with the likes of *Service for Ladies* (1932), *Tudor Rose* (1936) and an un-credited appearance in Hitchcock's *Sabotage* (1936), in which she was cast against type as the Professor's slatternly daughter. Later in her career, her grande dame arts perfected, she made welcome appearances in *The Prince and the Showgirl* (1957), *The Brides of Dracula* (1960), *The Unsinkable Molly Brown* (1964) and the Hitchcockian *Bunny Lake is Missing* (1965). **Hitchography:** *Sabotage* (1936)

HUNTER, EVAN (1926– , real name Salvadore Lombino) American novelist. Evan Hunter has had several of his books adapted for the screen, including *The Blackboard Jungle* and *Mister Buddwing*. He turned to screenwriting himself with *Strangers When We Meet* (1960), which led to *The Young Savages* (1961) and Hitchcock's *The Birds* (1963), for which he was paid $5000 a month for the seven month period it took to write. It was Hunter's idea to begin the film as a light romantic comedy. Commented the writer: 'I take full credit – or blame, as the case may be – for what I suggested to Hitch... a screwball comedy that gradually turns to stark terror. The idea appealed to him at once. I think he saw in it a challenge equal to the one the birds themselves presented. I think, too, that he saw in it a way of combining his vaunted sense of humour with the calculated horror he had used to great effect in *Psycho*.' [20]

Following the success of *The Birds*, Hitchcock asked Hunter to pen the script for *Marnie* (1964), but despite working on the project for a lengthy period, the director

was unhappy with the results, and so had him replaced with Jay Presson Allen. Recalled Hunter of the scene in which Sean Connery's Mark Rutland takes Tippi Hedren's Marnie Edgar by force on their honeymoon: '[Hitchcock] said, "Evan, when he sticks it in, I want that camera right on her face!" And I thought, "Oh, boy! We've got trouble here."' [21] Indeed, not long after, Hunter left the project. Recalled the writer, 'Many years later, when I told Jay Presson Allen how much his description of that scene had bothered me, she said, "You just got bothered by the scene that was his reason for making the movie. You just wrote your own ticket back to New York."' [22]

Hunter's other screen credits include *Walk Proud* (1979), while his television work includes such series as *87th Precinct* (1961), based on his crime novels written under the pseudonym Ed McBain, and *The Chisholms* (1978). He also had two of his short stories, *Number Twenty-Two* and *Vicious Circle*, adapted for *Alfred Hitchcock Presents*, and scripted another episode, *Appointment at Eleven* (1959, TV). He wrote about his experiences with Hitchcock in his 1997 book *Me and Hitch*. **Hitchography:** *Number Twenty-Two* (1957, TV), *Vicious Circle* (1957, TV), *Appointment at Eleven* (1959, TV), *The Birds* (1963)

HUNTER, IAN (1900–1975) South African–born actor. Ian Hunter made his stage debut in Britain in 1919 following military service in World War I. He broke into films in 1924 with *Not for Sale*, which he followed with *Confessions* (1925) and three successive Hitchcock silents in which he played leading roles: Archie in *Downhill* (1927), Bob Corby in *The Ring* (1927) and a court counsel in *Easy Virtue* (1927). His other films include *The Sign of Four* (1932), in which he played Dr Watson to Arthur Wontner's Sherlock Holmes, *Dr Jekyll and Mr Hyde* (1941) and *Northwest Frontier* (1959). **Hitchography:** *Downhill* (1927), *The Ring* (1927), *Easy Virtue* (1928)

HURLEY, JOSEPH (* –1982) American art director. Hurley's screen credits include Hitchcock's *Psycho* (1960), which he designed with Robert Clatworthy, earning an Oscar nomination in the process. He also acted as the production illustrator on *Altered States* (1980) and *Something Wicked This Way Comes* (1983). **Hitchography:** *Psycho* (1960)

HUTCHINSON, JOSEPHINE (1904–1998) American actress. In films from 1917 with *The Little Princess* following experience on stage as a dancer, Hutchinson returned to the theatre for another 17 years before making her adult debut in *Happiness Ahead* (1934). Though not quite a front rank star, she went on to become a popular leading actress in such films as *The Story of Louis Pasteur* (1936), *Son of Frankenstein* (1939) and *Tom Brown's School Days* (1940). In later years, she turned to character roles, appearing in Hitchcock's *North by Northwest* (1959), *Nevada Smith* (1966) and *The Homecoming* (1971, TV). **Hitchography:** *North by Northwest* (1959)

Montgomery Clift's Father Michael Logan is tried for a murder he did not commit in Hitchcock's I Confess *(1953).*

I

I Confess
(USA, 1953, 95m, bw) ★★

CREDITS

Production company:	Warner Bros.
Producer:	Alfred Hitchcock
Director:	Alfred Hitchcock
Screenplay:	George Tabori, William Archibald, based on *Nos Deux Consciences* by Paul Anthelme
Cinematographer:	Robert Burks
Music:	Dimitri Tiomkin
Music director:	Ray Heindorf
Editor:	Rudi Fehr
Art director:	Edward S Haworth
Costumes:	Orry-Kelly
Sound:	Oliver S Garretson

CAST

Montgomery Clift (Father Michael Logan), Anne Baxter (Ruth Grandfort), Karl Malden (Inspector Larrue), O E Hasse (Otto Keller), Dolly Haas (Alma Keller), Brian Aherne (Willy Robertson), Roger Dann (Pierre Grandfort), Ovila Legare (Villette), Charles Andre (Father Millars), Judson Pratt (Murphy), Gilles Pelletier (Father Benoit)

Following the commercial and critical success of *Strangers on a Train* (1951), which did much to restore his then-waning career, *I Confess* marked something of backwards step for Hitchcock. Even at the time of its release, its story must have seemed fairly passé: a young priest, Father Michael Logan (Montgomery Clift), hears the German caretaker of his church, Otto Heller (O E Hasse), confess to a murder, only to find *himself* accused of the crime, but unable to defend himself owing to the sanctity of the confessional ('If you knew what he knew, what would *you* do?' begged the film's poster).

For anyone but a devout Catholic, this concept will seem as illogical as it is ludicrous. Yet the ethical contradictions of its central notion aside (which no doubt appealed to Hitchcock because of his own strict devotion to Catholicism), *I Confess* is a thoroughly professional piece of work with many incidental pleasures for those willing to ignore the frustrations that its gimmicky plot engenders. That said, even Hitchcock had to admit that the film fell foul of its own conceit: 'That's the trouble with *I Confess*. We Catholics *know* that a priest cannot disclose the secret of the confessional, but the Protestants, the atheists, and the agnostics all say, "Ridiculous! *No* man would remain silent and sacrifice his life for such a thing."' [1]

Based on the 1902 play *Nos Deux Consciences* by Paul Athelme (real name Paul Bourde), the film was shot almost entirely on location in Quebec, with Robert

Burks's chiaroscuro photography and Hitchcock's eye-catching use of Quebec City's over-powering medieval-style architecture adding immeasurably to its brooding atmosphere (though the ads tried to play things differently, cheerfully stating that the movie had been 'Filmed in Canada's colourful Quebec by Warner Bros.').

Given the straightforward nature of its focal story, Hitchcock and his writers worked hard to disguise its basic simplicity, devising various subplots to distract attention. Consequently, it transpires that Heller had been disturbed while robbing a local lawyer, but as he'd been disguised in a cassock, this had led two schoolgirls who'd witnessed his departure from the scene of the crime to assume that the killer had been a priest, a conclusion with which the police investigator, Inspector Larrue (Karl Malden), seems to agree, especially given that Father Michael is either unable or unwilling to account for his whereabouts when the crime took place.

It further transpires (somewhat improbably) that Father Michael and his friend Ruth Grandfort (Anne Baxter) were being blackmailed by the murder victim, a lawyer named Villette, who knew of their previous romantic relationship and had threatened to tell Ruth's husband that the couple had briefly resumed their affair following Michael's return from the war just prior to his taking up orders, by which time Ruth had wed, thus damning the priest further by actually giving him a motive for the murder (it also gave Hitchcock the chance to stage a flashback featuring Michael and Ruth during their brief re-union, complete with a romantic clinch in a gazebo during a violent rainstorm, which at least offers some welcome respite from the general doom and gloom).

At the subsequent trial, all fingers seem to point to Michael (cue several shots of the priest juxtaposed against various crucifixes to suggest his impending martyrdom), yet the jury acquits him owing to a lack of concrete evidence (much to the judge's annoyance). A hostile crowd awaits Father Michael outside, yet Keller's wife Alma (Dolly Haas), who has seen her husband lie on the witness stand to cover his tracks, can no longer keep silent and runs to the priest's aid, declaring that she knows he is innocent, which prompts her husband to shoot her, conveniently sealing his own fate following a chase to a nearby theatre where he inadvertently gives the game away within earshot of the police ('So the priest talked!'), after which he is gunned down, asking Father Michael to give him the last rites as he lies dying.

The performances in *I Confess* are mostly top notch: O E Hasse is the perfect Hitchcock villain (cold-eyed, ruthless, *foreign*), Montgomery Clift offers quiet dignity as Father Michael, while Karl Malden's Inspector Larrue investigates the case with a convincing air of heartless efficiency ('With a murder, one has to jump from one detail to another. Maybe I jumped too suddenly for you?' he asks Father Michael accusingly during one interrogation sequence). The real star, though, is the Hitchcock, who subtly uses his close-ups to heighten tension and convey the feelings of his characters – particularly guilt. For example, note the breakfast scene in which Keller's wife serves coffee to Father Michael and his fellow priests on the morning following the murder; focusing on the back of Father Michael's head, Hitchcock has the maid pass him by several times, the slightly changing angle of the priest's head suggesting that he senses she is there, and that he knows that *she* knows that her husband committed the murder. Indeed, the guilt is plain to see on her face.

Hitchcock also makes excellent use of the locations in Quebec City, particularly during the opening title sequence which features examples of the city's austere architecture. Elsewhere in the film, Hitch further exploits the city backdrop by setting one liaison between Father Michael and Ruth on a ferry. Subtle touches also abound, among them a shot of Ruth descending a spiral staircase during the flashback sequence; seen from Michael's point of view, it is filmed with a gauzed lens, which gives the shot a fairytale quality, thus accentuating Michael's love for her.

Despite its various qualities, among them a driving score by Dimitri Tiomkin, *I Confess* was not a success and remains to be fully re-discovered. 'An interesting plot premise holds out considerable promise for this Alfred Hitchcock production, but *I Confess* is short of the suspense one would expect,' summed up *Variety*, though the *Monthly Film Bulletin* was more gracious, commenting, 'Whatever its shortcomings, it has the professional concentration of effect, the narrative control, of a storyteller who can still make most of his rivals look like amateurs.'

Hitchcock cameo Note that Hitchcock can be spotted crossing the top of a flight of imposing stone steps during the opening sequence.

IRENE (1901–1962, real name Irene Lenz-Gibbons) American costume designer. One of Hollywood's top costume designers and couturiers, Irene was contracted to MGM in 1942 and worked on such films as *Cabin in the Sky* (1943), *Bathing Beauty* (1944), *Weekend at the Waldorf* (1945), *The Postman Always Rings Twice* (1946) and *State of the Union* (1948). She began her film career as an extra and, following training at the Wolf School of Design, turned to costume design, among her early films being *The Animal Kingdom* (1932) and *Flying Down to Rio* (1933). In 1940, she did some un-credited work on Hitchcock's *Rebecca*, her main contribution being Joan Fontaine's voluminous ball gown. She also designed the costumes for Hitchcock's comedy *Mr and Mrs Smith* (1941), providing several sleek, 1940s-style outfits for Carole Lombard. Irene's other films include *B F's Daughter* (1948) and *Midnight Lace* (1960), both of which earned her Oscar nominations. She committed suicide in 1962 following years of alcoholism. **Hitchography:** *Rebecca* (1940), *Mr and Mrs Smith* (1941)

IRRGARTEN DER LEIDENSCHAFT see *The Pleasure Garden*

IRVINE, ROBIN British actor. Irvine appeared in a couple of Hitchcock's early silent films, notably *Downhill* (1927), in which he played Tim Wakely, the cad who allows his best school chum (played by Ivor Novello) to take the rap for getting a waitress pregnant. He also briefly popped up in the rather lighter *Easy Virtue* (1927) as a barrister. His other films include *The Ship of Lost Men* (1929), following which his film career wound down. **Hitchography:** *Downhill* (1927), *Easy Virtue* (1927)

ISLINGTON STUDIOS Following experience as a technical clerk at W T Henley Telegraph Company, where his skills as a graphic artist were put to use in the advertising department, Hitchcock applied for his first job in the film industry, working as a designer of inter-titles at Islington Studios, which was the London home of the American company Famous Players-Lasky (which eventually became Paramount, for which Hitchcock would later direct some of his best films). Work started on the studio, a former railway power station, in 1919, and its first production, released in 1920, was *The Great Day*, soon after followed by *The Call Of Youth*, both of which had inter-titles designed by Hitchcock.

Hitchcock remained at the studios for almost three years, designing the inter-titles for *Appearances* (1921), *Beside the Bonnie Brier Bush* (1921), *Dangerous Lies* (1921), *The Mystery Road* (1921), *The Princess of New York* (1921), *The Man from Home* (1922), *Perpetua* (1922), *The Spanish Jade* (1922), *Three Live Ghosts* (1922) and *Tell Your Children* (1922), the latter made independently for International Artists by Donald Crisp, one of Lasky's regular directors. Sadly, it appears that none of these films have survived. Hitchcock also made his first forays into direction at Islington Studios in 1922 with a two-reeler titled *Number 13* (aka *Mrs Peabody*), although the film was abandoned in mid-shoot. Hitchcock fared slightly better with his next assignment, *Always Tell Your Wife* (also 1922), a one-reel comedy starring Seymour Hicks, which he took over following the departure of the original director, Hugh Croise. Unfortunately, Hitchcock didn't receive a credit for the film.

IWERKS, UB (1900–1971) American animator and effects technician. Iwerks had a long association with Walt Disney, whom he first met in 1919. Their early collaborations included the *Alice* series (1923–1926), which blended animation with live action footage. Iwerks also animated the first Mickey Mouse cartoon *Plane Crazy* in 1928. He went independent in 1930 to work on the *Flip the Frog* series (1931–1933) as well as many other cartoon shorts, but returned to Disney in 1940, where he supervised the effects for such films as *The Reluctant Dragon* (1941), *Song of the South* (1946), *20,000 Leagues Under the Sea* (1954) and *The Parent Trap* (1961). He won Academy Awards in 1959 and 1965 for his technical achievements, which included advancing the capabilities of the travelling matte. He also earned an Oscar nomination for his work on Hitchcock's *The Birds* (1963), which included much matte and blue screen work. **Hitchography:** *The Birds* (1963)

J

JADE, CLAUDE French actress. This petite actress appeared in a handful of films in the 1960s and 1970s, among them *Stolen Kisses* (1968), *Uncle Benjamin* (1969), *Bed and Board* (1970) and *Love on the Run* (1969). She also appeared in Hitchcock's *Topaz* (1969) as the wife of journalist and sketch artist Michele Picard (Michel Subor).
Hitchography: *Topaz* (1969)

Jamaica Inn
(GB, 1939, 108m, bw film) ★

CREDITS
Production company: Mayflower Pictures
Producer: Erich Pommer
(and Charles Laughton)

Director: Alfred Hitchcock
Screenplay: Sidney Gilliat, Joan Harrison, J B Priestly, based on the novel by Daphne du Maurier
Cinematographers: Bernard Knowles, Harry Stradling
Music: Eric Fenby
Music director: Frederick Lewis
Editor: Robert Hamer
Art director: Tom Morahan
Costumes: Molly McArthur
Special effects: Harry Watts
Sound: Jack Rogerson
Camera operator: Jack Hildyard
Continuity: Alma Reville

Hitchcock and his cast pause between filming scenes for Jamaica Inn *(1939) to paste labels on collection tins for Lord Baldwin's Fund for Refugees. Taking part are (from left to right) Robert Newton, Marie Ney, Charles Laughton and Maureen O'Hara.*

CAST

Charles Laughton (Sir Humphrey Pengallan), Leslie Banks (Joss Merlyn), Maureen O'Hara (Mary Yelland), Robert Newton (Jim Trehearne), Marie Ney (Patience Merlyn), Emlyn Williams (Harr), Wylie Watson (Salvation), Frederick Piper (Broker), Hay Petrie (Sir Humphrey's groom), Herbert Lomas (Tenant), Clare Greet (Tenant), William Devlin (Tenant), Jeanne de Casalis (Guest), Basil Radford (Guest), Mabel Terry-Lewis (Guest), George Curzon (Guest), A Bromley Davenport (Guest), Edwin Greenwood (Dandy), Morland Graham (Lawyer), Mervyn Johns (Thomas), Stephen Haggard (Boy), Horace Hodges (Chadwick)

Video availability: Carlton

Jamaica Inn has long been regarded as one of Hitchcock's lesser efforts. However, though certainly dated, it doesn't entirely warrant its reputation. When Hitchcock made the film, he already knew he was going to America to work for producer David O Selznick. His first Hollywood film was to be *Titanic*, followed by an adaptation of Daphne du Maurier's *Rebecca*. When *Titanic* failed to materialize, Hitchcock found himself with time on his hands before his departure to America to work on *Rebecca*. 'Since the contract with Selznick wasn't due to start until April, 1939, I had time to make another British film, and that was *Jamaica Inn*,' [1] recalled the director.

Like the impending adaptation of *Rebecca*, *Jamaica Inn* was based on a novel (first published in 1936) by Daphne du Maurier, the daughter of stage star Gerald du Maurier, whom Hitchcock knew from *Lord Camber's Ladies*, which he'd produced back in 1932. By now, Hitchcock's contract with Gainsborough/Gaumont-British had run its course, and *Jamaica Inn* was to be produced by a new company called Mayflower Pictures, which was run by Erich Pommer (who had produced *The Blackguard* in 1925, on which Hitchcock had worked as a screenwriter, art director and assistant director) and the actor Charles Laughton. *Jamaica Inn* was the company's third film following *Vessel of Wrath* (1938) and *St Martin's Lane* (1938). It would also prove to be its last.

Set in 1819 Cornwall, the film follows the adventures of Mary Yelland (Maureen O'Hara), a young Irish woman who is travelling by coach to live with her uncle Joss (Leslie Banks) and aunt Patience (Marie Ney) following the death of her mother. However, the coachman refuses to drop Mary off at the inn ('There's queer things goes on there'), and instead dumps her and her box of belongings further down the pike, not far from the home of Sir Humphrey Pengallan (Charles Laughton), the local justice, whom Mary calls upon for help. Leaving a dinner party with his cronies, Sir Humphrey rides over to Jamaica Inn with Mary, dropping her off at the door, where she is met by her swarthy looking uncle and her meek aunt.

Mary's not been at the inn long when she realizes that its reputation is justified, for her uncle is the ringleader of a gang of smugglers. Worse than that, they're wreckers, luring ships on to the rocks by extinguishing the warning lights on the cliffs. Help is seemingly at hand, though, for one of the gang, Jim Trehearne (Robert Newton), is an undercover naval officer. When the rest of the gang discover Trehearne's true identity, they attempt to hang him, but he is saved at the last moment by Mary, who cuts through the rope. Escaping with Trehearne, the couple head for Sir Humphrey's home to inform him of the smugglers' activities. However, Jim and Mary are in for a surprise, for it transpires that the true ringleader of the smugglers is none other than Sir Humphrey himself, who soon after attempts to leave the country with Mary, whom he's kidnapped. Things eventually come to a rousing close when the authorities catch up with Sir Humphrey on his departing packet steamer. In a bid to escape, Sir Humphrey climbs the rigging, from whence he takes a suicidal leap with the words, 'Make way for Pengallan!'

Writing about the film in *The Spectator*, Graham Greene commented, 'I was irresistibly reminded of an all-star charity matinee.' Indeed, the film is packed with faces familiar from Hitchcock's previous films, among them Leslie Banks, Wylie Watson, Frederick Piper, Clare Greet, Basil Radford and George Curzon, all presumably onboard for a last hurrah before their director's departure to America. Meanwhile, Charles Laughton, with his coiffed hair and amazing stick-on eyebrows (surely the most ludicrous ever sported in a movie) reminds one of the barnstorming actor Tod Slaughter, thanks to his deliciously hammy rantings and ravings. In fact Laughton's dialogue was specially penned for him by none other than J B Priestley, whom the star brought on to the project to beef up his part, which was originally a cleric in the novel, thus making somewhat inevitable comparisons with Russell Thorndyke's *Christopher Syn*, filmed two years previously as *Dr Syn*. The novelist Clemence Dane had also worked on an early, rejected draft of the script, which was subsequently re-worked by Sidney Gilliat (fresh from the success of *The Lady Vanishes*) and Hitchcock's secretary and future associate producer Joan Harrison.

Laughton's isn't the only full-blooded performance in the film. Leslie Banks and Robert Newton both give their all to the proceedings. Meanwhile, the actors playing the wreckers look suitably grizzled (even if their accents tends towards Cockney rather than Cornish), while Maureen O'Hara makes a most attractive heroine, facing more perils than Pauline (she even gets to say the hoary line, 'He's mad, I tell you, *mad*!'). O'Hara began her career as an actress at Dublin's Abbey Theatre, making her debut in *Juno and the Paycock*, which Hitchcock had filmed back in 1930. The credits for *Jamaica Inn* claim to be 'introducing' O'Hara to the screen, though in fact she had already appeared in two films: *My Irish Molly* (1938) and *Kicking the Moon Around* (1938).

Despite a few *longueurs* here and there, the film rattles along at a reasonable pace, though save for a couple of expertly staged wrecking sequences (which benefit enormously from Harry Watts' model effects), the

Hitchcockian touches are few and far between, best among them being Mary's attempt to save Jim from the noose, which she does by breaking away the plaster on her bedroom wall and reaching through the hole to the beam in the hall beyond it with a conveniently sharp supper knife. Sir Humphrey's suicidal leap from the shrouds meanwhile benefits from some dizzying high angle shots.

Unfortunately, the critics were less inclined to be complimentary about the film following the high water mark of *The Lady Vanishes*. The *New York Herald Tribune* pretty much summed up the general consensus, proclaiming the film to be 'singularly dull and uninspired'. Even Hitchcock conceded that '*Jamaica Inn* was an absurd thing to undertake,' [2], while Daphne du Maurier declared herself to be less than satisfied with the results, which must have made her fear the worse for the impending adaptation of *Rebecca*. These views not withstanding, *Jamaica Inn* nevertheless makes for surprisingly tolerable viewing 60-odd years on, and is just the thing to while away a rainy afternoon for those in the mood.

Jamaica Inn
(GB, 1983, 3x60m TV episodes, colour)

CREDITS
Production company: HTV
Producer: Peter Graham Scott
Director: Lawrence Gordon Clarke

CAST
Jane Seymour (Mary Yelland), Patrick McGoohan (Sir Humphrey Pengallan), John McEnery, Trevor Eve, Billie Whitelaw

Forty-four years after Hitchcock's version of *Jamaica Inn*, along came this tepid television adaptation of the Daphne du Maurier novel. At £2.5 million, the production was one of the most expensive of its time, but like the Hitchcock film, it failed to inspire audiences. Note that Billie Whitelaw appeared in Hitchcock's *Frenzy* (1972).

JARRE, MAURICE (1924–   ) French composer. Following training at the Paris Conservatoire de Musique, Jarre became an arranger and conductor for the Jean Louis Barrault Theatre Company. He began writing music for the concert platform and the theatre while serving as the music director for the prestigious Theatre National Populaire. He scored his first film, the short *Hotel des Invalides*, in 1952, which he followed with a second short, *Toute la Memoire du Monde*, in 1956. He began scoring features in 1959 with *La Tete Contres les Murs*, which led to *Les Yeux Sans Visage* (1959), *The Longest Day* (1962), *Cybele ou les Dimanches de Ville d'Avray* (1962) and *Lawrence of Arabia* (1962), which won him his first Oscar. *Lawrence of Arabia* marked the first time Jarre worked with director David Lean, and their collaboration went on to include *Doctor Zhivago* (1965), *Ryan's Daughter* (1970) and *A Passage to India* (1984), with Jarre earning further Oscars

for *Zhivago* and *India*. His many other films include *The Professionals* (1966), *The Year of Living Dangerously* (1983), *Witness* (1985), *Ghost* (1990) and *Sunshine* (1999).

In 1969, he was asked by Hitchcock to score his Cold War thriller *Topaz*, but as Jarre revealed, this was not the first time he'd been approached by the director. 'He'd once asked me to do the music for a film called *Torn Curtain*, because at that time he had a big fight with Bernard Herrmann and he was looking for a different composer. But I couldn't do *Torn Curtain* because I was still working on *The Professionals*. So the next film he did, which was *Topaz*, he asked for me a long time in advance, and I thought it would be great to work with Hitchcock. I met him and we ran the film and I said I would like to do it. So I wrote a few themes, but when I told him I wanted to play these themes for him he asked, "Why?" And I said, "Well, because it's your film and I just want to know if we're on the same wavelength." He said, "Well, I've asked you to do the music, I trust you completely, and you do what you want." Finally he did listen and he said he liked it.' [3] Indeed, Hitchcock gave Jarre a full set of camera equipment by way of thanking him when the film came out. **Hitchography:** *Topaz* (1969)

JEANS, ISABEL (1891–1985) British actress. Though she spent much of her career on stage, where she made her debut in 1909, Jeans made several forays into film during her lengthy career, including three films for Hitchcock, among them two silents, in which she played leading roles. The more notable of these was that of Larita Filton in *Easy Virtue* (1927), a role that saw her twice divorced and accused of having loose morals during the course of the action. Her early films included *The Profligate* (1917), *Tilly of Bloomsbury* (1921), *The Rat* (1925) and *The Triumph of the Rat* (1926). In the late 1930s she moved to Hollywood for a brief period, appearing in *Tovarich* (1938) and Hitchcock's *Suspicion* (1941) Her other films include *Great Day* (1945), *Gigi* (1958), *Heavens Above!* (1963) and *The Magic Christian* (1969). Between 1913 and 1918, Jeans was married to the actor Claude Rains (1889–1967), who starred in Hitchcock's *Notorious* (1946) as well as five episodes of the *Alfred Hitchcock Presents* television series. **Hitchography:** *Downhill* (1927), *Easy Virtue* (1928), *Suspicion* (1941)

JOHNS, MERVYN (1899–1992) Welsh-born actor. On stage from 1923 and in films from 1934 with *Lady in Danger*, Johns went on to appear in a number of supporting roles in such films as *The Tunnel* (1935), *Storm in a Teacup* (1937) and Hitchcock's *Jamaica Inn* (1939), in which he appears briefly as Thomas. In the 1940s he graduated to leading man status and went on to appear in such classics as *Halfway House* (1944), *Dead of Night* (1945), *Scrooge* (1950) and *Moby Dick* (1956). He made his last film, *Ingrid* (1989), at the age of 90. He was the father of actress Glynis Johns (1923–   ). **Hitchography:** *Jamaica Inn* (1939)

JOHNSON, J MCMILLAN American designer. Much associated with the films of producer David O Selznick, J McMillan Johnson worked in various capacities throughout his career: as a production illustrator on *Gone with the Wind* (1939), as a production designer on *Duel in the Sun* (1946) and as a visual effects artist on *Portrait of Jennie* (1948), which earned him an Academy Award. He was also the production designer for Hitchcock's *The Paradine Case* (1947), among his sets for the film being an exact replica of the number one court at The Old Bailey, constructed at a cost of $400,000. Working with Hal Pereira, he also designed *Rear Window* (1954) for Hitchcock, which is noted for its enormous courtyard set, which featured over 30 individual apartments. His association with the director concluded with *To Catch a Thief* (1955), which made excellent use of glamorous French Riviera locations, among them The Carlton Hotel in Cannes. Again working with Pereira, Johnson received an Academy Award nomination for the film. **Hitchography:** *The Paradine Case* (1947), *Rear Window* (1954), *To Catch a Thief* (1955)

JOHNSON, NOEL British supporting actor. Johnson appeared in Hitchcock's *Frenzy* (1972) as one of the two misogynistic city gents discussing the crimes of the necktie killer. His other films include *The Partner* (1963). **Hitchography:** *Frenzy* (1972)

JONES, BARRY (1893–1981) British character actor. On stage from the early 1920s, Barry Jones turned to films in 1932 with *Women Who Play*, which he soon after followed with Hitchcock's *Number Seventeen* (1932), in which he played the duplicitous criminal Doyle. However, his best film role was as Professor Willingdon in the Oscar-winning *Seven Days to Noon* (1950), in which he threatens to blow up London in a bid to halt the misappropriation of his work. Interestingly, he also played the role of Professor Logan in the 1959 remake of Hitchcock's *The 39 Steps* (Geoffrey Tearle played the role of Professor Jordan in the original). Jones' other films include *Madeleine* (1959), *Plymouth Adventure* (1952) and *Brigadoon* (1954). **Hitchography:** *Number Seventeen* (1932)

JONES, CAROLYN (1929–1983) American actress. Best known for playing Morticia Addams in the much-revived sit-com *The Addams Family* (1964–1966), this quirky-looking actress came to films in 1952 with *The Turning Point* following stage and radio experience (as a DJ). Her other film appearances include *House of Wax* (1953), *The Seven Year Itch* (1955), *Invasion of the Body Snatchers* (1956) and Hitchcock's *The Man Who Knew Too Much* (1956), in which she had a few brief scenes as socialite Cindy Fontaine. Her other film work includes *The Bachelor Party* (1957), which earned her a best supporting actress Oscar nomination, *How the West Was Won* (1962) and *Eaten Alive* (1976). **Hitchography:** *The Man Who Knew Too Much* (1956)

JONES, HANNAH British supporting actress. This busy actress, who often appeared as landladies and housekeepers, popped up in four of Hitchcock's early films, beginning with *Downhill* in 1927. Her other films include *Piccadilly* (1929). Sadly, little else is known about her life and career. **Hitchography:** *Downhill* (1927), *Blackmail* (1929), *Murder!* (1930), *Rich and Strange* (1932)

JONES, HENRY (1912–1999) American supporting actor. In films from 1943 with *This is the Army*, this supercilious-looking actor had a busy career on stage, in films and on television. On the big screen, he can be seen in such diverse productions as *The Bad Seed* (1956), Hitchcock's *Vertigo* (1958), in which he played the Coroner, *Butch Cassidy and the Sundance Kid* (1969), *Tom Sawyer* (1973), *Deathtrap* (1982) and *Arachnophobia* (1990), while on television he was a regular in such series as *Channing* (1963–1964), *Phyllis* (1975–1977) and *Falcon Crest* (1985–1986). He also appeared in four episodes of *Alfred Hitchcock Presents* and an episode of *The Alfred Hitchcock Hour*. **Hitchography:** *Nightmare in 4D* (1957, TV), *The West Warlock Time Capsule* (1957, TV), *Vertigo* (1958), *The Blessington Method* (1959, TV), *Profit Sharing Plan* (1962, TV), *The World's Oldest Motive* (1965, TV)

JONES, JENNIFER (1919– , real name Phyllis Isley) American actress. Jones came to films in 1939 with *New Fontier*, in which she appeared under her real name, as she did in her second film, the serial *Dick Tracy's G-Men* (1939). In vaudeville as a child, Jones went on to study at New York's American Academy of Dramatic Art, where she met her first husband, actor Robert Walker (1918–1951), whom she married in 1939. The two went to Hollywood together the same year, where Jones met *Gone With the Wind* producer David O Selznick (1902–1965), who changed her name to Jennifer Jones, signed her to a contract and starred her in *The Song of Bernadette* (1943), which won her a best actress Oscar. Jones divorced Walker in 1945, and went on to marry Selznick in 1949, whose films she continued to star in, among them *Since You Went Away* (1944), *Duel in the Sun* (1947) and *Portrait of Jennie* (1949). She also appeared in war bonds promotion short in 1943, which was directed by Hitchcock, who surprisingly never worked with her on a feature, given that both were contracted to Selznick during the 1940s.

Jones' other films include *Carrie* (1952), *Beat the Devil* (1954), *Love is a Many-Splendored Thing* (1952), *Tender is the Night* (1962) and *The Towering Inferno* (1974). Note that her first husband also graduated to featured roles and star parts in the likes of *The Clock* (1945) and *One Touch of Venus* (1948), but his career was blighted by alcoholism and several nervous breakdowns. However, he briefly returned in triumph following a lengthy drying out period as the psychopath Bruno Antony in Hitchcock's *Strangers on a Train* (1951), for which he earned the best notices of his career. Tragically, he died the same year the film was released. Jones had two sons with Walker: Robert Walker Jr (1940–), himself an actor in *Ensign*

Pulver (1964) and *Easy Rider* (1969), and Michael Walker (1941–). **Hitchography:** *Buy War Bonds* (1943)

JOURDAN, LOUIS (1919– , real name Louis Gendre) French actor. This handsome French leading man made his film debut in 1939 in *Le Corsaire* following training at the Paris School of Drama. A popular draw in his home country, he went on to appear in *Premiere Rendez-Vous* (1941), *La Vie de Boheme* (1942) and *La Belle Aventure* (1945) before being invited to Hollywood by producer David O Selznick, where he made his English-speaking debut as the groom-turned-valet Andre La Tour in Hitchcock's *The Paradine Case* (1947), a role for which Hitchcock had originally wanted Robert Newton. Jourdan went on to carve himself a successful career in both America and Europe, appearing in such favourites as *Letter from an Unknown Woman* (1948), *Three Coins in the Fountain* (1954), *Gigi* (1958) and *The VIPs* (1963). Later on he made an excellent Dracula in the BBC's acclaimed *Count Dracula* (1977, TV) and a suitably oily villain in the James Bond epic *Octopussy* (1983). In the 1950s he also appeared in the television series *Paris Precinct* (1953–1955). **Hitchography:** *The Paradine Case* (1947)

JUNE see Tripp, June

JUNGE, ALFRED (1886–1964) German-born art director. Following experience at UFA in the 1920s, this important art director made key contributions to many notable British films of the 1930s and 1940s, including *The Good Companions* (1932), *King Solomon's Mines* (1938) and *Goodbye, Mr Chips* (1939). His best work was for director Michael Powell, for whom he designed *The Life and Death of Colonel Blimp* (1943), *I Know Where I'm Going* (1945), *A Matter of Life and Death* (1945) and *Black Narcissus* (1947), winning an Oscar for the latter. Meanwhile, for Hitchcock, he designed the disappointing *Waltzes from Vienna* (1933) and, more successfully, *The Man Who Knew Too Much* (1934), the popularity of which helped to re-establish Hitchcock's then-waning reputation. A third Hitchcock film followed three years later. **Hitchography:** *Waltzes from Vienna* (1933), *The Man Who Knew Too Much* (1934), *Young and Innocent* (1937)

Juno and the Paycock

(GB, 1930, 85m, bw) ★

CREDITS
Production Company:	British International Pictures
Producer:	John Maxwell
Director:	Alfred Hitchcock
Screenplay:	Alfred Hitchcock, Alma Reville (and Sean O'Casey) based on the play by Sean O'Casey
Cinematographer:	Jack Cox
Editor:	Emile de Ruelle
Art director:	J Marchant
Sound:	C Thornton
Assistant director:	Frank Mills

CAST
Sara Allgood (Juno Boyle), Edward Chapman (Jack 'the Captain' Boyle), John Laurie (Johnny Boyle), Kathleen O'Reagan (Mary Boyle), John Longden (Charles Bentham), Sidney Morgan (Joxer Daly), Barry Fitzgerald (Orator), Maire O'Neill (Mrs Madigan), Dave Morris (Jerry Devine), Dennis Wyndham (Mobiliser), Fred Schwartz (Mr Kelly), Donald Calthrop (Needle Nugent)

In the early 1930s, Alfred Hitchcock wasn't solely identified with making thrillers, as he would later be. Therefore, it was no surprise at the time that he should turn his attention to an 'All Talkie' version of Sean O'Casey's celebrated 1924 play. Indeed, Hitchcock had already filmed a number of plays, including *Downhill* (1927), *Easy Virtue* (1927), *The Farmer's Wife* (1928) and, most notably, *Blackmail* (1929).

Billed as 'A tragi-comedy of Irish life which reaches the highest pinnacle of dramatic intensity,' the film focuses on the Boyle family, which consists of the hardworking mother, Juno Boyle (Sara Allgood), her layabout husband Jack 'the Captain' Boyle (Edward Chapman) and their children, Johnny (John Laurie) and Mary (Kathleen O'Regan). Living in cramped poverty, they barely seem to get by. Then the family's luck changes when news comes of a legacy. A spending spree follows in which new furniture is bought and a celebratory party held. However, the Boyles have been premature in their expenditure, for the legacy evaporates in legal red tape. This is only the tip of the bad news, though. Johnny, who has lost an arm in 'the troubles' is murdered by the Republicans for informing, while Mary is revealed to be pregnant by Charles Bentham (John Longden), the solicitor who brought the family the news of their legacy, but who has since disappeared upon learning that it amounts to nothing.

Working with wife Alma on the screenplay adaptation, Hitchcock stuck pretty closely to O'Casey's original text (indeed, when it was deemed necessary that the piece needed an opening scene in the local pub – only mentioned in the one-set play – Hitchcock asked O'Casey himself to write the scene). In fact the only real cuts the text suffered were those needed to avoid confrontation with the censor. Consequently, Mary's illegitimate pregnancy – a major taboo at the time – is referred to as 'her shame' (hence the film's alternate American title, *The Shame of Mary Boyle*). References to the IRA also had to become euphemistic, while the suggestion that the Republicans have a right to attack the Royal Irish Constabulary was judiciously removed.

Working with the Irish Players, among them Sara Allgood who had appeared in Hitchcock's sound debut *Blackmail* (1929), Hitchcock fashioned a faithful rendering of the play, the inevitable static nature of which he and cinematographer Jack Cox attempted to disguise by avoiding camera angles that would suggest the proscenium arch of a theatre. However, though the critics admired Hitchcock's efforts – 'Bravo, Mr Hitchcock! Bravo the Irish Players… This is a magnificent British picture,' enthused James Agate in *The Tatler* – the director himself was less pleased with the end results, commenting, 'The film got very good notices, but I was actually ashamed, because it had nothing to do with cinema… I had the feeling I was dishonest, that I had stolen something.' [4]

Inevitably, given the passage of time, *Juno and the Paycock* does seem rather static today. Nevertheless, there are some impressive performances in the film, notably Sara Allgood's turn as Juno (her breakdown at the end following the death of her son is genuinely touching), while it's hard to believe that Edward Chapman, excellent as the layabout Captain, would later become famous as a stooge to comedian Norman Wisdom.

Interestingly, given Hitchcock's burgeoning reputation at the time, his photograph also appeared on the cover of the film's promotional press book, along with those of the cast. Already, the Hitchcock name had become a major selling point, and he was quickly becoming a star in his own right.

JYMPSON, JOHN British editor. Jympson has worked on a variety of notable productions, including *A Hard Day's Night* (1964), *Zulu* (1964), *The Bedford Incident* (1965), Hitchcock's *Frenzy* (1972), *Little Shop of Horrors* (1986) and *A Fish Called Wanda* (1988). It was Jympson's suggestion that Ron Goodwin score *Frenzy* after Henry Mancini's music was rejected, Jympson having worked with Goodwin previously on *Where Eagles Dare* (1969). **Hitchography:** *Frenzy* (1972).

'My American sponsors.' Lila Kedrova chats with Julie Andrews and Paul Newman in the coffee house scene from Hitchcock's Torn Curtain *(1966). The film was promoted as Hitchcock's official 50th production.*

K

KAZANJIAN, HOWARD American producer. Though just a humble first assistant director on Hitchcock's *Family Plot* (1976), Kazanjian had progressed to executive producer just one year later on the disaster flick *Rollercoaster*. His other credits include *More American Graffiti* (1979), *Raiders of the Lost Ark* (1981), which he executive produced with George Lucas, *The Rookie* (1990) and *Demolition Man* (1993). **Hitchography:** *Family Plot* (1976)

KEDROVA, LILA (1918–2000) Russian-born character actress. Living in France from the age of 10, Kedrova went on to make a wide variety of films in both Europe and Hollywood, among them *Weg Ohne Umkehr* (1953), *Montparnasse 19* (1957), *Zorba the Greek* (1964), which won her a best supporting actress Oscar, *A High Wind in Jamaica* (1965) and Hitchcock's *Torn Curtain* (1966), in which she played the eccentric Countess Luchinska, who helps Paul Newman's Professor Michael Armstrong and Julie Andrews' Sarah Sherman escape from East Germany in return for sponsorship to go to America. Her other films include *Penelope* (1966), *Soft Beds, Hard Battles* (1973), *Tell Me a Riddle* (1980) and *Getting Away with Murder* (1995). **Hitchography:** *Torn Curtain* (1966)

KEEN, MALCOLM (1887/8–1970) British actor. A respected stage star, Keen only occasionally ventured on to the screen, his handful of appearances including three leading roles for Hitchcock, the first being Fear O'God in *The Mountain Eagle* (1925), which he followed with the police detective Joe Betts in *The Lodger* (1926) and Philip Christian in *The Manxman* (1929). His other films include *Sixty Glorious Years* (1939), *The Mating Season* (1951) and *Francis of Assisi* (1960). His son, Geoffrey Keen (1916–), has meanwhile appeared in countless films, among them *Genevieve* (1953), *Taste the Blood of Dracula* (1970) and several James Bond adventures, as minister Frederick Gray. **Hitchography:** *The Mountain Eagle* (1925), *The Lodger* (1926), *The Manxman* (1929)

KELLY, GRACE (1928–1982) American actress. Following experience on stage from the age of 10 and a stint on Broadway in 1949, this glacially elegant star went on to make her film debut in 1951 in *Fourteen Hours*. Stardom followed with her second film, the classic western saga *High Noon* (1952), in which she played opposite Gary Cooper. Following the African-set *Mogambo* (1953), which earned her an Oscar nomination for best supporting actress, Kelly went on to make the first of three films for Hitchcock. This was *Dial M for Murder* (1954) in which she played Margot Wendice, who finds herself the subject of an elaborate murder plot by her greedy husband, who is keen to inherit her money. Originally filmed in 3D, the film contains one of Hitchcock's most iconographic images – that of Kelly's hand reaching for a pair of scissors so as to defend herself against her would-be murderer. Impressed with her work, Hitchcock invited the actress to return for his following film *Rear Window* (1954), in which

she played fashion model Lisa Carol Fremont, who finds herself actively involved in a grisly murder case. Wearing a number of beautifully designed Edith Head gowns, as befitting her character's occupation, Kelly never looked more glamorous. Commented assistant director Herbert Coleman, who worked with Kelly for the first time on *Rear Window*. 'Every man who was ever lucky enough to work with Grace Kelly fell in love with her.' [1]

By the time Kelly came to work for Hitchcock for the third and last time in *To Catch a Thief* (1955), she'd won an Oscar for her role in *The Country Girl* (1954) and made *Green Fire* (1954) and *The Bridges at Toko-Ri* (1954). Another glamorous film, *To Catch a Thief* sees Kelly play heiress Frances Stevens to Cary Grant's reformed cat burglar John Robie. 'Kelly… dresses up the sequences in more ways than one,' enthused *Variety* of her performance. Indeed, Kelly's banter with Grant is one of the film's highlights. Says Frances to Robie, who is trying to pass himself off as a lumber king, 'Name me three deciduous trees indigenous to the north west!'

It should be noted that it was *not* during the production of *To Catch a Thief* that Prince Ranier III of Monaco romanced the actress. That occurred in the following year when Kelly visited the Cannes Film Festival. The couple married in 1956, by which time Kelly had made her last two films: *The Swan* (1956) and *High Society* (1956). Though Hitchcock made attempts to lure Kelly back to the screen at various times, most notably for *Marnie* (1964), the princess acquiesced to her husband's wishes of entirely forgoing her onscreen career, although she did occasionally narrate a documentary, among them *The Children of Theatre Street* (1978). Tragically, Kelly died at the age of 52 following a car crash on the Cote d'Azur. Ironically, she died on the same stretch of road on which she had filmed scenes for *To Catch a Thief*. **Hitchography:** *Dial M for Murder* (1954), *Rear Window* (1954), *To Catch a Thief* (1955)

KELLY, ORRY see Orry-Kelly

KEMMERLING, WARREN J American supporting actor. Cast in Hitchcock's *Family Plot* (1976) as police investigator Grandison, Kemmerling can also be spotted in *Gun Street* (1961), *Convicts Four* (1962), *The Lawyer* (1969) and *Framed* (1975), although he is perhaps best known for playing army official Wild Bill in *Close Encounters of the Third Kind* (1977). **Hitchography:** *Family Plot* (1976)

KENDALL, HENRY (1897–1961) British actor. A major star of stage and screen in the 1930s, Kendall played the leading role of Fred Hill in Hitchcock's comedy drama *Rich and Strange*. Unfortunately, it wasn't one of the Master's better films, although its commercial and critical failure didn't adversely affect Kendall's career, as he went on to star in the likes of *The Ghost Camera* (1933), *The Girl in Possession* (1934), *Twelve Good Men* (1936) and many more. **Hitchography:** *Rich and Strange* (1932)

KENNEDY, MADGE (1891–1987) American actress. In films from 1917 with *Baby Mine* following stage experience (including Broadway), this popular silent star went on to appear in *A Perfect Lady* (1918), *The Highest Bidder* (1921) and *Oh, Baby!* (1926), after which she temporarily retired from the screen. However, she re-emerged as a character actress in the 1950s, appearing in *The Marrying Kind* (1952), *Lust for Life* (1956) and Hitchcock's *North by Northwest* (1959), in which she played a Washington agent, unable to help Cary Grant's Roger Thornhill, who has been mistaken for a decoy spy ('Goodbye, Mr Thornhill… wherever you are'). Her other films include *They Shoot Horses, Don't They?* (1969), *The Day of the Locust* (1975) and *Marathon Man* (1976). She also appeared in two episodes of *Alfred Hitchcock Presents*. **Hitchography:** *Help Wanted* (1956, TV), *North by Northwest* (1959), *Curtains for Me* (1959, TV)

KERN, HAL C (1894–1985) American editor. One of Hollywood's top film editors, Kern began his career working for director Thomas Ince, for whom he graduated from cutting shorts to features, among them *Civilization* (1916). In the 1920s he went to work for producer Joseph M Schenck at United Artists, for whom he cut such major productions as *The Eagle* (1925), while in 1933 he joined MGM, where he first worked with producer David O Selznick on *Night Flight* (1933). Kern cut several more pictures for Selznick at MGM, among them *Viva, Villa!* (1934), *David Copperfield* (1935), which earned him an Oscar nomination, and *Anna Karenina* (1935). When Selznick went independent and formed Selznick International in 1936, Kern went with him, editing many of the company's top productions (often in association with fellow editor James E Newcom, another defector from MGM), among them *Little Lord Fauntleroy* (1936), *The Garden of Allah* (1936), *A Star is Born* (1937), *Intermezzo* (1939) and *Gone with the Wind* (1939), which earned him (and Newcom) an Oscar. Kern also cut three films for Selznick's contracted director Alfred Hitchcock, beginning with *Rebecca* (1940), which earned him an Oscar nomination. His other films include *Puttin' on the Ritz* (1930), *Stage Door Canteen* (1943), *Since You Went Away* (1944), which earned him yet another Oscar nomination, and *Duel in the Sun* (1946). **Hitchography:** *Rebecca* (1940), *Spellbound* (1945), *The Paradine Case* (1947)

KIBBEE, MILTON (MILT) American supporting actor. Kibbee popped up in a handful of films in the 1940s, among them *Strange Holiday* (1942), *Betrayed* (1944) and *River Lady* (1948), although perhaps his most memorable role was his brief cameo in Hitchcock's *Saboteur* (1942), in which he played a jovial Radio City Music Hall patron who gets shot in the stomach during a shoot out. **Hitchography:** *Saboteur* (1942)

KIELING, WOLFGANG (1924–1985) German actor. In films from 1936 with *Maria die Magd*, Kieling went on to make films in both his homeland and America, among them *Falstaff in Wien* (1940), *Damsels in Paris* (1956), *Goya* (1966), *Dollars* (1971) and *Out of Order* (1985). He is perhaps best remembered

for playing the sinister, gum-chewing East German agent Hermann Gromek in Hitchcock's *Torn Curtain* (1966), in which he is memorably murdered in a farmhouse kitchen by Professor Michael Armstrong (Paul Newman), who has faked a defection to the East so as to steal a top secret nuclear formula. ('It's the big house for you, Professor,' comments Gromek when discovering Armstrong's duplicity.) Interestingly, Hitchcock also shot a scene at a factory featuring Professor Armstrong and Gromek's brother, who was also played by Kieling, but the scene, though shot, was cut from the release print because of over length and the director's dissatisfaction with Newman's performance in it. Commented Hitchcock: 'The actor who played Gromek was very good. I had him completely transformed for the brother's role. His hair was white, he had a moustache and wore glasses.' [2] **Hitchography:** *Torn Curtain* (1966)

KNIGHT, ESMOND (1906–1987) British actor. This noted stage star had a major West End success as Strauss the Younger at the Alhambra in *Waltzes from Vienna* between 1931 and 1932. He recreated the role on film for Hitchcock in 1933, but unfortunately lightening failed to strike twice. In films from 1928 with *The Blue Peter*, Knight's other film work includes notable supporting roles in *Contraband* (1940), *A Canterbury Tale* (1943), *Black Narcissus* (1947), *The Red Shoes* (1948) and *Peeping Tom* (1960), all for director Michael Powell. His last film was *Superman IV: The Quest for Peace* (1987). He was long married to actress Nora Swinburne (1902–2000, real name Elinor S Johnson). **Hitchography:** *Waltzes from Vienna* (1933)

KNOTT, FREDERICK British playwright. Knott is best remembered for his two classic thrillers, *Dial M for Murder* and *Wait Until Dark*, both of which have been filmed, the former by Hitchcock in 1954, for which Knott penned the screenplay adaptation. *Dial M for Murder* has also been filmed for television twice, in 1952 and 1981, and a further twice for the cinema, as *Aitbaar* (1985) and *A Perfect Murder* (1998). Its plot was also used for an episode of the TV series *77, Sunset Strip* (1958–1963) titled *The Fifth Stair*. **Hitchography:** *Dial M for Murder* (1954)

KNOWLES, BERNARD (1900–1975) British cinematographer. One of Britain's key cinematographers in the 1930s, Knowles began his career as an assistant to Percy Strong in the early 1920s, although by 1927 he was a fully-fledged cameraman himself, making his solo debut with *Mumsie* for director Herbert Wilcox. Knowles worked with a variety of directors on all manner of productions over the following years, among them *Auld Lang Syne* (1929), *The Hound of the Baskervilles* (1930), *The Good Companions* (1933) and *Jew Suss* (1934). However, in 1935 he began a five-picture association with Alfred Hitchcock which led to sterling work on such films as *The 39 Steps* (1935) and *Young and Innocent* (1937), the latter remembered for Knowles' incredible crane shot through a crowded ballroom, the camera finally coming to rest on the twitching eye of the murderer. Knowles' last film for Hitchcock was *Jamaica Inn* (1939), which he co-photographed with Harry Stradling. His other work as a cinematographer includes *Rhodes of Africa* (1936), *The Mikado* (1939) and *The Demi-Paradise* (1943), after which he turned to direction, helming *A Place of One's Own* (1945), *Jassy* (1947) and *Hell is Empty* (1968) among others. **Hitchography:** *The 39 Steps* (1935), *Secret Agent* (1936), *Sabotage* (1936), *Young and Innocent* (1937), *Jamaica Inn* (1939)

KOENEKAMP, HANS F (1891–1992) American cinematographer and photographic expert. Koenekamp began his film career in 1913 working for Mack Sennett. He went on to work for Fox and Vitagraph, but his best work was for Warner Bros., providing effects work for, among others, *High Sierra* (1941), *The Treasure of the Sierra Madre* (1948), *White Heat* (1949) and Hitchcock's *Strangers on a Train* (1951), the latter noted for its spectacular carousel climax, achieved through a mixture of rear projection and model work. His son is the cinematographer Fred Koenekamp (1922–), whose credits include *Patton* (1970), *Papillon* (1973), *The Towering Inferno* (1974), which won him an Oscar, and *Flight of the Intruder* (1991). **Hitchography:** *Strangers on a Train* (1951)

KONSTAM, PHYLLIS (1907–1976) British actress. Popular on the stage throughout her career, Konstam made too few films, the majority of them for Hitchcock in the late 1920s and early 1930s. Beginning as a supporting artist in *Champagne* (1928) and *Blackmail* (1929), she soon after graduated to larger roles in *Murder!* (1930) and *The Skin Game* (1931). Her other films include *Escape* (1930), *Tilly of Bloomsbury* (1931), *The Forgotten Factor* (1952) and *Voice of the Hurricane* (1960). **Hitchography:** *Champagne* (1928), *Blackmail* (1929), *Murder!* (1930), *The Skin Game* (1931)

KONSTANTIN, LEOPOLDINE (1886–1965) Czech-born stage actress. This respected actress made few films, among them Hitchcock's *Notorious* (1946), in which she played the cold-eyed Madame Sebastian, who prompts her neo-Nazi son Alexander (Claude Rains) into poisoning his duplicitous wife Alicia (Ingrid Bergman). **Hitchography:** *Notorious* (1946)

KOSLECK, MARTIN (1904–1994, real name Nicolai Yoshkin) Russian-born actor. Kosleck spent his early years as an actor on the German stage. He also made his film debut in Germany in 1927 with *Der Fahnenträger von Sedan*, which he followed with *Alraune der Singenden Stadt* (1930) and *Napoleon auf St Helena* (1931), after which he emigrated to America following the rise of the Nazis. Ironically, during the war years, he was frequently called upon to play Nazi agents, despite being Jewish, among them the 'tramp' who dirties his hands in Hitchcock's *Foreign Correspondent* (1940). He also played Goebbels three times, in *Confessions of a Nazi Spy* (1939), *The Hitler Gang* (1944) and *Hitler* (1961). His other films include *Espionage Agent* (1939), *Nazi Agent* (1942), *Berlin Correspondent* (1942), *The Flesh Eaters* (1967) and *Which Way to the Front?* (1970). **Hitchography:** *Foreign Correspondent* (1940)

KRAMPF, GUNTHER (1899–1955, some sources say 1956) Austrian cinematographer. Noted for his dramatic use of lighting, Krampf began his career in Germany, working as an assistant cameraman on the likes of *Nosferatu* (1922). His early films as a cinematographer include such classics as *The Student of Prague* (1924), *The Hands of Orlac* (1924) and *Pandora's Box* (1924). In Britain from 1931, Krampf continued his career with the likes of *The Outsider* (1931), *Rome Express* (1932), *The Ghoul* (1933) and *Black Eyes* (1939). In 1944, he photographed two French-language shorts for Hitchcock, made for the Ministry of Information as morale boosters for areas of France where the German occupation was weakening. However, the second of these films wasn't shown until 1993. Krampf's other films include *Latin Quarter* (1945), *Meet Me at Dawn* (1947) and *The Franchise Affair* (1950). **Hitchography:** *Bon Voyage* (1944), *Aventure Malgache* (1944)

KRASNA, NORMAN (1909–1984) American playwright and screenwriter. Though he occasionally tackled weighty drama in such films as *Fury* (1936), Krasna is best known for his comedy scripts, among them *Bachelor Mother* (1939), *The Devil and Miss Jones* (1941), *Princess O'Rourke* (1943), which earned him a best screenplay Oscar, and *Indiscreet* (1958), which was based on his play *Kind Sir*. He also penned *Mr and Mrs Smith* (1941) for Hitchcock, but the film is now considered one of the director's weaker efforts. Krasna also occasionally directed, helming *Princess O'Rourke* (1943), *The Big Hangover* (1950), which he also scripted and produced, and *The Ambassador's Daughter* (1956), which he again scripted and produced. **Hitchography:** *Mr and Mrs Smith* (1941)

KRUGER, ALMA (1868–1960) American actress. Memorable as the grandmother to whom dreadful revelations are whispered in *These Three* (1936) as well as head nurse Molly Byrd in the ongoing *Dr Kildare* series, Alma Kruger was frequently called upon to play matronly roles, among them society hostess Mrs Sutton in Hitchcock's *Saboteur* (1942). On stage from her childhood years, she didn't begin making films until well into her fifties, among them *Vogues of 1938* (1937), *One Hundred Men and a Girl* (1937), *Balalaika* (1939), *Our Hearts Were Young and Gay* (1944) and *Forever Amber* (1947), following which she retired from the screen. **Hitchography:** *Saboteur* (1942)

KRUGER, OTTO (1885–1974) American actor. Otto Kruger was the grandnephew of South African president Oom Paul Kruger. On stage from his mid-twenties, he went on to become one of Broadway's most sophisticated leading men. He began making films as early as 1915 with *When the Call Came*, the same year he made his Broadway debut. Film work was sporadic until the early 1930s, when he began to establish himself as an urbane supporting actor in the likes of *Beauty for Sale* (1933), *The Crime Doctor* (1934), *Dracula's Daughter* (1936) and *Another Thin Man* (1939). In 1942 he played the villainous Charles Tobin in Hitchcock's *Saboteur* (1942), about which *Variety* enthused that he 'barely seem[ed] to be acting.' His other films include *Hitler's Children* (1943), *Duel in the Sun* (1946) and *Sex and the Single Girl* (1964). **Hitchography:** *Saboteur* (1942)

L

LACEY, CATHERINE (1904–1979) British actress. Although she gave reliable performances in such notable British films as *I Know Where I'm Going* (1945), *The October Man* (1947) and *Whisky Galore* (1949), Lacey is perhaps best remembered for her film debut as the nun with high heels in Hitchcock's *The Lady Vanishes* (1938). Her other films include *The Fighting Prince of Donegal* (1966), *The Mummy's Shroud* (1966) and *The Sorcerers* (1967). **Hitchography:** *The Lady Vanishes* (1938)

The Lady Vanishes
(GB, 1938, 97m, bw) ★★★★

CREDITS
Production company: Gainsborough
Producer: Edward Black
Director: Alfred Hitchcock
Screenplay: Frank Launder, Sidney Gilliat, based on the novel *The Wheel Spins* by Ethel Lina White
Cinematographer: Jack Cox
Music: Charles Williams (un-credited)
Music director: Louis Levy
Editor: R E Dearing, Alfred Roome
Art director: Vetchinsky
Sound: S Wiles
Continuity: Alma Reville

CAST
Margaret Lockwood (Iris Henderson), Michael Redgrave (Gilbert Redman), Dame May Whitty (Miss Froy), Paul Lukas (Dr Hartz), Cecil Parker (Eric Todhunter), Linden Travers ('Mrs' Todhunter), Emile Boreo (Hotel manager), Basil Radford (Charters), Naunton Wayne (Caldicott), Mary Clare (Baroness), Googie Withers (Blanche), Sally Stewart (Julie), Josephine Wilson (Madame Kummer), Philip Leaver (Signor Doppo), Zelma Vas Dias (Signora

Hitchcock relaxes on the stairway of the hotel set with (from left to right) Sally Stewart, Margaret Lockwood and Googie Withers during the making of The Lady Vanishes *(1938). At this stage in production, the film was known as 'Lost Lady' hence the LL reference number at the bottom of the still.*

Doppo), Kathleen Tremaine (Anna), Charles Oliver (Badrikan Officer), Catherine Lacey (Nun)

DVD availability: Carlton
CD availability: *Psycho – The Essential Alfred Hitchcock* (Silva Screen), which contains *The Main Title*; *The Great British Film Music Album – Sixty Glorious Years 1938–1998* (Silva Screen) which contains the *Overture*

This is the great Hitchcock film that almost wasn't. As screenwriter Frank Launder recalled: 'This film was never intended for Hitchcock in the first place. It was meant for an American director called Roy William Neill. Well, he disappeared – I don't know why. His contract probably ended and he went back to America… Then one day Edward Black, the producer, discovered that Hitchcock had one more film to make under his contract, and they sent him the script round. Hitchcock was preparing another film at the time… but he suddenly abandoned everything else and took up the film.' [1]

Originally to have been titled *Lost Lady*, *The Lady Vanishes* is based on Ethel Lina White's 1936 novel *The Wheel Spins* and was filmed in just five weeks at Hitchcock's old haunt, the Islington Studios. Billed as containing 'Comedy! Chills! Chuckles!' in the distributor's handbook, it more than lives up to this claim.

By the time the film's original director, Roy William Neill, had left the project to return to Hollywood – where he went on to make several classic episodes in the Basil Rathbone Sherlock Holmes series, among them *Terror by Night* (1946), a train-bound thriller in the manner of *The Lady Vanishes* – some attempts to begin production on *The Lady Vanishes* had already been undertaken. According to screenwriter Sidney Gilliat, 'A second unit had been sent to Yugoslavia to shoot exteriors, and there was a real balls-up on location and the company was ordered out [of the country].' [2] Consequently, when Hitchcock was signed to the film, the script for which had already been completed, there was little time to prepare for shooting in his customary style, which included working out the action on storyboards. Yet given the brevity of the shooting schedule, this seems to have worked to his advantage in this case.

Like many of Hitchcock's films, the basic premise of *The Lady Vanishes* is fairly simple: a young woman named Iris Henderson (Margaret Lockwood) is befriended by an old lady, Miss Froy (Dame May Whitty), while travelling by train back to London through eastern Euorpe (Badrika, so we're told). However, when Miss Froy vanishes, no one will believe Iris that she ever existed, particularly given that the girl suffered a bump on the head at the station and may be hallucinating. In her quest to discover what's being going on, Iris is joined by an affable Englishman, Gilbert Redman (Michael Redgrave), who's been in Europe to research his book on folk dancing.

However, the reason for Miss Froy's disappearance proves to be slightly more complex, for it is revealed that she is not really a governess, as she has claimed, but a spy, her mission being to smuggle back to England a coded tune which contains the 'vital clause' in a pact between two European countries. As critic Leslie Halliwell later succinctly put it: 'Why the British Foreign Office should require an elderly lady to travel across Europe's more dangerous zones remembering a coded tune when the same information could have been conveyed more quickly and efficiently by morse tapper, telephone or pigeon post is a question with no possible answer,' though he goes on to conclude, 'but the film is so much fun that one does not begrudge its lunatic McGuffin.' [3] Hitchcock's simple explanation for all the nonsense was that, 'It's fantasy, sheer fantasy!' [4]

On board the train are various British types, and it is their involvement in the action that helps to pepper the more serious central situation with humour. Among them are two cricket-loving gents, Charters and Caldicott (Basil Radford and Naunton Wayne), who are desperate to get home to see the last days of the Test Match in Manchester, and a married barrister, Eric Todhunter (Cecil Parker), who has been vacationing with his illicit love (Linden Travers). Naturally, both parties, when asked about the disappearance of Miss Froy, whom they've all seen, have their own selfish reasons for denying her existence: Charters and Caldicott don't want the train stopped for a search, as it will delay their journey to the match, while Todhunter doesn't want to become involved, as he and his 'wife' might be called upon to give evidence.

Meanwhile, the Europeans onboard have a genuine reason for denying Miss Froy's existence – for it is they, led by the urbane surgeon Dr Hartz (Paul Lukas), who have kidnapped her and replaced her with a none too convincing lookalike, Madame Kummer (Josephine Wilson), who has been slipped on board the train in the guise of a bandaged car crash victim whose face is supposedly little more than 'lumps of flesh'. Among those keeping up the charade are the Baroness (Mary Clare), whose husband is a leading government minister, and a magician, Signor Doppo (Philip Leaver), who has pulled off the switch (although how he managed to smuggle Miss Froy's body through several carriages in order to wrap her in the bandages of the newly arrived decoy is never alluded to). And of course we mustn't forget the fake nun (Catherine Lacey) whose high heels give the game away.

There *are* clues as to Miss Froy's existence, such as her name, which she wrote for Iris in the steam of the dining car window, and a packet of the tea she always carries with her – Harriman's Herbal ('A million Mexicans drink it. At least that's what it says on the packet,' she tells Iris). Naturally, both clues disappear, although at least Gilbert gets a brief glimpse of the latter as it sticks to a window, having been thrown out with the rubbish by the cook. It is the sight of this that finally encourages him to believe Iris and help her unravel the mystery.

When they finally do uncover the conspiracy and discover Miss Froy beneath the bandages of the supposed accident victim, things start to turn nasty, with the train shunted on to a branch line, where armed government

(although it should be noted that Landis was actually 11 months *younger* than Grant!). While travelling in an elevator with her son, he informs her that two of the other passengers are enemy agents out to kill him, which elicits the cherished comment, 'You gentlemen aren't *really* trying to murder my son, are you?' Landis's other films include *Mr Belvedere Goes to College* (1949), *The Swan* (1956), *Bon Voyage* (1962) and *Airport* (1969). She also appeared in an episode of *Alfred Hitchcock Presents*. **Hitchography:** *To Catch a Thief* (1955), *North by Northwest* (1959), *Mother, May I Go Out to Swim?* (1960, TV)

LANE, PRISCILLA (1917–1995, real name Priscilla Mullican) American actress. Following experience as a dance band vocalist with Fred Waring's Pennsylvanians, Lane entered films in 1937 with the musical short *Swingtime in the Movies*, which led to a contract with Warner Bros. and a leading part in their musical *Varsity Show* (1937). She had a major hit in 1938 with the romantic drama *Four Daughters*, which co-starred her two sisters, Rosemary Lane (1914–1974, real name Rosemary Mullican) and Lola Lane (1909–1981, real name Dorothy Mullican). This led to two sequels, *Four Wives* (1939) and *Four Mothers* (1940), as well as a variation on the same theme, *Daughters Courageous* (1938). In 1942 Lane signed to be the leading lady in Hitchcock's *Saboteur*, although the director later learned, much to his chagrin, that she had been foisted upon him by the film's producers, Frank Lloyd and Jack H Skirball. Consequently, Lane comes across as one of Hitchcock's lesser leading ladies – adequate, but by no means memorable. Lane's other films include *The Meanest Man in the World* (1942), *Arsenic and Old Lace* (1943) and *Bodyguard* (1948), following which she retired from the screen. **Hitchography:** *Saboteur* (1942)

LANG, DOREEN American character actress. This distinctive-looking actress had the luck to appear in three Hitchcock films. In *The Wrong Man* (1956) she plays insurance clerk Ann James, who wrongly identifies Henry Fonda's Manny Balestrero as the man who's been carrying out a number of hold ups. In *North by Northwest* (1959) she plays Maggie, the long-suffering secretary of Cary Grant's Roger Thornhill, with whom she exchanges some amusing banter in the film's opening scene ('Do I look a little heavyish to you?' Thornhill asks her. 'I *feel* heavyish. Put a note on my desk in the morning. "Think thin"'). Meanwhile, in *The Birds* (1963), she can be seen as the concerned mother shielding her two frightened children in the Tides restaurant. Her other films include *Wild in the Country* (1961), *The Cabinet of Dr Caligari* (1962) and *The Group* (1966). She also appeared in an episode of *Alfred Hitchcock Presents*, in which she was again directed by Hitchcock. **Hitchography:** *The Wrong Man* (1956), *Dip in the Pool* (1958, TV), *North by Northwest* (1959), *The Birds* (1963)

LAPWORTH, CHARLES British production manager. Lapworth was associated with the early films of producer

Michael Balcon, for whom he provided the story for *The Mountain Eagle* (1925), Hitchcock's second film as a director. Prior to working for Balcon he helped to run Samuel Goldwyn's London office. **Hitchography:** *The Mountain Eagle* (1925)

LASKY, JESSE L (1880–1958) American film pioneer. Lasky formed several major film companies during his career, beginning in 1914 with the Feature Play Company, which had a huge commercial success with Cecil B de Mille's *Squaw Man* the same year. In 1916, the Feature Play Company merged with Adolph Zukor's Famous Players, subsequently becoming Famous Players-Lasky. In 1919 Lasky came to London to open a British branch of this company at Islington Studios, which went on to produce a busy programme of films, on many of which the young Alfred Hitchcock worked as an inter-title designer, including *The Great Day* (1920) and *Three Live Ghosts* (1922). Though the London branch of the company closed down as early as 1923, the American branch merged with several more companies over the following decade, finally emerging as Paramount Pictures Inc. in 1935, for which Hitchcock later made some of his most famous films in the 1950s. Films personally produced by Lasky during his career include *Yankee Doodle Dandy* (1941), *The Adventures of Mark Twain* (1944) and *Rhapsody in Blue* (1945), all of which were made at Warner Bros. Lasky's son, Jesse Lasky Jr (1910–1988), meanwhile became a successful screenwriter, penning 'additional dialogue' for Hitchcock's *Secret Agent* (1936) as well as authoring major productions for Cecil B de Mille, among them *Union Pacific* (1939), *Samson and Delilah* (1949) and *The Ten Commandments* (1956).

LATHAM, LOUISE American character actress. Latham made her screen debut in Hitchcock's *Marnie* (1964), in which she played the title character's domineering mother Bernice Edgar ('We don't talk smart about the bible in this house, Missy!'). Her other films include *Firecreek* (1967), *The Sugarland Express* (1974), *Mass Appeal* (1984), *Love Field* (1992) and *In Cold Blood* (1996, TV), while her TV work includes such series as *Sara* (1976) and *Scruples* (1980). **Hitchography:** *Marnie* (1964)

LAUGHTON, CHARLES (1899–1962) British actor. On stage from 1925 and in films from 1928 with the short *Bluebottles*, Laughton went on to become one of the screen's great character stars thanks to memorable performances in such landmark productions as *The Sign of the Cross* (1932), *The Private Life of Henry VIII* (1933), which earned him a best actor Oscar, *The Barretts of Wimpole Street* (1934), *Mutiny on the Bounty* (1935) and *Les Miserables* (1935). In fact so popular and powerful did he become that, in 1937, he formed his own production company, Mayflower Pictures, with the German producer Erich Pommer. The company made three films: *Vessel of Wrath* (1938), *St Martin's Lane* (1938) and *Jamaica Inn* (1939), the latter directed by Hitchcock just prior to his leaving for

Hollywood and a contract with David O Selznick. Hitchcock didn't particularly enjoy working on the film, and later commented: 'You can't direct a Laughton picture. In fact the best you can hope for is to referee.' [6] In fact Laughton gives one of his most deliciously hammy performances in the film as Sir Humphrey Pengallan, the leader of a gang of wreckers, about which *Variety* commented, 'Charles Laughton has a colourful, sinister part in the villainous squire with a strain of insanity.'

Following *Jamaica Inn*, Laughton returned to Hollywood to make *The Hunchback of Notre Dame* (1939), which was followed over the coming years by *It Started with Eve* (1941), *The Canterville Ghost* (1944), *Hobson's Choice* (1954), *Witness for the Prosecution* (1957), *Spartacus* (1960) and *Advise and Consent* (1962). In 1947 Laughton had a second encounter with Hitchcock on *The Paradine Case*, in which he played the lecherous Judge Lord Horfield. Another hammy star turn from Laughton was the result, prompting the critic of *The Times* to comment, 'Ripeness is all, ripeness and the relishing of it.' Added *Variety*, 'Charles Laughton gives a revealing portrait of a gross, lustful nobleman who presides at the trial.'

Laughton was married to actress Elsa Lanchester (1902–1986) from 1929 until his death. He also directed one film, the masterful *Night of the Hunter* (1955), which contains many Hitchcockian touches. **Hitchography:** *Jamaica Inn* (1939), *The Paradine Case* (1947)

LAUNDER, FRANK (1907–1997) British-born screenwriter, director and producer. Like Alfred Hitchcock, Launder began his screen career as a writer of inter-titles during the silent period. This led to work as a scriptwriter, among his early sound credits being *Under the Greenwood Tree* (1929), *The 'W' Plan* (1930) and *After Office Hours* (1931). However, it was his partnership with Sidney Gilliat (1908–1994), first as a screenwriter, and then as a director and producer, that produced a string of classic British films, among them *Night Train to Munich* (1940), *Millions Like Us* (1943), *I See a Dark Stranger* (1945), *Green for Danger* (1946), *The Happiest Days of Your Life* (1950) and *The Belles of St Trinian's* (1954). Perhaps their best screenwriting collaboration was for Hitchcock's *The Lady Vanishes* (1938), although the film was originally intended for another director, the American Roy William Neill. Said Launder of Hitchcock's reaction to their brilliant work: 'He always played things close to his chest, so we never really knew if he liked it or not.' [7] **Hitchography:** *The Lady Vanishes* (1938)

LAUNER S JOHN American supporting actor. Launer can be spotted in such films as *Creature with the Atom Brain* (1955), *The Werewolf* (1956), *Apache Rifles* (1964) and *Pendulum* (1969). He also appeared in Hitchcock's *Marnie* (1964), in which he played the role of Sam Ward. **Hitchography:** *Marnie* (1964)

LAURENTS, ARTHUR (1918–) American playwright. Laurent's successes include *Home of the Brave*, *The Time of the Cuckoo*, *West Side Story* and *Gypsy*, all of which have been filmed (*The Time of the Cuckoo* as *Summertime* aka *Summer Madness*). Although none of the aforementioned were scripted for the screen by Laurents, his own screenplay credits include Hitchcock's *Rope* (1948), *Caught* (1948), *Anastasia* (1956), *Bonjour, Tristesse* (1957), *The Way We Were* (1973), which was based on his novel, and *The Turning Point* (1977), the latter earning him an Oscar nomination for best original screenplay. **Hitchography:** *Rope* (1948)

LAURIE, JOHN (1897–1980) Scottish-born actor. Like Barry Fitzgerald and Edward Chapman, Laurie made his screen debut in Hitchcock's adaptation of Sean O'Casey's *Juno and the Paycock* in 1930, in which he played the one-armed Johnny Boyle who is shot for informing. Five years later he was cast as the suspicious crofter in Hitchcock's *The 39 Steps*. His scene is brief, yet it remains one of the film's many highlights. Laurie's many other films include *The Four Feathers* (1939), *The Life and Death of Colonel Blimp* (1943), *Richard III* (1955) and *The Prisoner of Zenda* (1979). However, he is perhaps best remembered as the dour funeral director Private James Fraser in TV's *Dad's Army*, which ran between 1968 and 1977 (catchphrase: 'We're all dooooooomed!'). **Hitchography:** *Juno and the Paycock* (1930), *The 39 Steps* (1935)

LAUTER, ED (1940–) American character actor. In films from 1970 with *Maybe I'll Come Home in the Spring* following experience as a stand up comic, Lauter frequently found himself cast as villainous types, among them his henchman Joseph Maloney, who comes to a tragic end when his car flies off the edge of a cliff while trying to run down Blanche Tyler (Barbara Harris) and George Lumley (Bruce Dern) in Hitchcock's *Family Plot* (1976). His many other films include *King Kong* (1976), *Death Hunt* (1980), *Youngblood* (1985), *The Rocketeer* (1991) and *Crash* (1996). **Hitchography:** *Family Plot* (1976)

LAWRENCE, GERTRUDE (1898–1952, real name Alexandra Dagmar Lawrence-Klasen) British revue artist. This celebrated artist is perhaps best remembered for her association with actor-playwright Noel Coward, who wrote the role of Sybil in *Private Lives* specifically for her. However, although she made a handful of films, beginning with *The Battle of Paris* in 1929, she remained essentially a stage personality. Her other films include *No Funny Business* (1932), *Aren't We All?* (1932), *Rembrandt* (1936), *Stage Door Canteen* (1943) and *The Glass Menagerie* (1950). She also appeared as Lady Camber in *Lord Camber's Ladies* (1932), which was produced by Hitchcock. In 1968 she was impersonated by Julie Andrews in the expensive but unsuccessful musical biopic *Star!* **Hitchography:** *Lord Camber's Ladies* (1932)

LEAVER, PHILIP British actor. Leaver, who played the oily magician Signor Doppo in Hitchcock's *The Lady*

Vanishes (1938) can also be spotted in two early Hammer films: *Dr Morelle – The Case of the Missing Heiress* (1949) and *Spaceways* (1953). Otherwise, little else seems to be known about his screen career. **Hitchography:** *The Lady Vanishes* (1938)

LEE, AURIOL (1880–1941) British-born actress. Lee was not only a descendant of Robert E Lee, but was also the first woman to fly across the equator. On the London stage from 1900, she later performed on Broadway and in the occasional Hollywood film, such as Hitchcock's *Suspicion* (1941), in which she had the minor role of Isobel Sedbusk. Like Hitchcock, she was a close friend of John Van Druten, and suggested to the playwright that he cast Hitchcock's daughter Pat in his 1941 play *Solitaire*. A meeting was arranged and Van Druten agreed to the idea, and so began Pat's acting career. Sadly, Lee died in a car crash soon after, following a visit to Van Druten's ranch in California. **Hitchography:** *Suspicion* (1941)

LEE, CANADA (1907–1952, real name Leonard Lionel Cornelius Canegata) American actor. This hulking actor was the first black person to have a major role in a Hitchcock film, appearing as the religious steward George Joe Spencer in *Lifeboat* (1944). However, this didn't prevent the movie's leading lady, Tallulah Bankhead, from nicknaming him Charcoal during the action. A former boxer, Lee began performing on stage in the mid-1930s, and had a major Broadway success with *Native Son* in 1941 (in which he was directed by Orson Welles). His other films are *Body and Soul* (1947), *Lost Boundaries* (1949) and *Cry the Beloved Country* (1952), following which he was blacklisted from the screen by the House of Un-American Activities Comittee for alleged communist activities. Lee also featured in the 1939 documentary *Keep Punching*. The only other black actor to feature prominently in a Hitchcock was Roscoe Lee Browne (1925–), who plays undercover agent Philippe Dubois in *Topaz* (1969). **Hitchography:** *Lifeboat* (1944)

LEHMAN, ERNEST (1920–) American screenwriter. With his work for *North by Northwest* (1959), Lehman gave Hitchcock not only his best script, but also one of the greatest screenplays ever written, every line of which has clearly been considered and rolled over the tongue for ultimate amusement and impact. Witty, complex and packed with jokes, it remains an industry high to this day (commented *Variety*, 'The complications are staggering, but they play like an Olympic version of a three-legged race,' to which Dylis Powell writing in the *Sunday Times* added, 'It is consistently entertaining, its excitement pointed by but never interrupted by the jokes'). Lehman came to films in 1948 with *The Inside Story* following experience as a short story writer and financial editor. He quickly earned respect for such scripts as *Executive Suite* (1954), *Sabrina* (1954), *Somebody Up There Likes Me* (1956) *The King and I* (1956) and *The Sweet Smell of Success* (1957). He originally joined forces with

Hitchcock to adapt the Hammond Innes novel *The Wreck of the Mary Deare* for the screen, but when Hitchcock became convinced that the film wouldn't work, they turned their attention to an idea the director had long harboured about a chase across the faces of Mount Rushmore tentatively titled *The Man in Lincoln's Nose.* This of course became *North by Northwest*, for which Lehman was rightly nominated for an Oscar (which he amazingly lost to the four-man army of Russell Rouse, Clarence Greene, Stanley Shapiro and Maurice Richlin for the innocuous Doris Day vehicle *Pillow Talk*). Recalled Lehman of the creation of the film's most famous scene, the crop duster sequence: '[It was] acted out, shot by shot, by Hitch and me in the living room of his home. I played the plane. He played the diesel truck.' [8]

Following *North by Northwest*, Lehman went on to pen the screenplays for *From the Terrace* (1960), *West Side Story* (1961), *The Prize* (1963), *The Sound of Music* (1965), *Who's Afraid of Virginia Woolf?* (1966) and *Hello, Dolly!* (1969), producing the latter two. In 1972, he wrote, produced and directed *Portnoy's Complaint*, but the film was not a success. In 1976, Lehman re-teamed with Hitchcock for what would prove to be the director's last film, *Family Plot*, which, though warmly enough greeted, was far from being in the same league as *North by Northwest*. Nevertheless, *Variety* described Lehman's screenplay as 'witty' and 'a model of construction.'

Following *Family Plot*, Hitchcock was determined to make one last film, and began to work on a project titled *The Short Night*, based on the novel by Ronald Kirkbridge. Lehman was again hired to write the screenplay, but when he disagreed with the director over a rape scene, the two parted company, with Lehman subsequently replaced by David Freeman. Lehman's other work includes the screenplay for *Black Sunday* (1977) and the novels *The French Atlantic Affair* and *Farewell Performance* (which opens with perhaps the longest sentence ever written). Following five Oscar nominations, he finally received a much-deserved honorary Oscar in recognition of his career in 2001. **Hitchography:** *North by Northwest* (1959), *Family Plot* (1976)

LEHN, JOHN American supporting actor. Lehn appeared in several films during the 1970s and early 1980s, among them *Who?* (1974), *Bound for Glory* (1976), *The Disappearance of Aimee* (1976, TV), Hitchcock's *Family Plot* (1976), in which he played Andy Bush, *The Darker Side of Terror* (1979) and *Carny* (1980). **Hitchography:** *Family Plot* (1976)

LEIGH, JANET (1927– , real name Jeanette Morrison) American actress. Discovered while still a student by MGM star Norma Shearer, Hollywood leading lady Leigh made her screen debut in 1947 with *The Romance of Rosy Ridge*, and quickly established herself with such films as *Words and Music* (1948), *Little Women* (1949) and *Scaramouche* (1951). Her third marriage to screen legend Tony Curtis (1925– , real name Bernard Schwartz), to

Hitchcock directs Janet Leigh in the much-discussed shower sequence from Psycho *(1960).*

Candidate (1962), Bye-Bye, Birdie (1
The House on Greenapple Road (19
mother of actress Jamie Lee Curtis (
she's worked in *The Fog* (1980) and
Years Later (1998), appearing in the
named Norma, whose appearance is g
Bernard Herrmann's musical motifs fror....   ...ign has also written about her experiences making *Psycho* in her 1995 book *Behind the Scenes of Psycho*, which she co-authored with Christopher Nickens. **Hitchography:** *Psycho* (1960)

LEIGH-HUNT, BARBARA (1935–) British stage actress. Familiar to television audiences as Catherine Parr in the series *The Six Wives of Henry VIII* (1970), Leigh-Hunt went on to make her film debut in Hitchcock's *Frenzy* (1972), in which she played Brenda Blaney, who is brutally raped and murdered by Barry Foster's neck-tie killer Robert Rusk in one of the most disturbing scenes the director ever filmed. Her other films include *Henry VIII and His Six Wives* (1972), *Bequest to the Nation* (1973) and *Paper Mask* (1990). **Hitchography:** *Frenzy* (1972)

LEIGHTON, MARGARET (1922–1976) British actress. This much-admired actress began her career on stage at the age of 16, and went on to achieve acclaim for her work at the Old Vic in the 1940s. Signed to producer Alexander Korda, she made her film debut in 1948 in *Bonnie Prince Charlie*, which she followed with *The Winslow Boy* (1948) and Hitchcock's *Under Capricorn* (1949), in which she played the Mrs Danvers-like house-keeper Milly, a role that prompted *The Tatler* to describe her as 'our most promising screen leading lady.' Leighton's subsequent films include *The Astonished Heart* (1950), *The Waltz of the Toreadors* (1962), *The Madwoman of Chaillot* (1969), *The Go-Between* (1970), *Lady Caroline Lamb* (1972) and *From Beyond the Grave* (1973), although it was on stage that she had her greatest successes, winning Tony awards for her work in *Separate Tables* and *The Night of the Iguana*. Married three times, her husbands were publisher Max Reinhardt, actor Laurence Harvey (1928–1973, real name Larushka Mischa Skikne), to whom she was married between 1957 and 1960, and actor Michael Wilding (1912–1979), to whom she was married from 1960, and with whom she'd co-starred in *Under Capricorn*. Commented Leighton of her film career, which she always viewed as secondary to her work in the theatre: 'I've made some terrible mistakes in accepting some roles and turning down others, but some good is bound to come of doing, rather than not doing, any role.' [10] She also appeared in an episode of *Alfred Hitchcock Presents* and an episode of *The Alfred Hitchcock Hour*. **Hitchography:** *Under Capricorn* (1949), *Tea Time* (1958, TV), *Where the Woodbine Twineth* (1965, TV)

LESLIE, JOAN (1925– , real name Joan Agnes Theresa Sadie Brodel) American actress. On stage professionally from the age of 9, Leslie began her career as a singer in

whom she was married between 1951 and 1962, was much-publicized, and helped her to move away from girl-next-door roles; the results were such films as *Houdini* (1953), *The Vikings* (1958) and *Touch of Evil* (1958), in which, interestingly, she is menaced in a motel room.

However, she is best remembered for the role of Marion Crane in Hitchcock's *Psycho* (1960), for which she received $25,000. Hitchcock surprised audiences the world over by having a star of Leigh's stature murdered so brutally in the now infamous shower scene less than halfway through the picture. Recalled the actress on first seeing the completed sequence: 'Even though I knew what was going to come, I screamed. And even though I knew I was sitting there in that screening quite alive and well, it was a very emotional thing to see your own demise.' [9] The actress earned a best supporting actress Oscar nomination for the film, which she followed with appearances in such diverse productions as *The Manchurian*

Three Brodels with her two sisters. Following experience as a model, she made her film debut in *Camille* (1937), following which she made several more minor appearances, among them an un-credited role in Hitchcock's *Foreign Correspondent* (1940) playing Johnny Jones' sister. She went on to achieve stardom in such films as *Sergeant York* (1941), *Yankee Doodle Dandy* (1942) and *Rhapsody in Blue* (1945). Her other films include *The Woman They Almost Lynched* (1953), *The Keegans* (1976, TV) and *Fire in the Dark* (1991, TV). She also has experience as a fashion designer. **Hitchography:** *Foreign Correspondent* (1940)

LEVERETT, WINSTON H American sound recordist. Long at Paramount, Leverett recorded the sound for a couple of Hitchcock's films in the 1950s. **Hitchography:** *The Trouble with Harry* (1955), *Vertigo* (1958)

LEVY, BENN W British dramatist and screenwriter. Benn Levy penned the dialogue for Hitchcock's debut talkie *Blackmail* (1929), following which he became friendly with the director. Hitchcock subsequently asked Levy to direct *Lord Camber's Ladies* in 1932, which Hitchcock produced. Unfortunately, the duo fell out during production and didn't speak for over 30 years. However, they were later reconciled in Hollywood and Hitchcock invited Levy to script an early version of *Frenzy*, although this was subsequently abandoned. **Hitchography:** *Blackmail* (1929), *Lord Camber's Ladies* (1932)

LEVY, LOUIS (1894–1957) British-born music director. In the 1930s and 1940s, it seemed that Louis Levy had a credit on every British film released. Indeed, between 1928 and 1947 he was the musical supervisor for both Gaumont-British and Gainsborough, composing, conducting and arranging scores for the likes of *Jack's the Boy* (1932), *The Good Companions* (1933), *Chu-Chin-Chow* (1934) and *The Wicked Lady* (1945). Given that Hitchcock was contracted to Gaumont in the 1930s, it was inevitable that the two should work together on several productions. Later, when Hitchcock returned to Britain to make the occasional film, it was Levy's services he called upon to direct the music, thus making him one of the director's most frequent collaborators. **Hitchography:** *Waltzes from Vienna* (1933), *The Man Who Knew Too Much* (1934), *The 39 Steps* (1935), *Secret Agent* (1936), *Sabotage* (1936), *Young and Innocent* (1937), *The Lady Vanishes* (1938), *Under Capricorn* (1949), *Stage Fright* (1950)

LEWIS, HAROLD C American sound recordist. Long with Paramount, Lewis won an Oscar for his work on *A Farewell to Arms* (1932). He also went on to record three of Hitchcock's five Paramount films in the 1950s. **Hitchography:** *To Catch a Thief* (1955), *The Trouble with Harry* (1955), *Vertigo* (1958)

Lifeboat
(US, 1944, 96m, bw) ★★

CREDITS

Production company:	Twentieth Century Fox
Producer:	Kenneth MacGowan
Director:	Alfred Hitchcock
Screenplay:	John Steinbeck (story), Jo Swerling
Cinematographer:	Glen MacWilliams
Music:	Hugo Friedhofer
Music director:	Emil Newman
Editor:	Dorothy Spencer
Art director:	James Basevi, Maurice Ransford
Costumes:	Rene Hubert
Sound:	Bernard Freericks, Roger Heman
Special effects:	Fred Sersen
Technical advisor:	Thomas Fitzsimmons

CAST

Tallulah Bankhead (Constance Porter), John Hodiak (John Kovac), William Bendix (Gus Smith), Walter Slezak (Willi, the German submarine captain), Hume Cronyn (Stanley Garrett), Canada Lee (George 'Joe' Spencer/Charcoal), Mary Anderson (Nurse Alice MacKenzie), Henry Hull (Charles D Rittenhouse/Ritt), Heather Angel (Mrs Higgins), William Yetter Jr (Baby-faced German sailor)

CD availability: *Psycho: The Essential Alfred Hitchcock* (Silva Screen) which contains the opening credits cue *Disaster*

Hitchcock always loved a technical challenge, and had often thought of making a film restricted to a single set. An early idea had been to film a story entirely in a telephone booth, and it was out of this concept that *Lifeboat* was eventually born. Described by Hitchcock as being 'a microcosm of the war,' [11] the film centres on a group of disparate people in a lifeboat, among them a glamorous Manhattan journalist, Constance Porter (Tallulah Bankhead), a tattooed crewman, John Kovac (John Hodiak), a millionaire factory owner, Charles D Rittenhouse (Henry Hull), a black steward, Joe Spencer (Canada Lee), a Cockney radio operator, Stanley Garrett (Hume Cronyn), a nurse, Alice MacKenzie (Mary Anderson), a seaman, Gus Smith (William Bendix), a young mother whose baby has died, Mrs Higgins (Heather Angel), and the captain of the U-boat responsible for the sinking of their ship (Walter Slezak), his submarine having also sunk in the aftermath of the torpedo explosion.

An abject lesson in 'know thy enemy,' the film sees the British and Americans manipulated throughout their mid-ocean ordeal by the devious Nazi captain. Having voted to allow him to remain onboard, they also elect that he takes charge of getting them to safety, given his seafaring experience. However, instead of steering the boat towards Bermuda by supposedly using the sun as a navigational tool, the captain instead uses a small compass secreted in his jacket to take his trusting fellow passengers further out to sea where he hopes to cross paths with a German supply boat (the captain may be fooling his fellow passengers, but Hitchcock reveals his true nature early on, when he yawns as the young mother mourns the loss of her baby, which is buried at sea).

On the voyage, during which they endure heat, storm and starvation, the survivors constantly argue and debate the meaning of their democratic actions in allowing the German to take charge of the boat, all the while enabling the Nazi to further deceive them. Indeed, Hitchcock intended the situation in the boat to represent the wider events in the world. 'We wanted to show that at that moment there were two world forces confronting each other, the democracies and the Nazis, and while the democracies were completely disorganized, all of the Germans were clearly headed in the same direction. So here was a statement telling the democracies to put their differences aside temporarily and to gather their forces to concentrate on the common enemy, whose strength was precisely derived from a spirit of unity and determination.' [12]

As well as exploiting the liberal attitudes of the democracies to his own advantage, the Nazi captain manipulates the weaknesses of others, such as those of the recently bereaved mother, whom he coaxes into committing suicide in the middle of the night. Meanwhile, he pushes seaman Smith, delirious following the amputation of a gangrenous foot, into the ocean as the others are sleeping, thus reducing the number of passengers he has to confront. However, when the democracies discover that he's been using his compass to purposely take them off course, and that he also has a concealed bottle of water (given away by the fact that he's sweating), they eventually beat him up and throw him overboard to drown, thus becoming the murderous savages they had strived to avoid becoming.

Yet they fail to learn their lesson, for soon after, a German supply ship arrives to pick them up; but when it is sunk by an allied vessel, arriving on the horizon at the last moment like the cavalry, they all too readily take aboard a baby-faced young German sailor, who immediately thanks them for saving his life by pulling a gun on them ('The baby has a toy,' quips Constance). Managing to disarm him, they sit to await their rescue, pondering over the plight they have endured and their reactions to it (says Rittenhouse of the enemy: 'You can't treat them as human beings. You have to exterminate them!').

As to be expected, when the film was released at the height of the war, several critics condemned it for its depiction of an evil Nazi as a good sailor, constantly outwitting the democracies onboard. But this was surely to miss the point. As the *Times* better observed, the captain 'owes his supremacy to fraud and lies…[as] it turns out that [he] is keeping up his strength and spirits by drinking water he has secreted, taking vitamin pills and setting a course by concealed compass.'

Given its single setting, the film is heavily reliant on its dialogue and performances, and generally they come up trumps. To script the film, Hitchcock had hoped to get literary heavyweight Ernest Hemmingway, but when he demurred, was equally ready to accept John Steinbeck as a substitute. Steinbeck provided the script's character and story basics, after which Hitchcock handed the treatment to Mackinlay Kantor – *Happy Land* (1943), *The Best Years of Our Lives* (1946) – for further development. Unsatisfied with Kantor's work, Hitchcock replaced him after two weeks with Jo Swerling, whose screenplays included *Platinum Blonde* (1932), *Pennies from Heaven* (1936) and *The Pride of the Yankees* (1942). Better satisfied with Swerling's work, to which he made his own amendments, Hitchcock thus proceeded with the film.

Performance-wise, the focus of the production is unquestionably Tallulah Bankhead, whose glamorous, self-centred Constance Porter dominates the action by sheer power of star personality. Discovered alone in the lifeboat at the top of the film, her first reaction to the death and chaos around her is to tut at her laddered stocking. Gradually she is joined by her fellow survivors, the first to haul himself onboard being John Hodiak's rough and ready seaman John Kovac. 'Lady, you certainly don't look like anyone that's just been shipwrecked,' he quips at her glamorous appearance. However, as the action progresses, Constance loses all her valuables, among them the cine-camera on which she's recorded the ship sinking, her typewriter, her fur coat and her bracelet. 'Little by little I'm being stripped of all my earthly possessions,' she observes at one point, although by the end of the film she is undeniably better off as a person because of this. She also has the love of Kovac, who earlier on has given her a pretty accurate summation of herself: 'Mrs Porter, I've read a lot of your stuff. Want to know what's a matter with it? You've been all over the world, you've met all kinds of people, but you never write about *them*, you only write about your*self*. You think this whole war's been a show put on for you to cover like a Broadway play, and if enough people die in the last act you *might* give it four stars!'

Perhaps the most telling line comes when Joe, the first major black character in a Hitchcock films, asks, 'Do I get to vote too?' when the passengers are deciding on the fate of the German captain. He *is* allowed to vote, but this doesn't prevent Constance from jokingly referring to him as Charcoal at one point.

Given the cramped conditions in which the film is set, opportunities for Hitchcock to embellish the proceedings with his customary touches are few and far between. Instead, he concentrates on the performances, and the film is all the better for it. He does nevertheless add a few visual flourishes, among them the sinking of the ship's smoke stack under the opening titles, a long dolly shot past the debris from the sunken ship (including wooden spoons, cards, a chess board, the odd body and a copy of the *New Yorker*), the discarding of Smith's boot with a thud on the deck following the amputation of his foot (made all the worse given his love of dancing), and the spectacularly explosive climax in which the German supply boat is literally blown out of the water by the allies. Elsewhere, he has to rely on the actors, the studio tank and some reasonably convincing back projection to get across the drama of the piece.

The film was not a major hit when released, and garnered a mixed response from the critics. 'Hitchcock has piloted the piece skillfully, ingeniously developing suspense and action,' praised *Variety*, though James Agee was less convinced, writing, 'As allegory the film is nicely knit, extensively shaded and detailed, and often fascinating, but the allegory itself is always too carefully slide-ruled… What disturbs me is the question whether Hitchcock has at last become so engrossed in the solution of pure problems of technique that he has lost some of his sensitiveness toward the purely human aspects of what he is doing.'

Note that the film promotes war bonds in its closing credits ('Buy your war bonds in this theatre,' audiences were encouraged). It went on to earn Oscar nominations for best screen story (John Steinbeck), best cinematography (Glen MacWilliams) and best director, making it Hitchcock's second nomination. None of the nominees took home the golden statuette, though. The film was adapted for radio in 1950 (with Tallulah Bankhead) and later remade as a science fiction piece titled *Lifepod* in 1993.

Hitchcock cameo Concerned that he wouldn't be able to make his customary cameo in the film, except perhaps as a body floating by, Hitchcock eventually came up with the ingenious solution of appearing in a newspaper ad for 'Reduco – Obesity Slayer,' which features him in before and after photos (said Hitch of his appearance: 'That's my favourite role, and I must admit that I had an awful time thinking it up' [13]).

Lifepod
(US, 1993, 84m, colour, TVM) ★

CREDITS
Production company:	Fox West/Trilogy/RHI
Producers:	Mark Stern, Tim Harbert
Executive producers:	Richard B Lewis, John Watson, Pen Densham
Director:	Ron Silver
Screenplay:	M Jay Roach, Pen Densham
Story:	Pen Densham
Cinematographer:	Robert Steadman
Music:	Hans Zimmer, Mark Mancina
Editor:	Alan Baumgarten
Production designer:	Curtis R Schnell
Costumes:	Katherine Dover
Special effects:	Starlight Films, Sam Nicholson
Sound:	Richard Lightstone

CAST
Ron Silver (Miles Terman), Robert Loggia (Daniel Banks), C C H Pounder (Lieutenant Janna Mayvene), Adam Storke (Kane), Jessica Tuck (Clair), Kelli Williams (Rena), Stan Shaw (Parker), Ed Gale (Q3)

In this ingenious TV movie re-working of Hitch's *Lifeboat* (1944), a group of survivors, who have abandoned their space cruiser, gradually come to realize while in a cramped lifepod that one of them is a murderer. But the question is: which one? The answer isn't hard to figure out, but the film remains intriguing, and makes the most of its claustrophobic setting.

LION, LEON M (1879–1947) British actor-manager. On stage from 1895, Lion had the 1925 play *Joyous Melodrama* specifically devised for him by playwright J Jefferson Farjeon; this was filmed by Hitchcock as *Number Seventeen* in 1932, in which Lion reprised his original stage role, that of the Cockney tramp Ben (who appeared in several other Farjeon plays). Lion also produced the film with John Maxwell. His other films include *Amazing Adventure* (1936), *Crackerjack* (1938) and *Strange Boarders* (1938). **Hitchography:** *Number Seventeen* (1932)

LIVINGSTON, RAY (1915–2002, real name Jacob Harold Levison) American songwriter. Long partnered with lyricist Ray Evans, this duo won best song Oscars for *Buttons and Bows* from *The Paleface* (1948), *Mona Lisa* from *Captain Carey USA* (1950) and the irritatingly sentimental *Que Sera Sera* from Hitchcock's *The Man Who Knew Too Much* (1956), for which they also penned *We'll Love Again*. The duo's other films include *My Friend Irma* (1949), *Son of Paleface* (1952) and *Houseboat* (1958), as well as the TV themes for *Bonanza* (1960–1973) and *Mr Ed* (1962–1965). In 1958, Livingston and Evans composed a song to promote Hitchcock's *Vertigo*, which was subsequently recorded by singer Billy Eckstine, but the record quickly disappeared. Then, in 1966, the duo added lyrics to John Addison's love theme from Hitchcock's *Torn Curtain*. Titled *Green Years*, it was again used as a promotional item and not actually heard in the film (although it features on the soundtrack album). **Hitchography:** *The Man Who Knew Too Much* (1956), *Vertigo* (1958), *Torn Curtain* (1966)

LLOYD, DORIS (1900–1968) British-born actress. Following stage experience in Britain, Lloyd moved to America in the mid-1920s, where she was much used as a supporting artist in Hollywood, usually in upper crust roles. Her many films include *The Lady* (1925), *Waterloo Bridge* (1930), *Becky Sharp* (1935), the second remake of Hitchcock's *The Lodger* (1944), *The Secret Life of Walter Mitty* (1947), *Mary Poppins* (1964) and *The Sound of Music* (1965). In 1941 she made an un-credited appearance in Hitchcock's *Suspicion* as one of the Miss Wetherbys. She also appeared in three episodes of *Alfred Hitchcock Presents*. **Hitchography:** *Suspicion* (1941), *The Impromptu Murder* (1958, TV), *Safety for the Witness* (1958, TV), *The Schartz-Metterlume Method* (1960, TV)

LLOYD, FRANK (1888–1960) Scottish-born actor and director. Best remembered for directing *Mutiny on the Bounty* (1935), Frank Lloyd began his career as an actor on the English stage in 1903. By 1910 he'd emigrated to Canada, where he continued his stage career. Then, in 1913, he made the move to Hollywood, where he appeared in a number of westerns. In 1914, he began to turn his attention to directing, helming the short *Billie's Baby*. Many shorts later, among them *For His Superior's Humor* (1914) and *Little Miss Fixer* (1915), Lloyd began to turn to more serious subjects with the likes of *A Tale of Two Cities* (1917), *Madame X* (1920) and *The Sea Hawk* (1924). In 1929, he won an Oscar for directing *The Divine Lady*. A second Oscar followed for *Cavalcade* in 1933. Yet despite further hits with *Mutiny on the Bounty* (1935), which won the best picture Oscar, and *Under Two Flags* (1936), Lloyd's career began to slip in the late 1930s. Nevertheless, he continued to direct and, occasionally, produce, among his credits being Hitchcock's *Saboteur* (1942), which he bought as a package from David O Selznick and made at Universal. Lloyd's final films include *Blood on the Sun* (1945), *The Shanghai Story* (1954) and *The Last Command* (1955). **Hitchography:** *Saboteur* (1942)

LLOYD, NORMAN (1914–) American actor. On stage as a child from 1919, Norman Lloyd played his most memorable role in his film debut, that of the real saboteur Frank Fry in Hitchcock's *Saboteur* (1942), about which *Variety* commented, 'Norman Lloyd is genuinely plausible as the ferret-like culprit who sets the fatal airplane factory fire.' Wisecracked screenwriter Ben Hecht – who penned Hitchcock's *Spellbound* (1945) and *Notorious* (1946) – of Lloyd's famous fall from the Statue of Liberty in the film: 'He should have had a better tailor!' [14]

Lloyd's subsequent films include *The Unseen* (1945), *The Southerner* (1945) and a further stint for Hitchcock in *Spellbound* (1945), in which he played Garmes, the mental patient with a guilt complex and a fascination for letter openers. Following the likes of *The Green Years* (1946), *The Flame and the Arrow* (1950) and *Limelight* (1951), Lloyd took a sabbatical from acting and turned to producing, among his credits being the television series *Alfred Hitchcock Presents* (1955–1961) and *The Alfred Hitchcock Hour* (1962–1965), of which he also appeared in three – *Design for Loving* (1958, TV), *The Little Man Who Was There* (1960, TV), *Maria* (1961, TV) – and directed 22 (see below). Lloyd began acting in films again in 1977 with *Audrey Rose*, which he followed with the likes of *The Nude Bomb* (1980), *Dead Poets Society* (1989), *The Age of Innocence* (1993) and *The Adventures of Rocky and Bullwinkle* (2000). He also had a recurring role in TV's *St Elsewhere* (1983–1989) as Dr Daniel Auschlander and *Seven Days* (1998–2001) as Isaac Mentnor. Recalled Lloyd of the *Alfred Hitchcock Presents* series: 'Hitch was The Star. And without Hitch, it would have been just another show... Those lead-ins which he appeared in were *very* much part of the draw of the show.' [15] **Hitchography:** *Saboteur* (1942), *Spellbound* (1945), *Design for Loving* (1958, TV), *The*

$2000 Defense (1958, TV), *Safety for the Witness* (1958, TV), *Six People, No Music* (1959, TV), *Your Witness* (1959, TV), *The Human Interest Story* (1959, TV), *No Pain* (1959, TV), *Anniversary Gift* (1959, TV), *Special Delivery* (1959, TV), *Man from the South* (1960, TV), *The Little Man Who Was There* (1960, TV), *The Day of the Bullet* (1960, TV), *Hooked* (1960, TV), *A Very Moral Theft* (1960, TV), *The Contest of Aaron Gold* (1960, TV), *Oh, Youth and Beauty* (1960, TV), *Incident in a Small Jail* (1961, TV), *Maria* (1961, TV), *You Can't Be a Little Girl All You're Life* (1961, TV), *I, Spy* (1961, TV), *The Faith of Aaron Menefee* (1962, TV), *Strange Miracle* (1962, TV), *Final Vow* (1962, TV), *The Jar* (1964, TV), *The Life and Work of Juan Diaz* (1964, TV)

LOCKWOOD, ALEXANDER American supporting actor. Lockwood played the disbelieving judge in Hitchcock's *North by Northwest* (1959). His other credits include *Beauty and the Beast* (1962), *Walk on the Wild Side* (1962) and *The Monkey's Uncle* (1965). He also popped up as a pastor in Hitchcock's last film, *Family Plot* (1976). **Hitchography:** *North by Northwest* (1959), *Family Plot* (1976)

LOCKWOOD, MARGARET (1916–1990, real name Margaret Day) British actress. Making her film debut in 1934 in *Lorna Doone*, Lockwood went on to become Britain's leading star actress in the 1940s, notably in such successes as *The Man in Grey* (1943), *Love Story* (1944) and, in particular, *The Wicked Lady* (1945). Though she excelled at villainous roles, it was as an *ingenue* in *Bank Holiday* (1938), Hitchcock's *The Lady Vanishes* (1938) and *Night Train to Munich* (1940) that she first cemented her appeal. Said Lockwood of working with Hitchcock on *The Lady Vanishes*, in which she played Iris Henderson, the young woman who is convinced that her travelling companion has disappeared: 'I found him most disconcerting because, having thoroughly worked out his film in script and sketch form, he rarely spoke to his players when actual shooting was in progress.' [16] Lockwood's other films include *Dr Syn* (1937), *The Stars Look Down* (1939), *Quiet Wedding* (1941), *Jassy* (1947) and *Cast a Dark Shadow* (1957), following which she retired from the big screen to concentrate on stage and television work, although she did return for one last appearance, as Cinderella's wicked stepmother in *The Slipper and the Rose* (1976). **Hitchography:** *The Lady Vanishes* (1938)

LODER, JOHN (1898–1988, real name John Lowe) British-born actor. Following experience as a cavalry officer, Loder turned to acting, first as an extra in German films, beginning with *Madame Wunscht Keine Kinder* in 1926, following which he appeared in films in Britain, Hollywood and Argentina, where he finally retired to become a cattle rancher. Loder made over 100 films despite being one of the most wooden leading men the movies has ever seen, among them such high profile works as *The Private Life of Henry VIII* (1933), *Sing as We Go* (1933), *How Green Was My Valley* (1941), *Now, Voyager* (1942) and *The Story of Esther Costello* (1957). He also

the *Secret Weapon* (1942) and *Sherlock Holmes in Washington* (1943), to B westerns such as *River Lady* (1948), *The Fargo Phantom* (1950) and *The Groom Wore Spurs* (1951). He was also occasionally let loose on A features, among them Hitchcock's *Saboteur* (1942). Yet despite its chase scenario and its multiple settings, the film lacks pace and feels bloated at 108 minutes. **Hitchography:** *Saboteur* (1942)

LUKAS, PAUL (1887–1971, real name Pal Lukacs) Hungarian-born actor. In films from 1915 with *A Man of the Earth*, Lukas found much employment in British, American and European films, more often than not as the villain of the piece, as per his role as the seemingly urbane Dr Hartz in Hitchcock's *The Lady Vanishes* (1938). His many other films include such classics as *Dodsworth* (1936), *Confessions of a Nazi Spy* (1939), *The Ghost Breakers* (1940), *Watch on the Rhine* (1943), which won him a best actor Oscar, *20,000 Leagues Under the Sea* (1954) and *55 Days at Peking* (1962). **Hitchography:** *The Lady Vanishes* (1938)

LUMMIS, DAYTON (1903–1988) American character actor. Following considerable stage and radio experience, Lummis found himself a useful support in a number of 1950s' films, among them *Les Miserables* (1952), *Ruby Gentry* (1953) and Hitchcock's *The Wrong Man* (1956), in which he played Judge Groat, who presides over the mistrial of Manny Balestrero (Henry Fonda). He also appeared in two episodes of *Alfred Hitchcock Presents*, in one of which, *Mr Blanchard's Secret* (1956, TV), he was again directed by Hitchcock. **Hitchography:** *The Wrong Man* (1956), *Mr Blanchard's Secret* (1956, TV), *Listen! Listen!* (1958, TV)

LYNCH, KEN American supporting actor. Lynch appeared in numerous films in the 1950s and 1960s, among them *The Bonnie Parker Story* (1958), *I Married a Monster from Outer Space* (1958) and *Apache Rifles* (1964). He can also be spotted in Hitchcock's *North by Northwest* (1959) as one of two Chicago cops sent to arrest Cary Grant's Roger Thornhill for causing a ruckus at an auction house in a bid to escape enemy agents out to kill him. **Hitchography:** *North by Northwest* (1959)

German character star Peter Lorre plays the piece of music to which Frank Vosper will assassinate a dignitary at the Albert Hall in Hitchcock's The Man Who Knew Too Much *(1934). Leslie Banks and Nova Pilbeam look on.*

M

MABRY, MOSS American costume designer. Resident at Warner Bros. in the 1950s, Mabry designed the wardrobe for such productions as Hitchcock's *Dial M for Murder* (1954) and *Giant* (1956). Recalled Hitchcock of Mabry's work on *Dial M for Murder*: 'We did an interesting colour experiment with Grace Kelly's clothing. I dressed her in very gay and bright colours at the beginning of the picture, and as the plot thickened, her clothes became gradually more sombre.' [1] **Hitchography:** *Dial M for Murder* (1954)

MCCALLUM, GORDON K British sound recordist. McCallum won an Oscar for his work on *Fiddler on the Roof* (1971) and a BAFTA for *Jesus Christ Superstar* (1973). He also recorded the sound for Hitchcock's last British picture, *Frenzy* (1972), which includes one scene in which all the peripheral sound is faded away, allowing Barry Foster's neck-tie killer Robert Rusk to quietly ask his next victim, 'Got a place to stay?' **Hitchography:** *Frenzy* (1972)

MCCOWEN, ALEC (1925–) British actor. On stage in rep from 1942, McCowen began appearing in films in 1953 with *The Cruel Sea*. He has since provided solid supporting work, sometimes as co-star, in the likes of *The Witches* (1966), *Travels with My Aunt* (1972), *Stevie* (1978), *Never Say Never Again* (1983), in which he played Q, *Personal Services* (1986) and *Henry V* (1989), while his television outings include *Angel Pavement* (1958) and *Mr Palfrey of Westminster* (1984–1985). In 1972, he played Chief Inspector Oxford in Hitchcock's *Frenzy*. Said McCowen of his casting: 'Hitchcock cast rather daringly, because people like myself, Anna Massey and Barry Foster weren't really known for our film work. But as far as the films I *have* made, I'd have to say it's probably the highlight, looking back.' [2] **Hitchography:** *Frenzy* (1972)

MCCREA, JOEL (1905–1990) American actor. One of Hollywood's most affable leading men, McCrea began his film career in 1927 with *The Fair Co-Ed*. By 1932 he was taking leading roles in *Bird of Paradise* and *The Most Dangerous Game*, and established himself as a more than capable actor in *These Three* (1936) and *Dead End* (1937). One of his best roles was that of the naïve newspaper reporter Johnny Jones in Hitchcock's *Foreign Correspondent* (1940), although Hitchcock made no bones about hiding the fact that his preferred choice had been Gary Cooper, who turned the part down. Commented *Variety* of his performance as Jones: 'Joel McCrea neatly blends the self-confidence and naïvité of the reporter-hero.' McCrea's many other films include *Sullivan's Travels* (1942), *The Palm Beach Story* (1942) and many westerns, the best of them being *Ride the High Country* (1961). He was married to actress Frances Dee (1907– , real name Jean Frances Dee) from 1933 to his death. **Hitchography:** *Foreign Correspondent* (1940)

MCDEVITT, RUTH (1895–1976) American actress. McDevitt had a busy old age playing character roles in a variety of films, including *The Parent Trap* (1962), Hitchcock's *The Birds* (1963), in which she can be seen as pet shop manageress Mrs MacGruder in the opening scenes, *The Out of Towners* (1969) and *Change of Habit* (1972), while her television work included the series *Pistols and Petticoats* (1966). **Hitchography:** *The Birds* (1963)

MACDONALD, PHILIP (1899–1980) British thriller writer. MacDonald's work includes *The List of Adrian Messenger* and *Twenty Three Paces to Baker Street*, both of which have been filmed. He also worked on many screenplays, among them Hitchcock's *Rebecca* (1940), contributing to the disastrous first draft, much criticized by producer David O Selznick ('I am shocked and disappointed beyond words by the treatment,' [3] he commented). MacDonald's other screen credits include *Raise the Roof* (1930), *Mr Moto's Last Warning* (1939) and *Ring of Fear* (1954). **Hitchography:** *Rebecca* (1940)

MCDONELL, GORDON American novelist. McDonell, who was married to Margaret McDonell, the head of David O Selznick's story department, came up with the original story on which the script for Hitchcock's *Shadow of a Doubt* (1943) was subsequently based. He earned an Academy Award nomination for best screen story for his efforts. **Hitchography:** *Shadow of a Doubt* (1943)

MCDONNELL, CLAUDE L British cinematographer. McDonnell photographed many of the silents on which Alfred Hitchcock worked as an assistant director. When Hitchcock himself became a director, he hired McDonnell to photograph two further films for him: *Downhill* and *Easy Virtue*, both made in 1927. Unfortunately, a disagreement over financial terms saw McDonnell replaced by Jack Cox for Hitchcock's next film, *The Ring* (1927). McDonnell's other films include *The Crooked Billet* (1929) and *City of Play* (1929). **Hitchography:** *Woman to Woman* (1923), *The White Shadow* (1924), *The Passionate Adventure* (1924), *The Prude's Fall* (1925), *The Blackguard* (1925), *Downhill* (1927), *Easy Virtue* (1927)

MACGOWAN, KENNETH (1888–1963) American producer. Following experience as a critic and theatre producer (working with Eugene O'Neill), MacGowan became a story editor for RKO in the early 1930s. This led to work as an associate producer and, eventually, producer, both at RKO and Fox. In this capacity MacGowan worked on *The Penguin Pool Murder* (1932), *Becky Sharp* (1935), *Young Mr Lincoln* (1939), *Stanley and Livingstone* (1939) and *Tin Pan Alley* (1940). In 1944 he produced Hitchcock's *Lifeboat*, for which he earned the director's thanks and approval for allowing him to make the film with little studio interference. Commented critic Herb Sterne of the film: 'The work has the advantage of the discriminating production guidance of Kenneth

MacGowan, Alfred Hitchcock's sensitive and restrained direction... and performances that both individually and collectively are just about precisely right.' Following work on *Jane Eyre* (1944) and *Easy Come, Easy Go* (1947), MacGowan retired from producing to become the chairman of UCLA's Department of Theatre Arts. He also wrote a number of books on film and theatre, including *Behind the Screen*. **Hitchography:** *Lifeboat* (1944)

MCGRAW, CHARLES (1914–1980) American character actor. This busy actor began appearing in films in the early 1940s following stage and radio experience. His many big screen appearances include *The Undying Monster* (1942), *The Narrow Margin* (1952), in which he took a rare leading role, *The Defiant Ones* (1958), *Spartacus* (1960) and Hitchcock's *The Birds* (1963), in which he played Sebastian Sholes. A familiar face on television, McGraw appeared in *Casablanca* (1955–1956) as Rick, and *The Smith Family* (1971–1972). He also starred in an episode of *The Alfred Hitchcock Hour*. **Hitchography:** *The Birds* (1963), *Diagnosis: Danger* (1963, TV)

THE 'MCGUFFIN' The much-mentioned 'McGuffin' was simply a device – usually irrelevant – to compel the action forward in a Hitchcock film. This could vary from the search for a secret organization, as in *The 39 Steps* (1935), to a non-existent decoy spy, as in *North by Northwest* (1959). Sometimes it was a formula, as in *Torn Curtain* (1966); sometimes it was a missing heir, as in *Family Plot* (1976). On one occasion, it was even something as simple as a missing overcoat belt, as in *Young and Innocent* (1937). However, once it had served its purpose, the McGuffin was quickly – almost contemptuously – explained or disposed of. The term was apparently coined by screenwriter Angus MacPhail from a joke about a device for trapping lions in the Scottish Highlands; as there are no lions in the Scottish Highlands, the McGuffin is of course irrelevant. However, it did prove handy as a catch-name for publicity purposes. It has since entered the public lexicon, and has even been used in film titles in its own right, as per *The Double McGuffin* (1979), in which a bunch of kids turn detective to prevent an assassination, and *The McGuffin* (1985, TV), in which a film critic suspects his neighbours of being involved in a murder plot (note that the latter film features former Hitchcock stars Ann Todd, Anna Massey and Bill Shine).

MCINTIRE, JOHN (1907–1991) American supporting actor. In films from the mid-1940s following experience as a seaman and a radio announcer, McIntire was frequently cast as a sheriff, his most famous being in Hitchcock's *Psycho* (1960), in which he played Sheriff Chambers ('You must remember that bad business out there about 10 years ago,' he comments of the Bates Motel, where Janet Leigh's Marion Crane appears to have gone missing). His many other films include *The Asphalt Jungle* (1950), *Apache* (1954), *Rooster Cogburn*

(1975) and *Cloak and Dagger* (1984), while on television he was a familiar face in such series as *The Naked City* (1959), *Wagon Train* (1961–1964) and *The Virginian* (1967–1969). He also appeared in two episodes of *Alfred Hitchcock Presents*. He was married to actress Jeanette Nolan (1911–1998) from 1935, and it should be noted that she dubbed some of Mother's lines in *Psycho*. Their son was the singer Tim McIntire (1943–1986). **Hitchography:** *Sylvia* (1958, TV), *Psycho* (1960), *Hitch Hike* (1960, TV)

MACLAINE, SHIRLEY (1934– , real name Shirley Maclean Beaty) American actress. This talented and vivacious singer, dancer and actress was discovered in the Broadway musical *The Pajama Game* by producer Hal Wallis while understudying leading lady Carol Haney who, in true Hollywood fashion, had broken her ankle. Later in the run, she was again spotted understudying the ill Haney by Hitchcock's associate producer Herbert Coleman and his unit manager Doc Erickson, who suggested that MacLaine would be perfect casting for the role of Jennifer Rogers in the director's up-coming black comedy *The Trouble with Harry* (1955), in which she went on to make her film debut. The film was poorly received, but nevertheless helped to launch the burgeoning star's film career. Hitchcock was particularly taken with MacLaine, as screenwriter John Michael Hayes recalled: 'When she came down on set and read her lines, Hitch said to me, "I'm not going to tamper with this girl. She has such an odd quality and it's delightful. I start giving her directions, and we're going to lose it."' [4] Added MacLaine of the incident: 'I remember the first script reading we had. Something came to me, like the mystery of acting does, and I just kind of invented this little part. And Hitch said to me, "My darling, you have the guts of a bank robber!"' [5]

In her subsequent career, MacLaine has appeared in such classics as *Ask Any Girl* (1959), *The Apartment* (1960), *Irma La Douce* (1963), *Sweet Charity* (1968), *Being There* (1979), *Terms of Endearment* (1983), which won her a best actress Oscar, *Steel Magnolias* (1989) and *Postcards from the Edge* (1990). Her television work includes the series *Shirley's World* (1971) plus many guest spots, while on stage and in cabaret she has successfully toured the world several times over. She is the sister of superstar Warren Beatty (1937– , real name Warren Beaty). **Hitchography:** *The Trouble with Harry* (1955)

MCLAUGHLIN, GIBB (1884–1960) British character actor. This emaciated-looking actor popped up as a supporting actor in countless productions, among them such key films as *Carnival* (1921), *The Private Life of Henry VIII* (1933), *The Scarlet Pimpernel* (1934), *Caesar and Cleopatra* (1945) and *Oliver Twist* (1948). A former stage monologuist, he also played the supporting role of Henry Coaker in Hitchcock's *The Farmer's Wife* (1927). His one leading role was in *Mr Reeder in Room Thirteen* (1940). **Hitchography:** *The Farmer's Wife* (1927)

MCNAUGHTON, GUS (1884–1969, real name Augustus Howard) British comedy actor. On stage from 1899 in musical hall, this former member of Fred Karno's Troupe supplied comedy relief in a number of British films in the 1930s and 1940s, most memorably in Hitchcock's *The 39 Steps* (1935), in which he and Jerry Verno played a couple of commercial travellers whose frank talk about the ladies' underwear they are pedaling made a memorable vignette. His other films include *Keep Your Seats, Please* (1937), *Much Too Shy* (1942) and an un-credited role in Hitchcock's *Murder!* (1930). **Hitchography:** *Murder!* (1930), *The 39 Steps* (1935)

MACPHAIL, ANGUS (1903–1962) British screen-writer. Though he first met Hitchcock in 1925 at the Film Society, MacPhail didn't work with the director until 1944, when he co-authored the scripts for two French-language shorts for the Ministry of Information that Hitchcock directed as part of the war effort. It was also during this period that MacPhail worked with Hitchcock on the first screenplay draft of *Spellbound* (1945), which was then further developed in Hollywood by Ben Hecht. Like Hitchcock, MacPhail began his career as a title writer during the silent period. However, with the coming of sound, he turned to scriptwriting, among his early credits being *The Wrecker* (1928), *The Ghost Train* (1931) and *My Old China* (1931).

In 1931 he became the story supervisor for Gainsborough, a post he retained until 1937. He took on the same post at Gaumont-British in 1939, remaining with the studio until 1948, after which he decamped to Ealing, where he scripted such classics as *It Always Rains on Sunday* (1947) and *Whisky Galore* (1948). He worked for Hitchcock again in Hollywood, firstly on an un-produced adaptation of Laurens van der Post's *Flamingo Feather*, which the director intended to film following *To Catch a Thief* (1955), then as a contributor to the script for the remake of *The Man Who Knew Too Much* (1956), but an arbitration brought about by writer John Michael Hayes saw MacPhail's credit removed. Nevertheless, MacPhail went on to co-write *The Wrong Man* (1957) for Hitch, and made some un-credited contributions to the development of the script for *Vertigo* (1958). He is also said to have been responsible for coining the much-used Hitchcock term 'McGuffin,' which the director used to describe the device (most often irrelevant) that compels the plot. **Hitchography:** *Bon Voyage* (1944), *Aventure Malgache* (1944), *Spellbound* (1945), *The Man Who Knew Too Much* (1956), *The Wrong Man* (1957), *Vertigo* (1958)

MACRORIE, ALMA American-born staff editor. Long at Paramount, MacRorie was asked to cut Hitchcock's black comedy *The Trouble with Harry* (1955) when his regular editor George Tomasini proved too busy on the director's previous film, *To Catch a Thief* (1955). MacRorie's other credits include *Lady in the Dark* (1944) and *The Bridges at Toko-Ri* (1954), for which she was nominated for an Oscar. **Hitchography:** *The Trouble with Harry* (1955)

MACWILLIAMS, GLEN (1898–1984) American-born cinematographer. MacWilliams began his career in Hollywood, where he photographed such productions as *Ever Since Eve* (1921), *Captain January* (1924) and *The Sea Wolf* (1930). In 1933 he was signed to work for Gaumont-British where he became associated with the musicals of Jessie Matthews, of which he photographed seven, beginning with Hitchcock's disappointing *Waltzes from Vienna* (1933), following which came such favourites as *Evergreen* (1934), *First a Girl* (1935) and *Gangway* (1937), to each of which MacWilliams gave a distinctive American gloss. Back in Hollywood, he continued his career with *Great Guns* (1941), *He Hired the Boss* (1943) and Hitchcock's *Lifeboat* (1944), for which he faced the challenge of photographing a film set entirely in an adrift lifeboat. For his efforts, MacWilliams earned an Academy Award nomination. **Hitchography:** *Waltzes from Vienna* (1933), *Lifeboat* (1944)

MADAGASCAR LANDING see *Aventure Malgache*

MAHIN, JOHN LEE (1902–1984) American-born scriptwriter. Responsible for writing some of the best films to come out of Hollywood in the 1930s, Mahin scripted such classics as *Scarface* (1932), *Red Dust* (1932), *Bombshell* (1933), *Captain Courageous* (1937) and *Too Hot to Handle* (1938). He also had a hand in the writing of Hitchcock's *Foreign Correspondent* (1940), but his work went un-credited. Mahin's other screenplays include *Quo Vadis?* (1951), *Elephant Walk* (1954) and *Heaven Knows, Mr Allison* (1957). He also produced one film, John Ford's *The Horse Soldiers* (1959), which he also wrote. **Hitchography:** *Foreign Correspondent* (1940)

MAIBAUM, RICHARD (1909–1991) American play-wright. From *Dr No* in 1962 through to *Licence to Kill* in 1989, Maibaum had a hand in the writing of 12 screen-plays for the James Bond series. His other work includes *We Went to College* (1936), *The Great Gatsby* (1949) and *The Day They Robbed the Bank of England* (1960). He also made un-credited contributions to the script of Hitchcock's *Foreign Correspondent* (1940). His plays include *The Tree*, *Sweet Mystery of Life*, which was filmed as *Gold Diggers of 1937* (1936), and *See My Lawyer*. **Hitchography:** *Foreign Correspondent* (1940)

MALDEN, KARL (1913– , real name Mladen Sekulovich) American actor. Known to television audiences the world over as Detective Lieutenant Mike Stone in *The Streets of San Francisco*, which ran from 1973 to 1980, this bulb-nosed actor of Yugoslavian parentage has also had a distinguished career on the big screen. On Broadway from 1937 and in films from 1940 with *They Knew What They Wanted*, he went on to contribute notable performances to the likes of *A Streetcar Named Desire* (1951), which won him a best supporting actor Oscar for re-creating his original stage role of Mitch, *On the Waterfront* (1954), *Baby Doll* (1956), *Bird Man of Alcatraz*

Leslie Banks and child star Nova Pilbeam in a tense moment from Hitchcock's The Man Who Knew Too Much *(1934)*

(1962) and *Patton* (1969). In 1953 he played Inspector Larrue in Hitchcock's *I Confess*, earning particular praise for his performance from the *Times*, whose critic commented that Malden 'acts everyone else off the screen.' Said Malden of the performance of his co-star Montgomery Clift, 'His ability to project mood and a held-back strength is quite extraordinary.' [6] Malden's many other films include *The Cincinnati Kid* (1965), *Nevada Smith* (1966), *Billion Dollar Brain* (1967), *Nuts* (1987) and *Back to the Streets of San Francisco* (1992, TV). He also directed one film, *Time Limit* (1957). **Hitchography:** *I Confess* (1953)

MALLESON, MILES (1888–1969, real name William Miles Malleson) British actor and writer. Malleson seems to have been on hand as either an actor or writer at all the key moments in the history of the British film industry. A playwright from 1915, his screenplay credits include *Nell Gwyn* (1934), *Victoria the Great* (1937) and *The Thief and Bagdad* (1940); as an actor he can be spotted in, among countless others, *Bitter Sweet* (1933), *Dead of Night* (1945), *Kind Hearts and Coronets* (1949), *The Importance of Being Earnest* (1952), *Dracula* (1958) and *I'm Alright, Jack* (1959). He also made a brief, un-credited appearance as the frustrated manager of the London Palladium at the climax of Hitchcock's *The 39 Steps* (1935) and later popped up in *Stage Fright* (1950) as Mr Fortescue, a short-sighted pub busy-body with bottle-bottom glasses. **Hitchography:** *The 39 Steps* (1935), *Stage Fright* (1950)

MALTBY, H F (1880–1963, real name Henry F Maltby) British character actor. This blustering actor first came to the screen in 1921 in *The Rotters*, although it would be 14 years before he appeared before the cameras again in *Facing the Music* (1935). His many other films include *I Spy* (1933), *Over the Garden Wall* (1934), *A Yank at Oxford* (1938), *Pygmalion* (1938) and *A Canterbury Tale* (1944). One of his best cameos came in Hitchcock's *Young and Innocent* (1937) in which he played the police sergeant forced to hitch a ride in a farmer's pig cart. Some sources state that he also had a part in Hitchcock's *Secret Agent* (1936). **Hitchography:** *Secret Agent* (1936), *Young and Innocent* (1937)

MALYON, EILY (1879–1961, real name Eily Lees-Craston) British-born character actress. This sepulchral bit-part player moved to Hollywood in 1931 following stage experience. Making her film debut in *Born to Love* (1931), she was subsequently much used as spinster types in the likes of *Great Expectations* (1934), *Clive of India* (1935), *Dracula's Daughter* (1936), *On Borrowed Time* (1938), *The Hound of the Baskervilles* (1939) and *Untamed* (1940). She can also be spotted as a hotel cashier in Hitchcock's *Foreign Correspondent* (1940) and as a stern librarian in *Shadow of a Doubt* (1943). Her other films include *Jane Eyre* (1943), *Going My Way* (1944), *She-Wolf of London* (1946) and *The Challenge* (1948), following which she retired. **Hitchography:** *Foreign Correspondent* (1940), *Shadow of a Doubt* (1943)

The Man from Home
(GB, 1922, 67m approx, bw, silent)

CREDITS

Production company:	Famous Players-Lasky
Director:	George Fitzmaurice
Screenplay:	Ouida Bergere, from the novel by Booth Tarkington and Harry Leon Wilson
Inter-titles:	Alfred Hitchcock

CAST

Anna Q Nilsson (Genevieve Granger-Simpson), James Kirkwood (Daniel Forbes Pike), Norman Kerry (Prince Leone Charmante), Dorothy Cumming (Princess Sabina), Geoffrey Kerr (Horance Granger-Simpson), John Milterne (King), Annette Benson (Faustina Riviere)

Released in 1922, this lost black-and-white silent centred round an American heiress and her fiancé who, while holidaying in Italy, help a fisherman who has been accused of stabbing his wife. Directed by George Fitzmaurice for Famous Players-Lasky, the film featured inter-titles designed by Hitchcock.

The Man in the Attic

(USA, 1953, 79m, bw)

CREDITS

Production company:	Twentieth Century Fox
Producer:	Robert L Jacks
Director:	Hugo Fregonese
Screenwriters:	Robert Presnell Jr, Barre Lyndon, based on the novel *The Lodger* by Marie Belloc-Lowndes
Cinematographer:	Leo Tover
Music director:	Lionel Newman

CAST

Jack Palance (The Lodger/Slade), Constance Smith (Lily Bonner), Rhys Williams (William Harley), Frances Bavier (Helen Harley), Byron Palmer (Paul Warwick)

In this third remake of Hitchcock's silent classic *The Lodger* (1926), Jack Palance plays the guilty party. Unfortunately, the proceedings are barely distinguished this time round, least of all by style or atmosphere, despite a reversion to the Victorian setting of the original novel and the previous 1944 version (which, incidentally, was also scripted by Barre Lyndon).

The Man Who Knew Too Much

(GB, 1934, 84m (some sources state 76m and 85m), bw)
AA

CREDITS

Production company:	Gaumont-British
Producer:	Michael Balcon
Associate producer:	Ivor Montagu
Director:	Alfred Hitchcock
Screenplay:	Charles Bennett, D B Wyndham-Lewis, A R Rawlinson, Emlyn Williams, Edwin Greenwood
Cinematographer:	Curt Courant
Music:	Arthur Benjamin
Music director:	Louis Levy
Editor:	Hugh Stewart
Art directors:	Alfred Junge, Peter Proud
Sound:	F McNally

CAST

Leslie Banks (Bob Lawrence), Edna Best (Jill Lawrence), Nova Pilbeam (Betty Lawrence), Peter Lorre (Abbott), Frank Vosper (Ramon), Pierre Fresnay (Louis Bernard), Hugh Wakefield (Clive), George Curzon (Gibson), Cicely Oates (Nurse Agnes), D A Clarke-Smith (Inspector Binstead)

Video availability: Carlton

Though he'd had a number of notable successes by 1934, among them *The Lodger* (1926) and *Blackmail* (1929), Hitchcock's career had suffered something of a downturn by the time he came to make *The Man Who Knew Too Much*, his most recent disappointment *Waltzes from Vienna* (1933).

Following the making of *Number Seventeen* (1932) and *Lord Camber's Ladies* (1932), Hitchcock was finally free of his contract with producer John Maxwell at British International Pictures, and so went to work on the Strauss film at Gaumont-British for the independent producer Tom Arnold. It was while he was filming *Waltzes from Vienna* that studio head Michael Balcon visited the set. The outcome was the offer of a new contract, which the director jumped at, Balcon having given Hitch his start as a director at Gainsborough with *The Pleasure Garden* back in 1925. Recalled Hitchcock, 'It's to the credit of Michael Balcon that he originally started me as a director and later gave me a second chance.' [7] In fact it was this second chance that would fully launch Hitchcock's career, forever identifying him with the thriller genre.

The story for *The Man Who Knew Too Much* (the title of which had been taken from a collection of G K Chesterton stories, the rights to which Hitchcock had purchased) can be traced back to an idea Hitchcock and screenwriter Charles Bennett had worked on a couple of years earlier titled *Bulldog Drummond's Baby*, in which the fictional adventurer swings into action when his child is kidnapped. This idea had been turned down by Hitchcock's then-producer John Maxwell. With his new contract with Michael Balcon, Hitchcock decided to rework the idea, again collaborating with Bennett and four new writers, among them playwright Emlyn Williams. This time, instead of Bulldog Drummond, it's Bob Lawrence (Leslie Banks) who finds himself the target of a ring of assassins. Holidaying in St Moritz with his wife Jill (Edna Best) and his daughter Betty (Nova Pilbeam), the family is befriended by a French skier named Louis Bernard (Pierre Fresnay). It transpires that Bernard is a government agent with information about the impending assassination of a world leader, and when he himself is shot, he manages to pass on this information to the Lawrences before dying. However, to ensure that the Lawrences don't go to the police their daughter is kidnapped by the assassins…

Back in London, Mr Lawrence, working with his friend Clive (Hugh Wakefield), attempts to track down the villains via the information Bernard has passed on. This consists of two names: a G Barbour, who can be found in Wapping, and an A Hall. Barbour, it turns out, is a dentist, and it is while at his surgery that Lawrence sees two men whom he and his wife had encountered in St Moritz: a Mr Abbott (Peter Lorre) and a Mr Ramon (Frank Vosper). Correctly figuring that they have something to do with the plot, Lawrence and Clive follow them to the Tabernacle of the Sun, where things turn nasty and a fight breaks out. However, during the fracas, Lawrence spots some tickets in Ramon's pocket for a concert at the Albert Hall, and puts two and two together, figuring that this is where the assassination is to take place.

Anny Ondra looks suitably downcast in this visually arresting close-up from Hitchcock's The Manxman *(1929). Ondra would go on to work with Hitchcock again on his first talkie,* Blackmail *(1929).*

from Switzerland to Morocco, the basic narrative of the remake remains pretty much the same as its predecessor. Hitchcock had actually discussed the possibility of a remake of *The Man Who Knew Too Much* as early as 1941, when producer David O Selznick, to whom he was contracted at the time, bought the rights to the story. Yet despite script conferences with John Houseman, during which it was decided to relocate the story to Sun Valley and South America, the project failed to materialize. Having re-purchased the rights for $45,000 in 1954, Hitchcock decided to have another stab at the enterprise, for which he went into partnership with his star James Stewart and his agent Lew Wasserman.

Having worked on the script's outline with Angus MacPhail, Hitchcock handed over his notes to screenwriter John Michael Hayes, who had penned the director's three previous films. Hayes himself worked on the script – for a brief period known as *Into Thin Air* – between late February and mid-May, by which time Hitchcock was already in Morocco, with shooting set to start on 13 May 1955. Commented Hayes of the situation: 'Hitch went off and the script wasn't even finished... They went to Marrakech, and I was sending pages by Pan American pilot to the set.' [11] This situation was hardly conducive to good work, and Hayes' witless dialogue for the film ranks among the worst of his career (in fact, this

would prove to be the last time Hayes and Hitchcock collaborated, as the two fell out over Hayes' screen credit, which Hitchcock wanted to split between Hayes and Angus MacPhail; consequently, when Hayes took Hitchcock to arbitration over the situation and won the case, Hitchcock washed his hands of the writer).

Hayes' contribution to the film is by no means its sole downfall. Robert Burks's static cinematography continually fails to capture the eye; Bernard Herrmann's non-descript score fails to generate any suspense or atmosphere; George Tomasini's editing seems lethargic at best; while Hitchcock's direction lacks both style and invention. Indeed, the director manages to make the very *least* of the Moroccan locations, badly fudging the use of local colour, while making much use of obvious back projection during certain scenes, making one wonder why he bothered to go to the expense of dragging his cast and crew to Morocco in the first place (at one point early in the action, Hank points out that the scenery looks identical to that of the Arizona desert, where Hitchcock could just have easily filmed these sequences which, in the finished picture, grind on for 50 tedious minutes).

The scenes in London aren't much better, with Hitchcock again resorting to poor rear projection work at entirely inappropriate moments. In fact it is only during the climactic assassination sequence at the Albert Hall that the film comes to anything like life. Carefully shot and edited, the sequence manages to generate some genuine suspense, with Arthur Benjamin's *Storm Clouds Cantata* (conducted onscreen by Bernard Herrmann) adding immeasurably to the sense of impending danger (the whole sequence runs some 12 minutes, during which no dialogue is spoken). Unfortunately, this all comes too late in the proceedings to compensate for the barely tolerable tedium that has gone before it (which is further compounded by a cringe-making rendition of the sentimental ditty *Que Sera, Sera* by Jo and Hank in their hotel bedroom early in the proceedings, this went on to become a major hit for Doris Day, earning its writers, Jay Evans and Ray Livingston, an Oscar in the process).

Performance-wise, James Stewart wanders through the proceedings seemingly without much interest, while the usually sunny Doris Day remains a curious choice as the heroine of the piece, her cardboard emotions failing to generate much sympathy for her plight. As for Christopher Olsen's precocious Hank, there are times when one is firmly on the side of the kidnappers who, as played by Brenda De Banzie and Bernard Miles, perhaps come off best, their sheer ordinariness ringing a welcome change on the expected perceptions of how villains should look and act (that said, Reggie Nalder's assassin looks suitably sinister, while Betty Bascomb's Edna, one of the Draytons' cronies, is given the wild hair and bottle-bottom glasses treatment).

At the end of the day, the remake of *The Man Who Knew Too Much* is something of an expensive self-indulgence, with Hitchcock seemingly forgetting all the subtleties of his craft. The film's xenophobia and the McKennas' general suspicion of Johnny Foreigner are also fairly hard to stomach today (even though the couple's initial perception of Louis Bernard as a mysterious Frenchman and the Draytons as dull Englanders is effectively turned on its head). The film was perhaps best summed up by the *Times*, whose discerning critic concluded: 'In spite of colour, wide screen devices and even louder sound, the Hitchcock technique has not changed greatly since the days of 1934 when the first *The Man Who Knew Too Much* was a high water mark of British production.' Nevertheless, despite its generally poor reviews, the movie turned a tidy profit when released following its Hollywood premiere on 22 May 1956.

The film was spoofed in the 1997 Bill Murray comedy *The Man Who Knew Too Little*; this was also the title of an episode of the 1980s revival series of *Alfred Hitchcock Presents*.

Hitchcock cameo Note that Hitchcock can be spotted in the market place in Marrakech.

MANDER, MILES (1888–1946, real name Lionel Mander, also known as Luther Miles) British-born actor, writer, director and producer. An aviator during World War I, this prolific actor entered films in 1918 with *Once Upon a Time*, following which he also became a busy writer, director and producer with the likes of *The Temporary Lady* (1921), *Half a Truth* (1922) and *Lovers in Araby* (1924). He first encountered Hitchcock on the set of *The Prude's Fall* in 1925, on which Hitchcock was working as an assistant director. When he became a director himself, Hitch hired Mander to play the villainous Levett in his debut *The Pleasure Garden* (1925). Mander also returned briefly to the Hitchcock fold for a smaller role in *Murder!* (1930), while in 1932 he co-scripted the remake of Hitchcock's breakthrough film *The Lodger* (1926), though this time Maurice Elvey was in the director's chair. In 1935, Mander emigrated to Hollywood, where he appeared in the likes of *The Three Musketeers* (1936 and 1939, both times as Richelieu), *Wuthering Heights* (1939), *Farewell, My Lovely* (1944) and *The Pearl of Death* (1944). He also popped up in the wartime propaganda film *Watchtower Over Tomorrow* (1945) on which Hitchcock did some un-credited directorial work. **Hitchography:** *The Prude's Fall* (1925), *The Pleasure Garden* (1925), *Murder!* (1930), *Watchtower Over Tomorrow* (1945)

MANNHEIM, LUCIE (1895–1976) German-born character actress. Long resident in Britain, Mannheim is best remembered for her role as the spy Annabella Smith in Hitchcock's *The 39 Steps* (1935), whose death at the hands of enemy agents propels Robert Donat's Richard Hannay on his adventures. Her other films include *The High Command* (1937), *Hotel Reserve* (1944) and *Bunny Lake is Missing* (1965). Her husband was the actor Marius Goring (1912–1998). **Hitchography:** *The 39 Steps* (1935)

MANTELL, JOE (1920–) American actor. Nominated for a best supporting actor Oscar for his performance as Angie in *Marty* (1955), Mantell also notched up supporting roles in such films as *Barbary Pirate* (1949), *Beau James* (1957), Hitchcock's *The Birds* (1963), in which he played the travelling salesman in the Tides restaurant scene, *Chinatown* (1974) and *The Two Jakes* (1990). He also appeared in an early episode of *Alfred Hitchcock Presents*. **Hitchography:** *Guilty Witness* (1955, TV), *The Birds* (1963)

The Manxman

(GB, 1929, 80m (some source state 90m and 100m), bw, silent) ★

CREDITS

Production company:	British International Pictures
Producer:	John Maxwell
Director:	Alfred Hitchcock
Screenplay:	Eliot Stannard, based on the novel by Sir Hall Caine
Cinematographer:	Jack Cox
Editor:	Emile de Ruelle
Art director:	Wilfred Arnold
Assistant director:	Frank Mills
Stills:	Michael Powell

CAST

Anny Ondra (Kate Cregeen), Carl Brisson (Pete Quilliam), Malcolm Keen (Philip Christian), Randle Ayrton (Caesar Cregeen), Clare Greet (Mrs Cregeen)

Hitchcock's last silent was another romantic triangle akin to *The Ring* (1927), with echoes of Tenyson's *Enoch Arden*. This time Kate Cregeen (Anny Ondra), the daughter of wealthy Isle of Man landowner Caesar Cregeen (Randle Ayrton), falls for poor fisherman Pete Quilliam (Carl Brisson), much to the consternation of her father. Quilliam consequently attempts to prove his worth, but apparently dies at sea. Soon after, Quilliam's friend, solicitor Philip Christian (Malcolm Keen), confesses his love for Kate, proposing that they marry. Kate agrees, but their plans are thrown into disarray when Quilliam returns. Kate subsequently marries Quilliam, only to discover that she is carrying Christian's child…

Based on the 1894 novel by Sir Hall Caine, *The Manxman* had actually been filmed before in 1916 by George Loane Tucker, with the hugely popular Elizabeth Risdon in the role of Kate (Risdon was voted Britain's most popular British star in a 1915 poll). Unfortunately, Hitchcock seems to have had little enthusiasm for the project. 'The only point of interest about that movie is that it was my last silent one,' he later said, adding, 'It was a very banal picture… It was not a Hitchcock movie.' [12] Filmed in the autumn of 1928 in and around the tiny Cornish fishing village of Polperro (as opposed to the Isle of Man itself), the film was only a modest success. As always, Hitchcock surrounded himself with familiar technicians and players, among them Carl Brisson, Malcolm Keen, Clare Greet, Jack Cox and Wilfred Arnold, although there was one important newcomer, German leading lady Anny Ondra, who of course went on to star in Hitchcock's next picture, his first sound film *Blackmail* (1929).

Recalled the film's stills cameraman, future director Michael Powell: 'When it came to shooting *The Manxman*, only two scenes were shot on the Isle of Man. Hitch was not enthralled by local colour, except in city streets. Mostly, we shot around Minehead in Somerset, and in North Cornwall. The truth is Hitch was bored.' [13]

MARLOWE, NORA American supporting actress. Marlowe played the stern housekeeper of Philip Vandamm in Hitchcock's *North by Northwest* (1959), holding up Cary Grant's Roger Thornhill with a gun loaded with blanks just prior to the climax of the film. Her other credits include *That Funny Feeling* (1965), *The Hostage* (1966), *Gaily, Gaily* (1969) and *Westworld* (1973). **Hitchography:** *North by Northwest* (1959)

MARMONT, PERCY (1883–1977) British-born actor. On stage since 1900, Marmont toured the world, apparently making his film debut in 1913 in either Australia or South Africa, depending on which source one believes (although the actual title of the film is apparently lost to the mists of time). Following a stint on Broadway, he made his Hollywood debut in 1917 in *The Monk and the Woman*. Many more films followed, among them *Dead Men Tell No Tales* (1920), *The Marriage Cheat* (1924) and *A Woman's Faith* (1925). In 1928 Marmont returned to Britain, where he resumed his stage career, and also appeared in countless films, including *The Squeaker* (1930), *No Orchids for Miss Blandish* (1948) and *Hostile Witness* (1968). He also directed one film, *The Captain's Table* (1936). Marmont made the first of his three appearances for Hitchcock in *Rich and Strange* in 1932, in which he played Commander Gordon, who whisks the much-married heroine off her feet. More spectacularly, he met a sticky end when pushed off a cliff by Peter Lorre in *Secret Agent* (1936), while in *Young and Innocent* (1937) he played the heroine's policeman father, Colonel Burgoyne. **Hitchography:** *Rich and Strange* (1932), *Secret Agent* (1936), *Young and Innocent* (1937)

Marnie

(US, 1964, 130m, Technicolor) ★

CREDITS

Production company:	Universal/Geoffrey Stanley
Producer:	Alfred Hitchcock
Director:	Alfred Hitchcock
Screenplay:	Jay Presson Allen (and Evan Hunter), based on the novel by Winston Graham
Cinematographer:	Robert Burks
Music:	Bernard Herrmann
Editor:	George Tomasini
Production design:	Robert Boyle
Costumes:	Edith Head
Costume supervisors:	Rita Riggs, Vincent Dee, James Linn
Special effects:	Albert Whitlock
Sound:	Waldon O Watson, William Russell
Camera operator:	Leonard J South

CAST

Tippi Hedren (Marion 'Marnie' Edgar/Rutland/Holland), Sean Connery (Mark Rutland), Diane Baker (Lil Mainwaring), Louise Latham (Bernice Edgar), Martin Gabel (Sidney Strutt), Bob Sweeney (Cousin Bob), Mariette Hartley (Susan Clabon), Milton Selzer (Pest at track), Alan Napier (Mr Rutland), Bruce Dern (Sailor), Edith Evanson (Rita), Meg Wyllie (Mrs Turpin), S John Launder (Sam Ward), Louise Lorimer (Mrs Strutt), Morgan Brittany (Girl)

Video availability: Universal
DVD availability: Universal
CD availability: *Marnie* (Varese), which contains the complete score as performed by conductor Joel McNeely and the Royal Scottish National Orchestra; *Psycho – The Essential Alfred Hitchcock* (Silva Screen), which contains the

Hitchcock and Tippi Hedren discuss a scene during the making of Marnie *(1964). The two fell out midway through production and thereafter spoke only through intermediaries.*

Prelude; *Hitchcock − Master of Mayhem* (Proarte), which contains a *Suite*; *A History of Hitchcock − Dial M for Murder* (Silva Screen), which contains the *Prelude*; *Citizen Kane − The Essential Bernard Herrmann Film Music Collection* (Silva Screen), which contains the *Prelude*; *Music from the Great Hitchcock Movie Thrillers* (Decca/Phase 4), which contains a *Suite* conducted by Bernard Herrmann

Billed as 'Alfred Hitchcock's suspenseful sex mystery', *Marnie* was intended as a comeback vehicle for former Hitchcock star Grace Kelly, who had married Prince Ranier of Monaco since making *Dial M for Murder* (1954), *Rear Window* (1954) and *To Catch a Thief* (1955) for the director. However, when the good subjects of Monaco objected to their princess returning to Hollywood, a greatly disappointed Hitchcock instead decided to cast his new find Tippi Hedren − whom he'd introduced in *The Birds* (1963) − in the title role.

Work on the script for *Marnie*, based on the 1961 novel

by Winston Graham, had begun a year after the release of *Psycho* (1960), at which point that film's screenwriter Joseph Stefano was on board. When Grace Kelly turned the project down, Hitchcock instead threw himself into *The Birds*, during the production of which he decided to have another crack at the project, thus assigning his current screenwriter Evan Hunter to begin the chore of adapting the book. However, Hunter and Hitchcock had a disagreement over one of the film's key scenes (which involves marital rape), and so the director instead turned to playwright Jay Presson Allen, who at the time was basking in the success of her stage adaptation of the Muriel Spark novel *The Prime of Miss Jean Brodie*.

The action in *Marnie* centres round Marion Edgar (Tippi Hedren), a compulsive thief who also happens to be frigid owing to a traumatic experience in her childhood, which has left her with an aversion to thunderstorms and the colour red, too. Changing her appearance by dyeing her hair and adopting a variety of aliases,

Marnie, as she is nicknamed, manages to wheedle her way into a number of secretarial jobs, despite a lack of proper references. Once she has gained the trust of her employer, she robs the company before moving on to her next job. 'Robbed! Cleaned out! $9,967 precisely... And that girl did it, Marion Holland. Marion Holland,' complains the recently robbed Sidney Strutt.

However, when a prospective employer, a widowed businessman named Mark Rutland (Sean Connery), recognizes Marnie from a previous encounter at Strutt's offices, he decides to take her on, his curiosity – and libido – having been aroused. In fact it was this fetishistic angle that attracted Hitchcock to the story. 'A man wants to go to bed with a thief because she is a thief, just like other men have a yen for a Chinese or a colored woman,' [14] he explained. But he went on to admit that he hadn't quite managed to relay this satisfactorily in the finished film: 'It's not as effective as *Vertigo*, where Jimmy Stewart's feeling for Kim Novak was clearly a fetishist love. To put it bluntly, we'd have had to have Sean Connery catching the girl robbing the safe and show that he felt like jumping at her and raping her on the spot.' [15]

Indeed, the film's pop psychology, which the director just about got away with in *Spellbound* (1945) and *Vertigo* (1958), is one of its major failings. One never fully appreciates Rutland's obsession with Marnie's criminal urges, especially when he blackmails her into marrying him following her robbery of his own company ('I was just curious at first, then things got out of control,' he tells her, adding later that, 'It seems to have been my misfortune to fall in love with a thief and a liar'). Compelled to get to the bottom of Marnie's psychosis ('Let's see if we can turn that Mount Everest of manure into facts'), Rutland replaces the money she has stolen from his company with money from his own account, after which he takes her on a honeymoon cruise, during which he forces himself upon her in their suite, having admitted that, had *he* not rescued her, 'Some *other* sexual blackmailer would have got his hands on you!' As a result, Marnie attempts to commit suicide by drowning herself in the ship's pool, but even Rutland is suspicious of her intentions here, wondering why she didn't simply throw herself overboard ('The idea was to kill myself, not to feed the damn fish,' comes the not entirely convincing reply).

Having run up against a wall with Marnie ('You Freud, me Jane,' she jokes of his attempts to analyze her), Rutland eventually gets to the bottom of things by hiring a private investigator to look into Marnie's past, which results in a trip to see her mother, whom she's told him was dead. During the ensuing confrontation with Mrs Edgar (Louise Latham), it is revealed that Marnie's mother used to be a prostitute, and that Marnie murdered one of her clients with a fire poker when he became aggressive with her during a thunderstorm – hence her aversion to storms and the colour red (for which read blood). One could hardly call these revelations surprising or subtle, and coming at the end of over two hours of dull chat, they are distinctly anti-climactic. As, in fact, is the whole film (if Hitchcock

was keen to explore the sexual hang-ups of Marnie, he might better have looked at her apparent obsession with her horse Forio, which she at one point rides bareback, and later has to shoot following a riding accident, comforting the dead animal with a, 'There, there now').

There are those who champion *Marnie*. Yet having sat through the film, one remains unconvinced by their enthusiasm, which is seemingly blind to the film's many faults. Chief among these is the production's artificial look, with much of the action taking place on what are obviously studio interiors (save for its sexual references, the film has the feel and attitude of a 1940s' 'woman's picture'). Even some of the outdoors scenes are shot on sound stages, among them the street on which Marnie's mother lives, the red brick frontage of which looks like it has come from a summer stock production, while the painted backdrop at the end of the terrace – that of a docked ship – is perhaps the worst in film history. If it had been Hitchcock's intention to recreate the surrealistic effect of a ship towering imposingly over the neighbourhood, then the poor execution of the artwork negates this ambition completely (some have argued that the painting represents the false world in which Marnie lives, though given the lazy rear projection work and poor matte photography to be found elsewhere in the film, this argument doesn't bear too much scrutiny; indeed, it betrays an overly literal interpretation of what is basically a bad piece of scenic painting by those keen to foist their own agenda upon the film).

One should also note the poorly painted corridor on board the curiously deserted ship on which Marnie and Mark spend their honeymoon; after forcing himself upon his wife, Mark goes to look for her, searching the corridors, one of which, painted in perspective, looks like it might have come from a fairground sideshow.

The film's overall pace is deadly slow, with one talkative scene following another. Performance-wise, Hedren has a good stab at Marnie, but despite her best efforts she isn't quite up to the task, while Sean Connery just doesn't convince as a Philadelphia businessman, never mind as a would-be psychologist with an unhealthy obsession with his 'patient'. In fact the best performance comes not from the leads, but from Diane Baker as Lil Mainwaring, the sister of Rutland's dead first wife. Lil has obviously set her cap at Mark and clearly sees Marnie as a threat to her plans (when she discovers that Marnie has a secret past, she comments, 'I'm queer for liars' a little too enthusiastically). Played with relish, perfectly capturing the character's spite, Baker has a field day with her supporting role (she also gets to say a line that clearly echoes Norman Bates's opinion in *Psycho*: 'I always thought that a girl's best friend is her mother').

In spite of being written by a woman, the screenplay seems curiously misogynistic. Aside from Rutland's attempt to cure his wife by literally raping some sense into her, there's also the curious scene following the injury of Marnie's horse Forio; running to a nearby farm to get a gun with which to put the creature out of its misery, she's informed by the woman there that she can't help because,

'My mister ain't home,' at which Lil, who has by now arrived on the scene, suggests that she'd better go 'back for one of the men.'

Like all bad Hitchcock films, though, there are good things in *Marnie*, chief among them Bernard Herrmann's throbbing score, the throat-grabbing *Main Title,* which promises much more than the movie ultimately delivers. Then there's the central robbery scene in which Marnie waits in the ladies' toilets until after office hours so as to clear out the Rutland safe. Filmed practically in split screen with neither dialogue nor music, we see Marnie on one side of a corridor stealing the money, while on the other a cleaner mops her way to where the crime is being committed. Naturally, one immediately identifies with Marnie, compelling her to leave before she's found out. Having finally noticed the cleaner, Marnie attempts to creep away. The twist in the scene comes when she drops one of her shoes, which she has taken off to better aid her escape. The cleaner doesn't register the noise, and it is only after Marnie has successfully crept away that we realize that the woman is deaf, given that a security guard has to shout at her to gain her attention shortly afterwards.

Other touches worth noting include the red filter (and dramatic music) Hitchcock resorts to whenever Marnie reacts to seeing something particularly red, including a bunch of gladioli at her mother's house, the spots on a jockey's shirt and an ink stain on her white chemise (yet the red bricks of her mother's house *don't* set her off, nor does Lil's scarlet dress during a party scene). A thunderstorm also arrives on cue while Marnie is working at Rutland's office over the weekend, sending a handy tree crashing through the window and through a glass case in which Mark has been keeping his late wife's pre-Columbian art. This seems to free Mark from his past ('Well, we've all got to go some time'), allowing him to kiss Marnie without any feelings of guilt. Then there's the sweeping crane shot across the hallway of the Rutland residence during the party scene. At first one wonders where the shot is heading, but the camera gradually hones in on the front door and the arriving guests, one of whom proves to be Sidney Strutt and his wife, thus making for a tense time in the ensuing scenes when Marnie wonders if her former boss will recognize her.

When it was released, *Marnie* was greeted indifferently by both critics and audiences, among them *Variety*, which noted that, although Tippi Hedren fulfilled her 'difficult assignment' satisfactorily, 'Hitchcock seldom permits a change of pace which would have made her character more interesting.' To add to the director's misery, he had a severe falling out with Hedren midway through production. Having grown weary of Hitchcock's continual and domineering manipulation of her career and private life, along with his apparent obsession with her, the actress finally snapped. Said Hitchcock of the incident: 'She did what no one is permitted to do. She referred to my *weight*.' [16] Consequently, from that point on, director and star spoke to each other through intermediaries, and once the film was over, they never worked together again. Revealed

Hedren: 'He kept me under contract and paid my little salary every week for a couple of years, and by that time all the people who did want to use me in films... they were just told I wasn't available... There was never a question of working together again. It was a very definite cut off, and it was by me. I am totally responsible for it. No – I'm not – *he* is!' [17]

If that weren't enough, the film marked Hitchcock's last collaboration with his cameraman Robert Burks (who died four years later) and his editor George Tomasini (who died following the film's release), both of them long-serving and trusted colleagues. The film also marked the director's last full collaboration with composer Bernard Herrmann, who was sacked from Hitchcock's next film, *Torn Curtain* (1966).

Hitchcock cameo Note that Hitchcock can be spotted coming out of a hotel room early in the picture.

MARSH, GARRY (1902–1981) British actor. Usually cast as exasperated types, Marsh popped up in countless British films down the decades, among them such favourites as *Bank Holiday* (1938), *Let George Do It* (1940) and *Mr Drake's Duck* (1950). He began his film career in 1930 with *Night Birds* and ended it in 1967 with a cameo in *Camelot*, between which he appeared in over 100 films, including Hitchcock's *Number Seventeen* (1932), in which his criminal, Sheldrake, comes to a nasty end in the spectacular train crash finale. **Hitchography:** *Number Seventeen* (1932)

MARSH, JEAN (1934–) British actress. Known to television audiences around the world for playing Rose the maid in *Upstairs, Downstairs* (1970–1975) – which she also created with fellow actress Eileen Atkins – Jean Marsh has made few films, among them *The Tales of Hoffman* (1951), *Cleopatra* (1963) and Hitchcock's *Frenzy* (1972), in which she played secretary Monica Barling, whose evidence sees the wrong man jailed for a series of sex killings. Marsh's subsequent films include *The Eagle Has Landed* (1976), *Return to Oz* (1985) and *Willow* (1988), while her other television work includes the sit-com *9 to 5* (1982–1983). She also created a second television series with Eileen Atkins titled *The House of Elliott* (1991–1994), but did not appear in it this time. She was married to the actor Jon Pertwee (1919–1996) between 1955 and 1960. **Hitchography:** *Frenzy* (1972)

MARSHALL, HERBERT (1880–1966) British actor. Though he came to films at the comparatively late age of 37, Marshall went on to become one of the most debonair leading men of the 1930s and 1940s, despite having lost a leg in action during World War I. He made his film debut in Britain in *Mumsy* (1927), which he followed with a role in *Dawn* (1928), the story of Nurse Edith Cavell. He went to America for his third film, *The Letter* (1929), but returned home to take the lead in Hitchcock's *Murder!* in which he played Sir John Menier, whose amateur sleuthing saves a beautiful murder suspect from the gallows. Following a handful of other films, Marshall returned to America, where he quickly made a name for himself in the likes of *Blonde Venus* (1932) and *Trouble in Paradise* (1932). In 1940, he teamed up again with Hitchcock for *Foreign Correspondent*, although this time he was on the wrong side of the law as the traitorous Stephen Fisher. The same year, he also performed in a radio adaptation of Hitchcock's 1926 film *The Lodger*, which Hitchcock himself scripted. A radio adaptation of *Rebecca* followed in 1942. Marshall also appeared in two episodes of *Alfred Hitchcock Presents*. His other films include the remake of *The Letter* (1940), *The Little Foxes* (1941), *Duel in the Sun* (1946), *The Fly* (1958) and *The Third Day* (1965). Marshall's wife, actress Edna Best (1900–1974), appeared in Hitchcock's *The Man Who Knew Too Much* (1934). **Hitchography:** *Murder!* (1930), *Foreign Correspondent* (1940), *The Lodger* (1940, radio), *Rebecca* (1942, radio), *A Bottle of Wine* (1957, TV), *Little White Frock* (1958, TV)

MARTINELLI, JEAN French actor. Much on stage and in films in his home country, Martinelli, something of an Eduardo Cianelli look-alike, can be seen in films such as *Le Rouge et le Noir* (1954) and *Heroines of Evil* (1979). He also popped up in Hitchcock's Riviera-set *To Catch a Thief* (1955) as the sinister-looking Foussard, distinguished by the gray streak in his hair. **Hitchography:** *To Catch a Thief* (1955)

Mary
(GB, 1930, 92m approx, bw)

CREDITS

Production company:	British International Pictures/Sud Film A G
Producer:	John Maxwell
Director:	Alfred Hitchcock
Screenplay:	Alma Reville, Herbert Juttke, Georg C Klaren, based on the play *Enter Sir John* by Helen Simpson and Clemence Dane (real name Winifred Ashton)
Cinematographer:	Jack Cox
Music:	John Reynders
Art director:	J F Mead
Editors:	Emile de Ruelle, Rene Marrison

CAST

Alfred Abel, Olga Tschechowa, Jack Mylong-Munz, Paul Graetz, Lotte Stein, Ekkehard Arendt, Louis Ralph, Hermine Sterler

Immediately after completing *Murder!* (1930), Hitchcock made *Mary*, the German language version of the story, this time with Alfred Abel replacing Herbert Marshall as the jury member unconvinced of the guilt of an actress accused of murder. Though the original star

and cast were all replaced, the technical crew remained the same, save for the addition of writers Herbert Juttke and Georg C Klaren, who assisted Alma Reville in refashioning the script.

MASON, JAMES (1909–1984) British-born actor. This urbane British star, remembered for his distinctive velvety voice, came to films in 1935 with *Late Extra* following stage experience and aspirations to become an architect (he left Cambridge in 1931 with a degree in the subject). Following years in low budget quota quickies, he became Britain's top box office draw in the 1940s thanks to villainous roles in such period melodramas as *The Man in Grey* (1943) and *The Wicked Lady* (1946), in which he co-starred with Margaret Lockwood. Personal triumphs in *The Seventh Veil* (1945) and *Odd Man Out* (1947) made Hollywood sit up and look, and he went on to make such hits as *The Prisoner of Zenda* (1952), *Julius Caesar* (1953), *A Star is Born* (1954) and *20,000 Leagues Under the Sea* (1954) in America.

In 1959 he played Philip Vandamm, his suavest villain yet, in Hitchcock's masterful *North by Northwest*, practically stealing the film from under Cary Grant's nose. Relishing the role, which *Variety* described as 'properly forbidding,' Mason made the very most of the polished lines provided for him by screenwriter Ernest Lehman ('The least I can do is afford you the opportunity of surviving the evening,' he informs Cary Grant's bemused Roger Thornhill, who has been mistaken for government agent George Kaplan). Following *North by Northwest*, Mason went on to appear in such successes as *Journey to the Center of the Earth* (1959), *Lolita* (1962), *Georgy Girl* (1966), *Heaven Can Wait* (1978), *The Boys from Brazil* (1978), *Salem's Lot* (1979, TV) and *The Verdict* (1982) among many others. He also starred in an episode of *The Alfred Hitchcock Hour*. Married twice, his wives were the actresses Pamela Kellino (1922– , real name Pamela Ostrer), to whom he was married between 1941 and 1964, and Clarissa Kaye, to whom he was married from 1971. **Hitchography:** *North by Northwest* (1959), *Captive Audience* (1962, TV)

MASSEY, ANNA (1937–) British actress. On stage from the mid-1950s, Massey made her film debut in *Gideon's Day* (1958) and went on to appear in the likes of *Peeping Tom* (1960), *Bunny Lake is Missing* (1965), *A Doll's House* (1973), *Five Days One Summer* (1981), *The McGuffin* (1985, TV) and *Haunted* (1995) and Hitchcock's *Frenzy* (1972), in which she meets her end being raped and strangled by Barry Foster's necktie killer Robert Rusk. Recalled Massey of her experiences on the latter film: 'It was fascinating working with Hitchcock, of course. You don't often get the chance to work with a legend, as he was... I thought he was extremely helpful. I found him completely and utterly approachable and delightful, full of irony – and a lot of people can't take irony... He was a brilliant technician. He wasn't a brilliant director insofar as knowing how to play a scene, but he would sure tell you if he didn't like it.' [18]

Hitchcock gets to grips with actress Anna Massey during the filming of Frenzy *(1972). Jon Finch looks on.*

Massey also played 'I' in the 1962 TV remake of Hitchcock's *Rebecca* (1940) and Mrs Danvers in the 1979 TV remake. She is the daughter of actor Raymond Massey (1896–1983), who appeared in *Road Hog* (1959, TV), an episode of *Alfred Hitchcock Presents*, and actress Adrianne Allen (1907–1993); she is also the sister of actor Daniel Massey (1933–1998). She was married to the actor Jeremy Brett (1935–1995, real name Jeremy Huggins) between 1958 and 1962. **Hitchography:** *Frenzy* (1972)

MATE, RUDOLPH (1898–1964) Polish-born cinematographer. Mate began his career in Hungary in 1919 as an assistant cameraman. Following further experience in Germany, he became a fully-fledged cinematographer in 1923 with *Der Kaufmann von Venedig*. In 1928 he went to work in France on such acclaimed films as *La Passion de Jeanne d'Arc* (1928), *Vampyre* (1932) and *Liliom* (1934). Then, in 1934, he made the move to America, resuming his career with *Metropolitan* (1935), *Dante's Inferno* (1935) and *Our Relations* (1936). In 1940 he photographed Hitchcock's *Foreign Correspondent*, which contains some of his best work, notably some well-framed interior shots in the windmill sequence. Mate's other work as a cinematographer includes *That Hamilton Woman* (1941), *To Be or Not to Be* (1942) and *Gilda* (1946). In 1947 he also began directing films, among them *It Had to Be You* (1948), *DOA* (1950) and *When Worlds Collide* (1951). **Hitchography:** *Foreign Correspondent* (1940)

MATHER, AUBREY (1885–1958) British-born actor. On stage from 1905, Mather made his film debut in 1931 with *Young Woodley*, following which he became a handy supporting actor, working in both Britain and Hollywood.

His credits include *As You Like It* (1936), *Jane Eyre* (1944) and *The Importance of Being Earnest* (152). He can also be spotted as a contact in Hitchcock's *Sabotage* (1936) and as Mr Webster in *Suspicion* (1941), but was not credited for either role. **Hitchography:** *Sabotage* (1936), *Suspicion* (1941)

MATHERS, JERRY (1948–) American actor. Best known for playing the mischievous 'Beaver' Cleaver in the sit-coms *Leave It to Beaver* (1957–1963), *Still the Beaver* (1985–1986) and *The New Leave It to Beaver* (1986–1989), child star turned adult performer Mathers began acting on television at the age of 2. In films from the age of 6 with *This Is My Love* (1954), he also appeared in Hitchcock's *The Trouble with Harry* (1955), as the equally mischievous Arnie Rogers, *That Certain Feeling* (1956) and *Back to the Beach* (1987). **Hitchography:** *The Trouble with Harry* (1955)

MATHIESON, MUIR (1911–1975, aka 'Doc' Mathieson) British (Scottish) conductor. Mathieson worked on literally hundreds of films during a relentlessly busy career. In films from 1931 as an assistant music director following training at the Royal College of Music, he went on to conduct the scores for *Catherine the Great* (1934), *Things to Come* (1936), *Dangerous Moonlight* (1941), *Brief Encounter* (1945), *Richard III* (1956) and *You Can't Win 'em All* (1970). He can be seen conducting the London Symphony Orchestra on screen in *The Seventh Veil* (1945), while in *The Magic Box* (1951) he appears briefly as Sir Arthur Sullivan. In 1958 Mathieson also conducted Bernard Herrmann's score for Hitchcock's *Vertigo* (1958) when a strike by musicians prevented it being recorded in Hollywood; however, when British musicians also walked out in support of their American colleagues, the recording had to be finished in Vienna. Surprisingly, this was the only time Mathieson worked for Hitchcock. **Hitchography:** *Vertigo* (1958)

MATHEWS, JESSIE (1907–1981) British actress. Britain's leading musical star of the 1930s, Jessie Matthews appeared in such classics as *The Good Companions* (1932), *First a Girl* (1935) and *Gangway* (1936). On stage from the age of 10, she later became a major attraction in the revues of impresario C B Cochran, most notably in *Evergreen*, which she filmed in 1934. When her film career began to fade in the late 1930s, she returned to the stage, occasionally popping up in character roles in such films as *Tom Thumb* (1958) and *The Hound of the Baskervilles* (1977). In the 1960s, she became known to millions of radio listeners as Mrs Dale in *The Dales* (1963–1969), while on television she portrayed Aunt Bessie in the hit series *Edward and Mrs Simpson* (1979). She also directed and narrated the wartime documentary short *Victory Wedding* (1944). She made only one film for Hitchcock, *Waltzes from Vienna* (1933), but their working relationship was not a comfortable one. The critics were non too impressed either, with *The Times* describing Matthews's role as Rasi, Strauss the Younger's sweetheart,

as 'a not too important part of the film's design.'
Hitchography: *Waltzes from Vienna* (1933)

MATTHEWS, LESTER (1900–1975) British-born
actor. On stage from 1916, Lester Matthews went on to
become a popular leading man in British films following
his debut in the short *Shivering Shocks* (1929). Among his
early features were *Creeping Shadows* (1931), *Her Night Out*
(1932) and *Blossom Time* (1934). He went to America in
1935, where he found much work as a supporting actor in
such films as *Werewolf of London* (1935), *The Prince and the
Pauper* (1937), *The Adventures of Robin Hood* (1938), *The
Sea Hawk* (1940) and *Gaslight* (1944). In 1947, he also had
a bit part in Hitchcock's *The Paradine Case*. His subsequent
films include *Anne of the Indies* (1951), *Niagara* (1953), *The
Prize* (1963) and *Star!* (1968). His second wife was the
actress Anne Grey (1907– , real name Aileen Ewing), to
whom he was married between 1931 and 1937.
Hitchography: *The Paradine Case* (1947)

MAXWELL, JOHN (1875–1940) British producer. A
major player in the British film industry of the 1920s and
1930s, the Scottish-born Maxwell began his career as a
solicitor in Glasgow. In 1912 he turned his hand to film
distribution and exhibition, and by the late 1920s his assets
were such that he was able to buy British National Studios
in Borehamwood, Hertforshire from its original founders,
J D Williams, W Schlesigner and Herbert Wilcox, whose
partnership had declined into litigation. Maxwell
completed the deal in 1927, and soon after renamed the
complex British International Studios, signing up a raft of
filmmaking talent in the process, among them Hitchcock,
who had grown weary of the financial restrictions
imposed upon him at Gainsborough.

Hitchcock, who was paid £13,000 per year for the
duration of his three-year contract, went on to make 12
pictures at BIP, 11 of which he directed, among them his
breakthrough sound film *Blackmail* (1929). Maxwell produced each of these 11 films, while Hitchcock himself
produced the 12th, *Lord Camber's Ladies* (1932), which was
directed by Benn W Levy. Hitchcock eventually left BIP
following a dispute with Maxwell over his proposition to
direct a Bulldog Drummond story titled *Bulldog
Drummond's Baby* ('It was never made, and that was the
end of my period with British International Pictures,' [19]
revealed the director many years later).

By this time, Maxwell had already formed Associated
British Cinemas, a chain at which he was able to showcase
his own product (by 1930, Maxwell had 130 cinemas
under his belt). Throughout the 1930s, BIP continued to
churn out a raft of 'quota quickies' and A features, many of
them featuring imported American stars such as Charles
Bickford and Douglas Fairbanks Jr. BIP also played host to
several other film companies, among them the Mayflower
Picture Corporation, which went on to produce
Hitchcock's *Jamaica Inn* (although Maxwell had no hand
in the film's production). Upon Maxwell's death in 1940,
by which time the studio was known as BIP Elstree, his

family gradually lost control of his empire (now collectively known as the Associated British Picture
Corporation), and by 1946 the majority of the company's
shares were in the hands of Warner Bros. **Hitchography:**
The Ring (1927), *The Farmer's Wife* (1928), *Champagne*
(1928), *The Manxman* (1929), *Blackmail* (1929), *Elstree
Calling* (1930), *Juno and the Paycock* (1930), *Murder!* (1930),
Mary (1930), *The Skin Game* (1931), *Number Seventeen*
(1932), *Rich and Strange* (1932), *Lord Camber's Ladies* (1932,
executive only)

MEGOWAN, DON American supporting actor.
Megowan can be spotted in films such as *The Werewolf*
(1956) and *Tarzan and the Valley of Gold* (1966), as well as
Hitchcock's *To Catch a Thief* (1955), in which he plays one
of the detectives investigating the activities of retired cat
burglar John Robie (Cary Grant). Megowan also played
the Frankenstein Monster in the pilot for the aborted
television series *The Tales of Frankenstein* (1957, TV).
Hitchography: *To Catch a Thief* (1955)

Memory of the Camps
(GB, 1944, 20m, bw) *

CREDITS

Production company:	Frontline/Ministry of Information
Producer:	Sergei Nolbandov, Stephanie Tapper
Executive producer:	Sidney Bernstein, David Fanning
Screenplay:	Colin Wills
Treatment:	Colin Wills, Richard Grossman,
Treatment advisor:	Alfred Hitchcock
Editors:	Stewart McAllister, Peter Tanner, Stephanie Tapper
Narrator:	Trevor Howard

This wartime documentary was one of the first films to
reveal the true horrors of the German concentration
camps to Allied audiences. Hitchcock worked as a treatment advisor on the film while in London directing two
French-speaking propaganda films for the war effort: *Bon
Voyage* (1944) and *Aventure Malgache* (1944). For
Hitchcock's other wartime work see *Men of the Lightship*
(1941), *Target for Tonight* (1941) and *Watchtower Over
Tomorrow* (1945).

Men of the Lightship
(GB, 1941, 10m, bw)

CREDITS

Production company:	Ministry of Information
Director:	David MacDonald
Editor:	Alfred Hitchcock (US version only)

This British-made information film about the important work of lightships during the war was re-cut by an uncredited Alfred Hitchcock for its American release in 1941. For Hitchcock's other wartime work see *Target for Tonight* (1941), *Memory of the Camps* (1944), *Bon Voyage* (1944), *Aventure Malgache* (1944) and *Watchtower Over Tomorrow* (1945).

MENZIES, WILLIAM CAMERON (1896–1957) American production designer. Menzies remains one of the cinema's great stylists, having won the very first Oscar for design for his work on both *The Dove* (1928) and *Tempest* (1928), as well as a 'special' Oscar for his work on *Gone with the Wind* (1939). Among his most visually arresting films are *Bulldog Drummond* (1929), *Our Town* (1940) and *King's Row* (1941). In 1940, he worked on Hitchcock's *Foreign Correspondent*, devising 'special production effects', among them the opening shot which sees the camera move from the (model) roof of the *New York Morning Globe*'s office block, down the side of the building and in through one of the windows, all in one seamless take. He also helped to devise the shot in which the camera moves from the exterior of a (model) clipper plane, in through one of the windows and then down the aisle inside, again in one seamless take.

In addition to his work as a designer, Menzies directed a number of films, but with the exception of *Things to Come* (1936) and *Invaders from Mars* (1954), they were mostly unexceptional, among them *Always Goodbye* (1931), *Address Unknown* (1944) and *The Maze* (1953), the latter a shocker about an heir who turns into a frog! In 1945, Menzies also did some un-credited work on *Spellbound* (1945), helping to make work the dream sequence designed by Salvador Dali. **Hitchography:** *Foreign Correspondent* (1940), *Spellbound* (1945)

MERCHANT, VIVIEN (1929–1982, real name Ada Thomson) British actress. This distinguished stage actress was noted for her performances in the plays of her one time husband Harold Pinter (1930–), to whom she was married between 1956 and 1980. Also much on television, her films were more infrequent, among them *Alfie* (1966), which earned her a best supporting actress Oscar nomination, *Accident* (1967), *Under Milk Wood* (1971) and Hitchcock's *Frenzy* (1972), in which she played Mrs Oxford, making the most of several comical domestic scenes in which she serves her hapless husband, Chief Inspector Oxford (Alec McCowen), a series of unappetizing *cordon bleu* meals, including a *soupe de poisson* that looks like a marine graveyard. Her other film appearances include *The Offence* (1973), *The Homecoming* (1973) and *The Man in the Iron Mask* (1977, TV). **Hitchography:** *Frenzy* (1972)

MERIVALE, PHILIP (1886–1946) British-born actor. This British stage actor, in films from 1914 with *Trilby*, later went to America where he appeared as a supporting actor in a number of Hollywood films, among them

Hitchcock's *Mr and Mrs Smith* (1941), in which he played Mr Custer, *This Land is Mine* (1943) and *Sister Kenny* (1946). He was the third husband of actress Dame Gladys Cooper (1888–1971), who had appeared in Hitchcock's *Rebecca* (1940). **Hitchography:** *Mr and Mrs Smith* (1941)

MERRITT, GEORGE (1890–1977) British supporting actor. Frequently cast as a policeman, Merritt can be spotted as such in Hitchcock's *Young and Innocent* (1937). On stage from 1909 and in films from 1930, his many appearances include *The 'W' Plan* (1931), *Brown on Resolution* (1935), *Rembrandt* (1936) and *The Day the Earth Caught Fire* (1962). He also appeared in the 1932 remake of Hitchcock's *The Lodger* (1926). **Hitchography:** *Young and Innocent* (1937)

MILES, SIR BERNARD (LORD MILES) (1907–1991) British character actor. On stage from 1930 following experience as a teacher, Bernard Miles became best known for his rural and everyman types. In films from 1933 with *Channel Crossing*, his key films include *In Which We Serve* (1942), *Tawny Pipit* (1944), which he also produced, co-wrote and co-directed, *Great Expectations* (1946), *Chance of a Lifetime* (1949), which he also produced, co-wrote and directed, *Moby Dick* (1956) and *Tom Thumb* (1958). He also appeared for Hitchcock twice, first in *Jamaica Inn* (1939) as a walk on, and secondly in the remake of *The Man Who Knew Too Much* (1956), in which he played the seemingly dull Mr Drayton, who turns out to be a lynchpin in a kidnapping and assassination plot. His greatest achievement, however, was the founding of the Mermaid Theatre in 1959. Miles was knighted in 1969 and created a Lord in 1978. **Hitchography:** *Jamaica Inn* (1939), *The Man Who Knew Too Much* (1956)

MILES, VERA (1929– , real name Vera Ralston) American actress. This strong leading lady, a former beauty contest winner, made her screen debut in 1950 in *When Willie Comes Marching Home*. Further minor parts in films followed, among them *Two Tickets to Broadway* (1951), *The Rose Bowl Story* (1952) and *So Big* (1953). Her big break came when she was cast in John Ford's *The Searchers* (1956), by which time she'd also notched up dozens of television appearances, including an episode of *Coca-Cola Playhouse*, in which she was spotted by Hitchcock, who subsequently cast her in the opening episode of his own television series *Alfred Hitchcock Presents*. Titled *Revenge* (1955, TV), the programme was directed by Hitchcock himself, who was so impressed by the actress that he placed her under a five-year contract. As a result, the director cast Miles in his next picture, *The Wrong Man* (1956), in which she played Rose Balestrero, who suffers a nervous breakdown when her husband Manny (Henry Fonda) is wrongly accused of carrying out a series of hold ups. The film was not a commercial success, but Miles's performance was generally admired.

Consequently, Hitchcock made plans to turn the actress into the next Grace Kelly, casting her as the duplicitous

In this still from Hitchcock's Psycho *(1960), Mort Mills' menacing patrolman looks on suspiciously as Janet Leigh's Marion Crane searches for her driving licence, coolly removing the $40,000 she has stolen to get to it. Mills also appeared in Hitchcock's* Torn Curtain *(1966) as a jovial spy.*

Judy Barton in his up-coming production of *Vertigo* (1958). Unfortunately for Hitchcock, Miles became pregnant by her then-husband, Tarzan star Gordon Scott, and so had to withdraw from the production, leaving the way open for Kim Novak. Commented Hitchcock: 'She became pregnant just before the part that was going to turn her into a star. After that I lost interest; I couldn't get the rhythm going with her again.' [20]

Nevertheless, Hitchcock did cast Miles in *Psycho* (1960), in which she played Lila Crane, the sister of Janet Leigh's Marion Crane, who has absconded with $40,000. However, as costumier Rita Riggs recalled, Miles, who was paid $1,700 per week for her work, was not happy during the shooting of the film. 'Vera was gorgeous, very bright, very independent, and very angry throughout the filming of *Psycho*. Mr Hitchcock made her look like a dowdy, old-maid schoolteacher, although Vera ended up having her things done at Paramount by Edith Head... I have great respect for Miss Head, but I remember thinking, "Gosh, that's a rather dowdy fabric and colour." But it was Mr Hitchcock's choice. He was very disappointed with Vera, on whom he had invested a lot of time, thought and emotion in preparing *Vertigo* for her before she got pregnant. That was some of his perversity coming through.' [21] Perhaps a part of this perversity was the fact that, in the trailer, it was not Janet Leigh who was attacked

in the shower, but Miles!

Miles' other films include *The Man Who Shot Liberty Valance* (1962), *Castaway Cowboy* (1974), *Brain Waves* (1982) and *Into the Night* (1984). She also appeared in an episode of *Ford Startime* titled *Incident at a Corner* (1960, TV), which was directed by Hitchcock, a further episode of *Alfred Hitchcock Presents* and an episode of *The Alfred Hitchcock Hour* (neither of them directed by Hitchcock). She returned to the *Psycho* franchise for *Psycho 2* (1983), in which she reprised her role of Lila Crane, now Lila Loomis, who comes to a sticky end in the Bates house while attempting to get Anthony Perkins' Norman Bates sent back to the asylum with the assistance of her daughter Mary (Meg Tilly). Married three times, Miles' husbands include actor Gordon Scott (1927– , real name Gordon M Werschkul), to whom she was married between 1955 and 1959, and director Keith Larsen (1925–), to whom she was married between 1960 and 1973. **Hitchography:** *Revenge* (1955, TV), *The Wrong Man* (1956), *Psycho* (1960), *Incident at a Corner* (1960, TV), *Don't Look Behind You* (1962, TV), *Death Scene* (1965, TV)

MILLAND, RAY (1907–1986, real name Reginald Truscott-Jones) British-born (Welsh) actor. In British films from 1929 following experience as a guardsman with the Royal Household Cavalry, Milland, made his screen debut under the name of Spike Milland in *The Plaything* (1929). Reverting to Raymond Milland for his next 15 films, among them *Piccadilly* (1929) and *Just a Gigolo* (1931), the actor finally became plain and simple Ray Milland in 1933 with *Orders is Orders*. By this time he had already made a handful of films in Hollywood, beginning with *Way for a Sailor* (1930), and after 1933 he made the place his permanent home, going on to establish himself as a light lead or support in such films as *We're Not Dressing* (1934), *Bulldog Drummond Escapes* (1937) and *The Major and the Minor* (1942).

However, it was his Oscar-winning performance as a desperate alcoholic in *The Lost Weekend* (1945) that established him as a dramatic actor of some note. Milland's subsequent films include *Kitty* (1945) and *Alias Nick Beal* (1949), while in 1949 he starred in a radio adaptation of Hitchcock's *Shadow of a Doubt*. He finally worked with Hitchcock five years later on *Dial M for Murder* (1954), in which he played former tennis pro Tony Wendice, whose plan it is to do away with his wealthy wife so that he can inherit. An assured performance, Milland's Wendice maintains his cool throughout the story, despite his elaborate plans going increasingly awry (when finally rumbled, his resigned reaction is simply to take a stiff drink). His subsequent films include *The Girl in the Red Velvet Swing* (1955), *The Man with X-Ray Eyes* (1963), *Gold* (1974) and *The Sea Serpent* (1985). He also directed five films, including *A Man Alone* (1955) and *Hostile Witness* (1968). In 1963, he appeared in an episode of *The Alfred Hitchcock Hour*. **Hitchography:** *Shadow of a Doubt* (1949, radio), *Dial M for Murder* (1954), *A Home Away from Home* (1963, TV)

MILLS, FRANK British assistant director. Following Hitchcock's marriage to Alma Reville, Mills took over her duties as assistant director, beginning with *Easy Virtue* in 1927. He held the position until 1932. **Hitchography:** *Easy Virtue* (1927), *The Ring* (1927), *The Farmer's Wife* (1928), *Champagne* (1928), *The Manxman* (1929), *Blackmail* (1929), *Juno and the Paycock* (1930), *Murder!* (1930), *Mary* (1930), *The Skin Game* (1931), *Number Seventeen* (1932), *Rich and Strange* (1932)

MILLS, MORT American supporting actor. Mort Mills is perhaps best remembered for playing the suspicious, sunglass-wearing Highway Patrolman in Hitchcock's *Psycho* (1960), in which role he bears an uncanny resemblance to Humphrey Bogart (he even sounds like him!). Mills returned to the Hitchcock fold for *Torn Curtain* (1966), this time as the cheerful farmer who proves to be a secret agent. His other films include *Davy Crocket and the River Pirates* (1956), *Ride a Crooked Trail* (1958), *Touch of Evil* (1958) and *The Outlaws is Coming* (1965). **Hitchography:** *Psycho* (1960), *Torn Curtain* (1966)

MILTON, FRANKLIN American sound recordist. Long at MGM, Milton won Oscars for his work on *Ben-Hur* (1959), *How the West Was Won* (1963) and *Grand Prix* (1966). He also recorded the sound for Hitchcock's *North by Northwest* (1959). **Hitchography:** *North by Northwest* (1959)

MINCIOTTI, ESTHER (1883–1962) Italian-American character actress. Esther Minciotti proved popular on television in the 1950s, where she became known for her appearances in the likes of the original production of *The Wrong Man* (1953, TV), which was transmitted as part of the *Robert Montgomery Presents* series. She re-created her role of Mamma Balestrero for Hitchcock's film version of 1956, prior to which her movie credits included *House of Strangers* (1949), *Strictly Dishonorable* (1951) and *Marty* (1955). Her husband was the actor Silvio Minciotti (1883–1961), who also appeared in *The Wrong Man* as her husband. **Hitchography:** *The Wrong Man* (1956)

MINCIOTTI, SILVIO (1883–1961) Italian-American character actor. Long married to actress Esther Minciotti (1883–1962), Silvio Minciotti made a handful of movies in the 1950s, among them *House of Strangers* (1949), *The Great Caruso* (1951) and Hitchcock's *The Wrong Man* (1956), in which he made an un-credited appearance as Mr Balestrero, the onscreen husband to his wife. **Hitchography:** *The Wrong Man* (1956)

MINOTIS, ALEX American supporting actor. Few credits for Minotis are available, among them Hitchcock's *Notorious* (1946), in which he played Joseph, *Land of the Pharaohs* (1955) and *Boy on a Dolphin* (1957). **Hitchography:** *Notorious* (1946)

MRS PEABODY see *Number 13*

Mr and Mrs Smith

(US, 1941, 94m, bw) ★

CREDITS

Production company:	RKO
Producer:	Carole Lombard (un-credited)
Executive producer:	Harry E Edington
Director:	Alfred Hitchcock
Screenplay:	Norman Krasna
Cinematographer:	Harry Stradling
Music:	Roy Webb
Editor:	William Hamilton
Art director:	Van Nest Polglase
Associate art director:	Lawrence P Williams
Costumes:	Irene
Sound:	John E Tribby
Special effects:	Vernon L Walker

CAST

Carole Lombard (Ann Smith), Robert Montgomery (David Smith), Gene Raymond (Jeff Custer), Jack Carson (Chuck Benson), William Tracy (Sammy), Philip Merivale (Mr Custer), Lucile Watson (Mrs Custer), Charles Halton (Mr Deever), Esther Dale (Mrs Krausheimer, Ann's mother), Emma Dunn (Martha), Patricia Farr (Gloria), Adele Pearce (Lili), William Edmunds (Proprietor), Betty Compson (Gertie), Beatrice Maude (Jeff's secretary), James Flavin (Escort), Emory Parnell (Conway)

Video availability: Universal

Following the success of his first two Hollywood films, *Rebecca* (1940) and *Foreign Correspondent* (1940), Hitchcock was hired out by David O Selznick to direct this rather uncharacteristic screwball comedy about Ann and David Smith (Carole Lombard and Robert Montgomery), a much-married couple who discover that their marriage isn't legal, thus raising the question of whether or not they should stay together.

The film, which bore the working titles *And So to Wed* and *Slightly Married*, was a pet project of actress Carole Lombard, who had befriended the Hitchcocks since their arrival in America (in fact they subsequently rented Lombard's former Bel Air home). Commented Hitchcock: 'That picture was done as a friendly gesture to Carole Lombard. At the time, she was married to Clark Gable, and she asked whether I'd do a picture with her. In a weak moment I accepted.' [22] Indeed, Hitchcock's interest in the film seems to have been minimal. 'All I did was to photograph the scenes as written,' [23] he admitted.

Consequently, given the subject matter, Hitchcockian touches are somewhat thin on the ground, among them a vertiginous sequence in which Mrs Smith and her new 'boyfriend' Jeff Custer (Gene Raymond) get stuck on a parachute ride at the New York World's Fair in the pouring rain, and a scene in which Jeff has a conversation with his parents in the bathroom of his office, their voices periodically drowned out by the banging of the pipes. Hitchcock had originally intended the sound to be that of a toilet flushing, but such noises were still taboo at the time and the front office nixed the idea, even though the Smiths are earlier shown to share a double bed, which was another taboo (even more so when one considers that they're not actually married!).

Despite Hitchcock's general disinterest in the film, he and Lombard nevertheless enjoyed working together, especially as they shared the same sense of humour. For example, on the first day of filming, Lombard had built on set a pen containing three cattle, each of which had a name card round its neck identifying them as Carole Lombard, Robert Montgomery and Gene Raymond in a clear reference to Hitchcock's alleged comment that 'All actors are cattle.' Hitchcock retaliated by having all of Lombard's lines chalked up on idiot boards.

Of all Hitchcock's early Hollywood films, *Mr and Mrs Smith* has dated the most. A rather strained affair, its frequently frenetic attempts to raise a laugh leave one exhausted, while the central characters are too childish and self-centred to make one entirely sympathetic to their so-called plight. Hitchcock was certainly no stranger to comedy, with many of his films containing a rich vein of humour (note the first 30 minutes of *The Lady Vanishes* [1938] and the first 15 minutes of *Rebecca* (1940)). However, when it came to an out and out farce, he seemed out of his depth. That said, the film is adequately made, benefiting from Harry Stradling's glossy black-and-white photography, some eye-catching interiors by art director Van Nest Polglase and a playful score by Edward Ward. As a Hitchcock film, though, it belongs to a list of aberrations that also numbers *Elstree Calling* (1930), *Juno and the Paycock* (1930), *Waltzes from Vienna* (1933) and the later *Under Capricorn* (1949). Reaction to *Mr and Mrs Smith* at the time was quite enthusiastic. Wrote *Variety*'s critic: 'Carole Lombard and Robert Montgomery are teamed successfully here in a light and gay marital farce... Alfred Hitchcock pilots the story in a straight farcical groove... Pacing his assignment at a steady gait, Hitchcock catches all of the laugh values from the above par script of Norman Krasna.' *Look* magazine was equally enthusiastic, describing the film as 'Another Hitchcock hit.' Otis Ferguson better hit the nail on the head, though, writing, 'I doubt that your interest or amusement will last as long as the picture.'

Hitchcock cameo Hitchcock watchers can spot the Master as a panhandler who passes David Smith in the street. Carole Lombard directed this scene herself, running up take after take in revenge for the various practical jokes Hitchcock had played on her during production. Also note that the film was adapted several times for radio, in 1941, 1942, 1944, 1946 and 1949.

MOHR, HAL (1894–1974) American cinematographer. An Oscar winner for his work on both *A Midsummer Night's Dream* (1935) and *The Phantom of the Opera*

(1943), Mohr began his career in 1918 with *Restitution*, prior to which he'd had experience with newsreels. His many subsequent films, which included pioneering work with cranes and dollies, include *The Golden Trail* (1920), *The Jazz Singer* (1927), *Broadway* (1929), *Captain Blood* (1935), *Destry Rides Again* (1939), *Rancho Notorious* (1952) and *The Bamboo Saucer* (1968). In 1969 he was the 'photographic consultant' on Hitchcock's *Topaz*, although the film was actually shot by Jack Hildyard. **Hitchography:** *Topaz* (1969)

THE MOLIERE PLAYERS This group of refugee French actors appeared in two wartime propaganda films for Hitchcock in 1944, both of which were made exclusively for showing in areas of France where the occupation forces were crumbling. However, the second film wasn't shown until 1993. **Hitchography:** *Bon Voyage* (1944), *Aventure Malgache* (1944)

MONTAGU, IVOR (1904–1984) British film historian, editor, writer, producer and director. Busy from the mid-1920s, initially as a critic (for *The Observer* and *New Statesman*), Montagu worked on several of Hitchcock's early films, most notably *The Lodger* (1926), which he helped to re-cut following its disappointing reception by several members of the Gainsborough board. He also edited *Downhill* (1927) and *Easy Virtue* (1927), re-working the screenplay, un-credited, for the former. Later, Montagu worked as Hitchcock's associate producer on *The Man Who Knew Too Much* (1934) and *The 39 Steps* (1935), and graduated to producer, with Michael Balcon, on *Secret Agent* (1936) and *Sabotage* (1936). As a director, his output included several wartime documentaries and propaganda films, among them *Behind Spanish Lines* (1938) and *Peace and Plenty* (1939), while his screenplays included *Blighty* (1926) and *Scott of the Antarctic* (1948). His published works include *Film Technique* (translated from the Russian original by Vsevolod I Pudovkin), *Film World* and *The Youngest Son*. He was also the co-founder, in 1925, of the Film Society, whose other co-founder, Sidney Bernstein, also went on to produce for Hitchcock. **Hitchography:** *The Lodger* (1926), *Downhill* (1927), *Easy Virtue* (1927), *The Man Who Knew Too Much* (1934), *The 39 Steps* (1935), *The Secret Agent* (1936), *Sabotage* (1936)

MONTGOMERY, ROBERT (1904–1981, real name Henry Montgomery Jr) American actor. On the New York stage from 1924 following experience as a railway mechanic, Montgomery went on to become one of Hollywood's most debonair leading men, beginning with *The Single Standard* in 1929. Among his subsequent films were *Riptide* (1934), *Ever Since Eve* (1937) and Hitchcock's *Mr and Mrs Smith* (1941), in which he co-starred with Carole Lombard as a much-married couple who discover that their marriage isn't legal (Montgomery also starred in two radio adaptations of the film). His other films include *Here Comes Mr Jordan*

(1941), *June Bride* (1948) and *Once More, My Darling* (1949), while on television he produced, hosted and occasionally directed the half-hour anthology drama series *Robert Montgomery Presents* (1950–1957), which included a version of *The Wrong Man* (1953, TV), later turned into a feature by Hitchcock in 1956. His film credits as a director meanwhile include *Lady in the Lake* (1946), noted for its subjective camera work, *Your Witness* (1950) and *The Gallant Hours* (1960). Politically active, Montgomery had been president of the Screen Actors' Guild between 1935 and 1939, while in 1947 he headed the Hollywood Republican Committee. During the war he earned a Bronze Star for his involvement in the D-Day landings. He was the father of *Bewitched* star Elizabeth Montgomery (1933–1995). **Hitchography:** *Mr and Mrs Smith* (1941), *Mr and Mrs Smith* (1946, radio), *Mr and Mrs Smith* (1949)

MOORE, BRIAN (1921–1999) Irish novelist. Moore has had several of his works adapted for the screen, among them *The Luck of Ginger Coffey* and *The Lonely Passion of Judith Hearne*. An occasional screenwriter, his scripts include Hitchcock's *Torn Curtain* (1966), which was subsequently polished by Keith Waterhouse and Willis Hall. Moore took the film to arbitration over whether or not he should receive sole credit for the script and won his case. **Hitchography:** *Torn Curtain* (1966)

MORAHAN, TOM (THOMAS M) (1906–) British art director. Following experience as an architect, Morahan went on to become one of Britain's leading art directors, working on such wide and varied films as *St Martin's Lane* (1938), *Treasure Island* (1950), *Sons and Lovers* (1960) and *Those Magnificent Men in Their Flying Machines* (1965). In 1939 he designed the sets for Hitchcock's *Jamaica Inn*, lending the film a suitably brooding atmosphere, his designs for the titular inn being particularly impressive. He went on to work with Hitchcock a further two times: in Hollywood on *The Paradine Case* (1947), notable for its re-creation of The Old Bailey's number one court, and back in Britain on the disappointing period melodrama *Under Capricorn* (1949). **Hitchography:** *Jamaica Inn* (1939), *The Paradine Case* (1947), *Under Capricorn* (1949)

MORELL, ANDRE (1909–1978, real name Andre Mesritz) British actor. An authoritative supporting actor with a sergeant-major persona (he was a major with the Royal Welsh Fusiliers during World War II), this distinguished-looking actor made his stage debut in 1934 following several years of amateur performing. In films from 1938 with *Many Tanks, Mr Atkins*, he went on to play small but noticeable roles in many major productions, among them *Madeleine* (1949), *Summer Madness* (1955), *The Bridge on the River Kwai* (1957) and *Ben-Hur* (1960). In larger roles he was even better, particularly in *Seven Days to Noon* (1950), *The Hound of the Baskervilles* (1959), in which he made an excellent Watson to Peter Cushing's Sherlock Holmes, *The Shadow of the Cat* (1961) and *The Plague of the Zombies* (1965). In 1950, he appeared briefly as Inspector Byard in Hitchcock's *Stage Fright*, in which he interrogates suspected murderess Charlotte Inwood (Marlene Dietrich). Unfortunately, given that the camera favoured the bigger star during the sequence, Morell for once failed to make much of an impact. His other films include *Cash on Demand* (1961), *She* (1965), *Barry Lyndon* (1975) and *The First Great Train Robbery* (1978). He was married to the actress Joan Greenwood (1921–1987) from 1960. **Hitchography:** *Stage Fright* (1950)

MORTON, MICHAEL British playwright and novelist. Morton had a major success with his stage play *Woman to Woman*, which to date has been filmed three times, in 1923, 1929 and 1946. The first version was adapted for the screen by director Graham Cutts and his then assistant Alfred Hitchcock. This association lasted a further two films, with Morton co-writing *The White Shadow* (1924) with Hitchcock (which was based on Morton's novel *Children of Chance*), and *The Passionate Adventure* (1924), both of which were helmed by Cutts. **Hitchography:** *Woman to Woman* (1923), *The White Shadow* (1924), *The Passionate Adventure* (1924)

The Mountain Eagle

(GB/Germany, 1925, 72m (some sources state 68m and 89m), bw, silent)

CREDITS

Production company:	Gainsborough/Munchener Lichtspielkunst
Producer:	Michael Balcon
Director:	Alfred Hitchcock
Screenwriter:	Eliot Stannard,
Story:	Charles Lapworth
Cinematographer:	Baron Ventimiglia
Art directors:	Willy Reiber, Ludwig Reiber
Assistant director/ script girl:	Alma Reville

CAST

Nita Naldi (Beatrice Talbot), Malcolm Keen (John Fulton/Fear O'God), Bernard Goetzke (Pettigrew), John F Hamilton (Edward Petigrew)

Made in 1925, but not actually released until 1927 following the success of *The Lodger*, *The Mountain Eagle* (also known as *Fear O'God* and *Der Bergadler*) is perhaps the most tantalizing of the lost Hitchcocks. The story of Beatrice Talbot, a young Kentucky schoolteacher who flees to the mountains so as to escape the unwanted attentions of a lecherous justice of the peace, it was a co-production between Gainsborough and Munchener Lichtspielkunst, and was shot in Munich and on location in the improbably named village of Obergurgl in the

Tyrolean Mountains. The film re-united Hitchcock with Nita Naldi, the co-star of his directorial debut *The Pleasure Garden* (1925), although according to Hitch, the glamorous actress made a less than convincing schoolmarm. 'Nita Naldi [was] the successor to Theda Bara. She had fingernails out to there. Ridiculous!' [24] he commented. He also described the film as, 'A very bad movie.' [25] Nevertheless, *The Bioscope* praised the film for its 'skilful direction and good acting,' while *The Kinematograph* described Hitchcock's work as 'thoroughly imaginative,' even if the reviewer was less impressed with the story, which was apparently 'too full of unconvincing twists' for his taste. Sadly, just a handful of stills survive of the film, among them a behind the scenes shot of Hitchcock directing, with script girl Alma Reville observing the action behind him.

As well as Naldi, *The Mountain Eagle* also re-united Hitchcock with several other colleagues from *The Pleasure Garden*, among them cinematographer Baron Ventimiglia, screenwriter Eliot Stannard and producer Michael Balcon. Malcolm Keen, who played Fear O'God, the hermit whom Beatrice falls in love with and marries, would return to the Hitchcock fold for *The Lodger* (1927) and *The Manxman* (1929), so already the director was building up a rep company of players and technicians even with his second film.

MOWBRAY, ALAN (1893–1969) British-born character actor. Frequently typecast as butlers and manservants in Hollywood films, Mowbray went to America at the age of 30 and, following stage experience, made his film debut in 1931 in *Leftover Ladies*. He went on to appear in some 200 films, among them *A Study in Scarlet* (1933), *Rose Marie* (1936), *My Man Godfrey* (1936), *His Butler's Sister* (1943) and *The King and I* (1956). His penultimate film was Hitchcock's remake of *The Man Who Knew Too Much* (1956), in which he played showbiz insider Val Parnell in a few brief scenes. Mowbray was also known for his television series *Colonel Humphrey Flack* (1953–1958). **Hitchography:** *The Man Who Knew Too Much* (1956)

MUDIE, LEONARD (1884–1965, real name Leonard M Cheetham) British character actor. One of many British ex-pats working in Hollywood in the 1930s and 1940s, Mudie can be spotted in such films as *The Mummy* (1932), *Dark Victory* (1939) and Hitchcock's *Foreign Correspondent* (1940), in which he cameos as Inspector McKenna. His other films include *Berlin Correspondent* (1942), *My Name is Julia Ross* (1945) and *Timbuktu* (1959). **Hitchography:** *Foreign Correspondent* (1940)

MULCASTER, G H (1891–1964) British character actor. Although he spent the majority of his career on stage, Mulcaster made the occasional foray into film, among them *The Dummy Talks* (1943), *Spring in Park Lane* (1948) and Hitchcock's *Under Capricorn* (1949), playing the role of Dr Macallister. **Hitchography:** *Under Capricorn* (1949)

Murder!

(GB, 1930, 92m (some sources state 100m), bw) ★

CREDITS

Production company:	British International Pictures
Producer:	John Maxwell
Director:	Alfred Hitchcock
Screenwriters:	Alfred Hitchcock, Alma Reville, Walter C Mycroft, based on the novel *Enter Sir John* by Clemence Dane and Helen Simpson
Cinematographer:	Jack Cox
Music director:	John Reynders
Editors:	Rene Marrison, Emile de Ruelle
Art director:	J F Mead
Assistant director:	Frank Mills
Sound:	Cecil V Thornton

CAST

Herbert Marshall (Sir John Menier), Norah Baring (Diana Baring), Esme Percy (Hanel Fane), Phyllis Konstam (Dulcie Markham), Edward Chapman (Ted Markham), Miles Mander (Gordon Druce), Donald Calthrop (Ian Stewart), Una O'Connor (Mrs Grogram), Joynson Powell (Judge), Esme V Chaplin (Prosecuting Counsel), Amy Brandon Thomas (Defending Counsel), R E Jefrey (Jury Foreman), Clare Greet, Alan Stainer, Guy Pelham, Kenneth Kove, Matthew Boulton, William Fazan, George Smythson, Ross Jefferson, Picton Roxborough, Drusilla Wills, Violet Farebrother, Robert Easton (Jury members)

Though it now seems quite dated, there are several points of interest in this whodunit based on the 1929 novel *Enter Sir John* by Helen Simpson and Clemence Dane (real name Winifred Ashton). In it, rep actress Diana Baring (Norah Baring) is accused of murdering fellow performer Edna Bruce. The trial that follows seems like an open-and-shut case, and the jury quickly concludes that Diana is guilty, based on the circumstantial evidence presented to them. However, one of the jury members, actor-manager Sir John Menier (Herbert Marshall) remains doubtful as to Diana's guilt, and while she is awaiting execution, he sets out to prove her innocence and discover the identity of the real killer. This turns out to be one Handel Fane (Esme Percy), an effete female impersonator who killed Edna Bruce to prevent her from revealing him to be half-caste (and, presumably, a homosexual). Facing exposure, Fane writes an explanatory note and commits suicide by hanging himself during the trapeze act he is currently performing in a circus. This leaves the way open for Diana to be released, following which she is cast by Sir John, who has fallen in love with her, in a stage version of the preceding events (thus forcing her to re-live her nightmare experience on a nightly basis – and twice on matinee days!).

Given its theatrical backdrop, it's interesting to note that

Norah Baring is visited in prison by Herbert Marshall in Hitchcock's Murder! *(1930).*

Hitchcock cast many of his own repertory company of players in *Murder!* among them Phyllis Konstam, Edward Chapman, Miles Mander, Donald Calthrop, Violet Farebrother and Clare Greet. New to the company was leading man Herbert Marshall, an up-coming star whom Hitchcock cast as Sir John Menier (and with whom he would later work again in Hollywood on *Foreign Correspondent* in 1940). As he had done on *Blackmail* the previous year, Hitchcock experimented with the new medium of sound on *Murder!* one of his ideas being to externalize Sir John's inner thoughts via a voice over in a scene in which he is shaving ('At the time, this was regarded as an extraordinary novelty,' [26] said Hitchcock later. Given that dubbing as such did not exist at the time, Hitchcock had Marshall pre-record his dialogue, which was then played back during the filming of the scene for the star to react to. The radio music to which Sir John is listening during this interior monologue – an extract from Wagner's *Tristan and Isolde* – also had to be recorded live, the 30-piece orchestra being hidden behind the set!

Hitchcock experimented for the first – and last – time with improvised dialogue in *Murder!* too. Unfortunately, this has the effect of making the actors look hesitant and uncertain ('The result wasn't good. There was too much faltering... We didn't get the spontaneity I had hoped for,' [27] the director admitted).

Hitchcock did better with his trademark visual touches, among them a dolly past the various rooms in the boarding house in which the murder takes place, the shot revealing the panicked guests scrambling into their clothes to see what's happened. A meeting between Sir John and Diana Baring in prison is also eye-catching, given that the two are sat at opposite ends of a lengthy table. Ditto several overhead shots as Diana awaits execution in her cell, the gallows looming in the background. Sir John's attempts to coerce the killer into confessing by persuading him to read for a part in a play based on the murder is also of note, if only for being so contrived (the idea was supposedly based on the play within the play in *Hamlet*).

In terms of present day political correctness the film

falls down pretty badly, its central plot device being completely racist ('Black blood!' exclaims Sir John upon discovering the guilty secret that has compelled Fane to murder). The sexual ambiguity of the killer no longer seems suitable either, though as Arthur Laurents, the screenwriter of *Rope* later commented of Hitchcock, 'He was fascinated by homosexuality.' [28] Indeed, in addition to *Murder!* allusions to homosexuality can also be found in *The Lodger* (1926), *Rebecca* (1940), *Rope* (1948), *Strangers on a Train* (1951), *North by Northwest* (1959) and *Psycho* (1960).

Despite its occasional failings, *Murder!* remains an interesting museum piece, and its commercial and critical success at the time certainly did Hitchcock's reputation no harm. Also note that Hitchcock directed a German language version of the film titled *Mary*, with Alfred Abel taking over the Herbert Marshall role.

Hitchcock cameo Note that Hitchcock can be spotted as Sir John leaves Diana's boarding house (the actor-manager having been there to see the scene of the crime for himself).

MURRAY, LYN (1909–1989) American composer. Murray wrote one of the gayest scores ever heard in a Hitchcock movie, his *Main Title* for *To Catch a Thief* (1955) being delightfully sunny and capricious. That said, his work elsewhere in the film has a remarkably Herrmannesque quality to it. Long at Paramount, Murray's other films include *Son of Paleface* (1952), *The Bridges at Toko-Ri* (1954) and *Promise Her Anything* (1966). It was also at Murray's suggestion that Hitchcock used his great friend Bernard Herrmann to score *The Trouble with Harry* (1955), which led to one of the great screen partnerships. Wrote Murray in his journal: 'I am writing *To Catch a Thief*. Hitchcock is shooting another picture, *The Trouble with Harry*. He told me he doesn't have a composer set for it yet. I now make what is probably the biggest mistake of my life. I recommended Herrmann for it. Hitch does not know Herrmann. I introduce them.' [29] **Hitchography:** *To Catch a Thief* (1955)

MUSE, CLARENCE (1889–1979) American actor. Like many black actors working in Hollywood in the 1930s and 1940s, Muse frequently found himself cast in subservient or menial roles, although in real life he was a graduate of law. Following stage and radio experience, Muse made his screen debut in 1928 in the short *Election Day*, which he followed with over 100 films, among them *A Royal Romance* (1930), *Broadway Bill* (1934), *Watch on the Rhine* (1943), *Porgy and Bess* (1959), *Car Wash* (1976) and *The Black Stallion* (1979). He can also be spotted in Hitchcock's *Shadow of a Doubt* (1943) as a railroad porter. An occasional scriptwriter and songwriter, Muse contributed to the script and score of *Way Down South* (1939)

and co-authored the screenplay for *Broken String* (1940) in which he also took the leading role. **Hitchography:** *Shadow of a Doubt* (1943)

MYCROFT, WALTER (1891–1959) British novelist and screenwriter. Mycroft, upon whose novel *Champagne* Hitchcock based his 1928 film, was the chief story editor for British International Pictures in the early 1930s, during the period Hitchcock was contracted to the studio. He also penned material for the musical revue *Elstree Calling* (1930) and collaborated with Hitchcock on the screenplay for *Murder!* (1930). He later became director of production at Elstree, but continued to write screenplays, occasionally directing and producing them, among them *Spring Meeting* (1940), *My Wife's Family* (1941), *Banana Ridge* (1941) and *The Woman's Angle* (1952). **Hitchography:** *Champagne* (1928), *Elstree Calling* (1930), *Murder!* (1930)

MYRTIL, ODETTE (1898–1978) French-born character actress. Myrtil made the move to Hollywood in the early 1930s, where she went on to provide support in many features, among them *Dodsworth* (1936), *Kitty Foyle* (1940), *Forever and a Day* (1943), *Devotion* (1946) and Hitchcock's *Strangers on a Train* (1951), in which she had the brief and almost irrelevant role of Madame Darville. **Hitchography:** *Strangers on a Train* (1951)

The Mystery Road

(GB, 1921, 68m approx, bw, silent)

CREDITS

Production company:	Famous Players–Lasky
Director:	Paul Powell
Screenplay:	Mary O'Connor, Margaret Turnbull, based on the novel by E Phillips Oppenheim
Inter-titles:	Alfred Hitchcock

CAST

Mary Glynne (Lady Susan Farrington), David Powell (The Honourable Gerald Dombey), Ruby Miller (Vera Lypasht), Nadja Ostrovska (Myrtle Sargot), Percy Standing (Luigi), Lewis Gilbert (Jean Sargot), Judd Green (Vagabond)

Yet another lost black-and-white silent with inter-titles designed by Hitchcock, this Nice-set drama told the story of a lord's son who has affairs with both a French peasant girl and an English girl who commits suicide. Directed at Islington Studios by Paul Powell for Famous Players–Lasky, it was one of many films made for the company in 1921 starring Mary Glynne.

N

NALDER, REGGIE Austrian-born character actor. This gaunt, sinister-looking actor was frequently cast in villainous roles, notable among them Rien the assassin in Hitchcock's 1956 remake of *The Man Who Knew Too Much* ('You have a very nice little boy, Madame. His safety will depend on *you* tonight,' he tells Doris Day's Jo McKenna in a bid to ensure her silence about a plot to kill a foreign dignitary during a concert at the Albert Hall). A former dancer, Nalder's other credits include *The Manchurian Candidate* (1962), *The Bird with the Crystal Plumage* (1969), in which he again played an assassin, *The Devil Don't Die* (1975, TV), *Zoltan, Hound of Dracula* (1977) and, most memorably, *Salem's Lot* (1979, TV), in which he played a terrifying Nosferatu-like vampire known as the Master. **Hitchography:** *The Man Who Knew Too Much* (1956)

NALDI, NITA (1899–1961, real name Anita Donna Dooley) American-born actress. Following experience as a dancer in The Ziegfeld Follies, this glamorous entertainer went on to appear in a number of key silent productions, notably *Dr Jekyll and Mr Hyde* (1920), opposite John Barrymore, *Blood and Sand* (1922), in which she was romantic fodder for screen idol Rudolph Valentino, and *The Ten Commandments* (1923), in which she was directed by Cecil B de Mille. She also appeared in Hitchcock's first two films as a director. In *The Pleasure Garden* (1925), she plays a native girl who is murdered by her colonial lover, while in *The Mountain Eagle* (1925) she is a young Kentucky schoolmarm who flees to the mountains to escape the unwanted attentions of a local lech. However, as Hitchcock recalled, she was not exactly ideal casting in the latter role. 'My heroine was a pleasant, simple, homely schoolmarm. My star was glamorous, dark, Latin, Junoesque, statuesque slinky, with slanting eyes, 4-inch heels, nails like a mandarin's, and a black dog to match her black swathed dress.' [1] Naldi was gradually persuaded to glam down for the role, though she did keep hold of one slinky item of apparel. Recalled Hitchcock: 'It was winter. But Nita under her frock wore just one garment: such scanties as even today would be considered – well, scanty.' [2] **Hitchography:** *The Pleasure Garden* (1925), *The Mountain Eagle* (1925)

NAPIER, ALAN (1903–1988, real name Alan Napier-Clavering) British actor. Best remembered for playing Alfred the butler in the TV series *Batman* (1966–1968), Napier made his film debut in *Caste* in Britain in 1930. Another eight British films followed, among them *Stamboul* (1932) and *Wings Over Africa* (1936), after which he went to Hollywood in 1939, making his first film there – *We Are Not Alone* – the same year. His subsequent credits include *The Invisible Man Returns* (1940), *The Uninvited* (1943), *Joan of Arc* (1948), *The Great Caruso* (1951) and *Journey to the Center of the Earth* (1959). In 1964 he played Mr Rutland, father of Mark Rutland (Sean Connery), in Hitchcock's *Marnie*. Like his daughter-in-law to-be, Mr Rutland has a great interest in horses. Comments Mark when he first takes Marnie to see him, 'If you smell anything like a horse, you're in!' Napier's other films include *My Fair Lady* (1964), *Batman* (1966), *The Paper Chase* (1973), *QB VII* (1974, TV) and *The Monkey Mission* (1981, TV). He also appeared in an episode of *Alfred Hitchcock Presents*. **Hitchography:** *The Avon Emeralds* (1959, TV), *Marnie* (1964)

NATWICK, MILDRED (1908–1992) American comedy character actress. On stage from 1932, Natwick made her film debut in *The Long Voyage Home* in 1940. Following her second film appearance in *The Enchanted Cottage* in 1945, she went on to become one of Hollywood's most reliable supporting stars, appearing in the likes of *Three Godfathers* (1948), *The Quiet Man* (1952), *The Court Jester* (1955), in which she took part in the memorable 'Chalice from the Palace' routine with Danny Kaye, and Hitchcock's *The Trouble with Harry* (1955), in which she played the spinster Miss Gravely ('What seems to be the trouble, Captain?' she nonchalantly enquires of Edmund Gwenn's Captain Wiles when she discovers him dragging the titular corpse through a field!). Her subsequent credits include *Barefoot in the Park* (1967), for which she was nominated for a best supporting actress Oscar, *If It's Tuesday It Must Be Belgium* (1969) and *Dangerous Liaisons* (1988), while on television she co-starred with Helen Hayes in *The Snoop Sisters* (1972, TV) and its subsequent series. She also appeared in two episodes of *Alfred Hitchcock Presents*. **Hitchography:** *The Trouble with Harry* (1955), *The Perfect Murder* (1956, TV), *Miss Bracegirdle Does Her Duty* (1958, TV)

NESBITT, CATHLEEN (1888–1982) British character actress. On stage from 1910, Nesbitt trod the boards for many years before making her film debut in 1932 with *The Frightened Lady*. The stage remained her first love, but she found time to make the occasional film in both Britain and America, among them *The Passing of the Third Floor Back* (1935), *Gaslight* (1940), *Nicholas Nickleby* (1947), *Three Coins in the Fountain* (1954), *Separate Tables* (1958), *Staircase* (1969), *French Connection II* (1975) and *Julia* (1977). In 1976, she also appeared as the wealthy Julia Rainbird, whose desire to track down her long lost nephew and heir sets the action in progress in Hitchcock's last film, *Family Plot* (1976). Nesbitt's television work includes *The Farmer's Daughter* (1965). She was long married to the actor Cecil Ramage (1895–1988). **Hitchography:** *Family Plot* (1976)

NEAME, RONALD (1911–) British director. Neame, whose films include *Take My Life* (1947), *The Prime of Miss Jean Brodie* (1969) and *The Poseidon Adventure* (1972), began his career as a cinematographer, noted for his work with director David Lean, which included *In Which We Serve* (1942), *This Happy Breed* (1944) and *Blithe Spirit* (1945). Neame joined the film industry in 1928 as an assistant in the camera department at BIP, and soon after found himself working on Hitchcock's *Blackmail* (1929), much of which he re-shot when sound came in mid-production. Commented Neame: 'Every conceivable kind of problem happened, all of which Hitchie took in his stride.' [3] Neame photographed his first film, *Drake of England*, in 1935. He has also produced several films, including *Brief Encounter* (1945) and *Great Expectations* (1946), for which he also contributed to the screenplays. **Hitchography:** *Blackmail* (1929)

NEWCOM, JAMES E American editor. Long associated with the films of David O Selznick, Newcom began to work for the producer in 1937 on *A Star is Born*. Often working in association with Hal C Kern, Newcom went on to cut *The Prisoner of Zenda* (1937), *Nothing Sacred* (1937), *Made for Each Other* (1939) and *Gone With the Wind* (1939), which earned him (and Kern) an Oscar. He also worked on Hitchcock's *Rebecca* (1940) as associate editor, again with Kern. **Hitchography:** *Rebecca* (1940)

NEWMAN, ALFRED (1901–1970) American-born musical director. One of Hollywood's key composer-conductor-administrators, Newman had a hand in over 250 film scores, beginning with the Irving Berlin musical *Reaching for the Moon* (1930), which he conducted, and ending with *Airport* (1969). Following training as a pianist from the age of 14 with Sigismond Stojowski, Newman got a job as a pit pianist at the Strand Theatre on Broadway, and by the age of 15 he was deputizing for the conductor on matinees. At the age of 19 he was conducting such major shows as *George White's Scandals of 1920*, while at the age of 25 he was invited to conduct the Cincinatti Symphony Orchestra. Having arrived in Hollywood, he established himself as a composer with his Gershwinesque score for *Street Scene* (1931), which led to his being appointed music director for United Artists and, later, for Twentieth Century Fox (between 1940 and 1960). Oscar-nominated an astonishing 45 times, he went on to win the statuette nine times, both for scoring and arranging such films as *Alexander's Ragtime Band* (1938), *The Song of Bernadette* (1943) and *The King and I* (1956). Newman's major works include *Wuthering Heights* (1939), *The Grapes of Wrath* (1940), *The Robe* (1953), *Anastasia* (1956) and *The Greatest Story Ever Told* (1965). He also provided a thrilling, cliffhanger-style score for Hitchcock's *Foreign Correspondent* (1940), which further enhances an already exciting film. The eldest of ten children, Newman's brothers include Emil Newman and Lionel Newman (1916–1989), both of them composer-conductors (Emil would conduct Hugo Friedhofer's score for Hitchcock's *Lifeboat* in 1944). His sons David Newman (1954–) and Thomas Newman have also entered the film business as composers, as has his nephew Randy Newman (1943–). **Hitchography:** *Foreign Correspondent* (1940)

NEWMAN, EMIL American music director. Long at Fox, Emil Newman was the brother of composer-conductor Alfred Newman (1901–1970). His many films include *Four Jills in a Jeep* (1944), *Pin Up Girl* (1944) and Hitchcock's *Lifeboat* (1944), for which he conducted Hugo Friedhofer's brief score (main and end credits only). **Hitchography:** *Lifeboat* (1944)

NEWMAN, PAUL (1925–) American actor. A product of the fabled Actor's Studio, this Hollywood legend made an inauspicious debut in films with the would-be epic *The Silver Chalice* (1955) following experience on Broadway, notably in the 1953 production of *Picnic*. Following a further flop, *The Rack* (1956), Newman hit a home run with his third film *Somebody Up There Likes Me* (1956), a biopic of boxer Rocky Graziano. Among Newman's subsequent films are *Cat on a Hot Tin Roof* (1958), *The Long, Hot Summer* (1958), *Exodus* (1960), *The Hustler* (1961), *Hud* (1963), the Hitchcockian thriller *The Prize* (1963), *Lady L* (1965) and *Harper* (1966). By 1966 Newman was one of Hollywood's top box office draws, and was cast as Professor Michael Armstrong in Hitchcock's Cold War thriller *Torn Curtain*, in which he fakes a defection to the East in order to steal a top secret nuclear formula. Along with leading lady Julie Andrews, who plays his fiancée Sarah Sherman, Newman was uneasily cast in the film, while their bedroom scene on board a freezing Norwegian cruiser caused some controversy at the time. The film was subsequently condemned by the National Roman Catholic Office For Motion Pictures for its 'gratuitous introduction of pre-marital sex between its sympathetic protagonists,' despite the fact that both are covered by layer upon layer of blankets. Commented Andrews of the scene: 'As it was necessary to the story to establish our close relationship, I saw no harm in it. Paul Newman was such a nice man; we didn't take it seriously, and had a lot of giggles over it. It didn't last long, so I don't see what all the fuss is about.' [4]

Paul Newman and Julie Andrews escape from behind the Iron Curtain in the tense bus chase sequence from Hitchcock's Torn Curtain *(1966), the director's last truly great film.*

Newman's subsequent films include *Cool Hand Luke* (1967), *Butch Cassidy and the Sundance Kid* (1969), *The Sting* (1973), *The Towering Inferno* (1974), *The Verdict* (1982), *The Color of Money* (1986), which won him a best actor Oscar, *The Hudsucker Proxy* (1993) and *Where the Money Is* (2000). He has also directed several films, among them *Rachel, Rachel* (1968), *The Shadow Box* (1980, TV) and *The Glass Menagerie* (1987). In 1986, Newman was given a special Oscar for his 'many memorable and compelling screen performances.' Active politically, he is also involved in much charity work, notably the Hole in the Wall Gang, a holiday retreat for disabled children which he funds through the post-tax profits of the Newman's Own product range (which has generated over $100 million since 1982). His first wife was the actress Jackie Witte, to whom he was married between 1949 and 1957. His second wife is the actress Joanne Woodward (1930–), to whom he has been married since 1958. **Hitchography:** *Torn Curtain* (1966)

NEWTON, ROBERT (1905–1956) British character actor. This swaggering star is best remembered for a series of eye-rolling parts, among them Bill Walker in *Major Barbara* (1941), James Brodie in *Hatter's Castle* (1941), Bill Sikes in *Oliver Twist* (1948) and pirate Long John Silver, whom he portrayed in two films and a television series respectively: *Treasure Island* (1950), *Long John Silver* (1953) and *The Adventures of Long John Silver* (1955, TV). Consequently, one is somewhat surprised to see him playing the hero in Hitchcock's *Jamaica Inn* (1939), his undercover naval officer Jim Trehearne bringing to book smuggler-in-chief Sir Humphrey Pangallan (Charles Laughton, himself doing a spot of the old eye rolling). On stage from 1920, Newton made his film debut in *The Tremane Case* (1932) and went on to appear in such highly regarded productions as *This Happy Breed* (1944), *Henry V* (1945), *Odd Man Out* (1946) and *The Beachcomber* (1954), despite the fact that his career was plagued with alcoholism. He also appeared in an episode of *Alfred Hitchcock Presents*. **Hitchography:** *Jamaica Inn* (1939), *The Derelicts* (1956, TV)

NEY, MARIE (1895–1981) British supporting actress. Ney appeared in a handful of British films in the 1930s, 1940s and 1950s, her most memorable role being that of timid Aunt Patience in Hitchcock's *Jamaica Inn* (1939). Her other films include *Escape* (1930), *Scrooge* (1935), *Night Was Our Friend* (1951) and *Simba* (1955). **Hitchography:** *Jamaica Inn* (1939)

NOIRET, PHILIPPE (1930–) French character actor. Noiret came to films following much stage experience, both as an actor and nightclub entertainer. Although he made his cinema debut in 1949 in *Gigi*, and went on to appear in the likes of *Olivia* (1950), *La Pointe Courte* (1956) and *Zazie dans le Metro* (1960), it wasn't until he was a little older that he began to leave his mark in such productions as Hitchcock's *Topaz* (1969), in which he livened up the last part of the film as double agent Henri Jarre, *Murphy's War* (1970), *La Grande Bouffe* (1973), *Le Cop* (1984), *Cinema Paradiso* (1988), *La Fille de D'Artagnan* (1993) and *Il Postino* (1994). **Hitchography:** *Topaz* (1969)

NOLAN, JEANETTE (1911–1998) American character actress. Familiar from such TV shows as *The Virginian* (1967) and *Dirty Sally* (1973), Nolan recorded several of Mother's lines for Hitchcock's *Psycho* (1960), although the majority of the dubbing was done by Virginia Gregg. Interestingly, Nolan's husband, actor John McIntire (1907–1991), whom she married in 1935, played Sheriff Chambers in the same movie. Recalled the actress: 'I had next to no contact with Mr Hitchcock. I simply went to the recording studio and looped some of the mother's lines.' [5] Nolan also dubbed Janet Leigh's scream in the shower and Vera Miles' scream in the fruit cellar. Nolan's other screen credits include *Macbeth* (1948), *The Guns of Fort Petticoat* (1957) and *Cloak and Dagger* (1984). She also appeared in three episodes of *Alfred Hitchcock Presents* and an episode of *The Alfred Hitchcock Hour*. She was the mother of singer Tim McIntire (1943–1986). **Hitchography:** *The Right Kind of House* (1958, TV), *The Morning After* (1959, TV), *Psycho* (1960), *Coming Home* (1961, TV), *Triumph* (1964, TV)

North by Northwest
(US, 1959, 136m, Technicolor, VistaVision) ★★★★

CREDITS

Production company:	MGM
Producer:	Alfred Hitchcock
Associate producer:	Herbert Coleman
Director:	Alfred Hitchcock
Screenplay:	Ernest Lehman
Cinematographer:	Robert Burks
Music:	Bernard Herrmann
Editor:	George Tomasini
Production design:	Robert Boyle
Art directors:	Merrill Pye, William A Horning
Special effects:	Lee LeBlanc, A Arnold Gillespie
Sound:	Franklin Milton
Titles:	Saul Bass

CAST

Gary Grant (Roger O Thornhill), James Mason (Philip Vandamm), Eva Marie Saint (Eve Kendall), Martin Landau (Leonard), Jessie Royce Landis (Clara Thornhill), Leo G Carroll (Professor), Philip Ober (Lester Townsend), Adam Williams (Valerian), Robert Ellenstein (Licht), Philip Coolidge (Dr Cross), Edward Platt (Victor Larrabee), Les Tremayne (Auctioneer), Pat McVey (Cop), Ken Lynch (Cop), Edward Binns (Captain Junket), Ernest Anderson (Porter), Malcolm Atterbury (Man at prairie crossing), John Beradino (Sergeant Emile Klinger), Tommy Farrell (Elevator operator), Ned Glass (Ticket teller), Doreen Lang (Maggie), Nora Marlowe

(Housekeeper), Maudie Prickett (Elsie the maid), Olan Soule (Assistant auctioneer), Carleton Young (Fanning Nelson), Josephine Hutchinson (Handsome woman), Madge Kennedy (Washington agent), Frank Wilcox (Weltner), Robert Shayne (Larry Wade), Casey Taggart (Shaving man)

Video availability: Warner Bros.
DVD availability: Warner Bros.
CD availability: *North by Northwest* (Turner Classic Movies/Rhino), which contains the complete score; *Music from The Great Hitchcock Movie Thrillers* (Phase 4/Decca) which contains the *Main Title*; *Hitchcock – Master of Mayhem* (Proarte), which contains the *Main Title*; *Bernard Herrmann – Film Scores* (Milan), which contains the *Prelude*; *A History of Hitchcock – Dial M for Murder* (Silva Screen), which contains the *Main Title*; *Psycho – The Essential Alfred Hitchcock* (Silva Screen), which contains the *Prelude* and *Conversation Piece*; and *Citizen Kane – The Essential Bernard Herrmann* (Silva Screen), which contains the *Prelude* and *Conversation Piece*

North by Northwest is the supreme Hitchcock package: an immaculately presented roller-coaster ride of wickedly ingenious thrills, laughs and surprises, it is quite simply the pinnacle of its director's career ('The Master of Suspense weaves his greatest tale!' boasted the film's strap line). At 136 minutes, it is also his longest; although such is its wit, pace and invention that it seems to speed by in half the time.

Hitchcock had been toying with the idea of a story climaxing with a chase across the presidential faces of Mount Rushmore for several years (one proposed title had been *The Man in Lincoln's Nose*). Indeed, during the writing of *The Trouble with Harry* (1955), John Michael Hayes recalled that he and Hitchcock would frequently discuss ideas for the film. 'In every spare moment we had, he kicked around ideas for something called *North by Northwest*. What Hitch really wanted to do was develop a story on which he could hang the Mount Rushmore scene and a few other unrelated ideas… I remember one idea involving an automobile production line that never made it into the completed picture. The hero would arrive to question a production foreman. As the scene would begin, the foreman would point out a frame coming on the line and talk for a minute about the wonders of the production line… But before the scene ended, the foreman would point to this car that the audience has seen assembled from a frame. The hero would go over, admire it, open the back door and a corpse would fall out.' [6]

While preparing to film *Vertigo* (1958), Hitchcock teamed up with an exciting new script writer named Ernest Lehman, whose credits already included such highly regarded pictures as *Executive Suite* (1954), *Sabrina* (1954), which had earned him an Oscar nomination, and *The Sweet Smell of Success* (1957). The intention had been to adapt the Hammond Innes novel *The Wreck of the Mary Deare* for the screen, but Hitchcock was dissatisfied with

the project almost from the start, and so abandoned it in favour of what eventually became *North by Northwest* (the *Mary Deare* film was subsequently made by other hands). At first, Hitchcock and the writer batted ideas about for a couple of months, until one day Lehman commented, 'All I want to do is write the Hitchcock picture to end all Hitchcock pictures.' When asked what that would be, he replied, 'Something with wit, glamour, sophistication, suspense, many different colourful locales, a real *movie* movie.' 'I always wanted to do a chase across the faces of Mount Rushmore,' responded the director, to which Lehman simply exclaimed, 'Hey!' [7]

Lehman continued to work on the project while Hitchcock filmed *Vertigo*, but the two remained in contact, with Hitchcock continually suggesting ideas for the project. 'I always wanted to do a scene where our hero is standing all alone in a wide open space and there's nobody and nothing else in sight for 360 degrees around, as far as the eye can see,' [8] Hitchcock told Lehman. Thus the crop duster scene was born.

Gradually, the plot began to take hold, with Hitchcock and Lehman centring their escapade around the exploits of a world-weary Madison Avenue advertising executive named Roger Thornhill (Cary Grant), who finds himself mistaken for a spy named George Kaplan. The irony of the situation is that George Kaplan doesn't actually exist; he's been created by members of a highly secret Washington agency as a decoy to keep an enemy operator, one Philip Vandamm (James Mason), from discovering that they have an agent placed in his very midst. This is a beautiful industrial designer named Eve Kendall (Eva Marie Saint), who fell in love with Vandamm at a party, but who has since been recruited by Washington to keep tabs on her lover, who is planning to smuggle top secret microfilm out of the country (this being a Hitchcock picture, we of course never discover what is actually *on* the microfilm). In order to prove his innocence, Thornhill makes his way across America from city to city, trying to track down the nonexistent Kaplan, only to be pursued by the bad guys, who try to kill him at every turn. Naturally, he and Kendall team up along the way and fall in love, with Thornhill saving her from the clutches of Vandamm at the last moment, having inadvertently exposed her true status to the other side. Everything ends on a happy note, though, with Thornhill and Kendall tying the knot (his previous two wives had left him because he led too dull a life, he informs her).

More than any other Hitchcock film, *North by Northwest* is a film of set pieces: the kidnapping of Thornhill at the Oak Bar ('What is this – a joke or something?' – 'Yes, a joke. We will laugh about it in the car'); Thornhill's drunken escape from Vandamm's house after having been force-fed a bottle of bourbon; the assassination of the hapless Lester Townsend at the United Nations, whose house Vandamm has appropriated for his activities; the astonishingly frank seduction scene between Thornhill and Kendall onboard the 20th Century Limited ('You wouldn't happen to have an extra pair of pajamas,

Hitchcock points Cary Grant and Eva Marie Saint in the right direction during the filming of North by Northwest *(1959).*

would you?'); the afore-mentioned crop-duster scene (which critic C A Lejeune predicted 'will be talked about as long as people talk about films at all');Thornhill's escape from an auction by making outrageous bids ('Would the gentleman *please* co-operate?' begs the exasperated auctioneer); the fake assassination of Thornhill by Kendall to help keep her cover; and that final clamber over Mount Rushmore that Hitchcock was so keen to make use of, even if he never did manage to show Thornhill having a sneezing fit in Lincoln's nose as he'd originally intended. Revealed Ernest Lehman, 'The US Department of National Parks refused to allow Hitch to shoot at Mount Rushmore, and the United Nations said no, too. No Problem. Gifted production designer Robert Boyle created the amazing Faces of the Presidents on the soundstages of MGM, and his magical sets also gave the film Vandamm's getaway house near the monument and the interior of the United Nations as well.' [9]

Hitchcock had of course tackled the theme of the innocent man on the run several times before, most notably in *The 39 Steps* (1935), *Young and Innocent* (1937) and *Saboteur* (1942). Some have accused *North by Northwest* of being little more than a compendium of his greatest hits (the auction house scene is little more than a re-working of the political rally at which Robert Donat's Richard Hannay finds himself unexpectedly speaking in *The 39 Steps*).That said, Hitchcock was working at the height of his powers, with each scene told with the maximum cinematic impact and arguably the most continually witty dialogue ever heard in a movie. Indeed, to list the best quotes would be to re-print practically the entire screenplay, but the cream is worth repeating. 'In the world of advertising there is no such thing as a lie, Maggie.There is only The Expeditious Exaggeration,' Thornhill tells his secretary. 'That's funny… That plane's dustin' crops where there ain't no crops,' observes a man prior to the crop duster scene. 'The three of you together. Now there's a picture only Charles Addams could draw,' quips Thornhill when encountering Vandamm, Miss Kendall and Vandamm's right-hand man Leonard (Martin Landau) at the auction house. 'War is hell, Mr Thornhill, even when it's a cold one,' explains the Professor to Thornhill. Then there's Vandamm's accusation that Thornhill/Kaplan has been overplaying his various roles – 'First you're the outraged Madison Avenue man who claims he has been mistaken for someone else.Then you play a fugitive from justice, supposedly trying to clear his name of a crime he knows he didn't commit. And now you play the peevish lover stung by jealousy and betrayal. Seems to me you fellows could stand a little less training from the FBI and a little more from the Actors' Studio.' Wrote critic Dylis Powell of the Lehman script in the *Sunday Times*:'It is consistently entertaining, its excitement pointed by but never interrupted by the jokes.'

The casting of the film is perfection itself. Cary Grant is at his absolute best as Thornhill (James Stewart lobbied hard for the part); though 50 at the time of filming, he couldn't be more debonair, while his joyous way with a *bon mot* in a tricky situation has caused some to regard his performance as a prototype for James Bond. In fact Hollis Alpert's comment in the *Saturday Review* that, 'It is only when you adopt the basic premise that Cary Grant could not possibly come to any harm that the tongue in Hitchcock's cheek becomes plainly visible,' could just as easily have been written about the exploits of Ian Fleming's 007. Meanwhile, Eva Marie Saint's Eve Kendall is Glamour personified (C A Lejeune described her as 'an elegant actress with a fine-drawn, exciting face'), while James Mason is the ultimate Hitchcock villain: suave, sophisticated, unruffled, and with a way with a sardonic put down that almost has us rooting for him.

All the supporting players are ideally cast, too, among them Hitchcock regular Leo G Carroll as the Professor, the head of the mysterious Washington bureau ('FBI, CIA, ONI, we're all in the same alphabet soup'), the delightful Jessie Royce Landis as Thornhill's wisecracking mother (even though she was 11 months *younger* than Cary Grant) and future *Mission: Impossible* star Martin Landau as Leonard,Vandamm's sneering assistant who, quite controversially for the time, is obviously a homosexual ('Call it my woman's intuition if you will,' he says of his suspicions about Eve being a double agent, to which Vandamm responds, 'You know what I think? I think you're jealous of her. I mean it. And I'm touched, dear boy. Really touched').

The *North by Northwest* shoot was a lengthy one, beginning in New York on 27 August 1958 and concluding on Christmas Eve later that same year. Even so, Hitchcock found time to direct two episodes of his television series during production (*Poison* and *Banquo's Chair*). Post-production was an even lengthier affair, which involved the addition of the dazzling title sequence by Saul Bass (the credits slide across the grid of a New York office block) and Bernard Herrmann's driving fandango-like score with its dancing rhythms (the music even manages to incorporate the roar of the MGM lion into its opening bars!).

The end results contain Hitchcock's most polished work, packed with self-references, in-jokes and dazzling camera work (for example, when Vandamm discovers Eve's duplicity, he comments: 'This is a matter best disposed of from a great height… over water,' at which Hitchcock slowly raises his camera above Vandamm's head so as to emphasize the threat). In addition to the jokes in the screenplay, also listen out for the rendition of *It's a Most Unusual Day* as Thornhill enters the Oak Room.The film concludes with the most phallic piece of imagery to be found in any Hitchcock film: this involves a cross fade from Thornhill and Eve dangling from the edge of Mount Rushmore to Thornhill pulling Eve – now the new Mrs Thornhill – up into the upper bunk of a Pullman compartment. Hitchcock then cuts to an exterior shot of the train as it disappears into a tunnel. Theorists have had a field day with this shot ever since!

Not all the critics were unanimous in their praise of the movie.Writing in *The New Republic*, Stanley Kaufman described the prairie crossroads scene as 'probably the low point of Hitchcock's career,' while Moira Walsh in *America* had concerns over the 'implications about the heroine's morals, the methods of American intelligence agencies and sundry other matters.' Elsewhere, though, the reaction was upbeat. 'That master magician has done it again,' enthused the *News of the World*, while *Variety* praised the 'delectable' mixture of 'suspense, intrigue, comedy, humour.' Audiences agreed, and the film went on to make in excess of $5 million in America alone, a huge sum for the period.

For all its polish, though, note that the film has one of the most amazing gaffes in any Hitchcock picture. During the scene in the Mount Rushmore cafeteria where Eve shoots Thornhill with the fake bullets, note the young boy sitting with his back to the action, for he puts his hands to his ears *before* the shots are fired! Meanwhile, Cary Grant refers to a picture of James Mason's Vandamm as 'Our man who's assembling the general assembly,' when he should have said, 'Our man who's *addressing* the general assembly.' Elsewhere, the shadow of the camera can be spotted moving past a newsstand in the opening scene. Ernest Lehman has also spotted a mistake: 'Thornhill is peering through binoculars at the faces of the presidents. "I don't like the way Teddy Roosevelt is looking at me," he says uneasily to the Professor, seated nearby. Go see the picture again. The way his face is positioned, Teddy Roosevelt isn't looking at *anyone*.' [10]

Note that the film was nominated for three Academy Awards: best screenplay (Ernest Lehman), best art direction (Robert Boyle, William Horning, Merrill Pye, Henry Grace, Frank McKelvy) and best editing (George Tomsini). It didn't win in a single category, although Ernest Lehman earned an honorary Oscar in 2001 for his body of work, including *North by Northwest*, which is quite simply the greatest screenplay ever constructed. The film was spoofed in the Gene Wilder vehicle *Hanky Panky* (1982).

Hitchcock cameo Hitchcock can be spotted at the climax of the opening titles, missing a departing bus.

Notorious
(US, 1946, 101m, bw) ★★★

CREDITS
Production company: RKO
Producer: Alfred Hitchcock
Director: Alfred Hitchcock
Screenplay: Ben Hecht, based upon *The Song of the Flame* by John Taintor Foote
Cinematographer: Ted Tetzlaff
Music: Roy Webb
Music director: Constantin Bakaleinikoff
Editor: Theron Warth
Art director: Carroll Clark, Albert S D'Agostino
Costumes: Edith Head
Special effects: Vernon L Walker, Paul Eagler

Sound: John E Tribi
Clem Portma
Terry Kellum
2nd unit photography: Gregg Toland

CAST
Cary Grant (T R Devlin), Ingrid Bergman (Alicia Huberman), Claude Rains (Alexander Sebastian), Leopoldine Konstantin (Madame Sebastian), Louis Calhern (Paul Prescott), Reinhold Schunzel (Dr Anderson), Moroni Olsen (Walter Beardsley), Ricardo Costa (Dr Barbosa), Ivan Triesault (Eric Mathis), Alex Minotis (Joseph), Wally Brown (Mr Hopkins), Charles Mendl (Commodore), Gavin Gordon (Ernest Weylin), Eberhard Krumschmidt (Emil Hupka), Fay Baker (Ethel), John Vosper (Reporter), Warren Jackson (District Attorney), Charles D Brown (Judge), Herbert Wyndham (Mr Cook), Frank Wilcox (Agent), Virginia Gregg (Clerk), William Gordon (Adams)

Video availability: Pearson
DVD availability: Pearson
CD availability: *The Curse of the Cat People – The Film Music of Roy Webb* (Cloud Nine), which contains a *Suite* and a *Dance Suite*

Given that it builds up to a fine climax of dramatic tension and contains some remarkable directorial flourishes, *Notorious* gets off to a fairly unremarkable start given its vaunted reputation (when interviewing Hitchcock for his book *Hitchcock by Truffaut*, the French critic turned director Francois Truffaut described the film as being 'the very quintessence of Hitchcock') In fact the best way to describe its early romantic scenes between Ingrid Bergman and Cary Grant is dull, dull, dull. But this is to jump ahead.

Having worked successfully with writer the Ben Hecht on *Spellbound* (1945), Hitchcock put him to work on a *Saturday Evening Post* short story titled *The Song of the Flame* by John Taintor Foote. Published in 1921, it was brought to Hitchcock's attention by David O Selznick, who intended to produce the resultant film, tentatively titled *Who Is My Love?* However, following various script revisions, Selznick went cold on the project, and sold it on for a whopping $800,000 (plus 50 per cent of the net profits!) to RKO, for whom Hitchcock had previously directed the 'comedy' *Mr and Mrs Smith* (1941).

In the original *Evening Post* story, an actress is coerced into sleeping with a spy so as to extract information from him. For the film, the basic notion remained the same, although instead of an actress, the notorious woman in question is Alicia Huberman (Ingrid Bergman), the daughter of a Nazi sympathizer who has just been convicted for treason. Although Alicia does not share her father's sympathies, she proves to be a valuable tool for the American government, which wishes to use her as a contact with further neo-Nazis hiding out in Brazil, among them one of Alicia's former suitors, one Alexander

Sebastian (Claude Rains).

Persuaded to accept the assignment by a handsome government agent named Devlin (Cary Grant), with whom she subsequently falls in love, Alicia travels to Rio with him, where a meeting with Sebastian is engineered at a riding club. Wooing Alicia with renewed vigour, Sebastian eventually proposes to her, much to the chagrin of his dominating mother (Leopoldine Konstantin), who is rightly suspicious of Alicia, who by now has discovered that Sebastian's work in Brazil is somehow connected to a number of wine bottles stored under lock and key in his cellar. Alicia agrees to put duty to country before her love for Devlin and agrees to marry Sebastian (thus effectively prostituting herself), and during a party thrown to celebrate their marriage, she and Devlin manage to sneak into the wine cellar with a key Alicia has purloined from her husband's key ring. Searching for clues, Devlin accidentally smashes one of the wine bottles, which turns out to be filled with sand. Having taken a sample before hiding the breakage, Devlin escorts Alicia from the cellar, only to hear Sebastian making his way there to get more champagne for the party. Grabbing Alicia, Devlin begins to kiss her, so as to throw Sebastian off the trail of what they've *really* been doing.

The rouse seems to have worked, and Alicia later returns the key to her husband's key ring. But Sebastian's suspicions (and jealousy) have now been aroused (he *had* noticed the disappearance and re-appearance of the key after all), and it's not long before he discovers the broken wine bottle in the cellar. Asking his mother for advice on what to do, he is persuaded to murder Alicia by gradually poisoning her with arsenic, so as not to raise suspicion. Meanwhile, Devlin has discovered that the sand in the wine bottle is in fact uranium ore, one of the vital components in the making of an atom bomb. Consequently, when Alicia fails to turn up for a meeting for further instructions, Devlin fears the worst and so goes to Sebastian's home where, in a nick-of-time climax, he rescues her, carrying her from her sick bed to his waiting car on the pretext that he is taking her to the hospital, leaving Sebastian behind to explain to his now suspicious Nazi cohorts why he – Alicia's husband, after all – hasn't gone with them to the hospital.

For Hitchcock, the thrust of *Notorious* was simple, it being 'the story of a man in love with a girl who, in the course of her official duties, had to go to bed with another man and even marry him.' [11] Indeed, the director attached very little importance to the activities of the Nazis and their intentions for the uranium ore. Instead, he concentrated on the stars, the romance and the visuals.

To be honest, over 50 years on, the early clinches between Bergman and Grant are a little tedious, particularly one scene in Alicia's Rio apartment, which contains one of the longest seduction scenes in screen history. Instead, one yearns for the plot to kick in and the thrills to start, which, after around 30 minutes, they finally do. However, this isn't to completely write off the first third of the movie, which contains some effective scenes and touches, among them Alicia's drunken midnight drive with Devlin and, the following morning, the tilted camera angle of Devlin standing in a doorway, taken from Alicia's point of view, as she lies hung over in bed. And what about the opening caption following the main credits, with its time and date written out in full ('Miami, Florida, three twenty-three pm, April the twenty-fourth, nineteen-hundred-and-forty-six')? Is this some kind of in-joke at the expense of overly detailed explanatory captions? Who knows!

Once Alicia has overcome her reservations about accepting Devlin's proposition to spy for the government ('I don't go for patriots or patriotism,' is her initial reaction), things begin to move at a more satisfactory speed, particularly once Alicia has duped Sebastian and is at last inside his house (comments Devlin's boss, Paul Prescott (Louis Calhern): 'She's good at making friends and we want someone inside his house'). Here, the drama really begins to grip, especially with the introduction of Sebastian's sinister mother. 'You didn't testify at your father's trial. We thought that unusual,' she comments when introduced to Alicia for the first time.

Once Alicia has won Sebastian's heart ('You can add Sebastian's name to my list of playmates,' she informs Devlin), and the wedding has taken place, the film moves into high gear with the party sequence, with much tension wrung from the stealing of Sebastian's key to the wine cellar. Then comes the celebrated crane shot from high across the dance floor down to a close-up of Alicia's hand in which she tightly clutches the key so as to pass it on to Devlin when he arrives (the crane shot recalls the similar one used by Hitchcock towards the climax of *Young and Innocent* nine years earlier). In 1979, when Hitchcock was honoured with a life achievement award by the American Film Institute, Bergman returned the key to the director, having kept it since the making of the film.

The scenes in which Alicia is gradually poisoned following Sebastian's discovery that she is a spy also compel ('I am married to an American agent,' Sebastian coolly informs his mother). During the poisoning sequences, Hitchcock makes much use of coffee cups, featuring them in close-ups and in the foreground of shots, for which giant plaster replicas had to be made, so as to keep everything in focus. Consequently, when Sebastian urges his wife to, 'Drink your coffee, darling, it's getting cold,' the well-meant suggestion takes on a much darker meaning. Alicia's discovery that she is being poisoned is also cleverly handled. When the doctor calls by to examine her, he mistakenly picks up Alicia's coffee cup instead of his own, producing an overly panicked reaction from Sebastian and his mother, from which Alicia puts two and two together. Finally, Devlin's rescue of Alicia in one long sweeping take as he carries her down the stairs and out to his car is the cherry on the cake, especially when he slams the door shut and drives off, leaving Sebastian with a lot of explaining to do and an uncertain future.

The performances by the entire cast are uniformly excellent throughout. Grant and Bergman are superbly matched in their scenes together (the film's poster bills

Ingrid Bergman and Cary Grant discover the McGuffin in the wine cellar in Hitchcock's Notorious *(1946).*

them as 'The screen's top romantic stars'). Even better are Bergman's scenes with Rains, in which she has to feign interest in him and avoid showing her revulsion at his touch (when she meets him for a dinner date and he kisses her hand, the smile momentarily vanishes from her face as he bows his head to do so). However, as good as the leads are, it is the supporting players who steal the film, notably Rains, who, for the want of our better judgment, manages to make us feel sympathetic towards Sebastian, despite his political leanings and his dastardly deeds, and Leopoldine Konstantin as Sebastian's cold, domineering mother (Sebastian's almost Oedipal relationship with her is practically worthy of a thesis in itself). For his efforts, Rains earned a best supporting actor Oscar nomination (Ben Hecht also earned a nomination for his screenplay).

Made for $2.3 million, *Notorious* went on to earn in excess of $7 million at the US box office, from which Selznick would have made around $3 million according to his deal (of course, he would have made much more had he kept faith with the project). The film also garnered mostly positive reviews. Praised *Variety*, 'Production and directorial skill of Alfred Hitchcock combine with a suspenseful story and excellent performances to make

Notorious force entertainment,' to which it added, 'The Ben Hecht scenario carries punchy dialogue, but it's much more the action and manner in which Hitchcock projects it on screen that counts heaviest... The terrific suspense maintained to the very last is also an important asset.' Commented James Agee in *Nation*: 'Hitchcock has always been as good at domestic psychology as at thrillers, and many times here he makes a moment in a party, or a lovers' quarrel, or a mere interior shrewdly exciting in ways that few people in films seem to know how.'

A radio version of the film was broadcast in 1948, while a TV movie remake followed in 1992 starring John Shea and Jenny Robertson.

Hitchcock cameo It's during the party scene that Hitchcock can be spotted, quaffing down a glass of champagne before quickly exiting the frame.

Notorious
(US, 1992, 95m, colour, TVM)

CREDITS
Director: Colin Bucksey
Screenplay: Douglas Lloyd McIntosh

CAST
John Shea (Devlin), Jenny Robertson (Alicia Velorus), Jean-Pierre Cassel (Alex Sebastian), Marisa Berenson (Katarina Sebastian), Ronald Guttman (Joseph), Paul Guilfoyle (Norman Prescott)

In this unremarkable and totally pointless remake of Hitchcock's 1946 classic neo-Nazis are replaced by Soviet spies. Otherwise, the story remains very much the same, with Jenny Robertson's Alicia Velorus sent off to an uncertain fate by John Shea's Devlin to romance Jean-Pierre Cassel's Alex Sebastian for his secrets. The results are rather less compelling this time round.

NOVAK, JANE (1896–1990) American actress. This busy silent star began her film career in 1913 and became a popular leading lady in countless shorts and features, among them *The Sign of Angels* (1913), *The Innocent Sinner* (1917) and *The Rosary* (1922). In 1923 she was contracted to appear in two films for Gainsborough, on which the young Hitchcock worked as an assistant director and art director. Many years later Hitchcock used Novak for a small role in *Foreign Correspondent* (1940), by which time she'd become a busy cameo actress, having lost the fortune she'd amassed from her silent career in the Wall Street crash of 1929. Her other sound films include *Hollywood Boulevard* (1936), *The File on Thelma Jordan* (1950) and *The Boss* (1956). Her sister, Eve Novak (1899–1988), was equally busy during the silent period, appearing in the likes of *The Speed Maniac* (1919), *The Man from Hell's River* (1922) and, later, *Sunset Boulevard* (1950) and *The Man Who Shot Liberty Valance* (1962). **Hitchography:** *The Blackguard* (1925), *The Prude's Fall* (1925), *Foreign Correspondent* (1940)

NOVAK, KIM (1933– , real name Marilyn Novak) American actress. One of the most glamorous Hollywood stars of the 1950s, Novak first appeared on screen in 1953 in *The Veils of Bagdad* following experience as a salesgirl and a refrigerator demonstrator (for which she was titled Miss Deepfreeze). Signed to Columbia in 1954, she was subsequently groomed for stardom, and just two years later was voted America's No. 1 female box office attraction thanks to leading roles in *Picnic* (1955), *The Eddy Duchin Story* (1956) and *The Man with the Golden Arm* (1956).

In 1958 she was loaned to Paramount to appear in Hitchcock's *Vertigo*, in which she played the duplicitous Judy Barton, whose impersonation of the mysterious Madeleine Elster sees James Stewart's Scottie Ferguson caught up in a bizarre murder plot. Rumour has it that Hitchcock and Novak didn't exactly see eye to eye ('At least I got the chance to throw her into the water,' [12] quipped the director), but apart from some concerns by Novak about her costumes for the film, their relationship seems to have been cordial enough. It certainly produced a career high performance from Novak. Commented the actress: 'When I read the script I thought it was absolutely incredible. I thought my playing the role was meant to

be, that that was why I had come to Hollywood... Time goes fast when you're really involved on a movie, and I never had time to think about *Vertigo* too much until it came out. I was really excited about it. I recognized right away that Hitchcock was a brilliant director because he never had you make a false move. When he wanted you to do something on camera I never needed to question it because I knew it was right.' [13]

Following *Vertigo*, Novak re-teamed with her co-star James Stewart for the fantasy comedy *Bell, Book and Candle* (1958), after which her career went on to include *Pal Joey* (1958), *Strangers When We Meet* (1960), *Kiss Me, Stupid* (1964), *The Legend of Lylah Clare* (1968), *Tales That Witness Madness* (1973), *Just a Gigolo* (1979), *The Mirror Crack'd* (1980), *The Children* (1990) and *Liebestraum* (1991), while her television work includes *Alfred Hitchcock Presents: The Movie* (1985), in which she appeared in the *Man from the South* segment with John Huston and Tippi Hedren. Linked romantically to Frank Sinatra, Sammy Davis Jr (whom she almost married) and Ally Khan, she became front-page news during the release of *Vertigo* when it was revealed that she had received a car from the son of the Dominican dictator Rafael Trujillo. Her husbands include British actor Richard Johnson (1927–), to whom she was married between 1964 and 1965. **Hitchography:** *Vertigo* (1958)

NOVELLO, IVOR (1893–1951, real name Ivor Davies) Welsh-born actor. This matinee idol was regarded as the British equivalent of Rudolph Valentino in the 1920s and 1930s. He made his film debut in 1919 in *The Call of the Blood*, which he followed with *The Bohemian Girl* (1922), *The Man Without Desire* (1923) and *Bonnie Prince Charlie* (1923) among others. In 1924 he had a major stage success with *The Rat* (which he also co-authored with Constance Collier). This was filmed in 1925 to even greater acclaim. He was then paid £100 per day to appear in Hitchcock's breakthrough film *The Lodger* (1926), in which he was suspected of being a serial killer known as The Avenger. However, due to concerns about the feelings of his army of female fans, the script was altered and he was proved innocent in the final reel. Yet by the time he appeared in the 1932 remake, which he also co-wrote, this decision was reversed and he *was* revealed to be the killer after all, as per the novel.

Novello also starred in *Downhill* (1927) for Hitchcock, which was based on the stage play he'd co-written with Constance Collier, with whom he'd also co-authored *The Rat*, while *Elstree Calling* (1930) contained several songs with lyrics by Novello. His other films include *The Return of the Rat* (1928), *Sleeping Car* (1933) and *Autumn Crocus* (1934). His greatest successes were on the stage, however, as both an actor and the composer/lyricist of such musicals as *Glamorous Nights*, *King's Rhapsody* and *Perchance to Dream*. He was also the composer of the World War I hit *Keep the Home Fires Burning*. Commented Novello of his film work: 'I love seeing films, but I hate doing them. I hate the hours one has to keep. I have never been able to get up early in the morning without a feeling of impending death.' [14] **Hitchography:** *The Lodger* (1926), *Downhill* (1927), *Elstree Calling* (1930)

Number 13

(GB 1922, 10m (approx), bw, silent)

CREDITS

Production company:	Famous Players-Lasky/Wardour & F
Producer:	Alfred Hitchcock
Director:	Alfred Hitchcock
Screenplay:	Anita Ross
Cinematographer:	Joe Rosenthal

CAST

Clare Greet, Ernest Thesiger

While working at Islington Studios as a graphic artist for Famous Players-Lasky, Hitchcock found himself offered his first job as a director. Unfortunately the film, a two-reeler, was never completed, and the footage shot has long been lost, although a still of its two stars in action has survived. According to Hitchcock, 'It wasn't very good, really. Aside from which, it was just at this point that the Americans closed their studio.' [15] Nevertheless, the film (also known as *Mrs Peabody*), seemingly a domestic drama, has some interesting credits. Screenwriter Anita Ross, who worked in the Lasky publicity office, had apparently worked for Chaplin in Hollywood ('In those days, anyone who had worked with Chaplin was top drawer,' [16] commented Hitchcock). Meanwhile, the film's cinematographer, Joe Rosenthal, had been a noted war cameraman. The cast was also top notch. Ernest Thesiger would go on to star in such horror classics as *The Old Dark House* (1932) and *The Bride of Frankenstein* (1935), while character actress Clare Greet would be used by Hitchcock in a further four films, concluding with *Jamaica Inn* (1939).

Number Seventeen

(GB, 1932, 63m, bw) ★

CREDITS

Production company:	British International Pictures
Producers:	John Maxwell, Leon M Lion
Director:	Alfred Hitchcock
Screenplay:	Alfred Hitchcock, Rodney Ackland, Alma Reville, based on the play *Joyous Melodrama* by J Jefferson Farjeon
Cinematographer:	Jack Cox
Model photography:	Bryan Langley
Music:	A Hallis
Editor:	A C Hammond
Art director:	Wilfred Arnold
Sound:	A D Valentine

CAST

Leon M Lion (Ben), John Stuart (Gilbert Allardyce/Detective Barton), Donald Calthrop (Brant), Barry Jones (Henry Doyle), Anne Grey (Nora), Anne Casson (Rose Ackroyd), Henry Caine (Mr Ackroyd), Garry Marsh (Sheldrake), Herbert Langley (Train guard)

With a running time of just 63 minutes, *Number Seventeen* has the feel of a 'quota quickie' to it. The title refers to the derelict house in which much of the action takes place. Here, various parties congregate to discover the whereabouts of stolen diamonds, among them a tramp named Ben (Leon M Lion, who also produced the film), a neighbour, Rose Ackroyd (Ann Casson), who is looking for her missing father, an undercover detective (John Stuart), and various criminals (Garry Marsh, Donald Calthrop, Barry Jones). The comings and goings of the various characters are not only complex, but often quite confusing, with several people not quite what they seem. Indeed, Hitchcock himself described the plot as 'a disaster.' [17]

Hitchcock worked on the film under duress, having instead wanted to film an adaptation of John Van Druten's stage play *London Wall*, on which he'd already begun work on the script with playwright Rodney Ackland. However, this was vetoed by studio head John Maxwell, who ordered him to make *Number Seventeen*, which Hitchcock and Ackland adapted from J Jefferson Farjeon's 1925 play *Joyous Melodrama*, which had already been filmed as a German silent by Geza von Bolvary in 1928.

To make up for his lack of enthusiasm for the project, Hitchcock decided to have some fun with the plot, piling improbability upon improbability, finally resolving everything in an exciting chase between a hijacked bus and a train, which climaxes with the train plunging into a cross channel ferry. This chase was filmed mostly using models with live action inserts, and though the models are obviously models, the sequence is quite excitingly staged. Certainly more so than the film's previous 55 minutes, the convoluted twists and turns in which quickly become tedious. That said, Hitchcock does make good use of the claustrophobic setting, occasionally enlivening things with an entertaining bit of incident, such as having the hero and heroine tied to a rickety banister, which collapses and leaves them dangling precariously at the top of a stairwell.

Reaction to the film was mixed, with American trade bible *Variety* criticizing the film's 'usual slow tempo British direction.' 'Wonder why they can't speed up a picture?' pondered the reviewer, coming to the conclusion that, 'Maybe it's the tea!'

Following his dispute with studio head John Maxwell, *Number Seventeen* proved to be the last picture Hitchcock directed for British International Pictures. He produced one more film, *Lord Camber's Ladies* (1932), which was directed by Benn W Levy, after which he decamped to Gaumont, where he made some of his very best films.

O

O'DEA, DENIS (1905–1978) Irish-born actor. Although he spent much of his career on stage, O'Dea made several films in both Britain and America, among them *The Informer* (1935), *Odd Man Out* (1947), *Fallen Idol* (1948), Hitchcock's *Under Capricorn* (1949), in which he played Corrigan, *Niagara* (1952) and *Esther and the King* (1962). **Hitchography:** *Under Capricorn* (1949)

O'DONOVAN, FRED (1889–1952) Irish actor. Like many Irish actors of his generation, O'Donovan was associated with the Abbey Theatre, from whence he launched a successful stage and film career. His many films include *The Food of Love* (1916), *The House of the Spaniard* (1936) and *The Vicar of Bray* (1937). He can also be spotted briefly in a supporting role in Hitchcock's *Young and Innocent* (1937). His work as a director includes *The Eleventh Hour* (1918) and *Willy Reilly and His Colleen* (1918). **Hitchography:** *Young and Innocent* (1937)

O'HARA, MAUREEN (1920– , real name Maureen Fitzsimmons) Irish-born actress. Though the opening credits for Hitchcock's *Jamaica Inn* (1939) claim to be 'introducing' Maureen O'Hara, the flame-haired actress had already made two films in Britain: *My Irish Molly* (1938) and *Kicking the Moon Around* (1938). A former player at Dublin's Abbey Theatre, where she had made her debut in *Juno and the Paycock*, O'Hara went to Hollywood following *Jamaica Inn* and starred in such successes as *The Hunchback of Notre Dame* (1939), which again headlined her *Jamaica Inn* co-star Charles Laughton, *How Green Was My Valley* (1940), *Miracle on 34th Street* (1947) and, most famously, *The Quiet Man* (1952). Her many other films include *Our Man in Havana* (1959), *Big Jake* (1971) and *The Red Pony* (1972, TV), following which she took a 19-year break, returning with *Only the Lonely* (1991). Said Charles Laughton's wife, Elsa Lanchester, of O'Hara, 'She looks as though butter wouldn't melt in her mouth – or anywhere else.' [1] **Hitchography:** *Jamaica Inn* (1939)

OAKLAND, SIMON (1922–1983) American supporting actor. In films from 1947 with *T-Men*, Oakland began his career as a violinist before turning his hand to the stage and, eventually, films. His many appearances include *The Brothers Karamazov* (1958), *West Side Story* (1961), *The Sand Pebbles* (1966), *The Night Strangler* (1972, TV) and *Evening in Byzantium* (1978, TV). He also played the psychiatrist Dr Richmond in Hitchcock's *Psycho* (1960), explaining the behaviour of Norman Bates at the end of the movie ('He was never all Norman, but he was *often* only Mother'). **Hitchography:** *Psycho* (1960)

OBER, PHILIP (1902–1982) American supporting actor. Ober appeared in several films in the 1950s and 1960s, including *From Here to Eternity* (1953), *Tammy* (1956) and *The Ghost and Mr Chicken* (1966), although

Hitchcock fans will best remember him for playing the unfortunate UNIPO delegate Lester Townsend who comes to a sticky end at the United Nations in *North by Northwest* (1959). He also appeared in an episode of *The Alfred Hitchcock Hour*, in which he was again directed by Hitchcock. **Hitchography:** *North by Northwest* (1959), *I Saw the Whole Thing* (1962, TV)

OLIVER, CHARLES British actor. Oliver had the brief but important role of the Badrikan Officer at the climax of Hitchcock's *The Lady Vanishes* (1938), in which he is hit over the head with a chair by leading man Michael Redgrave. He can also be spotted in supporting roles in *The Avenging Hand* (1936), *Midnight at Madame Tussaud's* (1936), *Sexton Blake and the Hooded Terror* (1938) and *Crook's Tour* (1941), the latter re-uniting him with his co-stars from *The Lady Vanishes*, Basil Radford and Naunton Wayne. **Hitchography:** *The Lady Vanishes* (1938)

OLIVIER, SIR LAURENCE (LORD OLIVIER) (1907–1989) British-born actor. The leading actor of his generation, British stage and film legend Olivier began performing at school at the age of 9, making his professional debut in 1926 at the Birmingham Repertory. He made his Broadway debut just three years later, and his film debut, back in Britain, in 1930 in *Too Many Crooks*. His film career was slow to take off, though, despite solid performances in films such as *As You Like It* (1936) and *The Divorce of Lady X* (1938), but on stage he reached the heights with his acclaimed interpretations of Shakespeare, among them *Hamlet*. His film career finally took hold in 1939 when he was cast as Heathcliffe in *Wuthering Heights*, which earned him a best actor Oscar nomination. His stardom was confirmed the following year when he played the brooding Maxim de Winter in Hitchcock's *Rebecca*, about which *Variety* commented, 'Laurence Olivier provides an impressionable portrayal as the master of Manderlay, unable to throw off the memory of his tragic first marriage while trying to secure happiness in his second venture.' However, the film's producer, David O Selznick, wasn't entirely happy with Olivier's performance during production, commenting to Hitchcock, 'Larry's silent action and reactions become slower as his dialogue becomes faster... For God's sake, speed him up... While you're at it, make sure that we know what the hell he's talking about, because he still has a tendency to speed up his words and to read them in such a way that an American audience can't understand them.' [2]

Olivier's many other films include *Pride and Prejudice* (1941), *Henry V* (1944), which he also adapted and directed, earning himself a special Academy Award for his efforts, *Hamlet* (1948), which he also produced and directed, earning Oscars for best picture and best actor, *Richard III* (1956), which he adapted, produced and directed, *Khartoum* (1966), *Sleuth* (1972), *The Boys from Brazil* (1978), *Dracula* (1979) and *War Requiem* (1988), while on television his work included *Brideshead Revisted* (1981) and *A Voyage Round My Father* (1982). In 1979, he was awarded an honorary Oscar for 'the unique achievements of his entire career.' Married three times, his wives were Jill Esmond (1908–1990), to whom he was married between 1930 and 1940; Vivien Leigh (1913–1967, real name Vivian Hartley), to whom he was married between 1940 and 1960; and Joan Plowright, to whom he was married from 1961 to his death. Esmond appeared in Hitchcock's *The Skin Game* (1932), whilst Leigh unsuccessfully screen tested for the role of the second Mrs de Winter in *Rebecca* while making *Gone with the Wind* for Selznick. However, Olivier did finally get to play opposite Leigh in *Rebecca* in a 1950 radio version of the story. **Hitchography:** *Rebecca* (1940), *Rebecca* (1950, radio)

OLSEN, CHRISTOPHER American actor. In Hitchcock's remake of *The Man Who Knew Too Much* (1956), young Christopher Olsen plays Hank McKenna, the kidnapped son of Ben and Jo McKenna (James Stewart and Doris Day). Unfortunately, Olsen is one of the silver screen's more wholesomely precocious child stars, and his duet with Doris Day of *Que Sera, Sera* is particularly cringe making. However, *Variety* was won over, commenting, 'Christopher Olsen plays the son naturally and appealingly.' **Hitchography:** *The Man Who Knew Too Much* (1956)

OLSEN, MORONI (1889–1954) American supporting actor. Following many years of stage experience, including running his own playhouse, this robust actor was lured to Hollywood at the age of 46 to play Porthos in *The Three Musketeers* (1935), a role he repeated in the 1939 musical remake. His many other films include *Mummy's Boys* (1936), *Rose of Washington Square* (1939), *The Song of Bernadette* (1943) and Hitchcock's *Notorious* (1946) in which he can be seen as Walter Beardsley. His other films include *The Fountainhead* (1949), *Father of the Bride* (1950), *Father's Little Dividend* (1951) and *Sign of the Pagan* (1954). He also provided the voice of the Magic Mirror in *Snow White and the Seven Dwarfs* (1937). **Hitchography:** *Notorious* (1946)

Once You Kiss a Stranger
(US, 1969, 105m, Perfectcolor)

CREDITS
Production company:	Warner Bros./Seven Arts
Producer:	Robert Goldstein
Director:	Robert Sparr
Screenplay:	Frank Tarloff, Norman Katkov, from the novel by Patricia Highsmith

CAST
Carol Lynley (Diana), Paul Burk (Jerry), Martha Hyer (Lee), Philip Carey (Mike), Stephen McNally (Lieutenant), Peter Lind Hayes (Peter)

The first of three remakes of Hitchcock's *Strangers on a Train* (1951), this version sees the psychotic Robert Walker

role played by Carol Lynley, who wants to swap murders with golf pro Paul Burke, the idea being that she murder his rival in return for his seeing off her psychiatrist. A box office flop, it quickly disappeared from view.

Once You Meet a Stranger
(US, 1996, 95m, colour)

CREDITS
Director:	Tommy Lee Wallace
Screenplay:	Tommy Lee Wallace, based on the novel by Patricia Highsmith

CAST
Theresa Russell (Margo Anthony), Jacqueline Bisset (Sheila Gaines), Celeste Holm (Clara), Robert Desiderio (Andy Stahl), Nick Mancuso (Aaron)

In this distaff but wholly unnecessary re-working of Hitchcock's *Strangers on a Train* (1951), Theresa Russell takes on the psycho role previously played by Robert Walker; wishing to be rid of her domineering mother, she plans to swap murders with Jacqueline Bissett's fading movie star, who in turn wishes to be rid of her husband. Unfortunately, the results are more tedious than intriguing.

ONDRA, ANNY (1903–1987, real name Aenny Ondrakova) Polish-born actress. Born in Poland but raised in Czechoslovakia, silent star Ondra began her film career in her home country in 1919 with *Zmizele Pismo*. Soon hugely popular, she went on to appear in many more Czech productions, among them *Setrle Pismo* (1920) and *Melenky Stareho Kriminalika* (1921). She married her most frequent director Karel Lamac (1897–1952) in the early 1920s and formed her own production company with him. In 1925 she began to make films in Germany, beginning with *Ich Liebe Dich* and, in 1927, Britain, with *A Chorus Girl's Romance*. Further films in Britain followed, including two productions for Hitchcock: *The Manxman* and *Blackmail* (both 1929). However, while she was acceptable as the daughter of an Isle of Man landowner torn between two lovers in the former, which was silent, her Czech accent made her unacceptable as the daughter of a London shopkeeper in the latter, which was Hitchcock's first sound film. Consequently she was dubbed, live on set, by Joan Barry. Following *Blackmail*, Ondra returned to Germany, where she married her second husband, boxer Max Schmeling, and continued to make films until 1957, among them *Die Kaviarprinzessin* (1929), *Narrem im Schnee* (1937) and *Die Zurcher Verlobung* (1957). Recalled future director Michael Powell, who was the stills cameraman on both *The Manxman* and *Blackmail*: '[Anny Ondra was a] tall, blonde, lovely girl with a sense of humour... She was a neat chick.' [3]

Interestingly, footage survives of Ondra making a sound test with Hitchcock on the *Blackmail* set. Hitchcock calls Ondra over to the camera and the delightful exchange goes as follows:

> **Hitchcock:** Now, Miss Ondra, we are going to do a sound test. Isn't that what you wanted? Now come right over here.
>
> **Ondra:** I don't know what to say I'm so nervous.
>
> **Hitchcock:** Have you been a good girl?
>
> **Ondra** (embarrassed): Oh, no!
>
> **Hitchcock:** No? Have you slept with men?
>
> **Ondra:** *No!*
>
> **Hitchcock:** Now come right over here, Miss Ondra, and stand still in your place, or it won't come out right, as the girl said to the soldier.
>
> **Ondra:** Oh, Hitch, you make me embarrassed!
>
> **Hitchcock** (laughing into camera): Cut! [4]

Hitchography: *The Manxman* (1929), *Blackmail* (1929)

Czech star Anny Ondra looks suitably disturbed having just murdered her date in Hitchcock's Blackmail *(1929), the director's first sound film.*

OPATOSHU, DAVID (1918–1996, real name David Opatovsky) American actor. Following experience on stage (in Yiddish theatre), Opatoshu went on to make several films as a supporting actor, among them *The Naked City* (1948), *Exodus* (1960), Hitchcock's *Torn Curtain* (1966), in which he played Jakobi, *The Defector* (1967) and *Masada* (1981, TV). He also appeared in three episodes of *Alfred Hitchcock Presents* and an episode of *The Alfred Hitchcock Hour*. **Hitchography:** *On the Nose* (1958, TV), *Strange Miracle* (1962, TV), *The Test* (1962, TV), *The Magic Shop* (1964, TV), *Torn Curtain* (1966)

ORMONDE, CZENZI American writer. Ormonde, an assistant to frequent Hitchcock collaborator Ben Hecht, contributed to the screenplay to Hitchcock's *Strangers on a Train* (1951). She also co-wrote the script for *Step Down to Terror* (1959), which was a remake of Hitchcock's *Shadow of a Doubt* (1943). **Hitchography:** *Strangers on a Train* (1951)

ORRY-KELLY (1897–1964, real name John Orry Kelly) Australian-born costume designer. Orry-Kelly moved to America in his late teens, gaining experience as an actor and a title designer for Fox in New York before going on to establish himself as a Broadway scenic and costume designer, noted for his elaborate revues, which inevitably led to a career in Hollywood as a costume designer. An Oscar winner for his work on *An American in Paris* (1951), *Les Girls* (1957) and *Some Like it Hot* (1959), his other films include *Maybe It's Love* (1930), *42nd Street* (1933), *Gold Diggers of 1933* (1933), *Dames* (1934), *Jezebel* (1938), *The Letter* (1939), *The Sea Hawk* (1940), *Casablanca* (1942), *Pat and Mike* (1952) and *Irma La Douce* (1963). He also designed the costumes for Hitchcock's *I Confess* (1953), one of his more sober assignments. **Hitchography:** *I Confess* (1953)

ORTON, J O C (MAJOR JOHN) (1889–1943) British director and screenwriter. Orton was noted for his comedy scripts, among them several for Jack Hulbert and Will Hay, including *Jack Ahoy* (1935), *Bulldog Jack* (1935), *Old Bones of the River* (1938) and *Where's That Fire?* (1939). He began his screen career in 1923 following 15 years of experience in the army and RAF, where he reached the post of Major. Following early credits in Sweden (where he worked as a scenarist and editor for Swedish Biograph), Orton began directing in Britain for British Instructional, which led to offers from British International Pictures and, in 1932, Gainsborough, where he remained for much of his career. In 1944, Orton co-scripted two French-language shorts for Hitchcock. Made for the Ministry of Information, they were intended for showing exclusively in France as morale boosters in those areas where the occupational forces were receding and the work of the Resistance was at last having some effect. However, the second of these films was not shown until 1993. **Hitchography:** *Bon Voyage* (1944), *Aventure Malgache* (1944)

OTTERSON, JACK American art director. Long at Universal, Otterson had a hand in all manner of productions, but is best remembered for his atmospheric sets for the studio's horror films, among them *Son of Frankenstein* (1939), *Tower of London* (1939), *The Mummy's Hand* (1940) and *The Wolf Man* (1941). He also designed the sets for several Sherlock Holmes films, among them *Sherlock Holmes and the Secret Weapon* (1942) and *Sherlock Holmes in Washington* (1943), as well as Hitchcock's *Saboteur* (1942), which includes recreations of the interior of the Statue of Liberty as well as the statue's torch arm, on which the vertiginous climax is set. Otterson's other films include *First Love* (1939), *Pirates of Monteray* (1947) and *Michigan Kid* (1949). **Hitchography:** *Saboteur* (1942)

P

PALMER, LILLI (1911–1986, real name Lilli Peiser) Austrian-born actress. Palmer made her screen debut in Britain in 1935 in *Crime Unlimited*. Following a number of further minor roles, including an appearance in Hitchcock's *Secret Agent* (1936) in which she played a chambermaid named Lilli, she went on to become a respected leading actress, working in both Hollywood and Europe. Her many films include *Good Morning, Boys* (1936), *The Rake's Progress* (1945), *Operation Crossbow* (1965), *The Boys from Brazil* (1978) and *The Holcroft Covenant* (1985). Her first husband was Rex Harrison (1908–1990), to whom she was married between 1943 and 1957. **Hitchography:** *Secret Agent* (1936)

The Paradine Case
(US, 1947, 131m (some sources state 125m and 115m), bw) ★★

CREDITS

Production company:	Selznick International
Producer:	David O Selznick
Director:	Alfred Hitchcock
Screenplay:	David O Selznick, Alma Reville, Alfred Hitchcock, James Bridie, Ben Hecht (un-credited), based on the novel by Robert Hichens
Cinematographer:	Lee Garmes
Music:	Franz Waxman
Editor:	John Faure, Hal C Kern
Art directors:	J McMillan Johnson, Thomas N Morahan
Costumes:	Travis Banton
Special effects:	Clarence Slifer
Sound:	James G Stewart, Richard Van Hessen

CAST

Gregory Peck (Anthony Keane), Valli (Mrs Maddalena Anna Paradine), Charles Laughton (Judge Lord Horfield), Ethel Barrymore (Lady Sophie Horfield), Ann Todd (Gay Keane), Charles Coburn (Sir Simon Flaquer), Joan Tetzel (Judy Flaquer), Louis Jourdan (Andre La Tour), Leo G Carroll (Counsel for the prosecution), Isobel Elsom (Inn landlady), John Williams (Mr Collins, Keane's assistant barrister), John Goldsworthy, Patrick Aherene, Colin Hunter, Lester Matthews

Video availability: Pearson
CD availability: *The Paradine Case* (Koch International Classics), which contains *Rhapsody for Piano and Orchestra from the film The Paradine Case*

Given its unwarranted reputation as one of the Master's lesser works, this courtroom drama with a dash of intrigue maintains its not insubstantial grip from first to last. The cast, which includes such names as Gregory Peck, Ann Todd, Charles Laughton, Charles Coburn, Ethel Barrymore, Alida Valli, Louis Jourdan and Leo G Carroll, is certainly one of Hitchcock's starriest, while the glossy black-and-white production, capped with a memorable Franz Waxman score, is as slick as any of the director's 1940s' work.

The film was very much a pet project of producer David O Selznick, whose seven-year contract with Hitchcock was about to come to an end, and consequently it proved to be their last together. In fact Hitchcock had longed to be free from Selznick's grip for some time, given the producer's frequently maddening penchant for controlling every aspect of a production, down to the tiniest detail. That Selznick also penned the screenplay for *The Paradine Case* must therefore have made Hitchcock feel even more suffocated than usual during production; nevertheless, this didn't prevent him from making a professional job of things.

Selznick bought the Robert Hichens novel on which the film is based from MGM, which had owned the rights since its publication in 1933. Indeed, when working at that studio in the mid-1930s Selznick had tried and failed to get Greta Garbo interested in the project. Hoping that Garbo, who'd retired six years earlier, could be persuaded to change her mind, Selznick approached the reclusive star again in 1946. Yet for a second time he faced disappointment. 'Unfortunately, Miss Garbo has always had an aversion to the story, and even today, she won't play in it,' [1] commented the producer, finally admitting defeat.

The role Selznick wanted Garbo to play was that of Maddalena Paradine, an elegant woman of social standing who finds herself accused of murdering her blind husband, one Colonel Richard Patrick Irving Paradine. When arrested, she calls upon the services of the family solicitor Sir Simon Flaquer, who instead refers her to the highly respected Anthony Keane, who agrees to take on the case. However Keane, increasingly convinced of Mrs Paradine's innocence, begins to fall in love with his client, much to the chagrin of his devoted wife of 11 years, Gay. Keane's obsession with Mrs Paradine also begins to cloud his judgement, and during the subsequent trial, he attempts to blame the murder on Andre La Tour, Colonel Paradine's groom-turned-valet. Given that La Tour has been left a substantial sum of money in the Colonel's will, and that he once used poison to put down one of his master's ailing dogs, the case looks cut and dried. But La Tour succumbs to the pressure placed upon him in court and commits suicide in his cell, which prompts Mrs Paradine to admit that yes, she did murder her husband after all, and all for the love of La Tour, with whom she'd been having a torrid affair, the revelation of which forces Keane to drop the case and, his career in shreds, return to his wife.

Given Garbo's reluctance to return to the screen, Selznick instead decided to cast his new find, Italian actress Alida Valli, in the role of Mrs Paradine. In films in her home country from 1935, Valli (as she was billed) was perfect casting, given her enigmatic good looks, which make it entirely believable that Keane should fall so heavily for her. However, Hitchcock was far less satisfied with several of Selznick's other casting choices for the picture. For the role of Anthony Keane, Hitchcock had hoped to bag either Laurence Olivier or Ronald Colman; instead Selznick saddled him with Gregory Peck, a more than able performer who was nevertheless just a shade too young for the role, which no doubt accounts for the rather theatrical-looking streaks of gray in his hair, the shades of which tend to vary somewhat alarmingly throughout the film (said Hitchcock: 'I don't think that Gregory Peck can properly represent an English lawyer' [2]).

If Hitchcock wasn't entirely convinced by the casting of Peck, he was even less enamoured of the handsome French heart-throb Louis Jourdan, another Selznick import whom the producer cast as the groom/valet Andre La Tour. Instead, Hitchcock had wanted the rather rougher looking Robert Newton, his reasoning being that the groom 'should have been a manure-smelling stable hand, a man who really reeked of manure,' [3] thus forcing Keane to accept that not only is his client a murderess, but also a nymphomaniac. 'This miscasting was very detrimental to the story,' [4] the director later admitted. He also had reservations about Ann Todd's performance as Keane's wife, but he blamed the script in this case, commenting, 'She was too coldly written, I'm afraid.' [5] Her cut glass accent may also have had something to do with it, giving the impression that sex to her was something one kept the coal in.

Despite these disappointments, Hitchcock was much happier with his supporting players, among them Charles Coburn as the jovial Sir Simon Flaquer, Charles Laughton as the trial judge Lord Horfield, and the regal Ethel Barrymore as the judge's dipsomaniac wife Lady Sophie Horfield.

After many delays, production on *The Paradine Case* finally began on December 23 1946. The hold-ups had generally been over the script, the first draft of which Hitchcock and his wife Alma Reville had worked on. This adaptation of the novel was subsequently re-worked by Scottish playwright James Bridie and Ben Hecht (the latter's contribution going un-credited), following which Selznick himself took over in a bid to hurry the process along. However, his commitments to other productions, notably his big budget western *Duel in the Sun* (1946), which was then being readied for release, continually kept him from concentrating on *The Paradine Case*. Consequently, the film went into production with half-completed dialogue, new versions of which Selznick sent down to the set when he found time to complete them. Said Selznick of the situation: 'I am on the verge of collapse and not thinking clearly, and am having under these conditions to try and patch up and re-write... I will simply have to hope that somehow we will be able to get together the cast for what will inevitably be costly re-takes.' [6]

Despite the problems with the script, which resulted in a slow shoot (which, amazingly, Selznick tried to blame on his director), Hitchcock managed to infuse the production with his usual professionalism. The early scenes of Mrs Paradine in her luxurious home before being arrested are particularly well handled, and contrast superbly with her arrival at the police cells, where she is stripped of her jewellery and her hairpins before the cell door is slammed shut behind her. In fact this sequence of events seems to have fascinated the director, who commented: 'What interested me in this picture was to take a person like Mrs Paradine, to put her in the hands of the police, to have to submit to all their formalities, and to say to her maid, as she was leaving the house between the two inspectors, "I don't think I shall be back for dinner." And then showing her spending the night in a cell, from which, in fact, she will never emerge... There's nothing to it when a habitual lawbreaker, like a drunk, is involved, but I am intrigued by the contrast in shading when it happens to a person of a certain social standing.' [7] However, despite his client being locked up in the slammer, Keane seems unusually upbeat about her prospects, telling her, 'A brief skirmish and you'll be lunching at The Savoy again!'

In fact the script is full of such frightfully glib lines. Says Gay when her husband informs her that he is going to take on Mrs Paradine's case, 'Nice people don't go about murdering other nice people,' while Keane himself later claims that his client couldn't possibly be a murderess because 'she's too fine a woman.' This at least produces a smart retort from Sir Simon Flaquer: 'Indeed? I was of the impression that she was a woman of low breeding and *very* easy virtue' (in fact Mrs Paradine reveals as much to Keane in her cell).

One of the most entertaining exchanges of dialogue comes during a dinner party, in which Keane, Gay, Sir Simon and his daughter Judy (Joan Tetzel) are being entertained by Lord Horfield and his wife. As everyone repairs to the drawing room for coffee, Lord Horfield attempts to make an advance on Gay, whom he joins on a settle, unnoticed by the others. 'You look very appetizing tonight, m' dear,' he oozes, gazing at her bare shoulders and placing his hand on top of hers, to which she replies, 'A charming compliment from such a gourmet as you,' before wrenching her hand free with a grimace and making a hasty exit to join the others.

Meanwhile, when Keane travels to Yorkshire to visit the Paradine estate and meet for himself Andre La Tour, an unashamedly xenophobic local says of the Frenchman, 'He's foreign. They never quite seem the same, do they, sir?' Then later, when Mrs Paradine learns of La Tour's death, she informs the still love-struck Keane, 'I loved La Tour and *you* murdered him. My life is finished. It is you yourself who has finished it. My only comfort is the hatred and contempt I feel for you!' At least Keane has his devoted wife to return to, who accepts him back with the mildly chiding comment, 'Incidentally, darling, you *do* need a shave!'

The sometimes risible dialogue aside, the film is nevertheless handsome to look at thanks to Lee Garmes's luminescent photography and the plush sets designed by J. McMillan Johnson and Thomas M Morahan, notable among them the Paradines' elegantly appointed London home (in which we first discover Mrs Paradine sipping sherry and playing the grand piano in the drawing room while awaiting dinner to be announced), and Mrs Paradine's bedroom at the family seat in Yorkshire, which bears an uncanny resemblance to Rebecca's bedroom in Manderley (note, too, the oppressively low ceiling in the Keanes' own bedroom). Johnson and Morahan also built an exact replica of the Old

Bailey's number one court for the film at a cost of some $400,000.

Despite the obstacles placed before him, Hitchcock is firmly in control of his material throughout the film, and his touches proliferate. For example, when Keane meets La Tour for the first time, Hitchcock keeps the groom's face in shadow for the entire encounter, and doesn't properly reveal the valet until later, when he visits Keane at his room in the nearby inn during a violent thunderstorm.

Hitchcock's handling of the courtroom scenes is also masterly, for which he used as many as four cameras to simultaneously capture the dialogue and actions of the various characters. He also pulls off an impressive shot with La Tour's arrival in court to give evidence. Hitchcock wanted Mrs Paradine to sense that the valet was passing behind her, while keeping both people in the same frame, which he achieved by photographing La Tour walking across court, on to which he then superimposed a shot of Mrs Paradine's face, which consequently moves with the turning camera.

Principal photography on *The Paradine Case* concluded in mid-March 1947, but the film, which cost just over $4 million, didn't receive its premiere – at two adjacent theatres in Westwood, Los Angeles – until 31 December, over a year after it went into production. Sadly, it was not a commercial success, and produced mixed reviews. Wrote critic James Agee of Selznick's screenplay: 'This is the wordiest script since the death of Edmund Burke.' *Variety*, however, was much more upbeat, commenting, 'Alfred Hitchcock's penchant for suspense, unusual atmosphere and development gets full play.' The reviewer even had some kind words for Selznick's script, adding, 'It is a job that puts much emphasis on dialogue, and it's talk that punches.'

Like a vintage wine, *The Paradine Case* seems to get better with each passing year, and is certainly well worth a look for its gleaming treatment and the performances of its stars who, though for the most part miscast, certainly give their all to the proceedings.

The film also earned Ethel Barrymore an Academy Award nomination for best supporting actress, despite the fact that she has only a handful of scenes in the film. A radio adaptation of the film was broadcast in 1949.

Hitchcock cameo Note that Hitchcock can be spotted leaving the train station in Yorkshire carrying a cello case.

PARKER, CECIL (1897–1971, real name Cecil Schwabe) British-born actor. One of the screen's most accomplished character comedians, Parker specialized in fallible upper-crust types, among them Eric Todhunter, the philandering barrister in Hitchcock's *The Lady Vanishes* (1938). Parker made his film debut in *The Silver Spoon* in 1933, and gradually built up to featured roles in *Storm in a Tea Cup* (1937) and *Bank Holiday* (1937). His many other films include *Quartet* (1948), *The Chiltern Hundreds* (1949), *The Man in the White Suit* (1951), *The Pure Hell of St Trinian's* (1960), *Carry On, Jack* (1963) and *Oh! What a Lovely War* (1969). He also worked for Hitchcock again on *Under Capricorn* (1949), but the production was bedeviled with problems and lightning

failed to strike twice. Recalled actress Linden Travers, who played opposite Parker in *The Lady Vanishes* and two other films: 'He was a very serious, dedicated actor. Once I asked him, "How do you manage all this? How do you approach parts?" He said, "I'm the dullest man on our street!" He was just a serious actor.' [8] Parker also appeared in one episode of *Alfred Hitchcock Presents*. **Hitchography:** *The Lady Vanishes* (1938), *Under Capricorn* (1949), *I, Spy* (1961, TV)

PARKER, DOROTHY (1893–1967) American writer. One of the great wits of the 20th century, Parker was noted as a writer of short stories, reviews, lyrics and cutting doggerel. She also contributed to a handful of screenplays, among them *Paris in Spring* (1935), *A Star is Born* (1937) and Hitchcock's *Saboteur* (1942), to which her major contribution was the sequence with the circus freaks. A noted member of the Algonquin Round Table, she once described the streets of Hollywood as being 'paved with Goldwyn.' Her second husband was actor/writer Alan Campbell (1905–1963), to whom she was married between 1933 and 1947. **Hitchography:** *Saboteur* (1942)

PARNELL, EMORY (1894–1979) American actor. Though familiar from the television western series *Lawman* (1958–1961), Parnell had by then clocked up over 200 supporting roles in films, 22 of them in 1939 alone, often as a policeman or prison warden. A former booking agent and vaudevillian, he had actually trained to become a concert violinist. In films from 1938 with *Doctor Rhythm*, his other appearances include *At the Circus* (1939), *Union Pacific* (1939), *The Maltese Falcon* (1941), *King's Row* (1942), *Call Me Madam* (1953) and *The Andromeda Strain* (1971). He was also a regular of the *Blondie* and *Ma and Pa Kettle* second feature series. He can be spotted in Hitchcock's *Foreign Correspondent* (1940) as the Captain of the Mohican. He worked for Hitchcock again two more times, in *Mr and Mrs Smith* (1941), as Conway, and *Saboteur* (1942), as an actor seen in a cinema screen, but both roles were un-credited. **Hitchography:** *Foreign Correspondent* (1940), *Mr and Mrs Smith* (1941), *Saboteur* (1942)

The Passionate Adventure
(GB, 1924, 79m approx, bw, silent)

CREDITS

Production company:	Gainsborough
Producer:	Michael Balcon
Director:	Graham Cutts
Screenplay:	Alfred Hitchcock, Michael Morton, based on the novel by Frank Stayton
Cinematographer:	Claude L McDonnell
Art director:	Alfred Hitchcock
Assistant director:	Alfred Hitchcock
Continuity girl:	Alma Reville

CAST

Clive Brook (Adrien St Clair), Marjorie Daw (Vickey), Mary Brough (Lady Rolls), Alice Joyce (Drusilla Sinclair), Lillian Hall-Davis (Pamela), Victor McLaglen (Herb Harris), John F Hamilton (Bill), J R Tozer (Inspector Stewart Sladen)

Following the commercial disappointment of *The White Shadow* (1924), Balcon-Freedman-Saville was dissolved by Michael Balcon and reformed as Gainsborough Pictures, through which a new raft of films was planned, among them this 1924 drama about a rich man who leaves his wife and later saves a poor factory girl from being exploited by a crook. The film re-united many of those who had worked on both *Woman to Woman* (1923) and *The White Shadow*, among them director Graham Cutts, star Clive Brook, and the young Hitchcock, who again took on multiple duties. Like most of the early films on which Hitchcock worked, this black-and-white silent has long been lost. However, it remains an important stepping-stone in his career, in that he met his agent, Myron Selznick, the brother of Hollywood producer David O Selznick, during its production. Visiting the set, Selznick fell for one of the film's stars, Majorie Daw, settled in England, and set up an agency with Frank Joyce, who was the brother of one of the film's other actresses, Alice Joyce. Selznick of course later introduced Hitchcock to his brother in Hollywood, which resulted in the director being signed to a seven-year contract with David O Selznick, resulting in such films as *Rebecca* (1940), *Spellbound* (1945) and *The Paradine Case* (1947).

PATON, CHARLES (1886–1950) British character actor. Paton, a former music hall performer, is perhaps best remembered for playing shopkeeper Mr White in Hitchcock's *Blackmail* (1929). He made his film debut in 1927 with two shorts: *John Citizen* and *John Citizen's Lament*. Featured in small roles until his death, his other films include *Piccadilly* (1929), *Major Barbara* (1941), *Uncle Silas* (1947) and *Portrait of Clare* (1950). **Hitchography:** *Blackmail* (1929)

PATRICK, LEE (1906–1982) American supporting actress. Best remembered for her role as Effie Perine, secretary to Sam Spade (Humphrey Bogart) in *The Maltese Falcon* (1941), Patrick came to films in 1929 with *Strange Cargo* following stage experience (she made her Broadway debut at the age of just 13). Her subsequent films include *Danger Patrol* (1937), *In This Our Life* (1942), *There's No Business Like Show Business* (1954), *Pillow Talk* (1959) and *The Black Bird* (1975), a sequel to *The Maltese Falcon* in which she reprised her role from the original. In 1958 she also had a walk on in Hitchcock's *Vertigo*, playing a woman whom James Stewart's Scottie Ferguson briefly mistakes for the dead Madeleine Elster. **Hitchography:** *Vertigo* (1958)

PECK, GREGORY (1916– , real name Eldred Gregory Peck) American actor. Following experience at the Neighborhood Playhouse in New York, Peck went on to make his Broadway debut in 1942. Two years later he was in Hollywood, where he made his first film appearance in *Days of Glory* (1944). He consolidated his stardom with his second film, *The Keys of the Kingdom* (1945), which led to a career as one of the screen's most reliable and endurable leading men. In 1945 he worked with Hitchcock for the first time on the psychological thriller *Spellbound* in which he played an amnesiac who may or may not have murdered the psychiatrist whose identity he has assumed. The film was the first Hollywood production to take a serious stab at the subject of psychiatry. A major commercial success, it further enhanced Peck's reputation. Revealed the film's producer David O. Selznick of the actor's impact in the film: 'We could not keep the audience quiet from the time his name came on the screen until we had shushed them through three or four sequences and stopped all the dames from "oohing" and "ahing" and gurgling.' [9]

Following *Spellbound*, Peck went on to appear in *The Yearling* (1946), *Duel in the Sun* (1946), *Gentleman's Agreement* (1947) and *The Macomber Affair* (1947) before returning to the Hitchcock fold for the courtroom drama *The Paradine Case* (1947). Hitchcock had wanted either Laurence Olivier or Ronald Colman for the film, but was overruled by the film's producer David O Selznick, to whom Peck, like Hitchcock, was under contract at the time. However, though Peck's performance is more than adequate, at 31 he seems a little young to be playing a noted barrister, hence the rather theatrical-looking gray streaks in his hair to help make him look older. Despite these drawbacks, *Variety* noted, 'Gregory Peck's stature as a performer of ability stands him in good stead among the extremely tough competition,' which included such stalwarts as Charles Laughton, Ethel Barrymore and Charles Coburn.

Peck's subsequent film work includes *Roman Holiday* (1953), *Moby Dick* (1956), *The Guns of Navarone* (1961), *Cape Fear* (1962), *To Kill a Mockingbird* (1963), which earned him a best actor Oscar, *Mirage* (1965), *Arabesque* (1966), *The Omen* (1976), *The Boys from Brazil* (1978), the remake of *Cape Fear* (1991) and *Other People's Money* (1991). He has also produced a handful of films, including *The Dove* (1974). **Hitchography:** *Spellbound* (1945), *The Paradine Case* (1947)

PEPPER, BARBARA (1912–1969) American actress. Familiar from the TV series *Green Acres* (1965–69), Pepper played a variety of supporting roles in the 1930s and 1940s, her speciality being floozies. She can be spotted in Hitchcock's *Foreign Correspondent* as Dorine, while her other films include *Our Daily Bread* (1933), *Lady in the Morgue* (1938) and *Kiss Me, Stupid* (1964), in which she played her best known floozy, Big Bertha. **Hitchography:** *Foreign Correspondent* (1940)

PERCY, ESME (1887–1957) British actor. Celebrated for his performances on stage in the plays of Shaw, Percy also appeared in several screen adaptations of Shaw's work, among them *Pygmalion* (1938), in which he played Henry Higgins' rival in phonetics, Count Aristid Karpathy, and *Caesar and Cleopatra* (1945). He made his screen debut in Hitchcock's *Murder!* (1930) in which he played the half-caste, homosexual, transvestite killer Handel Fane. His other films include *Nell Gwyn* (1934), *The Frog* (1936) and *Death in the Hand* (1947). **Hitchography:** *Murder!* (1930)

PEREIRA, HAL (1905–1983) American art director. At Paramount for his entire career, Pereira won an Oscar for his work on *The Rose Tattoo* (1955), and was nominated a further 18 times, among them two pictures for Hitchcock: *To Catch a Thief* (1955) and *Vertigo* (1958). A former stage designer, he joined Paramount in 1942, gaining his first official credit for *Double Indemnity* (1944). He first worked for Hitchcock on *Rear Window* (1954) for which, with Joseph MacMillan Johnson, he designed the impressive courtyard set which features over 30 apartments. His many other credits include *When Worlds Collide* (1951), *The Ten Commandments* (1956), *Breakfast at Tiffany's* (1961) and *The Odd Couple* (1968). Between 1950 and his retirement in 1968, he was Paramount's supervising art director, overseeing the design of every single production on the lot. **Hitchography:** *Rear Window* (1954), *To Catch a Thief* (1955), *The Trouble with Harry* (1955), *The Man Who Knew Too Much* (1956), *Vertigo* (1958)

A Perfect Murder
(US, 1998, 105m, Technicolor) ʌ

CREDITS
Production company: Warner
Producers: Arnold Kopelson, Anne Kopelson
Director: Andrew Davis
Screenplay: Patrick Smith Kelly, based on the stage play *Dial M for Murder* by Frederick Knott
Cinematographer: Dariusz Wolski
Music: James Newton Howard
Editor: Dennis Virkler, Dov Hoenig
Production designer: Philip Rosenberg
Costumes: Ellen Mirojnick
Sound: Lance Brown

CAST
Michael Douglas (Stephen Taylor), Gwyneth Paltrow (Emily Bradford-Taylor), Viggo Mortensen (David Shaw), David Suchet (Detective Mohamed Karaman), Sarita Choudhury (Raquel Martinez), Constance Towers (Sandra Bradford)

One of the better Hitchcock remakes, this re-fashions Frederick Knott's hit thriller, previously filmed by the Master as *Dial M for Murder* (1954), as a glossy, Manhattan set-melodrama of murder and greed. This time, instead of Ray Milland's retired tennis pro, it is Michael Douglas's commodities broker Stephen Taylor who wishes to do away with his wealthy wife Emily (Gwyneth Paltrow), said to be worth $100 million. However, in a twist on the original, he persuades his wife's lover, an ex-con turned artist named David Shaw (Viggo Mortensen) to carry out the deed for

$1/2 million. Again, there's the expected business with latchkeys and alibis, this time investigated by David Suchet's Detective Mohamed Karaman. However, despite some well-staged sequences in the first half and game performances from the cast (save for Suchet's rather hammy turn), the film doesn't quite go the distance, its real attraction being its slick photography and its beautifully designed interiors.

PERKINS, ANTHONY (1932–1992) American actor. This tall, gangly, handsome leading man was the son of actor Osgood Perkins (1892–1937). On stage from 1947, he made his film debut in 1953 in *The Actress*. Stage and television appearances followed, along with roles in such films as *Friendly Persuasion* (1956), which earned him a best supporting actor Oscar nomination, *Fear Strikes Out* (1957), *The Matchmaker* (1958), *On the Beach* (1959) and, of course, Hitchcock's *Psycho* (1960), in which he had his most memorable role as the schizophrenic motel keeper Norman Bates, who has the habit of bumping off the guests in the guise of his long dead mother ('She goes a little mad sometimes. We all go a little mad sometimes. Don't you?'). Commented *Variety* of his performance: 'Perkins gives a remarkably effective in-a-dream kind of performance as the possessed young man.'

Murder in mind – Anthony Perkins in his most celebrated role, that of transvestite serial killer Norman Bates in Hitchcock's Psycho *(1960). Janet Leigh's Marion Crane has a right to look suspicious.*

In fact so successful was Perkins in the role, for which he was paid $40,000, he remained identified with it for the remainder of his career, despite solid performances in such films as *The Trial* (1962), *Pretty Poison* (1968), *Murder on the Orient Express* (1974) and *Crimes of Passion* (1984). Recalled Paul Jasmin, a friend of Perkins' who also dubbed a handful of Mother's lines: 'Tony thought he was in the middle of making *the* career move of his life. And he was *right.*' [10] In fact so involved did Perkins become in the creation of the role he kept coming up with new bits of business with which to invest it. Recalled the actor: 'It was my idea to have Norman nervously chewing candy in the film.' [11] Ironically, Perkins wasn't on set during the shooting of the film's celebrated shower murder. Instead, he was in New York rehearsing the play *Greenwillow*. Recalled the actor, 'I said, "Look, I've got to take some of these rehearsals," and, through special graciousness on Hitchcock's part, he said, "Go ahead, we don't need you for this." [However], you only have to see the film to see that the silhouette coming in that door has as little resemblance to me as any silhouette could!' [12]

Perkins returned to the role of Norman Bates a further three times, in *Psycho 2* (1983), *Psycho III* (1986), which he also directed, and *Psycho IV: The Beginning* (1990, TV). Of his work in *Psycho 2*, *Variety* commented, 'Perkins is very entertaining, whether stammering over the pronunciation of "cutlery" or misleading the audience in both directions as to his relative sanity.'

In 1973, Perkins married Berinthia (Berry) Berenson, the sister of actress Marisa Berenson. He is the father of actor Osgood Perkins, who played the young Norman Bates in *Psycho 2* (1983). In addition to directing *Psycho III*, Perkins also helmed *Lucky Stiff* (1986) and, with famed composer-lyricist Stephen Sondheim, wrote the brilliantly witty and complex screenplay for the murder-mystery *The Last of Sheila* (1973). His final films included *A Demon in My View* (1991), *The Naked Target* (1991) and *In the Dark Woods* (1992). **Hitchography:** *Psycho* (1960)

Perpetua

(GB, 1922, 62m approx, bw, silent)

CREDITS

Company:	Famous Players-Lasky
Directors:	Tom Geraghty, John S Robertson
Screenplay:	Josephine Levett, Helen Blizzard based on the novel *Perpetua Mary* by Dion Clayton Calthrop
Inter-titles:	Alfred Hitchcock

CAST

David Powell (Brian McQueen), Ann Forrest (Perpetua Mary), Geoffrey Kerr (Saville Mender), Bunty Fosse (Young Perpetua Mary), John Milterne (Russell Felton), Frank Stanmore (Corn Chandler), Roy Byford (Lomballe)

This 1922 black-and-white silent with inter-titles designed by Hitchcock, was co-directed by Tom Geraghty and Hollywood import John S Robertson (best known for directing the 1920 version of *Dr Jekyll and Mr Hyde* starring John Barrymore). Sadly now lost, it told the story of a father who frames his daughter, who has seemingly poisoned her husband.

PERSOFF, NEHEMIAH (1920–) Israeli character actor. In America from 1929, Persoff made his film debut in 1948 in *The Naked City* following stage experience (from 1940) and training at the Actors' Studio, prior to which he'd worked as an electrician. His many films include *On the Waterfront* (1954), *Some Like it Hot* (1959), *The Girl Who Knew Too Much* (1969), *Psychic Killer* (1975), *Yentl* (1983) and *The Last Temptation of Christ* (1988). He also appeared in Hitchcock's *The Wrong Man* (1956) as Gene Conforti, and starred in two episodes of *Alfred Hitchcock Presents*. **Hitchography:** *The Wrong Man* (1956), *Heart of Gold* (1957, TV), *The Cure* (1960, TV)

PETERSON, DOROTHY (1900–1979) American actress. Familiar as a supporting actress during the 1930s and 1940s, Peterson popped up in such diverse films as *I'm No Angel* (1933), *Confession* (1937), *Dark Victory* (1939) and Hitchcock's *Saboteur* (1942), in which she played Mrs Mason. Her other films include *The Woman in the Window* (1945) and *That Hagen Girl* (1947). **Hitchography:** *Saboteur* (1942)

PETRIE, HAY (1895–1948, real name David Hay Petrie) British character actor. One of those actors who popped up regularly on the screen in the 1930s and 1940s, Petrie made his debut in *Suspense* in 1930, following which he went on to appear in *The Private Life of Henry VIII* (1933), *The Old Curiosity Shop* (1934), in which he took a rare leading role playing Quilp, *The Ghost Goes West* (1935), *The Four Feathers* (1939) and *A Canterbury Tale* (1944). He also played the small role of Sir Humphrey Pengallan's groom in Hitchcock's *Jamaica Inn* (1939), memorably bringing one of his master's horses into the dining hall. His many other films include *Contraband* (1940), *Great Expectations* (1946) and *The Queen of Spades* (1948). **Hitchography:** *Jamaica Inn* (1939)

THE PHANTOM FIEND see *The Lodger* (1932 remake)

PICCOLI, MICHEL (1925– , real name Jacques Daniel Michel Piccoli) French actor. On stage from the early 1940s and in films from 1944 with *Sortilèges*, Piccoli went on to become a distinguished character star in the 1960s and 1970s. His 150-plus films include *La Muerte en este Jardin* (1956), *Masquerade* (1964), *Les Demoiselles de Rochefort* (1966), *Belle de Jour* (1967), *The Discreet Charm of the Bourgeoisie* (1972), *The Phantom of Liberty* (1974), *Passion* (1982) and *Beaumarchais the Scoundrel* (1996). In 1969 he also appeared in Hitchcock's *Topaz* as top French government official Jacques Granville, also known as Columbine, the head of Topaz, a group of double agents who are passing on top-secret information to the Russians. Piccoli has also directed one film, *Alors Voila* (1997). The second of his three wives was singer–actress Juliette Greco (1927–). **Hitchography:** *Topaz* (1969)

PILBEAM, NOVA (1919–) British actress. A teenage star of the 1930s, Pilbeam was signed to Gaumont-British at the age of 15 and made her film debut in *Little Friend* (1934), in which she played a child driven to attempt suicide upon learning of her parents' plans to divorce. She followed this success by playing Betty Lawrence, the kidnapped child in Hitchcock's *The Man Who Knew Too Much* (1934). Recalling Hitchcock's working methods, the actress commented: 'Hitch had everything in his head before he went near the set; therefore one was rather moved around and manipulated. But, having said that, I liked him very much.' [13] In her next film, *Tudor Rose* (1936), Pilbeam played the doomed Lady Jane Grey, following which she was offered her first adult leading role in Hitchcock's *Young and Innocent* (1937). Said Pilbeam of the film, 'We did a lot in the country… I think it was quite the sunniest film I was involved with.' [14] However, not all was smooth sailing: 'We didn't use doubles; if you remember that scene in the mine, I did that, and it was my husband-to-be, Pen's, hand holding me up as I dangled there. I was terrified! Now, Hitch had this quirky sense of humour and he made it go on and on, so that I thought my arm would come out of its socket.' [15] Pilbeam's other films include *Cheer, Boys, Cheer* (1939), *Yellow Canary* (1943) and *Counterblast* (1948), after which she retired from the screen. Pilbeam's first husband, Pen Tennyson (1918–1941, real name Penrose Tennyson) was the aforementioned assistant director on *Young and Innocent*. He went on to become a director in his own right, but was killed in World War II before his career had a chance to truly take off. **Hitchography:** *The Man Who Knew Too Much* (1934), *Young and Innocent* (1937)

PIPER, FREDERICK (1902–1979) British actor. Piper began his career as a tea merchant, only to turn to acting in the 1930s, making his screen debut in *The Good Companions* (1933), following which he was much used as a supporting actor and bit part player, including four times by Hitchcock. His many films include *Jack of All Trades* (1936), *Passport to Pimlico* (1949), *The Lavender Hill Mob* (1951) and *Burke and Hare* (1971). **Hitchography:** *The 39 Steps* (1935), *Sabotage* (1936), *Young and Innocent* (1937), *Jamaica Inn* (1939)

PLATT, EDWARD (1916–1974) American supporting actor. Remembered for the TV sit-com *Get Smart* (1965–1969), in which he played Thaddeus ('The Chief'), Platt also popped up in numerous films, including *Stalag 17* (1955), which marked his debut, *The Proud Ones* (1956), *Designing Woman* (1957), *Polyanna* (1960) and *Bullet for a Badman* (1964). He also appeared in Hitchcock's

North by Northwest (1959) as Victor Larrabee, the exasperated lawyer of Roger Thornhill (Cary Grant), who has been arrested for drunk driving, having been purposefully intoxicated by the henchmen of Philip Vandamm (James Mason). Comments Larrabee to an incredulous judge: 'It was at this point that Mr Thornhill succeeded in escaping from his would-be assassins, and when they gave chase, he, naturally, had to drive as best he could under the, uh, circumstances. But unfortunately, the, uh, circumstances were a little more than he could handle, and so, well, here we are.' **Hitchography:** *North by Northwest* (1959)

The Pleasure Garden

(GB/Ger, 1925 (released 1927), 74m (some sources state 85m), bw, silent) ★

CREDITS

Production company:	Gainsborough/Emelka
Producers:	Michael Balcon, Erich Pommer
Director:	Alfred Hitchcock
Screenplay:	Eliot Stannard, based on the novel by Mrs Oliver Sandys
Cinematographer:	Baron Ventimiglia
Art directors:	C W Arnold, Ludwig Reiber
Assistant director/ continuity girl:	Alma Reville

CAST

Virginia Valli (Patsy Brand), Carmelita Geraghty (Jill Cheyne), Miles Mander (Levitt), John Stuart (Hugh Fielding), Nita Naldi (Native girl), C Falkenburg (Russian prince), George Snell (Oscar Hamilton), Florence Helminger, Frederick Martini

Video availability: Video Collection

Produced in 1925, although not released for almost two years owing to fears that it would fail at the box office, *The Pleasure Garden* marked Hitchcock's official debut as a director, an opportunity given to him by producer Michael Balcon, for whom he had worked as a screenwriter, art director and assistant director on a number of productions, including the highly successful *Woman to Woman* (1923).

Based on a novel by Mrs Oliver Sandys, the film was an Anglo-German co-production between Gainsborough Pictures and Emelka, and was shot on location in Germany and Italy, while interiors were filmed at Emelka's Berlin's studios, not far from the Neubabelsberg studios where Hitchcock had previously worked as an assistant director on *The Blackguard* (1925).

The story involves the romantic adventures of two chorus girls, Patsy Brand (Virginia Valli) and Jill Cheyne (Carmelita Geraghty), who are out to find wealthy husbands. This being a silent melodrama of the old school, things inevitably end in disillusionment and murder. Indeed, soon after Patsy's wedding, her husband Levett

(Miles Mander) leaves for the Far East on business with Jill's fiancé Hugh Fielding (John Stuart). Once there, Levett takes to drink, murders a native girl (Nita Naldi) with whom he's been having a *liaison*, then threatens to kill Patsy with a scimitar when she turns up on the scene, having learned that hubby has gone mad through a mix of guilt and fever. Luckily, Levett is shot dead by a local doctor before he can carry out his threat ('Oh, hello, doctor,' he says in a final moment of lucidity before hitting the deck). Meanwhile, Jill and Hugh are re-united and decide to make a go of things in light of everything that has happened to their friends.

The production of *The Pleasure Garden* was fraught with problems, among them the confiscation of film stock by customs officials in Italy and the theft of location expenses, which reduced the already tight budget yet further. Hitchcock was also nervous about directing Hollywood star Virginia Valli, whom producer Michael Balcon had brought over to boost the film's box office potential. A major star at the time, Hitchcock later said of Valli: 'She was at the height of her career... That she was coming to Europe to make a picture at all was something of an event... When we started shooting Virginia Valli's scenes, I was in a cold sweat. I wanted to disguise the fact that this was my first directorial effort. I dreaded to think what she, an established Hollywood star, would say if she discovered that she had been brought all the way to Europe to be directed by a beginner.' [16] Hitchcock seems to have disguised his worries well, though, for he added, 'Virginia Valli played her scenes sublimely unconscious of the emotional drama that was being enacted on the other side of the camera.' [17]

Despite the initial fears about the film's commercial prospects, *The Pleasure Garden* went on to do good business when released in 1927, by which time Hitchcock had already directed his second film, *The Mountain Eagle* (1925), which was similarly held back until the huge success of his third film, *The Lodger* (1926). Critically, the film was also lauded, with the *Daily Express* going so far as to describe Hitchcock as a 'young man with a master mind,' while *The Bioscope* found the film's cinematography 'enchanting'.

PLESHETTE, SUSANNE (1937–   ) American actress. Known for playing Bob Newhart's wife in the long-running sit-com *The Bob Newhart Show* (1972–1977), Pleshette came to films in 1958 with *The Geisha Boy* following experience on stage and television. Her subsequent films include *Rome Adventure* (1960), *The Ugly Dachshund* (1966), *The Return of the Pink Panther* (1975), *Hot Stuff* (1979) and *The Queen of Mean* (1990, TV). She is also remembered for playing the schoolteacher Annie Hayworth in Hitchcock's *The Birds* (1963) in which she comes to a sticky end following an attack from the titular creatures. She also appeared in an episode of *Alfred Hitchcock Presents*. Married twice, Pleshette was wed to actor Troy Donahue (1937– , real name Merle Johnson) for nine months in 1964. She

married her second husband, oil tycoon Thomas Joseph Gallagher III, in 1968. **Hitchography:** *Hitch Hike* (1960, TV), *The Birds* (1963)

PLOWRIGHT, HILDA American actress. Screen credits for Plowright are few and far between, though she did make an un-credited appearance as Miss Pimm in Hitchcock's *Foreign Correspondent* (1940), which led to the credited role of Postmistress in *Suspicion* (1941). Her other films include *Lover, Come Back* (1961), *Summer Magic* (1963), *My Fair Lady* (1964) and *36 Hours* (1965). **Hitchography:** *Foreign Correspondent* (1940), *Suspicion* (1941)

POLGLASE, VAN NEST (1898–1968) American art director. In films from 1919 working for Famous Players-Lasky, Polglase, who trained as an architect, went on to be noted for the art deco look of many of his sets, among them several musicals for Fred Astaire and Ginger Rogers. The supervising art director for RKO between 1932 and 1942, his many films for the studio include *Top Hat* (1935), *The Hunchback of Notre Dame* (1939), *Citizen Kane* (1941) and Hitchcock's *Mr and Mrs Smith* (1941), which again benefited from his art deco look. He also supervised the sets for Hitchcock's following film, *Suspicion* (1941), notable for the sweeping staircase up which Cary Grant's Johnnie Aysgarth takes the seemingly poisoned glass of milk at the climax. His other films include *A Song to Remember* (1945), *Gilda* (1946) and *The River's Edge* (1957). **Hitchography:** *Mr and Mrs Smith* (1941), *Suspicion* (1941)

POMMER, ERICH (1889–1966) German producer. Pommer began his film career in 1915 when he formed the Decla production company. He went on to have several silent successes, among them such landmark productions as *The Cabinet of Dr Caligari* (1919), *Dr Mabuse* (1922) and *Die Nibelungen* (1924). In 1925 he worked as an associate producer on *The Blackguard* for a visiting British unit, whose company included the young Hitchcock. The same year Pommer also co-produced, with Michael Balcon, Hitchcock's first major directorial effort, *The Pleasure Garden*, although its release was delayed by two years over fears that it would fail at the box office. In 1937 Pommer founded Mayflower Pictures with actor Charles Laughton, with whom he made *Vessel of Wrath* (1938), which he also directed, *St Martin's Lane* (1938) and *Jamaica Inn* (1939), the latter helmed by Hitchcock. However, Hitchcock wasn't entirely impressed with Pommer's contribution to *Jamaica Inn*, commenting, 'Erich Pommer? I'm not sure he understood the English idiom.' [18] Pommer's other film's include *The Last Laugh* (1924), *Variety* (1925), *Metropolis* (1926), *Faust* (1926), *The Blue Angel* (1930) *Fire Over England* (1937) and *They Knew What They Wanted* (1940). **Hitchography:** *The Blackguard* (1925), *The Pleasure Garden* (1925), *Jamaica Inn* (1939)

POWELL, DAVID (1883–1925) Scottish-born actor. On stage in America from 1904, David Powell made films on both sides of the Atlantic from 1917 onwards, among his British output being six films for Famous Players-Lasky, all of which the young Alfred Hitchcock worked on as an inter-titles designer. **Hitchography:** *The Princess of New York* (1921), *Appearances* (1921), *Dangerous Lies* (1921), *The Mystery Road* (1921), *Spanish Jade* (1922), *Perpetua* (1922)

POWELL, MICHAEL (1905–1990) British writer-producer-director. One of the great names in British cinema, Michael Powell was responsible for some of the greatest films ever made, among them *A Matter of Life and Death* (1946), *Black Narcissus* (1947) and *The Red Shoes* (1948), which were made in association with his longtime collaborator, Emeric Pressburger (1902–1988). Following experience as a bank clerk, Powell began his film career in 1925 as an assistant on *Mare Nostrum* in the South of France. Turning to stills photography, he went on to encounter Hitchcock on the set of *Champagne* (1928), for which he handled the publicity shots. Recalled Powell of his introduction to the great director: 'He really was the fattest young man I had ever seen. He had a fresh, rosy complexion, his dark hair was sleeked back, and he was correctly dressed in a suit with a watch-chain across his waistcoat. He wore a soft hat. He observed me out of the corner of his piggy eyes sunk in fat cheeks. There was not much Hitch missed with those piggy eyes.' [19]

Despite a slightly frosty reception from Hitchcock, he and Powell went on to become friends, and this led to a further stills asignment on *The Manxman* (1929), along with some un-credited work on the screenplay for *Blackmail* (1929), on which Powell helped Hitchcock script the film's chase finale. Wrote Powell of this opportunity: 'The invitation from Hitch, whose acute sense of cinema I admired, was the best thing that had happened to me in England. I started to make notes right away and discussed the part with Anny Ondra, while taking romantic still photographs of her charming face and body in the woods of Somerset.' [20]

Following *Blackmail*, Powell forsook the stills camera and turned to writing full time, next working on a handful of screenplays, among them *Caste* (1930) and *77, Park Lane* (1931), following which he got his directorial break with the 'quota quickie' *Two Crowded Hours* (1931). Many more B films followed, among them *Rynox* (1931), *Born Lucky* (1932) and *The Phantom Light* (1935). Powell finally broke into A features with *The Edge of the World* (1939). His many other films include *The Thief of Bagdad* (1940), *A Canterbury Tale* (1944), *The Battle of the River Plate* (1956), *Peeping Tom* (1959) and *Return to the Edge of the World* (1978). **Hitchography:** *Champagne* (1928), *The Manxman* (1929), *Blackmail* (1929)

POWELL, PAUL (1881–1944, full name Paul Mahlon Powell) American director. Following experience at Biograph under D W Griffith, Paul Powell went on to helm a number of high profile star vehicles in the late 1910s and early 1920s, among them *All Night* (1918) starring Rudolph Valentino, and *Pollyanna* (1920) starring Mary Pickford. In 1921, he travelled to London to helm two films for Famous Players-Lasky, on which Hitchcock worked as a graphic artist, designing the inter-titles. **Hitchography:** *Dangerous Lies* (1921), *The Mystery Road* (1921)

PRATT, JUDSON American supporting actor. Pratt can be seen in such low budgeters as *Monster on the Campus* (1958), *The Rise and Fall of Legs Diamond* (1960) and *Vigilante Force* (1975). He can also be seen in Hitchcock's *I Confess* (1953) as Murphy. **Hitchography:** *I Confess* (1953)

PREVIN, CHARLES American composer-songwriter-conductor. Long at Universal, Previn worked on countless scores for the studio, including *Tower of London* (1939), *Spring Parade* (1940), *A Little Bit of Heaven* (1940) and *The Wolf Man* (1941). He also conducted Frank Skinner's cliffhanger-style score for Hitchcock's *Saboteur* (1942) and Dimitri Tiomkin's rather more subtle music for *Shadow of a Doubt* (1943). **Hitchography:** *Saboteur* (1942), *Shadow of a Doubt* (1943)

PRICKETT, MAUDIE American character actress. Prickett popped up as a support, frequently in spinster roles, in a number of films, among them *I'll Take Sweden* (1965), *The Gnome-Mobile* (1967), *The Maltese Bippy* (1968), *Rascal* (1969) and *Sweet Charity* (1969). She can also be seen as Elsie the maid in the Plaza Hotel sequence in Hitchcock's *North by Northwest* (1959), sharing a couple of brief scenes with Cary Grant's Roger Thornhill. **Hitchography:** *North by Northwest* (1959)

PRIESTLEY, J B (1894–1984) British writer. The novels and plays of this highly admired and respected author have frequently been turned into films, among them *The Good Companions* (1933 and 1956), *The Old Dark House* (1932 and 1962, from *Benighted*), *When We Are Married* (1942) and *An Inspector Calls* (1954). Priestley's work as a screenwriter was less prolific, among his credits being one for 'additional dialogue' on Hitchcock's *Jamaica Inn* (1939), for which he was brought in at the behest of producer/star Charles Laughton to beef up his part as smuggler Sir Humphrey Pengallan. **Hitchography:** *Jamaica Inn* (1939)

PRINCE, WILLIAM (1913–1996) American stage actor. Prince began treading the boards in 1937. He turned to films in the early 1940s, and went on to appear in supporting roles in the likes of *Destination Tokyo* (1944), *Cyrano de Bergerac* (1950), in which he played Christian, *Macabre* (1958), *The Heartbreak Kid* (1972), *The Stepford Wives* (1975) and Hitchcock's *Family Plot* (1976), in which he played the bishop who is drugged and kidnapped in the middle of a church service. His other films include *Network* (1976), *The Gauntlet* (1977), *Nuts* (1987) and *The Paper* (1994). **Hitchography:** *Family Plot* (1976)

The Princess of New York
(GB, 1921, 64m approx, bw, silent)

CREDITS
Production company: Famous Players–Lasky
Director: Donald Crisp
Screenplay: Margaret Turnbull, based on the novel by Cosmo Hamilton
Inter-titles: Alfred Hitchcock

CAST
David Powell (Geoffrey Kingswood), Mary Glynne (Helen Stanton), Ivo Dawson (Alan Merstham), Dorothy Fane (Vilet Merstham), George Bellamy (Sir George Merstham), Wyndham Guise (Eardley Smith)

Released in 1921, this black-and-white silent, now apparently lost, told the story of a wealthy American steel king who pawns his daughter's jewels so as to keep them out of reach of her beau, a crook. Directed by Donald Crisp, it also had inter-titles designed by the young Hitchcock.

DIE PRINZESSIN UND DER GEIGER see *The Blackguard*

The Prude's Fall
(GB, 1925, 56m approx, bw, silent)

CREDITS
Production company: Gainsborough
Producer: Michael Balcon
Director: Graham Cutts
Screenplay: Alfred Hitchcock, based on the novel and play by Rudolf Besier and May Edginton
Cinematographer: Hal Young
Art director: Alfred Hitchcock
Assistant director: Alfred Hitchcock
Continuity girl: Alma Reville

CAST
Jane Novak (Beatrice Audley), Miles Mander (Sir Neville Moreton), Julanne Johnson (Sonia Roubetsky), Warwick Ward (Andre le Briquet), Hugh Miller (Marquis de Rocqueville), Gladys Jennings (Laura Westonry), Marie Ault (Mrs Masters), Henry Vibart (Dean Carey)

Made in 1925, this lost romantic drama about a French captain who romances a rich widow was one of several films on which Hitchcock worked for director Graham Cutts in the mid-1920s, among them *Woman to Woman* (1923), *The White Shadow* (1924), *The Passionate Adventure* (1924) and *The Blackguard* (1925). However, this proved to be the last time Hitchcock collaborated with Cutts, who informed him that he didn't want to work with him any more. The parting worked in Hitchcock's favour, however, for soon after he was offered *The Pleasure Garden* to direct by Michael Balcon, which helped to launch his career.

Psycho
(US, 1960, 109m, bw) ★★★★

CREDITS
Production company: Shamley (released by Paramount, filmed at Universal and Revue)
Director: Alfred Hitchcock
Screenplay: Joseph Stefano, based on the novel by Robert Bloch
Cinematographer: John L Russell
Music: Bernard Herrmann
Editor: George Tomasini
Art directors: Joseph Hurley, Robert Clatworthy
Costumes: Helen Colvig, Rita Riggs, Edith Head
Special effects: Clarence Champagne
Sound: Waldon O Watson, William Russell
Assistant director: Hilton A Green
Titles/pictorial consultant: Saul Bass

CAST
Anthony Perkins (Norman Bates/Mother), Janet Leigh (Marion Crane), Vera Miles (Lila Crane), John Gavin (Sam Loomis), Martin Balsam (Milton Arbogast), John McIntire (Sheriff Chambers), Vaughn Taylor (George Lowery), Simon Oakland (Dr Richmond), Frank Albertson (Tom Cassidy), Lurene Tuttle (Mrs Chambers), Pat Hitchcock (Caroline), Mort Mills (Patrolman), John Anderson (Charlie), George Eldredge (Police Chief), Virginia Gregg (Voice of Mother), Marli Renfro (Janet Leigh's body double)

Video availability: Universal
DVD availability: Universal
CD availability: *Psycho* (Varese), which contains a complete recording of the score by conductor Joel McNeely and the Royal Scottish National Orchestra; *Music from the Great Hitchcock Movie Thrillers* (Phase 4/Decca), which contains 'A narrative for orchestra'; *Bernard Herrmann – Film Scores* (Milan), which contains a *Suite* including *Prelude*, *The Murder* and *Finale*; *Citizen Kane – The Essential Bernard Herrmann* (Silva Screen), which contains *Prelude*, *The City*, *Rainstorm*, *Murder* and *Finale*; *A History of Hitchcock – Dial M for Murder* (Silva Screen), which contains *Prelude*, *The City*, *Rainstorm*, *Murder* and *Finale*; *Hitchcock – Master of Mayhem* (Proarte), which contains a *Suite* including *Prelude*, *The Murder*, *The City* and *Finale*; *Torn Curtain – The Classic Film Music of Bernard Herrmann* (Silva Screen), which includes a *Suite*; *Psycho – Horror and Fantasy at the Movies* (Silva Screen), which contains *Prelude*, *The Murder*, and *Finale*; and *Psycho – The Essential Alfred Hitchcock* (Silva Screen), which contains *Suite for String Orchestra*

Okay, this is the big one: *Psycho*, the most famous Hitchcock thriller of all. Allegedly made as a joke, it was

Just when you thought it was safe to go back in the shower. Guests are invited to join in the action at the Hitchcock pavilion at Universal Studios in Florida. The attraction closed in 2002.

the *Blair Witch Project* of its day; produced in black and white for $800,000 on the Universal back-lot, it went on to make $14m on its first run. Hitchcock certainly saw the funny side – he laughed all the way to the bank.

Over 40 years after its release, *Psycho* remains one of the most discussed films ever made, and is recognized not only as a genre classic but also as a *movie* classic. But not so at the time: 'Hitchcock may try to frighten me to death, but I draw the line at being *bored* to death,' sniped Alexander Walker in the *Evening Standard*, while Jympson Harmon of the *Evening News* described the film as 'More miserable than the most miserable peep show I have ever seen' (which would seem to suggest he *had* actually seen a certain number of peep shows). Meanwhile, the *Picturegoer's* critic simply commented, '*Psycho* is sicko.' Yet once the film started raking in the dough, some began to reassess the movie. 'You'd better have a pretty strong stomach and be prepared for a couple of grisly shocks,' wrote Bosley Crowther in the *New York Times* at the beginning of the year, later altering his view to acknowledge that the film 'represented [an] expert and sophisticated command of emotional development with cinematic techniques,' by the end of it.

In the late 1950s, Hitchcock had turned his attention to widescreen, Technicolor spectacle with the likes of *Vertigo* (1958) and *North by Northwest* (1959). Feeling the urge to do something simpler, he decided to make a movie utilizing the talents of the crew he had assembled to make his highly successful but modestly budgeted television series *Alfred Hitchcock Presents*, among them cinematographer John L Russell, who had photographed many of the episodes. If the experiment was a failure, he could always cut it down and present it as part of the TV series, he opined. The question was, what to film?

Hitchcock himself was noted for saying, 'The three most important things about a script are the story, the story, the story,' and he immediately recognized genius in Robert Bloch's tautly written 1959 pulp novel *Psycho*, which had been inspired by the true-life exploits of Ed Gein, a Wisconsin serial killer who, it was discovered in 1957, had filled his run down home with the body parts of his many female victims (including a cupful of noses, two pairs of lips on a string and four eviscerated face skins tacked to a wall). In the book, the story centres on Norman Bates, a pudgy 42-year-old whose mother apparently has a penchant for offing lone female guests at the motel they run together. However, a twist reveals that Mrs Bates died many years earlier, and that it is in fact Norman, dressed as his mother, who is actually the perpetrator of the ghastly crimes, which include the severing of a woman's head while she showers. Commented Hitchcock: 'I think that the thing that appealed to me and made me decide to do the picture was the suddenness of the murder in the shower, coming, as it were, out of the blue.' [21]

The book was brought to Hitchcock's attention by his long-time production assistant Peggy Robertson, and he made an anonymous bid for it in the autumn of 1959,

securing the screen rights for the astonishingly modest sum of $9000 (the only remuneration Bloch derived from the movie, although the film's success boosted his burgeoning career no end). Working through his own production company Shamley (named after his former home in the English village of the same name), Hitchcock began preparing *Psycho* for the screen, financing the film out of his own pocket and bringing in Paramount as a distributor (however, Paramount was unable to find studio space for the film, and so Hitchcock shot it on the Universal back-lot and at the Revue studios, home of *Alfred Hitchcock Presents*).

In keeping with his plan to make the film using his TV crew, Hitchcock first hired James P Cavanagh to write the script. Cavanagh had penned *One More Mile to Go* (1957, TV) for *Alfred Hitchcock Presents*, which the director had helmed himself, along with several other episodes. Unfortunately, Hitchcock was dissatisfied with Cavanagh's work, and subsequently handed the job to an up-coming writer named Joseph Stefano, with whom he overhauled the story, changing Norman Bates from the unsympathetic middle-aged slob of the book to a lonely young man to be played by the slender, good-looking Anthony Perkins, who had already begun to make a name for himself in such films as *Friendly Persuasion* (1956), for which he'd received a best supporting actor Oscar nomination, and *On the Beach* (1959).

Instead of introducing Norman Bates straight away, as Bloch does in the first paragraph book, Stefano hit upon the idea of beginning the Phoenix-set story with Marion Crane (Janet Leigh), a minor character in the novel, whose plight we initially follow after she steals $40,000 from her boss' client Tom Cassidy ('I never carry more than I can afford to lose,' Cassidy boasts, although he later changes his tune after the crime has been committed, commenting, 'I'll get it back, and if any of it's missing I'll replace it with her fine, soft flesh!'). Subsequently, Marion heads off to see her lover Sam (John Gavin) in Fairvale, but gets waylaid in a rain storm along the way, thus having to interrupt her journey with a stay at the lonely and deserted Bates Motel, run by the seemingly innocuous Norman Bates ('We have twelve vacancies, twelve cabins, twelve vacancies – they moved away the highway,' he explains).

The central story points now established, Stefano got to work on the dialogue, handing in his final draft in early November 1959, which allowed Hitchcock to begin production later that same month. In keeping with his plan to make a low budget picture, Hitchcock eschewed expensive stars, his one concession being Janet Leigh who would be playing Marion Crane, the director's reasoning being that audiences just wouldn't expect a star of her stature to be killed off so early in the proceedings, thus doubling the potential shock of her death, for which the director had something very special planned (that said, the film's titles *are* a slight giveaway, for Leigh is billed last in the actors' credits with the adjunct 'And Janet Leigh as Marion Crane').

As Marion's sister Lila, Hitchcock cast Vera Miles, with whom he'd already worked on *Revenge* (1955, TV), the first episode of *Alfred Hitchcock Presents*, and *The Wrong Man* (1956). The part of Marion's boyfriend Sam Loomis (owner of the screen's tidiest hardware shop) went to John Gavin, with the rest of the cast rounded out with Martin Balsam as the doomed Detective Arbogast, hired to discover the whereabouts of the missing Marion, and Hitchcock's daughter Pat, making her third and final film appearance for her father as Marion's fellow secretary Caroline.

The non-existent part of Mother was 'played' by various people doubling for Anthony Perkins, among them Margot Epper, Anne Dore, Paul Jasmine and Virginia Gregg, the latter giving Mother her distinctive voice. However, Hitchcock announced Judith Anderson and Helen Hayes for the role at various times during production, so as to keep the press off the track of the film's surprise twist. Astonishingly, the rouse worked, for it would appear that most journalists hadn't bothered to read the book to discover the true identity of Mother for themselves. Like many Hitchcock films before it, the casting of *Psycho* was spot on, and many of the actors, particularly Anthony Perkins and Janet Leigh, found themselves associated with their roles for the remainder of their careers (in fact Perkins went on to revive Norman Bates a further three times).

On the technical front, further members of Hitchcock's TV crew were recruited, among them costumiers Helen Colvig and Rita Riggs (although an uncredited Edith Head provided Vera Miles with her wardrobe), and assistant director Hilton Green, while Saul Bass, who'd worked on *Vertigo* (1958) and *North by Northwest* (1959), was brought in to design the titles and act as the film's 'pictorial consultant' which involved storyboarding the celebrated shower sequence in which Marion meets her demise. The editing was meanwhile in the hands of Hitchcock regular George Tomasini, while Bernard Herrmann was onboard as composer.

Principal photography began on 30 November 1959, and during production Hitchcock captured a number of controversial, never-before-seen sequences, among them the frank introductory post-coital scene between Marion and Sam, who have been seeing each other in a seedy downtown hotel during her lunch hour, and a shot of a toilet in Marion's room at the Bates Motel, which she not only flushes, but which her sister Lila later puts her hand down to retrieve a vital piece of evidence (ironically, despite this, Norman is unable to say the word 'bathroom' when showing Marion around her cabin). There were also several shots of suggested nudity both leading up to and during the shower sequence, with Norman spying through a hole in the wall, watching Marion disrobe. The hints of incest between Norman and his mother ('A boy's best friend is his mother'/'A son is a poor substitute for a lover') and the then-prickly subjects of necrophilia, transvestism and matricide ('the most unbearable crime of all') also added to the potent brew.

Given the fairly blunt nature of the story, Hitchcock was keen to add a number of subtleties to the proceedings, among them the number of mirrors in the Bates house, which helps to suggest Norman's dual personality; Marion's changing from a white bra and slip to black ones following her crime; the photo of Marion's parents on her bedroom wall watching over her as she packs to leave town; and the shower glimpsed through a doorway in Marion's bedroom as a taste of things to come. There are also several instances of black humour, among them Norman's love of taxidermy and his passion for stuffing birds (Hitchcock loved *double entendres* – it should also be noted that Marion's surname is that of a bird); Norman's stumbling over the word 'falsity' and his description of his mother as 'an invalid – er, invalid'; Norman hiding his mother's desiccated body in the fruit cellar ('You think I'm fruity, eh, boy?'); plus the fact that Marion's car, into which Norman has put her dead body and, unbeknownst to him, the stolen money, takes an awfully long time to sink into the swamp into which he has pushed it (we're actually rooting for Norman here).

Hitchcock also manages to disguise the true identity of Mother with some clever camera angles, thus making the art of cinema a completely complicit element in the telling of the story. For example, when Arbogast is stabbed on the stairs of the Bates house, the crime is shown from above, so that we don't see that Norman and Mother are one and the same (ditto when Norman carries Mother down to the fruit cellar).

However, The film's most important scene remains the much imitated shower sequence, and variations on its can be found in such films as *The Legend of Hell House* (1973), *Dressed to Kill* (1980), *Friday the 13th Part 2* (1981), *F/X 2: The Deadly Art of Illusion* (1991), *Body Double* (1984) and the Mel Brooks spoof *High Anxiety* (1977), in which Brooks finds himself stabbed with a newspaper by an irate bellhop during his ablutions.

The shower set was built so that all the walls could be removed, thus allowing the camera in close enough to photograph the elaborate montage sequence of 78 shots that the director needed to capture. The sequence took seven days to commit to film, using Janet Leigh, who wore moleskin 'pasties' to cover the intimate parts of her body, and body double Marli Renfro, who was paid $400 for the week's work. Recalled Leigh: 'There were many repeats of the same action, taken from different angles. Then there were delays due to moleskin problems or camera technicalities. We were fortunate that the cast and crew were patient and had a sense of humour, because these circumstances could have caused some flare-ups.' [22] Hitchcock kept a closed set during the filming, although as Janet Leigh went on to reveal: 'Security was a constant source of trouble. Even though I wore the moleskin, I was still pretty much on display, so to speak. I didn't want strangers lurking around, hoping to get a peek in case of any accidental mishap.' [23]

As shot, the sequence suggests not only that one sees a naked woman, but that one also sees a knife entering flesh.

However, close scrutiny of the sequence on video or DVD proves that this is not the case – one's eye is simply fooled by the rapidity of the cutting. In fact the scene is bloodless until the end, when we see Shasta chocolate sauce, which Hitchcock favoured in lieu of fake blood, famously trickle down the plughole. In fact so potent is the sequence that certain audience members at the time were convinced that the film switched to colour at this point (commented Hitchcock: 'It wasn't a message that stirred the audiences, nor was it a great performance or their enjoyment of the novel. They were aroused by pure film' [24]).

Yet despite Hitchcock's great care with the shower scene, it should be noted that, as Janet Leigh's Marion steps into the shower, a rubber mat can be plainly seen inside the bathtub, yet it disappears in all future shots. The soap wrapper that Marion so casually discards is also later missing when the camera cuts to the blood and water going down the plughole, as is the soap itself. Meanwhile, as Marion lies dead on the bathroom floor, Janet Leigh's eye flickers slightly (prior to release, Hitchcock's wife, Alma Reville, also noticed that Leigh swallowed during the shot, which was subsequently trimmed, while ophthalmologists pointed out that her pupils had not dilated).

Conspicuous by his absence during the filming of the shower scene, Anthony Perkins was actually in New York at the time rehearsing for the play *Greenwillow*. Consequently, stunt player Margot Epper stood in for him, her face blackened with make-up and shot in silhouette so as to keep Mother's true identity a secret.

Hitchcock wrapped filming on 1 February 1960, nine days over schedule. Following dubbing, re-shoots and effects work, a rough cut was ready by the end of April, at which stage the film was handed over to Bernard Herrmann to score. Amazingly, Hitchcock was convinced he had a turkey on his hands; however, once he saw the film with Herrmann's stabbing, strings-only 'black and white' score, he quickly changed his mind. Astonishingly, Herrmann wasn't even nominated for an Oscar for his ground breaking work on the movie, the *Main Title* for which alone leaves one wrung out before the story has even begun (by way of acknowledging Hermann's achievement, Hitchcock made the unprecedented move of giving the composer penultimate billing in the titles, just prior to his own screen credit).

During post-production, Hitchcock had several wrangles with the censor over the film's violence and implied nudity, but generally managed to have his own way, getting away with celluloid murder. The haggling done, the film was finally ready for its New York premiere on 16 June 1960.

Television audiences were of course by now used to welcoming Hitchcock into their living rooms every week with his TV show, which the director personally introduced. Consequently, Hitch decided to use this method to promote *Psycho* too, for which he filmed a special trailer penned by James Allardice, who wrote his TV intros. This features him walking about the back lot set of the Bates Motel. 'Here we have a quiet little motel, tucked away off the main highway, and as you see, perfectly harmless looking, whereas it has now become known as the scene of the crime,' he begins, going on to describe the 'sinister looking' house nearby, where 'the most dire, horrible events took place.' And then it's down to the motel itself: 'Let's go into cabin number one. I want to show you something there. All tidied up. The bathroom. Oh, they've cleaned this up now. Big difference. You should have seen the blood. The whole place was… well, it's too horrible to describe. Dreadful. And I tell you, a very important clue was found here [at which he indicates the toilet]; down there. Well, the murderer, you see, crept in here very slowly – of course, the shower was on, there was no sound, and…' [25] At this point, the trailer cuts to a brief shot of a woman being attacked in a shower. However, it should be noted that the screaming woman is not Janet Leigh, but Vera Miles!

The film, billed as 'A new and altogether different screen excitement,' was an instant commercial hit and a press sensation, thanks to Hitchcock's insistence that theatre managers only allow patrons to see it 'from the beginning – or not at all!' 'Please don't tell the ending. It's the only one we have,' pleaded the director in a further bid to keep the movie's big secret safe. Astonishingly, the public played the game, putty in the Master's hands. Indeed, for a whole generation, taking a shower would never be the same again…

Note that the film, which was Oscar nominated for best director, best cinematography (John L Russell), best supporting actress (Janet Leigh) and best art direction (Joseph Hurley and Robert Clatworthy), has so far produced four sequels, a television series and one remake: *Psycho 2* (1983), *Psycho III* (1986), *Bates Motel* (1987, TV, plus series), *Psycho IV: The Beginning* (1990, TV) and *Psycho* (1998). Meanwhile, *Dressed to Kill* (1980) owes much of its structure to *Psycho*, with Angie Dickinson's Kate Miller this time the unfortunate victim who finds herself bumped off halfway through the proceedings by Michael Caine's transvestite Dr Elliott.

Meanwhile, the Universal Studio Tour in California features a drive past the original *Psycho* house (moved to a different location on the lot since filming). Universal Studios in Florida also had a *Psycho* house, since demolished, which was built for the filming of *Psycho IV*. Until 2002, the theme park also boasted the 'Psycho Experience' in the Alfred Hitchcock pavilion, which featured clips from Hitchcock's films, a 3D recreation of *The Birds* (1963), props, exhibits and a live *Psycho* show introduced on film by Anthony Perkins.

Hitchcock cameo Hitchcock can be spotted making his customary gag cameo, this time outside Marion's office, wearing an over-sized stetson!

Psycho 2
(US, 1983, 113m, Technicolor, Dolby Stereo) ★

CREDITS

Production company:	Universal/Oak Industries
Producer:	Hilton A Green
Executive producer:	Bernard Schwartz
Screenplay:	Tom Holland
Director:	Richard Franklin
Cinematographer:	Dean Cundey
Music:	Jerry Goldsmith
Editor:	Andrew London
Production design:	John W Corso
Costumes:	Robert Ellsworth, Brian O'Dowd, Denise Schlom
Special effects:	Albert Whitlock
Make-up effects:	Michael McCracken, Chuck Crafts
Sound:	Jim Alexander, Roger Heman, Philip Fland, Rex Slinkard, Mark S Server, Andrew London

CAST

Anthony Perkins (Norman Bates), Vera Miles (Lila Loomis), Meg Tilly (Mary Loomis), Robert Loggia (Dr Raymond), Hugh Gillin (Sheriff Hunt), Claudia Byar (Mrs Spool), Dennis Franz (Toomey), Osgood Perkins (Young Norman), Virginia Gregg (Voice of Mother), Robert Alan Brown, Ben Hartigan, Tim Maier, Tom Holland

Twenty-three years is a long time to wait for a sequel, but *Psycho 2* (1983) by no means holds the record: *The Wizard of Oz* (1939) was followed by *Journey Back to Oz* (1964) 25 years later (35 years later if one adds on the decade the film lay on the shelf), while *National Velvet* (1945) was followed by *International Velvet* (1978) 33 years later. Given the enormous box office success of *Psycho* (1960), there were calls for some kind of follow up early on, but Hitchcock resisted the temptation. Thus it was left to Hitchcock devotee Richard Franklin to bring the project to life some three years after the death of Hitchcock.

Born in Australia, Franklin (1948–) came to study film at the University of Southern California in 1967, and it was during this period that the fledgling director first met Hitchcock at a retrospective of his work at the university, which Franklin chaired. 'It was the first time such a thing had been done, and the first time he'd appeared in front of students. In fact it was sufficiently significant in that it is referred to in the John Russell Taylor biography! Well, he subsequently invited me out to observe production on *Topaz*, which I did as much as I could, given that I was still in class at USC. I continued to keep in touch with him from different places, as I then came back to Australia.' [26]

Back in his homeland, Franklin's career took off with such films as *Belinda* (1972), *Patrick* (1978) and, most importantly, *Road Games* (1981), a Hitchcockian thriller starring Jamie Leigh Curtis – daughter of *Psycho*'s Janet Leigh – in a role named Hitch. It was this film that helped Franklin secure *Psycho 2*. 'I knew they were going to do a sequel to *Psycho* and I figured that it should be done well, and I like to think of *Psycho 2* not just as a sequel, but as a sort of dissertation on the original. Of course, it was never intended to be the second part in a four-part series. It was meant to be a sort of mirror reflection of the original, which took us back full circle.' [27]

In the film, the story – scripted by Tom Holland – sees Norman Bates let out of the asylum 22 years later ('It's 22 years later and Norman Bates is coming home!' proclaimed the posters), only to find himself at the centre of a bizarre plot to have himself re-committed. Back onboard were Anthony Perkins as Norman and Vera Miles as Lila Crane (now Loomis) who, with her daughter Mary (Meg Tilly), attempts to push Norman over the edge of sanity (the film, incidentally, was produced by *Psycho*'s assistant director, Hilton A Green, while sound recordist Roger Heman had worked on Hitchcock's *Lifeboat* back in 1944). Although slickly enough directed – Dean Cundey's camera makes some impressive moves – the film has the distinct look of being shot on the back lot (at times it resembles an episode of *Murder, She Wrote*). Nevertheless, there are several surprising twists in the plot-packed script, among them the appearance of Norman's real mother.

With an atmospheric score by Jerry Goldsmith, some eye-catching mattes by Hitchcock regular Albert Whitlock, and the inevitable re-working of the shower scene, the film passes the time entertainingly enough. Revealed Richard Franklin: 'My greatest achievement with *Psycho 2*, at least at the time, was that quite soon afterwards people started talking about *Psycho One* as opposed to *Psycho*! Can you imagine people going round talking about *Casablanca One* or *Gone with the Wind One*?' [28] Commented *Variety* of the results, 'Director Richard Franklin deftly keeps the suspense and tension on a high while doling out dozens of shock-of-recognition shots drawn from the audience's familiarity with *Psycho*.' Not everyone was impressed with the film, though. Sniped the *Sunday Times*, 'It's all very well having your tongue in your cheek, but it helps to have a brain in your head.'

Hitchcock cameo Note that Hitchcock makes his customary cameo, this time as a briefly seen shadow in Mother's bedroom!

Psycho III
(US, 1986, 93m, Technicolor, Dolby Stereo) ★

CREDITS

Production company:	Universal
Producer:	Hilton A Green
Director:	Anthony Perkins
Screenplay:	Charles Edward Pogue
Cinematographer:	Bruce Surtees
Music:	Carter Burwell
Editor:	David Blewitt

Production design: Henry Bumstead
Costumes: Peter V Saldutti,
Maria Denise Schlom
Special effects: Syd Dutton, Bill Taylor,
Karl G Miller,
Louis R Cooper, Dan Lester
Make-up effects: Michael Westmore
Sound: John Stacy, Jim Thompson

CAST

Anthony Perkins (Norman Bates), Diana Scarwid (Maureen Coyle), Jeff Fahey (Duane Duke), Hugh Gillin (Sheriff Hunt), Lee Garlington (Myrna), Roberta Maxwell (Tracy Venable), Robert Alan Browne (Staler), Virginia Gregg (Voice of Mother)

In this second follow up to *Psycho* (1960), Anthony Perkins took over the directorial reigns to provide a lively variation on the expected themes, which this time focus on a suicidal nun (Diana Scardwid) who takes refuge at the Bates Motel, where murder is the order of the day. A welcome dose of black humour is present this time. For example, as Norman ascends the stairs in the Bates house, with murder in mind, he takes a moment to straighten a picture as he does so; the film even opens with a tribute to the bell tower finale from Hitchcock's *Vertigo* (1958; note that Henry Bumstead, who designed *Vertigo*, is also the designer here). Well worth a look, this is actually an improvement on *Psycho 2* (1983). Commented *Variety*: 'Opening sequence is a full-fledged homage to Alfred Hitchcock's *Vertigo* and helps set the comic, in-joke tone of the rest of the picture... Main pleasure of the picture stems from Anthony Perkins' amusing performance.'

Psycho IV: The Beginning
(US, 1990, colour, TV) ★

CREDITS

Production company: Universal/Smart Money
Producers: George Zaloom, Les Mayfield
Executive producer: Hilton A Green
Director: Mick Garris
Screenplay: Joseph Stefano
Cinematographer: Rodney Charters
Music: Graeme Revell
Editor: Charles Bornstein
Production design: Michael Hanan
Costumes: Mary Ellen Winston
Special effects: Rick Jones, Bruce Block
Sound: Henri Lopez, Rick Alexander

CAST

Anthony Perkins (Norman Bates), Henry Thomas (Young Norman), Olivia Hussey (Norma Bates/Mother), C C H Pounder (Fran Ambrose), Warren Frost (Dr Leo Richmond), Donna Mitchell (Connie Bates), Thomas Schuster (Chet Rudolph), John Landis (Station owner)

In this TV movie addendum to the film series penned by original *Psycho* screenwriter Joseph Stefano, Norman Bates recalls his childhood years to a radio talk show host. The series had actually run its course by this time, but this is a mildly diverting effort, which begins promisingly before descending into a chase around the Bates house for the finale. Thankfully, Anthony Perkins retains his dignity throughout. Note that the film was made at Universal's then-new studio in Florida, at which a new version of the *Psycho* house was erected for the film. Used as a tourist attraction at the theme park, the set has since been torn down.

Psycho
(US, 1998, 104m, DeLuxe)

CREDITS

Production company: Universal/Imagine
Producers: Brian Grazer, Gus Van Sant
Director: Gus Van Sant
Screenplay: Joseph Stefano, based on the
novel by Robert Bloch
Cinematographer: Chris Doyle
Music: Bernard Herrmann,
adapted by Danny Elfman
Editor: Amy Duddleston
Production design: Tom Foden
Make-up effects: Rick Baker

CAST

Vince Vaughn (Norman Bates), Anne Heche (Marion Crane), Julianne Moore (Lila Crane), Viggo Mortensen (Sam Loomis), William H. Macy (Milton Arbogast), Robert Forster (Dr Simon), Philip Baker Hall (Sheriff Chambers), Anne Haney (Mrs Chambers), Chad Everett (Tom Cassidy), Rita Wilson (Caroline), James Remar (Highway patrolman), James LeGros (Car dealer), Rance Howard (Mr Lowery)

'We all go a little mad. Haven't you?' asks Norman Bates in *Psycho* (1960). It would certainly seem that art house director Gus Van Sant – known for such films as *Drugstore Cowboy* (1989), *My Own Private Idaho* (1991) and *Good Will Hunting* (1997) – went a little mad when he accepted the assignment to remake Hitchcock's shock classic more or less scene for scene and using the same script. The results are incongruous to say the least, with everything feeling just plain wrong, from the casting down to the colour photography. 'A new vision of the most frightening movie experience of all time,' boasted the posters. Critic Anthony Quinn writing in the *Independent* put it more succinctly: 'This version isn't sacrilege – it's just pointless.' Added *Variety*: 'The reason the conceit backfires is that the original depended on narrative surprises that can't possibly be surprising now, and on material that's long since lost its power to even raise an eyebrow (Hitch's single most shocking move was to show a toilet flushing, which had never been done in a major studio film).' Audiences, by now used to such ironic slasher fare as *Scream* (1996), stayed away in droves.

PUBLISHING There have, of course, been many books devoted to the life and films of Hitchcock. The director himself also had major ties with several publishing houses during his lifetime. In 1955 he made a deal with magazine publisher Richard E Decker to promote *The Alfred Hitchcock Mystery Magazine* (which actually survived its director by over a decade), while in 1957 he was approached by Simon & Schuster about endorsing a collection of short suspense and horror stories to be named after his then hugely popular TV show *Alfred Hitchcock Presents*. Titled *Alfred Hitchcock Presents: Stories They Wouldn't Let Me Do On TV*, it carried an introduction by the director himself. ('The reason why some of these stories cannot be produced on the home screen will be obvious on reading,' [28] he wrote.) An immediate success, the book was much re-printed, while two of the stories, *The Waxwork* by A M Burrage and *The Jokester* by Robert Arthur, were later filmed for the TV series.

Further deals with Random House and Dell followed, resulting in *Alfred Hitchcock Presents: Stories for Late at Night* in 1961. Another major success, it was followed by literally dozens of compilations, among them *Alfred Hitchcock's Witches' Brew*, *Alfred Hitchcock's Solve Them Yourself Mysteries*, *Alfred Hitchcock's 14 Suspense Stories to Play Russian Roulette By* and *Alfred Hitchcock Presents: More Stories My Mother Never Told Me*, all of which featured the director on their covers and carried introductions supposedly written by – though more often than not, ghost-written for – him. A series of children's mysteries titled *Alfred Hitchcock and the Three Investigators* was also produced, in which Hitchcock always turned up in the action at some stage to help his crime-solving young friends.

Q

QUAYLE, SIR ANTHONY (1913–1989) British actor. Knighted in 1985, Quayle made his stage debut in 1931 following training at RADA. At The Old Vic from 1932 and on Broadway from 1936, he made his film debut in a minor role in *Moscow Nights* in 1935. Another minor role in *Pygmalion* followed in 1938, after which he didn't appear before the cameras again until *Hamlet* in 1948, by which time he was also working as the manager of the Shakespeare Memorial Theatre Company, which he headed between 1948 and 1956. His film roles increased in stature during the 1950s, among them *The Battle for the River Plate* (1956) and Hitchcock's *The Wrong Man* (1956), in which he was surprisingly cast as the attorney Frank O'Connor. His film career now in full swing, Quayle's other credits went on to include *Woman in a Dressing Gown* (1957), *Ice Cold in Alex* (1958), *The Guns of Navarone* (1961), *Lawrence of Arabia* (1962), *The Fall of the Roman Empire* (1963), *Anne of the Thousand Days* (1969), *The Eagle Has Landed* (1976) and *Murder by Decree* (1979), while his television appearances included *The Strange Report* (1968, TV), *QB VII* (1974, TV) and the remake of Hitchcock's *Dial M for Murder* (1981, TV), in which he played Inspector Hubbard. An occasional novelist, his works include *Eight Hours from England* and *On Such a Night*, which were written during his experiences in World War II with the Royal Artillery, in which he reached the rank of major. His second wife was the American-born actress Dorothy Hyson (1914–1996, real name Dorothy Heisen), to whom he was married from 1947. **Hitchography:** *The Wrong Man* (1956)

R

RADFORD, BASIL (1897–1952) British actor On stage from the age of 25, Radford entered films in 1929 with *Barnum Was Right*, following which he appeared in the likes of *There Goes the Bride* (1932), *Broken Blossoms* (1936) and Hitchcock's *Young and Innocent* (1937), in which he played Nova Pilbeam's uncle in the tense birthday party scene. Radford worked for Hitchcock again the following year in *The Lady Vanishes*, in which he was partnered with Naunton Wayne (1901–1970) as the cricket-loving Englishmen Charters and Caldicott. An instant hit, they reprised the roles on radio and in two further films: *Night Train to Munich* (1940) and *Crook's Tours* (1941). In total, they went on to appear in 11 films together, among them *Dead of Night* (1945) and *It's Not Cricket* (1948). Radford's other films include *Quartet* (1948), *The Winslow Boy* (1948) and *The Galloping Major* (1951). Unlike Naunton Wayne, Radford truly was a cricket fanatic. Radford can also be spotted in a few brief scenes in Hitchcock's *Jamaica Inn* (1939), in which he played one of Sir Humphrey Pengallan's cronies. **Hitchography:** *Young and Innocent* (1937), *The Lady Vanishes* (1938), *Jamaica Inn* (1939)

RADIO Beginning in 1940 with *The Lodger*, a number of Hitchcock's more successful films were adapted for the radio in America, with several of the broadcasts featuring the original stars (or, sometimes, just stars generally associated with the director). The practice of adapting movies for the radio was commonplace throughout the 1940s and early 1950s, particularly on such programmes as *The Lux Radio Theatre*, *The Gulf Screen Guild Theatre* and *Academy Award Theatre*. This not only helped to promote the films themselves, but also kept contracted stars busy and in the public eye (ear?) when they were between making movies. Hitchcock's involvement in these broadcasts varied, from adapting and hosting *The Lodger* himself, to no involvement at all, save for the lure of his name. Some of the plays were broadcast several times with different casts, as was the case with *Rebecca*, *Mr and Mrs Smith* and *Shadow of a Doubt*. Also note that Hitchcock was to have hosted and supervised a series of mysteries titled *Once Upon a Midnight* in 1945, but the pilot episode, *Malice Aforethought*, was never broadcast, despite starring Jessica Tandy and Hume Cronyn.

The Lodger
Broadcast: 1940
Adaptation/host: Alfred Hitchcock
Music: Wilbur Hatch
Cast: Herbert Marshall, Edmund Gwenn, Lurene Tuttle

Rebecca
Broadcast: 1941
Cast: Ida Lupino, Ronald Colman

Mrs and Mrs Smith
Broadcast: 1941
Cast: Carole Lombard, Bob Hope

The Lady Vanishes
Broadcast: 1941
Cast: Flora Robson, Errol Flynn

Mr and Mrs Smith
Broadcast: 1942
Cast: Lana Turner, Errol Flynn

Rebecca
Broadcast: 1942
Cast: Herbert Marshall

Shadow of a Doubt
Broadcast: 1944
Cast: Teresa Wright, William Powell

Suspicion
Broadcast: 1944
Cast: Olivia De Havilland, William Powell

Mr and Mrs Smith
Broadcast: 1944
Cast: Victor Jory, Gertrude Warner, Betty Winkler

Rebecca
Broadcast: 1945
Cast: Victor Jory, Blanche Yurka, Gertrude Warner

Shadow of a Doubt
Broadcast: 1946
Cast: Brian Donlevy

Mr and Mrs Smith
Broadcast: 1946
Cast: Robert Montgomery

Foreign Correspondent
Broadcast: 1946
Cast: Joseph Cotten

The 39 Steps
Broadcast: 1946
Cast: David Niven

Rebecca
Broadcast: 1946
Cast: Joan Fontaine, Joseph Cotten

Suspicion
Broadcast: 1946
Cast: Cary Grant, Ann Todd

Notorious
Broadcast: 1948

Cast: Ingrid Bergman, Joseph Cotten, Gerald Mohr

Spellbound
Broadcast: 1948
Cast: Alida Valli, Joseph Cotten

Shadow of a Doubt
Broadcast: 1948
Cast: Joseph Cotten, Venessa Brown

Shadow of a Doubt
Broadcast: 1949
Cast: Ray Milland, Ann Blyth

The Paradine Case
Broadcast: 1949
Cast: Joseph Cotten

Rebecca
Broadcast: 1949
Cast: Audrey Totter

Mr and Mrs Smith
Broadcast: 1949
Cast: Robert Montgomery, Mary Jane Croft

Lifeboat
Broadcast: 1950
Cast: Tallulah Bankhead, Jeff Chandler, Sheldon Leonard

Rebecca
Broadcast: 1950
Cast: Laurence Olivier, Vivien Leigh

Spellbound
Broadcast: 1951
Cast: Joseph Cotten, Mercedes McCambridge

Shadow of a Doubt
Broadcast: 1952
Cast: Ann Blyth, Jeff Chandler

Rebecca
Broadcast: 1952
Cast: Melvyn Douglas

RAINS, CLAUDE (1889–1967, real name William Claude Rains) British-born actor. One of the screen's most charmingly sardonic stars, Rains began working in the theatre at the age of 11 as a call boy and eventually graduated to stage manager. He was taken under the wing of the legendary actor-manager Sir Herbert Beerbohm Tree, who encouraged him to turn his hand to acting. By 1911 Rains was touring Australia and, in 1914, America. Then in 1920, back home in England, he made his film debut in *Build Thy House*. By 1926 Rains was one of the Theatre Guild's leading actors, and in Hollywood in 1933 he made his 'official' film debut in *The Invisible Man*, in which he took the title

role, and although he was only seen for a few brief moments at the climax, the film turned him into a star. His subsequent films include such classics as *Anthony Adverse* (1936), *The Adventures of Robin Hood* (1938), *Mr Smith Goes to Washington* (1939), *The Wolf Man* (1941), *Casablanca* (1942) and *Mr Skeffington* (1944). In 1946, he appeared as the neo-Nazi Alexander Sebastian in Hitchcock's *Notorious*, though apparently the director's preferred choice for the role was Clifton Webb. At 5 feet 6 inches (168cm), Rains was somewhat shorter than the film's leading lady, Ingrid Bergman, about which Rains said: 'For *Notorious* I had to step up on a ramp to be near Miss Bergman. Every time the ramp was moved in, Mr Hitchcock would say, "There goes the shame of Rains."' [1]

Following *Notorious*, Rains went on to appear in *The Passionate Friends* (1947), *Lawrence of Arabia* (1962) and *The Greatest Story Ever Told* (1965). He also starred in five episodes of the *Alfred Hitchcock Presents* television series, one of which, *The Horseplayer* (1961, TV), was directed by Hitchcock. The first of Rains' six wives was the actress Isabel Jeans (1891–1985), to whom he was married between 1913 and 1918. She later appeared in three films for Hitchcock: *Downhill* (1927), *Easy Virtue* (1928) and *Suspicion* (1941). **Hitchography:** *Notorious* (1946), *And So Died Riabouchinska* (1956, TV), *The Cream of the Jest* (1957, TV), *The Diamond Necklace* (1959, TV), *The Horseplayer* (1961, TV), *The Door Without a Key* (1962, TV)

RANDOLPH, ELSIE (1901–1982, real name Elsie Florence Killick) British actress. A popular revue artist on the British stage in the 1930s, Randolph made her screen debut in Hitchcock's *Rich and Strange* (1932), in which she stole the film with her comic turn as an old maid whom the leading characters encounter on a cruise ship. Pleased with her performance, Hitchcock determined on using the actress again. However, she had to wait exactly *forty* years before being cast as Gladys, the snooty hotel receptionist at the Coburg Hotel in *Frenzy* (1972). Randolph's other infrequent screen credits include *That's a Good Girl* (1935), *This'll Make You Whistle* (1937) and *Charleston* (1977). **Hitchography:** *Rich and Strange* (1932), *Frenzy* (1972)

RANSFORD, MAURICE (1896–?) American art director. Long at Fox, Ransford began his career as an architect in the 1920s before turning to film design in the late 1930s. His many films include *The Pied Piper* (1942), *Panic in the Streets* (1950), *The Long, Hot Summer* (1958), and *Misty* (1960). One of his easier assignments was Hitchcock's *Lifeboat* (1944), which was set solely in the titular craft. Nevertheless, Ransford shared his screen credit with James Basevi. **Hitchography:** *Lifeboat* (1944)

RAPHAELSON, SAMSON (1896–1983) American playwright. Several of Raphaelson's works have been filmed, among them *Accent on Youth* and *Skylark*, although the most important of them was *The Jazz Singer*, which provided the basis for the screen's first talkie in 1927 (it was subsequently re-made in 1953 and 1980). Following this success, Raphaelson found himself in demand as a screenwriter, particularly by director Ernst Lubitsch, for whom he penned *The Smiling Lieutenant* (1931), *Trouble in Paradise* (1932) and *The Merry Widow* (1934). His other scripts include *The Last of Mrs Cheyney* (1937), *The Shop Around the Corner* (1940) and Hitchcock's *Suspicion* (1941), for which he provided the dialogue. **Hitchography:** *Suspicion* (1941)

RAYMOND, GENE (1908–1998, real name Raymond Guion) American actor. On stage from the age of 5 and on Broadway from the age of 12, Raymond turned to films in 1931 with *Personal Maid*. Long contracted to RKO, his films for the studio included *Flying Down to Rio* (1933), *Seven Keys to Baldpate* (1935) and Hitchcock's *Mr and Mrs Smith* (1941), in which he played Carole Lombard's 'boyfriend' Jeff Custer. Raymond's other films include *The Locket* (1946), *Million Dollar Weekend* (1948), which he also produced and directed, and *The Best Man* (1964). He was married to singing star Jeanette MacDonald (1901–1965) from 1937. **Hitchography:** *Mr and Mrs Smith* (1941)

Rear Window
(US, 1954, 107m, Technicolor) ****

CREDITS
Production company: Paramount
Producer: Alfred Hitchcock
Director: Alfred Hitchcock
Screenplay: John Michael Hayes, based on *It Had to Be Murder* by Cornell Woolrich (writing as William Irish)
Cinematographer: Robert Burks
Music: Franz Waxman
Editor: George Tomasini
Art directors: Hal Pereira, Joseph MacMillan Johnson
Costumes: Edith Head
Sound: Harry Lindren, John Cope, Loren L Ryder
Special effects: John P Fulton, Irmin Roberts
Assistant director: Herbert Coleman
Camera operators: William Schurr, Leonard J South

CAST
James Stewart (L B Jefferies), Grace Kelly (Lisa Carol Fremont), Thelma Ritter (Stella), Wendell Corey (Thomas J Doyle), Raymond Burr (Lars Thorworld), Irene Winston (Mrs Thorwald), Judith Evelyn ('Miss Lonelyhearts'), Georgine Darcy ('Miss Torso'), Ross Bagdasarian (Composer), Rand Harper, Mavis Davenport (Honeymooners), Frank Cady, Sara Berner (Couple with dog), Mike Mahoney (Cop), Anthony Warde (Detective)

Video availability: Universal
DVD availability: Universal
CD availability: *Hitchcock – Master of Mayhem* (Proarte), which contains a *Suite* comprising of *Prelude*, *Rhumba*, *Ballet* and *Finale*; *Psycho – The Essential Alfred Hitchcock* (Silva Screen), which contains the number *Lisa*

By the time he came to make *Rear Window* (1954), Hitchcock had already made three films set primarily in a single location: *Lifeboat* (1944), *Rope* (1948) and *Dial M for Murder* (1954). In each of these, he met the technical challenge of filming from such a confined viewpoint with variable effect. However, with *Rear Window*, which is set almost entirely within a New York apartment, he met the challenge with absolute mastery, revelling in the 'possibility of doing a purely cinematic film,' [2] as he put it.

The apartment belongs to *Life* photographer L B Jefferies (James Stewart), who is confined to a wheelchair, having broken his leg while on assignment. Bored with his situation, Jefferies finds himself idly gazing across the courtyard and into the homes of his neighbours to pass time, among them a composer, a voluptuous dancer whom he nicknames Miss Torso, a sculptress, a Miss Lonelyhearts, and a middle-aged couple who constantly seem to be bickering. Consequently, when the wife – an invalid confined to her bed – disappears, Jefferies begins to suspect that the husband, one Lars Thorwald (Raymond Burr), may have done away with her. Thus, with the help of his fiancée, fashion model Lisa Fremont (Grace Kelly), his day nurse, Stella (Thelma Ritter), and a policeman buddy, Thomas Doyle (Wendell Corey), Jefferies attempts to prove that Thorwald *has* indeed murdered his wife and disposed of the body.

Hitchcock based the film on the 1942 short story *It Had to Be Murder* by Cornell Woolrich (writing as William Irish), a screen treatment of which had already been prepared by the stage director Joshua Logan, who would go on to helm such films as *Picnic* (1956) and *Camelot* (1967). Logan had hoped to direct the film himself – at this stage in his career he had co-directed just one film, *I Met My Love Again* (1938) – but when this idea was nixed, he had to satisfy himself with the $15,000 he earned from selling the treatment (in total, Hitchcock paid $25,000 for the rights). Hitchcock then set to work on Logan's treatment with John Michael Hayes, a radio writer turned screenwriter whose work for the radio series *Suspense* had greatly impressed the director. The collaboration would prove to be fruitful, and Hayes would go on to write Hitchcock's next three films, too. Recalled Hayes of the writing process: 'We sat down in his office and he broke up all the scenes into individual shots, and made sketches of them, and laid out the picture.' [3]

Rear Window began filming on 27 November 1953. Hitchcock's first widescreen production, it was also his first film in a new nine-picture deal with Paramount (although he would ultimately make just six films for the studio). Art directors Hal Pereira and Joseph MacMillan Johnson built an entire courtyard inside Paramount's

The amazingly detailed courtyard set designed by Hal Pereira and Joseph MacMillan Johnson for Hitchcock's Rear Window (1954).

biggest soundstage. Comprising of over 30 individual apartments, each of these had to be lit, along with the courtyard itself, the skyline and the street that can be glimpsed through the alleyway. All this proved something of a headache for cinematographer Robert Burks, who used practically every lamp on the Paramount lot to achieve the required light levels. To save time during shooting, Burks pre-lit the entire set, which he could then fine tune for the requirements of each shot. Recalled Burks: 'I went on the soundstage about ten days prior to the starting date. Using a skeleton crew, we pre-lit every one of the 31 apartments for both day and night, as well as lit the exterior of the courtyard for the dual-type illumination required. A remote switch controlled the lights in each apartment. On the stage, we had a switching set up that looked like the console of the biggest organ ever made!' [4]

Perhaps more than most Hitchcocks, *Rear Window* is heavily reliant on script and performances as well as tech-

nique. To this end, the director couldn't have wished for a better cast to mouth the witty *bon mots* between the skillfully wrought thrills. James Stewart, with whom Hitchcock had already worked on *Rope* (1948), is utterly convincing as Jefferies, perfectly conveying his boredom at his inactivity; Grace Kelly never looked lovelier as Lisa, whose character Hayes based on his wife, herself a high-style fashion model; while Thelma Ritter's wisecracking Stella elicits every ounce of humour from the homespun philosophy she continually spouts. ('We've becomes a race of Peeping Toms,' she chides Jefferies, having caught him snooping on his neighbours. 'What people ought to do is get outside their own houses and look in for a change! How's *that* for philosophy?')

From the opening shot, it is absolutely clear that Hitchcock is completely in control of the film. Following the main titles, which play over the rising blinds of Jefferies' apartment window, Hitch treats us to a sweep of the courtyard and all its occupants. Commented Georgine

Darcy, aka Miss Torso, of the courtyard set: 'It was like a little village, with Mr Hitchcock playing with his dolls and placing them where he wanted them' [5]. The camera eventually comes to rest on Jefferies' sweating brow; it then moves on to take in his plaster-cast leg, on which is scrawled, 'Here lie the broken bones of L.B. Jefferies.' It then scans Jefferies' room, noting the camera broken in his accident and the framed action photos on his walls. Thus without a word being spoken, we know who Jefferies is, what he does for a living and how he came to break his leg – and all achieved through three carefully cut and composed shots. Said Hitchcock of the sequence: 'That's simply using cinematic means to relate a story.' [6]

Soon after, Jefferies begins to watch his neighbours, among them Miss Torso, who is exercising, Mr Thorwarld, who arrives home to his Shrewish wife, and a newly wed couple who have taken a hotel room, pulling down the blind as soon as the porter leaves. Comments Stella, who has arrived to give Jefferies his morning rub down: 'In the old days they used to put your eyes out with a red hot poker. Any of those bikini-clad bombshells you're always watchin' worth a red hot poker?' Through Stella we also learn about Jefferies' romance with Lisa and his reluctance to marry her: 'She's too perfect, she's too talented, she's too beautiful, she's too sophisticated, she's too everything but what I want,' he explains. That evening, as Jefferies dozes, we finally get to meet Lisa, who leans over him and, in extreme close-up, kisses him, in what has to be the screen's most perfectly photographed kiss. Responds Jefferies, 'Who are *you*?'

During the following exchanges between the two, we get to see more of Jefferies' neighbours, including Miss Loneleyhearts, who is serving dinner to herself, pretending that she has a gentleman caller, and Miss Torso, who is surrounded by men at a party she is throwing (comments Lisa, 'She's like the queen bee with the pick of the drones'). Said Hitchcock of the vignettes: '[They show] every kind of human behaviour… The picture would have been very dull if we hadn't done that. What you see across the way is a group of little stories that… mirror a small universe.' [7]

Later that night, once Lisa has gone, there is a scream, followed by a fade out. It is then that Jefferies' interest becomes genuinely aroused, for during a thunder storm he spies Thorwald go out with a suitcase at 1:55 am and not return until 2:35 am, after which he repeats the process. Could he be disposing of his wife's body? Convinced of this conclusion, he begins to watch Thorwald's apartment round the clock, using binoculars and a telephoto lens to gain a better view (said Hitchcock, 'Here we have a photographer who uses his camera equipment to pry into the back yard… I make it a rule to exploit elements that are connected with a character or location.' [8])

Having seen Thorwald wrap up a knife and a small saw in his kitchen, Jefferies now brings Stella in on the story. 'Why would a man leave his apartment three times on a rainy night with a suitcase and come back three times,' he asks, adding, 'Just how *would* you start to cut up a human body?' Equally intrigued, Lisa ponders why Thorwald's wife would leave her jewellery behind if, as has been suggested, she has simply gone away on a trip. Says Jefferies' policeman friend, whose advice the photographer has sought, 'That's a secret, private world you're looking into out there. People do a lot of things in private they couldn't possibly explain in public,' to which Lisa retorts, 'Like disposing of their wives?' However, when it looks like the trail has gone cold, Lisa perfectly sums up the situation for Jefferies: 'You know, if someone came in here, they wouldn't believe what they see! You and me with long faces, plunged into despair because we find out a man *didn't* kill his wife! We're two of the most frightening ghouls I've ever known!' At this stage in the proceedings, Lisa's comment would seem to apply equally to the audience, whose expectations have also been roused.

That night, there is a further scream. A couple's small dog has been strangled and left on the courtyard patio. The commotion brings out all the neighbours, and their shocked reactions to the crime are filmed in close-up, making this the only time the camera views the action from anywhere other than the point of view from Jefferies' apartment ('That was the only such scene,' [9] admitted Hitchcock). But one person hasn't come to his window: Lars Thorwald, whose presence is nevertheless noted by the cigarette glowing in his darkened window. Could he have killed the dog? And if so, why? Determined to get to the bottom of things, Jefferies eventually writes Thorwald a note, asking, 'What have you done with her?' Having persuaded Lisa to deliver it for him, he sees through his telephoto lens that the message has the desired effect. It would seem, after all, that Thorwald *does* have something to hide.

Having noted that the flowers in the courtyard bed have shrunk rather than grown, Jefferies surmises that perhaps parts of Mrs Thorwald are buried there, hence the reason for Thorwald disposing of the dog. To discover whether this is the case, Jefferies calls the murder suspect on the phone and sets up a meeting with him at the Albert Hotel. Believing he is about to be blackmailed, Thorwald agrees to the meeting, and while he is out, Lisa and Stella climb down to the courtyard with a spade to see if anything *is* buried under the azaleas. Finding nothing, Lisa rashly takes the opportunity to climb up the fire escape and into Thorwald's apartment, where she discovers Mrs Thorwald's wedding ring. Inevitably, Thorwald returns and finds the girl in his apartment. When things start to get rough, Jefferies calls the police, who arrive just in time. They arrest Lisa for breaking and entering, but before they take her away, Lisa turns her back to Jefferies and points to Mrs Thorwald's ring, which she has placed on her finger. Seeing what she is doing, Thorwald looks across the courtyard and puts two and two together, surmising that his blackmailer is just over the way!

Having sent Stella to bail out Lisa, Jefferies is left alone and vulnerable in the apartment, and as we suspect, it isn't long before Thorwald comes to pay a visit, his footsteps on the stairway heralding his imminent arrival. Writing instructions for his sound editor, Hitchcock advised that, 'The footsteps outside the door should clearly indicate the progression of the murderer. In other words, it should start with a faint door closing down below and the progression of the footsteps getting louder and louder... We should also get the effect of some caution on the part of the murderer as he comes up the stairs.' [10]

Once inside Jefferies' apartment, it quickly becomes clear that Thorwald's intentions are murderous, so again Jefferies uses the equipment of his trade to defend himself, blinding the approaching killer with his flashbulbs. To display the effect this has on him, Hitchcock shows us Thorwald's point of view, blurring it with a red filter (said Hitchcock, 'I would feel that I'd been remiss if I hadn't made maximum use of those elements' [11]). Unfortunately, the flash bulbs aren't enough to deter Thorwald, and in the ensuing fight, Jefferies finds himself being pushed from his window. To show Jefferies' fall to the ground, Hitchcock made effective use of a travelling matte, which involved photographing James Stewart lying against a black background and having the camera, shooting from overhead, quickly crane up; this shot was then combined with a shot of the courtyard taken from Jefferies' window, the result giving the very realistic impression that he is falling to the ground.

By this time the police have arrived, and all that is left to do is quickly wrap things up. 'Thorwald's ready to take us on a tour of the East River,' shouts a cop from Jefferies' window to his colleagues below, where Jefferies is being tended to by Lisa. The film then concludes as it began, with a sweep of the courtyard, where we now see that Miss Lonelyhearts is visiting the composer, the couple who lost their dog have acquired a new one, Miss Torso welcomes home a geeky-looking soldier who turns out to be her husband, and the newlyweds finally raise the blind of their hotel window. As before, the shot carries on into Jefferies' apartment, where it is revealed that he is now nursing *two* broken legs!

When it was released on 4 August 1954, *Rear Window* earned Hitchcock some of his best reviews yet, while its $5 million-plus gross ended his dry spell at the box office, making it the year's fifth most popular film. '*Rear Window* is one of the directorial masterpieces of recent years,' enthused *The Hollywood Reporter*, going on to praise Hitchcock's 'unsuspected flair for wisecracking comedy, particularly in the scenes where Miss Ritter and Corey make expert use of the bright dialogue in John Michael Hayes's screenplay.' Writing for the *New York Times*, Vincent Canby was equally taken, adding that the picture, 'Enchants us immediately, and need not be analyzed to death to achieve its place in the Pantheon.' Meanwhile, *Kine Weekly* described the film as 'fascinating and unique,' while *Variety* was impressed by the director's combination of 'artistic and technical skills' and Hayes' 'cleverly dialogued screenplay.' The Academy of Motion Pictures Arts and Sciences was also impressed, nominating the film in the best director, screenplay, sound and cinematography categories. Amazingly, the film didn't win a single Oscar, although John Michael Hayes did later pick up an Edgar Allan Poe Award from the Mystery Writers of America.

A brilliant combination of thrills and humour, *Rear Window* remains one of Hitchcock's key works, perfectly exploiting the fact that, to some extent, we're all *voyeurs*, even if only watching the actions of others on a cinema screen. Commented Michael Stragow in the *Boston Phoenix* upon the film's successful 1983 re-release: 'Hitchcock had already refined his use of subjective camera, putting the audience in the mind of the characters. In this film he pushes the technique to new heights. As our heroes gibe and quibble over the suspected murder (which we never see), we take refuge in the anonymity and safe distance of Jeff's flattening long lens – until the terrifying moment when Thorwald stares right back. It's an astonishing visual and psychological *coup*.'

Note that the film was the first of nine productions to be edited by George Tomasini who, like cinematographer Robert Burks and composer Bernard Herrmann, became one of Hitchcock's most valued collaborators during the 1950s and 1960s. The film was remade as a TV movie in 1998; elements from it can also be found in *Hi, Mom* (1969), *Sisters* (1973), *Someone's Watching Me* (1978, TV), *Body Double* (1984), *The Bedroom Window* (1986) and *What Lies Beneath* (2000).

Hitchcock cameo We see Hitchcock in his customary cameo, winding a clock in the composer's apartment during the collections of vignettes describing the lives of Jefferies' neighbours.

Rear Window
(US, 1998, 89m, colour, TVM)

CREDITS
Director: Jeff Bleckner
Screenplay: Larry Gross, Eric Overmeyer, from *It Had to Be Murder* by Cornell Woolrich (writing as William Irish)

CAST
Christopher Reeve (Jason Kemp), Daryl Hannah (Claudia Henderson), Ruben Santiago-Hudson (Antonio), Robert Forster (Detective Charlie Moore)

In this straightforward but otherwise passable TV movie remake, former Superman Christopher Reeve plays quadriplegic Jason Kemp who, like James Stewart's L B Jefferies before him, witnesses a murder from his apartment window. Naturally, no one believes his story at first, thus leaving Kemp defenceless when the killer comes to call ('Who's watching who?' ran the promotional strap line). Given extra resonance by the fact that Reeve is himself a quadriplegic following a tragic horse riding accident in 1995, this version of the story, though lacking the cinematic style of the Hitchcock original, is quite compelling in spots, particularly in the sequences in which Kemp has to defend himself from the killer by making use of all the high-tech gadgets he has at his disposal. For one scene, Reeve even insisted he be taken off his own respirator so as to achieve a realistic effect when the same thing happens to Kemp. Now that *is* devotion above and beyond the call of duty!

Rebecca
(US, 1940, 130m, bw) ★★★★

CREDITS

Production company:	Selznick International
Producer:	David O Selznick
Director:	Alfred Hitchcock
Screenplay:	Robert E Sherwood, Joan Harrison, Philip MacDonald, Michael Hogan, based on the novel by Daphne Du Maurier
Cinematographer:	George Barnes
Music:	Franz Waxman
Music director:	Lou Forbes
Editor:	Hal C Kern, James E Newcom
Art director:	Lyle Wheeler
Costumes:	Irene (un-credited)
Sound:	Jack Noyes
Special effects:	Jack Cosgrove, Arthur Johns

CAST

Laurence Olivier (Maxim de Winter) ('I'/the second Mrs de Winter), Joan Fontaine ('I'/the second Mrs de Winter), Judith Anderson (Mrs Danvers), George Sanders (Jack Flavell), Gladys Cooper (Beatrice Lacy), Nigel Bruce (Major Giles Lacy), C Aubrey Smith (Colonel Julyan), Melville Cooper (Coroner), Florence Bates (Mrs Van Hopper), Forrester Harvey (Chalcroft), Philip Winter (Robert), Lumsden Hare (Tabbs), Leonard Carey (Mad Ben), Leo G Carroll (Dr Baker), Reginald Denny (Frank Crawley), Billy Bevan (Policeman), Edward Fielding (Frith), Leyland Hodgson, Edith Sharpe

Video availability: Pearson
DVD availability: Pearson
CD availability: *Rebecca* (Marco Polo), *Psycho – The Essential Alfred Hitchcock* (Silva Screen), which contains a *Suite*, *Hitchcock – Master of Mayhem* (Proarte), which contains a *Suite*; and *A History of Hitchcock – Dial M for Murder* (Silva Screen) which contains a *Suite*, including *Prelude*, *After the Ball*, *Mrs Danvers*, *Confession Scene* and *Manderley in Flames*

Although he'd directed some classic films in Britain, among them *The Lodger* (1926), *The 39 Steps* (1935) and *The Lady Vanishes* (1938), Hitchcock's first Hollywood film leaves them standing for sheer professional gloss.

Hitchcock had long been hoping to make the move to America, and his agent, Myron Selznick, had fielded offers

from Paramount, MGM and RKO, the latter studio offering him the chance to direct *The Saint in New York* (which was later directed by Ben Holmes). However, it was an offer from Myron Selznick's brother, *Gone with the Wind* producer David O Selznick, which fully sparked Hitchcock's interest. The deal was a seven-year contract worth $40,000 per picture undertaken, beginning with a lavish account of the sinking of the *Titanic*, to be followed by an adaptation of Daphne Du Maurier's best selling 1938 novel *Rebecca* (the rights to which Hitchcock himself had tried to acquire during the making of *The Lady Vanishes*). As it turned out, the *Titanic* project fell by the wayside, and when Hitch finally moved out to America in April 1939, it was to concentrate fully on *Rebecca*.

Yet, despite being made in America, *Rebecca* could not have been more British. Commented Hitchcock: 'It's a completely British picture: the story, the actors and the director were all English. I've sometimes wondered what that picture would have been like had it been made in England with the same cast. I'm not sure I would have handled it in the same way. The American influence on it is obvious. First, because of Selznick, and then because the screenplay was written by the playwright Robert Sherwood, who gave it a broader viewpoint than it would have had if made in Britain.' [12]

As per Selznick's instructions, the script for *Rebecca* stuck as closely to the book as possible. Said the producer, 'It is my intention to do *Rebecca* and not some botched-up semi-original.' [13]

In it, a timid young woman (Joan Fontaine), working as a companion to a ghastly New York matron, Mrs Van Hopper (Florence Bates), meets and falls in love with a brooding Englishman, Maxim de Winter (Laurence Olivier), while holidaying in Monte Carlo with her employer. Accepting a proposal of marriage, the young woman returns to England with her new husband to his ancestral Cornish mansion Manderley, where, as the *second* Mrs de Winter, she finds herself living in the shadow of her much-admired predecessor, who died in a boating accident a year before.

The film opens with a portent of the drama to come. A young woman's voice (that of the heroine, never actually named and heretofore known as 'I') comments, 'Last night I dreamed I went to Manderley again,' at which the camera makes its way up a long, shadowy driveway to the ruins of the once-magnificent country house (the entire sequence was filmed with models at a cost of $25,000).

But this is to jump ahead, and the story quickly flashes back to the first meeting of 'I' and the brooding Maxim de Winter in Monte Carlo, he seemingly despondent over the death of his wife Rebecca some months before, and she in miserable servitude to the obnoxious Mrs Van Hopper ('Most girls would give their *eyes* for a chance to see Monte,' the old dragon chides her seemingly indifferent companion). Then, with Mrs Van Hopper out of the way with flu for a few days, the romance between Maxim and the young woman develops, 'I' accounting for her continued absence by telling her employer that she has

George Sanders makes an urgent call towards the end of Hitchcock's Rebecca *(1940). Although he shot it, the director cut his customary cameo appearance from the film, feeling that a laugh of recognition from the audience at this stage would ruin the tension he had carefully built up.*

been taking tennis lessons ('For the number of lessons you've had you ought to be ready for Wimbledon,' snipes old ma Hopper). Yet despite her growing love for him, 'I' never quite feels sure of herself in the presence of the mysterious Maxim.

Then comes the news that Mrs Van Hopper's daughter is to marry, and that she must travel back to America immediately to plan the wedding. Distraught at the thought of having to go to America, 'I' rushes to inform Maxim of her impending journey – a sequence which Hitchcock milks a good deal of tension from when she fails to locate him immediately – only to have her destiny forever altered by his proposal of marriage (note the microphone reflected in the top left-hand corner of the mirror in Maxim's hotel room during this exchange). Thus, having informed Mrs Van Hopper of her new plans ('Tell me, have you been doing anything you shouldn't?' enquires the old woman), 'I' and Maxim quickly wed and, following a brisk honeymoon, return to Manderley.

Yet despite her attempts to settle in as the new lady of the house, 'I' continually feels intimidated by the lingering presence of her predecessor, particularly as it seems that the housekeeper, the sinister Mrs Danvers (Judith Anderson), was and remains devoted to the first Mrs de Winter ('She absolutely *adored* Rebecca,' reveals Maxim's sister Beatrice (Gladys Cooper)). Indeed, this adoration – a lesbian obsession, it has been convincingly argued – is brilliantly put over in the scene in which Mrs Danvers shows 'I' Rebecca's vast bedroom. 'You've always wanted to see this room, haven't you?' asks Danvers, who proceeds to display her mistress' wardrobe. 'Feel this – it was a Christmas present from Mr de Winter,' she says of a mink coat. And then, 'I keep her underwear on this side. They were made specially for her by the nuns in the convent of St Chère.' Then, 'I embroidered this case for her myself and keep it here always.' And finally, with Rebecca's nightgown, 'Did you ever see anything so elegant? Look, you can see my hand through it…' at which 'I' makes a hasty exit from the room.

Despite this display of affection by Danvers for her former mistress (pretty near the knuckle for its day), when it is decided to revive the annual costume ball, 'I' fails to realize the housekeeper's sinister motives when she suggests that, for the occasion, the new Mrs de Winter has a dress made based on one of the portraits in the grand hall, which of course turns out to be exactly the same dress Rebecca wore at the previous ball ('*Rebecca!*' exclaims Beatrice upon seeing her sister-in-law in the dress, which Maxim orders her to change from before the rest of the guests arrive).

With 'I' upset and vulnerable, Mrs Danvers goes in for the kill, imploring her to jump from Rebecca's bedroom window. 'You're overwrought, madam. I've opened a window for you. A little air will do you good. Why don't you leave Manderley? He doesn't need you. He's got his memories. He doesn't love you. He wants to be alone again, with *her*. You've nothing to stay for. Nothing to live for, have you, really? Look down there. It's easy, isn't it? Why don't you? Go on. Go on. Don't be afraid.' However, Danvers' intentions are thwarted at the last moment by an exploding rocket signaling a wreck on the rocks in the bay beyond.

But the rescue effort churns up the past again, for a second wreck is found – the boat in which Rebecca met her end. And what's more, there is a woman's body inside it, which looks bad for Max, as he'd previously identified another body washed up on the shore some miles away as being that of his first wife. When it is revealed that the boat has been punctured with holes from the inside, an inquest is launched to discover how Rebecca truly met her end: an accident, suicide… or murder! Maxim is in no doubt. It's murder, for as he explains to his young wife, who wonders why he's sure, '*I* put the body there!' In fact it seems that Maxim was not as besotted with his first wife as we've been led to believe. 'You thought I loved Rebecca? You thought that? I *hated* her! Oh, I was carried away by her – enchanted by her, as everyone was. And when I was married, I was told I was the luckiest man in the world. She was so lovely, so accomplished, so amusing. "She's got the three things that matter in a wife," everyone said. "Breeding, brains and beauty." And I believed them completely. But I never had a moment's happiness with her. She was incapable of love, or tenderness, or decency.'

As it transpires, Maxim had an argument with Rebecca, who told him that she was pregnant by her cousin, car salesman Jack Flavell (George Sanders), who had been one of her many lovers (it turns out that Rebecca married Max purely for his money and that the couple were practically leading separate lives, with Rebecca maintaining things publicly for the sake of appearances). However, while goading Max further, telling him that it will be another man's son, and not his own, who will inherit Manderley, she slipped and fatally banged her head. In a panic, Max placed her body in the boat,

made the holes and pushed it out to sea, falsely identifying the body of another woman as that of his wife's when it conveniently washed up on shore.

Thus the scene is set for the inquest, during a break from which Flavell attempts to blackmail Maxim, informing him that he has in his possession a letter sent to him by Rebecca on the day that she died, the contents of which indicate that she wasn't remotely suicidal at the time. Flavell has also persuaded Mrs Danvers to testify against Maxim in court, prior to which she reveals that Rebecca had been seeing a Dr Baker in London. But a trip down to London by Flavell, Maxim, his estate manager Frank Crawley (Reginald Denny) and the local chief of police Colonel Julyan (C Aubrey Smith) to the doctor's office reveals that he is *not* the gynaecologist Flavell suspected Rebecca of seeing. Rather, the doctor was treating her for something far more serious: inoperable cancer ("The growth was deep-rooted…"). It seems, for appearances sake at least, Rebecca committed suicide after all.

With Maxim off the hook, he and Crawley drive back to Manderley, only to discover the mansion on fire ("That's not the dawn. It's Manderley!"). As "I" explains, at hearing the news of Rebecca's fatal illness via a phone call from Flavell, Mrs Danvers has finally gone mad and set the place alight, preferring to die in the home of her former mistress rather than see it pass on to the new Mrs de Winter, thus bringing to a close, *Jane Eyre*-style, one of the cinema's truly great romantic melodramas.

Filming on Rebecca began on 8 September 1939, just after the outbreak of World War II. Obviously, the war was much on Hitchcock's mind during shooting. In fact, many in the film community back in Britain felt that all nationals should return home, given the circumstances, and some even put their feelings in print, among them, surprisingly, Hitchcock's former producer Michael Balcon, who wrote scathingly: 'I had a plump young junior technician whom I promoted from department to department. Today he is one of our most famous directors and he is in Hollywood while we who are left behind short-handed are trying to harness the films to our great national effort.' [14]

Pre-production on *Rebecca*, as on most Selznick-produced films, had been a lengthy process. As early as September 1938, the script was under discussion, with Selznick suggesting as possible writers Ben Hecht, John Balderston and Clemence Dane (whose original script for Hitchcock's *Jamaica Inn* (19390 had been completely overhauled). Hitchcock meanwhile suggested Sidney Gilliat. Eventually, the director submitted an initial treatment worked on by himself, his secretary Joan Harrison (who was now also turning to screenwriting herself following her overhaul of *Jamaica Inn*) and Philip MacDonald, but this was rejected outright by Selznick, who found its quirky humour, which included scenes of sea sickness on an ocean voyage, 'cheap beyond words.' [15] In fact Selznick didn't mince words when communicating his disgust to Hitchcock. 'I regard it as a distorted and vulgarized version of a provenly successful work, in which, for no reason that I can discern, old fashioned movie scenes have been substituted for the captivatingly charming du Maurier scenes.' [16] Consequently, Selznick put playwright Robert Sherwood (*The Petrified Forest*, *Tovarich*) to work on the script, to give it a more professional sheen, and to rid it of Hitchcock's vulgarisms.

Thoughts were also turning to casting, with Ronald Colman, Leslie Howard and William Powell discussed for Maxim before Laurence Olivier was decided upon. At the time, Olivier was engaged to Vivien Leigh, who was then playing Scarlett O'Hara in Selznick's *Gone with the Wind* (1939). Leigh herself (whom Olivier would wed in 1940) was considered for the role of 'I' along with Anne Baxter (who would go on to work with Hitchcock on *I Confess* in 1953), Loretta Young, Margaret Sullavan and Olivia de Havilland, another *Gone with the Wind* alumnus. Instead, it was de Havilland's sister, Joan Fontaine, who finally, and rightly, took the role. It wasn't just the casting of people Selznick was concerned with, though. As his assistant Ray Klune recalled, 'David felt that Manderley was almost as important a character in *Rebecca* as any of the people... It was almost a living thing...' [17]

The shooting schedule for *Rebecca* was originally five weeks, but this almost doubled to nine. Longer, in fact, if one takes into consideration Selznick's penchant for retakes, which helped to push the film's budget from $767,000 to a then-whopping $1,280,000. The time and expense lavished upon the film were worth it, as the critics almost unanimously agreed. 'Alfred Hitchcock pilots his first American production with capable assurance and exceptional understanding of the motivation and story mood,' enthused *Variety*, continuing, 'Despite the psychological and moody aspects of the tale throughout its major footage, he highlights the piece with several intriguing passages that display inspired direction.' *The National Board of Review* agreed, describing the direction as, 'a masterly exhibition of the Hitchcock skill in creating suspense and shock with his action and his camera.'

Indeed, the mobile, chiaroscuro camerawork of cinematographer George Barnes cannot be underestimated when discussing the film's visual qualities, nor can Lyle Wheeler's sumptuous art direction, his brightly lit Riviera salons and hotel rooms contrasting sharply and effectively with the baronial gloom of Manderley. Franz Waxman's masterful score, with its haunting central theme and its eerie organ leitmotif played whenever Rebecca's name is mentioned, is also a major contribution to the film's impact. In fact, *Rebecca* was Hitchcock's first fully scored film (although *The 39 Steps* and *The Lady Vanishes* had contained a couple of jaunty tunes intrinsic to their plots, they almost completely lacked an accompanying score, as did all of Hitchcock's other early British films).

The performances in *Rebecca* are also perfect, from Olivier's guilt-ridden Maxim and Fontaine's cardigan-clad 'I' ('I can see by the way you dress you don't give a hoot,' comments Beatrice), through to Anderson's spiteful Mrs Danvers and Sanders' caddish Flavell ('I'd like to have your advice on how to live comfortably without hard work,' he says to Maxim, by way of blackmailing him). The script,

meanwhile, bristles with humour (the opening scenes with the dreadful Mrs Van Hopper are delightful), while Hitchcock's direction is never less than masterful.

Though by no means a typical Hitchcock picture, there are plenty of his touches on display, among them Mrs Van Hopper's stubbing out a cigarette in a jar of cold cream; the lap dog patiently waiting outside Rebecca's bedroom door for the mistress who will never return; the chest-high door handles in Manderley that serve to make 'I' seem even more insignificant; Mrs Danvers' penchant for suddenly appearing in a room ('Mrs Danvers was almost never seen walking and was rarely show in motion,' [18] said Hitchcock); and the final dolly across Rebecca's burning bedroom, the camera coming to rest on the embroidered R on her pillow.

A major commercial success, *Rebecca* went on to become the most successful film of 1940, earning $2.5 million in its first year of release. It also garnered an impressive 11 Oscar nominations, for best picture (Selznick), best director (Hitchcock), best screenplay (Robert E Sherwood, Joan Harrison), best music (Franz Waxman), best cinematography (George Barnes), best actor (Olivier), best actress (Fontaine), best supporting actress (Judith Anderson), best art direction (Lyle Wheeler), best special effects (Jack Cosgrove, Arthur Johns) and best editing (Hal C Kern). The film went on to win two of the awards: best cinematography and the much coveted best picture, making it two in a row for Selznick, who'd won the same award the previous year for *Gone with the Wind*. Hitchcock came away empty handed, but at least his talents had been recognized by the Academy. The best director award instead went to John Ford for *The Grapes of Wrath*.

Though the film has yet to be remade for the cinema, there have been three subsequent television versions of Du Maurier's book, which appeared in 1962, 1978 and 1997 (some sources claim a TV version also appeared as early as 1948); the film version was also adapted for radio in 1941, 1942, 1945, 1946, 1949, 1950 and 1952.

Hitchcock cameo Though filmed, Hitchcock's by now customary cameo appearance was cut from the final print of the film (he was to have been spotted standing by a telephone box towards the end of the film as Flavell makes a call to Mrs Danvers, but he removed the scene, feeling that a 'laugh of recognition' [19] from the audience at this point would destroy the tension he'd been building).

Rebecca
(US, 1962, 90m, bw)

CAST
James Mason (Maxim de Winter), Anna Massey ('I'/the second Mrs de Winter)

The first of three television versions of Du Maurier's much-loved novel, this adaptation starred James Mason as Maxim de Winter and Anna Massey as the second Mrs de

Winter. Interestingly, Massey would go on to play Mrs Danvers in the 1978 version. She would also appear in Hitchcock's *Frenzy* (1972); while Mason had co-starred in Hitchcock's *North by Northwest* (1959).

Rebecca

(GB, 1978, 3x50m episodes, colour TV)

CREDITS

Production company: BBC
Producer: Richard Beynon
Director: Simon Langton
Screenplay: Hugh Whitemore, based on the novel by Daphne Du Maurier

CAST

Jeremy Brett (Maxim de Winter), Joanna David ('I'/the second Mrs de Winter), Anna Massey (Mrs Danvers)

In this second, lavishly produced version of the story, Anna Massey graduates from playing the second Mrs de Winter, as she had done in the 1962 version, to the evil Mrs Danvers. Writing in the *Sunday Telegraph*, critic Philip Purser commented: 'Who would have thought of Anna Massey, an ingénue only yesterday, as the sinister Mrs Danvers? Richard Beynon or Simon Langton did, and she's great.' Though a ratings success, it nevertheless pales besides Hitchcock's version.

Rebecca

(GB, 1997, 96m, colour TV)

CREDITS

Production Company: Carlton

CAST

Charles Dance (Maxim de Winter), Diana Rigg (Mrs Danvers)

In this, the most recent adaptation of Du Maurier's novel, Maxim de Winter is played by Charles Dance, while the role of Mrs Danvers is portrayed by the highly respected Diana Rigg, who does her best to add a touch of malevolence to the proceedings. Nevertheless, despite her presence and an adequate production, the film again lacks the style and atmosphere of the Hitchcock version.

REDGRAVE, SIR MICHAEL (1908–1985) British actor. A former schoolteacher, Redgrave turned to the stage in 1934. He entered films in 1936 with a small, uncredited role in Hitchcock's *Secret Agent* as an army captain. He obviously made an impression on the director, for two years later he was elevated to leading man status in *The Lady Vanishes*, the success of which launched his career. He subsequently went on to star in *The Stars Look Down* (1939), *Kipps* (1940), *Dead of Night* (1945), *Mourning Becomes Electra* (1947), which earned him an Oscar nomi-

nation for best actor, *The Importance of Being Earnest* (1952), *The Dam Busters* (1954) and *Goodbye, Mr Chips* (1969). Recalled Redgrave of *The Lady Vanishes*: 'I respected Hitchcock's professionalism, yet secretly saw little to praise in it.' [20] Long married to actress Rachel Kempson (1910–), all of Redgrave's children – Vanessa (1937–), Corin (1939–) and Lynn (1943–) – turned to acting. He was knighted in 1959. **Hitchography:** *Secret Agent* (1936), *The Lady Vanishes* (1938)

Michael Redgrave's Gilbert Redman discusses the missing Miss Froy with the cricket-loving Englishmen Charters and Caldicott (played by Basil Radford, left, and Naunton Wayne, centre) in Hitchcock's much-loved The Lady Vanishes *(1938).*

REDMOND, MARGE American supporting actress. Redmond appeared in Hitchcock's last film *Family Plot* (1976) as Vera Hannagan. Her other films include *Sanctuary* (1961), *The Fortune Cookie* (1966), *The Trygon Factor* (1969) and *Adam at 6am* (1970). **Hitchography:** *Family Plot* (1976)

REMAKES There have been a number of remakes of Hitchcock's films, although not too surprisingly, none of them match the originals. Indeed, only a couple – *The Thirty-Nine Steps* (1978) and *A Perfect Murder* (1998), a remake of *Dial M for Murder* (1954) – come close to their predecessors. It is generally assumed that Hitchcock himself remade only one of his own films, *The Man Who Knew Too Much* (1956), which he had previously filmed in 1934. This is entirely true, though one could argue that *Saboteur* (1942) and *North by Northwest* (1959) are little more than remakes of *The 39 Steps* (1935). However, Hitchcock was involved in four other remakes of previously filmed dramas: these were *Always Tell Your Wife* (1922), which had been filmed in 1914; *The Manxman* (1929), which had been filmed in 1916; *The*

Skin Game (1931), which had been filmed in 1920; and *Number Seventeen*, which had been filmed in Germany in 1928. One could also argue that both *Dial M for Murder* (1954) and *The Wrong Man* (1956) are remakes, given that both had been broadcast on television before Hitchcock turned them into films. Also see Homages.

The list of Hitchcock remakes is:

Woman to Woman (1923) as *Woman to Woman* (1929 and 1946)

The Lodger (1926) as *The Lodger* (1932 and 1944) and *The Man in the Attic* (1953)

The Farmer's Wife (1928) as *The Farmer's Wife* (1940)

The Man Who Knew Too Much (1934) as *The Man Who Knew Too Much* (1956)

The 39 Steps (1935) as *The Thirty-Nine Steps* (1959 and 1978)

Sabotage (1936) as *The Secret Agent* (1996)

The Lady Vanishes (1938) as *The Lady Vanishes* (1979)

Jamaica Inn (1939) as *Jamaica Inn* (1983, TV)

Rebecca (1940) as *Rebecca* (1962, TV, 1978, TV and 1997, TV)

Suspicion (1941) as *Suspicion* (1987, TV)

Shadow of a Doubt (1943) as *Step Down to Terror* (1958) and *Shadow of a Doubt* (1991, TV)

Lifeboat (1944) as *Lifepod* (1993, TV)

Notorious (1946) as *Notorious* (1992, TV)

Rope (1948) as *Compulsion* (1959) and *Swoon* (1992)

Under Capricorn (1949) as *Under Capricorn* (1982, TV)

Strangers on a Train (1951) as *Once You Kiss a Stranger* (1969), *Throw Momma from the Train* (1987) and *Once You Meet a Stranger* (1996)

Dial M for Murder (1954) *The Fifth Stair* (episode of *77, Sunset Strip,* 1958–63, TV) as *Dial M for Murder* (1981, TV), *Aitbaar* (1985) and *A Perfect Murder* (1998)

Rear Window (1954) as *Rear Window* (1998, TV)

Psycho (1960) as *Psycho* (1998)

RENAVENT GEORGE(S) (1894–1969, real name Georges de Cheux) French-born character actor. Renavent moved to Hollywood in the late 1920s, where he carved out a career as a supporting actor in the likes of *Rio Rita* (1929), *Whipsaw* (1935) and Hitchcock's *Strangers on a Train* (1951), in which he played the almost irrelevant role of Monsieur Darville. **Hitchography:** *Strangers on a Train* (1951)

REVILLE, ALMA (1900–1982) British-born editor and screenwriter. Both Hitchcock's wife and his longest-serving and most valuable collaborator, British-born Reville began her film career at the age of 15 at Twickenham Film Studios, working as an assistant editor (rewind girl) and continuity girl (script girl) on such films as the first version of *The Prisoner of Zenda* (1915) also known as *Rupert of Hentzau.* Reville went to work for Islington Studios as a cutter in 1920, where she first became aware of Hitchcock's presence about the lot, at which point he was one of the studio's lowly graphic artists, providing films with their inter-titles. However, they did not work together until the making of *Woman to Woman* three years later,

Hitchcock and his beloved wife and collaborator Alma Reville arrive in France for the filming of To Catch a Thief *(1955). Hitchcock did nothing without her approval.*

on which Hitchcock had by then graduated to screen-writer, art director and assistant director; Alma was the continuity girl and editor. Revealed Reville: 'Since it is unthinkable for a British male to admit that a woman has a job more important than his, Hitch had waited to speak to me until he had a higher position.' [21]

Alma and Hitch continued to work together on such films as *The White Shadow* (1924), *The Passionate Adventure* (1924), *The Prude's Fall* (1925) and *The Blackguard* (1925), all of which, like *Woman to Woman,* were directed by Graham Cutts. Hitchcock and Reville became engaged during the production of *The Blackguard,* after which Hitch got his chance to make his official debut as a director with *The Pleasure Garden* (1925). Again, Alma was by his side as assistant director and continuity girl, as she was on his following film, *The Mountain Eagle* (1925). The couple married at Brompton Oratory on 2 December 1926 following the completion of Hitchcock's third film, *The Lodger* (1926), which was acclaimed following its delayed release in 1927.

Reville continued to assist her husband on his following films, contributing – un-credited – to the screenplay of *The Ring* (1927). She also worked for others too, co-scripting *The Constant Nymph* (1928) for director Adrian Brunel. However, she took a sabbatical from Hitchcock's next film, *The Farmer's Wife* (1928), so as to give birth to their only child, Patricia (Pat), who was born on 7 July 1928.

While Alma looked after Pat, she continued to help and advise her husband with his scripts, and she was recognized for her contributions to *Juno and the Paycock* (1930), *Murder!* (1930), *The Skin Game* (1931), *Number Seventeen* (1932), *Rich and Strange* (1932) and *Waltzes from*

Vienna (1933). She also worked on the continuity for *The 39 Steps* (1935), *Secret Agent* (1936), *Sabotage* (1936), *Young and Innocent* (1937), *The Lady Vanishes* (1938) and *Jamaica Inn* (1939). She even found time to work on such non-Hitchcock scripts as *The Passing of the Third Floor Back* (1935) during this period, which was produced by Ivor Montague, who had produced several of Hitchcock's 1930s' hits, including *The 39 Steps* (1935) and *Sabotage* (1936).

Once in Hollywood, Reville continued to contribute to her husband's films, either as a behind the scenes advisor or as a screenwriter, as was the case with *Suspicion* (1941), *Shadow of a Doubt* (1943) and *The Paradine Case* (1947), as well as the British-filmed *Stage Fright* (1950). She also continued to work on non-Hitchcock projects, among them *It's in the Bag* (1945), which she co-wrote. Her screenplay credits thinned out in the 1950s, although she did plot out – un-credited – the Corniche car chase in *To Catch a Thief* (1955) for Hitchcock. She also remained fully involved in every step of her husband's films (apparently, just before *Psycho* (1960) was shipped out, Reville spotted a couple of frames of Janet Leigh gulping after the shower murder, which were subsequently trimmed from the print). Commented Patricia Hitchcock, 'She was in on it all the way along.' [22] Added screenwriter Jay Presson Allen, who wrote *Marnie* (1964) for Hitchcock, '[Alma] was extremely smart and extremely knowledgeable about film.' [23]

Indeed, when Hitchcock accepted his Lifetime Achievement award from the American Film Institute in 1979, he dedicated the award to her. His speech ran: 'I beg permission to mention by name only four people who have given me the most affection, appreciation and encouragement, and constant collaboration. The first of the four is a film editor, the second is a script writer, the third is mother of my daughter, Pat, and the fourth is as fine a cook as ever performed miracles in a domestic kitchen, and their names are Alma Reville. Had the beautiful Miss Reville not accepted a lifetime contract, without options, as Mrs Alfred Hitchcock some 53 years ago, Mr Alfred Hitchcock might be in this room tonight – not at this table, but as one of the *slower* waiters on the floor. I share this award, as I have my life, with her.' [24]

Reville's health began to decline in the 1970s, and she suffered a minor stroke during the production of *Frenzy* (1972). Nevertheless, she survived her beloved husband by two years. **Hitchography:** *Woman to Woman* (1923), *The White Shadow* (1924), *The Passionate Adventure* (1924), *The Prude's Fall* (1925), *The Blackguard* (1925), *The Pleasure Garden* (1925), *The Mountain Eagle* (1925), *The Lodger* (1926), *The Ring* (1927), *Juno and the Paycock* (1930), *Murder!* (1930), *The Skin Game* (1931), *Number Seventeen* (1932), *Rich and Strange* (1932), *Waltzes from Vienna* (1933), *The 39 Steps* (1935), *Secret Agent* (1936), *Sabotage* (1936), *Young and Innocent* (1937), *The Lady Vanishes* (1938), *Jamaica Inn* (1931), *Suspicion* (1941), *Shadow of a Doubt* (1943), *The Paradine Case* (1947), *Stage Fright* (1950), *To Catch a Thief* (1955)

REYNDERS, JOHN British composer and conductor. Reynders worked on a handful of Hitchcock's early British sound films, most notably *Blackmail* (1929), for which he conducted the rather grandly titled British International Symphony Orchestra through Campbell and Connely's score. He also conducted several numbers for the musical revues *Harmony Heaven* and *Elstree Calling* (both 1930). **Hitchoghraphy:** *Blackmail* (1929), *Harmony Heaven* (1930), *Elstree Calling* (1930), *Murder!* (1930) *Mary* (1930), *Rich and Strange* (1932)

Rich and Strange

(GB, 1932, 83m (some sources state 87m), bw) ★

CREDITS

Production company:	British International Pictures
Producer:	John Maxwell
Director:	Alfred Hitchcock
Screenplay:	Alfred Hitchcock, Val Valentine, Alma Reville, based on the novel by Dale Collins
Cinematographer:	Jack Cox
2nd unit photographer:	Charles Martin
Music:	Hal Dolphe
Music director:	John Reynders
Editor:	Winifred Cooper, Rene Marrison
Art director:	Wilfred Arnold
Sound:	Alec Murray
Assistant director:	Frank Mills

CAST

Henry Kendall (Fred Hill), Joan Barry (Emily Hill), Betty Amann (Princess), Percy Marmont (Commander Gordon), Elsie Randolph (Old Maid), Hannah Jones (MrsPorter), Aubrey Dexter (Colonel), Billy Shine (Passenger)

Another curiosity from Hitchcock's early British period, this mildly entertaining comedy drama sees a married couple, Fred and Emily Hill (Henry Kendall and Joan Barry), suddenly come into money, which they use to travel the world in a bid to escape the suburban lives they are so discontent with. However, after a series of misadventures, among them romantic infidelities and a shipwreck, they finally come to the conclusion that there's no place like home.

The film's opening sequences, which depict the dull routine of Fred's office life, are inventively handled. So is the later shipwreck and the couple's subsequent attempts to get back home, which involve them being rescued by a passing Chinese junk, on which they are unwittingly fed the black cat they retrieved from the wreck (unwittingly, that is, until they see its skin being nailed out to dry by one of the crew!). In between, though, the couple's adventures onboard their cruise ship and in Paris tend to drag save for an excellent comic cameo by Elsie Randolph as an old maid whom they encounter on the voyage

(Hitchcock enjoyed working with Randolph so much he used her again in *Frenzy* – exactly *forty* years later!).

Rich and Strange made little headway at the box office, and the usually generous critics were less forthcoming with their praise this time, with *Variety* commenting that Hitchcock 'usually gets a rave as his pictures take the screen. Here's one where the admirers will have difficulty knowing what to say.' Meanwhile, present day viewers may balk at some of the xenophobic comments that spout forth from the hero ('Why, these damn Chinese breed like rabbits,' he observes after a woman gives birth in poor conditions on board the junk).

RICHARDS, ADDISON (1887–1964) American supporting actor. With some 200 credits to his name, Richards was one of Hollywood's busiest supporting artists, clocking up 20 appearances in 1939 alone. Following stage experience in Pasadena, he began his movie career in 1933 with *Lone Cowboy*, and went on to appear in *Ceiling Zero* (1935), *Boys' Town* (1938), *A Guy Named Joe* (1943), *The Courage of Lassie* (1946), *Last of the Badmen* (1957) and *For Those Who Think Young* (1964). He can also be spotted making an un-credited appearance in Hitchcock's *Spellbound* (1945) as the police captain. Also busy on television, Richards' work includes such series as *Fibber McGee* (1959) and *Cimarron City* (1958–1960). **Hitchography:** *Spellbound* (1945)

RIGBY, EDWARD (1879–1951, real name Edward Coke) British actor. Following experience as a farmer, Rigby turned to theatre and films, making his movie debut in 1907 with *The Man Who Fell by the Way*. Later in life he became one of Britain's most reliable character stars, specializing in old duffers, among them Old Will the China Mender in Hitchcock's *Young and Innocent* (1937). His many other films include *No Limit* (1935), *A Yank at Oxford* (1937), *A Canterbury Tale* (1944), *Don't Take it to Heart* (1944) and *The Happiest Days of Your Life* (1950), in which he played the hapless school caretaker, forever raising and dismantling the rugby posts. **Hitchography:** *Young and Innocent* (1937)

RIGGS, RITA American costume designer. Along with fellow costumier Helen Colvig, Riggs made her film debut with Hitchcock's *Psycho* (1960), prior to which they both worked on the director's TV series *Alfred Hitchcock Presents*, for which Riggs costumed Hitchcock's introductory cameos. Following *Psycho*, Riggs went on to assist costume designer Edith Head on two further Hitchcock projects, following which she went on to work on *Seconds* (1965), *Night Moves* (1975), *Yes, Giorgio* (1981) and *Mr North* (1987). Recalled Riggs of working with the Master: 'The real difference working with Hitchcock and his circle was that you had an entire, cohesive picture laid out before you on storyboards... You knew every angle in the picture, so there was not a lot of time wasted in talking an idea to death. We also didn't have to waste time worrying about things like shoes, for instance, because we knew he wasn't going to show them in the shot.' [25] **Hitchography:** *Alfred Hitchcock Presents* (1955–1962), *Psycho* (1960), *The Alfred Hitchcock Hour* (1962–1965), *The Birds* (1963), *Marnie* (1964)

RILLA, WALTER (1894–1980) German-born character actor. Busy in both Britain and Germany, this artist tended to major in sinister parts, among them the title role in *The Blackguard* (1925) on which the young Hitchcock worked as an assistant director and art director. His other films include *The Scarlet Pimpernel* (1934), *State Secret* (1950) and *The Testament of Dr Mabuse* (1962). His son, Wolf Rilla (1920–), directed such films as *Village of the Damned* (1960), *Piccadilly Third Stop* (1960) and *Cairo* (1963), the latter featuring an appearance by his father. **Hitchography:** *The Blackguard* (1925)

The Ring

(GB, 1927, 72m (some sources state 73m, 110m and 116m), bw, silent) ★

CREDITS

Production Company:	British International Pictures
Producer:	John Maxwell
Director:	Alfred Hitchcock
Screenplay:	Alfred Hitchcock, Eliot Stannard (Alma Reville, un-credited)
Cinematographer:	John (Jack) Cox
Art director:	C W Arnold
Assistant director:	Frank Mills
Continuity:	Alma Reville

CAST

Carl Brisson ('One Round' Jack Sander), Ian Hunter (Bill Corby), Lillian Hall-Davies (Mabel), Gordon Harker (Trainer), Forrester Harvey (Promoter), Harry Terry (Showman), Billy Wells (Boxer), Clare Greet (Gypsy)

In this love triangle drama penned by Hitchcock and Eliot Stannard (with un-credited assistance from Hitchcock's wife, Alma Reville), sideshow boxer 'One Round' Jack Sander (Carl Brisson) and an up-coming Australian fighter known as Bob Corby (Ian Hunter) fight it out in the ring for the affections of a ticket girl named Mabel (Lillian Hall-Davies). The story itself may not be too original, yet Hitchcock packed his film with enough incidental detail to make it intermittently very exciting. 'Challenges comparison with the best that America can produce,' enthused the *Daily Herald* of Hitchcock's labours, while *The Bioscope* claimed that the production was 'the most magnificent British film ever made.'

Among the more memorable sequences are a montage of 18 camera dissolves in the opening fun fair sequence, and the two fights that top and tail the film; the first in a cramped sideshow tent, the second in the cavernous Royal Albert Hall. Commented cinematographer Jack

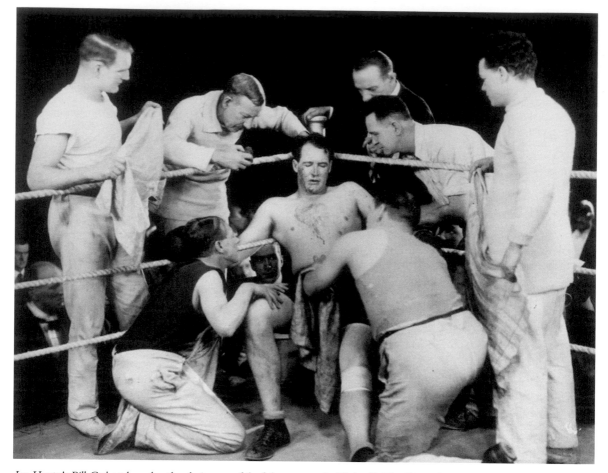

Ian Hunter's Bill Corby takes a breather during one of the fight sequences in Hitchcock's The Ring *(1927). The still was taken by future British cinematographer Eric Cross, who would go on to photograph such films as* The Bells *(1931)* and Private's Progress *(1956).*

Cox of the complex sequence of dissolves, which were achieved 'in camera': 'I sweated blood over that day's work and didn't sleep at all that night. But when they saw the rushes the next day, everything was the white-headed boy.' [26] The effort was worth it, as Hitchcock later recalled: 'At the premiere [that] elaborate montage got a round of applause. It was the first time that had ever happened to me.' [27]

Sleight of hand helped to produce a thrilling climax to the Albert Hall fight. Hitchcock instructed actor Carl Brisson (a real life Danish boxer) to attack his opponent, Ian Hunter, for real in the closing round. Recalled Hitchcock: '[Brisson] launched a blow at Hunter's body. Hunter caught his breath with a gulp… He swayed, tottered, sat down. He was congratulated on a brilliant piece of acting. I got some kudos for a good piece of direction. Actually, neither of us deserved any credit. I was not directing. Hunter was not acting. He really *was* out.' [28]

The film was a first for several reasons. It was the first of several films Hitchcock made for BIP (British International Pictures), which was based at Elstree Studios.

It also marked the first time he worked with producer John Maxwell (the owner of BIP) and cinematographer Jack Cox, who would film a total of 11 pictures for Hitchcock (Cox replaced Hitchcock's previous cinematographer, Claude L McDonnell, who left the film following a disagreement over financial terms). Character star Gordon Harker also made his film debut in the production as a wily trainer, his success as which led to several more pictures with Hitchcock.

RITCHARD, CYRIL (1896–1977) Australian-born stage actor. This song-and-dance man in the Jack Buchanan tradition rose to success on the London stage in the late 1920s, which led to a short-term contract with British International Pictures, for which he appeared in *Piccadilly* (1929) and, more importantly, Hitchcock's talkie debut *Blackmail* (1929), in which he played the artist Crewe, who is stabbed to death after attempting to rape shop girl Alice White (Anny Ondra). In the seduction scene, Hitchcock allowed Ritchard to display his song and dance abilities by performing snatches of his then hit song

Miss Up-to-Date at the piano. Ritchard later went to America, where he was equally successful on stage. His few other films include *I See Ice* (1937) and *Half a Sixpence* (1968), in which he re-created his stage role of Harry Chitterlow. **Hitchography:** *Blackmail* (1929)

RITTA, THELMA (1905–1965) American comedy actress. This sharp-talking star made her way into films with *Miracle on 34th Street* in 1947 following experience on stage and in radio. She went on to be nominated for the best supporting actress Oscar an incredible six times, for *All About Eve* (1950), *The Mating Season* (1951), *With a Song in My Heart* (1952), *Pickup on South Street* (1953), *Pillow Talk* (1959) and *Birdman of Alcatraz* (1962). One of her very best roles was as the wisecracking Stella in Hitchcock's *Rear Window* (1954). Guessing how a suspected killer disposed of his wife's body, she asks, 'Just where do you suppose he cut her up?' before going on to answer her own question with, 'Of course! The bathtub! It's the only place he could have washed away the blood,' to which she adds, 'He'd better take that trunk away before it starts to leak!' Ritter's other films include *A Letter to Three Wives* (1949), *Titanic* (1953), *The Misfits* (1961) and *What's So Bad About Feeling Good?* (1968). She also appeared in an episode of *Alfred Hitchcock Presents*. **Hitchography:** *Rear Window* (1954), *The Baby Sitter* (1956, TV)

RIVAS, CARLOS Hispanic supporting actor. Rivas has popped up in several films, including *The Beast of Hollow Mountain* (1956), *The King and I* (1956), *The Black Scorpion* (1957), *The Deerslayer* (1957) and Hitchcock's *Topaz* (1969), in which he played Hernandez. **Hitchography:** *Topaz* (1969)

ROBERTS, IRMIN American special effects technician. Roberts won an Oscar for his work on *Spawn of the North* (1938). He also worked on the visual effects for Hitchcock's *Rear Window* (1954). **Hitchography:** *Rear Window* (1954)

ROBERTSON, JOHN S (1878–1964) Canadian-born director. Robertson began his film career as an actor in 1915, but turned to direction in 1917 with *Intrigue*, which he followed with the likes of *Little Miss Hoover* (1918), *Here Comes the Bride* (1919) and, most importantly, *Dr Jekyll and Mr Hyde* (1920), starring John Barrymore. In 1922 he was hired by Famous Players-Lasky to helm two films at their London studio (which he co-directed with Tom Geraghty), for which Hitchcock provided the inter-titles. Back in Hollywood, Robertson directed *Tess of the Storm Country* (1922) starring Mary Pickford, *The Fighting Blade* (1923) and *The Road to Romance* (1927). His sound films included *Little Orphan Annie* (1932), *Wednesday's Child* (1934) and *Our Little Girl* (1935) starring Shirley Temple. **Hitchography:** *Perpetua* (1922), *The Spanish Jade* (1922)

ROBERTSON, PEGGY (? –1998) British-born editor-continuity girl. Robertson went on to be Hitchcock's long-time personal assistant following her work on *Under Capricorn* (1949) as a continuity girl (when she was known by her maiden name, Peggy Singer). She moved to America in the late 1950s with her husband and rejoined Hitchcock on *Vertigo* (1958), after which she remained with him throughout the rest of his career, during which she was never far from his side. Recalled Robertson: 'Hitchcock was very organized and very particular. We would often try to keep his name out of preliminary casting, because once an agent learned he was dealing with Hitchcock, the actor's price would begin to climb.' [29] **Hitchography:** *Under Capricorn* (1949), *Stage Fright* (1950), *Vertigo* (1958), *North by Northwest* (1959), *Psycho* (1960), *The Birds* (1963), *Marnie* (1964), *Torn Curtain* (1966), *Topaz* (1969), *Frenzy* (1972), *Family Plot* (1976)

ROBIN, DANY (1927–1995) French actress. In films from 1946 with *Lunegarde* following experience as a ballet dancer, Robin went on to appear in many films both at home and abroad, among them *Une Jeune Fille Savait* (1947), *Julietta* (1953), *Love and the Frenchwoman* (1960), *Waltz of the Toreadors* (1962), *Carry On – Don't Lose Your Head* (1966) and *The Best House in London* (1968). Her last film was Hitchcock's *Topaz* (1969), in which she played Nicole Devereaux who, unbeknownst to her husband, secret agent Andre Devereaux (Frederick Stafford), is having an affair with Jacques Granville (Michael Piccoli), a top French official who also happens to head the spy ring her husband is investigating. Robin's first husband was the French actor Georges Marchal (1920–1997, real name Georges-Louis Lucot); her second husband, whom she married in 1969, was the British producer Michael Sullivan, with whom she died in a fire. **Hitchography:** *Topaz* (1969)

ROMAN, RUTH (1923–1999, real name Norma Roman) American actress. Stardom came slowly for this striking looking star, who made her film debut in *Stage Door Canteen* in 1943 following stage experience. Her subsequent films include *Without Reservations* (1946), *Gilda* (1946) and *The Big Clock* (1948), after which she came to prominence in the likes of *The Window* (1949) and *Champion* (1949). By 1951 she was under contract to Warner Bros., who forced her upon Hitchcock for the role of Anne Morton in *Strangers on a Train*; nevertheless, the actress gave a committed performance as the senator's daughter who finds her lover falsely accused of murdering his shrewish wife (commented *Variety*, 'Roman's role as a nice, understanding girl is a switch for her, and she makes it warmly effective'). Her other films include *Tanganyika* (1954), *Joe Macbeth* (1955), *Love Has Many Faces* (1964), *The Baby* (1972) and *When in Rome* (1991). Her television work includes *The Long Hot Summer* (1965–1966) and *Knots Landing* (1986). **Hitchography:** *Strangers on a Train* (1951)

skyscraper – had several breakaway walls, so as to allow the camera to move from one room to another. Recalled Farley Granger: 'We had to have a lot of prop men to move the furniture out of the way… You'd go to sit down and you hoped he was going to put a chair under you, otherwise you'd end up on the floor!' [33]

Also adding to the technical challenge was the fact that the Manhattan skyline, almost constantly seen in the background, had to gradually darken and the buildings light up, given that the action is supposedly taking place between 7:30 and 9:15 in the evening. Clouds made of spun glass were also moved across the backdrop to help heighten the sense of reality.

Thus, Hitch and his cast and crew began filming the ten-minute takes, averaging one successful take of any given sequence per day. Not everything went to plan. Dialogue and bits of business were occasionally fluffed, furniture and props weren't reset in the right places and, occasionally, a technician would be caught on camera; and each time this happened, the sequence had to be started again from scratch. Eventually, though, after much concerted effort, the film was in the can, but not to Hitchcock's satisfaction. He felt that the lighting during the sunset was much too orange. Consequently, the cast was recalled and the last five reels of the film were completely re-shot. Even so, the shooting schedule ran to just 18 days.

The resultant film is a rather ponderous affair, and not much different from watching the play itself from the stalls, despite the mobility of the camera, the dexterity of which no longer seems as impressive as its must have done at the time. In fact, in this respect, the film is a bit of a cheat, for Hitchcock films the action from just one direction. The camera never does a complete 360-degree turn about the apartment, so that everything we see is from the same perspective, which *adds* to the sense of watching a filmed play rather than taking away from it. Said Hitchcock: 'When I look back, I realize it was quite nonsensical because I was breaking with my own theories on the importance of cutting and montage for the visual narration of a story. On the other hand, this film was in a sense pre-cut. The mobility of the camera and the movement of the players closely followed my usual cutting practice. In other words, I maintained the rule of varying the size of the image in relation to its emotional importance within a given episode.' [34]

Nevertheless, the film is still tedious to watch. Even the performances fail to add much spark to the action, though the occasional line of dialogue sticks in the mind. Comments Brandon to Philip of their murderous deed: 'Good Americans usually die young on the battlefield, don't they? Well, the Davids of this world merely occupy space, which is why he was the perfect victim for the perfect murder. Of course, he *was* a Harvard undergraduate. That might make it justifiable homicide!'

But the duo are mistaken; it *wasn't* the perfect murder, and by the end of the evening Rupert Cadell has discovered the body, his curiosity aroused by the absence of David from the party, the unexplained nervousness of Philip, Brandon's ramblings about intellectual superiors being above the law, and the occasional clue (when initially leaving, the maid hands him David's hat by mistake, which the men don't realize is still in the hall closet). 'These hands will bring you great fame,' says Mrs Atwater when reading Philip's palms after he has delighted her at the piano, and this indeed turns out to be the case (although in a rare continuity error for Hitchcock, the cut Philip received from a broken glass earlier in the evening has vanished, even though it was large enough to have warranted being wrapped in a handkerchief).

Of the actors, James Stewart perhaps comes off best, ably capturing the aroused inquisitiveness of his character, although he is given a good run for his money by Edith Evanson as the wisecracking maid ('If I were you I'd go easy on the paté, dear,' she whispers to Janet at one point, adding '*Calories!*'). Less effective is Sir Cedric Hardwicke as Mr Kentley who, as he was in *Suspicion* (1941), is given too little to do and consequently comes across as rather dull, and Constance Collier as Mrs Atwater, whose performance is all too obviously affected by nerves, the result of her genuine fear of having to perform the ten-minute takes (when she first appears, she seems unsteady on her feet, while later her dialogue is often quite slurred and hesitant). John Dall and Farley Granger are just about up to the job as the killers (based on the true life murderers Leopold and Loeb, whose exploits would also feature in *Compulsion* (1959) and *Swoon* (1992)), while Joan Chandler and Douglas Dick twitter about irritatingly as Janet and Kenneth, who we fully expect to be re-united as partners once they've learned of David's fate. Then there's Dick Hogan as the victim, glimpsed but for a few seconds at the top of the film before being unceremoniously dumped in the cassoni, which naturally doesn't give him much of a chance to register as an actor. That said, Hogan, along with Joan Chandler, *did* feature in the film's trailer, a brief prologue to the subsequent action in which the two characters plan their future together, only for James Stewart's voiceover to intone, 'That's the last time she ever saw him alive.' In fact no scenes from the film itself actually featured in the trailer.

As a director, Hitchcock is also severely restricted by the ten-minute take, although he does manage a few effective touches, among them of shot of the murder weapon hanging from the side of the chest; the shot of Brandon subsequently placing the rope in a kitchen drawer, the action of which we see through a swinging door; the close-up of David's initials inside the hat wrongly given to Rupert, thus alerting him to the fact that David has been to the apartment; the gradual build up of lights on the Manhattan skyline; and the gradual build up of sound outside the apartment building following Rupert's firing of a gun from the window to attract attention (Hitchcock sent out a sound crew specifically to record these sounds from the actual height at which they're heard in the film, including the approaching sound of a police siren, recorded over a distance of 2 miles (3.4km)). More glaring, however, are the occasionally wobbly movements of the camera and, at one point in the action when the floor is in shot, the revelation of white chalk marks for the placing of the furniture (these can be spotted during Rupert's speech about how he thinks the two men have carried out the murder).

When the film went on release, critical reaction was generally muted, with *Variety* perhaps best summing things up with: 'Hitchcock could have chosen a more entertaining subject with which to use the arresting camera and staging technique displayed in *Rope*.' The posters suggested otherwise. 'Nothing ever held you like Alfred Hitchcock's *Rope*,' read the strap line, although many thought it should have run, 'Nothing ever *bored* you like Alfred Hitchcock's *Rope*,' even though the film went on to recover its $1.5 million budget. At the end of the day, despite the freedoms granted to him with his contract with Sidney Bernstein, *Rope* was not the artistic success originally envisaged. Privately, David O Selznick must have been delighted.

Hitchcock cameo Note that Hitchcock can be spotted in the guise of a neon light.

ROZSA, MIKLOS (1907–1996) Hungarian-born composer. One of the cinema's most acclaimed composers, Rozsa began his film career in Britain in 1937 working for the Hungarian producer Alexander Korda, for whom he scored *Knight Without Armour* (1937), *The Four Feathers* (1939) and *The Thief of Baghdad* (1940), moving to Hollywood in 1941 with Korda to work on *That Hamilton Woman* and *The Jungle Book* (1942). A child prodigy, Rozsa was a gifted violinist by the age of 5 and began composing in his teenage years. His other credits, aside from ballet and concert works, include five films for Billy Wilder – *Five Graves to Cairo* (1943), *Double Indemnity* (1944), *The Lost Weekend* (1945), *The Private Life of Sherlock Holmes* (1970) and *Fedora* (1978) – and several large scale epics, among them *Quo Vadis?* (1951), *Ivanhoe* (1952), *Julius Caesar* (1953), *King of Kings* (1961), *El Cid* (1961) and *Sodom and Gomorrah* (1962).

Rozsa won the Oscar three times during his career, for Hitchcock's *Spellbound* (1945), *A Double Life* (1947) and *Ben-Hur* (1959). For *Spellbound*, one of his most unashamedly romantic scores, the composer made much effective use of the eerie-sounding theremin. Yet despite his sterling work for the film, Hitchcock didn't seem greatly impressed. Said the director of the famous scene in which Ingrid Bergman and Gregory Peck first kiss, to which he then cuts to a number of opening doors: 'Unfortunately, the violins begin to play just then. That was terrible.' [35] An interesting comment, this would seem to indicate that Hitchcock had no say in the spotting of the film's music, which was no doubt in the hands of its producer, David O Selznick. Rozsa's other scores include *Adam's Rib* (1949), *Lust for Life* (1956), *The VIPs* (1963), *The Golden Voyage of Sinbad* (1973) and *Dead Men Don't Wear Plaid* (1982). **Hitchography:** *Spellbound* (1945)

RUSSELL, JOHN L American cinematographer. Russell first came to note in 1948 when he photographed Orson Welles' low budget version of *Macbeth*. His other films include *Moonrise* (1948), *The Man from Planet X* (1951), *The City That Never Sleeps* (1953) and *Make Haste and Live* (1954). In the 1950s and 1960s, he also photographed several episodes of Hitchcock's TV series *Alfred Hitchcock Presents*. When Hitchcock decided to use his TV crew to shoot the low budget *Psycho* (1960), Russell was also invited along, earning an Oscar nomination for his efforts (he lost out to Freddie Francis, who won for *Sons and Lovers* (1960)). Russell's other films include *Billie* (1965) and *Jigsaw* (1968). **Hitchography:** *Psycho* (1960)

RYAN, EDMON(D) American supporting actor. Ryan appeared in a variety of films from the late 1930s onwards, including *Dark Eyes of London* (1939), *Side Street* (1950), *Two for the Seesaw* (1962) and Hitchcock's *Topaz* (1969), in which he played Thomas. He also appeared in an episode of *Alfred Hitchcock Presents*. **Hitchography:** *The Festive Season* (1958, TV), *Topaz* (1969)

RYAN, MADGE (1919–1994) Australian-born character actress. Working in Britain from the mid-1950s, Ryan did much stage work, particularly at the National Theatre. Her handful of films include *The Strange Affair* (1968), *I Start Counting* (1969), *A Clockwork Orange* (1971), the Hitchcockian *Endless Night* (1971), *Who Is Killing the Great Chefs of Europe?* (1978) and the remake of Hitchcock's *The Lady Vanishes* (1979). She can also be seen in Hitchcock's *Frenzy* (1972) as Mrs Davidson, the battle-axe who finds a companion in George Tovey's meek Mr Salt through the marriage bureau of Brenda Blaney (Barbara Leigh-Hunt). **Hitchography:** *Frenzy* (1972)

S

Sabotage
(GB, 1936, 76m, bw) ★★

CREDITS

Production company:	Gaumont–British
Producer:	Michael Balcon
Director:	Alfred Hitchcock
Screenplay:	Charles Bennett, Ian Hay, Helen Simpson, based on *The Secret Agent* by Joseph Conrad
Cinematographer:	Bernard Knowles
Editor:	Charles Frend
Art director:	Oscar Werndorff
Costumes:	J Strassner, Marianne
Music director:	Louis Levy
Cartoon sequence:	Walt Disney (segments from *Who Killed Cock Robin?*)

CAST

Oscar Homolka (Carl Verloc), Sylvia Sidney (Mrs Verloc), Desmond Tester (Stevie), John Loder (Ted Spencer), William Dewhurst (The Professor), Matthew Boulton (Superintendent Talbot), S J Warmington (Hollingshead), Charles Hawtrey (Schoolboy), Martita Hunt (Professor's daughter), Aubrey Mather (Conspirator), Torin Thatcher (Conspirator), Peter Bull (Conspirator), Clare Greet, Sara Allgood

Though not quite Hitchcock at his very best, there is much to admire in this mini-masterpiece of observation. Based on Joseph Conrad's 1907 novel *The Secret Agent*, the film was known as both *I Married a Murderer* and *The Hidden Power* at various stages during production before *Sabotage* was finally settled upon, presumably to avoid confusion with Hitchcock's previous picture, also called *Secret Agent*.

Set in and around a rundown London cinema, the film opens with the West End being plunged into darkness; an unknown party has sabotaged Battersea Power Station by putting sand in the turbines. We soon learn that this criminal act was perpetrated by the cinema's mild mannered owner, one Carl Verloc (Oscar Homolka), who now returns to his flat above the Bijou under the cover of darkness. Washing his hands before taking a nap, he leaves particles of sand in the wash basin.

Verloc arrives just in time for his young wife (Sylvia Sidney) to discover him dozing on their bed, where he says

Sylvia Sydney carves the meat as Oscar Homolka looks on in Hitchcock's Sabotage *(1936). In a few moments, the knife will be used for another purpose.*

he's been all afternoon, thus providing himself with an alibi. Not everyone is convinced of Verloc's innocence, though, for one of the assistants at the neighbouring green grocer's is an undercover police sergeant named Ted Spencer (John Loder) who has been watching Verloc for some time. He's also befriended Verloc's wife, whom he's been subtly quizzing to see if she knows anything about his double life.

The following day, under the pretence that he's going to see a trade show, Verloc leaves to meet a contact at the aquarium in London Zoo, where he learns of his next assignment, to blow up Piccadilly Circus. Told to visit a bird shop in Islington, Verloc discovers it to be a front for an explosives expert known as the Professor (William Dewhurst) who informs Verloc that two birds will be delivered to him the following Saturday, the cage of which will contain an explosive device to be planted in the cloakroom of the underground at Piccadilly Circus ready to go off at 1:45 pm. However, when Saturday arrives, Verloc finds that he is unable to leave his flat without being spotted by Ted, whom he and his wife by now know is a policeman. Consequently he has his wife's younger brother Stevie (Desmond Tester) take the device on the understanding that he is returning a two-reeler – *Bartholomew the Strangler* – to another cinema and dropping off the additional 'package' to be picked up by a colleague later in the day.

Unfortunately, though told to deliver the package by 1:30 pm at the latest, Stevie is delayed on his journey, not least by the Lord Mayor's Show, which he stands and watches on The Strand. Consequently, by the time he catches a bus to Piccadilly, he is woefully late, and the device goes off as planned, blowing up Stevie, the bus and the rest of the passengers.

Verloc has the perfect alibi again – he was being questioned by Ted at the time of the explosion – but when Stevie fails to return home and the evening paper reports that two film canisters were found in the bomb wreckage, Mrs Verloc collapses. This prompts Mr Verloc to tell her what really happened. Numb with grief, Mrs Verloc stabs her husband to death with a carving knife. Arriving soon after this, Ted confesses that he loves Mrs Verloc and offers to help her escape to the Continent, even though she is for coming clean to the police. Luckily for them, the Professor turns up to retrieve his bird cage, closely followed by the police, who evacuate the cinema fearing another explosion, which soon after follows when their attempts to arrest the Professor result in him blowing up the cinema – and the evidence of the murder – thus leaving Ted and Mrs Verloc free of any blame.

Many of Hitchcock's films take place on a large canvas, as per his two previous films *The 39 Steps* (1935) and *Secret Agent* (1936), which feature adventures in Scotland and Switzerland respectively. *Sabotage*, however, is very much a smaller, more interior film, its main focus being the almost dull *minutae* of everyday life (note the attention to domestic detail in the Verloc's flat, right down to the ritual of serving meat and two veg for dinner). Consequently, the film's main set pieces stand out all the more effectively, notable among them Verloc's aquarium assignation, the magnified fish and rippling shadows of which add to the atmosphere of the

sequence (in a stunning touch, Hitchcock also has one of the tanks turn into a screen on which Verloc sees projected Piccadilly Circus on the day of the proposed explosion, this image distorting like melted celluloid following the detonation of the bomb).

Even more impressive is the gradual build up to the explosion, with the unknowing Stevie being distracted by all manner of diversions on his way to Piccadilly, including a market hawker who uses him in a toothpaste demonstration and, of course, the staging of the Lord Mayor's Show, which was actually recreated on the back lot, with Hitchcock making use of a giant photograph (supposedly the biggest ever produced) of the law courts on The Strand as a backdrop. The editing during this sequence is also notable, particularly the inter-cutting of various clocks noting the passing time. The explosion of the bus, which spectacularly lifts from the ground with the force of the blast, is also memorable.

Yet despite the bravura staging of this entire sequence, Hitchcock came in for some critical flak for having an innocent boy killed in such a way (especially as he was stroking an old lady's playful puppy just prior to the explosion, thus making the scene all the blacker!). Wrote critic C A Lejeune: 'Discreet directors don't kill schoolboys and dogs in omnibuses. Believe me, it isn't done.' Hitchcock himself later admitted that the scene 'was a grave error on my part,' adding, 'The boy was involved in a situation that got him too much sympathy from the audience, so that when the bomb exploded and he was killed, the public was resentful.' [1]

The larger set pieces aside, there are some nicely detailed touches to be found in *Sabotage*, not least of which is Mrs Verloc's murder of her husband, which is shot via a series of close-ups, with Hitchcock paying particular attention to her hesitation in picking up the carving knife, and the look of realization on her husband's face as she finally does so. Then there is the detail of décor, with the Verlocs' homey flat offering a sharp contrast to the shabby cinema over which it is situated (and to the seedy rooms in which the Professor and his daughter live behind his bird shop).

Despite his one major miscalculation, *Sabotage* nevertheless did well at the British box office, with the majority of the reviews encouraging. 'Definitely a picture you should see,' enthused the *News of the World*, to which *The Evening Standard* added, 'Each scene knits into the whole as neatly as bits in a jig-saw puzzle.' Even Graham Greene, who had savaged Hitchcock's previous film *Secret Agent* had some positive things to say in his review for *The Spectator*, commenting: 'I have sometimes doubted Mr Hitchcock's talent… He has cared more for an ingenious melodramatic situation than for the construction and continuity of his story. In *Sabotage* for the first time he has really 'come off'… This melodrama is convincingly realistic [and] on a different level from his deplorable adaptation of Mr Maugham's *Ashenden*.'

Indeed, the film benefits enormously from some first rate playing, particularly from Sylvia Sidney and Oscar Homolka, with the only false note coming from John Loder as the undercover copper. In fact Hitchcock had hoped that

Robert Donat would play the part, but his hopes were dashed when Alexander Korda, to whom Donat was contracted, mixed the idea (said Hitchcock of Loder, '[He] wasn't suitable, and I was forced to rewrite the dialogue during shooting' [2]).

It should also be noted that the film features un-credited performances by the likes of Martita Hunt (as the Professor's slatternly daughter), future *Carry On* star Charles Hawtrey (as a schoolboy in the aquarium sequence who is telling his girlfriend about the mating habits of the oyster) and Peter Bull as one of Verloc's associates, while Hitchcock regulars Clare Greet and Sara Allgood can be spotted as extras. The film was later remade as *The Secret Agent* (1996), although this time the makers remained closer to the Joseph Conrad original; nevertheless, it wasn't a success.

Saboteur

(US, 1942, 108m, bw) ★★

CREDITS

Production company:	Universal
Director:	Alfred Hitchcock
Producers:	Frank Lloyd, Jack H Skirball
Screenplay:	Peter Viertel, Joan Harrison, Dorothy Parker
Story:	Alfred Hitchcock
Cinematographer:	Joseph A Valentine
Music:	Frank Skinner
Music director:	Charles Previn
Editor:	Otto Ludwig
Art director:	Robert F Boyle, Jack Otterson
Sound:	Bernard B Brown, William Hedgcock

CAST

Priscilla Lane (Patricia Martin), Robert Cummings (Barry Kane), Otto Kruger (Charles Tobin), Norman Lloyd (Frank Fry), Clem Bevans (Neilson), Alan Baxter (Mr Freeman), Alma Kruger (Mrs Sutton), Vaughan Glaser (Philip Martin), Dorothy Peterson (Mrs Mason), Ian Wolfe (Butler), Murray Alper (Truck driver), Frances Carson (Mrs Sutton's society friend), Kathryn Adams (Mother), Pedro de Cordoba (Bones), Marie LeDeaux (Fat Lady), Billy Curtis (The Colonel), Anita Sharp-Bolster (Lorelei, the bearded lady), Jeanne Roher, Lynn Roher (Siamese twins), Ralph Dunn (Detective), Charles Halton (Sheriff), Emory Parnell (Movie actor), Matt Willis (Sheriff), Milton Kibbee (Shoot out victim)

Video availability: Universal
DVD availability: Universal
Not to be confused with his 1936 British thriller *Sabotage*,

Saboteur is one of Hitchcock's 'innocent on the run' pictures, and though it doesn't quite reach the same cinematic heights of *The 39 Steps* (1935), *Young and Innocent* (1937) and *North by Northwest* (1959), it nevertheless contains some impressively staged sequences along the way.

Hitchcock began pre-production on the film under the aegis of producer David O Selznick, to whom he was contracted. However, Selznick sold the entire package. Consequently, Hitchcock made the film, based on his own story, on a loan out to Universal, hence the credit: 'Directed by Alfred Hitchcock, through courtesy of David O Selznick Productions, Inc.' Naturally, Hitchcock received his usual fee of $40,000 for the film, as per his contract with Selznick, while Selznick himself pocketed a tidy profit for the loan out (indeed, so great was Selznick's profit that it was said to have adversely affected the budget for *Saboteur*, much to Hitchcock's chagrin).

As had been the case with *Foreign Correspondent* (1940), Hitchcock's preferred choice for the film's hero was Gary Cooper. Coop had turned down *Foreign Correspondent*, and later admitted he'd made a mistake in doing so, although this didn't prevent him from turning down *Saboteur* as well. Consequently, after also considering Henry Fonda and Gene Kelly for the lead, Hitchcock plumped for Robert Cummings, an amiable 'nice guy' type, though hardly major league.

In the film, Cummings plays Barry Kane, a shift worker building aircraft at a California factory. However, when the plant goes up in flames and his buddy Ken is killed in the inferno, Kane finds himself accused of starting the blaze, for it transpires that the fire extinguisher he handed to his buddy to put out the blaze was filled with gasoline. Going on the run, Kane attempts to prove his innocence and find the guilty party, believing him to be a stranger whom he'd earlier bumped into at the factory, sending the chap's mail and money to the floor. Recalling the name and address on one of the envelopes, Kane thus sets off to find the man – one Frank Fry – who has of course disappeared ('I've got to get Fry, I've got to find him, or Ken won't be the last to die,' impassions Kane to Ken's grieving mother).

Hitching a lift across country to Deep Springs Ranch, Springville – the address on the envelope – Kane encounters the ranch's owner, Charles Tobin (Otto Kruger), who claims not to have heard of Fry. Yet when Tobin's baby granddaughter Susie throws some letters from his jacket to the ground, Kane spies a telegram that reads, 'All finished here. Joining Neilson in Soda City. Frank.' Realizing he's stumbled across the leader of a gang of saboteurs, Kane attempts to hotfoot it from the ranch, making his escape on horseback. But he's no match for Tobin's ranch hands, who quickly catch him on their own horses, lasso him and bring him back for the waiting cops, who naturally don't believe his story (this brief pursuit sequence at least allowed Hitchcock to direct his only cowboy chase).

Escaping from the cops by jumping from their car, the now handcuffed Kane again goes on the run, seeking shelter from a storm in the cottage of Phillip Martin (Vaughan Glaser), a blind man who offers him warmth and food (this scene is practically a replay of the similar scene in *The Bride of Frankenstein* (1935), in which the Monster seeks shelter from a blind hermit). Things are going well until the man's niece Patricia (Priscilla Lane) turns up and realizes that Kane is the man the radio has been reporting as on the run for the hangar fire. Placating her, her uncle tells Patricia he believes Kane to be innocent (blind eyes being more seeing and all that), and seemingly persuades her to take him to the local blacksmith (a trusted friend who'll ask no questions) to have his handcuffs removed. But once in the car, Pat shows her true colours by declaring that she's taking Kane straight to the police. Wresting control of the vehicle, Kane drives to an off-road in the desert, and after some verbal sparring with Pat finally persuades her that he's innocent, and that they need to get to Soda City to track down Fry.

But it's not long after this that the car breaks down (the fact that Kane has used the engine's fan to break the chain on his cuffs probably had something to do with this), and the couple is reduced to hitching a lift in a circus caravan, sharing the accommodation with the bearded lady, a midget and a pair of Siamese twins. When they finally reach Soda City, it seems to be a ghost town – that is until a phone in one of the shacks starts to ring. Kane and Pat reach it just as the line goes dead. Nevertheless, the room it is situated in reveals much, for it also contains a contact radio (hidden in the oven) and a telescope used for observing the nearby dam through a specially cut hole in the wall. Realizing they have stumbled across a saboteur's hideout, they start to leave, only to hear two men approaching. With Pat hidden, Kane confronts the men (one of them the Neilson mentioned in Fry's telegram), pretending that Toben has sent him following his successful sabotaging of the aircraft factory, and that they are to help him.

Leaving Pat behind to inform the local sheriff what's been going on, Kane finds himself on his way to New York, where he is offered a place to hide at the home of society matron Mrs Sutton (Frances Carson), who seems to be financing operations via her charity work. However, just as Kane seems to be getting away with his subterfuge, learning of another sabotage plot to be carried out the next day, Toben turns up, blowing his cover. Kane is also surprised to find Pat at Mrs Sutton's, learning that she's been brought there following a tip off from the sheriff, who is also in on the plot.

Undeterred, Kane manages to escape from Mrs Sutton's mansion the next morning and, learning from a newspaper that the USS *Alaska* is to be launched that day at the Brooklyn ship yard, puts two and two together and makes his way there to avert the planned atrocity. Once there he spies Frank Fry in the back of a newsreel van, ready to detonate a bomb under the ship by radio control. In the ensuing fight, Kane manages to prevent Fry from carrying out his task – that is until the ship has been safely launched, after which the bomb goes off and Fry makes a hasty exit. Meanwhile Pat, who has been moved to a room in a nearby tower block, also manages to escape, having attracted the attention of a group of cabbies on the road below by dropping them a help note scribbled in lipstick. Having informed the police of what's been going on, the chase is afoot to track down Fry, who turns up at the tower block only to find the police in wait.

Yet when he makes a run for it, it is Pat who manages to track Fry, following him on a boat to the Statue of Liberty.

Once there, she calls the police, who soon after arrive with Kane, who corners Fry with a police gun on the torch arm of the statue. Recoiling at the sight of Kane's gun, Fry steps back, only to tip over the edge of the railing. Grabbing on to an arm of Fry's jacket, Kane attempts to pull him to safety. Unfortunately, the stitching on the sleeve isn't strong enough to withstand Fry's weight and the jacket arm rips away, sending Fry falling to his death, but allowing Kane and Pat to be reunited in a warm embrace during the fadeout.

Like *The 39 Steps* before it, *Saboteur* covers a lot of ground (hence the poster strap line, '3000 miles of terror'). Yet at a bloated 108 minutes compared to its predecessor's brisk 81 minutes, the film seems to lack drive, despite its plethora of incidents. Admitted Hitchcock, 'I felt that it was cluttered with too many ideas; there's the hero in handcuffs leaping down from a bridge; the scene of the elderly blind man in the house; the ghost town with the deserted work yards; and the long shot of Boulder Dam. I think we covered too much ground.' [3]

Hitchcock also felt he'd been scuppered by his cast. Having had to settle for Robert Cummings instead of Gary Cooper, he additionally found himself lumbered with the just-about-adequate Priscilla Lane as his leading lady (thanks to the insistence of the film's producers, Frank Lloyd and Jack H Skirball), while his preferred choice for the villain, western star Harry Carey, turned down the role so as to protect his all-American screen image, leaving the path open for the reasonably effective Otto Kruger to take the part of Tobin. Meanwhile, for the role of Mrs Sutton, which was begging to be played by Florence Bates, who'd played the dragon-like Mrs Van Hopper in Hitchcock's *Rebecca* (1940), the director instead cast Alma Kruger, which isn't quite the same thing. Still, Norman Lloyd gives good value for money in his brief role as the elusive Frank Fry, taking that famous plunge from the Statue of Liberty, from which he's been hanging literally by a thread.

There are a few good lines of dialogue to compensate for the generally lacklustre casting. 'Sounds are my light and colour,' says the blind Philip Martin while playing the piano for his unexpected guest, to which Kane responds, 'I used to play the triangle in our high school band.' Then, later, Pat comments of their elusive quarry, 'Fry – he seems so small now. I'd almost forgotten about him,' thus enabling the writers to use the small fry gag they'd no doubt been storing up. However, when the truck driver who's been giving Kane a ride comments, 'Easy to see there's nothing on *your* mind,' one is inclined to agree with his assessment of our bland hero. Said Hitchcock of Cummings, 'He has an amusing face, so that even when he's in desperate straits, his features don't convey any anguish.' [4]

Still, Hitchcock gets to exercise his technique in a number of set pieces. Aside from the afore mentioned climax atop the Statue of Liberty, there's the amusing sequence aboard the circus caravan with the quarrelling Siamese twins and the bearded lady with her beard in curlers; the fire sequence at the factory (note the smoke appearing from the right hand side of the screen and the still shocking shot of Ken collapsing in the blaze); the shadowy figure walking across the screen during the credits; a chase across a studio-bound waterfall following Kane's escape from the police; the charity ball at Mrs Sutton's, with Pat and Kane trapped amidst the dancing; Kane's subsequent escape from Mrs Sutton's by setting off the sprinkler system; and the shoot out during a movie show at Radio City Music Hall. Hitchcock also slipped in a sly moment with Fry, having his cab drive past the recently capsized French liner the *Normandie*, the wry smile on his face seeming to suggest that he'd had something to do with it. Recalled Hitchcock: 'The Navy raised hell with Universal about these three shots because I implied that the *Normandie* had been sabotaged, which was a reflection on their lack of vigilance in guarding it.' [5] As good as these sequence are, though, they aren't presented with quite the same flair as the set pieces in *The 39 Steps* and *Foreign Correspondent*.

Despite its flaws, *Saboteur* was a commercial success, although the reviews were rather more mixed this time round. 'It's absurd, but it grips,' wrote William Whitebait in the *New Statesman*, adding that the film, 'just falls below the Master's best.' More enthusiastic was the *Monthly Film Bulletin*, commenting, 'The suspense and thrills in this highly melodramatic story are manifold, and the lighting and photography are worthy of special mention.' The *Motion Picture Herald* went even further: 'The drama of a nation stirred to action, of a people's growing realization of themselves and their responsibilities.' Indeed, the film's anti-Nazi stance and its suggestion that Fifth Columnists could already be at work in America, not to mention the script's constant platitudinising about freedom and liberty, were further attempts to cajole the US into World War II. However, on 7 December 1941, when *Saboteur* was already in mid-production, the Japanese attacked Pearl Harbor. Such clumsy devices were no longer necessary – America finally entered the war on 8 December, declaring hostilities against Japan, while on 11 December, Italy and Germany declared war on America. The world, it seemed, had much changed since Hitchcock's arrival in America just two years earlier.

Hitchcock cameo Note that Hitchcock can be spotted outside a New York drug store.

SAINT, EVA MARIE (1924–   ) American actress. This effortlessly elegant star won a best supporting actress Oscar for her first film, *On the Waterfront* (1954), prior to which she'd appeared on stage, notably in the Broadway production of *The Trip to Bountiful*. Her subsequent films include *Raintree County* (1957), *Exodus* (1960), *Grand Prix* (1966), *Loving* (1970), *Nothing in Common* (1986), *Titanic* (1996, TV) and *I Dreamed of Africa* (2000). She is best remembered for playing the cool but duplicitous Eve Kendall in Hitchcock's *North by Northwest* (1959), although MGM had wanted Cyd Charisse to play the role. In the film, Saint shares several romantic clinches with Cary Grant's Roger Thornhill, among them one aboard the 20th Century Limited ('You're an advertising man, that's all I know. You've got taste in clothes, taste in food,' she tells him as they caress, to which comes the response, 'Taste in women. I like your flavour'). Commented *Variety* of her performance in the film, 'Eva Marie Saint dives

head first into Mata Hari and shows she can be unexpectedly and thoroughly glamorous.' **Hitchography:** *North by Northwest* (1959)

ST JOHN, HOWARD (1905–1974) American actor. On stage from 1925 and in films from 1949 with *Shockproof*, St John carved out a niche for himself as official types, among his roles being Captain Turley in Hitchcock's *Strangers on a Train* (1951). His many other films include *The Undercover Man* (1949), *Born Yesterday* (1950), *Three Coins in the Fountain* (1954), *One, Two, Three* (1961) and *Don't Drink the Water* (1969). **Hitchography:** *Strangers on a Train* (1951)

SALA, OSKAR (1911–2002) German composer. Along with Remi Gassman, Sala provided the electronic 'bird music' for Hitchcock's *The Birds* (1963), which was played on their 'Trautonium'. Sala's other credits include *The Strangler of Blackmoor Castle* (1963) and *The Secret of Dr Mabuse* (1964). **Hitchography:** *The Birds* (1963)

SANDERS, GEORGE (1906–1972) British-born actor. Cornering the market in world-weary English bounders (his autobiography was titled *Memoirs of a Professional Cad*), Sanders, who was actually born in Russia, began his acting career in the early 1930s following experience in the textile industry and as a tobacco salesman in South America. He broke into British films with *Find the Lady* in 1936, prior to which he had gained experience in radio and revue. A handful of other films followed, among them *The Man Who Could Work Miracles* (1936) and *Love is News* (1936), following which he moved to Hollywood, making his debut in *Lloyd's of London* in 1937. Stardom beckoned in 1939 with *The Saint Strikes Back*, in which Sanders took over the role of Simon

Eva Marie Saint and her co-star James Mason get a closer look at the enormous VistaVision camera used to photograph Hitchcock's North by Northwest *(1959).*

Templar from Louis Hayward in RKO's popular second feature series (interestingly, Hitchcock had been offered the job of directing the first episode, *The Saint in New York* (1938)). In 1940, Sanders was cast as the blackmailing Jack Flavell in Hitchcock's *Rebecca* (' I say, marriage with Max is not exactly a bed of roses, is it?'), and his success in this role led to an appearance in the director's following film, *Foreign Correspondent* (1940), this time on the right side of the law as the improbably-named Scott ffolliott ('How do you say it – like a stutter?' he's asked, to which comes the reply, 'No, no, just straight ff!').

Sanders' many other films include the Hollywood remake of Hitchcock's *The Lodger* (1944), *The Picture of Dorian Gray* (1944), *All About Eve* (1950), which earned him a best supporting actor Oscar for his role as waspish theatre critic Addison de Witt, *Village of the Damned* (1960) and *Psychomania* (1972), shortly after which he committed suicide. He also presented the television series *George Sanders' Mystery Theatre* (1958). His four wives included Zsa Zsa Gabor (1919– , real name Sari Gabor), to whom he was married between 1949 and 1954 and Benita Hume (1906–1967), to whom he was married between 1959 and 1967. Hume appeared in both *Easy Virtue* (1927) and *Lord Camber's Ladies* (1932), the former directed by and the latter produced by Hitchcock. **Hitchography:** *Rebecca* (1940), *Foreign Correspondent* (1940)

SANFORD, ERSKINE (1880–1950) American actor. A frequent support in the films of Orson Welles, Sanford can be seen in films such as *Citizen Kane* (1941), *The Magnificent Ambersons* (1942) and *The Lady from Shanghai* (1948) as well as *Pop Always Pays* (1940), *Ministry of Fear* (1944) and Hitchcock's *Spellbound* (1945), in which he played the uncredited role of Dr Galt. **Hitchography:** *Spellbound* (1945)

SCHUNZEL, REINHOLD (1886–1954) German actor-director. Schunzel began his stage career during World War I following experience as a journalist. He made his first film as an actor, *Die Stricknadeln*, in 1916, and began directing three years later with *Maria Magdalena*, in which he also appeared. As an actor he went on to appear in such films as *Das Tagebuch einer Verlorenen* (1918), *Weltbrand* (1920) and *Die Dreigroschnoper* (1931), while as a director he helmed *Madchen aus der Ackerstrasse* (1921), *Don Juan in der Madchenschule* (1928) and *Viktor und Viktoria* (1933), the latter later musicalized by Blake Edwards as *Victor/Victoria* (1982). In 1938, Schunzel went to Hollywood, where he continued to work as an actor and director, helming *Rich Man, Poor Girl* (1938), *Ice Follies of 1939* (1939) and *New Wine* (1941). As an actor, however, his accent tended to restrict him to Nazi roles in films such as *The Hitler Gang* (1944) and Hitchcock's *Notorious* (1946), in which he played the chilling Dr Anderson. Schunzel's other American films as an actor include *The Plainsman and the Lady* (1946), *Golden Earrings* (1947) and *Washington Story* (1952). He returned to Germany for his last film, *Eine Liebesgeschichte* (1954). **Hitchography:** *Notorious* (1946)

Secret Agent

(GB, 1936, 86m, bw) ★

CREDITS

Production company:	Gaumont-British
Producer:	Michael Balcon
Associate producer:	Ivor Montague
Director:	Alfred Hitchcock
Screenplay:	Charles Bennett, Ian Hay, Alma Reville, Jesse Lasky Jr, based on the *The Traitor* and *The Hairless Mexican* by . Somerset Maugham and the play by Campbell Dixon
Cinematographer:	Bernard Knowles
Music director:	Louis Levy
Editor:	Charles Frend
Art director:	Oscar Werndorff
Costumes:	J Strassner, Marianne
Sound:	Philip Dorte

CAST

John Gielgud (Edgar Brodie/Richard Ashenden), Madeleine Carroll (Elsa Carrington/Mrs Ashenden), Peter Lorre (General), Robert Young (Robert Marvin), Percy Marmont (Caypor), Florence Kahn (Mrs Caypor), Lilli Palmer (Lilli), Charles Carson ('R'), Tom Helmore (Colonel Anderson), Michel Saint-Denis (Coach driver), Michael Redgrave (Army Captain), H F Maltby

Video availability: Carlton

Given that *Secret Agent* was made in the midst of Hitchcock's classic British period, one can't help but be disappointed by the film today. Based on two of W Somerset Maugham's 'Ashenden' stories and a play by Campbell Dixon, the film, set in 1916, centres round World War I hero and novelist Edgar Brodie (John Gielgud). Brodie has apparently died while at home on leave, and the film opens with friends and relatives filing past his coffin. However, once the gathering has dispersed, Brodie's one-armed manservant pulls the flag from the coffin and attempts to shift it, only to have it crash to the floor, empty. For Brodie's death has been faked so that he can travel to Europe undercover to assassinate an enemy agent.

Arriving in Switzerland where he is to meet a double agent who has information as to the identity of his victim, Brodie – now named Richard Ashenden – is surprised to learn that he has a 'wife' named Elsa Carrington (Madeleine Carroll) staying with him at his hotel, so as to help make his cover more convincing, while a Mexican agent nicknamed General (Peter Lorre) is on hand to help him with his assignment. Meanwhile, a tourist named Robert Marvin (Robert Young), also staying at the hotel, is making romantic advances to Ashenden's 'wife'. Unfortunately, Ashenden's arrival in Switzerland does not go unnoticed by the enemy, despite the elaborate precautions taken ('Novelist Brodie reported dead arrived today Hotel Excelsior on espionage work. Take steps,' reads an agent's instructions written on the inside of a chocolate bar wrapper).

Leaving his 'wife' at the hotel, Ashenden and General attempt to contact the double agent at a nearby church, only to find that he has been murdered (his body lies slumped over the organ, a single note echoing throughout the church). The only clue as to his killer is a button found in the dead man's hand. Later realizing that this belongs to a fellow hotel guest named Caypor (Percy Marmont), Ashenden and the General put two and two together, decide that he is the enemy agent, befriend him and tempt him into a day of walking in the mountains, where they plan to assassinate him by throwing him into a precipice. But Ashenden cannot bring himself to kill the man, and so leaves the task to General, preferring to watch him carry out the deed through a telescope in a nearby observatory.

But it transpires that Caypor was *not* the enemy Ashenden was assigned to kill, which leaves him wracked with guilt and determined to resign. In fact the true identity of the enemy agent is soon after revealed to be Robert Marvin, with whom Elsa has by now left on a train to Constantinople. Catching up with the couple, Ashenden again has to wrest with the idea of killing a man in cold blood. However, he is saved from carrying out the task, for the train is bombed by allied aircraft and Marvin is killed in the resulting crash, but not before putting a bullet into General. There is a happy ending, though, for Ashenden, who has fallen in love with Elsa, finally gets to make her his real wife, while the newspapers report a victory for the allies in Palestine, presumably thanks to their somewhat fumbled efforts.

There are several reasons why *Secret Agent* fails to work as a whole, paramount among them being the casting of John Gielgud, who simply fails to make the grade as a romantic hero (despite the fact that he was also playing an over-aged Romeo in an acclaimed stage production of *Romeo and Juliet* at the same time as filming). That said, even Robert Donat would have had problems making the Ashenden character work, given his Hamlet-like indecisiveness about the job he's been handed, not to mention the fact the audience is basically put into the position of rooting for him to commit a murder. Admitting he'd got things wrong, Hitchcock later said of this: 'In an adventure drama your central figure must have a purpose. That's vital for the progression of the film... The audience must be rooting for the character; they should almost be helping him to achieve his goal. John Gielgud, the hero of *Secret Agent*, has an assignment, but the job is distasteful and he is reluctant to do it... Therefore, because it's a negative purpose, the film is static – it doesn't move forward.' [6]

Indeed, aside from the intriguing opening with the fake funeral and the climactic train crash, there are acres of tedium in *Secret Agent*, including an interminable sequence set in The Excelsior's casino, which is a real endurance test. There are *some* notable scenes, among them the discovery of the murdered agent in the church, the assassination of Caypor, and a lively sequence in a chocolate factory, where Ashenden and General attempt to secure further informa-

tion about the true identity of the enemy agent, not realizing he's been underneath their noses all the time.

Hitchcock's love of risqué humour also rears its head again in various guises. For example, the womanizing General, who wears an earring long before it was fashionable for men to do so, picks up one young woman by throwing chocolate down her cleavage. Meanwhile, in an earlier scene set in their hotel bathroom, Ashenden and his wife banter away while General, annoyed at not having been assigned a 'wife' himself, throws toilet paper about the room in a tantrum (note that though the toilet paper dispenser is shown, there is of course no sign of a toilet – audiences would have to wait until Hitchcock's *Psycho* in 1960 to see one of those in a mainstream movie).

Performance-wise, Gielgud isn't the only cast member out of his depth. Peter Lorre (who at the time was addicted to morphine) is simply *too* flamboyant in his role as General, while Madeleine Carroll is woefully under used as the romantic interest. The idea of casting the usually likeable Robert Young as the chief villain no doubt seemed like a good idea at the time – he was the first of several charming Hitchcock villains. Unfortunately, he is given so much lightweight banter to perform in order to convince us of his charm, that his ultimate demise in the climactic train wreck can't come soon enough.

Though it was a reasonable commercial success, *Secret Agent* didn't entirely find favour with the critics. Writing in *The Spectator*, Graham Greene seemed to be on to Hitchcock's game. 'His films consist of a series of small "amusing" melodramatic situations: the murderer's button dropped on the baccarat board; the strangled organist's hands prolonging the notes in the empty church; the fugitives hiding in the bell-tower when the bell begins to swing. Very perfunctorily he builds up to these situations (paying no attention on the way to inconsistencies, loose ends, psychological absurdities) and then drops them: they mean nothing: they lead to nothing.'

Greene was right. The film *is* little more than a perfunctory series of set pieces, not too cleverly linked together. The highlights may be worth a look; elsewhere, though, video watchers will be grateful for the fast forward button.

The Secret Agent
(GB, 1996 (released 1998), 95m, Technicolor)

CREDITS

Production company:	Fox/Capitol
Producer:	Norma Heyman
Director:	Christopher Hampton
Screenplay:	Christopher Hampton, based on the novel by Joseph Conrad
Cinematographer:	Denis Lenoir
Music:	Philip Glass
Editor:	George Akers
Production designer:	Caroline Amies
Costumes:	Anushia Nieradzik

CAST

Bob Hoskins (Adolf Verloc), Patricia Arquette (Winnie
Verloc), Gerard Depardieu (Alexander Ossipon), Christian
Bale (Stevie), Jim Broadbent (Chief Inspector Heat), Eddie
Izzard (Vladimir), Robin Williams (The Professor),
Elizabeth Spriggs, Peter Vaughan

In this expensive, much-heralded all-star remake of the
Hitchcock classic *Sabotage* (1936), writer-director
Christopher Hampton reverts to the plotting and period of
the original 1907 Joseph Conrad novel on which Hitchcock
and his screenwriters based their version. Unfortunately,
despite this film's good intentions, it very quickly becomes a
chore to watch. Said *Variety* of the production:
'Appropriately gloomy and grim, but these are not qualities
that will recommend it to most audiences,' to which the *Film
Review Annual* added, 'This is an astonishingly ill-conceived
endeavour that, while clinging slavishly to Conrad's 1907
novel, sacrifices all credibility on the altar of commercialism.'
Though made in 1996, the film didn't receive a UK release
until 1998, when it quickly disappeared.

SEINE ZWEITE FRAU see *The Prude's Fall*

SELZER, MILTON American supporting actor. Selzer
appeared in a number of films from the 1950s onwards,
among them *A Big Hand for the Little Lady* (1966), *In Enemy
Country* (1968), *The Legend of Lylah Clare* (1968), *Lady Sings
the Blues* (1972), *Blue Collar* (1978) and *Miss Rose White*
(1992, TV). He can also be spotted in Hitchcock's *Marnie*
(1964) as a racetrack pest who thinks he recognizes Tippi
Hedren's Marnie Edgar from a previous encounter: 'Aren't
you Peggy Nicholson?' **Hitchography:** *Marnie* (1964)

SELZNICK, DAVID O (1902–1965) American producer.
This legendary Hollywood player, the son of producer and
distributor Lewis J Selznick (1870–1933), is best
remembered for producing *Gone with the Wind* (1939),
which earned him a best picture Oscar. In films from 1924
with *Roulette*, he went on to work for RKO (as Vice
President in Charge of Production) and MGM
(as Vice President) in the early 1930s before going
independent and founding Selznick International in 1936,
which produced the likes of *The Prisoner of Zenda* (1937),
Nothing Sacred (1937) and *Intermezzo* (1939).

In 1938, Selznick signed Alfred Hitchcock to a personal
seven-year contract, and their first film together, *Rebecca*
(1940), earned Selznick a second best picture Oscar.
However, in order to make a profit on his investment,
Selznick loaned Hitchcock out to other studios for a fee far
in excess of the $40,000 per picture Hitchcock received from
Selznick, which did much to frustrate the Director.
Subsequently, though Hitchcock remained busy during his
time under contract with Selznick, he actually made few
films that were personally supervised by Selznick, notable
among them *Spellbound* (1945) and *The Paradine Case* (1947),
the latter which Selznick wrote as well as produced. But the
production was a troubled one and by this time their

relationship had begun to sour. Commented Selznick at the
time: 'I am deeply concerned about the progress on *The
Paradine Case*... Hitch has slowed down unaccountably [and]
we are more than three days behind in the first six days of
shooting.' [7]

Selznick's many other films include *Dinner at Eight*
(1933), *A Tale of Two Cities* (1935), *Since You Went Away*
(1944), *The Third Man* (1949) and *A Farewell to Arms* (1957).
Married twice, his wives were Irene Mayer (daughter of
MGM executive Louis B Mayer) and actress Jennifer Jones
(1919– , real name Phylis Isley). Commented Hitchcock in
1965 of Selznick's penchant for lengthy memos, 'When I
came to America 25 years ago to direct *Rebecca*, David
Selznick sent me a memo. I've just finished reading it. I think
I may turn it into a motion picture. I plan to call it *The
Longest Story Ever Told*.' [8] Note that in 1943 Selznick also
produced a war bonds appeal film staring his wife-to-be
Jennifer Jones whom he had under contract; the 2-minute
short was directed by Hitchcock. **Hitchography:** *Rebecca*
(1940), *Buy War Bonds* (1943), *Spellbound* (1945), *Notorious*
(1946), *The Paradine Case* (1947)

SELZNICK, MYRON (1898–1944) American-born
agent. The elder brother of producer David O Selznick,
Myron Selznick was also a major player in the film
industry, but behind the scenes as a talent agent, among his
many clients being Constance Bennett, Fredric March,
Carole Lombard, Madeleine Carroll and directors William
Wellman and Alfred Hitchcock. Selznick first met
Hitchcock in 1924 at Islington Studios in London on the
set of *The Passionate Adventure*, on which Hitch was
working as screenwriter, editor, art director and assistant
director. Falling for and subsequently marrying (in 1925)
one of the film's stars, Marjorie Daw (1902–1979),
Selznick decided to stay in England, where he set up the
Joyce-Selznick talent agency with Frank Joyce, the brother
of Alice Joyce, one of *The Passionate Adventure*'s other
leading ladies. Representing Hitchcock from 1924 until
his death, it was Selznick who, in 1938, brokered
Hitchcock's seven-year, $40,000 per picture contract with
his brother David, which took the director to Hollywood,
where he made his debut with *Rebecca* (1940).

SEQUELS Although several Hitchcock's films have been
remade, only one film, *Psycho* (1960), has generated any
sequels. They are: *Psycho 2* (1983), *Psycho III* (1986), *Bates
Motel* (1987, TV, plus series), and *Psycho IV: The Beginning*
(1990). However, it should be noted that Hitchcock
considered filming John Buchan's *The Three Hostages*
following *Marnie* (1964); given that the novel features the
further exploits of Richard Hannay, this could well have
been seen as a sequel of sorts to *The 39 Steps* (1935), which
also features Hannay.

SERSEN, FRED (1890–1962) American special effects
technician. Sersen spent much of his career at Fox, where he
worked on films such as *In Old Chicago* (1937), *Suez* (1938),
The Rains Came (1939) and Hitchcock's *Lifeboat*

(1944), which involved much rear projection work.
Hitchography: *Lifeboat* (1944)

Shadow of a Doubt
(US, 1943, 106m, bw) ★★

CREDITS

Production company:	Universal
Producer:	Jack H Skirball
Director:	Alfred Hitchcock
Screenplay:	Thornton Wilder, Sally Benson, Alma Reville
Story:	Gordon McDonell
Cinematography:	Joseph A Valentine
Music:	Dimitri Tiomkin
Music director:	Charles Previn
Editor:	Milton Carruth
Art directors:	John B Goodman, Robert F Boyle
Costumes:	Vera West, Adrian
Sound:	Bernard B Brown, Robert Pritchard

CAST

Teresa Wright (Charlie Newton), Joseph Cotten (Charlie Oakley), Patricia Collinge (Emma Newton), Henry Travers (Joseph Newton), MacDonald Carey (Detective Jack Graham), Wallace Ford (Fred Saunders), Edna Mae Wonacott (Ann Newton), Charlie Bates (Roger Newton), Clarence Muse (Porter), Irving Bacon (Station Master), Estelle Jewell (Charlie's friend), Janet Shaw (Louise), Virginia Brissac (Mrs Phillips), Frances Carson (Mrs Potter), Edward Fielding (Doctor), Sarah Edwards (Doctor's wife), Eily Malyon (Librarian), Ruth Lee (Mrs MacCurdy), John McGuire (Detective), Grandon Rhodes (Reverend MacCurdy), Minerva Urecal (Mrs Henderson)

Video availability: Universal
DVD availability: Universal

One of Hitchcock's most intimate productions, *Shadow of a Doubt* (filmed under the working title of *Uncle Charlie*) is also one of his most 'American' thanks to its convincingly detailed depiction of small town life, stemming from the screenplay co-written by Thorton Wilder, the author of that most American of plays *Our Town*, and Sally Benson, author of that most American of books, *Meet Me in St Louis*.

Based on a story by Gordon McDonell, the film sees the seemingly affable Charlie Oakley (Joseph Cotten) arrive in the small town of Santa Rosa to visit his sister Emma (Patricia Collinge) and her family, among them his favourite niece Charlie (Teresa Wright), who's been named after him. However, nice Uncle Charlie is guarding a dark secret: in reality he's the so-called Merry Widow Murderer, a serial killer who has offed three rich widows for their savings, hence his being able to make a cash deposit of $40,000 at the bank where his brother-in-law Joseph works. However, when a couple of detectives turn up on the scene posing as survey tak-

ers, Uncle Charlie's amiable facade begins to crumble. So much so that he makes several attempts to murder his beloved niece who, having had her suspicions aroused by the detectives, has been making her own investigations into her uncle's life. Things eventually come to a head when, rather than risk facing exposure, Uncle Charlie finally agrees to leave town, only to fall to his death in front of an oncoming train while trying to push his niece from the door of his own departing train, on which he has held her against her will.

Made on location in the town of Santa Rosa itself, with only the interiors filmed at Universal Studios, *Shadow of a Doubt* was Hitchcock's attempt to fully capture the realism of actual settings. Consequently, a real house in the town was chosen for the exteriors of the Newton family home, with the local shops and library also made full use of. Hitchcock even cast some of the locals in the film, notably Edna Mae Wonacott, who plays Charlie's precocious younger sister Ann. Said Hitchcock, '[Thornton] Wilder and I went to great pains to be realistic about the town, the people, and the décor.' [9]

Reliant on atmosphere and performances rather than specific set pieces, the film generally comes up trumps, although there is the occasional Hitchcock touch, among them the use of waltzing couples during the title sequence, a shot which is superimposed over the action at various stages, the meaning of which only becomes apparent as Uncle Charlie's crimes are gradually revealed. Indeed, it's a case of extreme bad luck (or, rather, unexplained coincidence) that Young Charlie should start to hum the *Merry Widow Waltz* at the dinner table for no apparent reason, only to have Uncle Charlie purposely misidentify the tune as *The Blue Danube* so as to throw the family off the scent.

Throughout the film, Hitchcock goes to pains to paint Young Charlie and her Uncle as kindred spirits. The film opens with Uncle Charlie lying on his bed in the cheap Philadelphia rooming house at which he is staying (number 13, of course), the spoils from his latest crime scattered on the floor; meanwhile, several hundred miles away in Santa Rosa, his niece is lying on *her* bed, bored, and hoping that something will happen to liven up her dull life. Says Young Charlie to her father, 'We just go along and nothing happens. We're in a terrible rut.' However, the arrival of Uncle Charlie's telegram announcing his imminent arrival soon has the household in a flutter ('Telegram, huh? I knew there'd be an accident if your Aunt Sarah got her driving licence,' says Mr Newton before he's heard the contents of the message).

Uncle Charlie's arrival produces a frenzy of activity in the household. But even on his first night, there are portents of the drama to come. Says Young Charlie to her Uncle: 'I have a feeling deep inside of you there's something nobody knows about.' Nobody, that is, except the two detectives who turn up the following day, posing as survey takers, but who are really on the hunt for the killer and hoping to get a photograph of him for identification purposes ('I've never been photographed in my life, and I don't *intend* to be,' protests Uncle Charlie with perhaps a little too much vehemence at their request for a picture).

Meanwhile, a welcome dose of humour is brought into the proceedings with the introduction of Herbie Hawkins

(Hume Cronyn), the Newtons' neighbour, who shares a passion for crime stories with Mr Newton (who, it should be noted, is carrying a copy of *Unsolved Crimes* under his arm the first time we see him). Says Herbie during one of his many conversations with Joseph about the subject, 'That little Frenchman beats them all. You can talk all you like about Sherlock Holmes, but that little Frenchman beats them all' (of course, he really means that little *Belgian*!). Yet despite Herbie and Joseph's shared interest in the solving of crime puzzles, they both completely fail to pick up on the fact that a real life murderer is living under their noses. That falls to Young Charlie, who notices that her Uncle has removed a page from the evening newspaper; her suspicions further aroused, she hotfoots it down to the library to look at another copy, and is shocked to read the headline, 'Where is the Merry Widow Murderer?' which is followed by news of a 'Nation-wide search under way for strangler of three women.'

Naturally, it isn't long before Uncle Charlie realizes that his niece is on to him. 'Go away or I'll kill you myself,' she informs him, utterly betrayed. 'See, that's the way I feel about you!' Consequently, he decides to get rid of *her*, first by sawing away one of the steps on the back staircase that only she seems to use, then later by attempting to gas her with carbon monoxide in the garage. Both attempts fail – as does his bid to throw her from his train, which results in his own death, thus bringing the story to an ironic (albeit rather neat) close.

In a film not reliant on elaborate camera moves and angles, the performances in *Shadow of a Doubt* are all important. Teresa Wright and Joseph Cotten particularly shine in their roles, especially Wright, who develops from an excited girl with a crush on the uncle she's idealized, to a young woman betrayed by the grim reality, but determined on resolving the situation by doing what she sees as the right thing.

The supporting cast is also uniformly good, notably Henry Travers as the brow-beaten Joseph Newton, very much the underdog at the bank where he works as a lowly clerk; Edna Mae Wonacott as his younger daughter Ann, whose character very much resembles that of Tootie Smith in Sally Benson's *Meet Me in St Louis*; and Hume Cronyn as the crime-loving neighbour Herbie Hawkins, whose obsession with murder becomes more lurid with his every appearance. A word also for Janet Shaw's brief but telling turn as Louise, a cocktail waitress at a late-night drinking bar to which Uncle Charlie takes his niece to 'explain' things over a ginger beer and a double brandy. 'I never thought I'd see *you* in here, Charlie' says the slouching waitress, to whom life has obviously not been kind (when she spies the ring that Uncle Charlie has given her former classmate, she gasps, 'Why, I'd just *die* for a ring like that!'). However, the less said about Patricia Collinge's two-dimensional performance as Emma Newton the better. All toothy twittering, she very quickly becomes an irritation to watch.

Critical reaction to *Shadow of a Doubt* was mostly positive. 'One of the top spine-tinglers to come from Mr Hitchcock's well-stocked chamber of horrors,' enthused critic Herb Sterne, to which Harris Deans, writing in the *Sunday Dispatch*, added, 'Nothing much happens, but like a nervous girl going

down a dark alley, you've got your mouth open ready to scream if necessary.' Hmm, a bit over the top that one, given that the film has dated somewhat and does seem a little slow in places these days. Much more succinct, then, is James Agee's summation: 'I must admit that its skill is soft and that it is distinctly below the standard set by Hitchcock's best English work.'

Nevertheless, these minor reservations aside, the film was a commercial success and earned an Academy Award nomination for Gordon McDonell's original story (itself loosely based on the real life case of multiple strangler Earle Leonard Nelson, who was hanged in 1928). The film was adapted for radio in 1944, 1946, 1948, 1949 and 1952. It was remade for the big screen in 1959 (as *Step Down to Terror*) and in 1991 as a TV movie. However, the 1992 French film *A Shadow of a Doubt* (*L'Ombre du Doute*) is a different kettle of fish entirely.

Hitchcock cameo Note that Hitchcock can be spotted in an early scene on a train, playing cards with a doctor and his wife (he has the complete suit of spades in his hand!).

Shadow of a Doubt
(US, 1991, 96m, colour)

CREDITS
Director: Karen Arthur
Screenplay: John Gay

CAST
Mark Harmon (Charlie Spencer), Margaret Welsh (Charlie Newton), Diane Ladd (Emma Newton), William Lanteau (Henry Newton), Tippi Hedren (Mrs Mathewson), Rick Lenz (Herb Hawkins), Shirley Knight (Mrs Potter), Norm Skaggs (Gary Graham)

In this rather bland remake of the 1943 Hitchcock film, Mark Harmon takes over the Joseph Cotten role of serial killer Charles Spencer (previously Oakley), with Margaret Welsh as his devoted niece Charlie Newton. Of interest in the cast is Tippi Hedren, who of course starred in *The Birds* (1963) and *Marnie* (1964) for Hitchcock. Otherwise, this is typical television fodder, routine in almost every way.

SCHAFFER, ANTHONY (1926–2002) British playwright. The work of this noted playwright includes the hit thriller *Sleuth*, the screenplay for the 1972 film version of which he also penned. Following experience as a barrister, Shaffer turned to writing novels with his twin brother, playwright Peter Shaffer (1926–), in the 1950s, using the pseudonym Peter Anthony. He went on to form a partnership with director Robin Hardy in the 1960s, writing the scripts for commercials. He turned to screenwriting in 1971 with *Mr Forbush and the Penguins*, which was followed with, among others, *The Wicker Man* (1973), which was directed by Robin Hardy, *Murder on the Orient Express* (1974), on which he did an un-credited re-write, *Death on the Nile* (1978), *Absolution* (1978) and *Evil Under the Sun* (1982). In 1972 he wrote the screenplay for Hitchcock's *Frenzy*, having been offered the job on the back of *Sleuth*. Commented Shaffer: 'Hitch was always interested in writers from the thriller genre. He'd used Raymond Chandler before on *Strangers on a Train*, plus a number of other people who'd written thrillers. So I think it was the success of *Sleuth* that drew him to me... I got a call from him on New Year's Eve, and he said to me in that dark brown Cockney voice of his, "I wish you to work on a motion picture, dear boy" Of course, I thought it was a big gag. I was just off to a party and I thought, "Who *is* this joker?" I didn't take it seriously. So I said, "Why don't you come and join the party?" He then informed me that he was in Los Angeles and, as I was in New York at the time, he might be a few moments late! Well, a short while later, the book on which *Frenzy* was based arrived by special delivery at my door, and I must say it was one of the better New Year's presents one could have had!' [10] Added Shaffer: 'I think the success of *Frenzy* got him out of a bit of a hole, because his previous films had not succeeded. They were clinkers in a way. I'm talking of *Marnie*, *Torn Curtain* and *Topaz*. They didn't really work, so *Frenzy* got his audience back. Personally, I look back on it as a wonderful opportunity to work with Hitchcock. He was a legendary figure and you learn a lot from someone like that. Whether you use what you've learnt is another matter, but at least you've learnt it!' [11] Shaffer's third wife was the actress Diane Cilento (1933–). **Hitchography:** *Frenzy* (1972)

THE SHAME OF MARY BOYLE see *Juno and the Paycock*

SHAMLEY This was the name Hitchcock gave to the production company through which he produced his TV shows *Alfred Hitchcock Presents* (1955–1962) and *The Alfred Hitchcock Hour* (1962–1965). He also made *Psycho* (1960) and *Dark Intruder* (1965) through the company, the latter the pilot for another anthology series to have been titled *Black Cloak* (when the series failed to generate any interest from the networks, the pilot was released as a theatrical support). The name Shamley derives from the Tudor cottage the Hitchcocks bought in 1928 as a weekend retreat. Situated in Shamley Green not far from Guildford, it became the family's bolt hole during the 1930s. Hitchcock held on to the property as a safety net once he'd moved to America, but sold the place following the war (during which his mother lived there, so as to avoid the blitz).

SHARPE, EDITH British character actress. Sharpe had a small, un-credited role in Hitchcock's *Rebecca* (1940). Her other films include *The Guinea Pig* (1948), *Happy is the Bride* (1958) and *Satan Never Sleeps* (1962). **Hitchography:** *Rebecca* (1940)

SHAW, JANET (1919–2001) American small part actress. Shaw popped up in a handful of 1940s films, among them Hitchcock's *Shadow of a Doubt* (1943), in which she played Louise, *Ladies Courageous* (1944) and *Time Out of Mind* (1947). **Hitchography:** *Shadow of a Doubt* (1943)

SHEFFIELD, REGINALD (1901–1957) British-born actor. On stage and screen as a child, Sheffield went to appear in a number of Hollywood productions, among them *Of Human Bondage* (1934), *Cardinal Richelieu* (1935) and Hitchcock's *Suspicion* (1941), in which he played Reggie Wetherby. His other films include *Eyes of the Night* (1942), *Wilson* (1944) and *Kiss the Blood off My Hands* (1948). He was the father of Johnny Sheffield (1931–), child star of countless *Tarzan* and *Bomba* movies. **Hitchography:** *Suspicion* (1941)

SHERWOOD, ROBERT E (1896–1955) American playwright. This highly respected playwright, whose works include *Waterloo Bridge*, *The Petrified Forest*, *Tovarich* (adapted from the Jacques Deval original) and *Idiot's Delight*, also dabbled in screenwriting, among his credits being *The Scarlet Pimpernel* (1934), *The Adventures of Marco Polo* (1938) and Hitchcock's *Rebecca* (1940), for which he revised a disastrous first treatment submitted by Hitchcock, Joan Harrison and Philip MacDonald. Sherwood's other screenplays include *The Best Years of Our Lives* (1945), which earned him an Oscar, and *The Bishop's Wife* (1948). **Hitchography:** *Rebecca* (1940)

SHARP-BOLSTER, ANITA (1900–1985) Irish-born actress. This hatchet-faced performer popped up as a support in a variety of American films, most notably as Lorelei, the bearded lady in Hitchcock's *Saboteur* (1942). Her other credits include *The List of Adrian Messenger* (1963) and *The Boy Cried Murder* (1966). **Hitchography:** *Saboteur* (1942)

SHAYNE, CONSTANTIN (1888–1984) Russian-born character actor. Shayne is perhaps best remembered for playing bookstore owner Pop Liebel in Hitchcock's *Vertigo* (1958), in which he gets to tell the mysterious story of Carlotta Valdes, with whom Kim Novak's Madeleine Elster seems so obsessed ('He kept the child and threw her away. Men could do that in those days. They had the power... and the freedom...') **Hitchography:** *Vertigo* (1958)

SHAYNE, ROBERT (1900–1992, real name Robert Shaen Dawe) American actor. Although he took the lead role in *The Neanderthal Man* (1953), Shayne was more often cast in supporting roles in such films as *Keep 'em Rolling* (1934), *The Swordsman* (1947) and *Valley of the Redwoods* (1961). He can also be seen in Hitchcock's *North by Northwest* (1959) as businessman Larry Wade, sharing a scene with Cary Grant's Roger Thornhill in the Oak Room sequence. **Hitchography:** *North by Northwest* (1959)

SHINE, BILL (1911–1997, real name Wilfred Shine Jr) British supporting actor. Shine specialized in upper-class types. His many films, beginning with *High Seas* in 1929, include *The Scarlet Pimpernel* (1934), *Let George Do It* (1940), *Blue Murder at St Trinian's* (1957), *The Jigsaw Man* (1983) and

The McGuffin (1985, TV). He can also be seen in *Harmony Heaven* (1930), parts of which were allegedly directed by Hitchcock, as well as four subsequent Hitchcock pictures, all in minor supporting roles. **Hitchography:** *Harmony Heaven* (1930), *Rich and Strange* (1932), *Waltzes from Vienna* (1933), *Young and Innocent* (1937), *Under Capricorn* (1949)

SIDNEY, SYLVIA (1910–1999, real name Sophia Kosow) American actress. With a career spanning over 70 years, Sidney made her stage debut in 1926 and entered films in 1929 with *Thru Different Eyes*. She became a major star in the 1930s, appearing in such classics as *Street Scene* (1931), *Fury* (1936) and *You Only Live Once* (1937). In 1936 she travelled to Britain to appear in Hitchcock's *Sabotage*, in which she played the wife of an anarchist. However, she felt constricted by Hitchcock's method of direction, and later commented, 'What did Hitchcock teach me? To be a puppet and not try to be creative.' [12] In 1939, Sidney began to turn more to the stage, although she still occasionally appeared in films such as *The Wagons Roll at Night* (1941), *Love from a Stranger* (1947) and *Les Misérables* (1953) In later years she emerged as a respected character actress in a wide variety of films, among them *Summer Wishes, Winter Dreams* (1973), *Damien: Omen II* (1978), *The Shadow Box* (1980, TV), *Beetlejuice* (1988) and *Mars Attacks!* (1996). Her final appearance was in the 1990s' remake of the TV series *Fantasy Island* (1998–1999). **Hitchography:** *Sabotage* (1936)

THE SILENT STRANGER see *Step Down to Terror*

SIM, ALASTAIR (1900–1976) Scottish-born comedy character actor. This much-loved actor came to the profession at the comparatively late age of 30, following experience as an elocutionist. In films five years later with *The Case of Gabriel Perry* (1935), he went on to make the most of his lugubrious features in such cherished films as *Alf's Button Afloat* (1938), *This Man is News* (1938), *Inspector Hornleigh* (1938), *Green for Danger* (1946), *The Happiest Days of Your Life* (1950), *Laughter in Paradise* (1951) and *The Belles of St Trinian's* (1954), in which he memorably donned drag to play the headmistress Miss Fritton (as well as her ne'er do well brother Clarence). He was also the screen's finest *Scrooge* (1951), a role he repeated for the 1971 cartoon *A Christmas Carol*. In 1950 Sim appeared as the eccentric, accordion-playing Commodore Gill in Hitchcock's *Stage Fright*, bringing a welcome touch of humour to the proceedings (when asked what kind of a father he thinks he makes, the Commodore replies, 'Unique! Quite unique!' and one would have to agree). Astonishingly, Hitchcock was less than enamoured of Sim's performance. Sim's other films include *Folly to Be Wise* (1952), *An Inspector Calls* (1954), *School for Scoundrels* (1959), *The Ruling Class* (1971) and *Escape from the Dark* (1976). He also worked frequently on the stage, directing many of the productions he appeared in. **Hitchography:** *Stage Fright* (1950)

SIM, GERALD (1925–) British character actor. Noted for his flawed authority roles, Gerald Sim first came to films

at the age of 22 in *Fame is the Spur* (1947). He went on to appear in the likes of *Trio* (1955) and *Seven Days to Noon* (1950), but it was when he reached middle age that he finally came into his own in such films as *The Angry Silence* (1960), *Whistle Down the Wind* (1961), *Séance on a Wet Afternoon* (1964) and, best of all, *Ryan's Daughter* (1970). In 1972, he made a cameo appearance as one of two city gents discussing the crimes of a serial killer in a London pub in Hitchcock's *Frenzy*. His other films include *The Slipper and the Rose* (1976), *A Bridge Too Far* (1977) and *Shadowlands* (1993). He is also familiar to TV audiences as the rector in the sit-com *To the Manor Born* (1979–1981). **Hitchography:** *Frenzy* (1972)

SKALL, WILLIAM V (1898–1976) American cinematographer. Noted for his colour work, Skall filmed on both sides of the Atlantic, his credits including *Victoria the Great* (1937), for which he photographed the Technicolor finale, *Northwest Passage* (1940), *Quo Vadis?* (1955) and *The Silver Challis* (1955). In 1948 he photographed Hitchcock's *Rope* with Joseph Valentine, for which they were required to film in continuous ten-minute takes, which involved much prior rehearsal from both the actors and the crew. In 1948, Skall again teamed with Valentine (and Winton C Hoch) to photograph *Joan of Arc*, for which he won an Oscar for best colour cinematography. **Hitchography:** *Rope* (1948)

The Skin Game
(GB, 1932, 85m (some sources state 89m), bw) ★

CREDITS
Production company:	British International Pictures
Producer:	John Maxwell
Director:	Alfred Hitchcock
Screenplay:	Alfred Hitchcock, Alma Reville, based on the play by John Galsworthy
Cinematographer:	Jack Cox
Editor:	A Gobett, Rene Marrison
Art director:	J B Maxwell
Sound:	Alec Murray
Assistant director:	Frank Mills

CAST
Edmund Gwenn (Mr Hornblower), C V France (Mr Hillcrist), Helen Haye (Mrs Hillcrist), Jill Esmond (Jill Hillcrist), John Longden (Charles Hornblower), Phyllis Konstam (Chloe Hornblower), Herbert Ross (Mr Jackman), Frank Lawton (Rolf Hornblower), Dora Gregory (Mrs Jackman), Ronald Frankau (Auctioneer), R E Jeffrey (Stranger), George Bancroft (Second Stranger), Rodney Ackland (Extra)

Based on the 1920 play by John Galsworthy, *The Skin Game* is very much a talk piece and barely seems like a Hitchcock picture at all. The story centres round two feuding families, the Hillcrists and the Hornblowers, who fall out over a piece of land. The Hillcrists, who originally owned the land, have sold it on the understanding that those living on it should continue to do so, while the Hornblowers, who have bought the land, now want to evict the tenants and build a factory. The plot basically focuses on the arguments both for and against the proposed factory – country idyll vs jobs and security – with a pregnancy and suicide thrown into the brew to spice up the proceedings.

The play had actually been filmed before in 1920, with stage star Edmund Gwenn heading the cast. For his version, Hitchcock invited Gwenn back to play Mr Hornblower, casting character star C V France as his rival, Mr Hillcrist. The rest of the cast was filled out with such Hitchcock regulars as John Longden, Phyllis Konstam and Edward Chapman. Yet though he was surrounded by people he was comfortable working with, Hitchcock seems to have been pretty uninspired by the material, despite having adapted it himself, with assistance from his wife Alma. Commented Hitchcock later, 'I didn't make it by choice, and there isn't much to be said about it.' [13] Indeed, there is little to recommend the picture today, which is very slow and stiff, although it did at least introduce Hitchcock to Edmund Gwenn, whom he would later use to better effect in *Foreign Correspondent* (1940) and *The Trouble with Harry* (1955).

SKINNER, FRANK (1898–1968) American composer. Long at Universal, Skinner scored or co-scored hundreds of films, notable among them several of the studio's classic horrors, including *Son of Frankenstein* (1939), *Tower of London* (1939), *The Invisible Man Returns* (1940) and *Abbott and Costello Meet Frankenstein* (1948), as well as several Sherlock Holmes adventures, such as *Sherlock Holmes and the Voice of Terror* (1942) and *Sherlock Holmes and the Secret Weapon* (1942). He also scored Hitchcock's *Saboteur* (1942), but the music, full of cliffhanging melodramatics, was not among his more subtle efforts. His many other credits include *Destry Rides Again* (1939), *Hellzapoppin* (1941), *Harvey* (1950) and *Madame X* (1966). **Hitchography:** *Saboteur* (1942)

SKIRBALL, JACK H (1896–1985) American producer. Following experience as a salesman, Skirball turned to film, working his way up to executive in charge of production and distribution for Educational Pictures in 1932. He went independent in 1938, producing such films as *Miracle on Main Street* (1938), *It's in the Bag* (1945), *Payment on Demand* (1951) and *A Matter of Time* (1976). He also produced two films for Hitchcock: *Saboteur* (1942) and *Shadow of a Doubt* (1943), both of which were made for Universal. **Hitchography:** *Saboteur* (1942), *Shadow of a Doubt* (1943)

SLEZAK, WALTER (1902–1983) Austrian-born character actor. This burly-looking actor was discovered by director Michael Curtiz in 1922 while working as a bank clerk, and made his film debut in Curtiz's *Sodom und Gomorra*. Subsequently busy in Germany on both stage and screen, Slezak went on to appear in *Mein Leopold* (1924), *Aus des Rheinlands Schicksalstagen* (1926) and *Das Hannerl vom Rolandsbogen* (1928). In 1930 he moved to America, making his Broadway debut in 1931. However, he didn't appear in

his first American film, *Once Upon a Honeymoon*, until 1942. His best film role was as Willi, the Nazi submarine captain in Hitchcock's *Lifeboat* (1944). Ironically, Slezak was himself virulently anti-Nazi, but this didn't prevent the film's star, Tallulah Bankhead, from snidely referring to him as a 'God-damn Nazi' during production. Slezak's other films include *Born to Kill* (1947), *Abbott and Costello in the Foreign Legion* (1950), *Emil and the Detectives* (1964), *Wonderful Life* (1964) and *Black Beauty* (1971). He committed suicide in 1983. **Hitchography:** *Lifeboat* (1944)

SLIFER, CLARENCE American effects technician. Slifer worked on a number of films for producer David O Selznick, including *Duel in the Sun* (1946), Hitchcock's *The Paradine Case* (1947) and *Portrait of Jennie* (1948), which earned him an Oscar. **Hitchography:** *The Paradine Case* (1947)

SLOANE, OLIVE (1896–1963) British character actress. Sloane had her finest moment in the thriller *Seven Days to Noon* (1950), in which she played a middle-aged model caught up in a scientist's plot to blow up London. On stage from childhood as a singer and dancer, she made her film debut in *Greatheart* in 1921. She made a further six silent films, culminating with *Money Isn't Everything* (1925), after which she returned to the theatre for seven years. Back on screen with *The Good Companions* in 1933, she gradually built up a reputation for playing sympathe-tic floozies. Her subsequent films include *Sing As We Go* (1934), *Dreaming Lips* (1937), *Thunder Rock* (1942), *The Guinea Pig* (1948), *Serious Charge* (1959) and *Heavens Above!* (1963). She also appeared in Hitchcock's *Under Capricorn* (1949) as Sal, the drunken cook. **Hitchography:** *Under Capricorn* (1949)

SMITH, CYRIL (1892–1963, real name Cyril Bruce-Smith) Scottish-born actor. Busy on both stage and screen, Smith is best remembered for his stage and film role as the henpecked Pa Hornett in *Sailor, Beware!* (1956). On stage from the age of 8, Smith went on to make his film debut at the age of 16 in *The Great Fire of London* (1908). His other films include *The Good Companions* (1933), *One of Our Aircraft is Missing* (1943) and *She Knows Y' Know* (1962). He also made a brief appearance in Hitchcock's *Waltzes from Vienna* (1933). **Hitchography:** *Waltzes from Vienna* (1933)

SOULE, OLAN American supporting actor. Soule appeared in many films in the 1950s and 1960s, among them *Cash McCall* (1960), *13, West Street* (1962), *Shock Treatment* (1964), *The Cincinnati Kid* (1965), *The Bubble* (1966) and *The Destructors* (1967). He is perhaps best remembered, though, for playing the small but curiously memorable role of the assistant auctioneer in *North by Northwest* (1959). He also appeared in an episode of *The Alfred Hitchcock Hour*. **Hitchography:** *North by Northwest* (1959), *Ride the Nightmare* (1962, TV)

SOUTH, LEONARD J American cinematographer. Having operated the camera on many films for Hitchcock in the 1950s and 1960s, including several photographed by Robert Burks, cameraman South (who rarely received a screen credit) graduated to cinematographer proper with the director's final film, *Family Plot* (1976), by which time he'd also photographed *Hang 'Em High* (1968) and *I Sailed to Tahiti with An All-Girl Crew* (1969). His other credits include a handful of films for Disney, among them *Herbie Goes to Monte Carlo* (1977), *The North Avenue Irregulars* (1979) and *Amy* (1981). Not long before Hitchcock's death in 1980, South was preparing to go to Finland to shoot the second unit footage for the director's proposed final film *The Short Night*, but the project was subsequently cancelled. Said South of the director, 'Hitch was a rare combination of true artist, technician and businessman.' [14] **Hitchography:** *Rear Window* (1954), *To Catch a Thief* (1955), *The Trouble with Harry* (1955), *The Man Who Knew Too Much* (1956), *The Wrong Man* (1956), *Vertigo* (1958), *North by Northwest* (1959), *Psycho* (1960), *The Birds* (1963), *Marnie* (1964), *Torn Curtain* (1966), *Family Plot* (1976)

Spanish Jade
(GB, 1922, 67m approx, bw, silent)

CREDITS
Production company: Famous Players–Lasky
Directors: Tom Geraghty, John S Robertson
Screenplay: Josephine Lovett, based on the play by Louis Joseph Vance

CAST
Evelyn Brent (Manuela), David Powell (Perez), Marc MacDermott (Grandee), Harry Ham (Manvers), Charles de Rochefort (Esban), Frank Stanmore (Donkins)

Released in 1922, this lost melodrama about a Spanish girl whose lover kills her husband had inter-titles designed by Hitchcock. Starring American import Evelyn Brent, it was co-directed at Islington Studios by Tom Geraghty and John S Robertson for Famous Players–Lasky.

Spellbound
(US, 1945, 111m, bw) ★★

CREDITS
Production company: Selznick International
Producer: David O Selznick
Director: Alfred Hitchcock
Screenplay: Ben Hecht, Angus MacPhail, based on *The House of Dr Edwardes* by Francis Beeding
Cinematography: George Barnes
Music: Miklos Rozsa
Music director: Ray Heindorf (un-credited)
Editors: Hal C Kern, William H Ziegler
Production design: James Basevi, John Ewing

Costumes: Howard Greer
Special effects: Jack Cosgrove
Dream sequence: Salvador Dali

CAST
Ingrid Bergman (Dr Constance Peterson), Gregory Peck (Dr Anthony Edwardes/John Ballantine), Michael Chekhov (Dr Brulov), Leo G Carroll (Dr Merchison), Norman Lloyd (Garmes), Rhonda Fleming (Mary Carmichael), John Emery (Dr Fleurot), Bill Goodwin (Empire State Hotel house detective), Donald Curtis (Harry), Steven Geray (Dr Graff), Wallace Ford (Hotel bore), Art Baker (Lieutenant Cooley), Paul Harvey (Dr Hanish), Regis Toomey (Sergeant Gillespie), Jean Acker (Matron), Richard Bartell (Ticket collector), Edward Fielding (The real Dr Edwardes), Addison Richards (Police Captain), Erskine Sanford (Dr Galt), Joel Davis (Young Ballantine), Teddy Infuhr (Ballantine's brother)

Video availability: Pearson
DVD availability: Pearson
CD availability: *Spellbound* (Stanyan); *Psycho – The Essential Hitchcock* (Silva Screen), which contains *Concerto for Orchestra* derived from the score for *Spellbound*; *A History of Hitchcock – Dial M for Murder* (Silva Screen), which also contains the *Concerto for Orchestra*

'Will he kiss me or kill me?' So runs the poster strap line for Hitchcock's romantic psychological thriller, which the director himself described as 'just another manhunt story wrapped up in pseudo-psychoanalysis.' [15] Hitchcock was paid $150,000 to helm the $1.5 million production for producer David O Selznick, which was based on the 1927 novel *The House of Dr Edwardes* by John Leslie Palmer and Hilary Aiden St George Saunders (writing as Francis Beeding), although little of the book made it into the script by Ben Hecht and Angus MacPhail.

Hitchcock had been keen to make the first picture about psychoanalysis, and to this end he toned down some of the novel's more absurd goings on. 'The original novel... was about a madman taking over an insane asylum. It was melodramatic and quite weird... even the orderlies were lunatics and they did some very queer things,' [16] explained the director. Nevertheless, even in the finished film, the majority of the staff of Green Mansions psychiatric hospital appear to have as many emotional problems as the patients they are treating: Dr Constance Peterson (Ingrid Bergman) lacks human and emotional experience; her colleague Dr Fleurot (John Emery) is lovesick for her; Dr Edwardes (Gregory Peck), the new head of the institute, is an amnesiac who has assumed the role of a man he may or may not have killed; while Dr Murchison (Leo G Carroll), the outgoing head of the institute, has recently suffered a breakdown and is the real culprit of the death of his successor, brought about by psychotic jealousy. Compared to them, the patients – among them a man-hater named Mary Carmichael (Rhonda Fleming) and Garmes (Norman Lloyd), a young man with a guilt complex – seem to have but minor ailments.

Hitchcock began scripting the film with Angus MacPhail in Britain in 1944 while working on his two Ministry of Information films, *Bon Voyage* and *Aventure Malgache*, which were also written by MacPhail. Back in Hollywood, Hitch felt that the script needed further work, and so teamed up with Oscar winning writer Ben Hecht, who would go on to be involved in the scripting of several key 1940s films for the director (he'd already made some un-credited contributions to the script for *Foreign Correspondent* (1940)). Hecht was chosen because he had a personal fascination with psychiatry ('He turned out to be a very fortunate choice,' [17] commented Hitchcock). Nevertheless, Selznick was initially wary of the project, commenting, 'I don't think we should make this picture… it is somewhat of a waste of Hitchcock.' [18] However, given that his two stars, Ingrid Bergman and Gregory Peck, were due to be loaned out for another project in a couple of months time, *Spellbound* became the chosen film for want of a better project. Selznick needn't have worried, though; the film was a smash, earning in excess of $7 million on its release.

Almost 60 years on, the film, which began shooting on 7 July 1944, seems to have dated more than most Hitchcocks of its period. The psychological angle has lost much of its novelty value, while the endless scenes of chat consistently impede the forward pace. Very much an interior film, the story is set mostly in a series of interchangeable rooms, be they at the institute, a New York hotel or in the home of Dr Peterson's mentor, Dr Brulov (Michael Chekhov). Of course, some might argue that these interior scenes reflect the interior goings on in the mind of the central protagonist; if that keeps them quietly amused, then so be it.

That said, the Hitchcock touches are certainly memorable when they come, among them the fork lines drawn in a tablecloth that trigger Dr Edwardes's anxiety about his recent past; the first kiss between Dr Edwardes and Dr Peterson, which dissolves to a series of opening doors, symbolic of their growing trust and giving (which is reflected in the film's opening statement, 'The analyst seeks only to induce the patient to talk about his problems, to open the locked doors of his mind'); the constant referral to lines, be they the pattern on a robe, railway lines, sled tracks, or the design of a coverlet; the shot taken from inside Dr Edwardes's glass as he downs some milk spiked with bromide; and, best of all, the Salvador Dali-designed dream sequence, the interpretation of which reveals Dr Murchison to be the killer of the real Dr Edwardes, the witnessing of which has triggered John Ballantine – as we learn him to be – to assume the dead psychiatrist's identity.

Hitchcock was determined that the dream sequence should avoid the traditional swirling smoke look and be presented as a series of pin sharp images, among them a collage of eyes ('I seemed to be in a gambling house, but there weren't any walls, just a lot of curtains with eyes painted on them,' explains Ballantine), a faceless man ('He was hiding behind a tall chimney and he had a small wheel in his hand') and giant, winged creature ('I was running and heard something beating over my head…'). Selznick appreciated the publicity value that Dali's name would bring to the film, even though he was-

n't entirely appreciative of the artist's efforts. ('His work was a minor but still valuable contribution to the eventual success of the picture,' [19] he later commented.)

The small wheel in the hand of the faceless man cleverly turns out to be the revolver Dr Murchison shot the real Dr Edwardes with, the shock of which was enough for Ballantine to take over the dead doctor's personality in a bid to overcome the guilt *he* personally assumes for the crime, the trigger mechanism for this being his own accidental killing of his brother when they were children (in a rather gruesome flashback, we learn that he slid down a stoop wall, kicking his brother off the edge and onto some spiked railings below!). As far-fetched and involved as this explanation is, it is certainly effectively put over, even if it doesn't withstand much subsequent scrutiny.

Things finally conclude with Dr Murchison committing suicide using the same revolver he killed Dr Edwardes with; having threatened Dr Peterson with the weapon after she has 'solved' the case ('You forget that the punishment for two murders is the same as one,' he informs her), he goes on to commit suicide by turning the gun 180 degrees on himself once she has bluffed her way out of his office. Of course, such a hand manoeuvre is an impossible feat to accomplish, so Hitchcock had a giant plaster hand and gun created, which he filmed in close up from Murchison's point of view, complete with an animated explosion as the gun goes off. To complete this startling effect, Hitchcock had a few frames of the explosion hand-tinted red for the film's original release (prints of which occasionally show up on television, although viewers who videotape the film need to be extremely quick with the pause button to catch them).

To complete the film, Selznick hired the noted Hungarian composer Miklos Rozsa to provide the score. For it, Rozsa produced one of the cinema's most wildly romantic themes, the cherry on the cake being his use of a theremin for the more dramatic passages. Rozsa would go on to win a much-deserved Oscar for his efforts, which add immeasurably to the film's impact. However, when he again used a theremin for his score for *The Lost Weekend* (1945), Selznick objected. Responded Rozsa, 'Yes, I used the theremin – and also the violin, the oboe and the clarinet!' [20]

Despite the fairly far-fetched goings on in the film – we are expected to believe that a qualified psychiatrist will desert her professional code to protect an imposter and suspected murderer simply because she somewhat improbably falls in love with him – Peck and Bergman perform with conviction, even when delivering such lines as, 'I remember now – Edwardes is dead. I killed him and took his place. I'm someone else and I don't know who!' They even manage to enliven a series of mundane exchanges during a romantic picnic: 'Ham or liverwurst?' Edwardes asks Dr Peterson, regarding her preference of sandwich, to which comes the impassioned reply, 'Liverwurst!'

Given its frequently implausible developments, *Spellbound* received some fairly mixed reviews. 'Alfred Hitchcock handles his players and action in suspenseful manner and, except for a few episodes of much scientific dialogue, maintains a steady pace in keeping the camera moving,' opined *Variety*. Critic Herb Sterne was rather less forgiving, though, commenting: 'The hero of the film suffers from amnesia, a guilt complex, split personality and a form of paranoia that not only makes him believe that he killed a man, but on several occasions gives the impression he intends to commit murder again. With all that the matter with him, his psychiatrist sweetheart, who takes it on herself to cure him, snaps him out of it in what appears to be little more than three days.'

Audiences didn't care; when the film opened on 1 November 1945, they flocked to see its stars, hear the music and ponder the new psychological angle. The Academy of Motion Picture Arts and Sciences was also impressed, for in addition to earning Miklos Rozsa a best score statuette, the film was also nominated for best picture (Selznick), best director (Hitchcock), best supporting actor (Michael Chekhov), best cinematography (George Barnes) and best special effects (Jack Cosgrove).

The character Garmes, played by Norman Lloyd, was an in-joke: screenwriter Ben Hecht occasionally directed films himself, and his preferred cinematographer was Lee Garmes. Radio adaptations of the film were broadcast in 1948 and 1951.

Hitchcock cameo Note that Hitchcock can be seen exiting an elevator with a violin case in the Empire State Hotel.

SPENCER, DOROTHY (1909–) American editor. One of Hollywood's top editors, Spencer began her career in the late 1920s with *Married in Hollywood* (1929) and went on to cut many classic movies, among them *Stagecoach* (1939), *A Tree Grows in Brooklyn* (1945), *Cleopatra* (1963) and *Von Ryan's Express* (1965). She worked for Hitchcock twice, on *Foreign Correspondent* (1940), on which she had to keep a tight grip of the film's complex narrative, keeping the running time down to a brisk two hours, and *Lifeboat* (1944). **Hitchography:** *Foreign Correspondent* (1940), *Lifeboat* (1944)

Stage Fright

(GB, 1950, 110m, bw) ★★

CREDITS

Production company:	Warner Bros.
Producer:	Alfred Hitchcock
Director:	Alfred Hitchcock
Screenplay:	Whitfield Cook, Alma Reville, James Bridie, based on the novel *Man Running* (aka *Outrun the Constable* in America) by Selwyn Jepson
Cinematographer:	Wilkie Cooper
Music:	Leighton Lucas
Music director:	Louis Levy
Editor:	Edward Jarvis
Art director:	Terence Verity
Costumes:	Milo Anderson, Christian Dior
Sound:	Harold V King

CAST

Jane Wyman (Eve Gill/Doris Tinsdale), Marlene Dietrich (Charlotte Inwood), Michael Wilding (Inspector Wilfred Smith), Alastair Sim (Commodore Gill), Richard Todd (Jonathan Cooper), Sybil Thorndike (Mrs Gill), Kay Walsh (Nellie Goode), Joyce Grenfell ('Lovely Ducks'), Miles Malleson (Mr Fortescue), Hector MacGregor (Freddie), Andre Morell (Inspector Byard), Patricia Hitchcock (Chubby Bannister), Ballard Berkeley (Sergeant Mellish), Irene Handl (Mrs Mason), Alfie Bass (Stagehand)

CD availability: *Psycho – The Essential Alfred Hitchcock* (Silva Screen) which contains the *Rhapsody* inspired by the film's score; *The Great British Film Music Album – Sixty Glorious Years 1938–1998* (Silva Screen), which also contains *Rhapsody*.

Following his disappointing bid to become an independent filmmaker with the experimental *Rope* (1948) and the melodramatic *Under Capricorn* (1949), Hitchcock decided to return to safer ground with his next picture *Stage Fright*, an old-fashioned murder story that, like *Under Capricorn*, he shot in Britain. Astonishingly, the film, the first of four Hitchcock made for Warner Bros., was much criticized upon its release. Yet over 50 years later, it remains something of an un-acknowledged gem.

Based on the 1948 novel *Man Running* by Selwyn Jepson, as well as the true-life Thompson-Bywaters murder case of 1922, the film opens with a seemingly innocent man on the run for a murder he says he did not commit. As he explains it, Jonathan Cooper (Richard Todd) was at home in his flat when he was visited by his lover, stage legend Charlotte Inwood (Marlene Dietrich), who claims to have murdered her husband, the give away being the blood stain on the front of her dress. Begging Jonathan to return to her apartment to get her a clean dress, he reluctantly agrees to do so, staging things so that the murder looks like a break in. Unfortunately, when leaving the premises Jonathan is spotted by Charlotte's maid, Nellie Goode (Kay Walsh), who naturally reports him to the police. Consequently, when they pay a call on him, Jonathan makes a break for it, roping in his friend Eve Gill (Jane Wyman), a RADA drama student, who helps him by taking him to the seaside home of her father, Commodore Gill (Alastair Sim), so that he can lie low and figure out what to do next.

Examining the stained dress, which Jonathan has wisely kept, the Commodore concludes that the blood was deliberately smeared on it, which leads him to believe that Charlotte has somehow misled Jonathan, who, unwilling to believe this of his lover, foolishly throws the dress into the fire, thus destroying the vital piece of evidence. Determined to further help Jonathan, with whom she is secretly infatuated, Eve decides to see Charlotte Inwood herself and question her about the crime. However, when she reaches the star's home she discovers it to be surrounded by police and reporters. Consequently, she engineers a chance meeting with one of the detectives, Inspector Wilfred Smith (Michael Wilding), at the nearby pub, so that she can pump him for information about the case (comments one patron of the murder, 'I heard they clocked him so hard his false teeth went right across the room!'). Pretending to be a reporter, Eve also manages to bribe Inwood's maid Nellie – whom she also encounters in the pub – into allowing her to pose as her cousin Doris Tinsdale, so that she can cover for the supposedly ill maid, thus allowing her to get close to the star and expose her.

But given that Eve now knows Inspector Smith, whom she's agreed to meet again for tea, and is also posing as Doris the maid, it seems inevitable that their paths should cross at some point during the investigation, leaving Eve with a lot of explaining to do. In the meantime, though, disguised as Doris, Eve overhears Charlotte inform the police that she believes Jonathan to be obsessed with her, supposing that is why he killed her husband. This certainly seems to be the case, for Jonathan later turns up at the theatre where Charlotte is performing, telling her that he still has the blood stained dress; but when the police arrive on the scene, he again makes a run for it.

Things start to come to a head at a theatrical garden party at which Inwood is performing. Determined to expose the actress as a killer once and for all, Eve again poses as Doris Tinsdale, although things are once more complicated by the presence of Inspector Smith and the arrival of Nellie Goode, who is out for more money. Yet with the help of her father, Eve manages to placate Nellie and get a shock reaction from Charlotte by having a cub scout present the star with a blood stained doll (won by the Commodore at a shooting gallery) during her concert. But Eve's plan backfires when Charlotte's reaction to the doll prompts her to faint and subsequently ask for the help of Doris, who now has to explain herself to Inspector Smith, who is naturally curious as to why the star is calling Eve by another name.

With Smith now in on her role-playing deception, Eve determines to exploit it one last time by confronting Charlotte in a dressing room after that evening's show, telling her that *she* in fact has her blood stained dress. The star finally confesses to being in the room when the murder took place ('Some blood *did* splash on my dress,' she reveals) and offers money to buy the garment, at which point she is arrested by the police, who have been listening to the conversation via a hidden microphone. At last, Eve seems to have been vindicated.

But then comes the twist: Jonathan arrives at the theatre in the custody of the police, having been arrested at the home of Eve's mother, where he has been hiding out as 'Mr Robinson', Inspector Smith having put two and two together. Somehow, Jonathan breaks loose, bumps into Eve in one of the corridors and hides out with her in the basement in a prop stagecoach. And it is here, in the dark, that Eve hears her father's voice imploring her to

get away from Jonathan, as he *is* the murderer after all, having been provoked into the crime by Charlotte, so that she can be with her manager Freddie ('I hated to tell you that phony story in your car that time, but there was no other way,' Jonathan tells Eve by way of explanation). It also transpires that Jonathan has killed before, and that he now intends to strangle Eve to further bolster his case for an insanity plea ('There's nothing wrong with my mind. They can't prove there is – unless I do it a third time'). Luckily, Eve manages to escape, and in chasing her, Jonathan finds himself surrounded on the stage, only to have his one exit blocked by the descending safety curtain, under which he is crushed while trying to slip into the orchestra pit, thus bringing the film full circle, given that it opens with the rising of the safety curtain as the credits play.

Flashbacks don't lie! That was certainly the accusation hurled at *Stage Fright* by the critics, who felt that Jonathan's opening account of the murder was dishonest and misled the audience too much. In retrospect, though, this trick can be seen as the film's most effective device, perfectly setting up the deceptive plot, and effectively playing on audience expectations that flashbacks *do* tell the truth, especially when seemingly told by an innocent man wrongly accused of a crime, a contrivance already exploited to great effect by Hitchcock in the likes of *The 39 Steps* (1935) and *Young and Innocent* (1937). And anyway, why *shouldn't* a murderer lie? They do it all the time in real life! Indeed, the audience might better enquire as to why Jonathan's previous criminal record remains conveniently undisclosed until so late in the proceedings.

Packed with amusing incidents, *Stage Fright* very much recalls Hitchcock's British work in the 1930s in both plot and handling, albeit with more glamorous stars. In fact there were few more glamorous than the legendary Marlene Dietrich, whose vainglorious Charlotte Inwood seems to be little more than a sly send up of her own exaggerated stage and screen personality (comments the Commodore of Inwood at one point, 'I've seen her on the stage. She'd have made me laugh if I hadn't been strictly on my guard!'). This is most notable in Dietrich's superb rendition of Cole Porter's *The Laziest Girl in Town*, glamorously staged by Hitchcock on a series of *chaises-longue* amid an extravagant set of froufs and frills. Hitchcock apparently greatly enjoyed working with Dietrich, so much so that he allowed her more leeway than most in her performance, although one wonders if she was entirely in on the joke.

Less certain of herself is Jane Wyman, who doesn't quite convince as the RADA student-turned-detective (although *Variety* found her 'delightful as [the] embryo actress'). Nevertheless, her mousy Doris Tinsdale is an amusing creation, complete with *faux* Cockney accent, although Hitchcock had problems with the star over retaining her dowdy look (revealed the director, 'She couldn't accept the idea of her face being in character, while Dietrich looked so glamorous, so she kept improving her appearance every day and that's how she failed to

Punters cue up to see Hitchcock's Stage Fright (1950) at the Warner cinema in London's Leicester Square.

maintain the character' [21]). Even less convincing is Richard Todd as the suspected murderer; neither compelling enough in his claims of innocence nor dastardly enough when revealed as the true villain, he is unquestionably the weakest link in the piece ('The more successful the villain, the more successful the picture. That's the cardinal rule, and in this picture the villain was a flop!' [22] admitted Hitchcock). As for Michael Wilding's insipid Inspector Smith, there is little to say, except that it is an unusually bland performance even by Wilding's own standards (although again *Variety* found favour, commenting, 'Michael Wilding clicks as a debonair detective').

Consequently, it is left to the gallery of supporting characters to keep things afloat, which they do with aplomb. Alastair Sim, his usual lugubrious self, is delightful as the crusty Commodore ('Adventure in the mind or behind the footlights is much easier than actuality,' he sagely cautions his daughter); Joyce Grenfell makes the most of her brief revue-like cameo as the gauche proprietress of the shooting gallery at the garden party ('Do come and shoot some lovely ducks, only half-a-crown!'); while Kay Walsh is suitably thin-lipped and lank-haired as Charlotte Inwood's devious maid, herself a little hungry for the limelight ('I'm not saying a word to the reporters. Not a word. I'm going to be a star witness at that trial, and my story ought to be worth something, and I've no intention of giving it away,' she tells a rapt audience at the Shepherd's Pub). Also leaving their mark are Sybil Thorndike as Eve's mother ('This is Eve's father – we see him now and again,' she says by way of introducing the

Commodore to Inspector Smith) and Miles Malleson as a bespectacled busy body in the pub (Malleson had of course played the manager of the Palladium in Hitchcock's *The 39 Steps* 15 years earlier). One can even spot an un-credited and un-speaking Irene Handl as Mrs Gill's maid, Mrs Mason, while the young Alfie Bass pops up as a cheery stagehand.

The best moments go to Dietrich, though, who despite being billed second to Wyman, walks away with the film *and* some of the best lines. 'Isn't there some way we could let it plunge a little in front?' she asks her seamstress while being fitted for her widow's weeds, while of the enquiring Inspector Smith she quips, 'You can just stand so much of detectives – after all, they're just policemen with smaller feet.' She also makes the most of a running joke concerning Doris' name, miscalling her Elsie, Phyllis and Mavis at various points.

Meanwhile, Hitchcock has his customary fun with the set pieces, notable among them a dexterous camera move, which follows Jonathan Cooper from the street (a studio mock-up) through the front door of Charlotte Inwood's London flat and up the stairs to her bedroom in one continuous take. To achieve this, Hitchcock had Richard Todd pass through the front door, but only mime closing it behind him, as it obviously needed to remain open so that the camera crane could pass through it. However, to convince the audience that the door *had* closed behind the actor, Hitchcock passed a shadow across his back and had the sound of a barrel organ playing outside suitably diminished. Note also the scene in which Jonathan imagines the outcome of police inquiries into his connection with the murder; the brief scenes are combined with a shot of Jonathan's concerned face, thus giving the impression that we are seeing what he is thinking.

Elsewhere, Hitchcock delights in the staging of the rain-soaked garden party – this is a *British* garden party, after all – which even allows him the chance to re-use his sea of umbrellas shot, first seen in *Foreign Correspondent* (1940). He also successfully plays on theatrical conventions throughout the film by having practically all the characters assume roles other than their own: Charlotte Inwood plays the grieving widow; Eve pretends to be the Cockney maid Doris Tinsdale; Nellie Goode fancies herself as a star witness; Jonathan Cooper pretends to be an innocent man; while the Commodore describes himself as a smuggler (although his booty amounts to just two kegs of brandy!). Even the film's poster accentuated the theatrical metaphor with the strap line, 'The stage is set for Warner Bros.' most exciting hit yet!'

Though by no means a major hit, *Stage Fright* helped to diminish memories of *Rope* and *Under Capricorn* ('Gripping new greatness from Warner Bros.,' boasted the posters). It even managed to earn some good reviews amid the accusations of sleight of hand ('The dialogue has purpose, either for a chuckle or a thrill, and the pace is good,' concluded *Variety*). Indeed, the film seemed to bring to an end Hitchcock's brief dry spell and heralded one of his most creative periods, confirmed by his next outing, the superb *Strangers on a Train* (1951).

Hitchcock cameo Note that Hitchcock can be spotted in a London street, passing Eve Gill as she psyches herself up to play Doris Tinsdale. Hitchcock's daughter Pat can also be seen briefly at the garden party as Chubby Bannister, one of Eve's RADA chums (Pat herself was studying at RADA at the time). In fact *Stage Fright* marked the first of Pat's three film appearances for her father, the other two being *Strangers on a Train* (1951) and *Psycho* (1960). She also popped up in several episodes of her dad's television series, *Alfred Hitchcock Presents*.

STAFFORD, FREDERICK (1928–1979, real name Frederick Strobl von Stein) Austrian actor. This handsome but rather wooden leading man appeared in a number of James Bond-style action adventures in Europe in the 1960s, among them *Agent 505 – Todesfalle Beirut* (1965), *Furia a Bahia pour OSS 117* (1965), *A Tout Coeur A Tokyo Pour OSS 117* (1966) and *L'Homme Qui Valait des Milliards* (1967). Rather surprisingly, he was signed by Hitchcock in 1969 to appear as French undercover agent Andre Devereaux, the leading role in his Cold War thriller *Topaz*. The film was not a success, but represented the climax to Stafford's career. His other films include *Werewolf Woman* (1976). **Hitchography:** *Topaz* (1969)

STANNARD, ELIOT British screenwriter. A former Fleet Street journalist, Stannard scripted seven of Hitchcock's silents, including his directorial debut *The Pleasure Garden* (1925). Film maker Michael Powell, who shot the stills for a couple of early Hitchcocks, recalled meeting Stannard during the filming of *Champagne*, during which Hitchcock jokingly introduced the screenwriter to him as 'the author of this dreadful film.' [23] Powell himself remembered Stannard as being 'a dark, wildly handsome, untidy man.' [24] Stannard's other screenplays include *Ernest Maltravers* (1920), *Squibs* (1921), *The Harbour Lights* (1923) and *Blighty* (1926). **Hitchography:** *The Pleasure Garden* (1925), *The Mountain Eagle* (1925), *The Lodger* (1926), *Easy Virtue* (1927), *The Ring* (1927), *The Farmer's Wife* (1928), *Champagne* (1928), *The Manxman* (1929)

STEFANO, JOSEPH (1921–) American screenwriter. Stefano turned to writing for films and television following experience as a composer and lyricist. His first script was for *The Black Orchid* (1958), which was produced by Carlo Ponti and starred his wife Sophia Loren. Having soon after changed agencies to MCA, Stefano found himself offered the chance to work with Hitchcock on *Psycho* (1960), following the departure of screenwriter James P Cavanagh, whose work the director had not been happy with. It was Stefano's idea to revise the book's story line, concentrating on the exploits of Janet Leigh's Marion Crane for the first half of the film before introducing Anthony Perkins' Norman Bates into the action (which author Robert Bloch does in the first paragraph of the novel).

Recalled Stefano: 'I told him [Hitchcock], "I'd like to see Marion shacking up with Sam on her lunch hour." The moment I said "shack up" or anything like that, Hitchcock, being a very salacious man, adored it. I said, "We'll find out what the girl is all about, see her steal the money and head for Sam – on the way, this horrendous thing happens to her." He thought it was spectacular. I think that idea got me the job.' [25]

Stefano's other credits include *The Naked Edge* (1961), *Eye of the Cat* (1969), *Home for the Holidays* (1972, TV) and a return to the *Psycho* franchise with *Psycho IV: The Beginning* (1990, TV). It should also be noted that Stefano's *Psycho* screenplay was re-used for the ill-fated 1998 remake. His television work includes contributions to such series as *The Outer Limits* (1963–1964), which he also produced for a period, and *Mr Novak* (1963–1964), while his novels include *The Lycanthrope*. **Hitchography:** *Psycho* (1960)

STEINBECK, JOHN (1902–1968) American novelist and screenwriter. This celebrated writer, known for such landmark works as *The Grapes of Wrath* (which earned him the Nobel Prize) and *Of Mice and Men*, was called upon by Hitchcock to supply the screen story for *Lifeboat* (1944), which earned him an Academy Award nomination for best story. Given his literary stature, Steinbeck's name was featured on the posters for *Lifeboat* as prominently as Hitchcock's. **Hitchography:** *Lifeboat* (1944)

Step Down to Terror
(US, 1959, 76m, bw)

CREDITS

Production company:	Universal International
Producer:	Joseph Gershenson
Director:	Harry Keller
Screenplay:	Mel Dinelli, Chris Cooper, Czenzi Ormonde
Cinematographer:	Russell Metty
Music:	Joseph Gershenson

CAST

Charles Drake, Colleen Miller, Rod Taylor, Josephine Hutchinson, Jocelyn Brando

The first of two remakes of Hitchcock 1943 film *Shadow of a Doubt* (also see the 1991 TV movie with the same title as the original). Also known as *The Silent Stranger*, it replaces Joseph Cotten with Charles Drake as the murderous uncle, and Teresa Wright with Colleen Miller as his adoring niece. The results this time, however, are strictly boring, even at this abbreviated length. It should be noted that co-star Rod Taylor, who here plays the detective, went on to appear in Hitchcock's *The Birds* (1963), while Josephine Hutchinson, who here plays the mother, had a brief role in *North by Northwest* (1959). Meanwhile, screenwriter Czeni Ormonde worked on the script for *Strangers on a Train* (1951) while Mel Dinelli penned *And So Died Riabouchinska* (1956, TV) for *Alfred Hitchcock Presents*.

STEVENSON, EDWARD (1906–1968) American costume designer. Stevenson began his film career at the age of 16. By 1936 he was the head of RKO's wardrobe department. His many films for the studio include three for Orson Welles: *Citizen Kane* (1941), *The Magnificent Ambersons* (1942) and *Journey into Fear* (1942). He also designed the costumes for Hitchcock's *Suspicion* (1941). Stevenson left RKO in 1949 and went freelance. He returned to RKO in 1955, by which time it had been bought by Lucille Ball and Desi Arnaz and re-christened Desilu. Stevenson subsequently designed all of Ball's clothes for her TV sit-com *I Love Lucy* (1955–1961).
Hitchography: *Suspicion* (1941)

STEWART, HUGH (1910–) British producer. Though known today as the producer of a string of successful Norman Wisdom comedies, among them *The Square Peg* (1958), *On the Beat* (1962) and *The Early Bird* (1965), Stewart actually began his film career as an editor in the 1930s, working on such prestigious productions as *South Riding* (1938), *Q Planes* (1938) and *The Spy in Black* (1939). He also cut Hitchcock's *The Man Who Knew Too Much* (1934), on which he is credited as H St C Stewart. Recalled Stewart of Hitchcock's working methods: 'He knew exactly what he was going to do. In his mind, the film was already shot.' [26] **Hitchography:** *The Man Who Knew Too Much* (1934)

STEWART, JAMES (1908–1997) American actor. One of the silver screen's all time greats, Stewart began his professional career at the University Playhouse in Falmouth in 1932. Appearances on Broadway followed, after which Stewart, who'd planned to become an architect, made his Hollywood debut in the short *Art Trouble* in late 1934. Following another short, *Important News* (1935), he made his feature debut in *The Murder Man* (1935), performing opposite such stalwarts as Spencer Tracy and Lionel Atwill. Supporting roles in the likes of *Next Time We Love* (1936), *Rose Marie* (1936), *The Last Gangster* (1937) and *You Can't Take It with You* (1938) followed. However, the success of *Destry Rides Again* (1939) and *Mr Smith Goes to Washington* (1939), which earned him a best actor Oscar nomination, catapulted Stewart to the front ranks, a position he solidified by winning a best supporting actor Oscar for *The Philadelphia Story* (1940).

However, with the war in Europe deepening and America's involvement imminent, Stewart had just time to appear in *Ziegfeld Girl* (1941), *Come Live with Me* (1941) and *Pot o' Gold* (1941) before temporarily abandoning his career to join the US Air Force, in which he rose to the rank of Colonel thanks to his bravery flying 20 missions over Germany as a bomber pilot (by the time he officially retired from the service in 1968 he was a brigadier general). Upon his return to Hollywood, Stewart appeared in the classic heart-warmer *It's a Wonderful Life* (1946), which he followed with the likes of *Magic Town* (1947), *Call Northside 777* (1947) and Hitchcock's *Rope* (1948), which marked the first of four appearances for the Master. In this first encounter, Stewart played Rupert Cadell, a retired college professor who discovers that two of his former pupils have murdered a friend for the intellectual thrill of it. Hitchcock shot the film in a series of elaborate ten-minute takes, an approach that Stewart wasn't entirely comfortable with. Nevertheless, he delivered a customarily solid performance, about which *Variety* commented: 'James Stewart, as the ex-professor who first senses the guilt of his former pupils and nibbles away at their composure with verbal barbs, does a commanding job.'

Although Stewart hadn't enjoyed the experience of filming *Rope*, he and Hitchcock had got on well and agreed to work together again at some stage. However, it would be six years before they collaborated again, this time on *Rear Window* (1954), by which time Stewart had starred in such vehicles as *The Stratton Story* (1949), *Winchester '73* (1950), *Harvey* (1950), *The Greatest Show on Earth* (1952), *The Naked Spur* (1953) and *The Glenn Miller Story* (1953). For the entirety of *Rear Window*, the star had to perform from a wheelchair, his character - news photographer L B Jefferies - having broken his leg on an assignment. By the end of the film, he's broken his other leg too, having caught a wife murderer in the interim. *Variety* described *Rear Window* as 'an unusually good piece of murder mystery entertainment,' and the film went on to become a major box office draw.

For Stewart, *The Far Country* (1954), *Strategic Air Command* (1955) and *The Man from Laramie* (1955) fol-

James Stewart rescues Kim Novak from San Francisco Bay in Hitchcock's Vertigo *(1958). Note: is that someone leaning against the wall thinking they're out of shot?*

lowed, after which it was back to Hitchcock for the director's widescreen, Technicolor remake of his 1934 British hit *The Man Who Knew Too Much* (1956). Another box office success, the film has not survived well, although the critics found nice things to say about its star: 'James Stewart ably carries out his title duties,' enthused *Variety*, adding that he and co-star Doris Day 'both draw vivid portraits of tortured parents when their son is kidnapped.' By this time, Stewart was fairly accustomed to Hitchcock's working methods, unlike Doris Day, who found his lack of communication with actors unsettling. Remembered Stewart: 'I knew Hitch pretty well from having made *Rear Window* and *Rope* with him. He didn't believe in rehearsals. He preferred to let the actor figure things out for himself... Of course, this is confusing to an actor who is accustomed to a director who participates in the scene. In the beginning, it certainly threw Doris for a loop. Hitchcock believed that if you sat down with an actor to analyze a scene, you'd run the danger that the actor would act the scene with his head rather than his heart.' [27]

Two more films followed for the star – *Night Passage* (1957) and *Spirit of St Louis* (1957) – after which Stewart

made his fourth and final appearance for Hitchcock in the highly regarded *Vertigo* (1958), in which he played the acrophobic detective Scottie Ferguson, who finds himself embroiled in a complex murder plot when asked to trail the wife of a friend. Commented the star: 'After several years I saw the film again and I thought it was a fine picture. I myself had known fear like that [acrophobia], and I'd known people paralyzed by fear. It's a very powerful thing. I didn't realize when I was preparing for the role what an impact it would have, but it's an extraordinary achievement even for Hitch. I could tell it was a very personal film even while he was making it.' [28] Meanwhile, of his co-star Kim Novak, whom he would work with again immediately following *Vertigo* on *Bell, Book and Candle* (1958), Stewart recalled: 'When I was doing *Vertigo*, poor Kim Novak, bless her heart, said, "Mr Hitchcock, what is my character feeling in relation to her surroundings?" There was a silence on the set and Hitch said, "It's only a movie, for God's sakes." She never asked another question.' [29]

Following the conclusion of his working relationship with Hitchcock, Stewart went on to appear in the likes of

Anatomy of a Murder (1959), *The Man Who Shot Liberty Valance* (1962), *Shenandoah* (1965), *The Shootist* (1976), *The Big Sleep* (1978) and *An American Tail: Fievel Goes West* (1992), for which he provided the voice of Wylie Burp, while his TV work includes *The Jimmy Stewart Show* (1971) and *Hawkins on Murder* (1973). An amusing poet, he also authored *Jimmy Stewart and His Poems*, published in 1989. He received a special Academy Award in 1984 for 'fifty years of meaningful performances, [and] for his high ideals, both on an off the screen.' **Hitchography:** *Rope* (1948), *Rear Window* (1954), *The Man Who Knew Too Much* (1956), *Vertigo* (1958)

STEWART, JAMES G American sound technician. Long at RKO, James G Stewart worked on several of the studio's key films, notably *Citizen Kane* (1941) and *The Magnificent Ambersons* (1942). He also recorded a number of films for producer David O Selznick, including *Duel in the Sun* (1946), Hitchcock's *The Paradine Case* (1947) and *Portrait of Jennie* (1948), the latter earning him an Oscar for best audio effects. **Hitchography:** *The Paradine Case* (1947)

STONE, HAROLD J (1911–) American character actor. In films from 1956 with *Slander*, this tough-looking actor provided solid support in a number of films, among them Hitchcock's *The Wrong Man* (1956), in which he played Lieutenant Bowers, who leads the case against the wrongfully arrested Manny Balestrero (Henry Fonda). Stone's other film appearances include *Spartacus* (1960), *X – The Man with X-Ray Eyes* (1963) and *Hardly Working* (1981), while on television he was a fixture in *My World and Welcome to It* (1968) and *Bridget Loves Bernie* (1974). **Hitchography:** *The Wrong Man* (1956)

STORY, JACK TREVOR British actor. Working as Jack Trevor, this actor appeared in Hitchcock's 1928 comedy-drama *Champagne*. Later he changed his name to Jack Trevor Story and turned to writing, among his novels being the black comedy *The Trouble with Harry*, the film rights to which Hitchcock purchased, anonymously, for $11,000. The resultant movie was released in 1955. **Hitchography:** *Champagne* (1928), *The Trouble with Harry* (1955)

STRADLING, HARRY (1901–1970) British-born cinematographer. Stradling began his career in Hollywood, working on short films and undistinguished features, among them *The Devil's Garden* (1920), *The Great Adventure* (1921) and *The Substitute Wife* (1925). Moving to France in 1934, he photographed *La Kermesse Heroique* (1935) for director Jacques Feyder, who then took Stradling back to Britain with him to work on *Knight Without Armour* (1937). Several important British films followed, among them *South Riding* (1937), *Pygmalion* (1938), *The Citadel* (1938) and Hitchcock's *Jamaica Inn* (1939), which Stradling co-photographed with Hitchcock's then-regular cameraman, Jack Cox.

Stradling went back to Hollywood in 1939, where he worked twice with Hitchcock, on *Mr And Mrs Smith* (1941) and *Suspicion* (1941). A distinguished career followed, with Stradling winning Oscars for his work on *The Picture of Dorian Gray* (1945) and *My Fair Lady* (1964), the latter the musical version of *Pygmalion*, which he'd also photographed. His other credits include *Easter Parade* (1947), *A Streetcar Named Desire* (1951), *The Pajama Game* (1957) and *How to Murder Your Wife* (1965). He also photographed Barbra Streisand's first four films, *Funny Girl* (1968), *Hello, Dolly!* (1969), *On a Clear Day You Can See Forever* (1970) and *The Owl and the Pussycat* (1970). He died during the production of the latter, which was completed by Andrew Laszlo. Stradling's son, Harry Stradling Jr (1925–) is also a cinematographer, whose credits include *Welcome to Hard Times* (1967), *The Way We Were* (1973) and *Blind Date* (1987). **Hitchography:** *Jamaica Inn* (1939), *Mr And Mrs Smith* (1941) *Suspicion* (1941)

Strangers on a Train

(US, 1951, 101m/100m, bw) ★★★

CREDITS

Production company:	Warner Bros.
Producer:	Alfred Hitchcock
Director:	Alfred Hitchcock
Screenplay:	Whitfield Cook, Raymond Chandler, Czenzi Ormonde (and Ben Hecht), based on the novel by Patricia Highsmith
Cinematographer:	Robert Burks
Music:	Dimitri Tiomkin
Music director:	Ray Heindorf
Editor:	William Ziegler
Art director:	Edward S Haworth
Costumes:	Leah Rhodes
Special effects:	H F Koenekamp
Sound:	Dolph Thomas

CAST

Farley Granger (Guy Haines), Ruth Roman (Anne Morton), Robert Walker (Bruno Antony), Patricia Hitchcock (Barbara Morton), Leo G Carroll (Senator Morton), Maura Elliot (Miriam Haines), Marion Lorne (Mrs Antony), Jonathan Hale (Mr Antony), Norma Varden (Mrs Cunningham), Robert Gist (Hennessy), John Brown (Professor Collins), Howard St John (Captain Turley), Leonard Carey (Butler), Murray Alper (Boatman), Harry Hines (Old man under carousel), Georges Renavent (Monsieur Darville), Odette Myrtil (Madame Darville), Edna Holland (Mrs Joyce), Laura Treadwell (Mrs Anderson), Louis Lettieri (Boy)

Video availability: Warner Bros.
DVD availability: Warner Bros.
CD availability: *Psycho – The Essential Hitchcock* (Silva Screen), which contains a *Suite*

Following the misjudgements of both *Rope* (1948) and *Under Capricorn* (1949), Hitchcock partially restored his waning reputation with the quirky murder drama *Stage Fright* (1950). *Strangers on a Train*, however, would see his true return to form, both commercially and artistically. Based on Patricia Highsmith's 1950 debut novel, for which Hitchcock paid $7500, it was billed on the poster as '101 minutes of matchless suspense' (some posters also featured a still of Hitchcock playfully dangling a letter L over the word *Strangers*, thus transforming it into *Stranglers*).

Hitchcock worked on the screenplay adaptation with Whitfield Cook, with whom he'd previously collaborated on *Stage Fright*. This complete, the director then turned to acclaimed thriller writer Raymond Chandler to finesse the project. Unfortunately, this association was a troubled one, despite both Hitchcock's and Chandler's mastery of the thriller genre. Revealed Hitch: 'Our association didn't work out at all… The work he did was no good and I ended up with Czenzi Ormonde, a woman writer who was one of Ben Hecht's assistants.' [30] In fact as well as Ormonde, Hitchcock also had Hecht himself do some un-credited work on the screenplay, which finally went before the cameras in early October 1950.

The basic premise for the film is fairly simple: Guy Haines (Farley Granger), an amateur tennis player, accidentally bumps into Bruno Antony (Robert Walker) while travelling by train to his hometown of Metcalf. The two men get talking and share lunch together, and after a while the subject turns to murder, with Bruno suggesting that the perfect way to get away with one would be to swap crimes with a complete stranger, thus enabling each interested party to establish an alibi while the other carries out the deadly deed. Guy at first is amused by the notion, but becomes wary when Bruno reveals that he's read in the society pages that the tennis player is courting senator's daughter Anne Morton (Ruth Roman), and wishes to divorce his estranged wife Miriam (Laura Elliot) so that he can marry her. Might it not be mutually beneficial, Bruno suggests, that he kill Miriam for Guy in return for Guy killing Bruno's much-despised father? 'What is a life or two, Guy? Some people are better off dead – like your wife and my father, for instance,' Bruno opines. Thinking that Bruno is joking, Guy humours him. But unbeknownst to him, Bruno is in fact a psychopath, and deadly earnest. Consequently, Bruno tracks down Guy's wife and strangles her on the island of a fairground boating lake, following which he turns up at Guy's apartment building with the dead woman's glasses as proof, demanding that the horrified Guy now keep his part of the supposed bargain.

The remainder of the film centres round Guy's desperate attempts to prove his own innocence to the police (a drunk he met on a train while the murder was being committed fails to recognize him the next day), and Bruno's further attempts to coerce Guy into keeping his side of the deal, his bargaining chip being the distinctive cigarette lighter Guy left behind after their first meeting, which he now plans to plant at the scene of the crime as evidence of Guy's supposed guilt.

There were several raised eyebrows in Hollywood when Hitchcock announced that he would be filming *Strangers on a Train*, the dissenters claiming that the story wouldn't work in film terms. Yet Hitchcock proved his detractors wrong, producing one of his most tightly structured thrillers, with sheer cinematic skill papering over the general lack of logic, making the very most of a basically absurd situation ('You may not take it seriously, but you certainly don't have time to think about anything else,' wrote Richard Mallett of the film in *Punch*).

The film opens in style, with the camera following the feet of both Guy and Bruno as they arrive at the station and make their way to the train. It is only after Guy accidentally kicks Bruno's foot when sitting down that the faces of the two protagonists are revealed (note, too, that it is *Guy's* action and not Bruno's that instigates the plot). It quickly becomes apparent to the audience, if not Guy, that Bruno is slightly off the rails, especially when he boasts, 'Have you ever driven a car blindfolded at 150 miles an hour? *I* have!' This is further confirmed at Bruno's home, when his father can be heard telling his mother, 'He should be sent somewhere for treatment, before it's too late!'

We get to meet Guy's shrewish wife at the record shop where she works. Mean, bespectacled and something of a tramp (she is expecting another man's baby, it is revealed), she does little to earn our sympathy ('I'd like to break her neck,' Guy tells Anne over the phone, a comment he will later come to regret). In fact so despicable is Miriam that the audience is actually on Bruno's side as he stalks her at the fairground, where she's gone to spend the evening with not one, but two men.

The fairground sequence is particularly well handled, with Miriam clearly giving Bruno the come on, while he remains coolly steadfast is his pursuit of her, ignoring all distractions, among them a young boy dressed as a cowboy. 'Bang, bang, you're dead,' squeals the kid, at which Bruno nonchalantly bursts the child's balloon with his cigarette. Hitchcock even works a false climax into the sequence; when Bruno follows Miriam and her two beaus into the Tunnel of Love, he has the shadow of Bruno and his boat catch up with Miriam's; a scream follows, but it is quickly revealed to be a scream of laughter, as one of the men makes a pass at Miriam. On the island, however, Bruno finally catches up with his quarry. 'Is your name Miriam?' he enquires. 'Why, yes,' comes the slightly surprised reply, at which he dispassionately places his hands round her neck and strangles her, the act of which is shown reflected in Miriam's glasses, which have fallen to the ground, the result being one of Hitchcock's most iconographic images. 'It was very quick, Guy. She wasn't hurt in any way,' Bruno later informs Guy.

Hitchcock later returns to the fairground for the film's climax, with Guy, trailed by the police, attempting to catch Bruno before he plants the incriminating cigarette lighter on the island. Before leaving for the fair, Guy has to play a scheduled tennis match in Washington, thus adding to the tension (not playing would arouse suspicion, Anne concludes), after which he has to hot foot it by train to Metcalf (when Guy arrives at the station to buy his ticket, note the extras on the ascending escalator behind the two undercover cops following him – one of them turns round and looks directly at the camera; noticing this misdemeanour, another extra points at him, motioning that he should look the other way!). Meanwhile, on *his* way to the fairground, Bruno accidentally drops the lighter down a drain, through the grating of which he has to painfully squeeze his hand in order to retrieve it. Here, Hitchcock cleverly causes something of a dilemma for the audience, in that they will Bruno to reach the lighter, knowing that he is going to use it to incriminate Guy.

Things finally come to a head in a fight between Guy and Bruno on the fair's carousel. One of the cops fires his gun at Guy, believing him to be attacking Bruno, only to have the bullet instead kill the ride's operator, who falls against the gear stick, sending it spinning out of control (this idea was lifted by Hitchcock from Edmund Crispin's 1946 novel *The Moving Toyshop*, the rights to which the director had Warner Bros purchase). The subsequent sequence is a masterpiece of montage, with Bruno and Guy's punches being inter-cut with shots of the carousel's horses, their faces and hooves lurching towards the camera. Hitchcock also edits in reaction shots of the screaming observers, among them a concerned mother. 'My little boy!' she yells, at which the director cuts to the boy in question, who is beaming with pleasure over the carousel's extra speed. Finally, a toothless old man offers to crawl under the ride to reach the control stick. Though much of the carousel sequence was filmed using models and rear projection, this part was actually done for real, Revealed Hitchcock: 'My hands still sweat when I think of that scene today. You know, that little man actually crawled under the spinning carousel. If he'd raised his head by an inch, he'd have been killed.' [31]

By the time the old man reaches the gear stick, Guy is holding on to one of the ride's outer support poles, his body flying through the air; wanting him to fall to his death, Bruno begins to kick Guy's clutching hands, an idea Hitchcock would later re-use at the climax of *North by Northwest* (1959), as Cary Grant clings to the edge of Mount Rushmore. But as the old man tries to stop the ride, the engine explodes and the carousel collapses in spectacular fashion, killing Bruno in the process, but not before the fairground's boatman reveals to the police that he saw Bruno follow Miriam to the island the night she was murdered. Guy's innocence is further confirmed when one of the cops discovers the incriminating lighter in Bruno's hand.

These compelling sequences aside, Hitchcock also crams the film with his customary gallery of eye-catching supporting characters. Notable among them are Laura Elliot's delightfully grotesque Miriam and Patricia Hitchcock's turn as Anne's plain-speaking sister, Barbara ('Daddy doesn't mind a little scandal. He's a senator!' she informs Guy when it is revealed that Miriam has been

murdered, and possibly by her brother-in-law to be). One of Hitchcock's favourite actors, Leo G Carroll, is meanwhile on hand to play Senator Morton ('Never lose any sleep over accusations – unless they can be proved, of course,' he advises Guy), while Bruno's dotty mother is in the expert hands of professional ditherer Marion Lorne ('She's a little, how shall I say, confused,' says Bruno of her).

Of the leading performances, Ruth Roman is more than adequate if a little distant as Guy's love interest, Anne (Hitchcock was forced to use the actress by Warner Bros., who had her under contract at the time); Farley Granger also performs well as Guy, although Hitchcock had hoped to bag William Holden for the role (*Variety* described Roman's work as 'warmly effective' and Granger's as 'excellent'). However, everyone pales besides Robert Walker's masterful work as the charmingly psychotic Bruno. 'You don't mind if I borrow your neck for a moment?' he asks a clearly smitten matron at a party he has gatecrashed at the Senator's, before demonstrating how best to commit murder. Unfortunately, his demonstration goes awry when he spots Barbara, who just happens to be wearing glasses similar to Miriam's, thus reminding him of the murder and almost turning his light-hearted demonstration into a repeat performance. 'He looked at me. His hands were on *her* throat, and he was strangling *me*,' says a distressed Barbara, prompting her sister, somewhat incredulously, to conclude that Bruno must have murdered Miriam ('He killed Miriam, didn't he?' she asks Guy, who subsequently comes clean with her).

Elsewhere, other interesting touches include a shot of Bruno watching Guy at a tennis match not long after the murder; the heads of the spectators move from left to right following the ball, except for Bruno's, which remains still, his gaze fixed firmly on Guy (Hitchcock later manages to suggest that Bruno might actually have homosexual feelings for Guy: 'But, Guy. I like you!' he tells the tennis player, prompting Guy to punch him in the face, which Hitchcock stages by having Guy punch directly into the camera, then cutting to Bruno, who falls away from it onto a conveniently placed sofa). Hitchcock also cranks up the suspense by having Guy at one stage seemingly agree to keep his side of the murderous bargain by paying Bruno's father a nighttime visit, his intention being to tell the old boy exactly what his son has been plotting. The director elicits the maximum suspense from the scene by placing a giant mastiff on the stairs, which Guy has to pass in order to reach Mr Antony's bedroom. The twist is that Bruno's father is away on business, and that Bruno himself is waiting for Guy in his father's bed, having suspected that Guy was planning to trick him all along.

A commercial and critical success when released in June 1952, *Strangers on a Train* immediately restored Hitchcock's reputation. 'In spite of its many lapses, the film will certainly be classed as one of the successes of the year – and rightly so,' enthused Richard Winnington in *Sight and Sound*, while in *Time and Tide*, Margaret Hinxman proclaimed the film as 'Undoubtedly an improvement on

[his] last three or four.' The movie even earned an Oscar nomination for Robert Burks's crisp photography, thus launching an association with Hitchcock that would last for a total of 12 films.

Note that the film has been re-made three times: as *Once You Kiss a Stranger* (1969), *Throw Momma from the Train* (1987) and *Once You Meet a Stranger* (1996). It should also be noted that the American and British release prints of the film differ slightly, the British print containing a lengthier version of Guy and Bruno's first meeting on the train, while the American print features a coda with Guy and Anne on a train – when a minister recognizes Guy, he moves away from the clergyman with his wife to be, wishing to have no more with strangers on trains.

Hitchcock cameo Hitchcock gets his customary cameo out of the way early on in the film: as Guy alights the train at Metcalf, the director struggles to get on with a double bass!

STRAUSS'S GREAT WALTZ see *Waltzes from Vienna*

STUART, JOHN (1898–1979, real name John Croall) Scottish-born actor. Busy as a leading man in silents, Stuart began his film career in 1920 with *Her Son*, *The Great Gay Road* (1920), *The Little Mother* (1922) and *The Loves of Mary Queen of Scots* (1924) followed, along with a leading role – that of Hugh Fielding – in Hitchcock's debut, *The Pleasure Garden* (1925). He also popped up in *Elstree Calling* (1930), although not in the segment directed by Hitchcock, and played the detective in Hitchcock's *Number Seventeen* (1932). Stuart's other films, among many, include *The Show Goes On* (1937), *The Quatermass Experiment* (1955), *The Revenge of Frankenstein* (1958), *The Mummy* (1959) and *Superman* (1978). **Hitchography:** *The Pleasure Garden* (1925), *Elstree Calling* (1930), *Number Seventeen* (1932)

SUBOR, MICHEL French actor. Subor has appeared in a handful of films since the early 1960s, including *Le Petit Soldat* (1960), Hitchcock's *Topaz* (1969), in which he played journalist and sketch artist Francois Picard, and *Beau Travail* (1999). **Hitchography:** *Topaz* (1969)

Suspicion

(US, 1941, 99m, bw) ★

CREDITS

Production company:	RKO
Producer:	Alfred Hitchcock
Director:	Alfred Hitchcock
Screenplay:	Joan Harrison, Alma Reville, Samson Raphael, based on the novel *Before the Fact* by Francis Iles
Cinematographer:	Harry Stradling
Music:	Franz Waxman
Editor:	William Hamilton
Art directors:	Van Nest Polglase,
	Carroll Clark
Costumes:	Edward Stevenson
Special effects:	Vernon L Walker
Sound:	John E Tribby

CAST

Joan Fontaine (Lina McLaidlaw/Aysgarth), Cary Grant (Johnnie Aysgarth), Nigel Bruce (Beaky), Sir Cedric Hardwicke (Mr McLaidlaw), Dame May Whitty (Mrs McLaidlaw), Leo G Carroll (Captain Melbeck), Isabel Jeans (Mrs Newsham), Auriol Lee (Isobel Sedbusk), Heather Angel (Ethel), Reginald Sheffield (Reggie Wetherby), Gertrude Hoffman (Mrs Wetherby), Billy Bevan (Ticket collector), Ben Webster (Registrar), Hilda Plowright (Postmistress), Lumsden Hare (Inspector Hodgson), Faith Brook (Alice Barham), Leonard Carey (Butler), Edward Fielding (Antique shop owner), Aubrey Mather (Mr Webster), Doris Lloyd (Miss Wetherby), Elsie Weller (Miss Wetherby)

Video availability: Universal
CD availability: *Psycho – The Essential Alfred Hitchcock* (Silva Screen), which contains the *Prelude* and *Sunday Morning* from *Suspicion*

Despite its reputation, and the fact that it earned Joan Fontaine a best actress Oscar and was also nominated for best picture and best score statuettes, *Suspicion* is a surprisingly bland affair. Indeed, its story of a shy young woman who increasingly believes that her debonair husband is trying to murder her for her money, is, for the most part, highly unconvincing, while Hitchcock's directorial flourishes are somewhat thin on the ground.

In it Fontaine plays the bookish Lina McLaidlaw, who is romantically pursued by a penniless playboy called Johnnie Aysgarth (Cary Grant), whom she first encounters while travelling home by train, he with a third-class ticket, for which he has to borrow money from *her* to upgrade to the first-class compartment in which they are travelling. Given her withdrawn nature, it seems improbable that Johnnie should have any interest in Lina, whom he nicknames 'monkey face', and so when he begins to woo her, our suspicions are naturally aroused. Yet Lina, herself somewhat incredulous, seems happy to be romanced by Johnnie, given the cloistered existence in which she has been living with her parents ('Have you ever been kissed in a car?' he asks her as they leave a party. She shakes her head. 'Would you like to be?' he ventures, to which the answer is an emphatic, 'Yes'). However, once married, Lina's concerns continue to grow regarding Johnnie's intentions, to the point that she fully believes that he is aiming to murder her so as to inherit ('Each time they kissed there was the thrill of love... the threat of murder!' screamed the posters).

Throughout the film, the script, based on the novel *Before the Fact* by Francis Iles, heavily signposts that Johnnie's intentions *are* strictly dishonourable, with incident upon incident pointing to his seeming guilt, including the apparent murder of his best friend Beaky (Nigel Bruce in buffoonish Dr Watson overdrive). In the novel, Johnnie *is* the cad we suspect him of being. Consequently, to help divert attention from this fact (despite the aforementioned signposting), Hitchcock decided to cast the role against type, persuading the executives at RKO to allow him to have Cary Grant, Hollywood's most eligible leading man, as Johnnie. All was going well during filming, until the front office realized the error of their ways and requested that Hitchcock alter the ending, revealing Johnnie not to be guilty after all, Lina's suspicions being the result of various wild coincidences and her own overwrought imagination.

Sixty-odd years on, this double bluff actually works in the film's favour, but at the time Hitchcock – not the front office, note – was much criticized for having altered Iles's book. Commented William Whitebait in the *New Statesman*: 'The fact that Hitchcock throws in a happy end during the last five minutes, like a conjuror explaining his tricks, seems to me a pity; but it spoils the film only in retrospect, and we have already had our thrills' (although what these thrills are he fails to mention).

Said Hitchcock of the production: 'You might say *Suspicion* was the second English picture I made in Hollywood. The actors, the atmosphere, and the novel on which it's based were all British.' [32] Yet the film is almost a catalogue of exaggerated incidents and missed opportunities, with Dame May Whitty and Sir Cedric Hardwicke, cast as Lina's disapproving parents, particularly wasted. As the 'villain' of the piece, Cary Grant is completely unconvincing (almost as unconvincing as the film's English atmosphere, with its mix of hunt balls and 'gor-blimey, guv'nor' supporting characters), while Joan Fontaine is more irritating than sympathetic as the imperiled Lina, making one wonder whether she received the Oscar as compensation for not having won it for her far superior performance in *Rebecca* the previous year.

Hitchcock's grip on the narrative also seems fairly lacklustre. Of course, everyone remembers Cary Grant walking up the staircase with the apparently poisoned glass of milk at the climax. To make sure our attention is focused on the glass, Hitchcock had a light bulb placed inside it, to give the milk a luminous quality. Shot in one sweeping take, this is without doubt the most memorable moment in the film. However, one should also note the shot in which Lina, cast in the shadow of an ornate window frame, looks as if she's caught in a giant spider's web, and the early shot in which she snaps the clasp of her handbag shut to indicate to Johnnie that, at that stage of his courting her, she has no interest in him (some commentators have likened this brief shot to the snapping shut of Lina's genitalia, which would certainly tie in with the kind of sexual innuendo Hitchcock revelled in).

Despite its faults, *Suspicion* (known as *Last Lover*, *Love in Irons* and *Fright* at various stages of production) was a box office success, while the reviews were generally favourable. *Variety* pretty much summed up the general consensus,

commenting, 'Alfred Hitchcock's trademark cinematic development of suspenseful drama, through mental emotions of the story principals, is vividly displayed,' although the reviewer did have reservations about the film's 'leisurely pace.'

The film was adapted for radio in 1944 and 1946, and remade for television in 1987, while in 1957 Hitchcock executive produced a television anthology series with the same title.

Hitchcock cameo Note that Hitchcock can be spotted at the village post office, posting a letter about halfway through the film.

Suspicion
(US, 1957–1958, 21x50m episodes, bw) ★

In 1957, Hitchcock executive produced this anthology of suspense stories bearing the umbrella title of his 1941 film. Unlike his other television series, *Alfred Hitchcock Presents* (1955–1961) and *The Alfred Hitchcock Hour* (1962–1965), the presentation was rather more serious, lacking Hitchcock's jaunty introductions. Given the Hitchcock name, the show was nevertheless able to attract a variety of top stars for its weekly episodes. It should be noted that Hitchcock's involvement with the series ended after the first ten episodes; the second season ran to 11 episodes, but was made by other hands. The episodes executive produced by Hitchcock are listed below, of which the first, *Four O'Clock* was directed by Hitchcock himself.

GENERAL CREDITS
Production company: NBC/Revue/Shamley
Executive producer: Alfred Hitchcock

EPISODE CREDITS

Four O'Clock
Director: Alfred Hitchcock
Teleplay: Francis Cockrell, based on a story by Cornell Woolrich
Cast: E G Marshall, Nancy Kelly, Richard Long, Tom Pittman, Harry Dean Stanton

Rainy Day
Director: James Neilson
Cast: Robert Flemyng, George Willi

Lord Arthur Savile's Crime
Director: Robert Stevens
Cast: Ronald Howard, Sebastian Cabot

Heartbeat
Director: Robert Stevens
Cast: David Wayne

Meeting in Paris
Director: James Neilson
Cast: Rory Calhoun

The Eye of Truth
Director: Robert Stevens
Cast: Joseph Cotten

The Bull Skinner
Director: Lewis Milestone
Cast: Rod Steiger, John Beal

The Way Up to Heaven
Director: Herschel Daugherty
Cast: Sebastian Cabot, Marian Lorne

The Voice in the Night
Director: Arthur Hiller
Cast: Barbara Rush, James Donald

The Woman Who Turned to Salt
Director: Stirling Silliphant
Cast: Michael Rennie, Pamela Brown

Suspicion
(GB, 1987, 96m, colour TV)

CREDITS
Production company:	HTV
Producers:	Barry Levinson, Sebastian Robinson
Screenplay:	Jonathan Lynn, Barry Levinson, from the novel *Before the Fact* by Francis Iles
Director:	Andrew Grieves
Music:	Larry Grossman
Costumes:	Jane Robinson

CAST
Anthony Andrews (Johnnie Aysgarth), Jane Curtin (Lina McLaidlaw/Aysgarth), Michael Hordern (Mr McLaidlaw), Vivien Pickles (Mrs McLaidlaw), Jonathan Lynn (Beaky), Betsy Blair

In this flat, ill-advised television remake of Hitchcock's less than perfect original, Anthony Andrews now plays the debonair Johnnie Aysgarth, seemingly out to murder his bookish wife (Jane Curtin) for her money. Typically bland TV movie fare, it completely fails to rise to the occasion.

SWEENEY, BOB American supporting actor. The film credits of this actor number several 1960s' productions, among them three for Disney: *Toby Tyler* (1960), *Moon Pilot* (1961) and *Son of Flubber* (1962). He can also be seen in Hitchcock's *Marnie* (1964) as busybody cousin Bob, who reveals that Marnie's engagement ring cost, '$42,000 – *plus* tax!' He also co-starred in *Incident at a Corner* (1960, TV), the episode of *Ford Startime* that Hitchcock directed, and an episode of *Alfred Hitchcock Presents*.

Hitchography: *Incident at a Corner* (1960, TV), *Letter of Credit* (1960, TV), *Marnie* (1964)

SWENSON, KARL American supporting actor. Swenson can be spotted in a number of films from the 1950s onwards, among them *Kings Go Forth* (1958), *Lonely Are the Brave* (1962) and *Ulzana's Raid* (1972). He played the annoying doom mongering drunk in the Tides restaurant in Hitchcock's *The Birds* (1963), a role the director admitted was 'straight out of an O'Casey play.' [33] He also co-starred in an episode of *Alfred Hitchcock Presents*. **Hitchography:** *A Very Moral Theft* (1960, TV), *The Birds* (1963)

SWERLING, JO (JOSEPH) (1897–1964) Russian-born playwright and screenwriter. Swerling emigrated to America as a child. Following experience as a journalist, he turned to screenwriting, among his many scripts being several for director Frank Capra, including *Dirigible* (1931), *Platinum Blonde* (1931) and *It's a Wonderful Life* (1946). In 1944 Swerling was hired by Hitchcock to work on the script for *Lifeboat*, which was based on a screen treatment by John Steinbeck. Swerling's many other screenplays include *Pennies from Heaven* (1936), *The Westerner* (1940), *The Pride of the Yankees* (1942) and *King of the Roaring Twenties* (1961). His plays number *The Kibitzer*, *Guys and Dolls* and *The Understander*. **Hitchography:** *Lifeboat* (1944)

SWIFT, CLIVE (1936–) British character actor. Best known for playing the put upon Richard Bucket in the TV sit-com *Keeping Up Appearances* (1990–1995), Swift has spent much of his career on television in a variety of programmes, from *Doctor Who* to *Inspector Morse*. His films have been less frequent, among them *Catch Us if You Can* (1965), Hitchcock's *Frenzy* (1972), in which he played Johnny Porter, the friend of wrongly suspected neck-tie killer Richard Blaney (Jon Finch), and *A Passage to India* (1984). **Hitchography:** *Frenzy* (1972)

SYLBERT, PAUL American production designer. An Oscar winner for his work on *Heaven Can Wait* (1978), Sylbert began his career in the mid-1950s, among his early credits being Hitchcock's *The Wrong Man* (1956), which made much use of the original locations in which the true-life story of musician Manny Balestrero, wrongly arrested of a series of robberies, took place. Sylbert's other design credits include *The Manchurian Candidate* (1962), *Riot* (1969), *One Flew Over the Cuckoo's Nest* (1975), *Kramer vs Kramer* (1979), *The Prince of Tides* (1991) and *Sliver* (1993). An occasional writer and director, his credits here include *The Steagle* (1969). He is the brother of production designer Richard Sylbert (1928–) and costume designer-turned production designer Anthea Sylbert. **Hitchography:** *The Wrong Man* (1956)

T

TABORI, GEORGE (1914–) Hungarian novelist-playwright. Remembered for such works as *Leo the Last* and *My Mother's Courage*, Tabori has also contributed to several screenplays, among them *Crisis* (1950), Hitchcock's *I Confess* (1953), *No Exit* (1962) and *Secret Ceremony* (1968). He has also directed one film, *Frohes Fest* (1981) and appeared in *Bye Bye, America* (1994). **Hitchography:** *I Confess* (1953)

TALTON, ALICE see Talton, Alix

TALTON, ALIX American supporting actress. Talton appeared in a handful of films in the 1950s and 1960s, among them *The Great Jewel Robber* (1950), *Rock Around the Clock* (1956) and Hitchcock's *The Man Who Knew Too Much* (1956), in which she played Helen Parnell, the socialite wife of showbiz entrepreneur Val Parnell (Alan Mowbray). Her other films include *The Deadly Mantis* (1957) and *Romanoff and Juliet* (1961). She was also occasionally billed as Alice Talton. **Hitchography:** *The Man Who Knew Too Much* (1956)

TANDY, JESSICA (1907–1994) British-born actress. Acclaimed as Blanche du Bois in the original 1948 Broadway run of Tennessee Williams' *A Streetcar Named Desire*, which won her the first of three Tony awards, Tandy made her stage debut in Britain at the age of 16 and was appearing on Broadway just five years later. In films in Britain from 1932 with *The Indiscretions of Eve*, she went on to appear in such Hollywood productions as *The Seventh Cross* (1944), *Forever Amber* (1947) and Hitchcock's *The Birds* (1963), in which she had the rather thankless role of the disapproving mother Lydia Brenner. Tandy's film work became more frequent in old age, and she contributed character roles to the likes of *The World According to Garp* (1982), *Cocoon* (1985) and *Driving Miss Daisy* (1989), the latter winning her a best actress Oscar, making her the oldest actress ever to do so. She also appeared in three episodes of *Alfred Hitchcock Presents*. Tandy's first husband was the British screen star Jack Hawkins (1910–1973), to whom she was married between 1932 and 1940. She married her second husband, actor-writer Hume Cronyn (1911– , real name Hume Blake), with whom she appeared many times on stage and in films, in 1942. He appeared in Hitchcock's *Shadow of a Doubt* (1943) and *Lifeboat* (1944), as well as two episodes of *Alfred Hitchcock Presents*; he also contributed to the screenplays for *Rope* (1948) and *Under Capricorn* (1949). **Hitchography:** *The Glass Eye* (1957, TV), *Toby* (1956, TV), *The Canary Sedan* (1958, TV), *The Birds* (1963)

Target for Tonight
(GB, 1941, 48m, bw) ★★★

CREDITS

Production company: The Crown Film Unit
Director: Harry Watt
Screenplay: Harry Watt, B Cooper

This superb wartime documentary about an RAF bombing raid over Germany earned a special Academy Award and rave notices in America, where *Variety* described it as 'One of the must-see films of 1941.' The film was slightly modified for its American release, on which Alfred Hitchcock worked as an un-credited editorial supervisor. For Hitchcock's other wartime work see *Men of the Lightship* (1941), *Bon Voyage* (1944), *Aventure Malgache* (1944), *Memory of the Camps* (1944) and *Watchtower Over Tomorrow* (1945).

TAYLOR, GILBERT (1914–) British cinematographer. Taylor began his career in 1929 as an assistant at Gainsborough, and following a lengthy appreticeship which saw him work as an assistant and an operator, he photographed his first film, *The Guinea Pig*, in 1948. The director of this film was Roy Boulting, and Taylor went on to work with him and his brother John on a further six films, including *Seven Days to Noon* (1950) and *Seagulls Over Sorrento* (1954). Taylor also notched up nine films for director J Lee-Thompson, among them such classics as *Yield to the Night* (1956) and *Ice Cold in Alex* (1958). Noted for his black-and-white work, Taylor went on to contribute sterling work to Stanley Kubrick's *Dr Strangelove* (1963), Richard Lester's *A Hard Day's Night* (1964) and Roman Polanski's *Repulsion* (1965). In 1972, Taylor filmed Hitchcock's last British production *Frenzy*, which is noted for its London location photography, including sequences in the old Covent Garden market. In the 1970s, Taylor worked on such blockbusters as *The Omen* (1976), *Star Wars* (1977) and *Dracula* (1979). His other films include *Flash Gordon* (1980), *Lassiter* (1983), *The Bedroom Window* (1986) and *Don't Get Me Started* (1993). **Hitchography:** *Frenzy* (1972)

TAYLOR, ROD (1929– , real name Robert Taylor) Australian actor. This ruggedly handsome actor came to acting following experience as a painter. In films from 1951 in his home country, he appeared in *The Stuart Expedition* (1951) and *Long John Silver* (1954) before making the move to Hollywood, where he went on to appear in such productions as *The Virgin Queen* (1955), *Raintree County* (1957), *The Time Machine* (1960) and Hitchcock's *The Birds* (1963), in which he played Mitch Brenner. Screenwriter Evan Hunter described Taylor's performance in the film as being 'So full of machismo, you expect him to have a steer thrown over his shoulder.' [1] Taylor's other films include *The VIPs* (1963), *Hotel* (1966), *The Picture Show Man* (1977) and *Welcome to Woop Woop* (1997), while his TV work includes such series as *The Bearcats* (1971). **Hitchography:** *The Birds* (1963)

TAYLOR, SAMUEL (1912–2000) American play-wright. Best known for his play *Sabrina Fair*, which has been filmed twice (in 1954 and 1995), Samuel Taylor has also had such works as *The Happy Time*, *The Pleasure of His Company* (co-written with Cornelia Otis Skinner) and *First Love* (as *Promise at Dawn*) filmed. As a screenwriter, his credits include *The Eddy Duchin Story* (1955), Hitchcock's *Vertigo* (1958), *Three on a Couch* (1966), a return to Hitchcock for *Topaz* (1969) and *The Love Machine* (1971). He also directed one film, *The Monte Carlo Story* (1956).

Recalled Taylor of working with Hitchcock on *Vertigo*: 'We discovered as soon as we met that our minds worked alike and that we had a rapport. It seemed to be a rapport that didn't have to be announced. So, when we worked, especially at his house, we would sit and talk. We would talk about all sorts of things; talk about food, talk about wives, talk about travel. We'd talk about the picture and there would be a long silence and Hitchcock would say, "Well, the motor is still running." And then all of a sudden we would pick up again and talk some more.' [2] It was during these sessions that Taylor suggested the title *To Lay a Ghost* for the movie! Taylor also commented of Hitchcock: 'He wanted fame, he wanted fortune and he wanted the right to make his own art in his own way, and he got all those things.' [3] Sadly, Taylor's second collaboration with the director on *Topaz* was not a happy affair; Hitchcock asked Taylor to completely re-write the film's original script by Leon Uris, upon whose novel it was based. However, by this time, pre-production on the film had already begun, and Taylor had to continue writing throughout shooting. **Hitchography:** *Vertigo* (1958), *Topaz* (1969)

TEARLE, SIR GODFREY (1884–1953) British stage actor. On stage from 1893 and in films from 1906 with *Romeo and Juliet* (in which he played Romeo), Tearle made too few film appearances, among his more memorable roles being that of the nefarious Professor Jordan in Hitchcock's *The 39 Steps* (1935), in which half of his character's right-hand little finger is shown to be missing. Tearle's other films include such favourites as *One of Our Aircraft is Missing* (1942), *Mandy* (1952) and *The Titfield Thunderbolt* (1952). **Hitchography:** *The 39 Steps* (1935)

Television see *Alfred Hitchcock Presents*, *The Alfred Hitchcock Hour* and *Suspicion*

Tell Your Children
(GB, 1922, 55m approx, bw, silent)

CREDITS

Production company:	International Artists
Producer:	Martin Sabine
Director:	Donald Crisp
Screenplay:	Leslie Howard Gordon, based on the novel *Lark's Gate* by Rachel McNamara
Inter-titles:	Alfred Hitchcock

CAST
Walter Tennyson (John Haslar), Doris Eaton (Rosny Edwards), Margaret Halstan (Lady Sybil Edwards), Gertrude McCoy (Maudie), Warwick Ward (Lord Belhurst), Mary Rorke (Susan Haslar), A Harding Steerman (Vicar)

This lost black-and-white silent film about a woman who prevents her daughter from eloping with a farmer was filmed at Islington Studios for Famous Players-Lasky and featured inter-titles designed by Hitchcock.

TENNYSON, PEN (1918–1941, real name Penrose Tennyson) British director. Tennyson was killed in World War II before his career had a chance to truly take off. However, he did direct three films: *There Ain't No Justice* (1939), *The Proud Valley* (1939) and *Convoy* (1940), prior to which he worked as an assistant director, among his credits being Hitchcock's *Young and Innocent* (1937), which co-starred his soon to be wife Nova Pilbeam (1919–). **Hitchography:** *Young and Innocent* (1937)

TESTER, DESMOND (1919–) British actor. In films from his early teenage years, Tester is best remembered for playing Stevie, the boy who gets blown up on a London bus in Hitchcock's *Sabotage* (1936). Hitchcock later regretted filming the sequence ('The bomb must never go off,' [4] he said in retrospect) and several critics chastised him for it. Not *all* the critics were sympathetic, however. Wrote Graham Greene of Tester's performance in *The Spectator*: 'For Master Desmond Tester's prep school accent I feel an invincible distaste (it glares out at you, like a first-fifteen muffler, from every disguise).' Tester's other films include *Tudor Rose* (1936), *The Drum* (1938), *Barry Mackenzie Holds His Own* (1974) and *Wild Duck* (1984). **Hitchography:** *Sabotage* (1936)

TETZEL, JOAN (1924–1977) American stage actress. Tetzel made all too few films, among them an appearance in Hitchcock's *The Paradine Case* (1947) as Judy Flaquer, Sir Simon Flaquer's plain-speaking daughter. Her other films include *Duel in the Sun* (1946), *The File on Thelma Jordan* (1950) and *Joy in the Morning* (1965). She also co-starred in an episode of *Alfred Hitchcock Presents*. She was married to the character actor Oscar Homolka (1898–1978) from 1949 until her death. He starred in Hitchcock's *Sabotage* (1936), plus three episodes of *Alfred Hitchcock Presents*. **Hitchography:** *The Paradine Case* (1947), *Guest for Breakfast* (1958, TV)

TETZLAFF, TED (1903–1995, real name Theodore Tetzlaff) American cinematographer. Working his way up from lab assistant, to camera assistant to director of photography, Tetzlaff received his first screen credit for *Atta Boy* in 1926, following which he went on to photograph *Eager Lips* (1926), *My Man Godfrey* (1936), *Easy Living* (1937), *I Married a Witch* (1942) and Hitchcock's *Notorious* (1946). Wrote Dilys Powell in *The Sunday Times* of the photography in *Notorious*: 'The movement of the camera is overruling; and possible distaste for the elements of Ben Hecht's script is most of the time lost in the interest of watching the rhythm of motion, the sliding or the sudden approaches, the swoops and swerves and horizontal swings.' Following the completion of *Notorious*, Tetzlaff turned to direction, having already made his debut with *World Premiere* in 1941. He subsequently went on to helm *Riff-Raff* (1947), *The Window* (1949), *Son of Sinbad* (1955) and *The Young Land* (1959), following which he retired. **Hitchography:** *Notorious* (1946)

THATCHER, TORIN (1905–1981, real name Torren Thatcher) British character actor. Born in India, Thatcher became noted for his villainous roles, the most memorable of them being Sokurah the Magician in *The 7th Voyage of Sinbad* (1958) and Pendragon in *Jack the Giant Killer* (1962). A former schoolmaster, he made his film debut in 1932 in *But the Flesh is Weak*. His many other films include *Drake of England* (1935), *Major Barbara* (1941) and *Hawaii* (1966). He can also be spotted in minor roles in two Hitchcocks: as an anarchist in *Sabotage* (1936) and as a surly doss house manager in *Young and Innocent* (1937), although both performances were un-credited. However, he did go on to star in an episode of *Alfred Hitchcock Presents* and an episode of *The Alfred Hitchcock Hour*. **Hitchography:** *Sabotage* (1936), *Young and Innocent* (1937), *Relative Value* (1959, TV), *Bed of Roses* (1964, TV)

THESIGER, ERNEST (1878–1961) British character actor. Remembered chiefly for his roles in James Whale's *The Old Dark House* (1932) and *The Bride of Frankenstein* (1935), in which he played Horace Femm and Dr Praetorius respectively, this equine star began his lengthy career as an actor on stage in 1909 following work as an artist (as well as being a noted watercolourist, Thesiger was also an accomplished embroiderer, a passion for which he shared with his friend Queen Mary). He made his first film appearance in *The Real Thing at Last* in 1916, which he followed with *Nelson* (1918), *A Little Bit of Fluff* (1919) and *Bachelor Club* (1921) among others. In 1922 he appeared in Hitchcock's aborted first film, *Number 13*. Sadly he never worked for Hitch again, although he did go on to make welcome appearances in such classics as *Henry V* (1944), *The Man in the White Suit* (1951) and *Father Brown* (1954). **Hitchography:** *Number 13* (1922)

The 39 Steps
(GB, 1935, 81m, bw) ★★★★

CREDITS

Production company:	Gaumont-British
Director:	Alfred Hitchcock
Producer:	Michael Balcon
Associate producer:	Ivor Montague
Screenplay:	Charles Bennett, Ian Hay, Alma Reville, based on the novel by John Buchan
Cinematographer:	Bernard Knowles
Music:	Hubert Bath, Jack Beaver (un-credited)
Music director:	Louis Levy
Editor:	D N Twist
Art director:	Oscar Werndorff
Costumes:	Marianne, J Strassner
Sound:	A Birch

CAST
Robert Donat (Richard Hannay), Madeleine Carroll (Pamela), Lucie Mannheim (Annabella Smith), John Laurie (John, the crofter), Peggy Ashcroft (Margaret, the crofter's wife), Godfrey Tearle (Professor Jordan), Helen Haye (Mrs Jordan), Wylie Watson (Memory), Gus MacNaughton (Commercial traveller), Jerry Verno (Commercial traveller), Peggy Simpson (Maid), Miles Malleson (Palladium stage manager)

Video availability: Rank; Cinema Club
CD availability: *Psycho – The Essential Hitchcock* (Silva Screen), which contains a *Suite* featuring the *Main Title*, *Highland Hotel*, *Mr Memory* and the *Finale*

With a running time of just 81 minutes, *The 39 Steps* is one of Hitchcock's most tightly plotted and fast moving thrillers. Or as critic Otis Ferguson aptly described it, 'A miracle of speed and light.'

The script, penned by Hitchcock regular Charles Bennett, is loosely based on John Buchan's 1915 novel and follows the plight of the Canadian Richard Hannay (Robert Donat) who, while visiting London, finds himself implicated in the murder a young woman in his Portland Place flat. What the authorities don't know is that the woman, Annabella Smith (Lucie Mannheim), whom Hannay met at a music hall where a memory act had been playing, was a freelance agent who had discovered that top secret plans, vital to Britain's air defence, are about to be smuggled out of the country by a secret organization known as The 39 Steps. Taking refuge in Hannay's rooms for the night, Annabella only has enough time to tell him the sketchiest of details before she is knifed in the back by enemy agents while Hannay sleeps. Consequently, with the barest information – a map of Scotland retrieved from the dead woman's hand on which the mountain Alt-na Shellach has been circled, and a clue as to the identity of the organization's ringleader, who is apparently missing part of a finger – Hannay has no option but to make his way to Scotland, find the villains himself and clear his name.

However, this proves easier said than done, given that the law is in hot pursuit. Indeed, Hannay finds himself cornered by the police on the Flying Scotsman, from which he makes a daring escape on the Forth Bridge when a lady passenger refuses to help conceal his identity. Finding brief salvage in a crofter's cottage, Hannay finally makes it over the moors to the home of one Professor Jordan (Godfrey Tearle), who reveals that it is *he* who is the

Hitchcock directs Madeleine Carroll and Robert Donat in The 39 Steps *(1935) as the assistant director and continuity girl look on.*

half-fingered ringleader. With no other option, Jordan shoots Hannay, who miraculously survives the ordeal thanks to a well-placed hymnbook in the breast pocket of the longcoat the crofter's wife has given him!

Now that he knows the identity of the ringleader, Hannay approaches the police. Unfortunately, the local sheriff fails to believe his story, given that the Professor is one of his closest friends. Consequently, Hannay has no option but to go on the run again, hiding out in a passing Salvation Army parade, and then at a political rally, at which he is mistaken as the guest speaker and forced to address the impatient audience! This is by no means the end of his troubles, though, for the young woman whose help he failed to attain on the train now arrives with the real speaker. Identifying Hannay to the police, the woman – Pamela (Madeleine Carroll) – is forced to travel to the police station with Hannay and the officers to make a formal identification. But it turns out that these particular police officers are in fact enemy agents, and the couple

find themselves on their way back to the Professor's home, where a sticky end no doubt awaits them.

Luckily, when the agents' car is held up by a flock of sheep ('Oh, look, a flock of detectives,' jokes Hannay), Hannay and Pamela – who by now have been handcuffed together – manage to escape, hiding out at a nearby inn, informing the landlady not to give them away as they're a runaway couple. During the night, Pamela manages to squeeze her hand from the cuffs. Making her escape from the bedroom that she's been forced to share with Hannay, she is about to make a run for it when the 'police' turn up at the reception desk asking if the couple are staying there. Overhearing their conversation, which includes mention of a pick up at the London Palladium, Pamela finally realizes that Hannay is innocent and, once the agents have been shooed out of the inn by the landlady for ordering drinks after hours, makes her way back to the bedroom, where she falls asleep at the foot of the bed.

Though Hannay is at first surprised to find that Pamela

has not only escaped the handcuffs, but has remained with him when she so easily could have run away, his joy soon turns to anger when she tells him that the agents called at the inn during the night looking for them; he is even more irked when she tells him of the pick up at the Palladium. Thus Hannay and Pamela hotfoot it to London, where she attempts in vain to convince the police of the plot to smuggle secrets (but no papers have actually been stolen, she is told), and he goes to the Palladium to try and figure out how the information is going to be passed on.

It's only when an act called Mr Memory makes his appearance that Hannay puts two and two together and realizes how the top secret information is going to be smuggled out of the country ('I've got it, I've got it! There are no papers missing – all the information's inside Memory's head!' he exclaims). Consequently, when Memory asks for questions from the audience Hannay shouts, 'What are The Thirty-Nine steps?' Unable to resist answering, Memory begins to spill the beans, only to be shot by the Professor, who has been watching in a stage box, ready to escort him out of the country. In the fracas that follows the police capture the Professor, and Memory finally gets to tell Hannay about the plans he had to memorize, which apparently enable aeroplane engines to be rendered silent. As Memory finally dies and the dancing girls are urged on to the stage to placate the audience by the manager, Hannay and Pamela hold hands, each no longer concerned about being shackled to the other.

Very much a series of connected vignettes, *The 39 Steps* proceeds at a rare speed once the basic plotline has been established. Said Hitchcock of this approach: 'I saw it as a film of episodes, and this time I was on my toes... I made sure the content of every scene was very solid, so that each one would be a little film in itself.' [5] Indeed, each of these little films is perfectly cast and executed. Among the best of them is the opening music hall sequence, where Hannay first sees Mr Memory's act, the jaunty, introductory music to which he later can't get out of his head (this piece of music was composed by an uncredited Jack Beaver, and proves to be the first memorable piece of music to feature in a Hitchcock film). Memory (Wylie Watson) was based on a real music hall personality named Datas whom Hitchcock had seen years earlier. Hitchcock's love of the halls is shown throughout the sequence, the rowdy audience featuring comical types from all walks of life ('How old's Mae West?' one punter keeps shouting before things descend into a riot). This scene is partially replayed at the end of the film, this time at the London Palladium, when Hannay finally asks Memory about The Thirty-Nine Steps, and Memory is shot when he begins to answer. Said Hitchcock of this: 'The whole idea is that the man is doomed by his sense of duty. Mr Memory *knows* what The Thirty-Nine Steps are, and when he is asked the question, he is *compelled* to give the answer.' [6]

On a more intimate scale, the episode in the crofter's cottage (which does not exist in Buchan's book) is perfectly formed, with the sour, middle-aged crofter (John Laurie) mistakenly believing that Hannay is trying to make love to his young wife (Peggy Ashcroft). Hitchcock even resorts to silent techniques when Hannay has to convince the crofter's wife – who has just read of the Portland Place murders in the newspaper – of his innocence merely by facial expression, given that her husband is saying grace over their evening meal at the same table.

Rather more action-packed is Hannay's escape across the Scottish moors, which involves police, tracker dogs, much splashing about in streams and, at one point, a rather curious looking helicopter.

Meanwhile, the scene at the inn, with Hannay and Pamela shackled together in the bedroom, is both comical and risqué. The comedy comes from the fact that neither can accomplish the simplest of tasks without assistance from the other. The risqué element derives from the fact that the film was made in 1935, when it was taboo for an unmarried couple to share a bedroom in the movies. Yet so deft are the direction and performances that, in addition to having Hannay and Pamela share the same bed, Hitchcock even gets away with the moment when Pamela removes her wet stockings, Hannay's shackled hand brushing down her leg as she does so. This must surely have raised an eyebrow or two at the time.

In fact the film is fairly full of risqué moments. Early on, when Hannay meets Annabella Smith at the music hall, she boldly asks him, 'May I come home with you?' More importantly, Hannay instantly accepts her apparent offer of free love! Meanwhile, the following morning, Hannay has a fairly ribald conversation with a passing milkman whose uniform he borrows in order to make his escape, informing the milko that he's been paying a married woman a visit, and that it is her husband and brother rather than two enemy agents who are waiting for him outside. This bold admission of extramarital sex, albeit a lie on Hannay's part, must have been quite a shocker at the time. Then there are the two travelling salesmen (Gus MacNaughton and Jerry Verno) whom Hannay encounters on the Flying Scotsman, who are discussing in almost lurid detail their wares, which just happen to be ladies' underwear. There's also the crofter's scene, which has a heavy air of adultery to it, with the crofter suspecting that he is about to be cuckolded (indeed, the crofter's wife receives Hannay's farewell kiss with an almost rapturous look).

What Hitchcock is really obsessed with in the film, though, is speed. 'What I like in *The 39 Steps* are the swift transitions,' [7] he later commented. However, logic doesn't always follow. For example, having shown Hannay being shot by the Professor, Hitchcock then cuts to a police station, with Hannay explaining away not only how he dodged death, but also how he escaped the Professor's house and got to the station, none of which is shown. It seems that the coat that the crofter's wife gave Hannay had a hymnbook in its breast pocket, and it was this mild form of divine intervention that saved Hannay's life. All a bit hard to swallow, but at least it prompts the Sheriff (Frank Cellier) to comment, 'Some of those hymns are terrible hard to get through!'

'The rapidity of those transitions heightens the excitement,' explained Hitch, adding, 'I'm not concerned with plausibility; that's the easiest part of it, so why bother?' [8] It is this pre-occupation with speed that no doubt precludes there being any overtly flamboyant stylistic touches in the film, although Bernard Knowles' camera is always in the right spot to make the most of each scene. Nevertheless, a couple of touches are worth pointing out. Following Hannay's escape on the Forth Bridge, a montage of sound featuring radio news broadcasts and police reports about Hannay play over a lengthy shot of the bridge. Given that only five years earlier Hitchcock had to have a live orchestra hidden behind a set when Herbert Marshall turned on his radio in *Murder!* (1930), this is a pretty impressive advance in sound editing. Later in the film, as Hannay and Pamela are being driven to the Professor's house by the pseudo policemen, Hitchcock dollies the camera from an interior shot of Hannay and Pamela in the back of the car (shot at the studio with back projection plates) to an exterior shot (filmed on location), seamlessly melding the two. The effect is so subtle it's very easy to miss this extremely accomplished piece of sleight of hand. Rather more obvious is the shot of Hannay's landlady in Portland Place screaming as she discovers the body of Annabella Smith, which Hitchcock blends with the whistle of the Flying Scotsman.

Thematically, the film marked Hitchcock's first full use of the 'innocent man on the run' motif, already alluded to in *The Lodger* (1926), and which he would return to again and again in the likes of *Young and Innocent* (1937), *Saboteur* (1942), *To Catch a Thief* (1955) and *North by Northwest* (1959), the latter being practically a remake of *The 39 Steps*. In exploiting this motif, the director is here superbly aided by Robert Donat's amiable performance, which helps to glue together the various predicaments Hannay finds himself in (Donat would later comment that he and Hitchcock 'understood each other so perfectly in the making of that film.' [9]. Madeline Carroll, whom producer Michael Balcon personally flew to Hollywood to secure for the film, makes the perfect Hitchcock heroine: glacial at first, she gradually succumbs to the hero's charms once she learns of his true innocence. The supporting gallery of character parts is also flawlessly cast, with John Laurie, Peggy Ashcroft, Wylie Watson and Godfrey Tearle deserving credit for creating such fully rounded and memorable characters given their comparatively brief time on screen.

Critics and audiences in both Britain and America were highly impressed by the labours of Hitchcock and his colleagues. 'The story twists and spins artfully from one high-powered sequence to another while the entertainment holds like steel cable from start to finish,' enthused *Variety*, while the *London Evening Standard* described the film as 'A grand mixture of comedy, melodrama and character study.' Elsewhere, *The Daily Mail* likened the film's speed to 'the Flying Scotsman, which is one of its stars.'

Note that a radio adaptation of the film, starring David Niven as Hannay, was broadcast in 1946. Two big screen remakes followed, in 1959 (with Kenneth More) and 1978 (with Robert Powell), while a television series titled *Hannay* (again starting Powell) ran between 1988 and 1989. In the late 1990s, a superb stage spoof of the Hitchcock film toured Britain, with Simon Ward as Hannay (Simon Williams took over the role in a later tour).

Hitchcock cameo Note that Hitchcock can be spotted early on outside the music hall as Hannay and Annabella Smith leave amid the commotion.

The Thirty-Nine Steps
(GB, 1959, 93m, Eastmancolor) ★

CREDITS

Production company:	Rank
Producer:	Betty E Box
Director:	Ralph Thomas
Screenwriter:	Frank Harvey, based on the novel by John Buchan
Cinematographer:	Ernest Steward
Music:	Clifton Parker
Music director:	Muir Mathieson
Editor:	Alfred Roome
Art director:	Maurice Carter
Costumes:	Yvonne Caffin
Sound:	John W Mitchell, Gordon K McCallum

CAST

Kenneth More (Richard Hannay), Tania Elg (Miss Fisher), Brenda de Banzie (Nellie Lumsden), Reginald Beckwith (Mr Lumsden), James Hayter (Mr Memory), Barry Evans (Professor Logan), Faith Brook (Nanny/Miss Robinson), Michael Goodliffe (Brown), Sid James (Truck driver), Leslie Dwyer (Milkman), Joan Hickson (Schoolmarm), Andrew Cruickshank, Betty Henderson, Wally Patch

Produced and directed by the husband and wife team who gave us the popular 'Doctor' comedies (*Doctor in the House* (1954), *Doctor at Sea* (1955), etc.), this unimaginatively handled remake of the Hitchcock classic at least has the saving grace of a personable leading performance by Kenneth More as Richard Hannay. Otherwise, the results, filmed at Pinewood Studios and on location in London and Scotland, completely lack atmosphere, thanks mostly to Ernest Steward's overly bright Eastmancolor cinematography. The story is practically the same as the Hitchcock version (i.e., little to do with Buchan), save for one or two variations. Hannay's female accomplice is this time a school teacher named Miss Fisher (Tania Elg), whose class he ends up lecturing on the finer points of botany. Meanwhile, instead of hiding out at a crofter's cottage, Hannay beds down at a roadside café, whose middle-aged proprietress, Nellie Lumsden (Brenda de Banzie), has the hots for him. He meanwhile makes his way across the moors under the cover of a group of cyclists. As before, though, things come to a climax with the shooting of Mr

Memory (James Hayter) at the music hall. Though by no means an unwatchable film, one can't help feeling disappointed by its lack of ambition. Said Hitchcock of the film: 'They miss the whole point.' [10]

Note that Barry Jones, who here plays Professor Logan, appeared in Hitchcock's 1932 film *Number Seventeen*, that Brenda de Banzie, who here plays Nellie Lumsden, played Mrs Drayton in Hitchcock's 1955 remake of *The Man Who Knew Too Much*, and that Faith Brook, who here plays Nanny, played Alice Barham in *Suspicion* (1941). Music director Muir Mathieson conducted Bernard Herrmann's score for *Vertigo* (1958), editor Alfred Roome cut *The Lady Vanishes* (1938) and was an assistant camera operator on *Blackmail* (1929), while art director Maurice Carter was an assistant art director on *The Lady Vanishes* (1938).

The Thirty-Nine Steps

(GB, 1978, 102m, Eastmancolor) ★★

CREDITS

Production company:	Rank/Norfolk International
Producer:	Greg Smith
Executive producer:	James Kenelm Clarke
Director:	Don Sharp
Screenplay:	Michael Robson, from the novel by John Buchan
Cinematographer:	John Coquillon
Music:	Ed Welch
Editor:	Eric Boyd-Perkins
Production design:	Harry Pottle
Costumes:	Joyce Stoneman
Sound:	Peter Sutton, Vernon Messenger, Terry Poulton, Ken Barker
Stunt co-ordinator:	Colin Skeaping
Additional photography:	Harry Waxman, Jimmy Bawden

CAST

Robert Powell (Richard Hannay), Karen Dotrice (Alex Mackenzie), Eric Porter (Inspector Lomas), John Mills (Scudder), David Warner (Edmund Appleton), Timothy West (Porton), Ronald Pickup (Bayliss), George Baker (Sit Walter Bullivant), Andrew Keir (Lord Rohan), Miles Anderson (David Hamilton), Robert Flemyng (Magistrate), Donald Pickering (Marshall), William Squire (Harkness), David Collings (Tilloston), John Welsh (Lord Belthane), Edward de Souza (Woodville), Robert Gillespie (Crombie)

This third refashioning of the John Buchan novel sees Robert Powell take on the role of Richard Hannay, a role he was to repeat in the later TV series *Hannay* (1988–1989). Despite reverting to the original 1914 period of the book, the script follows the plotting of the Hitchcock version fairly closely. Unlike the 1959 remake, though, the action is inventively handled by director Don

Sharp, who is aided immeasurably by John Coquillon's carefully framed photography, the convincing period art direction of Harry Pottle and – the icing on the cake, this – Ed Welch's sweeping score, which fully captures the adventure of the piece.

Performance-wise, Powell is the equal of Robert Donat as Hannay, while Karen Dotrice is suitably decorative as his aid and romantic interest, Alex Mackenzie. John Mills also leaves his mark as Scudder, the spy whose death sets Hannay off on his journey to the Scottish Highlands to prove his innocence and unearth the enemy agents. The film also benefits from a fine gallery of supporting players, among them such stalwarts as Eric Porter, David Warner and Donald Pickering. A note should also be made of the vertiginous, Harold Lloyd-style finale, which sees Hannay hanging from the minute hand of Big Ben in a bid to prevent it from setting off a bomb (though surely the enemy agents could have found an easier way of blowing up the Houses of Parliament?). The idea for this scene was lifted from the 1943 Will Hay comedy *My Learned Friend* (which was co-written by Hitchcock regular Angus MacPhail), for which a giant replica of the clock face was recreated on the Pinewood back lot (this clock face was also used in the titles for ITN's *News at Ten* for many years).

A superbly managed piece of entertainment, this is undoubtedly the best of all the Hitchcock remakes.

THOMAS, JAMESON (1892–1939) British actor. A popular leading man in the late 1920s, Thomas made his film debut in 1923 in *Chu Chin Chow*, which he followed with *Decameron Nights* (1924), *The Apache* (1925) and *The White Sheik* (1928) among others. In 1928 he took the leading role of widower farmer Samuel Sweetland in Hitchcock's *The Farmer's Wife*. He briefly went to Hollywood in the 1930s where he appeared in supporting roles in such classics as *It Happened One Night* (1934), *Lives of a Bengal Lancer* (1935) and *Mr Deeds Goes to Town* (1936). His other films include *One-Hundred Men and a Girl* (1937) and *Death Goes North* (1938), soon after which he died from tuberculosis. He also made a cameo appearance in *Elstree Calling* (1930) on which Hitchcock worked. **Hitchography:** *The Farmer's Wife* (1928), *Elstree Calling* (1930)

THORNDIKE, DAME SYBIL (1882–1976) British actress. One of the *grande dames* of the British theatre, Thorndike made her acting debut in 1904 following experience as a concert pianist, which was curtailed when she broke her wrist. A notable Saint Joan (a role penned for her by the great George Bernard Shaw), she was created a Dame for her work on stage in 1931. Her film appearances were less frequent, beginning with *Moth and Rust* in 1921, but included eye-catching cameos in *Major Barbara* (1941), *Nicholas Nickleby* (1947) and Hitchcock's *Stage Fright* (1950), in which she played the mother of RADA student Eve Gill (Jane Wyman), gaining one of the film's biggest laughs when confronted by her heavily disguised daughter, which prompts her to comment, 'Oh, there you are! Help me find my glasses, Eve, darling. I can't see a thing.' Her other films include *The Magic Box* (1951), *The Prince and the Showgirl* (1957) and *The Big Gamble* (1961). She was married to the actor Sir Lewis Casson (1875–1969) from 1908, and their daughter, the actress Anne Casson (1915–1990), appeared in Hitchcock's *Number Seventeen* (1932). **Hitchography:** *Stage Fright* (1950)

Three Live Ghosts
(GB, 1922, 66m approx, bw, silent)

CREDITS
Production company: Famous Players-Lasky
Director: George Fitzmaurice
Screenplay: Margaret Turnbull, Ouida Bergere, from the play by Max Marcin and Frederick Isham
Inter-titles: Alfred Hitchcock

CAST
Norman Kerry (Edward Foster), Anna Q Nilsson (Ivis), Edmund Goulding (Jimmy Gubbins), John Milterne (Jimmy Larne), Dorothy Fane (Duchess), Clare Greet (Mrs Gubbins), Wyndham Guise (Briggs)

This comedy about the ghosts of three dead prisoners of war who find themselves involved in a murder was one of several black-and-white silents for which Hitchcock designed the inter-titles. Unfortunately, this 1922 production, filmed at Islington Studios for Famous Players-Lasky by George Fitzmaurice, is currently missing, believed lost.

Throw Momma From the Train
(US, 1987, 88m, DeLuxe) ★

CREDITS
Production company: Orion
Producer: Larry Brezner
Director: Danny de Vito
Screenplay: Stu Silver
Cinematographer: Barry Sonnenfeld
Music: David Newman
Editor: Michael Jablow
Production design: Ida Random
Costumes: Marilyn Vance

CAST
Danny de Vito (Owen Lift), Billy Crystal (Larry Donner), Anne Ramsey (Mrs Lift), Kate Mulgrew (Margaret), Kim Greist (Beth), Brandford Marsalis (Lester), Rob Reiner (Joel), Bruce Kirby (Detective De Benedetto), Oprah Winfrey

In this fitfully amusing though sometimes overly aggressive variation on Hitchcock's *Strangers on a Train* (1951),

Danny de Vito stars as Owen Lift, a mother-dominated bachelor who wishes to be rid of his ma (Anne Ramsey), and so suggests swapping murders with aggrieved writer Larry Donner (Billy Crystal), whose ex-wife (Kate Mulgrew) has since become a millionaire by passing off one of her former husband's manuscripts as her own. Directed with occasional vigour by the debutant de Vito, the film earned Ramsey a best supporting actress Oscar nomination and met with a certain box office success (*Variety* described it as 'fun and delightfully venal').

TIOMKIN, DIMITRI (DMITRI) (1899–1979) Russian-born composer and conductor. Tiomkin began his career in music in 1919 as a pianist and conductor, having graduated from the St Petersburg Conservatory of Music and St Petersburg University (he also gained a law degree from the University of St Mary's). Tiomkin emigrated to America in 1925 and began scoring films in 1929, providing ballet music for a number of early musicals, among them *Devil-May-Care* (1929), *Lord Byron of Broadway* (1929), *The Rogue Song* (1930) and *Our Blushing Brides* (1930). He wrote his first dramatic score for *Resurrection* in 1931, and over the next 40 years went on to score such films as *Lost Horizon* (1937), *Mr Smith Goes to Washington* (1939), *It's a Wonderful Life* (1946), *Red River* (1948), *The Thing* (1951), *Giant* (1956), *Gunfight at the OK Corral* (1957), *55 Days at Peking* (1963) and *The Fall of the Roman Empire* (1964), earning Oscars for his work on *High Noon* (1952) – winning for both best score and best song, *Do Not Forsake Me – The High and the Mighty* (1954) and *The Old Man and the Sea* (1958).

He also scored four films for Hitchcock, beginning with *Shadow of a Doubt* in 1943. Tiomkin's work for Hitchcock is often overlooked in favour of Bernard Herrmann's more flamboyant music, but it should be noted that he wrote particularly strong scores for both *Strangers on a Train* (1951) and *Dial M for Murder* (1954), their intensity adding immeasurably to the tension (his scoring of the murder scene in *Dial M for Murder* is particularly noteworthy, the on screen violence being reflected by some equally violent brass work). In 1969, Tiomkin briefly turned to the production side of filmmaking, co-producing *MacKenna's Gold* with Carl Foreman, while in 1970 he produced, directed and orchestrated the music for *Tchaikovsky*, an American-Russian co-production about the famous composer. **Hitchography:** *Shadow of a Doubt* (1943), *Strangers on a Train* (1951), *I Confess* (1953), *Dial M for Murder* (1954)

To Catch a Thief
(US, 1955, 107m, Technicolor, VistaVision) ★

CREDITS
Production company: Paramount
Producer: Alfred Hitchcock
Director: Alfred Hitchcock
Screenplay: John Michael Hayes

(and, un-credited, Alec Coppel, who worked on a few retake shots), based on the novel by David Dodge

Cinematographer: Robert Burks
Music: Lyn Murray
Editor: George Tomasini
Art director: Hal Pereira,
Joseph MacMillan Johnson
Costumes: Edith Head
Sound: John Cope, Harold C Lewis
Special effects: Farciot Edouart, John P Fulton
2nd unit director: Herbert Coleman
2nd unit cinematography: Wallace Kelly

CAST

Cary Grant (John Robie/The Cat), Grace Kelly (Frances Stevens), Jessie Royce Landis (Jessie Stevens), John Williams (H H Hughson), Brigitte Auber (Danielle Foussard), Charles Vanel (Bertani), Jean Martinelli (Foussard), Georgette Anys (Germaine, Robie's maid), John Alderson (Detective), Rene Blancard (Inspector Lepic), Frank Chelland (Chef), Lewis Charles (Kitchen hand), William 'Wee Willie' Davis (Portly kitchen hand), Dominique Davray (Antoinette), Don Megowan (Detective), Louis Mercier (Croupier), Philip Van Zandt (Jewellery clerk), Gladys Holland (Woman at casino)

Video availability: Paramount
CD availability: *Psycho – The Essential Hitchcock* (Silva Screen), which contains a *Suite*, including Nathan Van Cleave's heraldic *Paramount VistaVision Fanfare*

The disappointing thing about *To Catch a Thief* is that one's memories of it tend to be better than the experience of actually watching it. The film boasts an excellent cast and features some of the most ravishing locations of any Hitchcock film, yet by equal measure, it is uncertainly paced, has a handful of talky *longueurs* and is somewhat variably made (some of the dubbing is atrocious). Perhaps everyone was having too good a time enjoying the hospitality of the French Riviera. Hitchcock and his company certainly took advantage of the world-class restaurants and casinos at hand, although it should be noted that it wasn't until the *following* year, during a trip to the Cannes Film Festival, that leading lady Grace Kelly found herself being romanced by Monaco's Prince Ranier III, whom she went on to marry in 1956.

Based on David Dodge's 1952 novel, the film follows the exploits of retired cat burglar John Robie (Cary Grant), whose life on the Riviera comes under threat when another thief commits a series of jewel robberies using his *modus operandi*. Naturally, the authorities suspect Robie, who now, like so many Hitchcock heroes before him, has to take on the job of proving his own innocence before being wrongly incarcerated ('What I can't understand is how this thief could imitate me so perfectly – it has to be someone who knew every detail of my tech-

nique,' muses Robie as to who the culprit could be).

In addition to the authorities, among those also suspecting Robie of the crimes are his former comrades from the French Resistance, now working as cooks at a chic restaurant ('I wouldn't put it past any of them to be doing the robberies themselves,' sniffs Robie), an English insurance investigator, H H Hughson (John Williams), and a visiting American heiress, Frances Stevens (Grace Kelly), and her plain-talking mother, Jessie (Jessie Royce Landis). By the end of the picture, Robie has, as we fully expected, exposed the real thief – Danielle Foussard (Brigitte Auber), the daughter of one of his wartime comrades – and won the girl, by which time we've also been treated to some ravishing local colour and a fair amount of amusing banter between the stars.

Dodge based his book on the true-life crimes of cat burglar Dario Sambucco, and Hitchcock takes every opportunity to point up the story's feline motifs: a cat slinks across a moonlit roof at the start of the film to signify the first robbery (cut to the inevitable shot of a screaming woman following the crime); Robie's nickname is The Cat; Robie's own cat sharpens its claws on a newspaper reporting the imposter's crimes; and a smirking kitchen hand pours out a saucer of milk for Robie when he visits the restaurant run by his comrades. The feline motif is also taken up in the dialogue: 'Did I brush your fur the wrong way?' enquires Danielle of Robie, whom she later takes to Cannes in her speedboat. 'You're getting me wet,' complains Robie as the boat skips along the back projected waves. 'It must be true what they say – cat's don't like water,' comes the retort. Meanwhile, Bertani, the restaurant proprietor, accuses Robie of being 'as nervous as a cat.' Robie even receives a note from the imposter, which reads, 'Robie, You've already used up eight of your nine lives. Don't gamble your last one.' Finally, when Frances is convinced of Robie's innocence and determines on helping him expose the imposter, she tells him, 'The Cat has a new kitten!'

The writing of the screenplay was a fairly leisurely affair, for which John Michael Hayes (with whom Hitchcock had just made *Rear Window* (1954)) was on salary for some 23 weeks. Recalled Hayes: 'Most of my conferences with Hitch were concerned with his reminiscing about how he had solved some cinematic problem. It was very enjoyable to sit and have him ramble through 30 years of film-making.' [11] Among the sequences thought up for the film was the fight between Robie and the police at the flower market, and the scenes at Bertani's restaurant, during which an anonymous hand throws an egg at Robie, which smashes against a window. Hitchcock had a personal hatred of eggs, and this is further exploited when Jessie later stubs out a cigarette in a fried egg. Hitchcock also built up the finale, staged during a costume ball, with Robie's masked blackamore fooling the cops by swapping places with Hughson so that he can wait on the roof and wait for the impostor to strike.

Filming on the $3 million production, for which Hitchcock was paid $150,000, began in France on 31 May

1954, and although there were initial delays owing to bad weather (which caused a carnival scene to be cut from the schedule), things generally went smoothly, although the schedule ultimately overran by 22 days. Cary Grant had agreed to come out of semi-retirement to play Robie, the carrot on the stick being a chance to work with the beautiful Grace Kelly, with whom he would become a lifelong friend. Revealed Grant: 'I really didn't want to do the film. I told Hitch that I was too old to play a leading man and that I was old fashioned. It was only when Hitch told me that I would be playing opposite Grace Kelly that I accepted.' [12] Hitchcock couldn't have been more delighted, though it should be noted that, far from retiring, Grant made a further *12* films following *To Catch a Thief*, including Hitchcock's *North by Northwest* (1959).

Having secured Grant and Kelly, Hitchcock made the most of the pairing during the romantic clinches, among the film's highlights being the seduction scene between the two stars, during which the screen erupts with fireworks when they finally kiss. This device has, of course, become something of a cliché since then, but, amazingly, was enough to cause concerns from the censor at the time!

In fact the script is packed with sexual innuendo: 'Look. Hold them!' Frances invites Robie during the seduction scene; *she* is referring to the diamonds in her necklace, but the *camera* is firmly fixed on her cleavage. Hitchcock also worked in a joke involving Robie dropping a 10,000-franc chip down a woman's cleavage at the casino by way of having him introduce himself to Frances and Jessie, who have been watching in amusement. Meanwhile, in a scene in which Robie swims at the Carlton beach with Frances and Danielle, Frances accuses Robie of flirting with the younger woman: 'From where I was standing it looked like you were conjugating some irregular verbs!' Then later, as Robie and Frances picnic together on chicken, she asks him if he'd prefer 'a leg or a breast.' It is also during this scene, shot overlooking the principality of Monaco, that Frances comments, 'Have you ever seen any place in the world more beautiful?' Two years later, Kelly would of course be Princess Grace of Monaco.

The performances in *To Catch a Thief* are all fairly easy-going. Indeed, during the swimming scene at the Carlton beach, Cary Grant visibly corpses during the banter between Danielle and Frances (having been accused by Frances of being a mere child, Danielle retorts, 'Shall we stand in shallower water and debate that?'). As glamorous as Grant and Kelly are, though, it is John Williams, as the strait-laced insurance investigator Hughson, and Jessie Royce Landis as Jessie, Frances' plain-speaking mother, who give the most memorable performances ('Just what *did* he steal from you?' Jessie asks her daughter of her romantic involvement with Robie). The film also benefits from Robert Burks' colourful VistaVision photography (the scenes at the flower market are particularly vibrant) and a bright score by Lyn Murray, which perfectly captures the *joi de vivre* of the Riviera (although it should be noted that the music becomes surprisingly Herrmannesque during the tenser moments, among them Robie's trip to the comrades' restaurant).

Though noting that it was basically a piece of fluff, the critics were generally upbeat about *To Catch a Thief* when it was released on 4 August 1955 (even Hitchcock described it as 'lightweight' [13]). '*To Catch a Thief* does nothing but give out a good, exciting time. If you'll settle for that at a movie, you should give it your custom right now,' enthused Bosley Crowther in the *New York Times*, while the London *Times* described the film as being 'as good as a holiday in itself.' Audiences agreed, and flocked to admire the stars and the sunny locations. If that weren't enough, the movie had the honour of being selected for the Royal Film Performance that year. It was also nominated for three Oscars: best costume design (Edith Head), best art direction (Hal Pereira, Joseph MacMillan Johnson) and best cinematography (Robert Burks), of which it won the latter.

Hitchcock cameo Note that Hitchcock can be spotted sitting next to Cary Grant on a bus early on in the film. The director celebrated his birthday (13 August) during the film's making with cake and champagne. A secretary apparently announced to the cast and crew, 'Would you all come into the other room, please, and have a piece of Mr Hitchcake's cock?' The story could well be apocryphal, for it sounds suspiciously like another incident said to have taken place at a Hollywood party. As the evening drew to a close, a butler began to announce the arrival of the guests' cars. Having successfully called Miss Deborah Kerr's car and Mr John Kerr's car, he went on to announce Mr Hitch's cock.

TODD, ANN (1909–1993) British actress. This immaculate-looking actress with a cut glass accent made her stage debut in 1928. In films from 1931 with *Keepers of Youth*, she went on to appear in the likes of *The Ghost Train* (1931), *Things to Come* (1936), *South Riding* (1938) and *Poison Pen* (1939) before finally hitting the big time with *The Seventh Veil* (1945). In 1946 she went to America where she performed in a radio adaptation of *Suspicion* with Cary Grant and, a year later, co-starred in Hitchcock's *The Paradine Case*, in which she played Gregory Peck's faithful wife, about which *Variety* commented, 'Ann Todd delights as his wife, giving the assignment a grace and understanding that tug at the emotions.' Todd's third husband was the acclaimed director David Lean (1908–1991) to whom she was married between 1949 and 1957. He directed her in three films: *The Passionate Friends* (1948), *Madeleine* (1949) and *The Sound Barrier* (1952). Todd's other films include *The Green Scarf* (1954), *Taste of Fear* (1961), *The Fiend* (1971), *The McGuffin* (1985, TV) and the Hitchcock, *il Brividio del Genio* (1985). In the mid-1960s she also produced and directed three travelogues: *Thunder in Heaven* (1965), *Thunder of the Gods* (1966) and *Thunder of the Kings* (1967). Her television credits include an episode of *Alfred Hitchcock Presents*. **Hitchography:** *Suspicion* (1946, radio), *The Paradine Case* (1947), *Sylvia* (1958, TV)

Hitchcock holds on to a wooden post for support whilst filming a vertiginous shot for To Catch a Thief *(1955).*

TODD, RICHARD (1919– , real name Richard Palethorpe-Todd) Irish-born actor. On stage from 1937, Todd was signed to films in 1948, and following his debut in *For Them That Trespass*, he went on to earn an Oscar nomination for his second film, *The Hasty Heart* (1949), which secured his stardom. The archetypal stiff-upper-lip-type, he went on to appear in *The Sword and the Rose* (1953), *The Dam Busters* (1954), *Chase a Crooked Shadow* (1958), *Operation Crossbow* (1965), *Asylum* (1972) and *House of the Long Shadows* (1982). In 1950 he appeared as the murderer Jonathan Cooper in Hitchcock's *Stage Fright*, but the director regarded the character as a flop. Nevertheless, Todd was thrilled to have been asked to star in the film: 'It was a terrific surprise and a feather in my cap to have Hitchcock wanting me… He was a strange man, not a lot of help to his actors. He didn't rehearse you. He just gave his first assistant a diagram of what he wanted, and then he would go off to his office. Once we had rehearsed together and worked out our moves, he would come down to have a look at it, say if it was okay or not, and then shoot it. I think he took the view that you only hire people who know what they're doing. However, he said I had expressive eyes and spent a lot of time doing shots on me where only the eyes were lit, because they tell the story.' [14] **Hitchography:** *Stage Fright* (1950)

TOLAND, GREGG (1904–1948) American cinematographer. One of the great Hollywood cinematographers, Toland graduated to lighting cameraman in 1929 with *Bulldog Drummond* (which he co-photographed with George Barnes) following experience as a camera assistant. He went on to photograph such classics as *Les Misérables* (1935), *These Three* (1946), *Dead End* (1937), *Wuthering Heights* (1939), which won him an Oscar, *The Grapes of Wrath* (1940), *Citizen Kane* (1941), *The Little Foxes* (1941) and *The Best Years of Our Lives* (1946). He also did some un-credited second unit photography for Hitchcock's *Notorious* (1946), photographing the scenes in Brazil for the rear projection plates. **Hitchography:** *Notorious* (1946)

TOMASINI, GEORGE (1909–1964) American editor. Tomasini became one of Hitchcock's key collaborators in the 1950s and 1960s, cutting a total of nine films for the Master, beginning with *Rear Window* (1954). He earned an Oscar nomination for editing *North by Northwest* (1959), but surprisingly not for *Psycho* (1960), despite the complexities of the shower sequence (78 cuts within this one scene alone). Tomasini's other credits include *Wild Harvest* (1947), *Cape Fear* (1961), *The Time Machine* (1960) and *The Seven Faces of Dr Lao* (1964). **Hitchography:** *Rear Window* (1954), *To Catch a Thief* (1955), *The Man Who Knew Too Much* (1956), *The Wrong Man* (1957), *Vertigo* (1958), *North by Northwest* (1959), *Psycho* (1960), *The Birds* (1963), *Marnie* (1964)

TOOMEY, REGIS (1901–1991) American supporting actor. In films from 1929 with *Rich People*, Toomey went

on to notch up over 150 film appearances in films such as *Perfect Alibi* (1931), *Illegal Traffic* (1938), Hitchcock's *Spellbound* (1945), in which he played Sergeant Gillespie, *The Tall Target* (1951), *Voyage to the Bottom of the Sea* (1961) and *Won Ton Ton, the Dog Who Saved Hollywood* (1976). He also proved popular in such series as *Burke's Law* (1963–1965) and *Petticoat Junction* (1968–1969). **Hitchography:** *Spellbound* (1945)

Topaz
(US, 1969, 127m, Technicolor) ★

CREDITS
Production company:	Universal
Producer:	Alfred Hitchcock
Associate producer:	Herbert Coleman
Director:	Alfred Hitchcock
Screenplay:	Samuel Taylor (and Leon Uris), based on the novel by Leon Uris
Cinematographer:	Jack Hildyard
Photographic consultant:	Hal Mohr
Music:	Maurice Jarre
Editor:	William H Ziegler
Production designer:	Henry Bumstead
Costumes:	Edith Head
Special effects:	Albert Whitlock
Sound:	Waldon O Watson, Robert R Bertrand

CAST
John Forsythe (Michael Nordstrom), Frederick Stafford (Andre Devereaux), Dany Robin (Nicole Devereaux), Karin Dor (Juanita de Cordoba), John Vernon (Rico Parra), Michel Piccoli (Jacques Granville/Columbine), Philippe Noiret (Henri Jarre), Per-Axel Arosenius (Boris Kusenov), Roscoe Lee Browne (Philippe Dubois), Claude Jade (Michael Picard), Michel Subor (Francois Picard), Edmon Ryan (McKittreck), Sonja Kolthoff (Mrs Kusenov), Tina Hedstrom (Tamara Kusenov), Don Randolph (Luis Uribe), John Van Dreelen (Claude Martin), John Roper (Thomas), Lew Brown (US official), Carlos Rivas (Hernandez), George Skaff (Rene d'Arcy), Sandor Szabo (Emile Redon), Lewis Charles (Mr Mendoza), Anna Navarro (Mrs Mendoza), Roger Til (Jean Chabrier)

Video availability: Universal
DVD availability: Universal
CD availability: *Psycho – The Essential Alfred Hitchcock* (Silva Screen), which contains the *Main Title March*; *The Essential Maurice Jarre Film Music Collection* (Silva Screen), which contains the *Main Title March*; *A History of Hitchcock – Dial M for Murder* (Silva Screen), which also contains the *Main Title March*

Like several of Hitchcock's maligned films, among them *Marnie* (1964) and *Torn Curtain* (1966), *Topaz* doesn't entirely justify its poor reputation. It is undeniably the weakest of the director's 1960s' films. It also suffers from an unnecessarily complex plot, a surfeit of minor characters, a confused ending and several talky *longueurs*. But one shouldn't dismiss it entirely, for it is made with the director's customary professionalism (despite the fact that he lost interest in the production during filming) and contains a number of touches worthy of his better films.

Based on the 1967 best seller by Leon Uris – whose contract stipulated that he should script any subsequent film adaptations – *Topaz* is loosely based on an actual political crisis from 1962 in which it was revealed by a KGB official who had defected to America that spies working on behalf of Russia had managed to penetrate the French government. Here, the spies are revealed to be members of a secret organization named Topaz, which is the codename for a group of French officials in high circles who work for the Soviet Union.

Unfortunately, although intrigued by the story, Hitchcock was dissatisfied with Uris' script and subsequently hired Samuel Taylor, who'd penned *Vertigo* (1958) for him, to do a complete re-write. But Hitchcock was already in advanced pre-production by this stage, and actually had to begin shooting before Taylor had completed his task. Consequently, some scenes were shot just days, sometimes even hours, after Taylor had finished working on them. For Hitchcock this was anathema, for he was used to planning his camera angles months ahead of shooting. Consequently, he had to improvise several sequences on the hoof. This might have been fine for a small, low budget film, but *Topaz* was a major $4 million studio production, with complex location scenes in Copenhagen, Paris, New York and Cuba (for which read the back lot).

Having worked with Paul Newman and Julie Andrews, two of Hollywood's biggest stars, on his previous film *Torn Curtain* (1966), Hitchcock decided to eschew name actors for *Topaz*, his one concession being John Forsythe, who had starred in *The Trouble with Harry* for him back in 1955. In the film, Forsythe plays Michael Nordstrom, a US intelligence expert who helps KGB official Boris Kusenow (Per-Axel Arosenius) escape to the West while holidaying with his family in Copenhagen. This lengthy sequence, shot mostly without dialogue as Kusenow and his family try to dodge three Soviet agents in a pottery and a busy department store, gets the film off to an exciting start, climaxing with a particularly tense moment when Kusenow's daughter stumbles in the street and almost gets left behind when her parents are finally bundled into a car by the Americans. Shot in the director's best style – lots of furtive looks, good use made of angles and locations – this is Hitchcock operating somewhere near his best.

Sadly, once this ten-minute sequence has concluded, the plot proper kicks in, and things become increasingly confusing as French agent Andre Devereaux (Frederick Stafford) is asked by Nordstrom, an old family friend, to question his contact in Cuba as to whether or not Kusenow's revelations are true. Things are further compli-

cated by the fact that Devereaux is having an affair with his Cuban contact, Juanita de Cordoba (Karin Dor), the widow of a hero in Castro's revolution, who in turn is having an affair with Cuban military leader Rico Parra (John Vernon). Devereaux's wife Nicole (Dany Robin) is meanwhile having an affair with top French official Jacques Granville (Michel Piccoli), aka Columbine, who turns out to be the head of Topaz. The film concludes with the exposure of Granville and his subsequent suicide, although by this time one cares very little about what who has been doing to whom or why.

This is a shame, for there are some neat scenes and touches worth catching along the way. Among them is a sequence involving Philippe Dubois (Roscoe Lee Browne), a black undercover agent who operates out of a Harlem florist shop, whom Devereaux hires on behalf of Nordstrom to photograph some papers belonging to Parra, who is visiting New York and staying in a nearby hotel. Helped in his task by Luis Uribe (Dona Randolph), who is part of Parra's entourage, Dubois is initially successful in his goal, posing as a journalist keen to interview Parra, during which Uribe manages to lift the briefcase containing the papers. However, when Parra soon after notices that the case has disappeared, he quickly tracks Dubois and Uribe to a room down the corridor where they are photographing the documents. In the ensuing fracas, Dubois jumps out of the hotel window, lands on a convenient awning below and makes his way back to his shop, passing his camera on to Devereaux, whom he purposely bumps into in the street. Directed with style and economy, the sequence manages to generate a good deal of suspense as Uribe attempts to lift Parra's case, while Dubois' jump from the hotel window is a completely unexpected development (note that when the camera dollies down the hotel corridor, one of the overhanging lamps lifts out of the way to make room for it to do so!).

Elsewhere, Juanita's death at the hands of Parra, who shoots her while embracing her in her villa for betraying him, is superbly handled. Once the shot has been fired, Hitchcock cuts to an overhead angle as Juanita collapses to the floor, her long purple dress splaying out beneath her like a pool of blood.

Frederick Stafford's rather wooden Deveraux aside, there are some good performances in the film, among them those by Roscoe Lee Browne, Per-Axel Arosenius, John Forsythe, Karin Dor, John Vernon and Don Randolph, while the late arrival of Philippe Noiret as Henri Jarre, Columbine's second in command who inadvertently gives the game away, livens up several of the film's later scenes. Unfortunately, none of the film's plus points helped to entice audiences, who this time failed to be lured by the poster's claim that 'Hitchcock takes you behind the actual headlines to expose the most explosive spy scandal of this century!' Perhaps surprisingly, then, some critics were quite enamoured with the film. '*Topaz* tends to move more solidly and less infectiously than many of Alfred Hitchcock's best remembered pix, yet Hitchcock brings in a full quota of twists and tingling moments,' enthused *Variety*. Writing in *The Village Voice*, Andrew Sarris also found things to admire, commenting: '[For] all its blemishes and drawbacks, *Topaz* is a haunting experience, both inspired and intelligent, convulsive and controlled, passionate and pessimistic.'

Note that three endings were filmed, all of which can be found on the Universal DVD. The first involved Devereaux and Granville sorting out their differences with a duel at a deserted sports stadium, with Granville being shot by a Russian sniper before Devereaux fires his pistol. Hitchcock spent a good deal of time on the sequence, but when test audiences found the scene wanting, Hitchcock was persuaded to remove it by the front office and replace it with a scene in which Devereaux and Granville go their separate ways at an airport having bid each other farewell. Hitchcock himself found this lacking, and so replaced it with the released ending, which has Granville shooting himself in his apartment (Hitchcock didn't actually shoot any new footage for this sequence, but instead re-cut an earlier scene in which Jarre arrives at Granville's flat for a meeting; trimming the shot of Jarre entering the front door, the director used this to imply that it was instead Granville returning home, which he then followed with the sound of a gun shot).

Hitchcock cameo Note that Hitchcock can be spotted in an airport scene, getting out of a wheelchair to greet a friend.

Torn Curtain
(US, 1966, 119m, Technicolor) ★★

CREDITS

Production company:	Universal
Producer:	Alfred Hitchcock
Screenplay:	Brian Moore (and Keith Waterhouse and Willis Hall)
Cinematographer:	John F Warren
Music:	John Addison
Lyrics:	Jay Livingston, Ray Evans
Editor:	Bud Hoffman
Production design:	Hein Heckroth
Art director:	Frank Arrigo
Costumes:	Edith Head, Grady Hunt
Special effects:	Albert Whitlock
Sound:	Waldo O Watson, William Russell
Camera operator:	Leonard J South

CAST

Paul Newman (Professor Michael Armstrong), Julie Andrews (Sarah Sherman), Wolfgang Kieling (Hermann Gromek), Lila Kedrova (Countess Luchinska), Tamara Toumanova (Prima ballerina), Hansjoerg Felmy (Heinrich Gerhard), Ludwig Donath (Professor Gustav Lindt), Gunter Strack (Professor Karl Manfred), David Opatoshu (Jakobi), Mort Mills (Farmer), Carolyn Conwell (Farmer's wife), Arthur Gould-Porter (Freddy), Gloria Gorvin (Fraulein Mann), Gisela Fischer (Dr Koska)

Video availability: Universal
DVD availability: Universal
CD availability: *Torn Curtain* (Varese), which contains John Addison's score; *Torn Curtain* (Varese), which contains a new recording of Bernard Herrmann's unused score by conductor Joel McNeely and the National Philharmonic Orchestra; *Torn Curtain – The Classic Film Music of Bernard Herrmann* (Silva Screen), which contains the *Main Title*, *Gromek* and *The Killing* from Herrmann's unused score; *Citizen Kane – The Essential Bernard Herrmann Film Music Collection* (Silva Screen), which contains the *Main Title*, *Gromek* and *The Killing* from Herrmann's unused score; *Psycho – The Essential Alfred Hitchcock* (Silva Screen), which contains a *Suite* from Herrmann's unused score and Addison's *Main Title*

Although he would make another three films, *Torn Curtain* (1966) is Hitchcock's last truly good film, containing some well-wrought scenes in his best manner. 'It tears you apart with suspense,' promised the poster. It may seem a little old fashioned now and lacking in humour, but it does exactly what it says on the tin. In fact, despite some casting misjudgements, it doesn't deserve its reputation as one of the director's weaker films, and certainly ranks as one of the more entertaining Cold War thrillers to emerge from the 1960s (commented *The Times*, one of the few newspapers to praise it, 'The film remains great fun for most of its length, and it would be silly to let regret for what it *might* have been and is *not* blind us to the considerable advantages of what it actually *is*').

Hitchcock's inspiration for the film was the defection of British diplomats Guy Burgess and Donald MacLean to Russia. What, he wondered, did Mrs MacLean think of the whole thing? Consequently, he and screenwriter Brian Moore concocted a plot involving an American nuclear physicist, one Professor Michael Armstrong (Paul Newman), who seemingly defects to East Germany when the funding for his anti-nuclear missile project, Gamma 5, is cut. Much to his chagrin, his fiancée and assistant Sarah Sherman (Julie Andrews) decides to follow him into the eastern bloc, having decided that, no matter what his political affiliations now are, she still loves him and wants to be with him. However, the twist is that the Professor has *not* defected; he is in fact a member of a top-secret spy ring – codename Pi – hoping to steal a new formula from Professor Gustav Lindt (Ludwig Donath), with whom he is now expected to work at the Leipzig University. With the formula acquired, Armstrong and Sherman try to make their way out of East Germany, helped and hindered along the way by a variety of people, among them the University's doctor (Gisela Fischer), a disaffected Polish countess (Lila Kedrova), a Russian ballerina (Tamara Toumanova) and members of the Pi underground.

For Hitchcock, the film was full of compromises, chief among them the casting of Paul Newman and Julie Andrews, then the two biggest stars Hollywood had to offer, whose presence in the film the Universal front office insisted upon. The director felt that the stars were ill suited to their roles, while their salaries of $750,000 ate somewhat heavily into the film's $5 million budget (despite a solid effort, Newman's Actors' Studio approach is at odds with Hitchcock's rather more artificial style, while the mumsy Andrews – the second major musical star to be cast in a Hitchcock film following Doris Day's outing in *The Man Who Knew Too Much* in 1956 – never begins to convince, though at least, unlike Day, she doesn't burst into song at inappropriate moments). Hitchcock also had the script re-worked at the last moment by Keith Waterhouse and Willis Hall, known for their screenplays for *Whistle Down the Wind* (1961), *A Kind of Loving* (1962) and *Billy Liar* (1963), the latter based on the novel by Waterhouse.

Hitchcock was also now working without some of his most trusted collaborators. His long-time cinematographer Robert Burks was away on another project – he would die in a house fire tragedy before the two could work together again – while his editor George Tomasini had also recently died. Hitchcock even famously fell out with his longtime composer Bernard Herrmann during the production. Hitchcock and the front office had wanted a lighter, more commercially exploitable score for the movie than Herrmann customarily provided. However, Herrmann eschewed the demands for a strong love theme and instead scored the film as he saw fit, using 16 French horns, nine trombones, two tubas, 12 flutes, eight cellos and eight basses. When Hitchcock attended the recording session and heard Herrmann's bombastic *Main Title* theme, he removed him from the picture, and the two never spoke to each other again. Commented fellow composer Elmer Bernstein, a close friend of Herrmann's: 'He was greatly disturbed by the *Torn Curtain* incident, and in a curious way I'm sure he felt betrayed by Hitchcock, despite the fact that evidence seems to indicate that Hitchcock had warned Herrmann that he didn't want the kind of score that Herrmann ultimately wrote. But I think Herrmann himself thought he – the dramatist – was doing what was best for the film. Hitchcock didn't agree'. [15]

Herrmann was subsequently replaced by John Addison, an Oscar winner for his work for *Tom Jones* (1963), although Hitchcock had first approached Maurice Jarre, who was at the time busy with *The Professionals* (1966) and so had to decline the director's invitation (the two did get together for Hitchcock's next production, though, *Topaz* (1969)). Addison managed to provide the love theme Hitchcock so desperately wanted; titled *Green Years*, it had lyrics by *Que Sera, Sera* Oscar winners Jay Livingston and Ray Evans, and was used to promote the film, even though only an orchestral version of it can be heard in the film. Elsewhere, Addison's score is decidedly Herrmannesque, even if in a slightly more humorous vein (note that Herrmann's unused score has subsequently been recorded and is currently available on CD, while the DVD restores his music in the extras section).

Filming on *Torn Curtain* began in mid-November 1965 and took in location work in Copenhagen and Berlin (where Hitchcock had filmed in the 1920s), as well as on the Universal back lot. The two leads may not have been ideally cast, but Hitchcock made sure to surround them with many eye-catching supporting actors, among them Lila Kedrova as the eccentric and flamboyantly dressed Countess Luchinska who helps Armstrong and Sherman

Hitchcock observes Tamara Toumanova as she prepares to film the highly effective freeze-frames for the ballet in Torn Curtain *(1966).*

in their escape in return for their sponsoring her to go to America ('My American sponsors,' she wails when they have to make a run for it); Tamara Toumanova as the haughty prima ballerina whose limelight Armstrong steals when he arrives in East Berlin; Ludwig Donath as the crotchety Professor Lindt, eager to cut the chat and get down to business, only to realize he'd been duped by Armstrong ('You told me *nothing*! You *know* nothing!'); and, best of all, Wolfgang Kieling as the sinister Hermann Gromek, the gum-chewing 'personal guide' the East German authorities have provided to shadow Professor Armstrong's every move.

In fact Gromek features in two of the film's key set pieces: in order to meet up with a fellow double agent, Armstrong attempts to shake off his 'guide' in the Berlin museum, through the deserted galleries of which he quickly makes his way, followed all the time by Gromek's echoing footsteps. Having shaken off his tail, Armstrong makes his way by taxi to a farm on the outskirts of the city, where he receives further instructions from the owner. But Gromek has managed to follow him on his motorbike, and having spotted the Pi sign Armstrong has made in the dirt by way of identifying himself to the farmer's wife, looks set to blow the Professor's cover. Consequently, Armstrong realizes that if he is to keep his mission a secret, he will have to kill Gromek, which he does with the help of the farmer's wife.

Hitchcock had long wanted to film a sequence showing how hard it is to actually kill a man (commented the director, 'I thought it was time to show that it was very difficult, very painful, and it takes a very long time to kill a man' [16]). Given that the taxi driver is waiting outside the farmhouse for Armstrong, he and the woman – who speaks no English – have to kill Gromek as quietly as possible, which Hitchcock has them do by making full use of the household objects available to them in the kitchen, among them a kettle full of soup (which is thrown at Gromek's head), a carving knife (which breaks when the farmer's wife plunges it into his collar bone), a shovel (used to smash his shins and incapacitate his legs) and, finally, the cooking range (to which he is slowly hefted and gassed in the oven). Herrmann had originally scored this sequence, but in the finished film it is played without music, which makes it all the more shocking (note that John Addison also scored the sequence, but the music was again removed by the director; however, the cue remains on the CD and is titled *The Murder of Gromek*). In fact Hitchcock almost spent as much time committing this sequence to film as he did the shower scene in *Psycho*; shot from a variety of carefully inter-cut angles so as to maximize its impact, it is one of the best scenes to be found in *any* of the director's films.

Other touches and set pieces in the film worth pointing out include the opening scenes on board the Norwegian cruise ship on which the heating has broken down (in the dining room, one passenger is shown breaking the ice atop his glass of water with a fork); the ripple effect across the screen which represents Sherman's tears

when she realizes her fiancé isn't the man she thought he was; the halo of chalk dust on the blackboard behind Armstrong's head as he is interviewed by the academics at Leipzig University (at this stage, we don't know that he is duping them); Professor Lindt's shocked realization that Armstrong is a fraud (Hitchcock cuts to a high-angle shot of Lindt's classroom as he dramatically pulls the cover down over his top-secret blackboard calculations); the escape of Armstrong and Sherman on a bus owned and peopled by the Pi underground (despite some poor rear projection work – something Hitchcock *never* licked in any of his pictures – the tension builds superbly here, particularly when the scheduled bus starts to catch up behind, thus alerting the authorities); the prima ballerina's realization that Armstrong and Sherman, by now exposed in the newspapers, are in the audience for her ballet, waiting to be smuggled out of the country in the company's costume baskets (as the ballerina pirouettes, Hitchcock freeze-frames her face to show the realization sinking in); and the couple's subsequent escape from the auditorium as the alerted authorities close in (Armstrong shouts 'Fire' and the couple escape amid the ensuing chaos, recalling the political rally in *The 39 Steps* and the auction house scene in *North by Northwest*).

The film's washed out colour scheme should also be noted, which emphasizes the drab greys and browns during certain of the East Berlin scenes, especially in Sherman's echoing hotel bedroom, in which the only note of colour is her bright red nightgown (this de-saturation of colour also emphasizes her emotional reaction to Armstrong's defection).

It is frequently assumed that *Torn Curtain* was a flop for Hitchcock, marking the downward turn of his career, but nothing could be further from the truth. In fact the film grossed a healthy $7 million in America alone, despite a lukewarm reaction from the press. 'Some good plot ideas are marred by routine dialogue, and a too-relaxed pace contributes to a dull over-length,' commented *Variety*, adding that, 'Hitchcock freshens up his bag of tricks in a good pot-pourri which becomes a bit stale through a noticeable lack of zip and pacing.' Writing in *Punch*, Richard Mallett better assessed the situation: 'The film as a whole may be a bit diffuse… but it has some brilliant scenes, it's pleasing to the eye, and it is *continuously* entertaining.' Indeed, *Torn Curtain* is a gem of a film – a little unpolished in places and in need of some shaping perhaps, but well worth seeing, with much to reward viewers prepared to overlook the miscasting of its stars.

Hitchcock cameo Note that Hitchcock can be spotted in the hotel lobby of the Hotel D'Angleterre in Copenhagen, bouncing a baby on his knee, which subsequently wets itself (Hitchcock's brief appearance is accompanied by a burst of his TV theme, Gounod's *Funeral March of the Marionette*).

TOUMANOVA, TAMARA (1919–1996) Russian ballet star. Long in America, Toumanova made a number of film appearances either as a dancer or in supporting roles, among them *Deep in My Heart* (1954), *Invitation to the Dance* (1956) and *The Private Life of Sherlock Holmes* (1970). Her most memorable film was Hitchcock's *Torn Curtain* (1966), in which she played a haughty prima ballerina who turns informer when she spots Paul Newman's double agent Professor Michael Armstrong in her audience. She was at one time married to the Hollywood screenwriter-producer Casey Robinson (1902–1979) in whose film *Days of Glory* (1943) she appeared. Robinson also penned an episode of *Alfred Hitchcock Presents*; titled *Poison* (1958, TV), it was helmed by Hitchcock himself. **Hitchography:** *Torn Curtain* (1966)

TOVEY, GEORGE British supporting actor. Tovey has popped up in a handful of films, including *The Secret Partner* (1961), *Never Back Losers* (1967), *Poor Cow* (1968) and Hitchcock's *Frenzy* (1972), in which his meek Mr Salt shares a scene with Madge Ryan's battleaxe Mrs Davidson in the marriage bureau of Brenda Blaney (Barbara Leigh-Hunt). **Hitchography:** *Frenzy* (1972)

TRACY, WILLIAM (1917–1967) American actor. Specializing in dumb-wits, Tracy began his career on stage in the early 1930s, going to Hollywood in 1938 to re-create his role in the military comedy *Brother Rat*. His subsequent films include *Angels with Dirty Faces* (1938), *Tobacco Road* (1941) and a turn for Hitchcock in *Mr and Mrs Smith* (1941) as Sammy. **Hitchography:** *Mr and Mrs Smith* (1941)

TRANSATLANTIC PICTURES Formed in 1948 by Alfred Hitchcock and Sidney Bernstein following the expiration of Hitchcock's contract with David O Selznick, the intention of this independent production company was to allow Hitchcock the autonomy to make the kind of pictures he wanted with complete artistic control. The company's first production was *Rope* (1948), for which Hitchcock employed the ten-minute take. Although admired in some quarters for its (then) technical audacity, the picture was not deemed a success (though it did manage to break even at the box office). Even less successful was the company's second film, *Under Capricorn* (1949). An Australian-set period melodrama, it was filmed in Britain with vestiges of the ten-minute take, and was a commercial and critical disaster. Following this disappointment, Hitchcock and Bernstein wound up the company, although they remained friends until the end of their lives.

TRAVERS, HENRY (1874–1965) Irish-born character actor. Henry Travers made his stage debut at the age of 20. He moved to America at the age of 25 and continued to work in the theatre, but didn't make his first film, *Reunion at Vienna* (1933), until he was 59. He went on to appear in over 50 films, among them *The Sisters* (1939), *Ball of Fire* (1941) and *Mrs Miniver* (1942), although he is best remembered for playing Clarence the Angel in *It's a Wonderful Life* (1946). In 1944 he appeared in Hitchcock's *Shadow of a Doubt* as Joseph Newton, his character bringing a touch of

humour to the proceedings with his love of murder mysteries, not realizing that he is sheltering a serial killer known as the Merry Widow Murderer. **Hitchography:** *Shadow of a Doubt* (1943)

TRAVERS, LINDEN (1913–2001, real name Florence Lindon-Travers) British actress. On stage from the age of 18, Travers made her film debut in *Children of the Fog* in 1935, following which she developed into a reliable supporting actress in the likes of *Bank Holiday* (1938), *Almost a Honeymoon* (1938) and, in particular, *The Lady Vanishes* (1938), in which she played Margaret, the illicit inamorata of the married Eric Todhunter (Cecil Parker). Recalled the actress on how she got the role: 'He [Hitchcock] made a test, though I think he'd already decided on me. You see, he was a very subtle man. He said to me, "Can you speak with your mouth closed?" And I thought, "I know what he means. He doesn't want big mouthing." He asked me a few questions and I answered them with my mouth closed. Of course, I made an absolute fool of myself, but I think he enjoyed it. He liked to make you uncomfortable... Anyway, I got the part and I was delighted. He had this thing about making you want to wriggle a bit.' [17] Travers later said of Hitchcock: 'He wasn't the sort of person everyone would go up to and chat to all the time. He was quite remote and self-contained.' [18] Travers's other films include *The Ghost Train* (1941), *No Orchids for Miss Blandish* (1948) and *Quartet* (1948). She retired from films in 1955 following an appearance in the short *The Schemer*. Her brother was the actor Bill Travers (1922–1994). **Hitchography:** *The Lady Vanishes* (1938)

TREMAYNE, LES (1913–) British-born character actor. Long in Hollywood, Tremayne can be spotted in such films as *The Racket* (1951), *The Fortune Cookie* (1966) and *Snakes* (1974), as well as the TV series *Shazam* (1974–1977). He also played the flustered auctioneer in Hitchcock's *North by Northwest* (1959), in which he has to contend with some outrageous bidding from Cary Grant's Roger Thornhill, who is attempting to cause a distraction so that he can escape enemy agents ('I wonder if I could respectfully ask the gentleman to get into the spirit of the proceedings here'). He also appeared in two episodes of *Alfred Hitchcock Presents* – in one of which, *Mrs Bixby and the Colonel's Coat* (1960, TV), he was again directed by Hitchcock – and an episode of *The Alfred Hitchcock Hour*. **Hitchography:** *North by Northwest* (1959), *Mrs Bixby and the Colonel's Coat* (1960, TV), *Deathmate* (1961, TV), *Isabel* (1964, TV)

TREVOR, AUSTIN (1897–1978, real name A T Schilsky) British actor. Best remembered for playing the screen's first Hercule Poirot in the 1930s – in *Alibi* (1931), *Black Coffee* (1931) and *Lord Edgware Dies* (1934) –Trevor was a much-used character actor whose fluency in German made him a popular choice for accented roles. Beginning with *Escape* in 1930, his many films include *As*

You Like It (1936), *Goodbye, Mr Chips* (1939) and *Horrors of the Black Museum* (1959). His last film was the Poirot mystery *The Alphabet Murders* (1965), in which the Belgian sleuth was this time played by Tony Randall. Trevor can also be spotted briefly in Hitchcock's *Sabotage* (1936) as an anarchist. **Hitchography:** *Sabotage* (1936)

TREVOR, JACK see Story, Jack Trevor

TRIPP, JUNE (1901–1985, real name June Howard Tripp) British actress. Popular on stage in musicals in the 1920s and 1930s, Tripp was frequently billed solely by her Christian name June. Her films were few, numbering *Auld Lang Syne* (1917), *Tom Jones* (1917), *Forever and a Day* (1943) and *The River* (1951), which she narrated. Her most notable film is Hitchcock's *The Lodger* (1926) in which she played landlord's daughter Daisy Bunting. She later married Lord Inverclyde, only to divorce him several years later. **Hitchography:** *The Lodger* (1926)

The Trouble with Harry
(US, 1955, 100m, Technicolor, VistaVision)

CREDITS

Producer:	Alfred Hitchcock
Associate producer:	Herbert Coleman
Director:	Alfred Hitchcock
Screenplay:	John Michael Hayes, based on the novelette by Jack Trevor Story
Cinematographer:	Robert Burks
Music:	Bernard Herrmann
Song:	*Flaggin' the Train to Tuscaloosa* by Raymond Scott (music), Mack David (lyrics)
Editor:	Alma MacRorie
Art directors:	Hal Pereira, John B Goodman
Costumes:	Edith Head
Special effects:	John P Fulton
Sound:	Harold C Lewis, Winston H Leverett

CAST

Edmund Gwenn (Captain Albert Wiles), John Forsythe (Sam Marlowe), Shirley MacLaine (Jennifer Rogers), Mildred Natwick (Miss Gravely), Mildred Dunnock (Mrs Wiggs), Royal Dano (Calvin Wiggs), Jerry Mathers (Arnie Rogers), Dwight Marfield (Dr Greenbow), Barry Macollum (Tramp), Parker Fennelly (Millionaire), Leslie Wolff (Art critic), Philip Truex (Harry Worp)

DVD availability: Universal
CD availability: *The Trouble with Harry* (Varese; entire score as played by the Royal Scottish National Orchestra conducted by Joel McNeely); *Music from the Great Hitchcock Movie Thrillers* (London/Phase 4), which contains *A Portrait of Hitch*, based on *The Trouble with Harry* score;

Psycho – The Essential Alfred Hitchcock (Silva Screen), which also contains *A Portrait of Hitch*; *Citizen Kane – The Essential Bernard Herrmann Film Music Collection* (Silva Screen), which again contains *A Portrait of Hitch*

The trouble with *The Trouble with Harry* is that, as a comedy thriller, it is neither very funny nor very thrilling. In fact it is quite possibly Hitchcock's weakest film. 'The unexpected from Hitchcock!' boasted the posters. Unfortunately, when it came to Hitchcock, audiences wanted the *expected* – thrills. Consequently, they stayed away from the picture.

Hitchcock anonymously bought the rights to Jack Trevor Story's 1949 novelette on which the film is based for just $11,000, which he subsequently sold on to Paramount for $78,000 (a one-time actor known as Jack Trevor, Story had previously worked with Hitchcock on *Champagne* back in 1928, in which he had played an officer). The book had been set in the English countryside; Hitchcock altered this to autumnal Vermont, but otherwise the plot remained pretty much the same. This involves the discovery of a body on a hillside, revealed to be one Harry Worp. However, in the course of events, he is hidden, buried and unearthed several times by a handful of locals, each of whom believes that he or she may have caused his death. Among those believing themselves guilty of the crime is Captain Albert Wiles (Edmund Gwenn), who has been out shooting rabbits ('a harmless pot shot at a rabbit and I'm a murderer'); Jennifer Rogers (Shirley MacLaine), the dead man's estranged wife, who hit him over the head with a milk bottle when he unexpectedly came to call; and the prim Miss Gravely (Mildred Natwick), who confesses to having struck Harry with her hiking boot when he came lurching towards her in the woods. Also involved in the cover up is a local artist, Sam Marlowe (John Forsythe) and Harry's young son, Arnie (Jerry Mathers).

Commented screenwriter John Michael Hayes of the modestly budgeted $1 million production: 'It was a relief from the pressures of trying to make a big box office success. We were just trying to make a good picture and enjoy it. I don't think Paramount really wanted to make it, because they didn't see much future in it commercially. But Hitch had done so well with them, they couldn't quarrel with him.' [18] In fact the main attraction for the director seems to have been to film a dark story in broad daylight. Said Hitchcock: 'I've always been interested in establishing a contrast, in going against the traditional and breaking away from clichés. With *Harry* I took a melodrama out of the pitch-black night and brought it out into the sunshine.' [19]

Filming began on 20 September 1954 in Vermont, but after a month of variable weather, the unit returned to Hollywood, where additional exteriors were mocked up on a soundstage. However, Hitchcock did return to Vermont for the premiere on 30 September 1955, following which the film went on general release on 17 October. Unfortunately, public reaction to the film was poor, while the reviews tended to be variable. Though

Variety described the film as, 'A blithe little comedy, produced and directed with affection by Alfred Hitchcock,' Dylis Powell, writing in the *Times*, rather better hit the nail on the head when she wrote, 'Has, I fear, neither the desperation which makes the predicament of its characters wryly enjoyable, nor the urbanity which would make their actions sympathetic... Everybody carries on in a manner to describe which I am driven to use a word I generally deny myself: whimsical.'

Indeed, the performances throughout the film do little to involve the audience in their rather absurd actions, which generate little in the way of suspense, although the dialogue does occasionally sparkle. For example, when talking about Miss Gravely to Sam Marlowe, the Captain says of her, 'She's a well preserved woman. Yes, well preserved. And preserves have to be opened some day.' Later, when told that he is drinking from her late father's coffee cup, the Captain enquires of Miss Gravely, 'I trust he died peacefully,' to which comes the reply, 'He was caught in a threshing machine.' Meanwhile, once he realizes that he *didn't* kill Harry (who, it eventually transpires, had a heart seizure), the Captain queries of Marlowe, 'If it's murder, whodunit?' '*Did* it,' corrects Marlowe, to which the Captain responds, 'That's what I said. Who*dunit*?' Finally, once everything is resolved, a caption reads, 'The trouble with Harry is over.' Unfortunately, it doesn't come soon enough.

Yet despite its lack of pace and directorial flourishes, the film does have its pluses. Robert Burks' otherwise uninventive VistaVision cinematography makes good use of the autumnal backgrounds, while Bernard Herrmann's delightfully breezy music jollies things along as best it can. This proved to be the first in a long line of collaborations with Hitchcock for the composer, who went on to produce landmark scores for *Vertigo* (1958), *North by Northwest* (1959) and *Psycho* (1960). The film also introduced the young Shirley MacLaine to audiences, while it re-united Hitchcock with character actor Edmund Gwenn, with whom he'd previously worked on *The Skin Game* (1931), *Waltzes from Vienna* (1933) and *Foreign Correspondent* (1940). Otherwise, it is distinctly one of the director's lesser efforts, lacking his usual cinematic vigour and inventiveness. Even Hitchcock described the film as 'an expensive self-indulgence.' [20]

The film's central premise has also been re-used in a handful of films, among them *The Busy Body* (1966), *Weekend at Bernie's* (1989) and *Weekend at Bernie's II* (1993).

Hitchcock cameo Note that Hitchcock can be spotted walking past an outdoor exhibition of Sam Marlowe's artwork.

TRUMAN, RALPH (1900–1977) British character actor. With over 5000 broadcasts to his credit, Truman was something of a radio stalwart. He also made around 100 films, beginning with *City of Song* (1930), which he followed with *Catherine the Great* (1934), *Fire Over England* (1936), *South Riding* (1937), *Henry V* (1945), *Oliver Twist* (1948) and *Quo Vadis?* (1952). In 1956 he appeared in Hitchcock's remake of *The Man Who Knew Too Much*, in which he played Inspector Buchanan of Scotland Yard, whose attempts to recover a kidnapped boy proves somewhat fruitless. Truman's other films include *The Good Companions* (1956), *Ben-Hur* (1959) and *Lady Caroline Lamb* (1972). **Hitchography:** *The Man Who Knew Too Much* (1956)

TUTTLE, LURENE (1906–1986) American character actress. A busy performer in films, television and radio, Tuttle appeared in many movies, among them *Mr Blandings Builds His Dream House* (1946), *Niagara* (1953) and *The Sweet Smell of Success* (1957), as well as such TV shows as *Life with Father* (1953–1955), *Father of the Bride* (1961–1962) and *Julia* (1968–1970). She first worked with Hitchcock on his 1940 radio adaptation of his 1926 film *The Lodger*, though she is perhaps best remembered for playing Sheriff Chambers's twittery wife in *Psycho* (1960), in which she at one point recalls helping Norman Bates to pick out his mother's 'periwinkle blue' burial dress. Recalled the actress of her experiences on *Psycho*: '[Hitchcock] trusted actors and didn't give a lot of direction, except to tell me to be sure to stand on my mark. He staged scenes like blueprints. He told me, "If you move one inch either way, you'll be out of my light," then slumped over in his chair like he'd dozed off.' Tuttle's other films include *The Fortune Cookie* (1966), *Walking Tall* (1973) and *The Adventures of Huckleberry Finn* (1981). **Hitchography:** *The Lodger* (1940, radio), *Psycho* (1960)

TWIST, DEREK N (1905–1979) British director. Twist helmed such low budgeters as *Green Grow the Rushes* (1951), *Police Dog* (1955) and *Family Doctor* (1957), prior to which he worked as an editor, cutting such films as Hitchcock's *The 39 Steps* (1935), for which he was billed as D N Twist. **Hitchography:** *The 39 Steps* (1935)

TYNER, CHARLES American actor. In Hitchcock's last film *Family Plot* (1976) in the supporting role of Wheeler, Tyner's other films include *Lilith* (1964), *Cool Hand Luke* (1967), *The Reivers* (1969), *Monte Walsh* (1970) and *Bad Company* (1972). **Hitchography:** *Family Plot* (1976)

U

Under Capricorn
(GB, 1949, 117m, Technicolor)

CREDITS

Production company:	Transatlantic Pictures
Producers:	Alfred Hitchcock, Sidney Bernstein
Director:	Alfred Hitchcock
Screenplay:	James Bridie (and Hume Cronyn), based on the novel by Helen Simpson
Cinematographer:	Jack Cardiff
Music:	Richard Addinsell
Music director:	Louis Levy
Editor:	A S Bates
Production design:	Thomas N Morahan
Costumes:	Roger Furse
Sound:	Peter Hadford, A W Watkins

CAST

Ingrid Bergman (Henrietta Flusky), Joseph Cotten (Sam Flusky), Michael Wilding (Charles Adare), Cecil Parker (Governor Bourke), Margaret Leighton (Milly), Jack Watling (Winter), Denis O'Dea (Corrigan), Harcourt Williams (Coachman), Olive Sloane (Sal), John Ruddock (Potter), Bill Shine (Banks), Victor Lucas (Reverend Smiley), Francis De Wolff (Major Wilkins), Julia Lang (Susan), Betty McDermott (Martha), Ronald Adam (Riggs), G H Mulcaster (Dr Macallister), Maureen Delaney (Flo)

CD availability: *Psycho – The Essential Alfred Hitchcock* (Silva Screen), which contains a *Suite*; *The Great British Film Music Album – Sixty Glorious Years 1938 – 1998* (Silva Screen) which also contains the *Suite*

As much as one wants to be charitable to *Under Capricorn*, or even re-evaluate it as some kind of overlooked masterpiece, there is little in this rather tedious melodrama to be enthusiastic about. It was the second film to be made under the Transatlantic Pictures banner following the disappointing *Rope* (1948). Hitchcock and his partner Sidney Bernstein had formed the company in 1948 following the expiry of the director's contract with David O Selznick, the intention being that it would allow Hitchcock to make the kind of films he wanted to in the style that he saw fit. Unfortunately, following the experimental *Rope*, which was shot in a series of lengthy ten-minute takes, Hitchcock's previously uncanny ability to hit on the right story must have seemed a little vulnerable (commented critic C A Lejeune: 'I can't feel that the choice of subject is a very happy one, for either Hitchcock or his actors').

Based on the novel by Helen Simpson (co-author of the novel *Enter Sir John*, filmed by Hitchcock as *Murder!*

in 1930), the £2.5 million production was shot in England, making it Hitchcock's first film in his home country since *Jamaica Inn* back in 1939. Set in Sydney, Australia in 1831, the story centres on Sam Flusky (Joseph Cotten), a former stable hand and an ex-convict who has made his fortune Down Under, having been originally deported there for the alleged murder of his brother-in-law. Flusky's wife Henrietta (Ingrid Bergman), the sister of the murdered man, believes in her husband's innocence absolutely – so much so that she left their home in Ireland to follow him half way around the world so as to be with him, much to the consternation of her family, who feel she has married beneath herself. However, upon Flusky's release, their marriage begins to crumble, despite the wealth he manages to amass for her. Indeed, Henrietta becomes a dipsomaniac, as her visiting cousin Charles Adair (Michael Wilding) discovers.

Determined on helping his cousin, who has apparently been seeing things, Adair attempts to cheer her up by spending time with her, but his actions are misinterpreted by the Fluskys' malicious housekeeper, Milly (Margaret Leighton), who is subsequently sacked for spreading her rumours. But the seeds of doubt have been sown, and when Adair gets permission to take Henrietta to the Irish Society Ball at Government House, imagination gets the better of Flusky, who gatecrashes the event and takes his wife home where, having been so publicly humiliated, she teeters on the edge of sanity, confessing to Adair, who has followed her home, that it was in fact *she* who accidentally killed her beloved brother. With Milly now back working at the house, Henrietta continues to decline, until it is discovered that the housekeeper has been manipulating her mistress' health with sleeping potions, and by placing objects in her room, such as shrunken skulls, to help convince her that she is going mad. Yet things come to a relatively happy ending, with the Fluskys somewhat improbably re-united at the picture's close following several further unnecessary twists that find Sam wrongly accused of attempting to murder Adair in a jealous rage.

Hitchcock's main objective in making *Under Capricorn* seems to have been to work with Ingrid Bergman again. Bergman was the biggest star in America at the time, and getting her services was something of a coup for him. In fact the director seems to have been more concerned about this one-upmanship than with the film itself, as he later confessed: 'I must admit that I made the mistake of thinking that to get Bergman would be a tremendous feat; it was a victory over the rest of the industry, you see... All I could think about was: "Here I am, Hitchcock, the one time English director, returning to London with the biggest star of the day." I was literally intoxicated at the thought of the cameras and flashbulbs that would be directed at Bergman and myself at the London airport. All of these externals seemed to be terribly important. I can only say now that I was being stupid and juvenile.' [1]

In fact newsreel footage of Bergman's arrival at London airport survives, and Hitchcock's pleasure amid the popping flashbulbs is plain to see. Yet when it came to the nitty gritty of actually making the picture, the director's enthusiasm quickly waned. As scriptwriter Hume Cronyn recalled: 'I remember one day we were working and Hitchcock said, "This film is going to be a flop," and he disappeared. This wasn't like him. It was a temperamental outburst.' [2] Hitchcock's prediction proved prescient. The film *did* turn out to be a flop, except in Australia, where the novelty of its local setting, combined with the names of Hitchcock and Bergman, turned it into a minor hit – but not enough of one to recoup its hefty outlay.

Seen today, *Under Capricorn* lacks pace, humour, tension and originality (its plot plays like a poor man's rehash of *Rebecca* with elements of *Notorious* and *The Paradine Case* thrown in for good measure). Indeed, its staging is frequently dull, with too many long, uncut scenes devoted to tedious chat. That said, Jack Cardiff's chalky colour photography is occasionally attractive to look at, while some of the elaborate camera movements (a holdover from *Rope*) are well executed, among them a lengthy shot that takes in both floors of the Flusky household. Other tracking shots do wobble somewhat, though, while in one kitchen scene, the shadow of the microphone can be seen on the chimney breast; one can also clearly see that the elaborately laid table in the Fluskys' dining room is made up of three sections, so as to be ready to split for when the camera dollies in for a close-up. Even more unforgivably, the map of Australia featured during the main credits is missing the island of Tasmania, while the editing in the opening scene, which sees the arrival of the new Governor (Cecil Parker), is uncertain to say the least, with one character clearly stepping forward to speak, but not featured in a close up until several shots later.

Performance-wise, Bergman's descent into madness is well handled, bringing to mind her work in both *Gaslight* (1944) and *Notorious* (1946), although her Irish brogue completely disappears at times, notably during the Irish Society Ball sequence. However, Margaret Leighton's devious Milly offers an entertaining variation on *Rebecca*'s Mrs Danvers, while Cecil Parker also provides some welcome exchanges as Governor Bourke, playing one lengthy scene in a bathtub. Less convincing is Joseph Cotten's emanthropist and Michael Wilding's visiting cousin, neither of them seeming well suited to their roles.

Like the public, the critics of the day were unimpressed. '*Under Capricorn* is overlong and talky, with scant measure of the Alfred Hitchcock thriller tricks,' commented *Variety*, neatly summing up the film's failures, while *Time* described the film as 'a florid, historical romance.'

Following its premiere at New York's Radio City Music Hall on 8 September 1949, the film was such a commercial disaster that the financing bank reclaimed it and didn't license it for re-issue until the 1960s (Ingrid Bergman's subsequent adulterous affair with the Italian director Roberto Rossellini also harmed *Under Capricorn*'s box office chances, the resultant scandal prompting various Catholic organizations to boycott the film). Thus Hitchcock's dreams of being a truly independent film maker came screeching to a halt after just two productions. Transatlantic Pictures was liquidated, and the director found himself having to make some serious decisions about his future. The film was remade for television in 1982.

Hitchcock cameo Note that Hitchcock can be spotted twice in *Under Capricorn*, first in Sydney's town square and later on the steps of Government House.

Under Capricorn
(Australia, 1982, 1982, 150m, colour)

CREDITS
Director: Rod Hardy
Screenplay: based on the novel
by Helen Simpson

CAST
Lisa Harrow (Henrietta Flusky), Peter Cousens, John Hallam

In this lengthy TV movie remake of one of Hitchcock's least interesting films, Lisa Harrow takes on the Ingrid Bergman role of the dipsomaniac Henrietta Flusky, who has a dark secret to hide from her visiting cousin. The film benefits from being shot in Australia, but is otherwise a fairly routine time filler – as, indeed, is the Hitchcock version.

UNFILMED HITCHCOCK Among the many projects Hitchcock considered for filming, but which never came to fruition for one reason or another, were:

The Wall
In 1931, during the filming of *The Skin Game*, Hitchcock met playwright Rodney Ackland, and together they decided to make a film of John Van Druten's play *The Wall*. However, though scripted, the proposed production never materialized. Instead, Hitchcock and Ackland worked together on *Number Seventeen* (1932), an adaptation of J Jefferson Farjeon's play *Joyous Melodrama*.

Bulldog Drummond's Baby
Working with writer Charles Bennett, Hitchcock conceived this story involving the kidnapping of the fictional adventurer's child while still under contract to BIP in 1932. BIP subsequently bought the property, but producer and studio head John Maxwell eventually baulked at the now seemingly miniscule £10,000 budget. Wrote Maxwell to Hitch, 'It's a masterpiece of cinematics, old boy, but I'd rather have the £10,000.' [3] Nevertheless, elements of the script turned up in *The Man Who Knew Too Much* (1934), which was co-written by Bennett.

271

The Park

Following his successful adaptation of *Juno and the Paycock* in 1930, Hitchcock teamed up with its author, Irish playwright Sean O'Casey, to work on a story about the comings and goings one day in a park. Work was started on the script, but enthusiasm seems to have waned at some point, though O'Casey did go on to re-work the idea for his play *Within the Gate*.

Greenmantle

After the success of *The Man Who Knew Too Much* (1934), Hitchcock briefly considered filming this novel by John Buchan, but instead turned his attention to the same author's *The 39 Steps* (1935).

Florodora

Having had a major success with *The 39 Steps* (1935), Gaumont-British executive C M Woolf attempted to get Hitchcock interested in this musical on the life of composer Leslie Stuart, whose hits included *Florodora*. Though some work was apparently done on the film, Hitchcock never took the idea seriously enough to fully develop it, no doubt discouraged by the disappointing outcome of his previous musical, *Waltzes from Vienna* (1933).

The Saint in New York

Prior to signing a seven-year contract with David O Selznick to go to Hollywood, Hitchcock also sounded out the possibility of working for Paramount and MGM. Overtures were also made to RKO, who offered him the first episode in their new series of second feature mystery thrillers based on the novels by Leslie Charteris. Hitchcock turned the offer down, although the film still went ahead. Released in 1938, it starred Louis Hayward as The Saint, was produced by William Sistrom and directed by Ben Holmes, from a script by Charles Kaufman and Mortimer Offner. The supporting cast included Kay Sutton, Sig Rumann and Jack Carson.

Titanic

When Hitchcock signed his seven-year contract with David O Selznick, the idea was to present a lavish account of the sinking of the *Titanic*, followed by an adaptation of Daphne du Maurier's *Rebecca*. However, the *Titanic* project, set to start filming in August 1938, began to disintegrate when Selznick's plans to buy a real ocean liner – the *Leviathan* – to double for the stricken vessel, came to nothing. Hitchcock nevertheless had an interesting idea how to begin the film, with a close-up of a single rivet, from which the camera would slowly pull back to reveal the entire ship.

Forever and a Day

Following the completion of *Foreign Correspondent* (1940), Hitchcock had planned to direct a sequence in the multi-drama *Forever and a Day*, the story of a London house from 1804 through to the blitz of World War II. Produced by Herbert Wilcox and Victor Saville for RKO, it was intend-ed that the profits generated by the film should go to various war charities. Hitchcock's contribution was to have been a brief sequence starring Ida Lupino as a Cockney maid unable to see a passing parade due to the density of the watching crowds. Unfortunately, though he supervised the scripting and planning of the scene, Hitchcock's commitment to direct *Mr and Mrs Smith* (1941) meant that he had to hand over this particular assignment to another director, Rene Clair. Long in production, *Forever and a Day* was eventually released in 1943. Among those contributing to the film were screenwriter Charles Bennett and actors Dame May Whitty, C Aubrey Smith, Edmund Gwenn, Jessie Matthews, Charles Laughton, Nigel Bruce, Gladys Cooper and Donald Crisp, all of who had previously worked with Hitchcock.

The Man Who Knew Too Much

In 1941, producer David O Selznick secured the rights to Hitchcock's 1934 British hit with a view to remaking it in Hollywood with the director. Unfortunately, the film failed to materialize, despite initial story conferences between Hitchcock and John Houseman. Nevertheless, Hitchcock remained keen on the idea of a remake, which finally came to fruition in 1956, although the resultant film is one of his most disappointing efforts.

Dark Duty

After the debacle of *Under Capricorn* (1949), Hitchcock considered filming this story about a prison governor, but eventually decided to play safe with the murder drama *Stage Fright* (1950).

Jack Sheppard

Like Dark Duty, this story about the legendary 18th-century highwayman who consistently managed to elude the authorities was considered as a possible project following *Under Capricorn* (1949). It was eventually made as *Where's Jack?* in 1969, starring Tommy Steele, Stanley Baker and Fiona Lewis, with James Clavell directing.

The Bramble Bush

Following the tepid reception of *I Confess* (1953), Hitchcock intended to film this Mexican-set story by David Duncan concerning a man who assumes the identity of a stranger while south of the border, only to discover that the man he has become is on the run for murder. Hitchcock had hoped to cast Alec Guinness in the leading role, yet the project never materialized owing to scripting problems. Consequently, Hitchcock filmed *Dial M for Murder* (1954) instead.

Flamingo Feather

After the box office success of *To Catch a Thief* (1955), Hitchcock announced as his next project an adaptation of this Laurens van der Post novel about the training of a secret army in South Africa by the Russians. Unfortunately, despite a script being started by Hitchcock regular Angus MacPhail, the planned location shoot presented too many problems, so the project was abandoned, leaving Hitchcock to concentrate instead on *The Trouble with Harry* (1955).

The Wreck of the Mary Deare

Following *Vertigo* (1958), Hitchcock began work on a script with Ernest Lehman for this drama – based on a novel by Hammond Innes – involving a salvage ship and an insurance fraud. However, things weren't developing satisfactorily. As Hitchcock put it, 'When you're involved in a project and you see it isn't going to work out, the wisest thing is to simply throw the whole thing away.' [4] Consequently, Hitchcock and Lehman instead turned their attention to *North by Northwest* (1959). The *Mary Deare* project didn't disappear, however; instead it was handed to producer Julian Blaustein, who made it for MGM, with Michael Anderson directing from an Eric Ambler script. The film was a starry affair, headlining Charlton Heston, Gary Cooper, Virginia McKenna and Richard Harris, as well as such Hitchcock alumni as Michael Redgrave, Cecil Parker and Emlyn Williams.

No Bail for the Judge

Hitchcock intended to film this Henry Cecil novel following the completion of *North by Northwest* (1959), and gave that film's screenwriter, Ernest Lehman, the job of adapting it. Hitchcock planned to make the film in Britain, with Audrey Hepburn and Laurence Harvey, but the project failed to jell. Hitchcock tried to resurrect it following the release of *Psycho* (1960), again without success.

Village of the Stars

After the huge international success of *Psycho* (1960), Hitchcock put a number of projects into development, among them this story about a pilot who finds himself saddled with a bomb set to detonate when it drops below a certain altitude. An interesting premise, but Hitchcock failed to develop a script to showcase the dilemma satisfactorily.

Trap for a Solitary Man

Based on the stage play by Robert Thomas, this thriller was to tell the story of a man whose wife disappears, only to later re-appear in the guise of an impostor. Like *Village of the Stars*, it was put into development following *Psycho* (1960), but stalled at the scripting stage.

Untitled Disneyland Project

Another idea considered after *Psycho* (1960) was this untitled story about a man who receives a cornea transplant (then the stuff of science fiction), only to discover that his donor didn't die in a car crash, as he had been told, but had been murdered. A trip to Disneyland triggers the story, with the lead character apparently recognizing someone he has never seen before. Hitchcock began developing a script with Ernest Lehman, who had written *North by Northwest* (1959) for him, but the project began to fall apart when Walt Disney nixed the prospect of Hitchcock filming in his theme park.

Kaleidoscope Frenzy

Hitchcock began work on this idea about a young man who finds himself compelled to murder whenever near large bodies of water – lakes, rivers, the sea – around 1962. He tentatively titled the project *Frenzy* and began work on a script with Benn W Levy, who had penned *Blackmail* for him back in 1929, but with whom he had had a falling out over *Lord Camber's Ladies* (1932), which Hitchcock had produced and Levy directed. The film was to feature a murder in Central Park, an action scene in the Shea Stadium and a chase sequence set on board a mothballed Liberty ship at the Maritime Harbor. Levy suggested calling the film *Waters of Forgetfulness*, but the project failed to come together to Hitchcock's satisfaction. Consequently, Hitchcock brought in several other writers to work on it during the 1960s, including playwright Hugh Wheeler, later known for the musical *A Little Night Music*, and historical novelist Howard Fast, best known for *Spartacus*. By this time the story was known as *Kaleidoscope Frenzy*. Unfortunately, none of the writers could lick the story's outcome. Hitchcock himself even wrote a script, but it was considered too violent, even by the standards he'd set with *Psycho*. Consequently Hitchcock shelved the idea, despite having had stills and some test footage made for the film by acclaimed photographer Arthur Schatz. Nevertheless, he retained the title *Frenzy* for his 1972 film, which was based on the Arthur La Bern novel *Goodbye, Piccadilly, Farewell, Leicester Square*.

Mary Rose

Following *Marnie* (1964), Hitchcock began to work on an adaptation of this J M Barrie play about a young woman who disappears on her belated honeymoon, only to re-appear many years later completely unchanged, despite the fact that her husband is now middle-aged and her son has grown up. Despite having fallen out with Tippi Hedren during the filming of *Marnie*, Hitchcock tailored the script with her in mind. But Universal was unconvinced that the story was commercial enough, and so rejected Hitchcock's plans to make it. He tried to resurrect the project several times, but always ran up against the studio, which eventually had a clause inserted into his contract stating that he would *never* make the film.

The Three Hostages

Another project considered after *Marnie* (1964) was this novel by John Buchan featuring the further exploits of Richard Hannay, the hero of *The 39 Steps*, with which Hitchcock had had a major success in 1935. The story centred round the kidnapping of three children by a hypnotist, but the director abandoned the idea when he concluded that he wouldn't be able to make the hypnotism angle convincing on screen. 'You cannot put hypnotism on screen and expect it to hold water. It is a condition too remote from the audience's own experiences... Visually speaking, there would be no difference between someone who is really hypnotized and someone who is pretending,' [5] concluded the director.

R.R.R.R.R.

Hitchcock also began developing this intriguingly titled project following *Marnie* (1964). Set in a large hotel, it focuses on an Italian immigrant who works his way up from bellboy to manager, only to have his family – a gang of thieves – descend upon the place with the idea of robbing the rich clients. Hitchcock hired two Italian writers, Age & Scarpelli, to develop the script, but the language barrier scuppered proceedings early on. Commented Hitchcock: 'Italians are very slipshod in matters of story construction. They just ramble on.' [6] Hitchcock briefly returned to the idea following the release of *Torn Curtain* (1966), after which it was dropped.

The Short Night

Following the release in 1976 of *Family Plot*, Hitchcock was determined on making one final film, even if only to keep his morale going. Based on two books – *The Short Night* by Ronald Kirkbridge and *The Springing of George Blake* by Sean Bourke – it was to tell the story of a daring escape from prison by a British spy working for the Russians. He subsequently makes his way to Finland to meet up with his wife and children; however, his wife has fallen in love with an American agent who, unbeknownst to her, has been sent to assassinate her husband. Hitchcock began work on the script with Ernest Lehman, his screenwriter for both *North by Northwest* (1959) and *Family Plot* (1976). However, the two disagreed over the inclusion of a rape scene, and so Lehman left the project and was replaced by playwright David Freeman. Recalled Freeman of the scripting process: 'He [Hitchcock] would never move around during a story meeting. He would sit like a Buddha and just make his decrees.' [7] Preparation on the film reached the storyboard stage, with cinematographer Leonard J South poised to fly to Finland to begin shooting second unit footage. Meanwhile, Catherine Deneuve, Walter Matthau, Sean Connery and Liv Ullmann were being actively considered for the cast. But in May 1979, even Hitchcock had to admit defeat, and so abandoned the project. Recalled Hilton Green, Hitchcock's former assistant director who was to be the film's associate producer: 'I got a call from Mr Hitchcock's assistant Sue to go to his office. He said to me, "I want you to do me a favour. I want you to call Mr Wassermann [the studio head] and tell him I'm never going to make another movie." It was very sad. Something that I'll never forget.' [8] A few days later, Hitchcock closed his office at Universal. Thirteen months later he was dead.

URECALL, MINERVA (1896–1966, real name Minerva Holzer) American character actress. Urecall had featured roles in well over 200 films, beginning with *Meet the Baron* in 1933 and ending with *That Funny Feeling* in 1965. In 1941 alone she made 21 films, among them *Billy the Kid*, *Dressed to Kill* and *Never Give a Sucker an Even Break*. In 1943 she appeared briefly in Hitchcock's *Shadow of a Doubt* as Mrs Henderson, but like much of her work, it was un-credited. She also appeared in the television series *The Adventures of Tugboat Annie* (1956) in which she played the title role. **Hitchography:** *Shadow of a Doubt* (1943)

URIS, LEON American novelist. Best known for his epic *Exodus*, Uris adapted his own 1967 best seller *Topaz* for Hitchcock's subsequent 1969 film version (as per a clause in his publishing contract). Unfortunately, the director was less than impressed with Uris' script, and had it completely re-written by Samuel Taylor, who had previously penned *Vertigo* (1958) for him. **Hitchography:** *Topaz* (1969)

V

VALENTINE, JOSEPH (1900–1949, real name Giuseppe Valentino) American cinematographer. Of Italian parentage, Valentine began his career in 1920 as an assistant, but quickly made the jump to lighting cameraman in 1924 with *My Husband's Wives*. Following experience at Fox, he moved to Universal, where he photographed many of the studio's key productions, including several Deanna Durbin vehicles, among them *Three Smart Girls* (1936), *One-Hundred Men and a Girl* (1937), *Mad About Music* (1938) and *First Love* (1939). His other films include *My Little Chickadee* (1940), *The Wolf Man* (1941) and *Joan of Arc* (1948), the latter earning him an Academy Award for best cinematography. He also photographed three films for Hitchcock: *Saboteur* (1942), *Shadow of a Doubt* (1943) and – with William V Skall – *Rope* (1948), which is noted for its lengthy, ten-minute takes, the result of much rehearsal by both cast and technicians. *Rope* was also Hitchcock's first colour film. **Hitchography:** *Saboteur* (1942), *Shadow of a Doubt* (1943), *Rope* (1948)

VALLI, ALIDA (1921– , real name Alida Maria Altenburger) Italian actress. Alida Valli began making films at the age of 15 with *Il Capello a Tre Punte*, following which she gradually rose to become a popular home-grown star in such films as *Manon Lescaut* (1939), *Luce Nelle Tenebre* (1940) and *Il Canto della Vita* (1945).

In 1947, she was signed to a contract by Hollywood producer David O Selznick and, billed simply as Valli, made her English-speaking debut in Hitchcock's *The Paradine Case* (1947), in which she played the duplicitous Mrs Maddalena Anna Paradine. Although the film was not a commercial success, 'Valli' made a mark, and went on to star in *Miracle of the Bells* (1948) and, most famously, *The Third Man* (1949), following which her career took on an international flavour, with appearances in *Ultimo Incontro* (1951), *Il Grido* (1957), *Les Yeux sans Visage* (1960), *The Spider's Stratagem* (1970), *1900* (1976), *Suspiria* (1976), *Inferno* (1980), *Aspern* (1982) and *Il Dolce Rumore della Vita* (1999). Note that Valli also starred in a radio adaptation of Hitchcock's *Spellbound* in 1948 with Joseph Cotten. **Hitchography:** *The Paradine Case* (1947), *Spellbound* (1948, radio)

VALLI, VIRGINIA (1898–1968, real name Virginia McSweeney) American-born actress. One of the silent period's most glamorous stars, Valli appeared in several highly popular 1920s' productions, among them *The Storm* (1922) and *A Lady of Quality* (1923). In 1925, she was contracted by producer Michael Balcon to be the leading lady in Hitchcock's first film, *The Pleasure Garden*. Upon returning to America Valli made several more films, among them *Paid to Love* (1927) and *Isle of Lost Ships* (1932), after which she retired from the screen to devote more time to her husband, actor Charles Farrell (1901–1988), who himself retired from films in 1941, following which he ran a number of sports clubs and, later, became Mayor of Palm Springs. **Hitchography:** *The Pleasure Garden* (1925)

VAN ZANDT, PHILIP (1904–1958) Dutch-born actor. In America from 1927, Van Zandt did much stage work during a busy career, which also saw him appear as a supporting actor in well over 100 films, beginning with *Those High Gray Walls* in 1939. His other credits, among them many villainous roles, include *Citizen Kane* (1941), *Sherlock Holmes and the Secret Weapon* (1942), *House of Frankenstein* (1944) and *The Desert Fox* (1951). He also made an un-credited appearance in Hitchcock's *To Catch a Thief* (1955) as a jewellery clerk. **Hitchography:** *To Catch a Thief* (1955)

Alida Valli's beautiful Mrs. Maddalena Anna Paradine meets Gregory Peck's Anthony Keane for the first time in Hitchcock's underrated The Paradine Case *(1947).*

VANEL, CHARLES (1892–1989) French actor. Remembered for his roles in *The Wages of Fear* (1953) and *Les Diaboliques* (1955), this distinguished actor began performing on stage in 1908. Four years later he made his first film, *Jim Crow* (1912), although it would be another eight before he made his second, *Miarka la Fille a l'Ourse* (1920). This led to a busy career in almost 200 films, among them *Waterloo* (1928), *Les Miserables* (1934), *Le Feu aux Poudres* (1957) and *La Puce et le Prive* (1979). Vanel also directed two films: *Dans la Nuit* (1929) and *Le Coup de Minuit* (1935). In 1955, he appeared in Hitchcock's *To Catch a Thief* as the French underground leader turned restaurateur Bertani. Unfortunately, Hitchcock didn't check whether Vanel could speak English prior to filming, and when it transpired that he could not, much of his dialogue had to be revised. Recalled screenwriter John Michael Hayes: 'They tried to teach him phonetically, and that inhibited all the scenes we wanted to do with him, because he hardly moved and talked in simple sentences. We couldn't get the subtlety in his part... They had his lines on a blackboard, and he tried to look offstage and read the lines. It was too bad, because he was an accomplished actor.' [1] Hitchcock also tried shooting the actor from the side and with his mouth partially obscured, so as to disguise the fact that he couldn't speak English properly; ultimately, the director had him entirely re-dubbed in post-production by fellow Frenchman Jean Duval. Unfortunately, the job wasn't as professional as it could have been, and badly lets down all the scenes in which Vanel appears. **Hitchography:** *To Catch a Thief* (1955)

VARDEN, NORMA (1898–1989) British character comedienne. A popular member of the Aldwych farce team in the 1920s and 1930s, Varden was frequently cast in snooty roles. On stage following experience as a concert pianist, she made her film debut in 1932 in *A Night Like This*, which she followed with *Turkey Time* (1933), *Evergreen* (1934) and *Boys Will Be Boys* (1935). She moved to Hollywood in 1939, where she appeared in the likes of *Waterloo Bridge* (1940), *Random Harvest* (1942), *Casablanca* (1942) and *Forever Amber* (1947). In 1951, she appeared in Hitchcock's *Strangers on a Train* as Mrs Cunningham, the society lady who is almost strangled to death at a Washington soirée by Robert Walker's psychopath Bruno Antony ('You don't mind if I borrow your neck for a moment?' Antony asks the initially intrigued woman). Varden's other films include *Elephant Walk* (1953), *Witness for the Prosecution* (1957) and *The Sound of Music* (1965). She also appeared in an episode of *Alfred Hitchcock Presents*. **Hitchography:** *Strangers on a Train* (1951), *The Schartz-Metterlume Method* (1960, TV)

VARLEY, BEATRICE (1896–1969) British character actress. Beginning in 1936 with *Tomorrow We Live*, Varley appeared in countless supporting roles, more often than not as spinster types. One of her earliest films was Hitchcock's *Young and Innocent* (1937), in which she briefly appears as Mrs Vessons. Her other films include *Poison Pen* (1939), *Hatter's Castle* (1941), *Hell Drivers* (1957) and *Night Without Pity* (1962). **Hitchography:** *Young and Innocent* (1937)

VENTIMIGLIA, BARON GIOVANNI Italian-born cinematographer. A busy and respected cinematographer, Ventimiglia was a mainstay of the British film industry in the 1920s and 1930s, working chiefly for Gaumont-British. He photographed Hitchcock's first three films, including, most importantly, *The Lodger* (1926). **Hitchography:** *The Pleasure Garden* (1925), *The Mountain Eagle* (1925), *The Lodger* (1926)

VERNO, JERRY (1895–1975) British comedian. On stage from 1907 as a singer, Verno later became a respected music hall comedian, experience as which he later put to good use in countless comic supporting roles on screen. One of the most memorable of these was in Hitchcock's *The 39 Steps* (1935), in which he played one of two commercial travellers whose frank discussion of the ladies' underwear they are pedaling provides a few easy chuckles at an otherwise particularly tense moment in the film. He can also be spotted in Hitchcock's *Young and Innocent* (1937) as a lorry driver, as well as *Pagliacci* (1936), *Old Mother Riley in Paris* (1938), *The Belles of St Trinian's* (1954) and *The Plague of the Zombies* (1966). **Hitchography:** *The 39 Steps* (1935), *Young and Innocent* (1937)

VERNON, JOHN (1932–) Canadian character actor. Equally adept at villainous or comedic roles, Vernon began his film career in Britain in 1956 following training at RADA, providing the voice of Big Brother for *1984*. Although much stage and television work in his home country followed, Vernon didn't make his on-screen debut until 1964 in the Canadian *Nobody Waved Goodbye*, after which he finally broke into Hollywood with *Point Blank* (1967) and *Justine* (1969). In 1969, he was signed by Hitchcock to appear as the ruthless Cuban revolutionary leader Rico Parra in *Topaz*, a performance that *Variety* found to be 'powerful'. Vernon's many other films include *Dirty Harry* (1971), *The Black Windmill* (1974), *The Outlaw Josey Wales* (1976), *National Lampoon's Animal House* (1978), *Killer Klowns from Outer Space* (1988) and *Class Act* (1994). **Hitchography:** *Topaz* (1969)

Vertigo
(US, 1958, 128m, Technicolor) ★★

CREDITS

Production company:	Paramount (1984 re-release by Universal)
Producer:	Alfred Hitchcock
Associate producer:	Herbert Coleman
Director:	Alfred Hitchcock
Screenplay:	Samuel Taylor, Alec Coppel (and, un-credited, Angus MacPhail, Maxwell Anderson),

James Stewart finds himself surrounded by images of Kim Novak in this eye-catching publicity shot for Hitchcock's Vertigo *(1958)*

	from the novel *D'Entre les Morts* by Pierre Boileau and Thomas Narcejac
Cinematographer:	Robert Burks
Music:	Bernard Herrmann
Conductor:	Muir Mathieson
Editor:	George Tomasini
Art directors:	Henry Bumstead, Hal Pereira
Costumes:	Edith Head
Special effects:	Farciot Edouart, John P Fulton, W Wallace Kelley
Sound:	Harold Lewis, Winston Leverett
Titles:	Saul Bass
Dream sequence designed by:	John Ferren

CAST

James Stewart (John 'Scottie' Ferguson), Kim Novak (Madeleine Elster/Judy Barton), Barbara Bel Geddes (Midge Wood), Tom Helmore (Gavin Elster), Ellen Corby (Hotel manageress), Henry Jones (Coroner), Raymond Bailey (Doctor), Konstantin Shayne (Pop Leibel), Lee Patrick (Madeleine lookalike), Margaret Brayton (Ransohoff salesperson), Joanne Genthon (Dream Carlotta), Sara Taft (Nun)

Video availability: Universal
DVD availability: Columbia/Tri-Star
CD availability: *Vertigo* (Varese Sarabande), which contains the complete original score; *Vertigo* (Varese Sarabande), which contains a new recording of the complete score by conductor Joel McNeely and the Royal Scottish National Orchestra; *Torn Curtain – The Classic Film Music of Bernard Herrmann* (Silva Screen), which contains a *Suite*, including *Prelude*, *The Nightmare* and *Scene D'Amour*; *A History of Hitchcock – Dial M for Murder* (Silva Screen), which contains *Scene D'Amour*; *Psycho – The Essential Alfred Hitchcock* (Silva Screen), which contains *Prelude* and *The Nightmare*; *Hitchcock – Master of Mayhem* (Proarte), which contains a *Suite*; *Citizen Kane – The Essential Bernard Herrmann* (Silva Screen), which contains the *Prelude*, *Nightmare* and *Scene D'Amour*; *Bernard Herrmann Film Scores* (Milan), which contains *Scene D'Amour*; and *Music from the Great Hitchcock Movie Thrillers* (Phase 4/Decca), in which Herrmann himself conducts *Prelude*, *The Nightmare* and *Scene D'Amour*

The critical reaction to *Vertigo* has gone from one extreme to another since its release. Though regarded by many as something of a masterpiece today, back in 1958 it was a commercial and critical disappointment. 'Alfred Hitchcock, who produced and directed the thing, has never before indulged in such far-fetched nonsense,' damned John McCarten in *The New Yorker*, to which Arthur Knight in the *Saturday Review* added, 'Technical facility is being exploited to gild pure dross… by the time the climactic cat is let out of the bag, the audience has long since had kittens.' *Time* also got in on the attack, commenting, 'The mystery is not so much who done it as who cares.' Even those who praised the film did so with reservations, such as Dylis Powell in the *Sunday Times*: 'The plot is a brilliant bag of tricks. And yet the film disappoints. It seems too long, too elaborately designed; the narration of this kind of criminal intrigue sags under such luscious treatment.'

The film has since been re-evaluated, with critical reaction reaching almost hysterical proportions. 'Of all Hitchcock's films, the one nearest to perfection,' wrote Robin Wood in *Hitchcock Revisited* in 1989, adding, 'Its profundity is inseparable from the perfection of form: it is a perfect organism, each character, each sequence, each image, illuminating each other. Form and technique here become the perfect expression of concerns both deep and universal.' The film was also much re-evaluated during its 1983 re-release and 1998 restoration: 'For more than a few people, *Vertigo* is the ultimate movie,' wrote J Hoberman in *The Village Voice*, to which Kenneth Turan in the *L.A. Times* added, '*Vertigo* stands today as what it probably always was, an audacious, brilliantly twisted movie, infused with touches of genius and madness… it's more impressive today than forty years ago.'

The truth is that *Vertigo* lies somewhere between these two camps of reaction. '*Vertigo* has its moments, all right, but between them stretches a lot of wasted time,' summed up Philip Oakes in the *Evening Standard* at the time of the film's British release, perfectly hitting the nail on the head. Of course, the film *is* sumptuous to look at, the locations *are* breathtaking, the music *is* sublime and the story *is* intriguing. At the end of the day, though, 128 minutes is a *lot* of time to spend on what is basically no more than an elaborate after dinner anecdote with *Pygmalion* overtones.

For Hitchcock, *Vertigo* was an extremely personal project. A few years earlier he had hoped to film *Celle Qui n'Etait Plus* by Pierre Boileau and Thomas Narcejac, but was beaten to the rights by French director Henri-Georges Clouzot, who filmed the 1952 book as *Les Diaboliques* (1954), which was much admired by the critics, as well as Hitchcock himself. Consequently, when the two authors penned *D'Entre les Morts* in 1954, the director was quick to snap up the rights this time.

Having just worked with Maxwell Anderson on the screenplay for *The Wrong Man* (1956), Hitchcock handed the book over to the playwright to adapt for the screen, for which Anderson was paid a whopping $65,000. Unfortunately Hitchcock was far from satisfied with Anderson's work, which had been tentatively titled *Darkling, I Listen*. Consequently, he turned to Alec Coppel, who had penned a couple of un-credited retake scenes for *To Catch a Thief* (1955), to take up the job. Still dissatisfied with the results, Hitchcock next had his old friend Angus MacPhail do some work on the project before finally handing it over to Samuel Taylor, who did a complete re-write (recalled Taylor, 'Hitchcock recognized what he called a good yarn' [2]).

In the finished draft, a police detective named Scottie Ferguson (James Stewart), who has retired following a rooftop chase which has left him suffering from vertigo, finds himself hired by an old friend, Gavin Elster (Tom Helmore), to follow his wife Madeleine (Kim Novak), who has been suffering from a series of trance-like states brought about by her maudlin obsession with her great-grandmother Carlotta Valdes, who committed suicide at the age of 26, having been abandoned by her lover and separated from her child. Fearing that his wife may also try to kill herself ('I'm afraid some harm may come to her'), Elster manages to persuade Scottie to trail the blonde beauty. Initially intrigued, Scottie carries out the assignment, only to find himself drawn into Madeleine's world; this eventually turns into his own obsession when he rescues Madeleine from attempting to drown herself and falls in love with her. But even her romance with Scottie seems unable to snap Madeleine out of her dream-like state, and she eventually succeeds in killing herself by throwing herself from the tower of the San Juan Bautista mission. Scottie is naturally devastated by the whole episode, especially given that he was unable to follow Madeleine all the way up the tower and prevent her from doing this owing to his vertigo. Consequently, he is institutionalized for a lengthy period, much to the concern of his friend and former fiancée Midge (Barbara Bel Geddes).

Over a year later, Scottie is walking the streets of San Francisco, convinced that he sees Madeleine at every turn, when a brunette captures his attention. Her name is Judy Barton, and Scottie feigns an introduction at her hotel, given her remarkable similarities to the dead Madeleine. Scottie persuades the girl to meet him for a drink later, to which she eventually agrees. However, once he has left her room, Judy sits down to write Scottie a letter, revealing that she had been hired by Elster to pose as his wife in an elaborate murder plot. Full knowing that, owing to his vertigo, Scottie wouldn't be able to follow the fake Madeleine up the mission tower, Elster waited at the top with the real Madeleine, whom he had already killed, throwing her body from the tower in her stead. But Judy doesn't give the letter to Ferguson; instead she meets him for the drink as arranged, hoping that he will fall in love with her again, for while playing Madeleine, she had also fallen in love with him.

Though Scottie is clearly smitten with Judy, it is only because of her resemblance to the 'dead' Madeleine. Consequently, he tries to mould Judy to look more like her by buying her the clothes Madeleine wore and persuading her to dye her hair blonde. Judy reluctantly agrees to each of the increasingly outlandish requests made of her, simply because of her love for Scottie, which reaches fruition when the transformation is finally completed. It appears that Scottie has finally got his wish – that is until he spots that Judy, while getting ready for dinner, is putting on the identical necklace that Madeleine wore the day she 'died'. Concluding that Judy and Madeleine must be the same person, Scottie coaxes Judy into a drive before they eat, but instead takes her to San Juan Bautista, where he confronts her with his suspicions while dragging her up the bell tower. Judy begs to be forgiven for her role in the deceit, and the couple embrace, but when a figure emerges from the shadows, Judy steps back in horror and falls to her death. The figure turns out not to be the ghost of Madeleine, though, but a concerned nun who had heard all the commotion. Thus for a second time, Scottie has lost his 'Madeleine', the shock of which ironically cures him of his vertigo, enabling him to stand on the ledge of the tower and look down on the broken body of his lover.

Hitchcock and Taylor battled to make this far-fetched story as believable as they possibly could. To help put it over, Taylor created the character of Midge, to act as a sounding board for Scottie at key moments in the film. Nevertheless, certain discrepancies remain, key among them the fact that Scottie isn't asked to identify Madeleine's body at the death scene, which would surely have given the game away. It would also appear that Elster and Judy were able to sneak back down the bell tower following the crime and make their escape undetected. One also finds oneself wondering what Judy got out of impersonating Madeleine, given that when Scottie discovers her as Judy, she is living in a run down hotel on a clearly limited income. And why would she wear such an obviously incriminating piece of jewellery, full knowing that Scottie would be bound to recognize it? Even more importantly, how does Scottie get down from the roof on which he finds himself clinging so precariously at the top of the picture?

But these are thoughts for the cold light of day, for the film has other imperfections, notably its undue length, its slow pace (which defenders are quick to attribute to its dream-like quality) and the decision to disclose that Judy and Madeleine are one and the same person two thirds of the way through the film via the rather clumsy device of the letter. Hitchcock defended the disclosure, commenting: 'Everyone around me was against this… they all felt that the revelation should be saved for the end of the picture… But now we give the public the truth about the hoax so that our suspense will hinge around the question of how [Scottie] is going to react when he discovers that Judy and Madeleine are actually the same person.' [3] But in this instance Hitchcock was wrong, for Scottie reacts in *exactly* the way we would expect him to react in such a situation. Hitchcock certainly wasn't infallible – as his decision to make such films as *Mr and Mrs Smith* (1941) and *Under Capricorn* (1949) proves – and that is certainly the case here, for once the plot gimmick (and it *is* purely a gimmick) has been revealed, the film has no place to go.

Given that it has been revealed that Judy is Madeleine, we now know that she is resisting being made over by Scottie to look like Madeleine for a reason: self-preservation (which begs the question, why would she succumb to the process full knowing that it could expose her?). Surely more

tension could have been created if the audience was kept in the dark longer, making one wonder why Judy would allow herself to be subjected to Scottie's necrophiliac fantasies. Commented screenwriter Samuel Taylor, whose idea the disclosure originally was: 'We finally fastened on what we did, which is the writing of the letter and the flashback. I always felt it was a weakness that we had to do it that way, but there was no other way to do it.' [4]

During the lengthy writing process, Hitchcock became ill and had to undergo surgery twice, for a hernia and gallbladder problems, so filming didn't begin until 30 September 1957, by which time second unit and rear projection footage had been filmed and a contract dispute with Kim Novak had been resolved (Novak also raised concerns over the gray suit she had to wear as Madeleine, but was overruled by Hitchcock, who had carefully planned the film's colour scheme down to practically the last thread). As with all Hitchcock productions, the film was heavily storyboarded, and so filming went as smoothly as one would expect, with the director making excellent use of the carefully chosen locations in San Francisco and its environs, including Mission Dolores (where Scottie trails Madeleine to the grave of Carlotta Valdes), the Palace of the Legion of Honor (where Scottie finds Madeleine gazing at the portrait of Carlotta Valdes), Fort Point under the Golden Gate Bridge (where Madeleine fakes her suicide attempt), Big Basin Redwoods State Park (doubling for Muir Woods, where Scottie and Madeleine take their romantic walk), Cypress Point on Seventeen-Mile Drive near Carmel (where Scottie and Madeleine first kiss), Mission San Juan Bautista (where the 'real' Madeleine falls to her death from the bell tower) and the York Hotel (where Scottie discovers Judy).

For the scenes at San Juan Bautista, a matte painting of the bell tower had to be added to the exteriors, for the mission's own tower had perished in the great 'quake of 1906. The interior of the tower was meanwhile created back at the studio, along with an elaborate model, which was used to create the film's celebrated vertigo effect, which was achieved by having the camera dolly backwards at great speed while the focus zoomed forward, thus giving the impression of stretched peripheral vision while the point of focus remains the same (Steven Spielberg later re-used the effect in *Jaws*, when Roy Scheider witnesses a shark attack from his beach chair; since then, the shot has been somewhat overused by a number of lesser directors, which has subsequently lessened its impact).

The film is full of subtle touches, less ostentatious than most Hitchcocks. Note the overpowering red décor of Ernie's Restaurant, where Scottie first sees Madeleine; the gradually dimming light in the scene at the Argosy bookshop where Scottie and Midge learn about the real Carlotta from the owner; the continual reflection of Madeleine/Judy in mirrors which points to her duplicity; the dream sequence, designed by John Ferren, which pushes Scottie into his breakdown; the use of a green filter in Judy's hotel room from which she emerges as the recreated Madeleine; and the circular camera move which seamlessly changes from Judy's hotel room to the stables of San Juan Bautista as Scottie and the recreated Madeleine finally kiss.

Filming completed on 19 December 1957, after which post-production began, which included the scoring by Bernard Herrmann (the composer was paid $17,500 for his efforts). However, a musicians' strike meant that Herrmann couldn't conduct the score in America; consequently, the score was recorded in London, where it was conducted by the prolific Muir Mathieson. Unfortunately, the musicians in London subsequently walked out in support of their American comrades half way through the sessions, and so the rest of the score was recorded in Vienna. Jay Livingston and Ray Evans, who had penned the Oscar-winning hit *Que Sera, Sera* for Hitchcock's *The Man Who Knew Too Much* (1956) were also hired to pen a song titled *Vertigo* to help promote the movie. A demo' was recorded by singer Billy Eckstine, but – perhaps thankfully – the end result was not used (Livingston and Evans would later work with Hitchcock again on *Torn Curtain* [1966]). A song titled *Madeleine*, based on Herrmann's central theme, was instead used to promote the film. Arranged and with lyrics by Larry Orenstein and Jeff Alexander, it sank without trace.

The film premiered in San Francisco on 9 May 1958. A variety of promotional campaigns were used to launch the film, including a poster designed by Saul Bass that featured the swirling graphics from his memorable main title design (*Vertigo* would mark the first of three collaborations between Hitchcock and Bass). Other posters meanwhile accentuated the mystery of the piece: 'Somewhere, somehow, he'd loved her and let her slip through his fingers. *He had seen her die.* And now here she was, looking into his eyes again...' ran the enticing strap line for one, which also featured Madeleine falling from the bell tower.

The film went on to earn $3.2 million in the US on its initial release; the production outlay had been just under $2.5 million. By no means a flop, but by the same token, far from being one of Hitchcock's most commercial enterprises. For audiences of the time, the film was much too slow and languorous compared to the snappily cut thrillers they were used to. Commented *Cue* magazine: 'There was a time when Alfred Hitchcock did nothing but turn out 70-80-90 minute movie masterpieces. They were taut, terrifying exercises in suspense-manhunt melodramas, eerie tales of murder done and detected, killings thwarted, dangers evaded, and horrifying fights into the miasmic maze of disordered minds. As director Hitchcock grew more successful, his producers grew more generous. They put more footage in his films, and greater production values... His pictures became elaborate chess problems, in which frequently the beauty of the pieces rather than their moves seemed to fascinate him... *Vertigo* is a two-hour-and-eight-minutes case in point.' Of course, critical reaction has since changed. But really, can so many esteemed critics of the day have been so entirely wrong?

An additional ending was filmed: following Judy's fall from the tower at the climax, Hitchcock cut to Midge's apartment some time later. Midge is listening to the news on the radio and hears that Gavin Elster has been arrested for the murder of his wife. Scottie then enters the apartment. Midge mixes him a drink, but no words are exchanged. Fadeout. This scene can be found on the restored DVD of the movie (the film was fully restored in 1998 by Bob Harris and Jim Katz).

The film was more or less remade by Brian de Palma as *Obsession* (1976), which was also scored by Bernard Herrmann. The bell tower sequence is also referenced in *Psycho III* (1986), which was designed by *Vertigo's* art director, Henry Bumstead, and directed by Anthony Perkins, the star of Hitchcock's original *Psycho* (1960). *Vertigo* was nominated for two Oscars: for Henry Bumstead's art direction and the sound recording by Harold Lewis and Winston Leverett. Neither category won.

Hitchcock cameo Hitchcock can be spotted passing a shipyard gate carrying a cornet case when Scottie goes to visit Elster early in the film.

VETCHINSKY, ALEX British art director. Often billed simply as Vetchinsky, this busy designer worked on many films for Gaumont-British and its sister company Gainsborough in the 1930s and 1940s, chief among them

"You don't mind if I borrow your neck for a moment?" Robert Walker demonstrates the art of strangulation to Norma Varden in Hitchcock's Strangers on a Train *(1951). A worried Pat Hitchcock looks on.*

Hitchcock's *The Lady Vanishes* (1938), for which, in addition to designing the cramped carriages of the steam train, he also provided the train station and the rustic hotel seen at the beginning of the film. Recalled Vetchinsky's assistant on the film, Maurice Carter (1913–), who himself went on to become a respected designer: 'He had a very good perception of shooting and he could put it over to a director – except when he came to Hitchcock, because, as you can imagine, Hitchcock took little instruction from anyone! We worked for Hitchcock on *The Lady Vanishes*, a phenomenal film, and we were trying to pack this huge station and train by building it in perspective in a tiny studio which was only 90 feet long.' [5] Vetchinsky's many other films include *Foreign Affairs* (1935), *Beware of Pity* (1946), *The Mark of Cain* (1947), *House of Secrets* (1956), *A Night to Remember* (1958), *Carry On, Nurse* (1959), *Carry On Up the Khyber* (1968) and *Carry On Up the Jungle* (1970) **Hitchography:** *The Lady Vanishes* (1938)

VIERTEL, PETER (1920–) German-born novelist. Viertel began his screenwriting career on Hitchcock's *Saboteur* (1942). Like Hitchcock, he was under contract to David O Selznick at the time, as was his mother, actress/screenwriter Salka Viertel (1889–1978), whose screenwriting credits included Selznick's *Anna Karenina* (1935). The collaboration between Hitchcock and Viertel went well, so much so that Hitchcock proposed that Viertel make his debut as a director under his aegis with *Rope*, a project Hitchcock had been toying with for some time. Eventually, Hitchcock directed the film himself in 1948. Viertel's other screen credits include *We Were Strangers* (1949), *Blood and Roses* (1960) and *White Hunter, Black Heart* (1990), the latter based on his experiences with director John Huston in Africa during the shooting of *The African Queen* (1951). Viertel's father was writer/director Berthold Viertel (1885–1953). His second wife is the actress Deborah Kerr (1921– , real name Deborah Kerr-Trimmer). **Hitchography:** *Saboteur* (1942)

VOSPER, FRANK (1899–1937) British character actor. Vosper had the misfortune of falling from a transatlantic liner and drowning in mid-ocean at the height of his career! He began on stage in 1919 and entered films in 1926 with *Blinkeyes*, which he followed with appearances in *Strange Evidence* (1932) and *Dick Turpin* (1933) among others. He also made two films for Hitchcock: *Waltzes from Vienna* (1933) in which he played the Prince, and *The Man Who Knew Too Much* (1934) in which he played the assassin Ramon, who gets shot by the rifle-toting heroine. His other films include *Jew Suss* (1934), *Heart's Desire* (1935) and *Spy of Napoleon* (1936). He was also an occasional writer, penning the play *Murder on the Second Floor*, which was filmed in 1932 and 1941, latterly as *Shadows on the Stairs*. He also co-authored the screenplay for *No Funny Business* (1933). **Hitchography:** *Waltzes from Vienna* (1933), *The Man Who Knew Too Much* (1934)

WAKEFIELD, HUGH (1888–1971) British-born character actor. On stage from 1898, Wakefield later became a reliable actor specializing in upper-class roles. He made his film debut in 1930 in *City of Song*, which led to a busy decade on screen in the likes of *The Man They Could Not Arrest* (1931), *Aren't We All?* (1932) and Hitchcock's *The Man Who Knew Too Much* (1934), in which he played the supporting role of Clive, the hero's best friend. His other films include *Blithe Spirit* (1945), *Love's a Luxury* (1952) and *The Million Pound Note* (1953) **Hitchography:** *The Man Who Knew Too Much* (1934)

WALKER, ROBERT (1918–1951) American actor. In bit parts from 1939 following training at the Academy of Dramatic Arts in New York, this leading man's early film career was initially overshadowed by that of his first wife, Jennifer Jones (1919– , real name Phyllis Isley), to whom he was married between 1939 and 1945 (she went on to marry producer David O Selznick, to whom Hitchcock was contracted to for much of the 1940s). Walker graduated to featured roles and star parts in films such as *Since You Went Away* (1944), *Till the Clouds Roll By* (1945), *The Clock* (1945) and *One Touch of Venus* (1948), but his career was blighted by alcoholism and several nervous breakdowns. Following a lengthy period drying out, he returned in triumph as the psychopath Bruno Antony in Hitchcock's *Strangers on a Train* (1951), for which he earned the best notices of his career. Sadly, he died the same year the film was released after doctors sedated him following a violent outburst on the set of his last film *My Son John*, which was released posthumously. His second wife was Barbara Ford, the daughter of director John Ford, to whom he was married for just six weeks in 1948. Walker had two sons by Jones: Robert Walker Jr (1940–), himself an actor in the likes of *Ensign Pulver* (1964) and *Easy Rider* (1969), and Michael Walker (1941–). **Hitchography:** *Strangers on a Train* (1951)

WALKER, VERNON L (1894–1948) American special effects technician. At RKO from the early 1930s, Walker provided effects for several of the studio's key films, among them *Flying Down to Rio* (1933), *She* (1935) and, most importantly, *Citizen Kane* (1940). He also contributed effects to Hitchcock's three films for RKO in the 1940s. His other films include *None But the Lonely Heart* (1944), *The Spiral Staircase* (1946) and *Sinbad the Sailor* (1947). **Hitchography:** *Mr and Mrs Smith* (1941), *Suspicion* (1941), *Notorious* (1946)

WALSH, KAY (1914–) British actress. Walsh began her film career in 1934 with a small role in *How's Chances?* following experience on stage as a dancer. Further roles in *Get Your Man* (1934), *The Luck of the Irish* (1935) and *The Secret of Stamboul* (1936) followed, but it was a contract with Ealing and two co-starring appearances with the ukulele-playing George Formby in *Keep Fit* (1937) and *I See Ice* (1938) that helped to raise her profile. However, it was her role as Freda Lewis in the David Lean-Noel Coward co-production *In Which We Serve* (1942) that secured her name. The second of Lean's six wives, she was married to the director between 1940 and 1949, during which period she also worked with him on *This Happy Breed* (1944) and *Oliver Twist* (1948). She also contributed to the scripts of Lean's *Great Expectations* (1946) and *Oliver Twist* (1948), the former earning her an Oscar nomination. Walsh's subsequent films include *Last Holiday* (1950), *Cast a Dark Shadow* (1955), *A Study in Terror* (1965), *The Witches* (1966) and *Night Crossing* (1982). In 1950 she made an excellent cameo in Hitchcock's *Stage Fright* as the mealy mouthed maid Nellie Goode. Recalled Walsh of working with the director: 'Hitchcock gave me a good part in his not very good film *Stage Fright*. By now I had met such giants that I gave up thinking I was dreaming. Watching Marlene Dietrich tuck into the steak and kidney pudding in the canteen was something!' [1] Walsh also appeared in an episode of *Alfred Hitchcock Presents*. **Hitchography:** *Stage Fright* (1950), *I, Spy* (1961, TV)

Jessie Matthews gets to grips with the dishes in Hitchcock's Waltzes from Vienna *(1933). Matthews and Hitchcock reportedly did not get on well together during filming.*

Waltzes from Vienna
(GB, 1933, 80m, bw) ★

CREDITS
Production company:	Gaumont-British
Producer:	Tom Arnold
Director:	Alfred Hitchcock
Screenplay:	Guy Bolton, Alma Reville, based on the play *Waltzes from Vienna* by Guy Bolton, itself based on the German play *Waltzkrieg* by Heinz Reichhart, A M Wilmer, Ernest Marischka
Cinematographer:	Glen MacWilliams
Music:	Johann Strauss Jr, Johann Strauss Sr
Music director:	Louis Levy
Editor:	Charles Frend
Art director:	Alfred Junge, Oscar Werndorff, Peter Proud
Sound:	Alfred Birch
Assistant director:	Richard Beville

CAST
Esmond Knight (Johann Strauss Jr), Edmund Gwenn (Johann Strauss Sr), Jessie Matthews (Rasi), Fay Compton (Countess), Marcus Barron (Drexter), Frank Vosper (Prince), Sybil Grove (Madame Fouchette), Hindle Edgar (Leopold), Robert Hale (Ebezeder), Betty Huntley-Wright (Maid), Cyril Smith (Secretary), Bertram Dench (Engine driver), Charles Heslop (Valet), B M Lewis (Domeyer), Billy Shine Jr (Carl), Berinoff & Charlot

Perhaps the most curious of all Hitchcock pictures, this mild romantic comedy with music revolves around the attempts by Viennese composer Johann Strauss Jr (Esmond Knight) to get one of his compositions performed, despite opposition from his eminent father, Johann Strauss Sr (Edmund Gwenn), who fears the competition from his son. Helped by his fiancée Rasi (Jessie Matthews) and a benevolent Countess (Fay Compton), Strauss the Younger finally succeeds, and his composition, *On the Beautiful Blue Danube*, launches a career that sees him appointed the Imperial-Royal Director of Music for Balls by Emperor Franz-Joseph I by the time he's 25.

Having left British International Pictures following a series of disappointing assignments, Hitchcock arrived at Gaumont-British, where he would initially be working with independent producer Tom Arnold, in high expectation. Indeed, he would go on to make some of his most notable British productions at Gaumont, among them *The Man Who Knew Too Much* (1934), *The 39 Steps* (1935) and *Sabotage* (1936), all of which would be produced by Michael Balcon, who had already produced his first five films at Gainsborough back in the 1920s. However, this inaugural production did little to light the director's creative fire, prompting him to comment, 'I hate this sort of stuff. Melodrama's the only thing I can do.' [2] Indeed, judging by the flippancy frequently on display here, it's clear that Hitchcock's mind *was* on other things. That said, the production, based on a long-running West End success also starring Esmond Knight, has a charmingly dated air to it, and though Hitch flexes his style very little, the film passes its running time amiably enough. Yet like Hitchcock's first three films, the release of *Waltzes from Vienna* was delayed in Britain until 1934, and in America, it didn't appear until 1935, following the success of his next film, *The Man Who Knew Too Much*, which helped to re-establish his waning reputation.

Interestingly, the Strauss story featured here has been remade twice: first in Hollywood by Julien Duvivier as *The Great Waltz* (1938), with Fernand Gravet and Luise Rainer, and later in Europe by Andrew L Stone, also as *The Great Waltz* (1972), with Horst Buchholz and Mary Costa. Disney also had a bash at the story with *The Waltz King* (1963), with Kerwin Matthews and Senta Berger. There has also been a British television series, *The Strauss Family* (1973), with Eric Woolfe, Stuart Wilson and Anne Stallybrass.

WANGER, WALTER (1894–1968, real name Walter Feuchtwanger) American producer. Working both independently and as part of the studio system, Wanger was responsible for such classics as *Queen Christina* (1933), *Algiers* (1938), *Stagecoach* (1939), Hitchcock's *Foreign Correspondent* (1940) and *Invasion of the Body Snatchers* (1955). Following experience as a Broadway producer and an Army Intelligence Officer during World War I, Wanger turned to film in the early 1920s, gaining experience at Paramount as a producer and, eventually, production chief, a post he also later held at MGM and Columbia. His final film was the much-troubled *Cleopatra* (1963), the cost of which almost bankrupted Twentieth Century Fox. **Hitchography:** *Foreign Correspondent* (1940)

WARD, EDWARD (*–1971) American composer-conductor. In films from the early 1930s, Ward worked for a variety of studios on such productions as *Kismet* (1931), *Great Expectations* (1934) and *Stablemates* (1938). In 1941 he scored Hitchcock's comedy *Mr and Mrs Smith*. His other credits include *Phantom of the Opera* (1943), which earned him an Oscar nomination, *The Climax* (1944) and *The Babe Ruth Story* (1948). **Hitchography:** *Mr and Mrs Smith* (1941)

WARD, ANTHONY American supporting actor. Warde appeared in a handful of films in the 1950s and 1960s, including two Hitchcocks: *Rear Window* (1954), in which he played a detective, and *The Man Who Knew Too Much* (1956) in which he played a French policeman. His other credits include *The Carpetbaggers* (1964). **Hitchography:** *Rear Window* (1954), *The Man Who Knew Too Much* (1956)

WARREN, JOHN F American cameraman. Hitchcock turned to Warren to photograph his Cold War thriller *Torn Curtain* (1966) when his regular cinematographer Robert Burks proved unavailable. Yet despite Warren's best efforts, this was the only time the two collaborated on a feature (Warren had, however, photographed several episodes of *Alfred Hitchcock Presents*). Commented Hitchcock: 'We shot the whole film through a grey gauze. The actors kept asking, "Where are the lights?" We almost attained the ideal... shooting with natural light.' [3] Warren's other films include *The Love-Ins* (1967), *Tammy and the Millionaire* (1967), *For Singles Only* (1968), *The Counterfeit Killer* (1968) and *The*

Young Runaways (1968). Warren also photographed *Dark Intruder* (1965), a Shamley production originally intended as a TV pilot for a series to be titled *Black Cloak*. When the series failed to materialize, the pilot was released as a theatrical supporting programme. Shamley was of course Hitchcock's own production company, through which he made *Alfred Hitchcock Presents*, *The Alfred Hitchcock Hour* and *Psycho* (1960). **Hitchography:** *Torn Curtain* (1966)

Watchtower Over Tomorrow
(US, 1945, 15m, bw)

CREDITS
Production company:	Department of State/Office of War Information
Directors:	John Cromwell, Harold Kress, Elia Kazan, Alfred Hitchcock
Screenplay:	Ben Hecht, Karl Lamb
Cinematographer:	Lester White
Narrator:	Jon Nesbitt

CAST
Miles Mander, George Zucco, Grant Mitchell, Jonathan Hale, Secretary of State Edward Stettinius Jr

This wartime propaganda film, made for the Department of State, chronicles the formation of the United Nations. Though officially directed by John Cromwell and Harold Kress, the film also contains un-credited directorial contributions from Elia Kazan and Alfred Hitchcock. For Hitchcock's other wartime work also see *Men of the Lightship* (1941), *Target for Tonight* (1941), *Bon Voyage* (1944), *Aventure Malgache* (1944) and *Memory of the Camps* (1944).

WATERHOUSE, KEITH (1929–) British novelist, screenwriter and journalist. Waterhouse is best known for his novel *Billy Liar*, which he adapted for both the stage and the screen (1963) with his longtime collaborator Willis Hall (1929–). Their screenplays include *Whistle Down the Wind* (1961), *A Kind of Loving* (1962) and Hitchcock's *Torn Curtain* (1966), for which they did a re-write, but failed to gain a screen credit for their efforts when the original scriptwriter, Brian Moore, took them to arbitration over it. **Hitchography:** *Torn Curtain* (1966)

WATLING, JACK (1923–) British supporting actor. Watling made his screen debut in 1938 in *Sixty Glorious Years*, which he followed with roles in such key films as *Goodbye, Mr Chips* (1939), *Major Barbara* (1941), *The Way Ahead* (1944), *The Winslow Boy* (1948) and *Quartet* (1948). In 1949 he played the role of Winter in Hitchcock's *Under Capricorn*, the director's first British film for ten years. Watling's other films include *Meet Mr Lucifer* (1953), *The Admirable Crichton* (1957), *A Night to Remember* (1958), *The Nanny* (1965) and *11, Harrowhouse* (1974), following which he retired from the screen. His children include the actress Dilys Watling. **Hitchography:** *Under Capricorn* (1949)

WATSON, LUCILLE (1879–1962) Canadian-born character actress. On stage from 1900, Lucille Watson made her film debut in 1916 with *The Girl with Green Eyes*, but didn't make another film until *What Every Woman Knows* in 1934. Busy throughout the 1930s and 1940s, she appeared in *The Garden of Allah* (1936), *Waterloo Bridge* (1940), Hitchcock's *Mr and Mrs Smith* (1941), in which she played Mrs Custer, *Song of the South* (1946), *Little Women* (1949) and *My Forbidden Past* (1951), following which she retired from the big screen and returned to the stage. **Hitchography:** *Mr and Mrs Smith* (1941)

WATSON, WALDON O American sound recordist. Long at Universal, Watson worked on all of Hitchcock's 1960s' films, from *Psycho* (1960) onwards. **Hitchography:** *Psycho* (1960), *The Birds* (1963), *Marnie* (1964), *Torn Curtain* (1966), *Topaz* (1969)

WATSON, WYLIE (1889–1966, real name John Wylie Robertson) British actor. Beginning in 1932 with *For the Love of Mike*, this former music hall singer popped up in cameo roles in dozens of British films, among them such classics as *Waterloo Road* (1945), *Brighton Rock* (1947), *London Belongs to Me* (1948) and *Whisky Galore* (1948), usually as a henpecked husband or underdog. However, to most he will always be remembered for his role as Mr Memory in Hitchcock's *The 39 Steps* (1935), whose brain, it transpires, carries the secret designs for a new silent aircraft engine around which the whole film revolves (though this doesn't prevent him from having to answer such mundane questions as, 'Where's my old man?' and 'How old's Mae West?' twice nightly). Four years later he also appeared as Salvation in Hitchcock's *Jamaica Inn*. Watson retired from British films in the early 1950s and moved to Australia, where he made one final appearance before the cameras in *The Sundowners* (1960). **Hitchography:** *The 39 Steps* (1935), *Jamaica Inn* (1939)

WATTIS, RICHARD (1912–1975) British comedy actor. This much-loved, bespectacled actor, known for his dithering upper-class types, made his film debut in 1937 in *A Yank at Oxford*. His subsequent films include such favourites as *The Happiest Days of Your Life* (1950), *The Belles of St Trinian's* (1954), *Blue Murder at St Trinian's* (1957), *The VIPs* (1963), *Carry On Spying* (1964) and *Chitty Chitty Bang Bang* (1968). In 1956, he also appeared briefly in Hitchcock's *The Man Who Knew Too Much* as the frustrated front of house manager of the Albert Hall. Wattis was also known for playing Mr Brown in the long-running sit-com *Sykes* (1960–1979). **Hitchography:** *The Man Who Knew Too Much* (1956)

WAXMAN, FRANZ (1906–1967, real name Franz Wachsmann) German-born composer. One of Hollywood's greatest composers, Waxman began his career as a jazz pianist with the Weintraub Syncopators following training at the Dresden Music Academy. Waxman started working in films in 1930 when the Weintraub Syncopators were asked to play on the soundtrack for *The Blue Angel*, accompanying some of Marlene Dietrich's numbers. This in turn led to work as an arranger/conductor on the film. Waxman began scoring three years later with *Liliom*. Following a period in Paris, he next moved to America at the suggestion of Erich Pommer, the producer of *The Blue Angel*, who commissioned him to arrange the music for the Jerome Kern operetta *Music in the Air* (1934).

Waxman secured his reputation the following year with his score for *The Bride of Frankenstein* (1935), which led to his being appointed head of Universal's music department, from which he soon after resigned so as to be able to concentrate on his own scores. His many subsequent films include *The Philadelphia Story* (1940), *Objective Burma* (1945), *Alias Nick Beal* (1949), *Sunset Boulevard* (1950), which earned him an Oscar, and *A Place in the Sun* (1951), which brought a second Oscar. Waxman also scored four films for Hitchcock, beginning with the Oscar-nominated *Rebecca* (1940), which proved to be Hitchcock's first fully scored movie, notable for its haunting main theme and its eerie organ motif, played whenever the late Rebecca's name is mentioned. Waxman's second score for Hitchcock, for *Suspicion* (1941), was also nominated for an Oscar, no doubt thanks to its sweepingly romantic main theme, first heard in the impressive *Main Titles*. Equally impressive is Waxman's work for *The Paradine Case* (1947), which was written in the style of a piano concerto, while his score for *Rear Window* (1954) kicks off with a superb *Main Title*, clearly influenced by his roots in jazz (the remainder of the film was scored with source music, however). **Hitchography:** *Rebecca* (1940), *Suspicion* (1941), *The Paradine Case* (1947), *Rear Window* (1954)

WAYNE, NAUNTON (1901–1970, real name Naunton Davies) British actor. Along with fellow actor Basil Radford (1897–1952), Wayne became forever known as the cricket mad Englishmen Charters and Caldicott in Hitchcock's *The Lady Vanishes* (1938). They reprised the roles in a radio series and two further films: *Night Train to Munich* (1940) and *Crook's Tour* (1941), and went on to appear in a total of 11 films together, among them *Dead of Night* (1945) and *It's Not Cricket* (1948). On stage from the age of 19, Wayne entered films in 1930 with *The First Mrs Fraser*. His other films include *Passport to Pimlico* (1948), *The Titfield Thunderbolt* (1953), *Operation Bullshine* (1959) and *Nothing Barred* (1961). **Hitchography:** *The Lady Vanishes* (1938)

WEAVER, DOODLES (1911–1983, real name Winstead Sheffield Weaver) American character actor. Weaver can be spotted in Hitchcock's *The Birds* (1963) as the fisherman who loans Tippi Hedren's Melanie Daniels a boat so that she may deliver two love birds to the farm of Rod Taylor's Mitch Brenner. A former member of Spike Jones's City Slickers, Weaver's other films include *Topper* (1937), *Gentlemen Prefer Blondes* (1952) and *The*

Great Gundown (1977), while on television he had his own series in 1951. He was the uncle of actress Sigourney Weaver (1949– , real name Susan Alexandra Weaver). **Hitchography:** *The Birds* (1963)

WEBB, RITA (1904–1981) British comedy character actress. This diminutive (4-foot 10-inch (147cm), rotund, red-haired, actress was the archetypal old bag in scores of films and television shows. Among her films were *Oliver!* (1968), *Zeta One* (1969), *Up the Chastity Belt* (1971), in which she played a most unlikely Maid Marion, *Percy* (1971), Hitchcock's *Frenzy* (1972), in which she briefly appeared as the mother of necktie killer Robert Rusk (Barry Foster), *Confessions of a Pop Performer* (1975) and *Venom* (1982). **Hitchography:** *Frenzy* (1972)

WEBB, ROY (1888–1982) American composer. Following music studies at Columbia University and experience on Broadway as a conductor, Webb was signed by RKO in 1929 as an orchestrator for the musical *Rio Rita*. Webb remained with the studio until 1953, when it was sold to Lucille Ball's television company, Desilu, for which Webb stayed on as composer/music director. One of the cinema's most prolific composers, Webb churned out over 300 scores, notable among them his work for *films noir* and Val Lewton shockers, including *Cat People* (1942), *Journey into Fear* (1942), *The Body Snatcher* (1945), *Bedlam* (1946), *The Spiral Staircase* (1946) and *Crossfire* (1947). Webb also worked on two of Hitchcock's three films for RKO, conducting Edward Ward's jaunty score for *Mr and Mrs Smith* (1941) and scoring *Notorious* (1946), for which he provided a darkly romantic *Main Title* theme as well as a series of vibrant big band pieces for the film's Rio set sequences. **Hitchography:** *Mr and Mrs Smith* (1941), *Notorious* (1946)

WEBSITES As you'd expect, given his cult status, there are *many* websites devoted to Hitchcock and his films, and it's just a matter of exploring the web to find them. Among those worth checking out are (Please note the Publisher takes no responsibility for the contents of web-sites.):

www.labyrinth.net.au/~muffin/
The home of the Alfred Hitchcock Scholars/'McGuffin' site, this is unquestionably the best of all the websites, containing – literally – everything you could possibly wish to know about Hitchcock and his films. Indeed, the detail is both scholarly and obsessive (no simple filmography, this), and includes a news page, essays, articles, a comments section, a bibliography and an editor's diary, which contains a wide variety of musings. Thoroughly addictive, this is what the internet was invented for!

www.uib.no/herrmann/db/
Equally worthy of attention is this site devoted to Hitchcock's most celebrated collaborator, composer Bernard Herrmann. The official home of The Bernard Herrmann Society, it explores and details every facet of the composer's life and work, and contains a biography, album reviews and an deliriously thorough database of compositions and recordings, taking in Herrmann's work for opera, radio, the concert platform, film and television.

www.tdfilm.com/hitchcock/hitchmain2.html
A subsection of tdfilm.com this site contains sections on essays, posters, book reviews, CD information and links, as well as a complete filmography. Well worth exploring.

www.homestead.com/alfredhitchcockpresents/home.htm
The home of the *Alfred Hitchcock Presents* site, this tells you everything you could wish to know about Hitchcock's long-running TV show.

http://users.netreach.net/treyl/hitchcock.htm
Nothing too surprising here, with sections devoted to Hitchcock's films and television programmes. The best segment details all of Hitchcock's movie cameos.

www.qumulus.nl/hitchcock/
This Dutch site gives you all the basics you wish to know about Hitchcock, and includes the expected biography, film and cameo sections.

http://personal.redestb.es/hailbrath/
This Spanish homepage is another meat and potatoes site with all the basics, although one can't deny the enthusiasm of its creator.

WEBSTER, BEN (1864–1947) British actor. A stalwart stage actor, Webster played character parts in a number of films, beginning with *The House of Temperly* in 1913, which he followed with the likes of *Enoch Arden* (1914), *The Vicar of Wakefield* (1916) and *The Call of Youth* (1921), the latter of which had inter-titles designed by the young Alfred Hitchcock. In 1927, he was cast as Dr Dowson in Hitchcock's fourth film *Downhill*. Webster's wife, Dame May Whitty (1865–1948), later played Miss Froy in Hitchcock's *The Lady Vanishes* in 1938. When Hollywood called for Whitty following her success in this film, Webster went with her, appearing in several supporting roles himself, among them a small part in Hitchcock's *Suspicion* (1941), in which his wife also appeared. His other films include *The Old Curiosity Shop* (1934) and *Drake of England* (1935). **Hitchography:** *The Call of Youth* (1921), *Downhill* (1927), *Suspicion* (1941)

WELD, TUESDAY (1943– , real name Susan Weld) American actress. A former child model, Weld made her screen debut at the age of 13 in an un-credited role in Hitchcock's *The Wrong Man* (1956) as a giggling school-girl, the same year she also appeared in the teen flick *Rock, Rock, Rock*. Initially known for nymphet roles, she later matured into an actress far better than the critics would have her be. Her subsequent films include *Rally Round the Flag, Boys* (1959), *Sex Kittens Go to College* (1960), *Pretty*

Poison (1968), *Looking for Mr Goodbar* (1977), which earned her a best supporting actress Oscar nomination, and *Falling Down* (1993). Married three times, her husbands include comedy star Dudley Moore (1935–2002), to whom she was married between 1980 and 1985. **Hitchography:** *The Wrong Man* (1956)

WERNDORFF, OSCAR M (1886–1938, aka Otto Werndorff, Oscar Friedrich Werndorff) Austrian-born art director. Prior to entering the film industry, Werndorff actually held the prestigious post of chief architect to the last Emperor of Austria. In the 1920s he went to work at UFA in Germany, designing such films as *Variety* (1925) for director E A Dupont. His first British film, currently lost, was *The Bells* (1931), which, as well as designing, he also co-directed with Harcourt Templeman. Shot in three languages (English, French and German), it was an adaptation of the 1896 French play *Le Juif Polonais* by Alexandre Chatrian and Emile Erckmann, and told the story of a wealthy burgomaster whose conscience leads him to confess to the murder of a Polish Jew for his money belt. Photographed by Gunther Krampf and Eric Cross, and scored by no less than Gustav Holst, the film starred Hitchcock regular Donald Calthrop as the guilt-ridden burgomaster. In the mid-1930s, Werndorff designed several key films for Hitchcock, notably *The 39 Steps*, the sets for which included studio re-creations of the Scottish highlands, complete with running streams. **Hitchography:** *Waltzes from Vienna* (1933), *The 39 Steps* (1935), *Secret Agent* (1936), *Sabotage* (1936)

WEST, MARTIN African-American actor. West is best remembered for playing Dawson in *Assault on Precinct 13* (1976), the same year he also had a couple of brief lines as a cop named Sanger in Hitchcock's last film *Family Plot* (1976). His other films include *Lord Love a Duck* (1966), *Sweet November* (1968), *The Price of Survival* (1980) and *Mac and Me* (1988). **Hitchography:** *Family Plot* (1976)

WEST, VERA (1900–1947) American costume designer. West spent the majority of her career at Universal, where she started working in 1927. She designed and supervised the costumes of many films, among them *Showboat* (1936), *Mad About Music* (1938), *Son of Frankenstein* (1939), *Destry Rides Again* (1939), *Sherlock Holmes and the Secret Weapon* (1942), *Sherlock Holmes in Washington* (1943), *Son of Dracula* (1943) and *Cobra Woman* (1944). She also worked on Hitchcock's *Shadow of a Doubt* (1944), sharing her credit with Adrian. A year later she committed suicide. **Hitchography:** *Shadow of a Doubt* (1943)

WHEELER, LYLE (1905–1990) American art director. Nominated for an incredible 27 Oscars, Wheeler went on to win five of the golden statuettes, for *Gone with the Wind* (1939), *Anna and the King of Siam* (1946), *The Robe* (1953), *The King and I* (1956) and *The Diary of Anne Frank* (1959). Following experience as an architect and an industrial

designer, Wheeler entered films in the 1930s, first gaining recognition for his work for producer David O Selznick, for whom he designed such films as *The Garden of Allah* (1936), *A Star is Born* (1937), *The Adventures of Tom Sawyer* (1938) and, of course, *Gone with the Wind*, on which he worked closely with the film's production designer in chief, William Cameron Menzies. Wheeler also designed the sets for the Selznick-Hitchcock collaboration *Rebecca* (1940), which earned him one of his many Oscar nominations. In 1944, Wheeler was invited to head the art department at Twentieth Century Fox where, over the following 16 years, it is estimated that he either oversaw or directly worked on some 500 productions, among them *All About Eve* (1950), *The Snows of Kilimanjaro* (1952) and *Journey to the Center of the Earth* (1959), all of which received Oscar nominations for their art direction. Wheeler's other films include *The Cardinal* (1963), *Tell Me That You Love Me, Junie Moon* (1969) and *Posse* (1975). Said Wheeler of the overlapping schedules of *Gone with the Wind* and *Rebecca*: 'The sets on *Gone with the Wind* were still up [for retakes] when we started *Rebecca*... I remember we couldn't wait to strike the Twelve Oaks hallway to make room for Manderlay.' [4] **Hitchography:** *Rebecca* (1940)

WHEN THE BOYS LEAVE HOME see *Downhill*

The White Shadow
(GB, 1924, 50m approx, bw, silent)

CREDITS

Production company:	Balcon-Freedman-Saville
Producers:	Michael Balcon,
	John Freedman, Victor Saville
Director:	Graham Cutts
Screenplay:	Alfred Hitchcock,
	Michael Morton, based on
	Morton's novel, *Children of*
	Chance
Cinematographer:	Claude L McDonnell
Editor:	Alfred Hitchcock
Art director:	Alfred Hitchcock
Assistant director:	Alfred Hitchcock
Continuity girl:	Alma Reville

CAST

Betty Compson (Nancy/Georgina Brent), Clive Brook (Robin Field), Henry Victor (Louis Chadwick), Daisy Campbell (Elizabeth Brent), Olaf Hytten (Herbert Barnes), A B Imeson (Mr Brent)

One of several black-and-white silents on which Hitchcock worked in various production capacities, this 1924 drama about a wild young woman who becomes possessed by the soul of her twin sister who died to save her, re-united practically the entire cast and crew of the previous year's success, *Woman to Woman*, although lightning failed to strike twice at the box office.

WHITE SHADOWS see *The White Shadow*

WHITELAW, BILLIE (1932–) British actress. On radio from the age of 11, this stage star, acclaimed for her work in the plays of Samuel Beckett among others, began her theatre career in 1950. She started making films soon after, appearing in small roles in the likes of *The Fake* (1953) and *The Sleeping Tiger* (1954) before going on to greater acclaim in the likes of *No Love for Johnnie* (1960), *Charlie Bubbles* (1968), which won her a BAFTA, *Twisted Nerve* (1968), *Gumshoe* (1972), *Night Watch* (1973), *The Omen* (1976), *Maurice* (1987), *The Krays* (1990) and *Quills* (2000). In 1972 she played the small, rather thankless role of Hettie Porter in Hitchcock's *Frenzy*. She has also appeared in a remake of Hitchcock's *Jamaica Inn* (1983, TV). **Hitchography:** *Frenzy* (1972)

WHITLOCK, ALBERT (1915–1999) British matte painter and special effects technician. Whitlock won Oscars for his work on both *Earthquake* (1974) and *The Hindenburg* (1975). He also provided the mattes for several of Hitchcock's later films, beginning with the 1956 remake of *The Man Who Knew Too Much*. His other credits, often in collaboration, include *The War Lord* (1965), *The Forbin Project* (1969), *Diamonds Are Forever* (1971), *The Wiz* (1978) and *The Never-Ending Story II: The Next Chapter* (1990). In 1977 he provided the mattes for Mel Brooks's Hitchcock parody *High Anxiety*, in which he made a brief cameo appearance. He also provided the matte shots for *Psycho 2* in 1983. The highpoint of his association with Hitchcock was unquestionably *The Birds* (1963), on which he collaborated with effects supervisor Ub Iwerks, providing 12 matte paintings for the film; the low point was *Marnie* (1964), which includes a dockyard matte, one of the poorest seen in *any* film. Some sources indicate that, as a sign painter, Whitlock also worked on Hitchcock's *The 39 Steps* (1935) and *The Lady Vanishes* (1938). **Hitchography:** *The 39 Steps* (1935), *The Lady Vanishes* (1938), *The Man Who Knew Too Much* (1956), *The Birds* (1963), *Marnie* (1964), *Torn Curtain* (1966), *Topaz* (1969), *Frenzy* (1972), *Family Plot* (1976)

WHITTY, DAME MAY (1865–1948) British character actress. On stage from the age of 16, Whitty went on to forge a distinguished career for herself on the boards, for which she was created a Dame in 1918. She had made her screen debut four years previous to this in *Enoch Arden*, but it wasn't until the late 1930s, when she was already in her seventies, that her film career took off in Hollywood with roles in *Night Must Fall* (1937), which earned her an Oscar nomination as best supporting actress, *Conquest* (1937) and *I Met My Love Again* (1937). In 1938, she returned to England to make *The Lady Vanishes* for Hitchcock, in which she played the kindly Miss Froy, who is abducted by Balkan spies. Recalled co-star Linden Travers: 'She was 72 at the time, and she said to me, "I've just got a contract to go to Hollywood. It's on account of my voluptuous lips!"' [5] Indeed, Whitty did soon after return to Hollywood,

Dame May Whitty and Hitchcock go over the script as Emile Boreo looks on during the filming of the opening hotel sequence in The Lady Vanishes *(1938). Note the roughly finished back of the reception desk, not seen by the cameras.*

where she went on to appear in *Raffles* (1940), Hitchcock's *Suspicion* (1941), *Mrs Miniver* (1942), which earned her a second best supporting actress Oscar nomination, *Gaslight* (1944) and *My Name is Julia Ross* (1945). Her last film was *The Return of October* (1948). Said Whitty, 'So long as I can do my bit, I'll keep on doing it.' [6] Whitty's husband, actor Ben Webster (1864–1947), also had a few brushes with Hitchcock, appearing in *The Call of Youth* (1921), which had inter-titles designed by Hitchcock, as well as *Downhill* (1927) and *Suspicion* (1941), which Hitchcock directed. **Hitchography:** *The Lady Vanishes* (1938), *Suspicion* (1941)

WILCOX, FRANK (1907–1974) American supporting actor. Wilcox appeared in many films from the mid-1930s onwards, including *The Fighting 69th* (1939), *Across the Pacific* (1942), *Gentleman's Agreement* (1947) and *Samson and Delilah* (1949). He can also be spotted as an FBI agent in Hitchcock's *Notorious* (1946) and as businessman Weltner in *North by Northwest* (1959). **Hitchography:** *Notorious* (1946), *North by Northwest* (1959)

WILDER, THORNTON (1897–1975) American playwright and novelist. Wilder is best known for such works as *Our Town*, *The Matchmaker* and *The Bridge at San Luis Rey*, all of which have been filmed (*The Matchmaker* also served as the source for the musical *Hello, Dolly!*). In 1943, Wilder was asked to script Hitchcock's *Shadow of a Doubt*, no doubt to bring a touch of his own brand of Americana to the film's small town setting. **Hitchography:** *Shadow of a Doubt* (1943)

WILDING, MICHAEL (1912–1979) British actor. This debonair leading man came to acting following experience as a portrait painter. In 1933 he joined the art department of British and Dominican, the same year he made his screen debut as an extra in *Bitter Sweet*. A variety of walk on roles followed, along with stage experience, and by the early 1940s he was making gains as a supporting actor in the likes of *Secret Mission* (1942) and *In Which We Serve* (1942). Stardom beckoned with *Dear Octopus* in 1943, which was soon after confirmed with a number of co-starring vehicles with Anna Neagle, among them *Piccadilly Incident* (1946), *The Courtneys of Curzon Street* (1947), *Spring in Park Lane* (1948) and *Maytime in Mayfair* (1949). In 1949 Wilding made the first of two films for Hitchcock: *Under Capricorn*, in which he played Charles Adair who, while visiting his cousin in Australia, discovers that she has become a mentally unhinged dipsomaniac. Unfortunately the film, a period piece, was a commercial disaster and ended Hitchcock's plans of being an independent filmmaker. Despite the film's lack of success, Hitchcock invited Wilding back for his following feature, *Stage Fright* (1950), an amusing murder mystery and one of the director's most underrated films. In it, Wilding played Inspector Wilfred Smith. Wilding's other films include *The Lady with a Lamp* (1951), *The Egyptian* (1954), *The World of Suzie Wong* (1960), *Waterloo* (1970) and *Lady Caroline Lamb* (1972). Married four times, Wilding's wives included Elizabeth Taylor (1932–), to whom he was married between 1952 and 1957, and Margaret Leighton (1922–1964), whom he married in 1964, and with whom he'd co-starred in Hitchcock's *Under Capricorn*. **Hitchography:** *Under Capricorn* (1949), *Stage Fright* (1950)

WILLIAMS, ADAM (1929–) American actor. Williams became a familiar support in the 1950s and 1960s in such films as *Queen for a Day* (1950), *Darby's Rangers* (1958) and *The Last Sunset* (1961). He also appeared in Hitchcock's *North by Northwest* (1959) as Valerian, one of the henchmen of James Mason's arch villain Philip Vandamm, and two episodes of *Alfred Hitchcock Presents*. **Hitchography:** *Listen! Listen!* (1958, TV), *North by Northwest* (1959), *What Frightened You, Fred?* (1962, TV)

WILLIAMS, EMLYN (1905–1987, real name George E Williams) British-born actor. Born into poverty in a Welsh mining village, Williams not only went on to win a scholarship to Oxford, but also became one of the leading actor-playwrights of his generation, among his classics being *The Corn is Green* (loosely based on his own experiences) and *Night Must Fall* (both of which have been filmed twice). On stage from 1927, he made his film debut in 1932 with *The Frightened Lady*, which was followed by performances in *Broken Blossoms* (1936), *They Drive by Night* (1938), *Major Barbara* (1941), *Hatter's Castle* (1941), *Ivanhoe* (1952) and *The Walking Stick* (1970) among others. His screenplays include *Friday the Thirteenth* (1933), *Evergreen* (1934) and Hitchcock's *The Man Who Knew Too Much* (1934), on which he did a dialogue polish without actually meeting with the director. He did, however, later

act for Hitchcock in *Jamaica Inn* (1939), in which he played the supporting role of Harr, one of the murderous wreckers. He also wrote, directed and appeared in *The Last Days of Dolwyn* (1949). **Hitchography:** *The Man Who Knew Too Much* (1934), *Jamaica Inn* (1939)

WILLIAMS, HARCOURT (1880–1957) British stage actor. Respected for his work in the classics, Williams only occasionally ventured into films, among his credits being *Henry V* (1944), *Brighton Rock* (1947), *Hamlet* (1948) and *Roman Holiday* (1953). He also had a small role in Hitchcock's *Under Capricorn* (1949) as a coachman. **Hitchography:** *Under Capricorn* (1949)

WILLIAMS, JOHN (1903–1985) British-born actor. On stage from 1916, Williams was the archetypal Englishman, a role he played to perfection in many films and television productions. He made his film debut in 1919 in *Edge o' Beyond*, but didn't make another film until 1942 with the Will Hay comedy *The Goose Steps Out*, which he followed with *The Foreman Went to France* (1942), *Next of Kin* (1942) and *He Snoops to Conquer* (1944). Williams was working in America as early as 1924, the year he made his Broadway debut, but he didn't make a film in Hollywood until 1947 with *A Woman's Vengeance*. The same year he also worked for Hitchcock the first time on *The Paradine Case*, in which he played the barrister Mr Collins. Unfortunately, much of his role ended up on the cutting room floor, and though he appears throughout the climactic courtroom scene, he is little more than a glorified extra.

Williams had better luck with his next film for Hitchcock, *Dial M for Murder* (1954), in which he played Inspector Hubbard, a role he'd already played on television in 1952 and in the play's original stage run, thus making the part truly his own. The following year, Williams returned to the Hitchcock fold for *To Catch a Thief* (1955), in which he played insurance investigator H H Hughson. Along with Jessie Royce Landis, Williams stole the picture, prompting *Variety* to comment, 'Support from Landis and Williams is first rate, both being major assets to the entertainment in their way with a line or a look.'

Williams' other films include *The Student Prince* (1954), *Sabrina* (1954), *The Solid Gold Cadillac* (1956), *Witness for the Prosecution* (1957), *Midnight Lace* (1960), *A Flea in Her Ear* (1968) and *The Swarm* (1978). He also appeared in a record ten episodes of *Alfred Hitchcock Presents*, three of which were directed by Hitchcock: *Back for Christmas* (1956, TV), *Wet Saturday* (1956, TV) and *Banquo's Chair* (1959, TV). **Hitchography:** *The Paradine Case* (1947), *Dial M For Murder* (1954), *To Catch a Thief* (1955), *The Long Shot* (1955, TV), *Back for Christmas* (1956, TV), *Whodunnit* (1956, TV), *Wet Saturday* (1956, TV), *The Rose Garden* (1956, TV), *I Killed the Count* (1957, TV, three episodes), *The Three Dreams of Mr Findlater* (1957, TV), *Banquo's Chair* (1959, TV)

WILLIAMS, JOHN (1932–) American composer and conductor. This much-Oscared composer, celebrated for his work for directors Steven Spielberg and George Lucas, has so far won the golden statuette five times, for *Fiddler on the Roof* (1971), *Jaws* (1975), *Star Wars* (1975), *E.T.* (1982) and *Schindler's List* (1993); he has been nominated a further 36 times. Following training at the prestigious Juilliard School of Music he became a jazz pianist; he also worked as a session musician on a number of film and television scores. He began scoring for television and then films in the late 1950s, among his early scores being those for *I Passed for White* (1960), *Bachelor Flat* (1961) and *Diamond Head* (1962). Williams's many subsequent scores include *The Rare Breed* (1966), *The Cowboys* (1972), *The Towering Inferno* (1974), *Close Encounters of the Third Kind* (1977), *Superman* (1978), *Raiders of the Lost Ark* (1981), *Born on the Fourth of July* (1989), *Home Alone* (1990), *Jurassic Park* (1993), *The Patriot* (2000) and *Harry Potter and the Sorcerer's Stone* (2001). He also provided the music for Hitchcock's last film *Family Plot* (1976), his playful score doing much to enliven the often lethargically paced and handled comedy-thriller. **Hitchography:** *Family Plot* (1976)

WILLIAMS (J) TERRY American editor. Long at Universal, Williams cut Hitchcock's final film, *Family Plot* (1976). His other credits include *House of Cards* (1969), *Airport 1975* (1974), *Airport 1977* (1977) and *Raise the Titanic* (1980). **Hitchography:** *Family Plot* (1976)

WILLMAN, NOEL (1918–1988) Irish-born character actor. Willman was frequently cast in sinister roles in the movies, most notably as the vampire Dr Ravna in Hammer's *Kiss of the Vampire* (1963). On stage from the age of 20, he carved out a solid theatrical career, augmented by the occasional film, beginning with *The Pickwick Papers* (1952) and including *Beau Brummell* (1954), Hitchcock's *The Man Who Knew Too Much* (1956), in which he briefly appears as Woburn, *Doctor Zhivago* (1965) and *The Odessa File* (1974). **Hitchography:** *The Man Who Knew Too Much* (1956)

WITHERS, GOOGIE (1917– , real name Georgette Withers) British actress. On stage from 1930, Withers became a name to watch with her first film, an early Michael Powell quota quickie titled *Girl in the Crowd* (1934), from which she was promoted from supporting artist to leading lady when the original star walked from the production. A string of supporting roles followed in the likes of *Crime Over London* (1936), *Convict 99* (1938) and Hitchcock's *The Lady Vanishes* (1938), in which she played Blanche, one of the heroine's friends in the film's early scenes. Following further support work, Withers headed for the front ranks following an appearance as a Dutch resistance fighter in *One of Our Aircraft is Missing* (1942), also for Michael Powell. Following this she went on to star in such hits as *On Approval* (1944), *Dead of Night* (1945), *It Always Rains on Sunday* (1949), *Miranda* (1948)

and *The Magic Box* (1951). Withers also had a major success in the 1970s with the prison-set television drama *Within These Walls* (1974–1978), in which she played governess Faye Boswell. Withers has long been married to the Australian-born actor John McCallum (1917–), with whom she emigrated Down Under in the 1970s. Her more recent films include *Country Life* (1994) and *Shine* (1996). **Hitchography:** *The Lady Vanishes* (1938)

WOLFE, IAN (1896–1992) American character actor. Wolfe appeared in over 150 films, beginning with *The Fountain* in 1934 and ending with *Dick Tracy* in 1990. In between, his gaunt features appeared in such classics as *Mutiny on the Bounty* (1935), *Mrs Miniver* (1942), *Random Harvest* (1942), *The Great Caruso* (1951) and *Reds* (1981). A regular in the Sherlock Holmes second features of the 1940s, among them *Sherlock Holmes in Washington* (1943), *Pearl of Death* (1944) and *Dressed to Kill* (1946), he also found time to work for Hitchcock twice, on *Foreign Correspondent* (1940) as Stiles, and *Saboteur* (1942) as Robert (the butler). In 1944 alone, he made 14 films and a serial. **Hitchography:** *Foreign Correspondent* (1940), *Saboteur* (1942)

A WOMAN ALONE see *Sabotage*

Woman to Woman

(GB, 1923, 74m approx, bw, silent)

CREDITS

Production company:	Balcon-Saville-Freedman
Producers:	Michael Balcon, John Freedman, Victor Saville
Director:	Graham Cutts
Screenplay:	Graham Cutts, Alfred Hitchcock, based on the play by Michael Morton
Cinematographer:	Claude L McDonnell
Editor/continuity girl:	Alma Reville
Art director:	Alfred Hitchcock

CAST

Betty Compson (Louise Boucher), Clive Brook (David Compos), Marie Ault (Henriette), Josephine Earle (Mrs Anson-Pond), Mytle Peter (Davy), A Harding Steerman (Doctor)

NB: Some sources also suggest that Victor McLaglen appeared in the film disguised as a Nubian.

This 1923 drama, about a British army officer who has an affair with a dancer while on leave in Paris during World War I, was the first film to be shot at Islington Studios for the newly formed production company Balcon-Saville-Freedman, so named after its founders Michael Balcon, Victor Saville and John Freedman. Having seen him at work, helping Seymour Hicks complete *Always Tell Your Wife*, the triumvirate hired Hitchcock to be their film's assistant director. Having further impressed his employees with a script adaptation of a play he'd done purely as an exercise, Hitchcock was also hired to co-write the film's script with its director, Graham Cutts, which was based on a play by Michael Morton. Hitchcock's skills as a draughtsman earned him the position of art director, too! Commented Hitchcock: 'On *Woman to Woman* I was the general factotum. I wrote the script. I designed the sets, and I managed the production. It was the first film that I had really got my hands on to.' [7]

Also involved in the film, which was made between June and August, was a young editor and continuity girl named Alma Reville, who would become Hitchcock's wife.

Hitchcock went on to work with the film's star, American import Betty Compson, on two further silents for Balcon-Freedman-Saville: *The White Shadow* (1924) and *The Prude's Fall* (1925). Much later he also directed her in *Mr and Mrs Smith* (1941) in Hollywood. Compson also appeared in the 1929 remake of *Woman to Woman*, which was directed by the first film's producer, Victor Saville. A third remake, directed by Maclean Rogers, appeared in 1946, although this time the leading lady was Adele Dixon. Sadly, no prints of the first version are known to survive, which is a pity, as it was a major commercial success, and was described by the *The Daily Express* as being, 'The best American picture made in England.'

WORDSWORTH, RICHARD (1915–1993) British character actor. Wordsworth was the great-great-grandson of the celebrated poet William Wordsworth. Although on stage from 1938, he didn't make his film debut until 1955, when he played the astronaut-turned-monster in Hammer's breakthrough shocker *The Quatermass Experiment*. The following year he appeared as taxidermist Ambrose Chappell Jr in Hitchcock's remake of *The Man Who Knew Too Much*, but the director badly fumbled what few comic opportunities Wordsworth's scene held. Wordsworth's other films include *The Camp on Blood Island* (1958), *Curse of the Werewolf* (1961) and *Lock Up Your Daughters* (1969), while his television work includes *R3* (1964) and *The Regiment* (1972). **Hitchcography:** *The Man Who Knew Too Much* (1956)

WRIGHT, TERESA (1918–) American actress. After training as an actress in Provincetown, Wright made her Broadway debut in 1938 as an understudy in Thornton Wilder's *Our Town*, which she followed with a leading role in *Life with Father* the next year. This earned her a contract with producer Samuel Goldwyn, for whom she made her screen debut in *The Little Foxes* (1941), for which she was nominated for a best supporting actress Oscar. She followed this film with *Mrs Miniver* (1942) and *The Pride of the Yankees* (1942), and was nominated again in the best supporting actress category for both films, winning for *Mrs Miniver*. She also won plaudits for her role as Charlie Newton in Hitchcock's *Shadow of a Doubt* (1943), in which she plays a teenager who discovers that her much-loved uncle is a serial killer. Commented

Variety of her performance: 'Wright provides a sincere and persuasive portrayal.' Wright also starred in a radio adaptation of the film in 1944 (in which Joseph Cotten was replaced by William Powell). Her other films include *The Best Years of Our Lives* (1946), *The Actress* (1953), *Roseland* (1977) and *The Rainmaker* (1997). She also appeared in two episodes of *The Alfred Hitchcock Hour* and contributed to the 1999 documentary *Dial H for Hitchcock*. **Hitchography:** *Shadow of a Doubt* (1943), *Shadow of a Doubt* (1944, radio), *Three Wives Too Many* (1964, TV), *Lonely Place* (1964, TV)

The Wrong Man
(US 1953, 25m, bw) ★

CREDITS
Production company: NBC
Producer/host: Robert Montgomery
Story: Herbert Brean

CAST
Robert Ellenstein (Manny Balestrero), Esther Minciotti (Mamma Balestrero)

Produced as part of the half-hour anthology series *Robert Montgomery Presents* (1950– 1957), this potted version of Manny Balestrero's real life ordeal as a man wrongly accused of carrying out a series of hold-ups was filmed three years later by Hitchcock under the same title. In this version Robert Ellenstein starred as the unfortunate Stork Club musician while Esther Minciotti played his concerned mother. Minciotti made it to the movie, in which she played the same role; Ellenstein did not, being replaced by the rather more bankable Henry Fonda.

The Wrong Man
(US, 1956, 105m, bw) ★

CREDITS
Production company: Warner Bros.
Producer: Alfred Hitchcock
Associate producer: Herbert Coleman
Director: Alfred Hitchcock
Screenplay: Angus MacPhail, Maxwell Anderson, based on the *Life* article 'A Case of Identity' by Herbert Brean
Cinematography: Robert Burks
Music: Bernard Herrmann
Editor: George Tomasini
Art director: Paul Sylbert
Sound: Earl Crain Sr

CAST
Henry Fonda (Manny Balestrero), Vera Miles (Rose Balestrero), Anthony Quayle (Frank O'Connor), Esther Minciotti (Mamma Balestrero), Nehemiah Persoff (Gene Conforti), Peggy Webber (Miss Dennerly), Harold Stone

Henry Fonda and Vera Miles pose for a striking publicity still for Hitchcock's downbeat docu-thriller The Wrong Man *(1957).*

(Lieutenant Bowers), John Heldabrand (Tomasini), Lola D'Annunzio (Olga Conforti), Doreen Lang (Ann James), Laurinda Barrett (Constance Willis), Robert Essen (Gregory Balestrero), Dayton Lummis (Judge Groat), Norma Connolly (Betty Todd), Charles Cooper (Detective Matthews), Kippy Campbell (Robert Balestrero), Richard Robbins (Daniell), Barry Atwater (Mr Bishop), Anna Karen (Miss Duffield), Tuesday Weld (Laughing girl)

CD availability: *Bernard Herrmann Film Scores* (Milan), which contains the *Prelude*

One could hardly call *The Wrong Man* an entertaining film. Like the situation in which the central character finds himself, it's something of an ordeal. Yet scene by-scene, it is extremely well made and remains one of Hitchcock's most underrated ventures.

Based on a 1953 *Life* feature by Herbert Brean titled 'A Case of Identity', it chronicles the true story of double bass player Manny Balestrero (Henry Fonda) who, having been wrongly identified, finds himself arrested for a string of robberies he did not commit. Unable to prove that he was elsewhere when the crimes were committed owing to the fact that his witnesses have either died or moved away, Balestrero finds himself having to prove his innocence in the face of mounting circumstantial evidence. Bailed out by his brother-in-law, Manny and his wife Rose (Vera Miles) hire a local lawyer, Frank O'Connor (Anthony Quayle), to help them with the case, but things go from bad to worse, for O'Connor's inexperience contributes to the trial being declared a mistrial, by which time Rose has suffered a breakdown and has been placed in an institution. It is only with the inadvertent capture of the real criminal that Balestrero's ordeal comes to a close.

Balestrero's story had already been presented as a teleplay by NBC in 1953. Produced by Robert Montgomery – the co-star of Hitchcock's *Mr and Mrs Smith* (1941) – the drama had starred Robert Ellenstein. Impressed by both the *Life* article and the teleplay, Hitchcock decided to film the piece for the big screen. 'I thought the story would make an interesting picture if all the events were shown from the viewpoint of the innocent man, describing his suffering as a result of a crime committed by someone else,' [8] explained Hitchcock. Determined to make the picture as authentic as possible, Hitchcock and his crew returned to the actual locations at which the events occurred; the director even cast some of those actually involved in the case, while the use of lesser known actors in supporting roles helped to make the unfolding events appear as authentic as possible (Hitchcock even used the actual psychiatric home in which Rose was placed and had some of the doctors play themselves).

Hitchcock's own fear of the police was reflected in the care he undertook to depict Balestrero's Kafkaesque arrest and imprisonment. Shot mostly from Balestrero's point of view, this involves his being fingerprinted, handcuffed and transported to prison with other felons, which is all the more humiliating for the musician given his innocence, hence his inability to look anyone in the eye while he endures the procedure.

By the time Hitchcock came to make *The Wrong Man*, the film industry was in something of a crisis, as a result of the increasing popularity of television, which kept potential audiences away from the cinemas, despite such come-ons as widescreen, Technicolor, 3D and stereophonic sound. Consequently, Hitchcock offered to make the film for nothing, given that Warner Bros., its producing studio, had financed four of his early 1950s' films. The studio was more than happy to take Hitch up on his offer, even though the film's stark docudrama approach didn't ultimately appeal to audiences. 'The all-round biggest Hitchcock hit ever to hit the screen,' proclaimed the poster somewhat extravagantly. Hitchcock himself even felt the need to 'explain' the picture, and so filmed a brief introduction.

Shot in a deserted studio, the director stands a distance from the camera, ominously backlit. 'This is Alfred Hitchcock speaking,' he announces from the shadows. 'In the past I have given you many types of suspense pictures, but this time I want you to see a different one. The difference lies in the fact that this is a true story – every word of it – and yet it contains elements that are stranger than all the fiction that has gone into many of the films that I've

made before.' But, as had been the case with such pictures as *Mr and Mrs Smith* (1941), *Rope* (1948) and *Under Capricorn* (1949), audiences didn't want a 'different' Hitchcock picture – they wanted from him what they knew best: laughs, thrills, glamorous stars and edge-of-your-seat suspense. Instead, they got an unrelentingly grim slice of life – hardly the kind of thing to attract a Saturday night audience away from the TV (on which, coincidentally, Hitchcock himself was now appearing weekly).

Yet despite its failings as a piece of entertainment, the film is made with Hitchcock's accustomed care, and directed with a calm and focused eye (commented *Variety*: 'Hitchcock drains the dramatic possibilities with often frightening overtones, as the spectator comes to realize that the very same thing could happen to him if he fell into such a situation').

Robert Burks' *noir*-style black-and-white cinematography is suitably claustrophobic (note the consistent use of close-ups and the inclusion of ceilings in many shots), while Bernard Herrmann's understated score, with its effective double bass motif, underlines the hopelessness of the protagonist's situation. Even the script, by Hitchcock regular Angus MacPhail and noted playwright Maxwell Anderson, is suitably spare. In fact, given the stark reality of the piece, directorial flourishes are kept to a minimum, notable among them a spinning camera shot in Balestrero's cell, used to show his state of mind as things spin beyond his control, and the re-use of a dolly shot through a front door, previously seen in *Stage Fright* (1950), which Hitchcock here resorts to twice, with Balestrero miming closing the door behind him as the camera follows him into his home. Finally, there is the bravura shot of Balestrero, praying in close-up, on to which Hitchcock overlays a shot of the 'right' man walking up a street into equal close-up, his face juxtaposed on top of that of his unfortunate look-alike.

The performances in the film are uniformly excellent. Henry Fonda, whom Hitchcock had long wanted to work with, is never less than convincing as Balestrero, perfectly capturing the man's weary resignation to his fate, while Anthony Quayle, a surprise choice as the lawyer O'Connor, presents the right degree of concern and optimism. The greatest revelation, however, is Vera Miles' performance as Rose Balestrero. The actress had first caught Hitchcock's eye in an episode of *The Coca-Cola Playhouse*, following which he cast her in *Revenge* (1955, TV), the first episode of his *Alfred Hitchcock Presents* series. The director quickly signed Miles to a five-year contract, his hope being to turn her into the next Grace Kelly. Ultimately this didn't work out, yet in *The Wrong Man* she gives a career high turn as Balestrero's troubled wife, most notably in the scene in which she fully breaks down, attacking her husband with a hair brush in their bedroom, breaking the dressing table mirror in two in the process, resulting in her husband being twice reflected in the cracked glass. 'Do you realize what you've done to my wife?' says the selfless Balestrero to the 'right' man when they finally cross paths.

The film tries to end on a positive note. 'Suspect in holdups cleared by "double"' declares a newspaper headline, while a title card informs us that, 'Two years later, Rose Balestrero walked out of the sanatorium – completely cured. Today she lives happily in Florida with Manny and the two boys... and what happened seems like a nightmare to them – but it did happen...' Yet despite these sops, there remains the lingering doubt that the Balestreros didn't *quite* live happily ever after following their ordeal...

Note that John Heldabrand plays a character named Tomasini, which is surely an in-joke, given that Hitchcock's editor during this period was George Tomasini.

Hitchcock cameo In addition to his appearance during his introduction, Hitchcock also filmed his customary cameo, reading a newspaper behind Henry Fonda in a diner. However, given the serious nature of the film, the director cut the scene, fearing a laugh of recognition would divert from the drama.

WYLLIE, MEG American character actress. Wyllie popped up in an occasional film, among them *The Flight That Disappeared* (1961), *Beauty and the Beast* (1963) and Hitchcock's *Marnie* (1964), in which she played Mrs Turpin. **Hitchography:** *Marnie* (1964)

WYMAN, JANE (1914– , real name Sarah Jane Faulks) American actress. Following experience as a radio singer under the name of Jane Durrell, Wyman broke into movies as a chorus girl in *The Kid from Spain* (1932), by which point she had reverted to her real name. Following further bit parts in the likes of *Elmer the Great* (1933), *King of Burlesque* (1935) and *Anything Goes* (1936), she changed her name to Jane Wyman and began a very gradual climb

to stardom in such films as *Cain and Mabel* (1936), *Stage Struck* (1937), *Torchy Plays with Dynamite* (1939) and *Princess O'Rourke* (1943), but it wasn't until she was cast as the love interest in *The Lost Weekend* (1945) that her star began to shine.

Roles in *The Yearling* (1946) and *Magic Town* (1947) followed, but it wasn't until she won an Oscar for playing a deaf mute in *Johnny Belinda* (1948) that Wyman truly came into her own. In 1950, the actress travelled to London to star in Hitchcock's *Stage Fright* (1950), an entertaining if somewhat old-fashioned murder melodrama in which she played a RADA student who has to pretend to be a Cockney maid in order to investigate a murder. Despite being a little out of her depth in both roles, *Variety* nevertheless described Wyman's efforts as 'delightful'. Hitchcock himself was less enamoured of the actress, though, revealing that, 'I had lots of problems with Jane Wyman.' [9] Wyman's many subsequent films include *The Glass Menagerie* (1950), *Magnificent Obsession* (1954), *All That Heaven Allows* (1955), *Miracle in the Rain* (1958), *Polyanna* (1960) and *Wild Bill: Hollywood Maverick* (1996), while on television she has appeared in *The Jane Wyman Theatre* (1956–1960) and *Falcon Crest* (1981–1990). The second of her four husbands was the actor and US president Ronald Reagan (1911–), to whom she was married between 1940 and 1948. **Hitchography:** *Stage Fright* (1950)

WYNDHAM-LEWIS, D B British scenarist. Wyndham-Lewis worked with Charles Bennett on Hitchcock's 1934 hit *The Man Who Knew Too Much*, which was later revamped in Hollywood by the director in 1956, although to rather less effect. **Hitchography:** *The Man Who Knew Too Much* (1934), *The Man Who Knew Too Much* (1956)

Y

Young and Innocent
(GB, 1937, 82m, bw) ★★★★

CREDITS

Production company:	Gainsborough/ Gaumont-British
Producer:	Edward Black
Director:	Alfred Hitchcock
Screenplay:	Charles Bennett, Edwin Greenwood, Anthony Armstrong, Gerald Savory, based on *A Shilling for Candles* by Josephine Tey
Cinematographer:	Bernard Knowles
Music director:	Louis Levy
Song:	*The Drummer Man* by Al Goodhart, Samuel Lerner, Al Hoffman
Editor:	Charles Frend
Art director:	Alfred Junge
Costumes:	Marianne
Sound:	A O'Donoghue
Assistant director:	Pen Tennyson
Continuity:	Alma Reville

CAST

Nova Pilbeam (Erica Burgoyne), Derrick De Marney (Robert Tisdall), Edward Rigby (Old Will the China Mender), Percy Marmont (Colonel Burgoyne), Mary Clare (Aunt Margaret), Basil Radford (Uncle Basil), George Curzon (Guy), Pamela Carme (Christine Clay), John Longden (Detective Inspector Kent), H F Maltby (Sergeant), John Miller (Constable), Jerry Verno (Lorry driver), George Merritt (Detective Sergeant Miller), J H Roberts (Henry Briggs, solicitor), Torin Thatcher (Doss house manager), Gerry Fitzgerald (Bandleader), Bill Shine (Bill), Beatrice Varley (Mrs Vessons), Frank Atkinson (Venner), Frederick Piper, Peggy Simpson, Jack Vyvian, Pamela Bevan, Syd Crossley, William Fazan, Richard George, Albert Chevalier, Anna Konstam, Fred O'Donovan, Humberston Wright

Video availability: Hollywood Classics
DVD availability: Carlton

Ask anyone about Hitchcock's classic British period and films such as *The Man Who Knew Too Much* (1934), *The 39 Steps* (1935) and *The Lady Vanishes* (1938) are quickly mentioned. *Young and Innocent* is almost always overlooked, however, despite being their equal. Indeed, it contains some of Hitchcock's most assured work of the period, as well as that incredible tracking shot that identifies the killer.

Following the completion of *Sabotage* (1936), Gaumont-British, to whom Hitchcock was contracted, closed down its film-making division so as to concentrate solely on distribution. Hitchcock's contract was subsequently taken over by Gaumont's sister company Gainsborough. However his producers, Michael Balcon and Ivor Montague, with whom he'd had some of his greatest successes, found themselves out of a job. Balcon soon after went to work for MGM's British arm as director of production, where he oversaw such hits as *A Yank at Oxford* (1937), while in 1937 he was appointed chief of production at Ealing. Ivor Montague turned to documentaries and propaganda films. Thus Hitchcock began work with a new producer, Edward Black, and at a new studio, Pinewood.

Young and Innocent is based on Josephine Tey's novel *A Shilling for Candles*. Like *The 39 Steps*, it follows the exploits of a young man out to prove himself innocent of a murder he's been is accused of committing; and just as *The 39 Steps* has little to do with Buchan, so *Young and Innocent* has little to do with Tey. Indeed, the plot, which is simplicity itself, is little more than a hook for some of Hitchcock's better set pieces.

The film opens in a somewhat melodramatic fashion, with a screaming row between a man and his actress wife during a raging thunderstorm, he accusing her of infidelity with a series of 'boys' since her success. The brief scene concludes with a close up of the man's twitching eyes in the flashes of lighting.

We then cut to the beach the next morning. It seems that a young woman is swimming in the surf. However, it quickly becomes clear that she is dead, having been strangled with the belt from a raincoat. A young man, screenwriter Robert Tisdall (Derrick De Marney), happens to be walking along the cliffs when he spots the body. Rushing down to the beach, he is horrified to learn that it is that of his actress friend Christine Clay (Pamela Carme), whom we'd seen arguing at the top of the film. Rushing to get help, Robert is spotted by two young women, who accuse him of running away from the crime scene when he returns with the police. Thus he is arrested on this plainly obvious circumstantial evidence. Yet once at the police station, the case against him grows stronger with the revelation of several further seemingly damning facts: Robert had sold Christine a script idea in the past and is presumably one of the 'boys' her husband has accused her of dallying with; it transpires that the belt used to strangle Christine came from Robert's coat, which he claims was stolen some time ago; and finally, Christine has left him £1,200 in her will, thus giving him a financial motive to kill her. It's no wonder, then, that Robert faints, only to be brought round by Erica Burgoyne (Nova Pilbeam), the pretty young daughter of the local police chief Colonel Burgoyne (Percy Marmont).

To help him with his case, Robert is appointed a solicitor (J H Roberts), who seems equally convinced of his client's guilt. Consequently, realizing that things look pretty bad, Robert escapes amid the bustle of the courthouse, using his solicitor's glasses as a disguise. Unfortunately, the car he chooses to hide out in turns out to belong to none other than Erica, whom Robert now cajoles into helping him prove his innocence. Thus the scene is set for the various adventures that follow, all of them leading to the revelation of the real killer, Christine's husband Guy (George Curzon), who is working at an hotel as a drummer in a blackface band (of course, the police never get in touch with him during the action to inform him and question him about his wife's murder, which would have saved everyone concerned a lot of time and effort!).

Said Hitchcock of the film: 'It was an attempt to do a chase story with very young people involved. The point of view is that of a young girl who is bewildered when she becomes involved.' [1] To play the girl, Hitchcock cast 18-year-old Nova Pilbeam, who had previously impressed him as the kidnapped child in *The Man Who Knew Too Much* back in 1934. *Young and Innocent* was her first adult role, and it must be said that she performs admirably under Hitchcock's guidance. Ditto Derrick De Marney (13 years Pilbeam's senior), who brings much natural sympathy to his role as the accused killer, whom Pilbeam gradually realizes is innocent.

The focus of the film becomes the recovery of Robert's raincoat, which first leads Erica and Robert to Tom's Hat, a transport café where the coat was apparently stolen. Here Erica learns that a tramp named Old Will the China Mender recently acquired a new coat, and so they set out to track the vagrant down at a doss house. But when Erica and Robert finally catch up with Old Will and the raincoat, they discover that yes, it is missing the belt, and that Will received the coat from a man with twitching eyes. The trail seems to have gone cold, but when a book of matches from the nearby Grand Hotel is discovered in one of the coat's pockets – to which neither Robert nor Will have been – Robert and Erica correctly surmise that the real killer must have been there recently... and may even still be there. Consequently, with Old Will kitted out in a new set of clothes befitting a wealthy hotel guest, the trio stake out the hotel. However, the police have by now caught up with Robert. Luckily, their presence leads the killer, playing the drums at a *the dansant*, to believe that they have come for him. This sets off a twitching fit, allowing Will to identify him and the police at last to arrest the real killer, who also handily confesses to the murder in the midst of his fit (asks Erica, 'You gave an old tramp a raincoat, didn't you? What did you do with the belt that belonged to it?' to which comes the reply, 'What did I do with the belt? Ha, ha, ha, ha, ha! I twisted it round her neck and choked the life out of her! Ha, ha, ha, ha, ha!').

A closer examination of the plot of *Young and Innocent* reveals it not to make much sense (why Guy would trail Robert to Tom's Hat, steal his coat undetected, remove the belt and then give the coat to Old Will is never alluded to). But this really doesn't matter, for the set pieces more than compensate. Highlights include a birthday party at the home of Erica's aunt (Mary Clare) in which Erica and Robert find themselves caught, Erica having gone there to give herself an alibi for being away from home, forgetting

that the party was on. Here, Hitchcock has his two protagonists itching to escape, only to find themselves involved in the frivolity, including a game of blind man's buff, with Erica's increasingly suspicious aunt as 'it'. This was Hitchcock's favourite scene in the movie; unfortunately, when the film was released in America (as *The Girl Was Young* in 1938), it was cut in its entirety.

Other highpoints include an astonishing scene in a disused mine, into which Erica drives her car so that she, Robert and Old Will can hide from the police. Unfortunately, as soon as the car enters the mine the ground collapses beneath its weight, and as the vehicle begins to descend into the void, its occupants have to scramble out, Robert pulling Erica to safety at the very last moment. The scene serves no particular narrative point; nevertheless, it is extremely well staged and all the more surprising for coming so completely out of the blue.

The most discussed set piece in the film is of course the incredible one-minute-ten-second crane shot across the lobby and dance floor of the Grand Hotel, finally coming to rest on the killer's twitching eyes. Recalled Hitchcock: 'There are lots of people there, and the tramp says, "Isn't it ridiculous to try and spot a pair of twitching eyes in a crowd of this size." Just then, right on that line of dialogue, I place the camera in the highest position, above the lounge, next to the ceiling, and we dolly down, right through the lobby, into the big ballroom, and past the dancers, the bandstand, and the musicians, right up to a close-up of the drummer. The musicians are all in blackface, and we stay on the drummer's face until his eyes fill the screen. And then, the eyes twitch. The whole thing was done in one shot.' [2]

In fact so complex was the timing of this shot, what with the musicians, dancing extras and elaborate camera moves, that it took two days to rehearse and shoot. Nearly 65 years later it remains a bravura piece of cinema. A pity then that George Curzon is so out of beat with the music being played by the rest of the orchestra (the song being played is titled *The Drummer Man*, and though the soundtrack features some energetic drum and cymbal work, Curzon's playing couldn't be more offbeat, making this one of the bigger continuity errors to be found in a Hitchcock film).

In addition to the strong performances from the two leads, the film is full of excellent cameos, best among them Edward Rigby's turn as Old Will. Exploiting the old man's full comic potential, the actor provides plenty of amusing moments, none more so than his attempts to dance with Erica in the ballroom of the Grand Hotel. Elsewhere, Percy Marmont provides just the right amount of kindly authority as Erica's policeman father, while J H Roberts has some amusing comedy business as Robert's solicitor. Meanwhile, Mary Clare is suitably suspicious of Robert in the tense birthday party scene (she, along with Basil Radford, who plays Erica's uncle, would both go on to appear in Hitchcock's next film, *The Lady Vanishes* (1938)).

The tone of the film is light and airy throughout, much of it being set on sunlit country roads ('I think it was quite the sunniest film I was involved in,' [3] recalled Nova Pilbeam). One never really doubts that Robert will fail to prove his innocence. So it's best just to sit back and enjoy the ride and the jokes, which include several jabs at the police, the best of them involving two coppers who have to hitch a ride on a farmer's pig cart ('Can't you give us a bit more room?' asks one of the policemen, to which comes the classic reply, 'Cart don't reckon to hold more than ten pigs').

Hitchcock cameo Note that Hitchcock makes his cameo appearance outside the courthouse as a press photographer holding a camera.

YOUNG, CARLETON (1906–1971) American character actor. Following experience in radio, Young went on to make many film appearances in minor supporting roles, including *The Glory Brigade* (1953), *Billy Mitchell* (1955) and Hitchcock's *North by Northwest* (1959), in which he plays the deaf business executive Fanning Nelson in the Oak Room sequence. His other credits include *Armored Command* (1961), *The Big Show* (1961) and *How the West Was Won* (1962). He was the father of actor Tony Young (1938–), known for the TV series *Gunslinger* (1961). **Hitchography:** *North by Northwest* (1959)

YOUNG, MARY (1879–1971, full name Mary Marsden Young) American character actress. Mary Young popped up in a variety of minor supporting roles from the 1930s onwards, among them Hitchcock's *Foreign Correspondent* (1940) as Auntie Maude (un-credited), *Address Unknown* (1944), *The Stork Club* (1945) and *The Murder Clinic* (1966). **Hitchography:** *Foreign Correspondent* (1940)

YOUNG, ROBERT (1907–1998) American actor. In films from 1931 with *The Sin of Madelon Claudet*, Young went on to become an affable leading man in over 100 films, among them *The Bride Wore Red* (1937), *The Mortal Storm* (1940) and *The Canterville Ghost* (1944), although he is best remembered for the television series *Father Knows Best* (1954–1960) and *Marcus Welby MD* (1969–1975). Unfortunately, one of his least affecting performances was in Hitchcock's *Secret Agent* (1936), in which he played enemy agent Robert Marvin, spending much of the movie mouthing un-amusing quips penned by the writers in a bid to disguise the fact that he's really the bad guy. **Hitchography:** *Secret Agent* (1936)

Z

ZIEGLER, WILLIAM (1909–1977) American editor. Ziegler cut four films for Hitchcock, working with him both before and after the decade his films were cut chiefly by George Tomasini. His work for *Strangers on a Train* (1951) is particularly noteworthy, especially during the tense carousel climax. By contrast, however, he had an easy time with *Rope* (1948), which was filmed in long continuous takes which were then simply spliced together (said Hitchcock, 'This film was, in a sense, precut' [1]). Ziegler's other films include *The Housekeeper's Daughter* (1939), *The Desert Song* (1953), *Rebel Without a Cause* (1955), *The Music Man* (1962), *My Fair Lady* (1964) and *The Omega Man* (1971). **Hitchography:** *Spellbound* (1945), *Rope* (1948), *Strangers on a Train* (1951), *Topaz* (1969)

Appendix

Stills sources:

British International Pictures: The Ring *(1927)*, Champagne *(1928)*, The Manxman *(1929)*, Blackmail *(1929)*, Elstree Calling *(1930)*, Murder! *(1930)*

Gainsborough: The Lady Vanishes *(1938)*

Gaumont British: Waltzes from Vienna *(1933)*, The Man Who Knew Too Much *(1934)*, The 39 Steps *(1935)*, Sabotage *(1936)*, Secret Agent *(1936)*

Mayflower: Jamaica Inn *(1939)*

MGM: North by Northwest *(1959)*

Paramount: Rear Window *(1954)*, To Catch a Thief *(1955)*, The Man Who Knew Too Much *(1956)*, Vertigo *(1958)*

RKO: Notorious *(1946)*

Selznick International: Rebecca *(1940)*, Spellbound *(1945)*, The Paradine Case *(1947)*

Transatlantic: Rope *(1948)*

Universal: Shadow of a Doubt *(1943)*, Alfred Hitchcock Presents *(1955–1962)*, Psycho *(1960)*, The Birds *(1963)*, Marnie *(1964)*, Torn Curtain *(1966)*, Frenzy *(1972)*, Family Plot *(1976)*

Walter Wanger Productions: Foreign Correspondent *(1940)*

Warner Bros.: Stage Fright *(1950)*, Strangers on a Train *(1951)*, I Confess *(1953)*, Dial M for Murder *(1954)*, The Wrong Man *(1957)*

The majority of stills were provided by the Joel Finler Collection.

Bibliography

Aachen, George and Reid, John Howard: Popular Films of the Forties (Rastar Press, 1988)

Auiler, Dan: Hitchcock's Secret Notebooks (Bloomsbury, 1999)

Auiler, Dan: Vertigo: The Making of a Hitchcock Classic (Titan, 1999)

Bergan, Ronald and Karney, Robyn: Bloomsbury Foreign Film Guide (Bloomsbury, 1992)

Brownlow, Kevin: The Parade's Gone By (Columbus, 1989)

Cameron-Wilson, James: Film Review 1999–2000 (Reynolds & Hearn, 1999)

Cardiff, Jack: Magic Hour (Faber, 1996)

Condon, Paul and Sangster, Jim: The Complete Hitchcock (Virgin, 1999)

Conrad, Peter: The Hitchcock Murders (Faber & Faber, 2000)

Cook, Pam: Gainsborough Pictures (Cassell, 1997)

De Rosa, Steven: Writing with Hitchcock (Faber & Faber, 2002)

Elley, Derek (ed.): Variety Movie Guide 1999 (Boxtree, 1999)

Evans, Jeff: The Penguin TV Companion (Penguin, 2001)

Fane-Saunders, Kilmeny: Radio Times Guide to Films (BBC Worldwide, 2001)

Filmer, Alison J and Golay, Andre: Harrap's Book of Film Directors and Their Films (Harrap, 1989)

Fox, Ken and McDonagh, Maitland: The Tenth Virgin Film Guide (Virgin, 2001)

Freeman, David: The Last Days of Alfred Hitchcock (Overlook, 1984)

Gifford, Denis: The British Film Catalogue, Volume 1, Fiction Film, 1895–1994, 3rd Edition (Fitzroy Dearborn, 2001)

Gottlieb, Sidney (ed): Hitchcock on Hitchcock (Faber & Faber, 1995)

Halliwell, Leslie: Halliwell's Hundred (Granada, 1982)

Halliwell, Leslie: Halliwell's Harvest (Grafton, 1986)

Halliwell, Leslie: Halliwell's Television Companion (Grafton, 1986)

Halliwell, Leslie and Walker, John (ed): Hallwell's Who's Who in the Movies (Harper Collins, 2001)

Halliwell, Leslie and Walker, John (ed): Halliwell's Film & Video Guide 2002 (Harper Collins, 2001)

Hammer, Tad Bentley: International Film Prizes (St. James Press, 1991)

Haver, Ronald: David O. Selznick's Hollywood (Bonanza, 1980)

Hunter, Evan: Me and Hitch (Faber, 1997)

Hurley, Neil P: Soul in Suspense – Hitchcock's Fright and Delight (Scarecrow, 1993)

Kapsis, Robert E: Hitchcock – The Making of a Reputation (University of Chicago, 1992)

Katz, Emphraim: The Film Encyclopedia (Harper Perennial, 1994)

Petrie, Duncan: The British Cinematographer (BFI, 1996)

Klepper, Robert K: Silent Films, 1877–1996 (McFarland, 1999)

La Valley, Albert: Focus on Hitchcock (Prentice-Hall, 1972)

Leff, Leonard J: Hitchcock and Selznick – The Rich and Strange Collaboration of Alfred Hitchcock and David O. Selznick (Weidenfeld & Nicolson, 1987)

Lehman, Ernest: North by Northwest, Classic Screenplays (Faber, 1999)

Leigh, Janet and Nickens, Christopher: Behind the Scenes of Psycho (Harmony, 1995)

Leitch, Thomas M: Find the Director and Other Hitchcock Games (University of Georgia, 1991)

Lentz III, Harris M: Feature Films, 1960–1969 (McFarland, 2001)

McFarlane, Brian: An Autobiography of British Cinema (Methuen, 1997)

Maltin, Leonard: Maltin's 1997 Movie & Video Guide (Signet, 1996)

Maxford, Howard: The A–Z of Horror Films *(Batsford, 1996)*

Maxford, Howard: The A–Z of Science Fiction & Fantasy Films *(Batsford, 1997)*

McDermott, Andy: DVD Review Presents: The Ultimate DVD Guide *(Titan/Paragon, 2000)*

Modleski, Tania: The Women Who Knew Too Much – Hitchcock and Feminist Theory *(Methuen, 1988)*

Mogg, Ken: The Alfred Hitchcock Story *(Titan, 1999)*

Morecambe, Gary and Sterling, Martin: Cary Grant – In Name Only *(Robson, 2001)*

Nelson, Craig: The Very Best of the Very Worst Bad TV *(Delta, 1995)*

Nourmand, Tony and Wolff, Mark H: Hitchcock Poster Art *(Aurum, 1999)*

Petrie, Duncan: The British Cinematographer *(BFI, 1996)*

Pfeiffer, Lee and Lisa, Philip: The Films of Sean Connery *(Citadel, 1993)*

Powell, Michael: A Life in Movies *(Faber, 2000)*

Quinlan, David: Quinlan's Illustrated Directory of Comedy Stars *(Batsford, 1992)*

Quinlan, David: Quinlan's Illustrated Directory of Character Actors *(Batsford, 1995)*

Quinlan, David: Quinlan's Film Directors *(Batsford, 1999)*

Quinlan, David: Quinlan's Film Stars *(Batsford, 2000)*

Rebello, Stephen: Alfred Hitchcock and the Making of Psycho *(Marion Boyars, 1990)*

Ryall, Tom: Alfred Hitchcock and the British Cinema *(University of Illinois, 1986)*

Scheuer, Steven H (ed.): Movies on TV and Videocassette *(Bantam, 1991)*

Sheridan, Simon: Keeping the British End Up *(Reynolds & Hearn, 2001)*

Soister, John T: Claude Rains – A Comprehensive Illustrated Reference *(McFarland, 1999)*

Sigolof, Marc: The Films of the Seventies *(McFarland Classics, 2000)*

Sloan, Jane E: Alfred Hitchcock: A Guide to References and Resources *(G.K. Hall, 1993)*

Smith, Susan: Hitchcock – Suspense, Humour and Tone *(BFI, 2000)*

Spotto, Donald: The Dark Side of Genius – The Life of Alfred Hitchcock *(Ballantine, 1983)*

Taylor, John Russell: Hitch *(Berkley, 1980)*

Thomas, Nicholas (ed): International Dictionary of Films and Filmmakers – 1: Films *(St. James, 1990)*

Thomas, Nicholas (ed.): International Dictionary of Films and Filmmakers – 3: Actors and Actresses *(St. James, 1992)*

Tookey, Christopher: The Critics' Film Guide *(Boxtree, 1994)*

Truffaut, Francois: Hitchcock by Truffaut *(Paladin, 1986)*

Vazna, Eugene Michael: Silent Film Necrology, Second Edition *(McFarland, 2001)*

Warren, Patricia: British Film Studios – An Illustrated History *(Batsford, 2001)*

Walker, Mark: Gramophone Film Music *(Gramophone/Arcam, 1998)*

Weaver, Tom: I Was a Monster Movie Maker *(McFarland, 2001)*

Windeler, Robert: Julie Andrews – A Life on Stage and Screen *(Aurum, 1997)*

Wood, Robin: Hitchcock's Films Revisited *(Columbia University, 1989)*

Yacower, Maurice: Hitchcock's British Films *(Shoestring, 1977)*

Periodicals

The Cine Technician *(1943)*

Cinefantastique *(Fall 1980, Volume 10, Number 2, The Making of Alfred Hitchcock's The Birds, by Kyle B Counts and Steve Rubin)*

Film Review *(June 1997, Call Sheet: Vertigo by Anwar Brett)*

Film Review *(September 1999, Call Sheet: Frenzy by Howard Maxford)*

Film Weekly *(6 March, 1937)*

Music from the Movies *(Issue 2, Spring 1993)*

Picturegoer *(1 April 1950)*

Shivers *(No. 38, February 1997, Psycho by Howard Maxford)*

Starburst *(1991)*

What's On in London *(December 1993, Citizen Herrmann by Howard Maxford)*

Newspapers

London Evening News *(16 November 1927)*

London Evening News *(25 June 1929)*

Sunday Express *(17 September 1946)*

Los Angeles Times *(20 October 1946)*

Videography

Hitchcock Tribute *(Channel Four, 1989)*

Music for the Movies: Bernard Herrmann *(Les Films d'Ici/Alternate Current International/La Sept/Channel Four, 1993)*

Omnibus *(BBC, 1986)*

Reputations: Hitchcock *(BBC/Arts and Entertainment Network, 1999)*

Legends: Alfred Hitchcock *(Carlton, 2001)*

Discography

The Trouble with Harry *(Varese, 1998, liner notes by Christopher Husted)*

Websites
http://www.labyrinth.net.au/~muffin/
http://www.uib.no/herrmann/db/

Quotation Sources

Auiler, Dan: **Hitchcock's Secret Notebooks**
(Bloomsbury, 1999)
N1, N2, R29

Auiler, Dan: **Vertigo: The Making of a Hitchcock
Classic** *(Titan, 1999)*
B2, B3, T2, V4

Cardiff, Jack: **Magic Hour** *(Faber, 1996)*
C3

Cook, Pam: **Gainsborough Pictures** *(Cassell, 1997)*
B28, L19

De Rosa, Steven: **Writing with Hitchcock** *(Faber &
Faber, 2002)*
A8, B34, D4, D5, H1, H2, K1, M4, M5, M11, N6, R3,
R4, R10, R24, S27, T11, T18, T20, V1

Gottlieb, Sidney (ed): **Hitchcock on Hitchcock** *(Faber &
Faber, 1995)*
B32, B33, P16, P17, W7

Halliwell, Leslie and Walker, John (ed): **Halliwell's Film &
Video Guide 2002** *(Harper Collins, 2001)*
G1, P25, W2

Halliwell, Leslie: **Halliwell's Hundred** *(Granada, 1982)*
L3

Halliwell, Leslie and Walker, John (ed): **Hallwell's Who's
Who in the Movies** *(Harper Collins, 2001)*
A5, A6, B10, D6, F7, F8, F11, F12, H3, H19, L6, N14,
O1, S8, S12, S29, W6

Haver, Ronald: **David O. Selznick's Hollywood**
(Bonanza, 1980)
D1, D2, F10, F13, M3, O2, P1, P6, P9, R15, R17, S7,
S18, W4

Hunter, Evan: **Me and Hitch** *(Faber, 1997)*
B16, B17, B18, B19, B26, H20, H22

Katz, Ephraim: **The Film Encyclopedia** *(Harper
Perennial, 1994)*
F9

Lehman, Ernest: **North by Northwest, Classic
Screenplays** *(Faber, 1999)*
L8, N7, N8, N9, N10

Leigh, Janet and Nickens, Christopher: **Behind the Scenes
of Psycho** *(Harmony, 1995)*
L9, P22, P23

McFarlane, Brian: **An Autobiography of British
Cinema** *(Methuen, 1997)*
G2, L2, L5, L10, M8, M18, P8, P13, P14, P15, R20,
R30, T14, T17, V5, W1, W5, Y3

Mogg, Ken: **The Alfred Hitchcock Story** *(Titan, 1999)*
M6, P28, R13, R14, R16

Morecambe, Gary and Sterling, Martin: **Cary Grant – In
Name Only** *(Robson, 2001)*
G7, G9, G10, T12

Petrie, Duncan: **The British Cinematographer** *(BFI,
1996)*
C2

Pfeiffer, Lee and Lisa, Philip: **The Films of Sean
Connery** *(Citadel, 1993)*
C10, C11

Powell, Michael: **A Life in Movies** *(Faber, 2000)*
C4, C6, C12, M13, O3, P19, P20, S23, S24

Quinlan, David: **Quinlan's Illustrated Directory of
Character Actors** *(Batsford, 1995)*
A4

Rebello, Stephen: **Alfred Hitchcock and the Making
of Psycho** *(Marion Boyars, 1990)*
B4, B5, B6, B7, C8, C9, G11, G12, M21, N5, P10, P11,
P12, R25, S14, S25, T21

Taylor, John Russell: **Hitch** *(Berkley, 1980)*
B1, C7, D8, F1, H16, M16, R21, U3

Truffaut, Francois: **Hitchcock by Truffaut** *(Paladin, 1986)*
B8, B12, B15, B29, B30, B31, C5, C15, D7, D10, D11,
E1, E2, F2, F4, F14, F15, G6, I1, J1, J2, J4, K2, L4, L11,
L12, L13, L17, L18, L20, L21, L22, L23, L24, M1, M7,
M9, M10, M12, M14, M15, M19, M20, M22, M23,
M24, M25, M26, M27, N11, N15, N16, N17, P2, P3,
P4, P5, P7, P18, P21, P24, R2, R6, R7, R8, R9, R11,
R12, R18, R19, R27, R28, R31, R34, R35, S1, S2, S3,
S4, S5, S6, S9, S13, S15, S16, S17, S19, S20, S21, S22,
S30, S31, S32, S33, T5, T6, T7, T8, T10, T13, T16, T19,
U1, U4, U5, U6, V3, W3, W8, W9, Z1

Weaver, Tom: **I Was a Monster Movie Maker**
(McFarland, 2001)
A1, A2, A3, L14, L15

Windeler, Robert: **Julie Andrews – A Life on Stage
and Screen** *(Aurum, 1997)*
A7, N4

Periodicals

The Cine Technician *(1943)*
C13, R26

Cinefantastique *(Fall 1980, Volume 10, Number 2, The Making of Alfred Hitchcock's The Birds, by Kyle B Counts and Steve Rubin)*
B13, B20, B21, B23, B25, B27, H4, H5, H6, H7, T1

Film Review *(June 1997, Call Sheet: Vertigo by Anwar Brett)*
B9, N12, N13, S28

Film Review *(September 1999, Call Sheet: Frenzy by Howard Maxford)*
F5, F6, F16, F17, F18, F19, F20, F21, F22, F23, F24, F25, G3, G4, M2, S10, S11

Film Weekly *(6 March 1937)*
D9, T9

Music from the Movies *(Issue 2, Spring 1993)*
J3

Picturegoer *(1 April 1950)*
L16

Starburst *(1991)*
P26, P27, P28

What's On in London *(December 1993, Citizen Herrmann by Howard Maxford)*
H15, T15

Newspapers

London Evening News *(16 November 1927)*
F3

London Evening News *(25 June 1929)*
C1

Sunday Express *(17 September 1946)*
G8

Los Angeles Times *(20 October 1946)*
R1

Videography

Hitchcock Tribute *(Channel Four, 1989)*
L1, L7

Music for the Movies: Bernard Herrmann *(Les Films d'Ici/Alternate Current International/La Sept/Channel 4, 1993)*
H9, H11, H12, H13, H14

Omnibus *(BBC, 1986)*
B11

Reputations: Hitchcock *(BBC/Arts and Entertainment Network, 1999)*
Intro 1, Intro 2, B14, B22, B24, C11, D3, G5, H8, H16, H17, H18, H21, M17, M28, N3, O4, S26, T3, T4, T18, U2, U7, U8, V2

Discography

The Trouble with Harry *(Varese, 1998, liner notes by Christopher Husted)*
M29

Bernard Herrmann – Film Scores *(Milan, 1993, interview with Bernard Herrmann)*
H10